New Club Kids

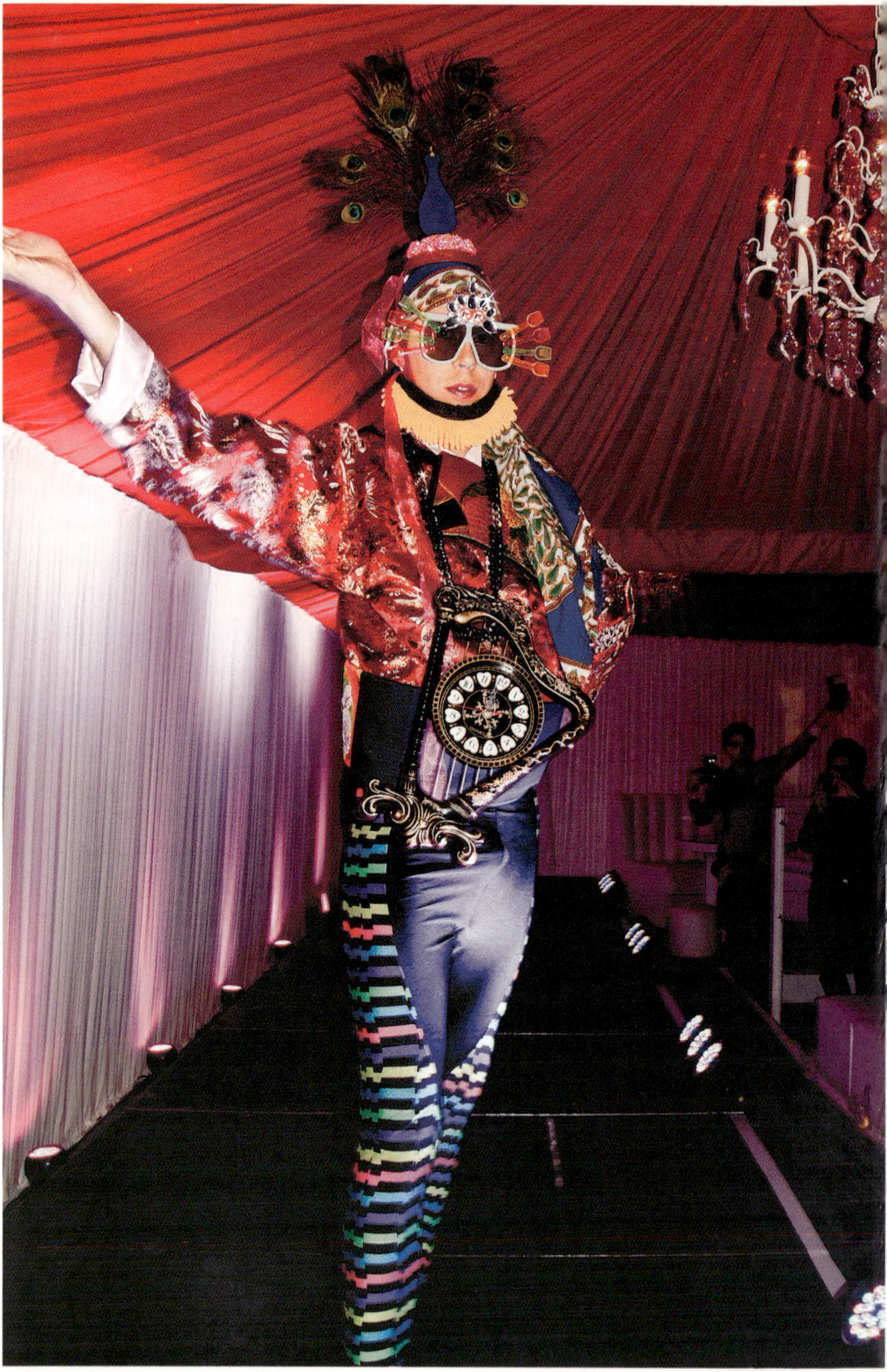

London Party Fashion in the Noughties

New Club Kids

Prestel

Munich • London • New York

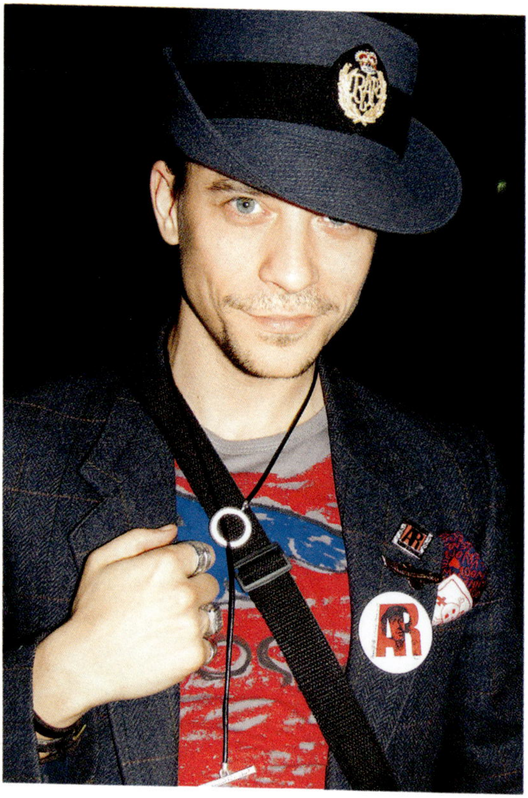

Oggy Yordanov is a Bulgarian-born photographer based in London's Soho district. A party kid himself, he has been documenting the exuberance of London's avant-garde club scene since 2001.

While selecting the photographs for this book, I reviewed thousands of images shot over the past decade. The incredible memories flooded back, all those parties and amazing people that made my years in the great city of London so phenomenal. I want you to share these memories.

At the time I moved to London, in early 2001, the party scene was still dominated by the super-clubs – places like Fabric, Ministry of Sound, Fridge, Heaven and Turnmills – providing a vibrant playground for the young clubber. These were huge capacity venues with great DJ line-ups that pulled in massive crowds of energetic party-goers, but one breed of party animal was missing – the club kid. It was the time of "less is more" and dressing down was the ongoing trend. For a while I believed that the avant-garde fashion of the real underground London had disappeared, somehow vanished with the modern transformation of clubland. Thankfully, things were starting to change.

In 2002, the musical "Taboo" opened in Leicester Square, Boy George's tribute to a bygone era – the New Romantics – London's original "dressers".

The New Romantics were a group of creative and very ambitious individuals, bored with the Punk that had ruled the London scene since the mid '70s - these kids were looking for something new and different. What started as "Bowie Night", a small gathering at Billy's in Soho, quickly progressed into a new wave of party style. It then moved to the now legendary Blitz Club in Covent Garden in 1979. Started by Steve Strange of *Visage*, Blitz became a hotspot for new talent and attracted a great deal of attention from both the media and the music world. With their outrageous dress-sense, black lipstick, heavy eyeliner and asymmetric hairdos, the Blitz Kids started a nightclub revolution. They drew inspiration from the unlikeliest of places and would go to extraordinary lengths to look different, anything to stay ahead of the pack.

The musical "Taboo" did much more than revive the New Romantics. It centred around one of the most eminent figures of '80s nightlife, the very heart and soul of London's alternative fashion scene – Leigh Bowery.

A true innovator – performance artist, club promoter, model, fashion designer – Leigh started the now infamous polysexual club, Taboo, in 1985. It quickly established itself as the wildest, most fashionable night in town. With his body-morphing costumes, a taste for the bizarre and a deep desire to shock, Bowery radically challenged the boundaries between figure, gender, fashion, beauty and art. With his premature death in the early '90s, London lost its brightest, most extraordinary star and arguably the single-most influential figure for the New Club Kid generation.

A year after "Taboo", the musical, a movie about the New York Club Kids of the '80s hit the big screens worldwide. "Party Monster" brought to life the most outrageous and daring party characters from across the Atlantic, in all their glory and hedonistic debauchery. Partly influenced and often joined by Leigh, these kids took the scene to new heights. They partied harder, dressed wilder, became the underground superstars to a generation worldwide and coined the term Club Kids.

By 2003 London had already witnessed the first signs of a new wave of underground "art-clubbing". Nag Nag Nag, a mid-week mash-up at the small Soho backstreet club, The Ghetto, and the more challenging Kashpoint, were both gaining popularity. Kashpoint, with its very strict door policy, encouraged extreme dress-up and reignited London's alternative clubbing. Suddenly the New London Club Kids generation had arrived.

Kashpoint attracted some of the original founders of the New Romantics scene, along with fresh new artists, fashion students and up-and-coming musicians – the usual bunch. Not surprisingly, its most memorable night was a Leigh Bowery tribute – imagine a club packed with hundreds of Boweries. The scene was thriving and an array of new clubs were popping up on a weekly basis. Kashpoint and Nag Nag Nag championed a low-fi, electroclash sound that soon became synonymous with the scene. Jonny Slut told *The Guardian* in 2005 "One reason I started Nag Nag Nag was that music was becoming more interesting again. Anyone who thinks club culture is dead should come and see the queue on Wednesday night."

Another breakthrough club that started around the same time was Act Art, which focused on live performances merging art, fashion, pop and club culture. It established itself as the ultimate underground event to challenge creativity and make people feel like they belonged. It is, to this day, a platform for emerging artists showcasing some of the most radical, experimental and risqué performances imaginable.

The mid-noughties were the new '80s. Music and fashion were reviving the styles of the decade in its entirety and inevitably, it reflected in the club-scene. There were the Neo-Romantics, the New Punks and the Voguers but perhaps the most original of all revivals was the Nu Rave, advocating DIY style over fashion. Though short-lived, it made its mark on the scene. Labels were being ripped off in favour of personally customized outfits. Plastic neon toys became the ultra-chic, must-have accessory, matched with brightly coloured jeans and gold trainers.

Throughout 2006-2008 London was overtaken by the Voguing revival. Though started as an underground dance movement in '80s New York, it was brought to the mainstream with Madonna's 1990 hit single 'Vogue'. Almost completely wiped out by the AIDS epidemic in the '90s, Voguing was brought back to life on this side of the Atlantic through the advanced popularity of YouTube and the documentary "Paris Is Burning". Voguing "Houses" were formed and for a couple of years many a Voguing Ball and dance-off took place around London.

Embracing this amalgam of styles – old and new, was the club Boombox, based in the new fashion hot-spot of Hoxton in the East End. It was the brainchild of Richard Mortimer and just like its predecessor Family, it was never advertised but always spoken about. Boombox attracted a cult following and became the hottest ticket in town. It was particularly favoured by the youth 'bible' – *i-D* magazine - and regularly featured in their pages. With its eclectic style and iconic status Boombox became the symbol of the contemporary London look. Favoured for spotting new talent, it was the place to be seen and soon magazines from all over the world were referencing the scene. Editorials in *V* magazine, *WAD* and *POP* magazine followed, but by far the most serious recognition of their fashion came when Italian *Vogue* "borrowed" Molaroid's signature disco ball accessory for their cover. The Club Kids were getting serious attention from the media, a lot were casted in music videos and commercials, others kick-started their careers as fashion designers, stylists, make-up artists, musicians or DJs. Some started their own club-nights, most famously Jodie Harsh, who emerged in 2006 with Circus, and Daniel Lismore, whose latest venture Shabba-Dabba-Da has just made *i-D* magazine's "Hottest Night in Town" list.

Fashion has always walked hand in hand with music and London has a rich history of dressing-up. Club Kids or "dressers", as some would prefer, encapsulate the creative London as I know it. Fabulous, yet trashy, beautiful and scary, glamorous or freaky – meet the New London Club Kids.

Oggy Yordanov

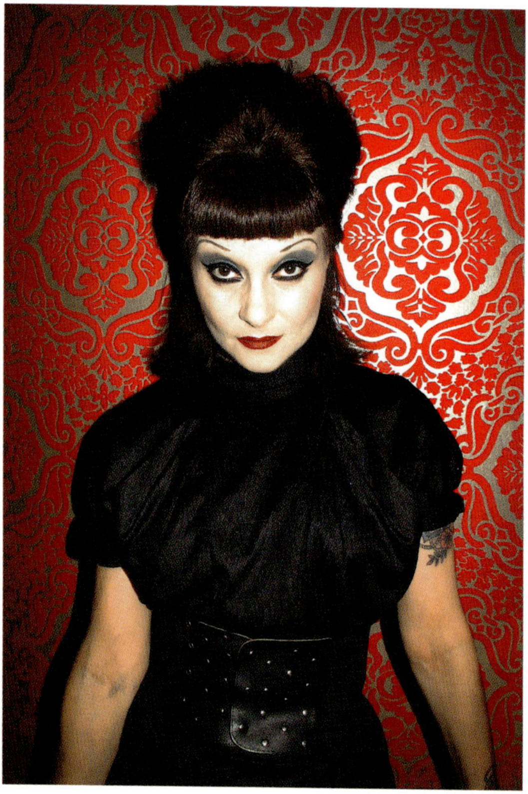

Princess Julia is an acclaimed London DJ and music editor for *i-D* magazine, who emerged on the London social party scene in the early '80s as part of the Blitz Kids alongside Boy George, Steve Strange and Marc Almond.

Oggy Yordanov: Let's talk about the scene back in the day and how it all started, how it transformed from trashy Punk into the fashionable New Romantics.

Princess Julia: We're talking about a club scene that started in the mid-1970s with clubs like The Roxy. This was the pivotal moment for the Punk scene, which was anti-fashion and anti-style. It was all about making yourself look kind of awful, but in a very stylized way. The core of the Punk scene was a group of art students, designers and musicians – much in the way that creative people are on the club music scene now. Most of the people that gravitated towards The Blitz Club had been part of the Punk scene but were now more interested in a dandified form of beautification. One day I got a call from Steve Strange, who had been residing in Wales for a while – he was coming back to town and was asking what was going on. And I was like, "Well there's not really a lot going on." The whole punk scene had gone mainstream quite quickly and Steve took up the opportunity to do a one-night club at a place called Billy's in Meard Street. And basically we just used to hang out at Steve Strange's night.

OY: And then it moved to the Blitz and the scene expanded.

PJ: Yes, Steve loved the attention from the media and I think he enjoyed the notoriety, as we all did, because we were quite a bunch of poseurs. We were serious about our individual looks at the Blitz but we had humour about what we were doing. References came from all directions, from *film noir*, camp movies, black and white movie stars, from art movements like Surrealism. It was a great time to research and experiment.

OY: Do you think that was happening anywhere else at the time? For me it's really a London thing.

PJ: The conversation between New York and London was apparent. The music was very important: new electronic music, like *Kraftwerk*, was filtering in from Europe that wasn't being played in other clubs, only ours. We crossed over with other things like Eurodisco, Electronica. The sort of music that Rusty Egan was playing was a really important part of the club and the atmosphere.

OY: I remember Philip Sallon telling me it wasn't a very big scene, but when I read about it, it always seems like it was massive – the queues outside, people not being able to get in, even people like Mick Jagger not being able to get in. A big influence on the new generation Club Kids is Leigh Bowery who emerged on the scene a little later with his extreme dressing and body-morphing costumes.

PJ: There was a real direct thread running from The Blitz Club in 1979 through to Taboo, Leigh's club, in 1984. Leigh turned up in London in 1982 to 1983 and having studied fashion he was inspired by London and the energy he was hearing about through magazines such as *i-D*, *The Face* and *The Blitz*. Leigh soon became a regular of a club called Cha Cha's which was a back room of Heaven. He was experimenting with his early collections like 'Pakis from Outer Space'. Leigh and Trojan would go out with the blue face, a bit Picasso, lips to one side and all the rest of it. Very, very quickly Leigh and Trojan became installed on the London club scene.

OY: A lot of people from The Blitz turned into artists, musicians and designers.

PJ: As with Punk, there were a lot of fashion students, designers, stylists. Everyone went on to do his or her respective jobs. I lived on Warren Street with Stephen Jones, Kim Bowen, Jeremy Healy – a whole group of creative people. And then later on I lived on Great Titchfield Street with Boy George. We were all doing creative things, all just having a go and having a laugh. One of my favourite subjects is the dressing-up box – the way people decide what they're going to reference or look into and what they take with them. Leigh Bowery made the most amazing costumes – he became art in a way. It's just a matter of experimenting. We have a history in this country and especially in London, of embracing the Avant-garde and even if you don't carry it through your whole life, if you just have a moment, when you're twenty, of dressing up and just letting it all go, it's very exciting.

OY: I think there was a gap between the early 1990s and the new revival of the Club Kids.

PJ: After Taboo finished there were still clubs going on, but the late 1980s were very interesting from a musical point of view: bedroom technology came along and people could sample music. New dance music was coming through which was soon called House Music. Club life was becoming a global phenomenon. I remember deejaying at a club called The Daisy Chain that Leigh Bowery did a lot of installations at, including his famous Enema show. Then I started working with Michael and Gerlinde Costiff who started up the club Kinky Gerlinky which was a total dressing-up extravaganza. Once again, Leigh Bowery always used to come there. Then there was Trade.

OY: What is interesting about Trade is that it started as another place that was extravagant and stylish, but by the late 1990s it was all about dressing down.

PJ: That whole rave culture was about dressing down, but it was very label-conscious because it was the beginning of branding. The moment people got a bit of money they'd buy designer clothes and wear them with the tag still on. Branding really peaked in the 1990s – even the clubs branded themselves, like the Ministry of Sound. That went for the music as well – everything had to have a label. By the end of the 1990s people were becoming bored with it.

OY: So by the early noughties people started looking back and dressing-up again.

PJ: There was a shift away, in the demographic of London, from the West End towards the East End. The scene in East London was packed with artists and students, because it was very run down around there and people could live there quite cheaply. People were taking over some of the bars and clubs and it was starting to be a bit more refreshing. Fashion places like Kokon to Zai and Pineal Eye started up; and with music one of the most notable moments was the *Fischerspooner* moment. That album was floating around in very specific places and it was so different from the stuff that was being played in clubs. You also had people like *Soulwax* doing their mash up.

OY: And when Electroclash started making it big, that was a change to the whole scene. Kashpoint and The Ghetto pioneered the sound.

PJ: Simon Hobart opened The Ghetto and I was resident at a club night there called The Cock. There were all manner of bands and different kinds of new music coming through. *Scissor Sisters* did their debut gig at The Cock: they were considered an art band but were doing this amazing pop disco music. And then, of course, there was Nag Nag Nag – those two nights were pioneering the new music that was coming through. The Ghetto became quite a showcase for people to experiment with performance and we actively encouraged it.

OY: And later came Boombox.

PJ: One of the first incarnations of Boombox was the club Golf Sale: the music would be rock 'n' roll, pop and disco. People weren't interested in being pigeonholed so dressing-up was majorly encouraged; it was a place to experiment again.

OY: If we had to compare the current Club Kids scene to the original one, how different is it, how much is history repeating itself and how much is new and original?

PJ: I always feel there is a thread of creativity – people enquiring about ideas and concepts, about how they look, how they want to present themselves, how they want their lifestyle to be and where it's all going. It's interesting to see the things that people glean from their retro archives and the modern things they put these together with. There are some amazing looks that I've not seen before. Maybe I could sit there and go, 'Well that's a bit this and that,' but not put together in quite that way and that's the personality of the person, because we're all unique so we all put things together in different ways and I think that goes with art, with music – it goes with everything about being alive.

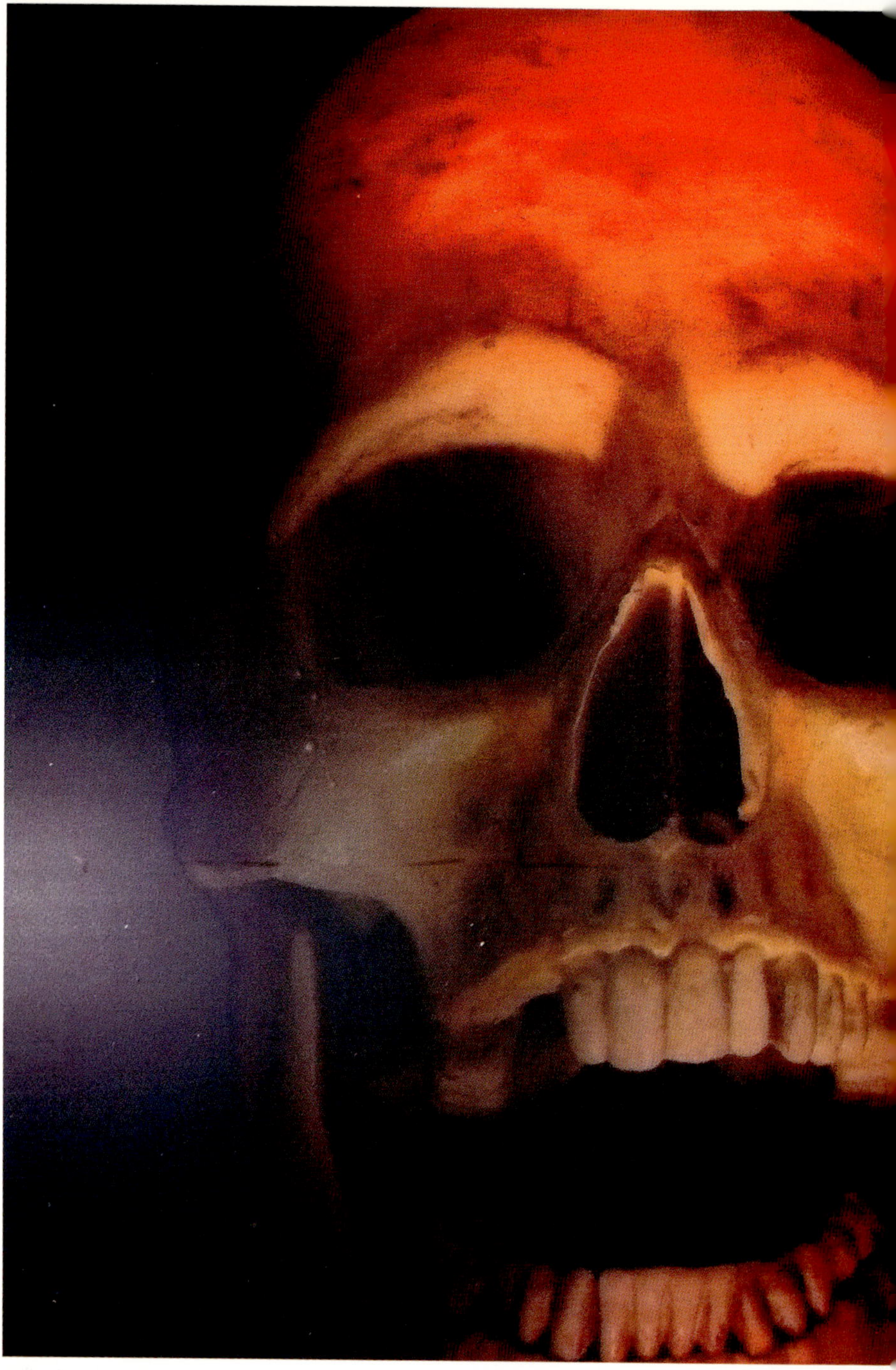

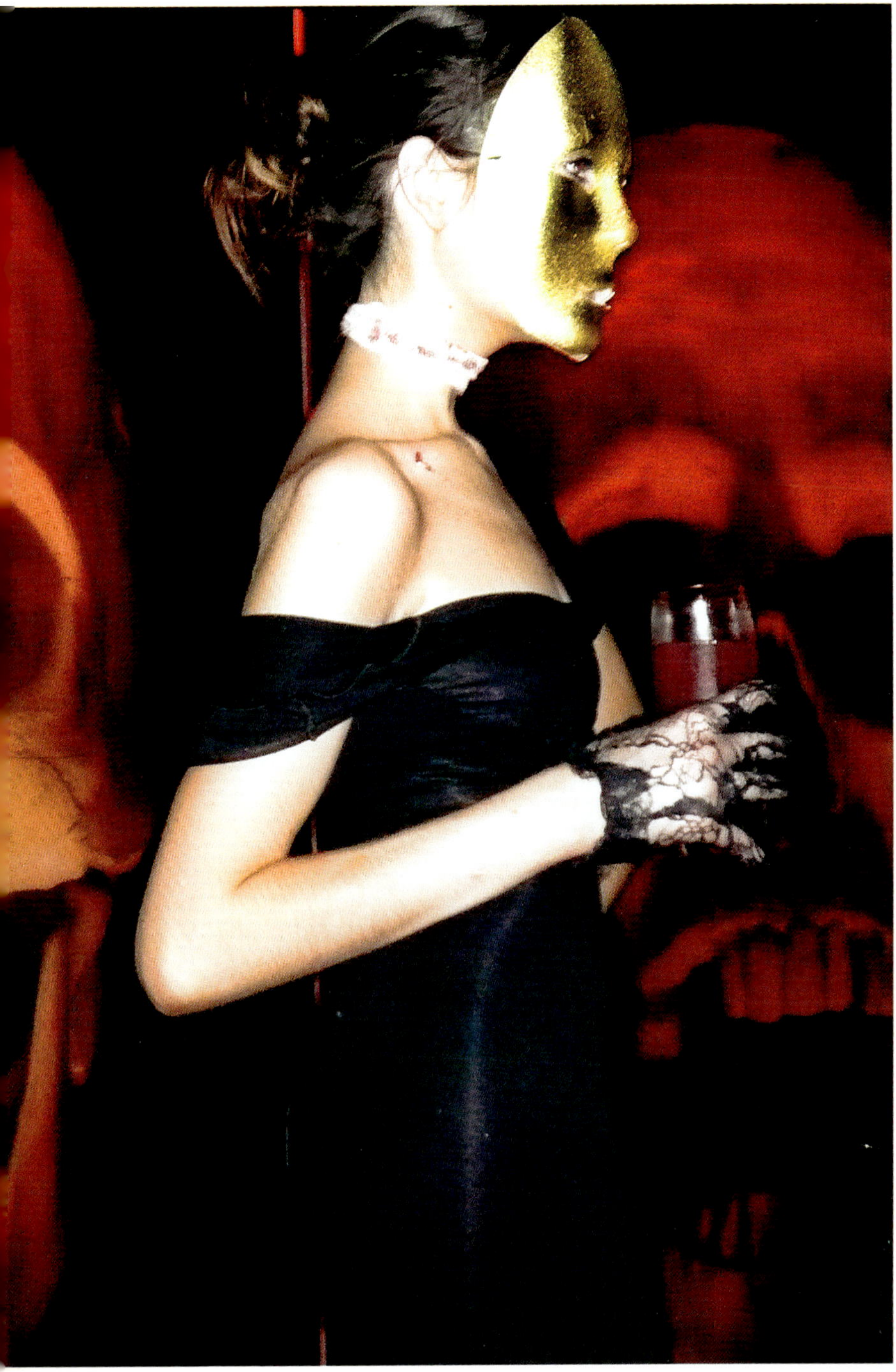

Maddox Club – Nov 2001

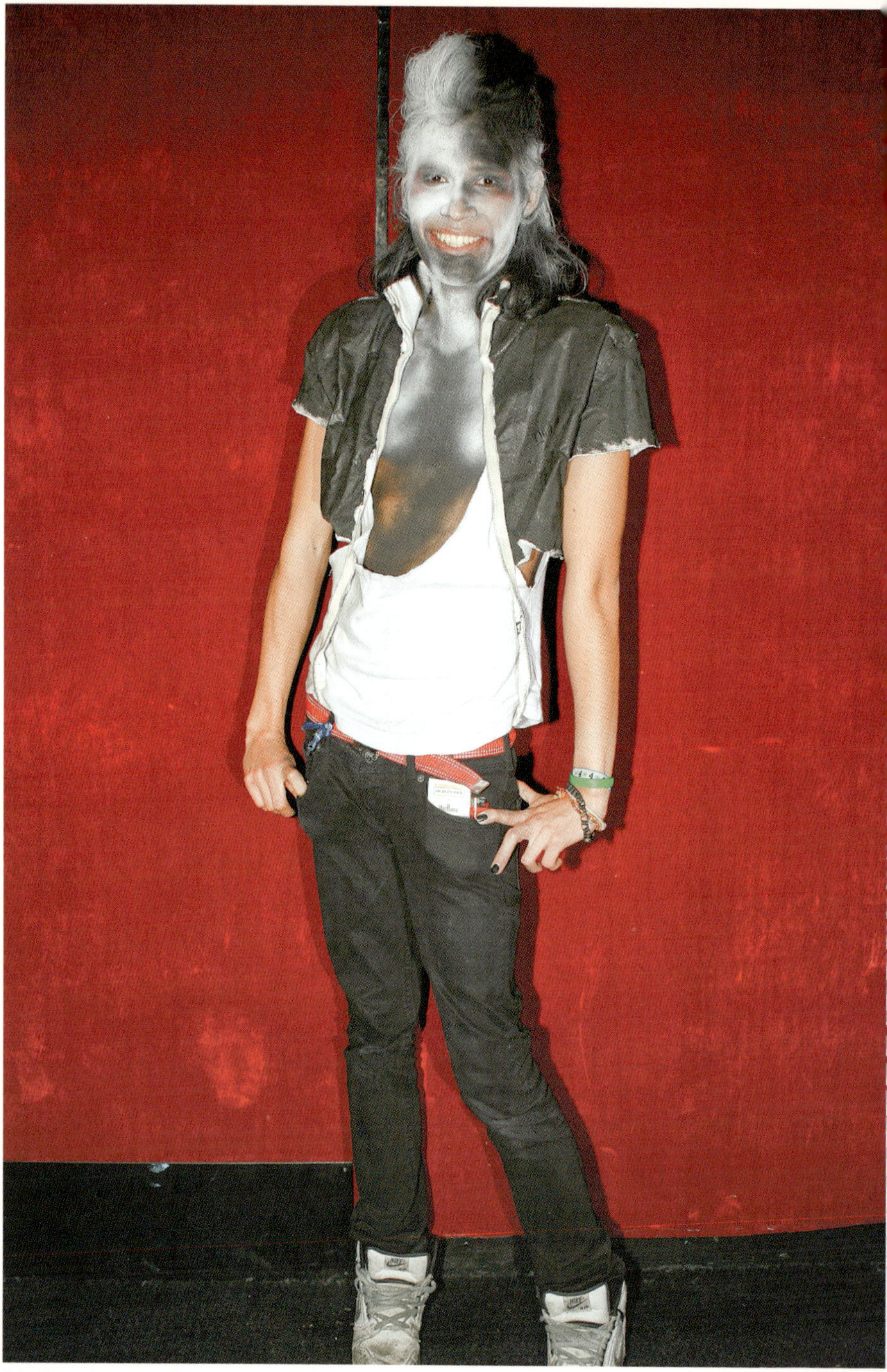

Soho Revue Bar – Nov 2007

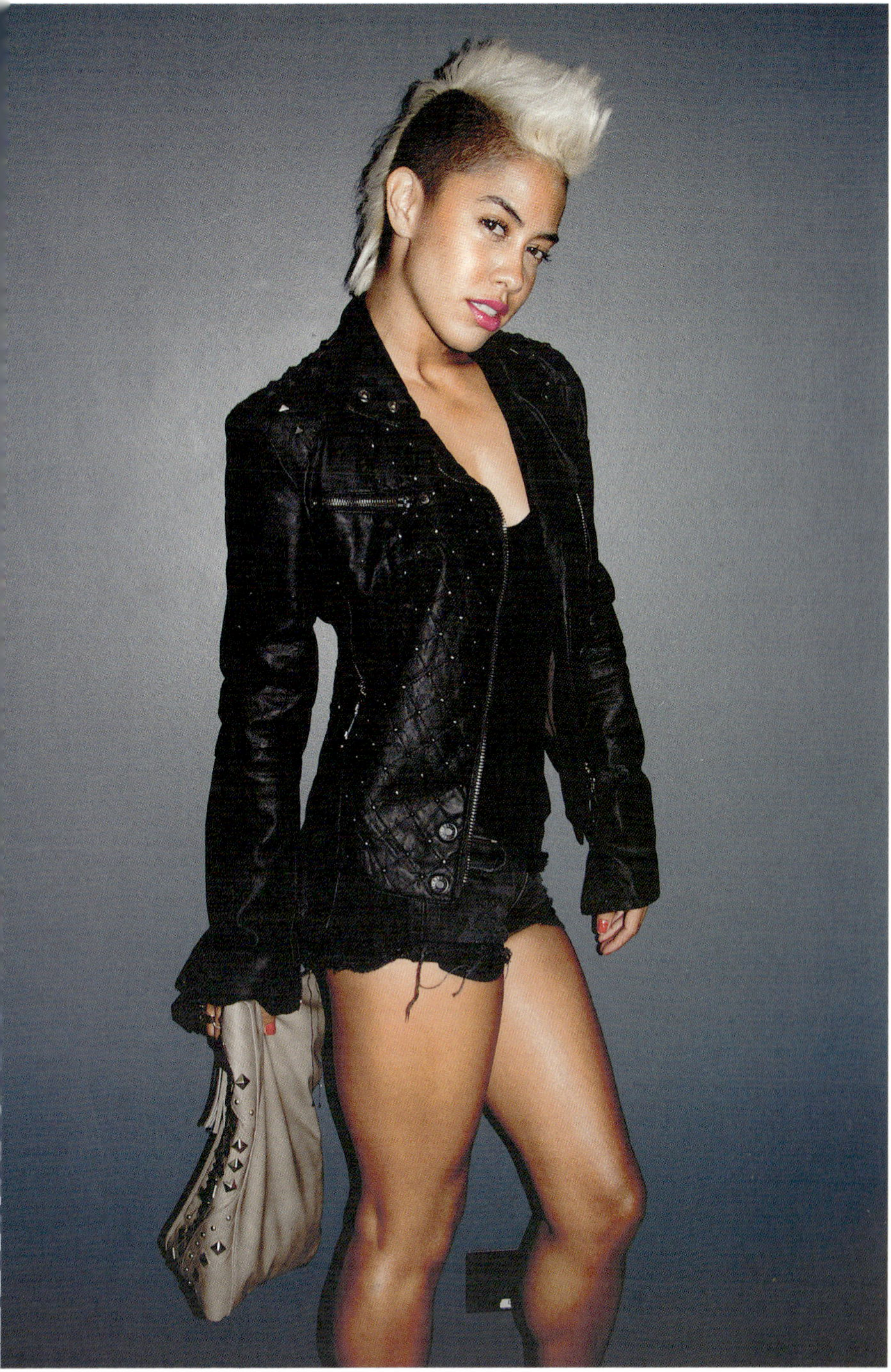

Paramount – Sept 2010

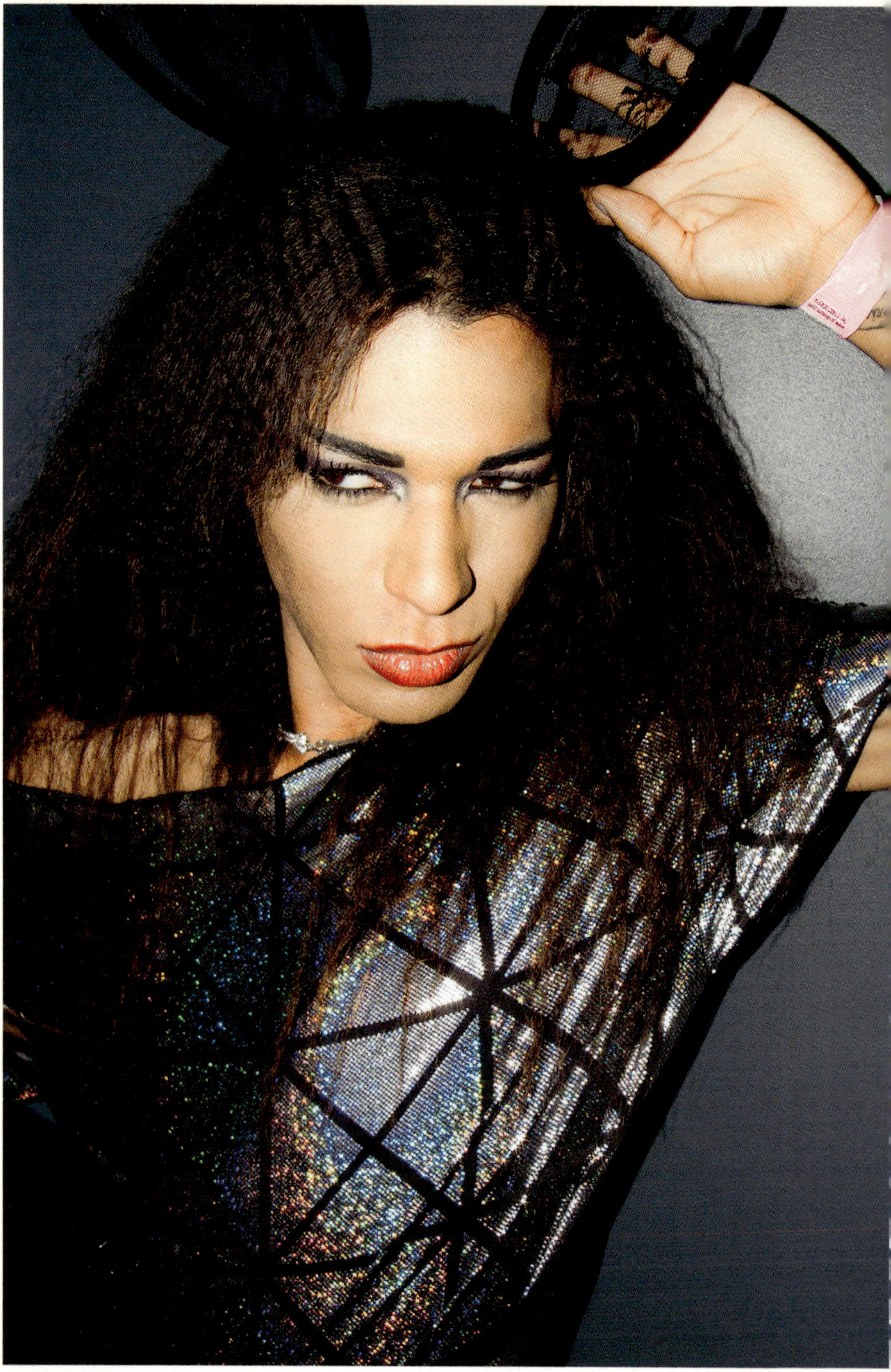

Circus – Nov 2009

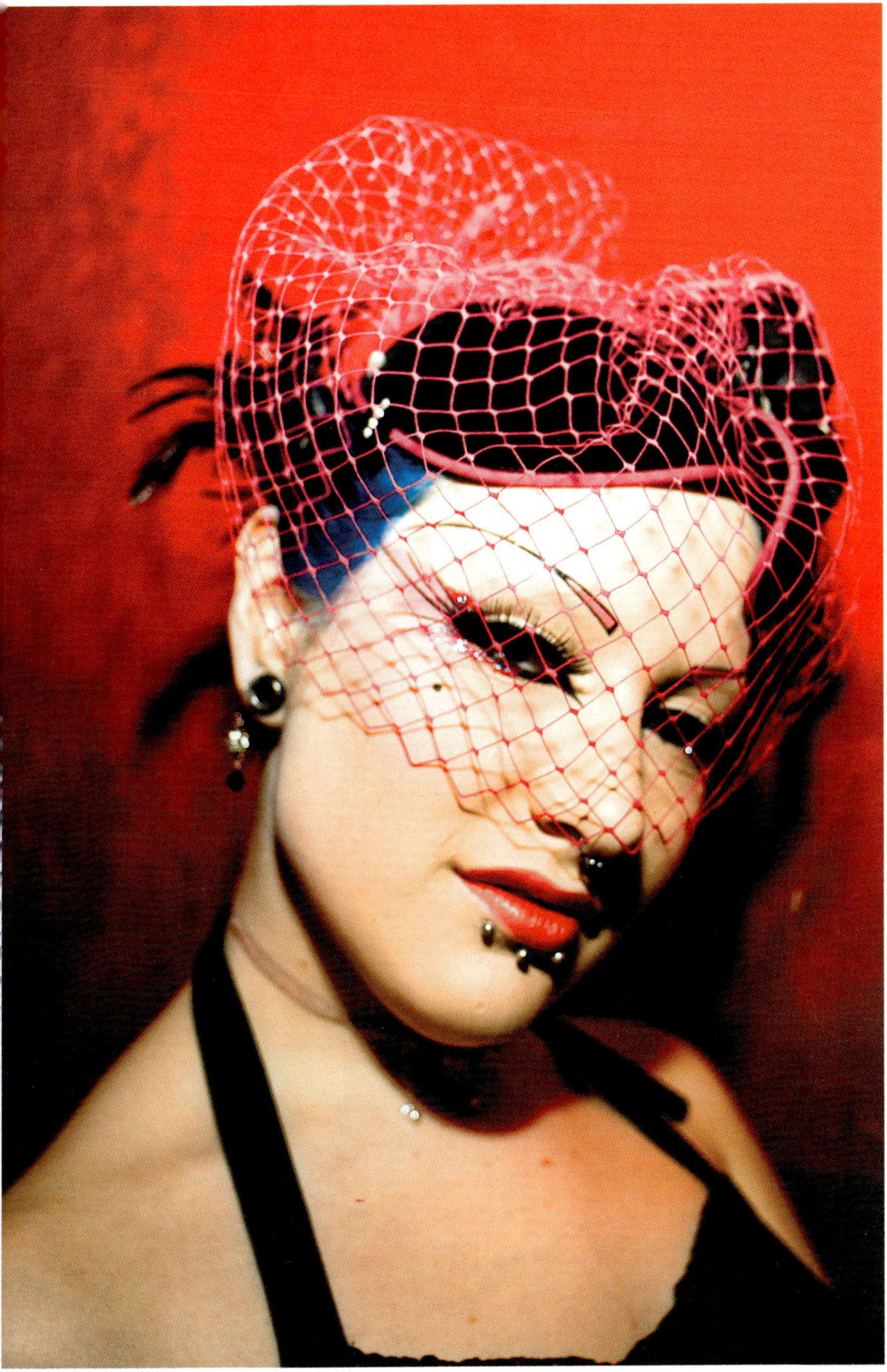

Too2Much – Nov 2005

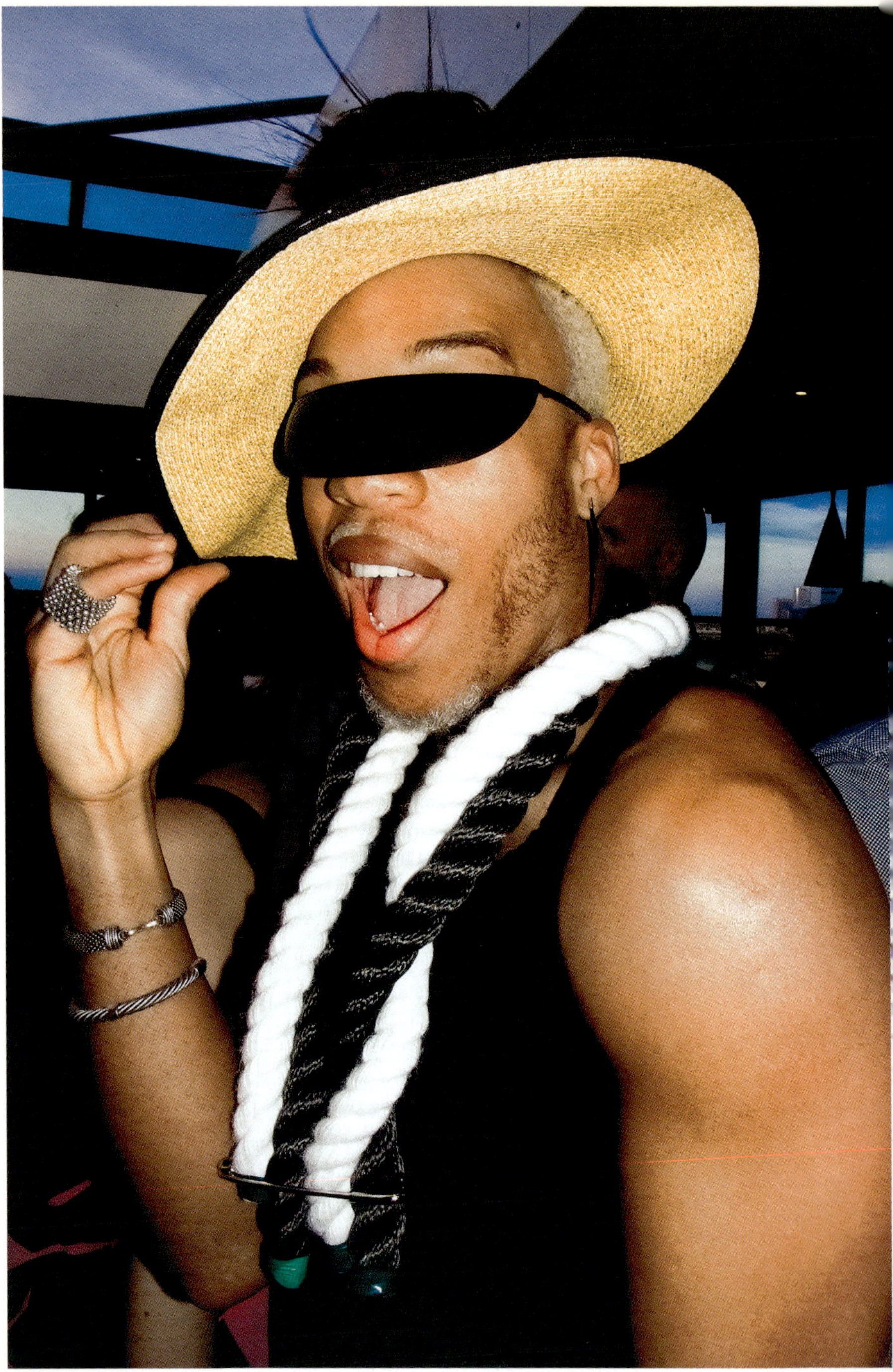

Shoreditch House – Sept 2010

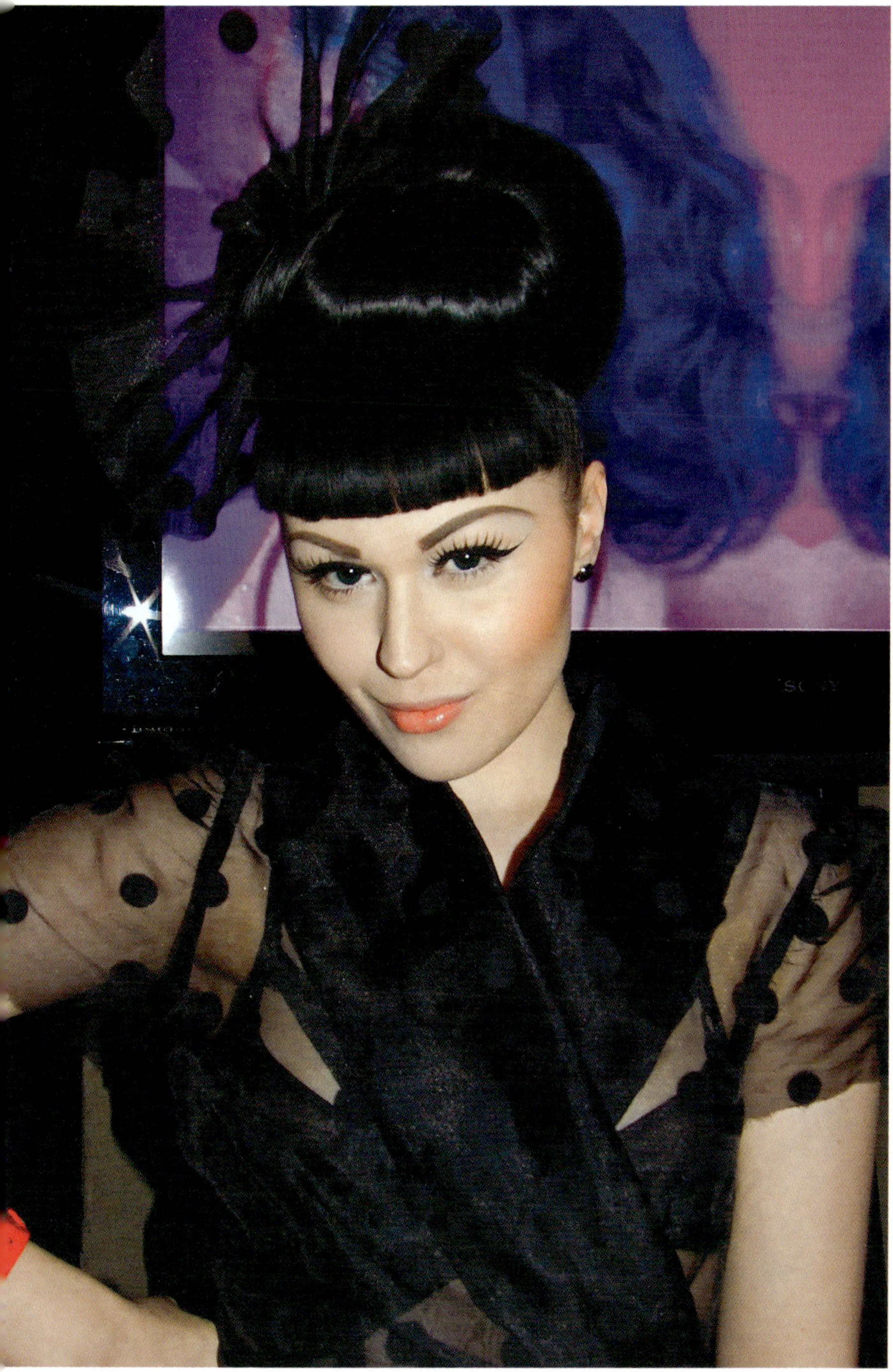

Paramount – Sept 2010

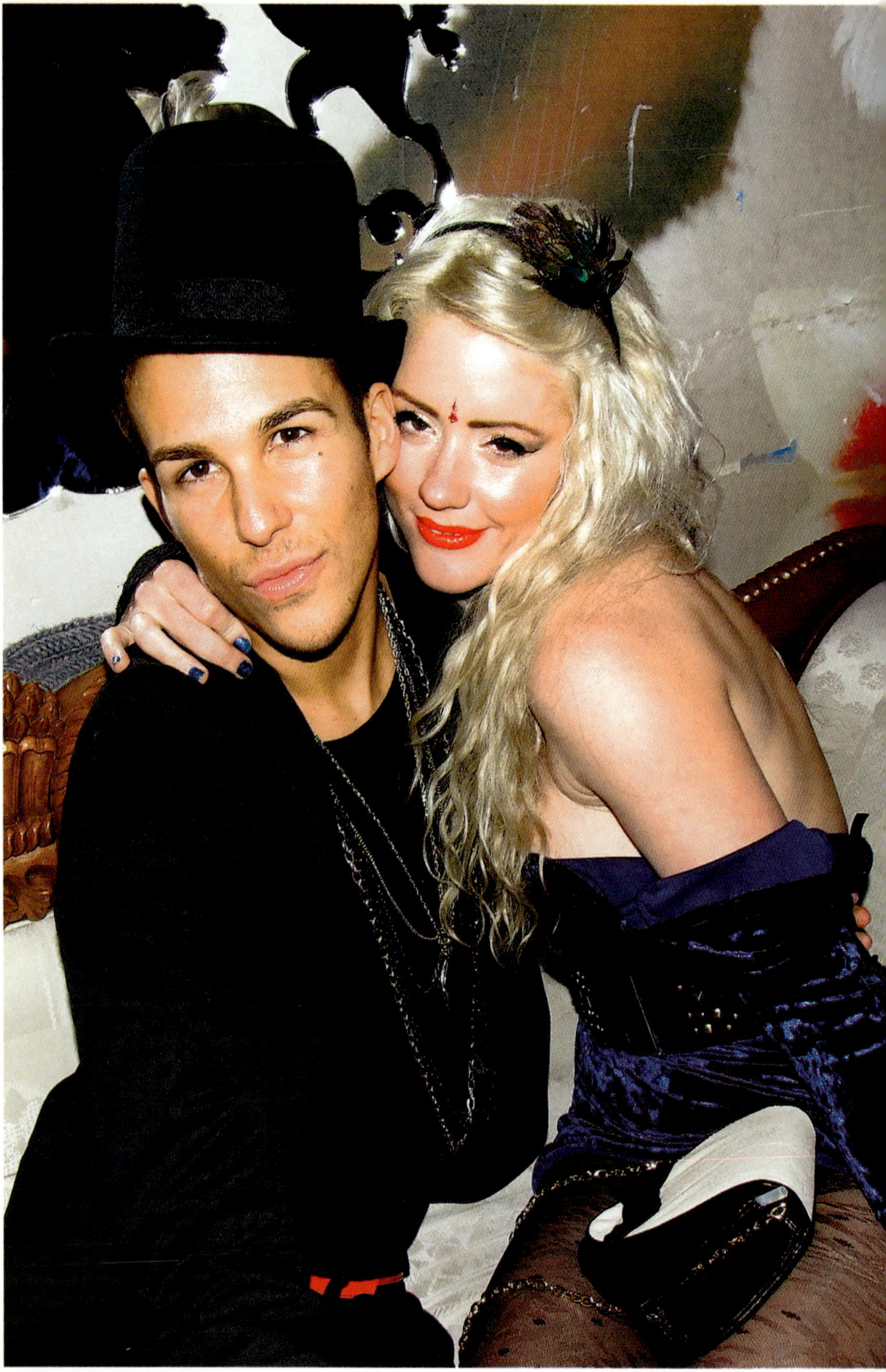

Your Mum's House – Dec 2009

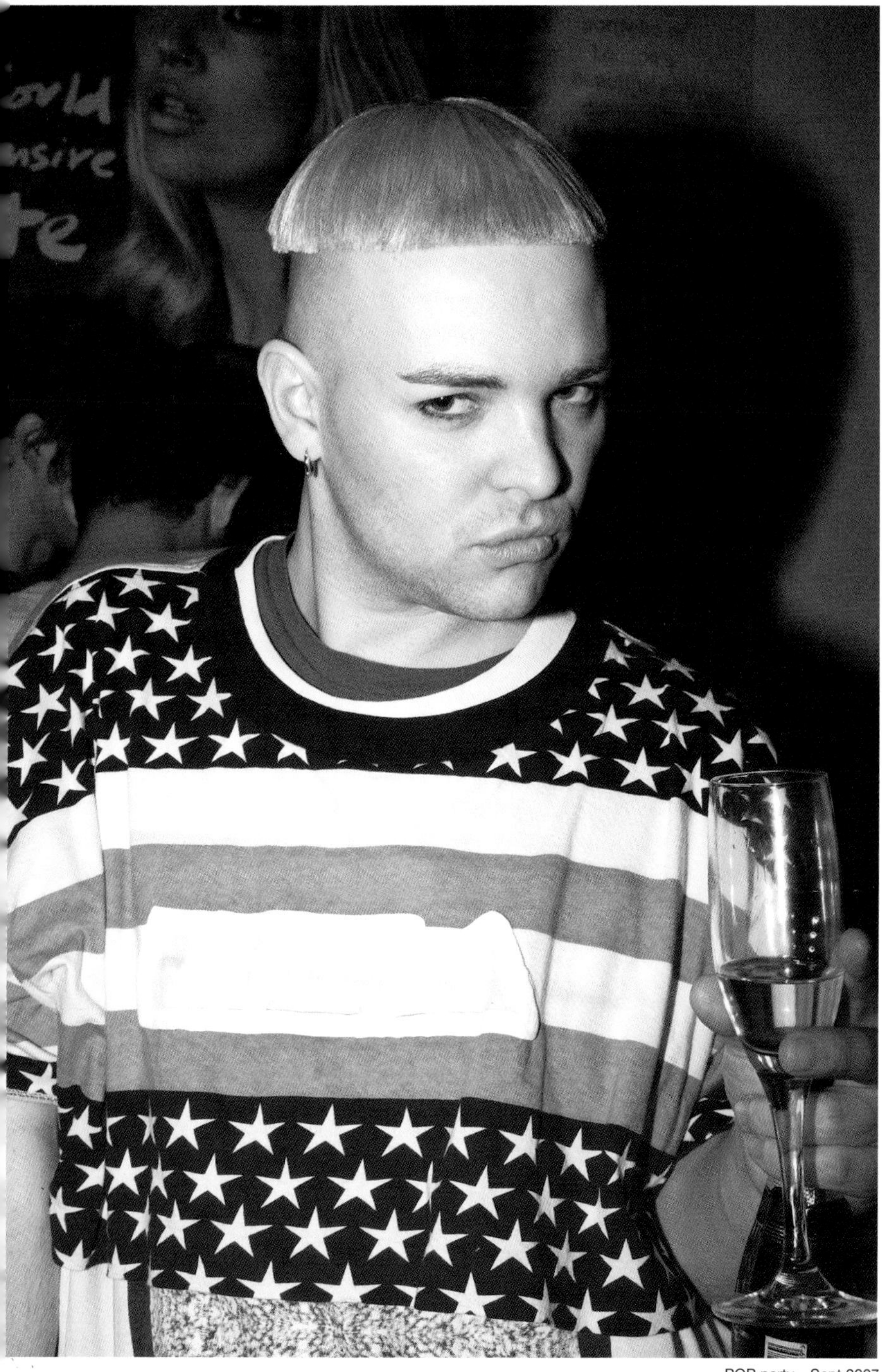

POP party – Sept 2007

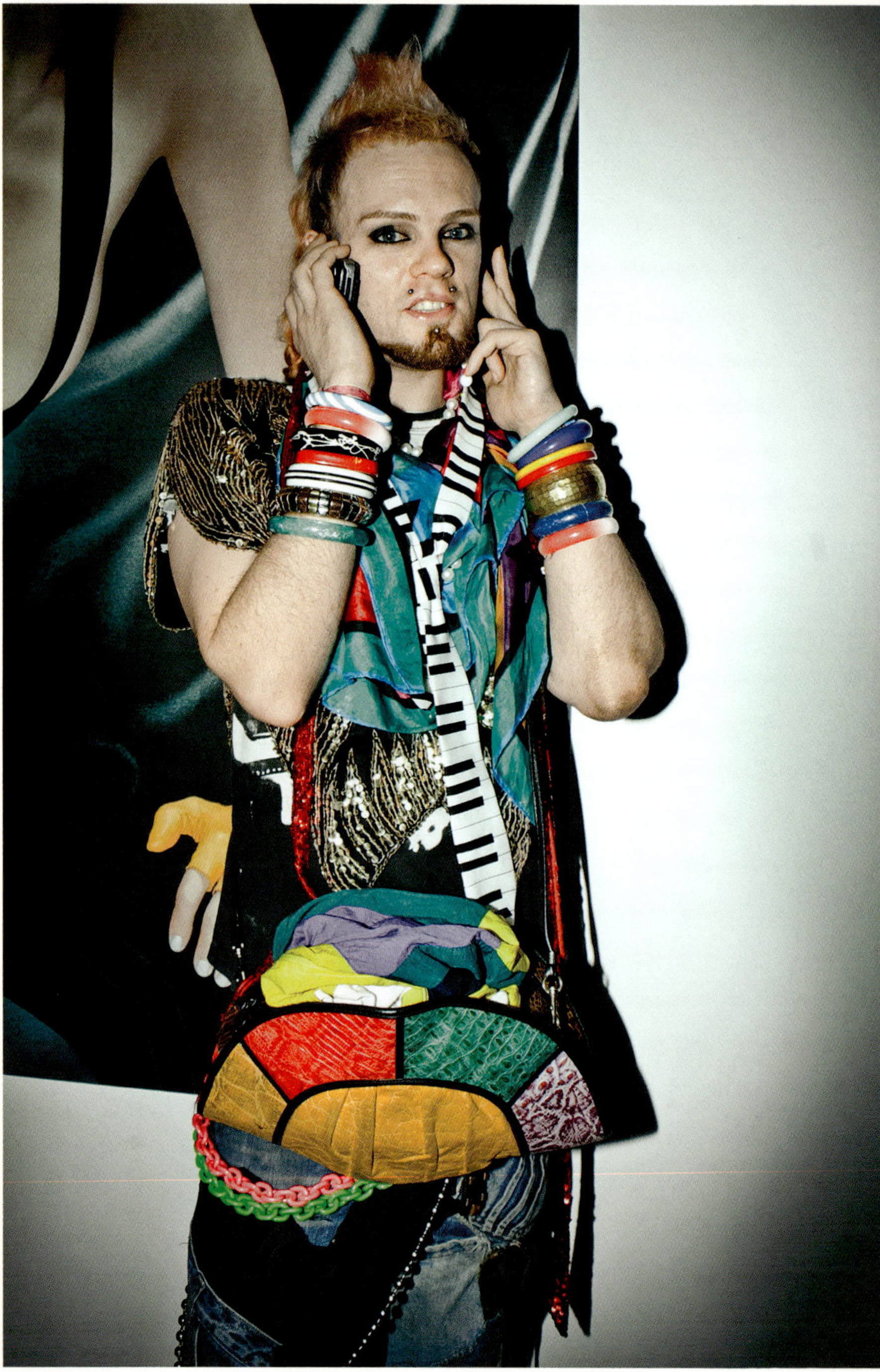

POP party – Sept 2007

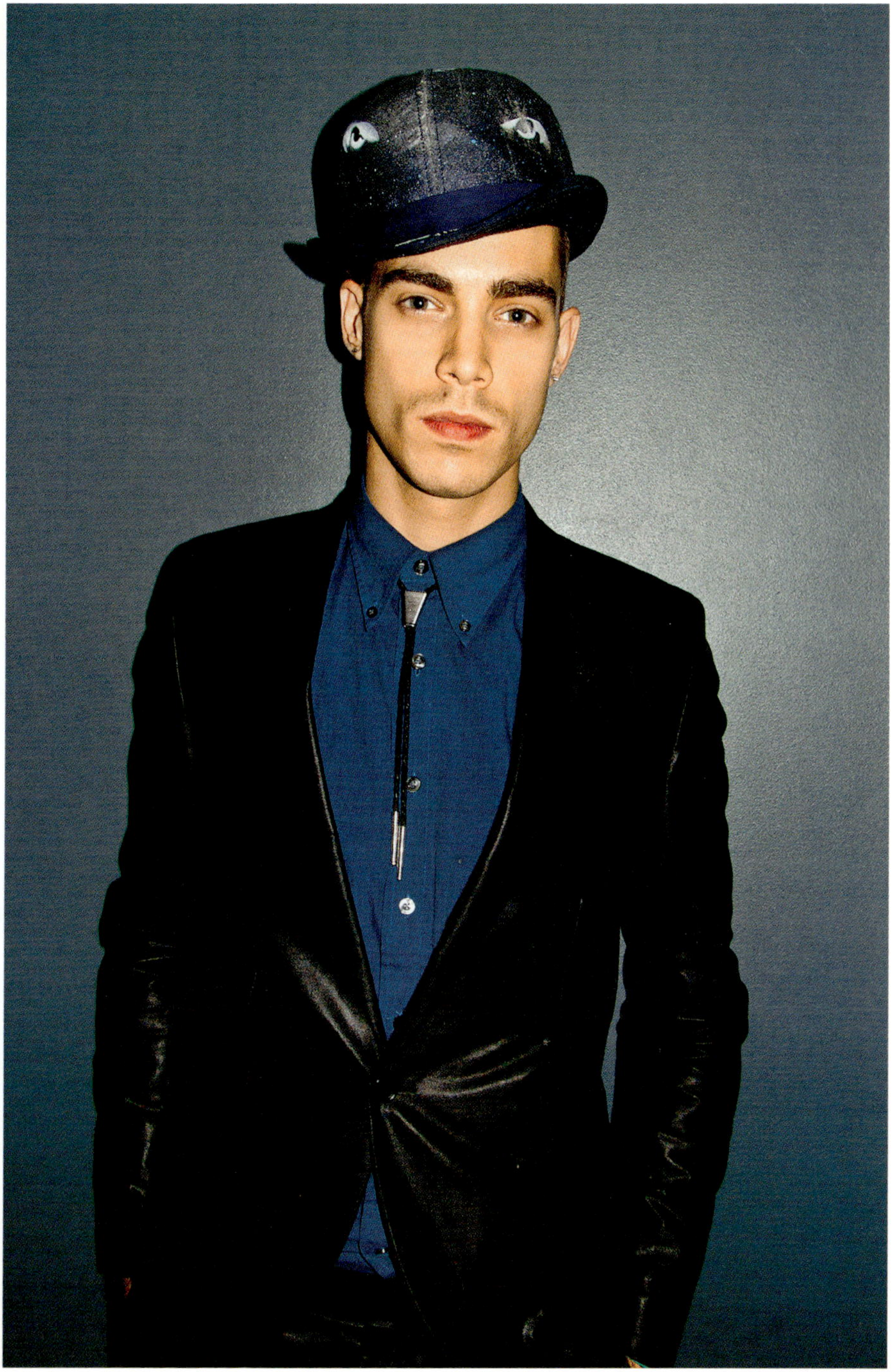

Circus – Oct 2009

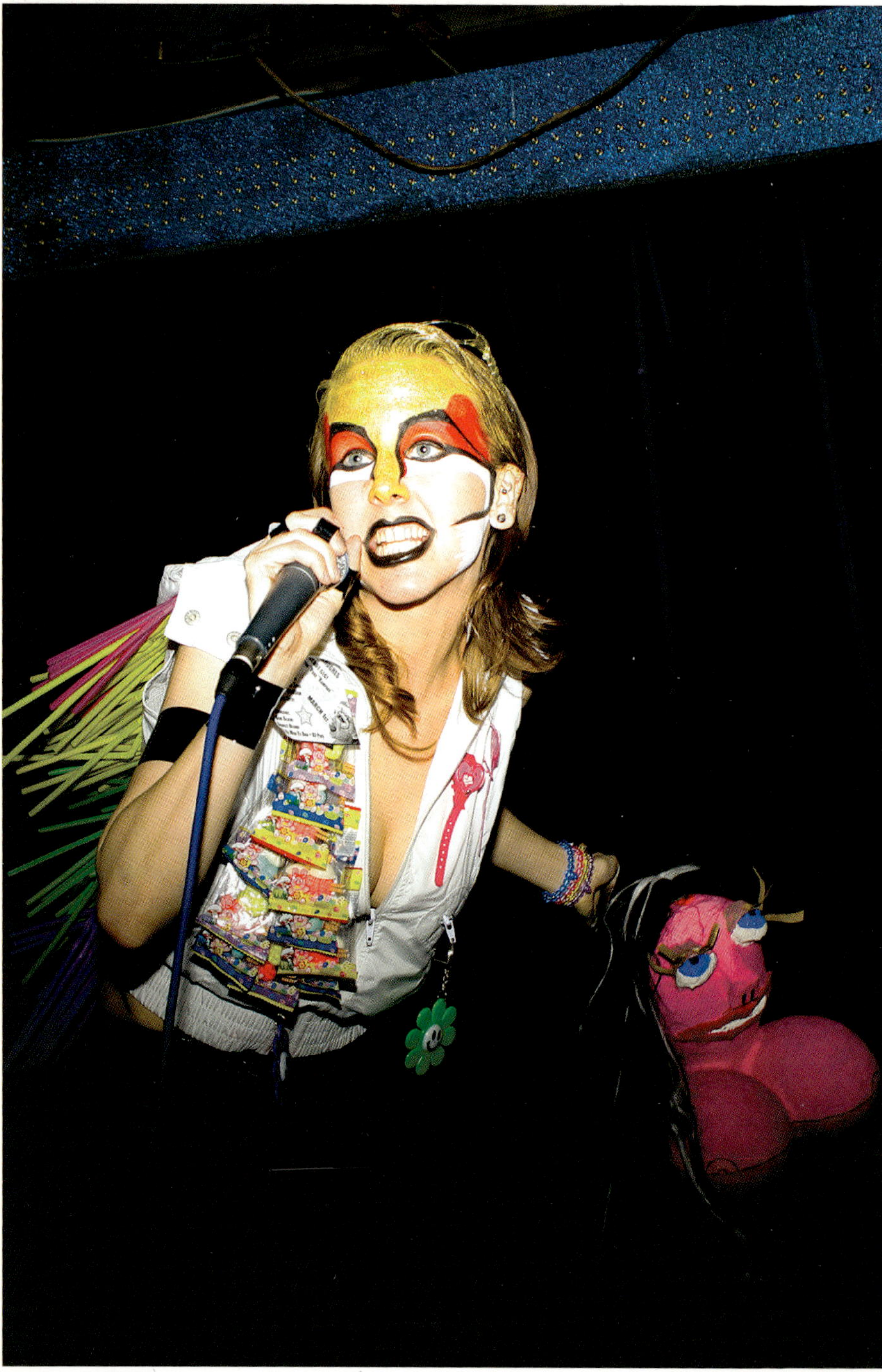

Too2Much – Feb 2006

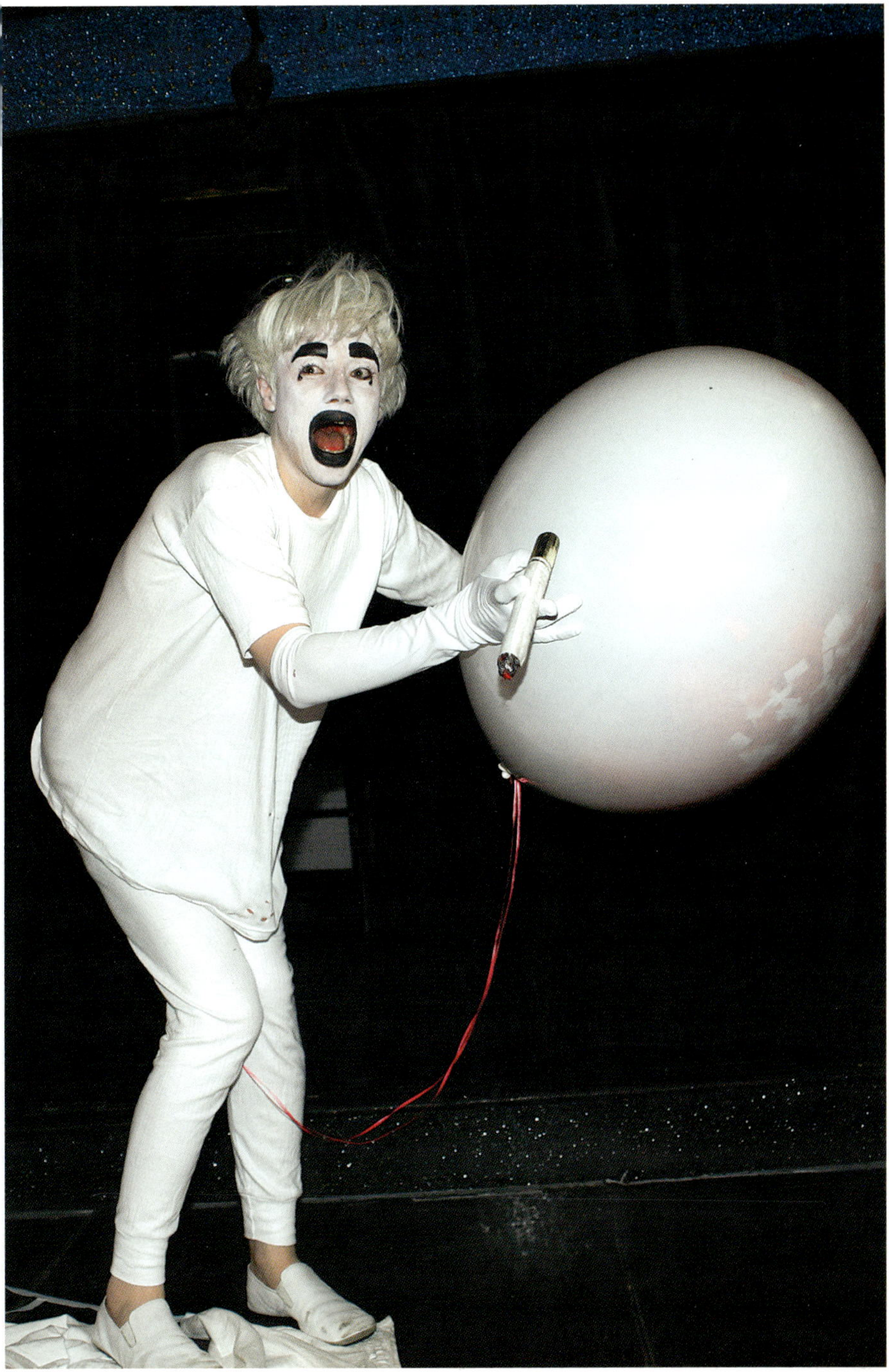

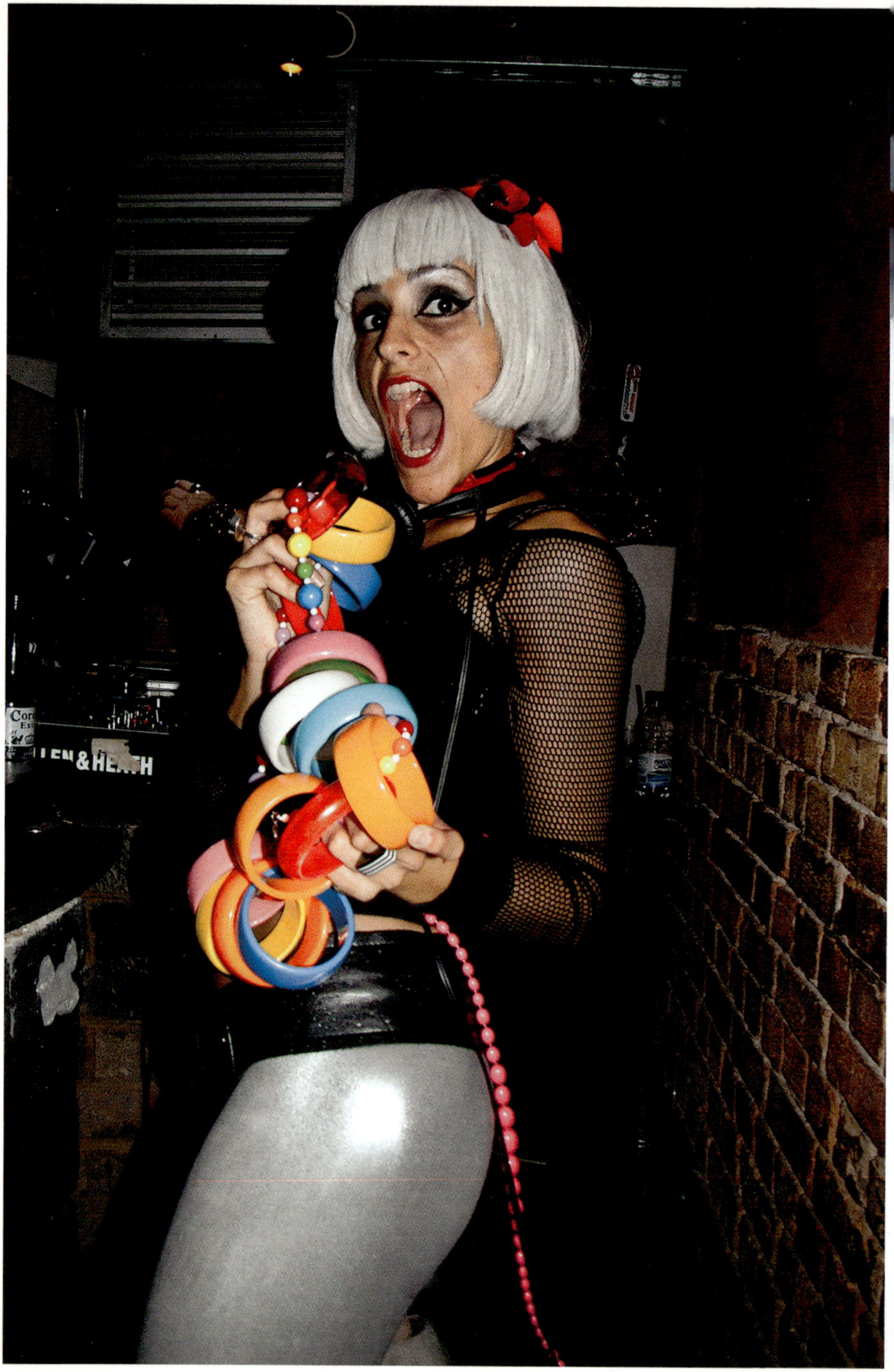

Wearable Art@Egg – Sept 2010

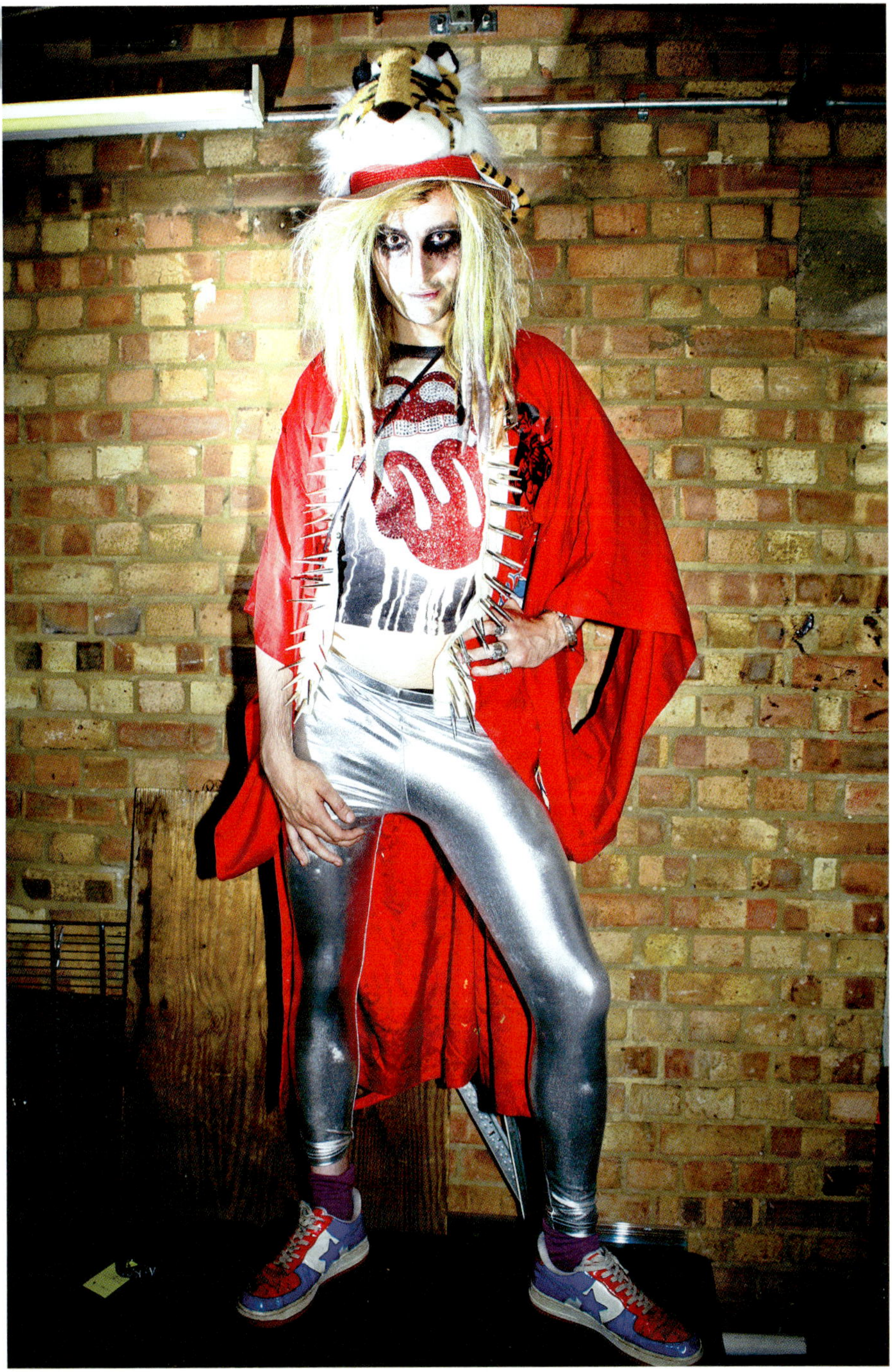

Year Zero@Crystal – June 2007

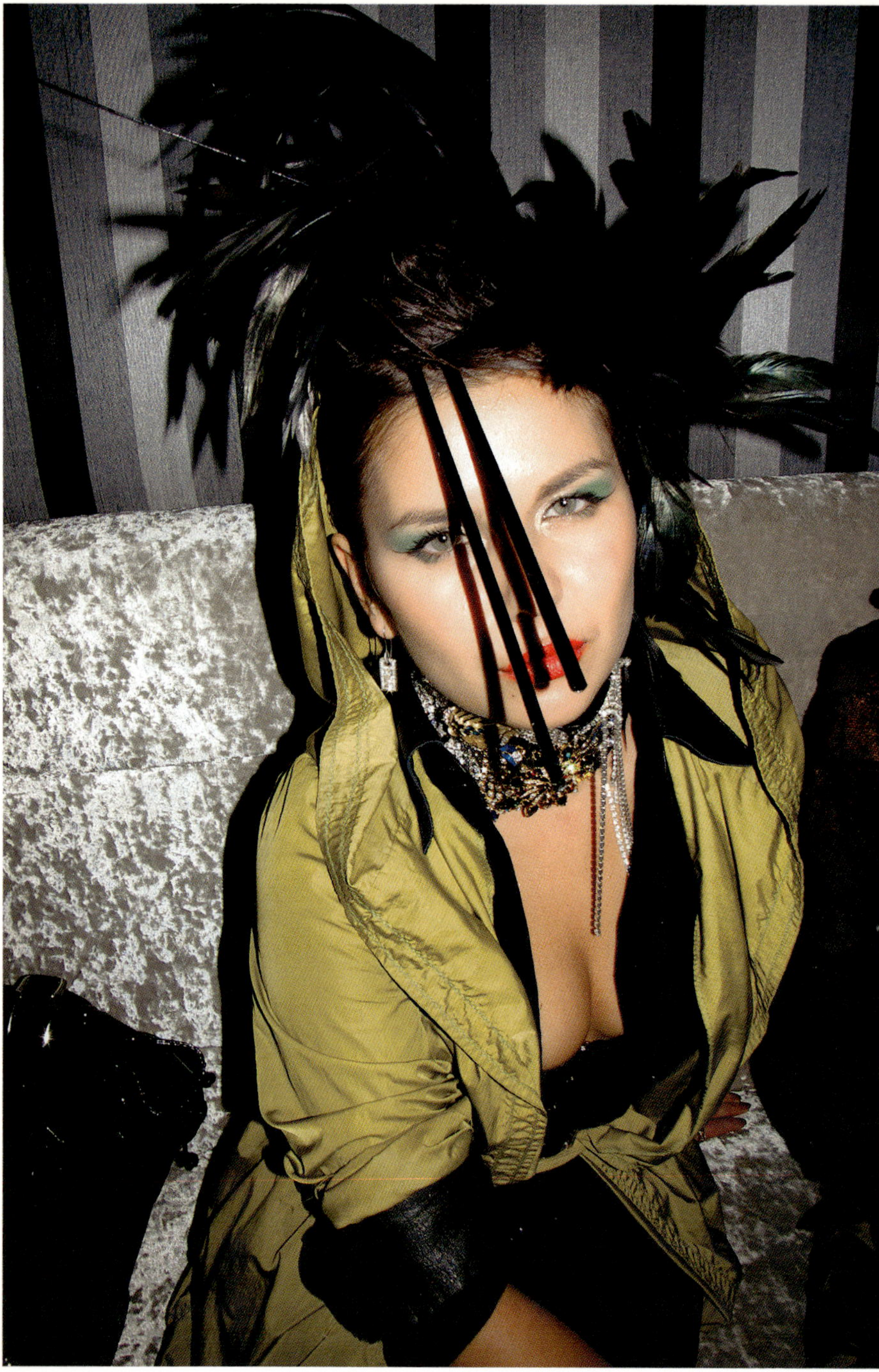

Shabba Dabba Da – Oct 2010

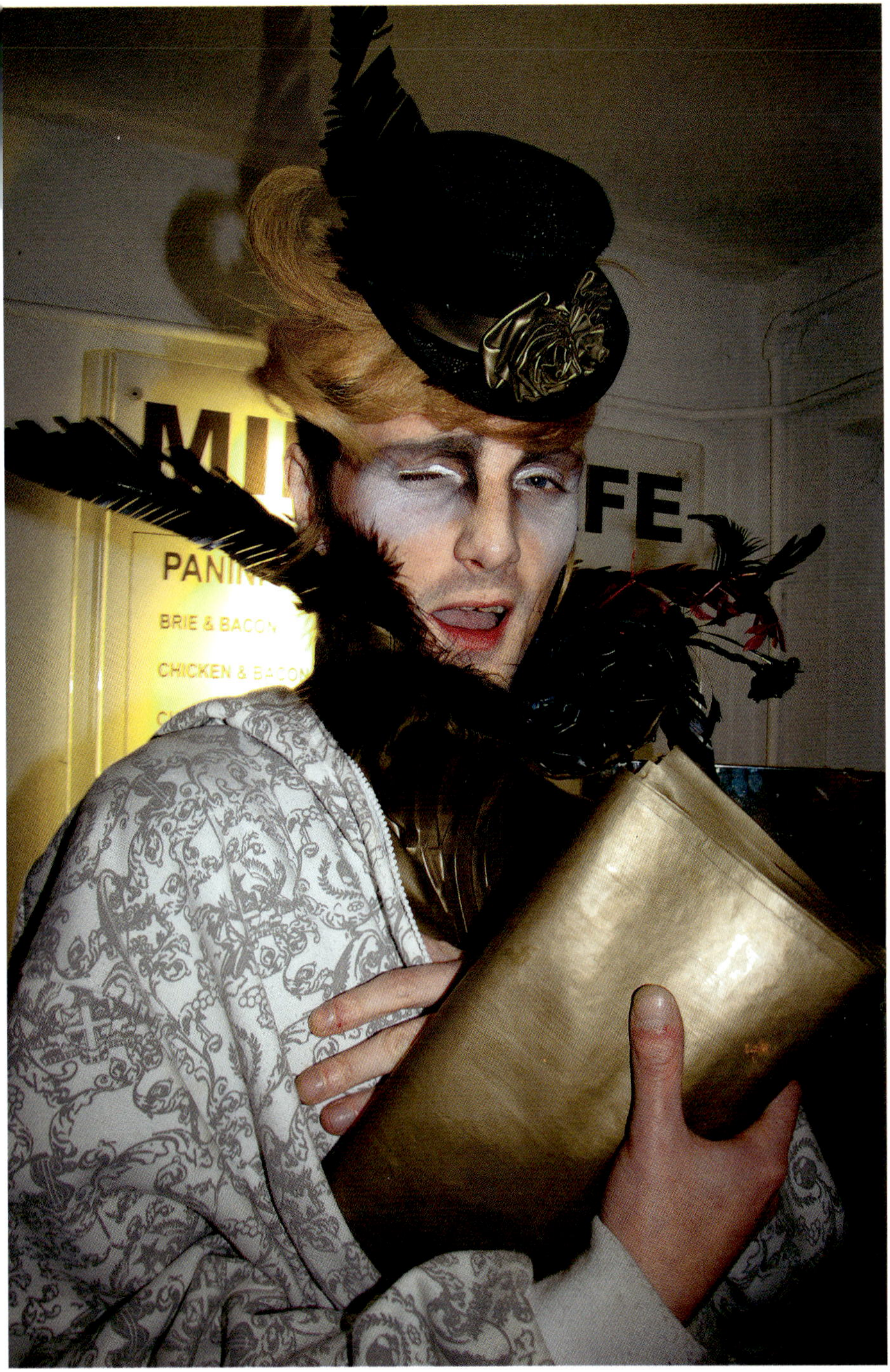

Wearable Art@Egg – Sept 2010

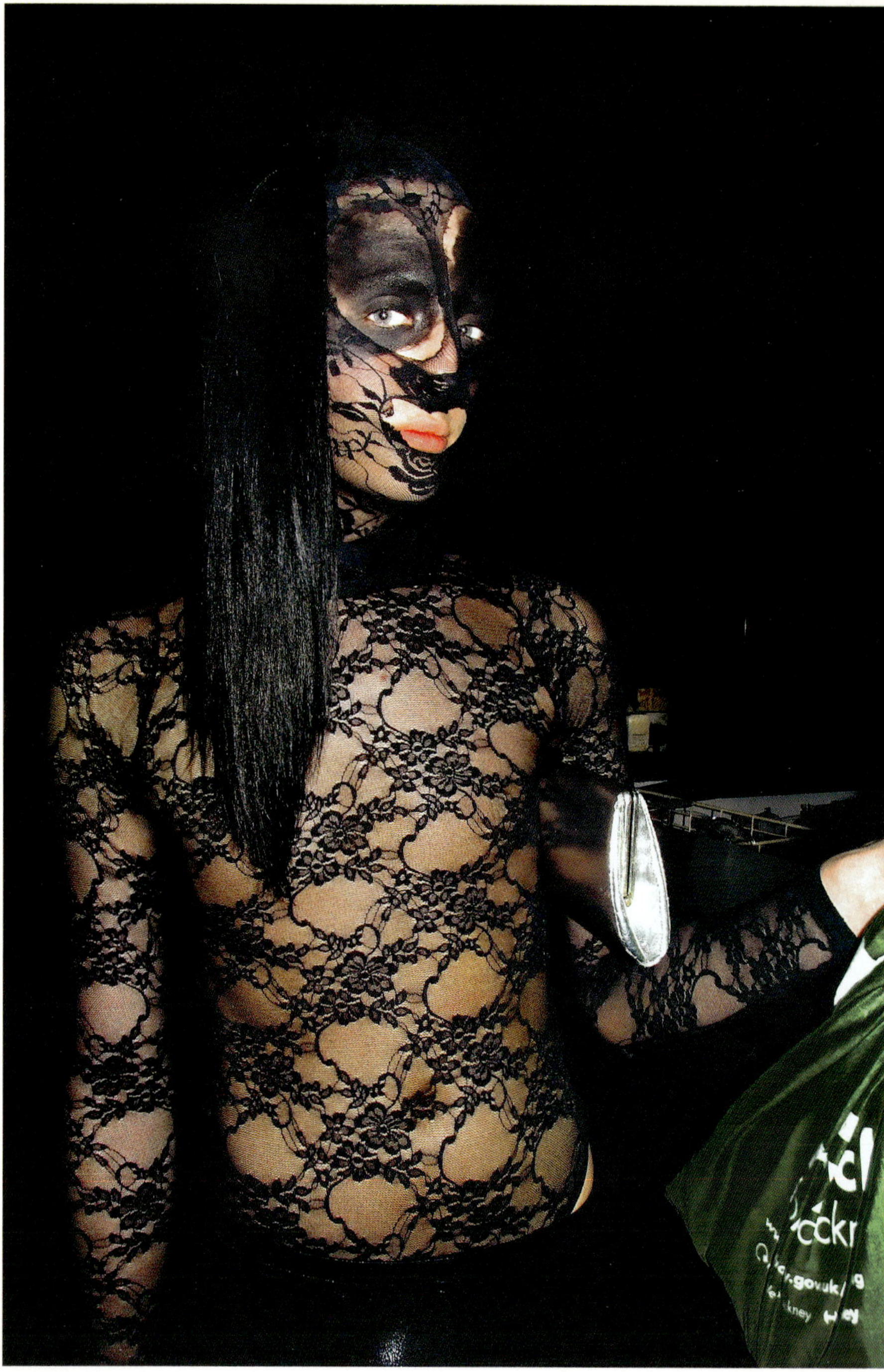

GutterBall – Oct 2010

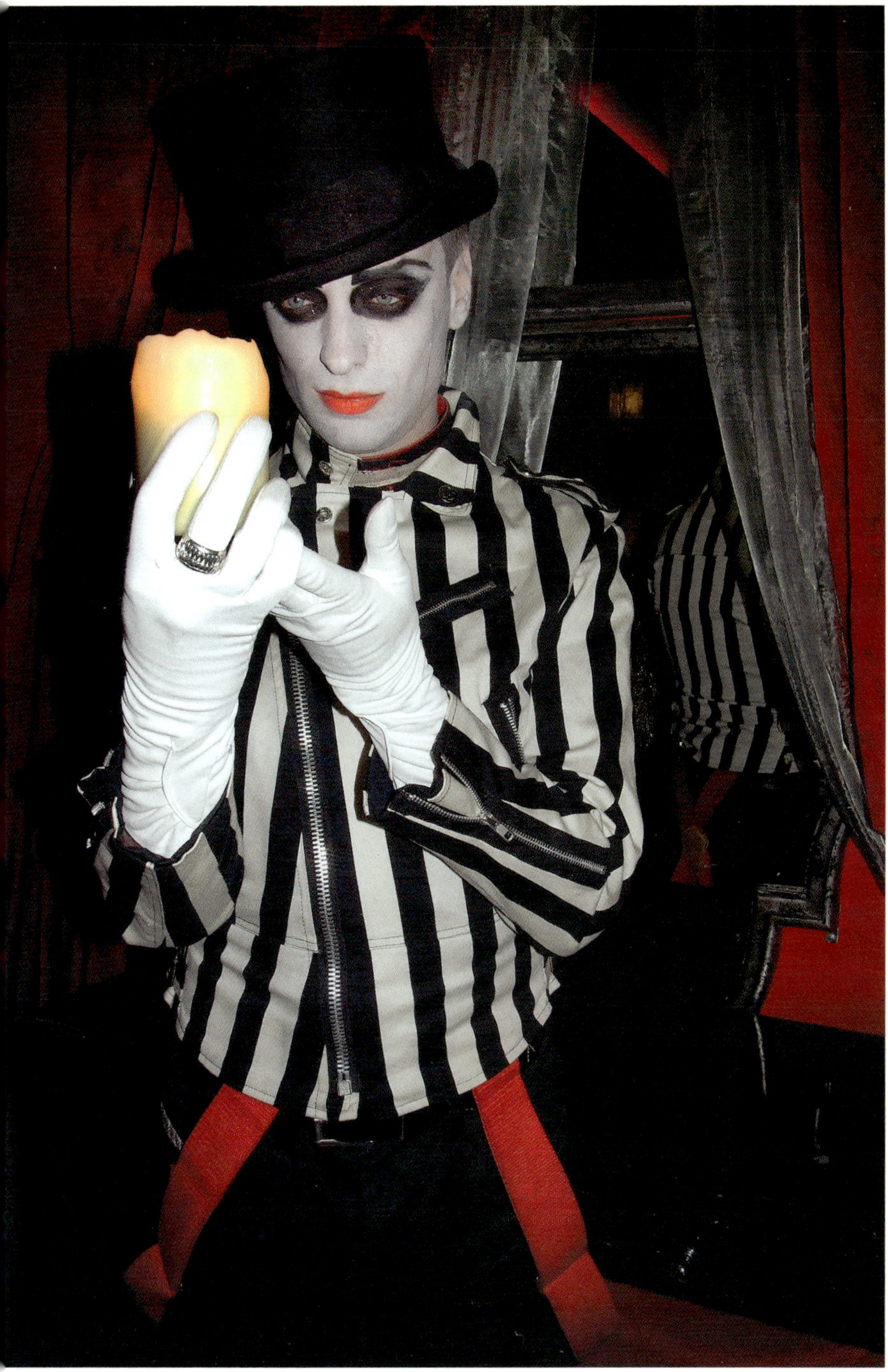

Shabba Dabba Da – Nov 2010

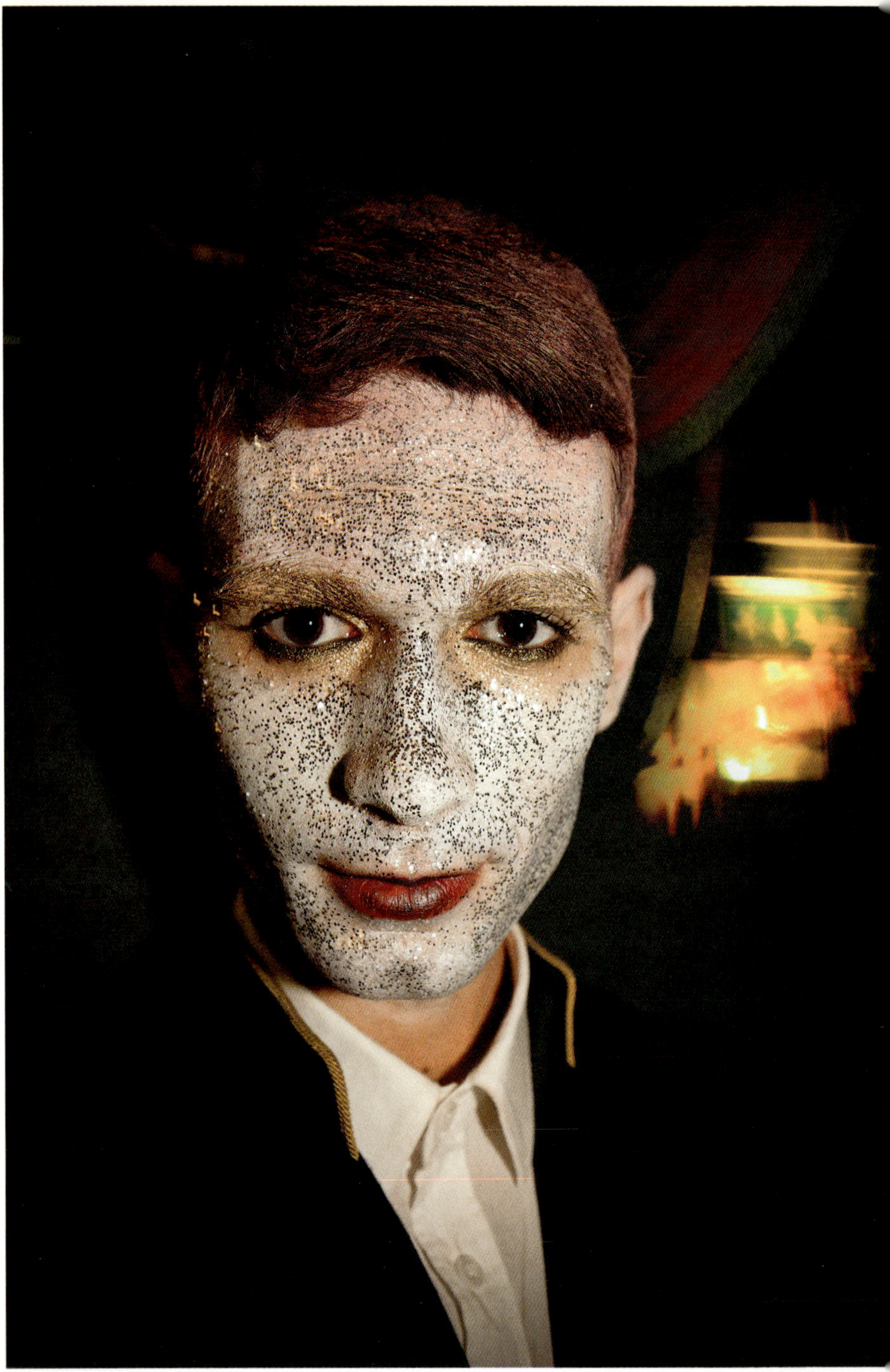

Circus@Paramount – April 2010

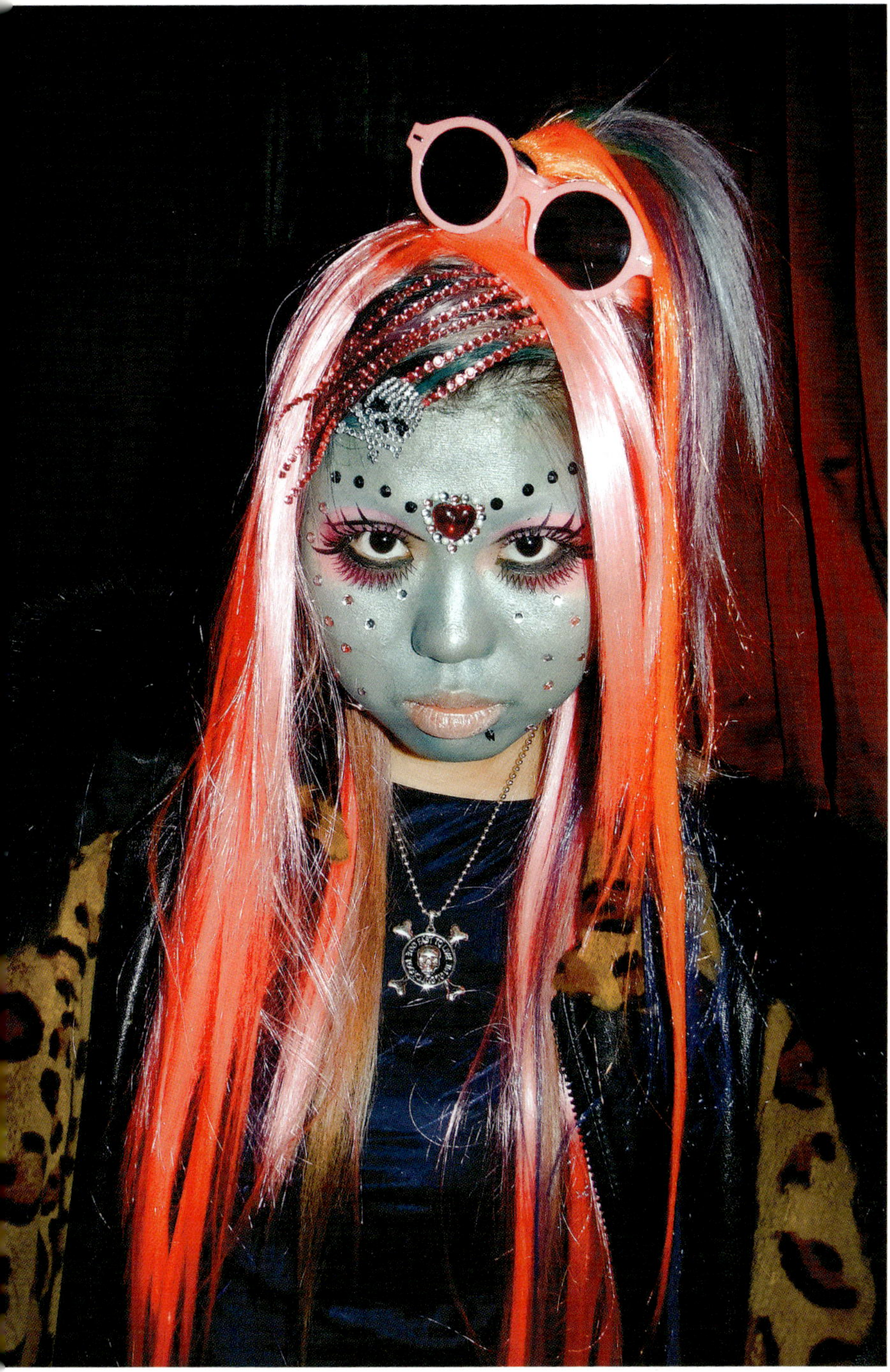

Shabba Dabba Da – Nov 2010

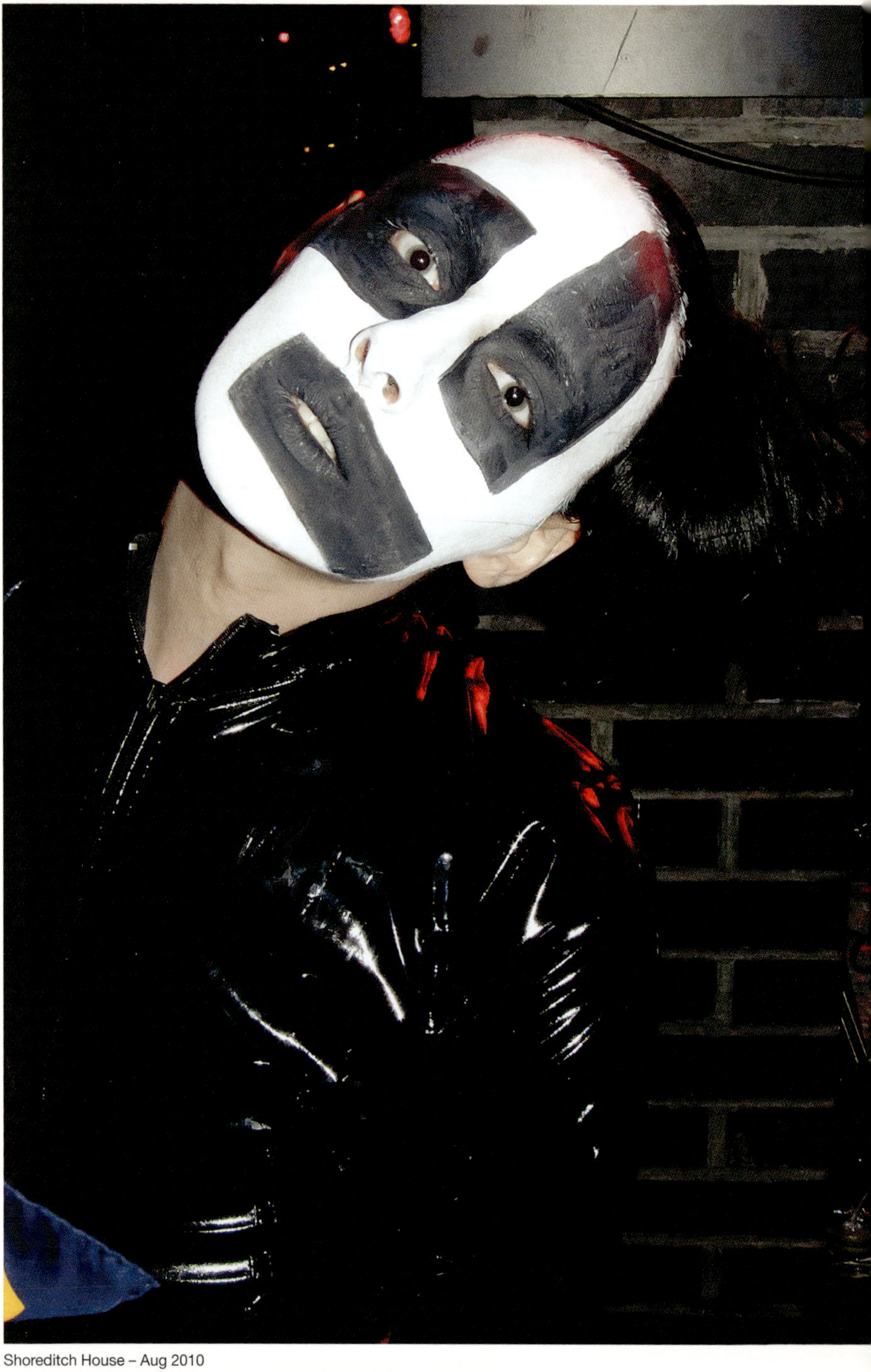
Shoreditch House – Aug 2010

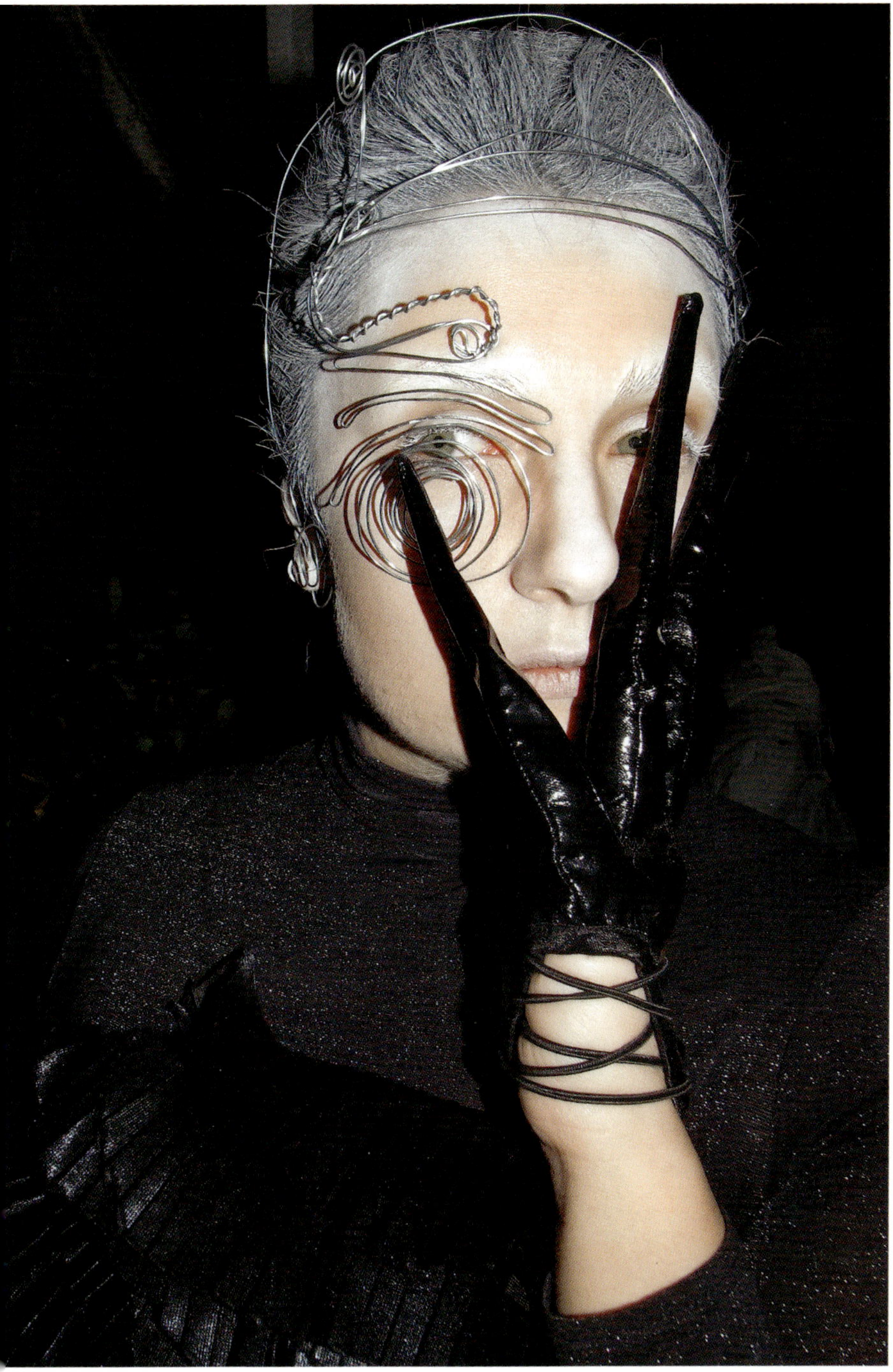

Caligula – Sept 2010

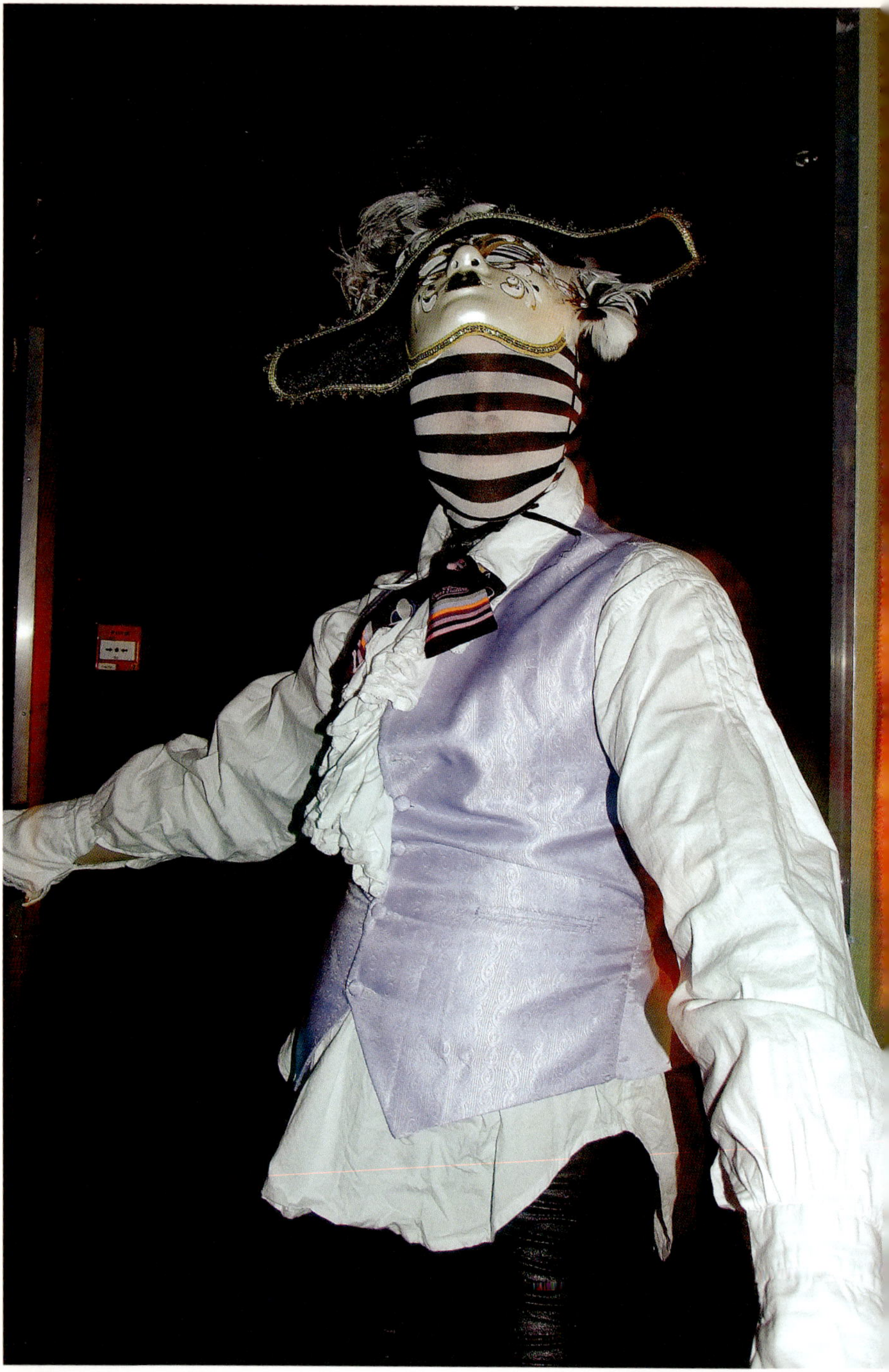

Your Mum's House – March 2010

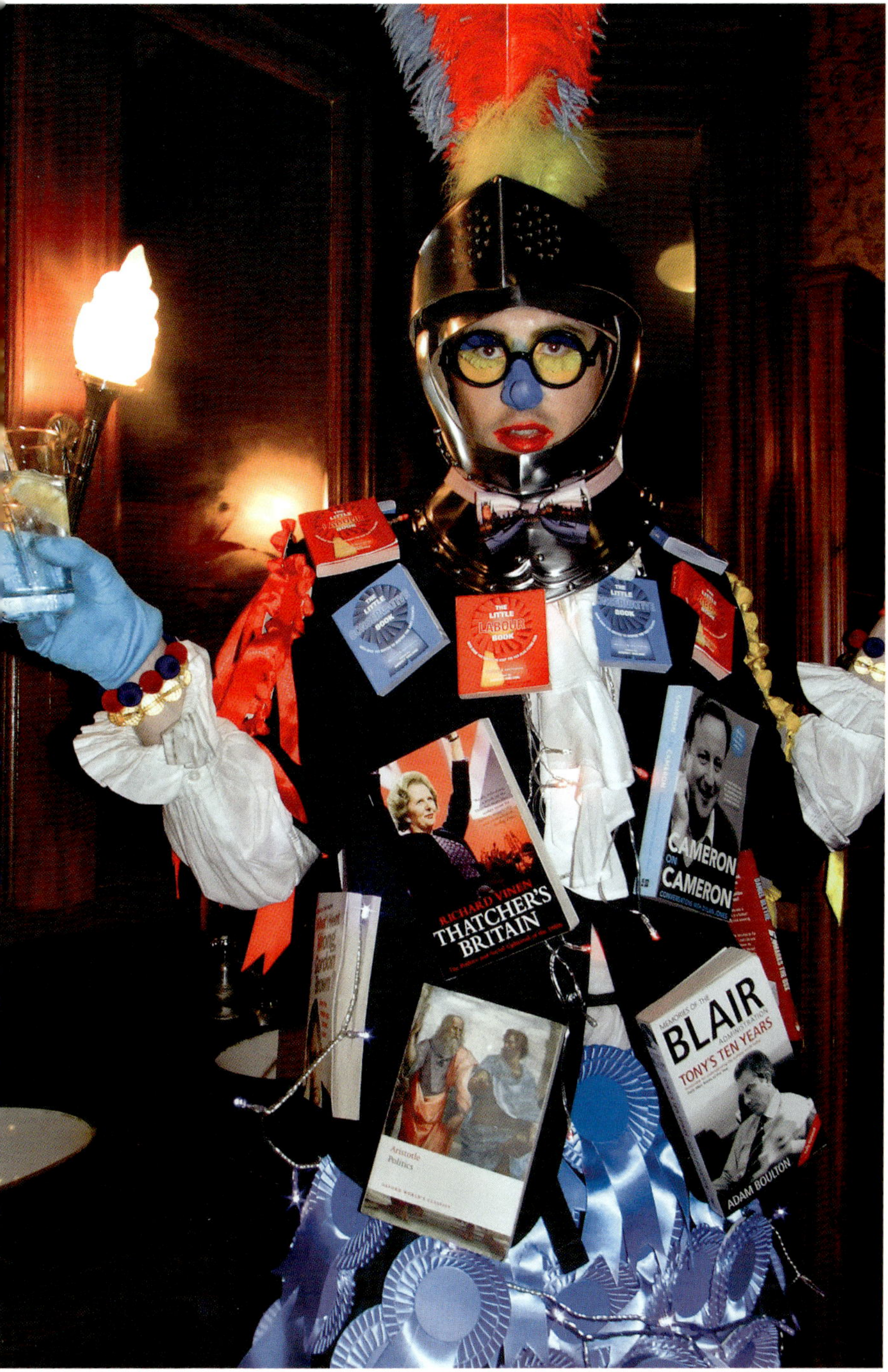

Mayday@Home House – May 2010

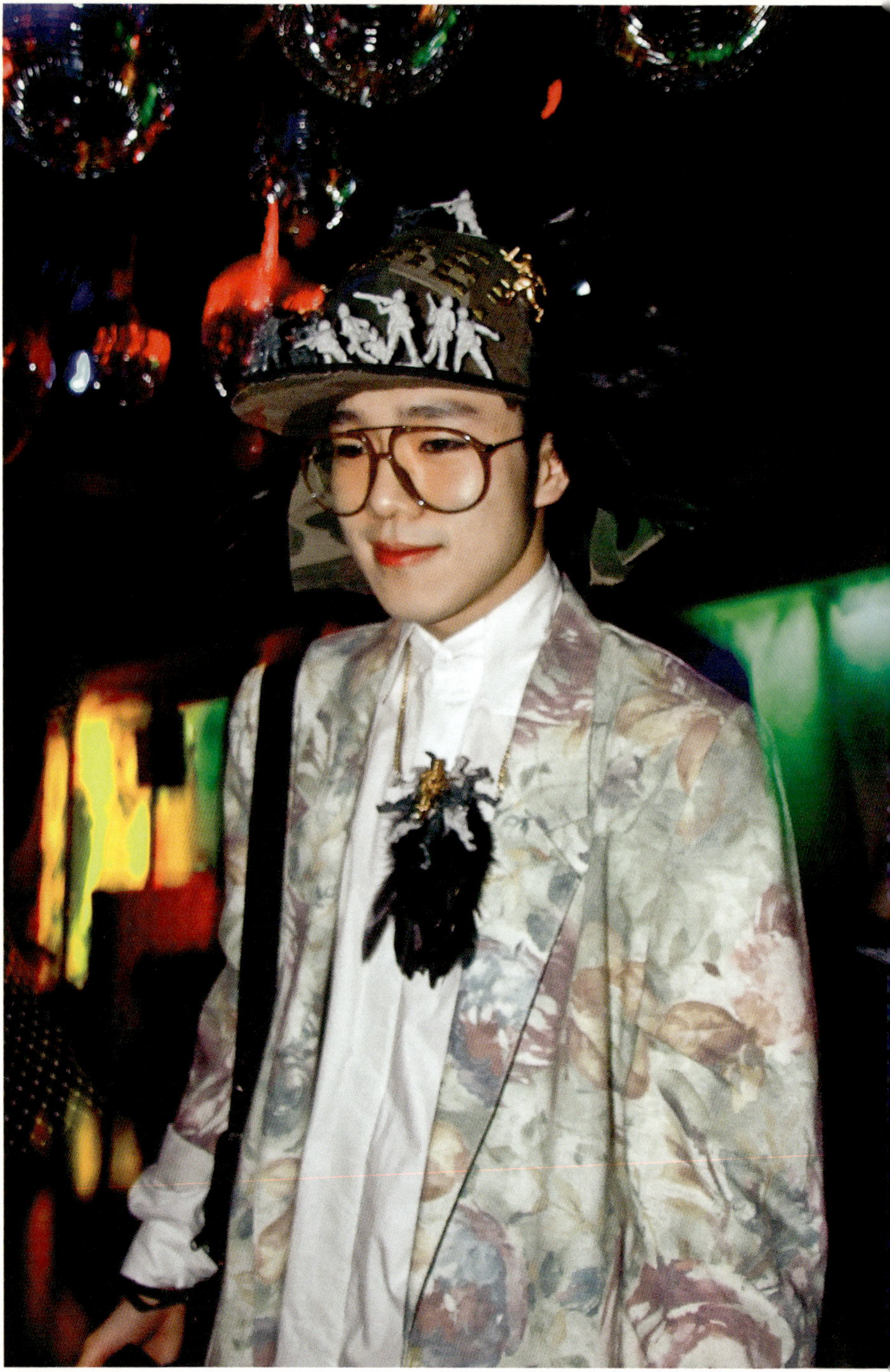

Your Mum's House – Feb 2010

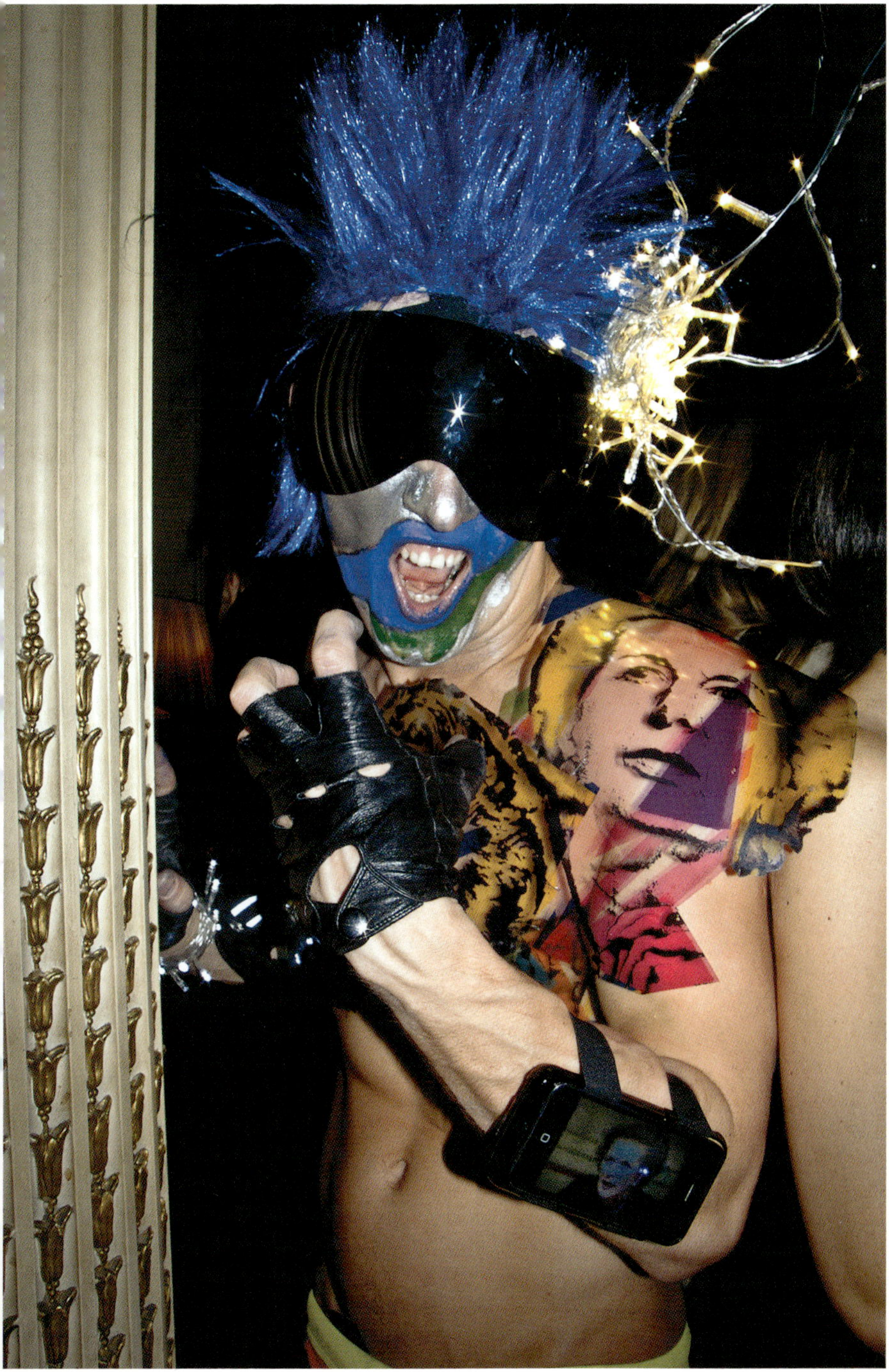

Mayday@Home House – May 2010

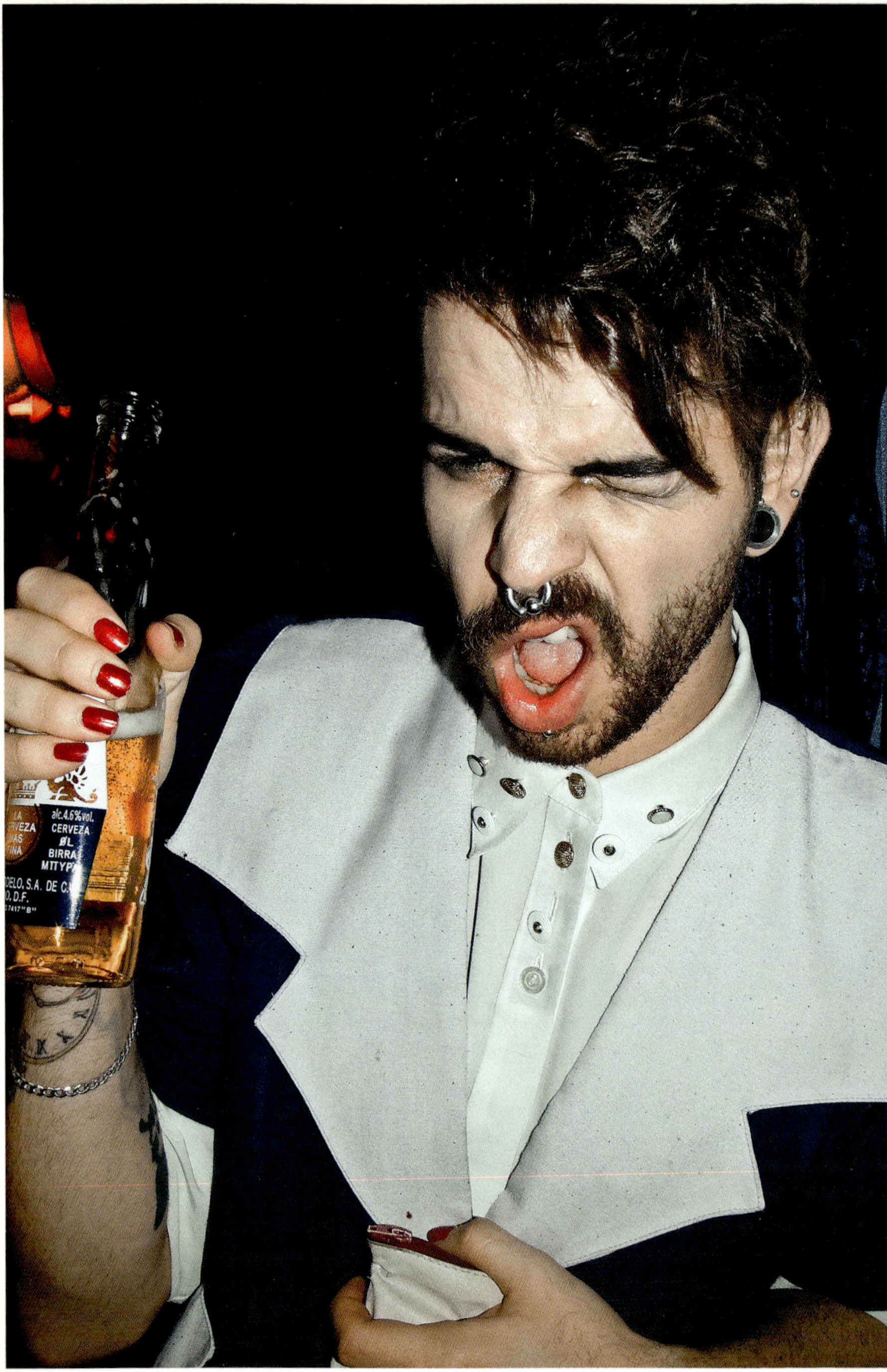

Paradise@Cafe De Paris – Sept 2010

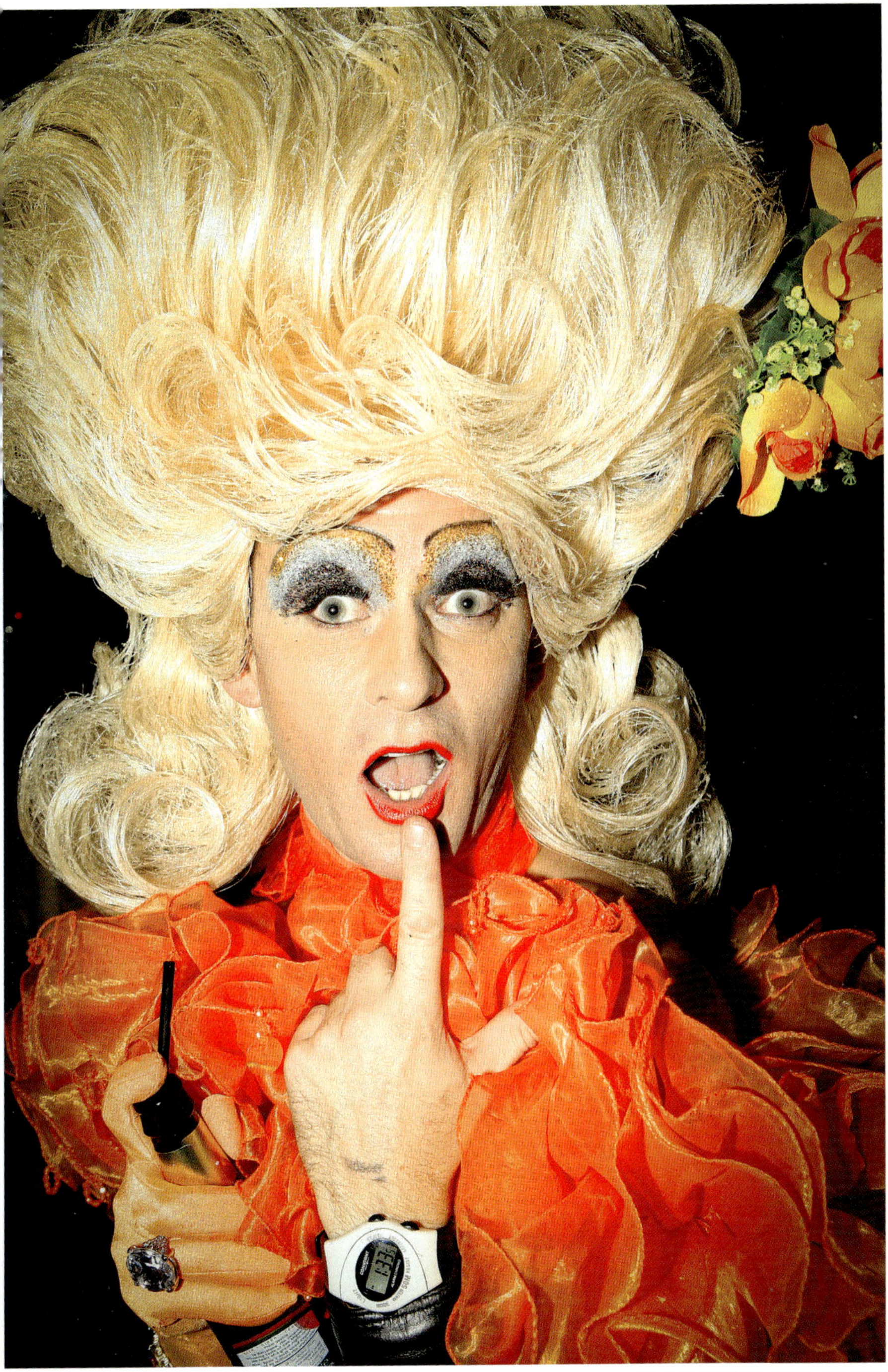

Wig Party@Cafe De Paris – Oct 2007

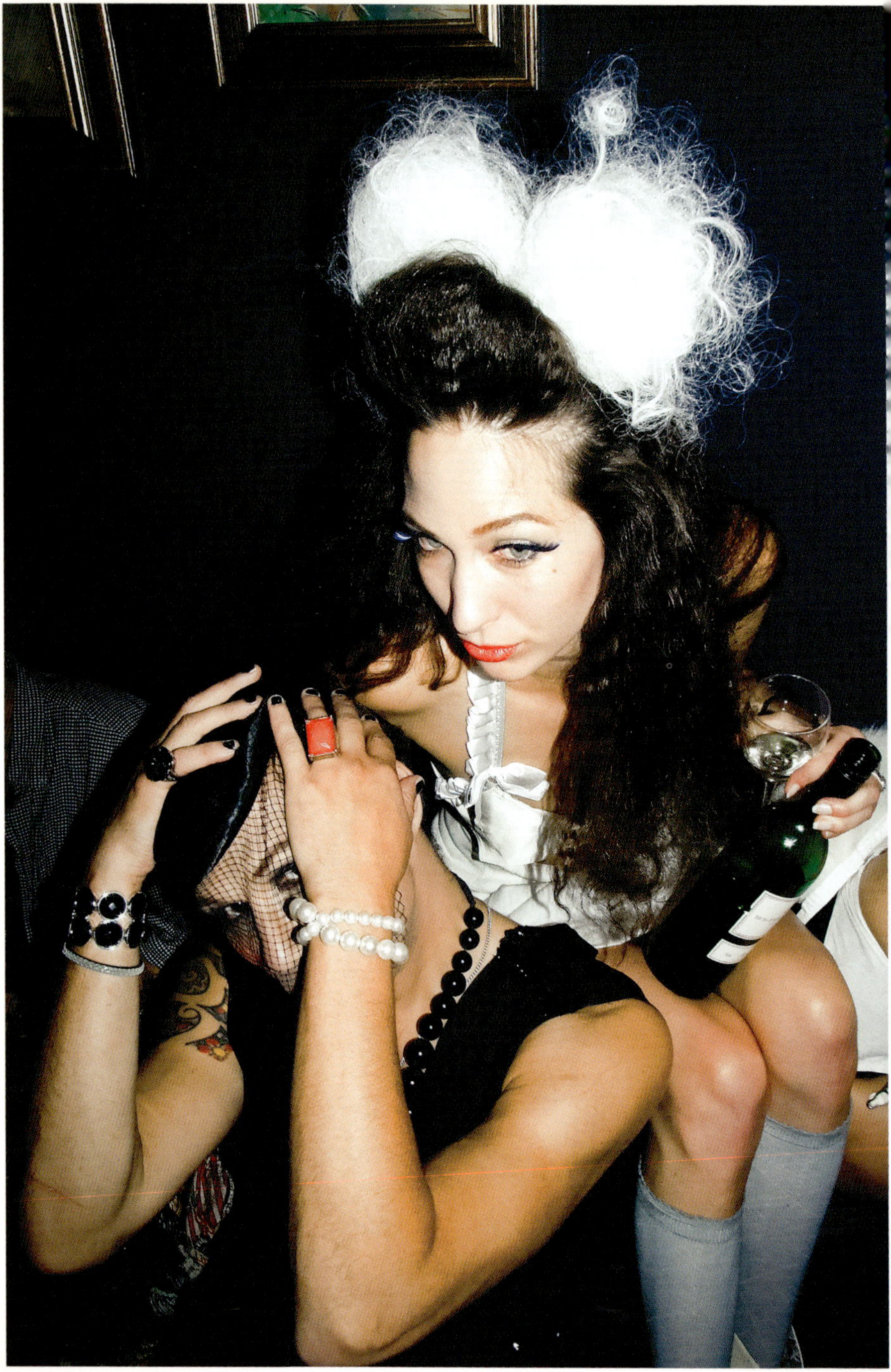
Paradise@Cafe De Paris – Sept 2010

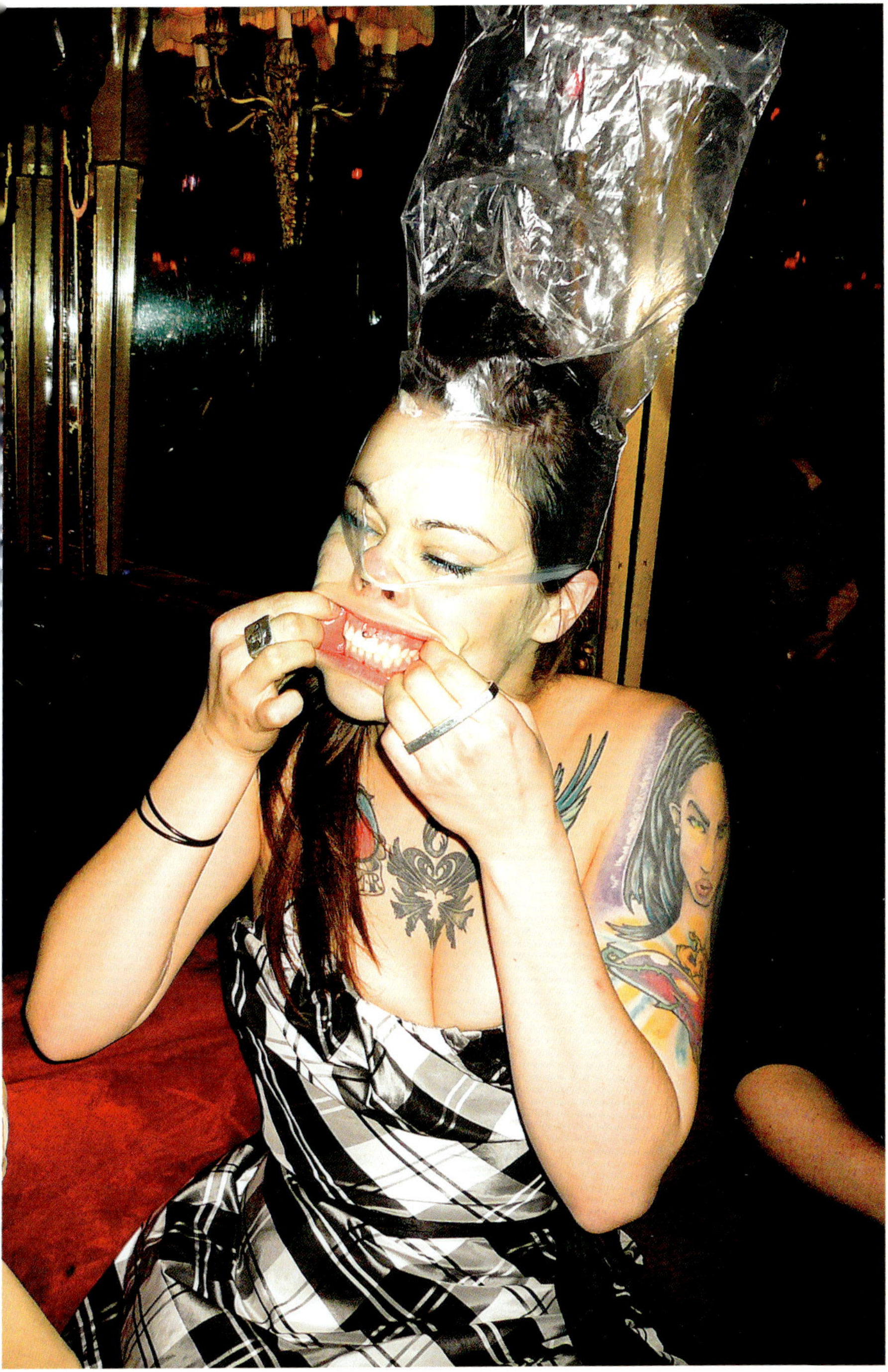

Cafe Royal – Sept 2005

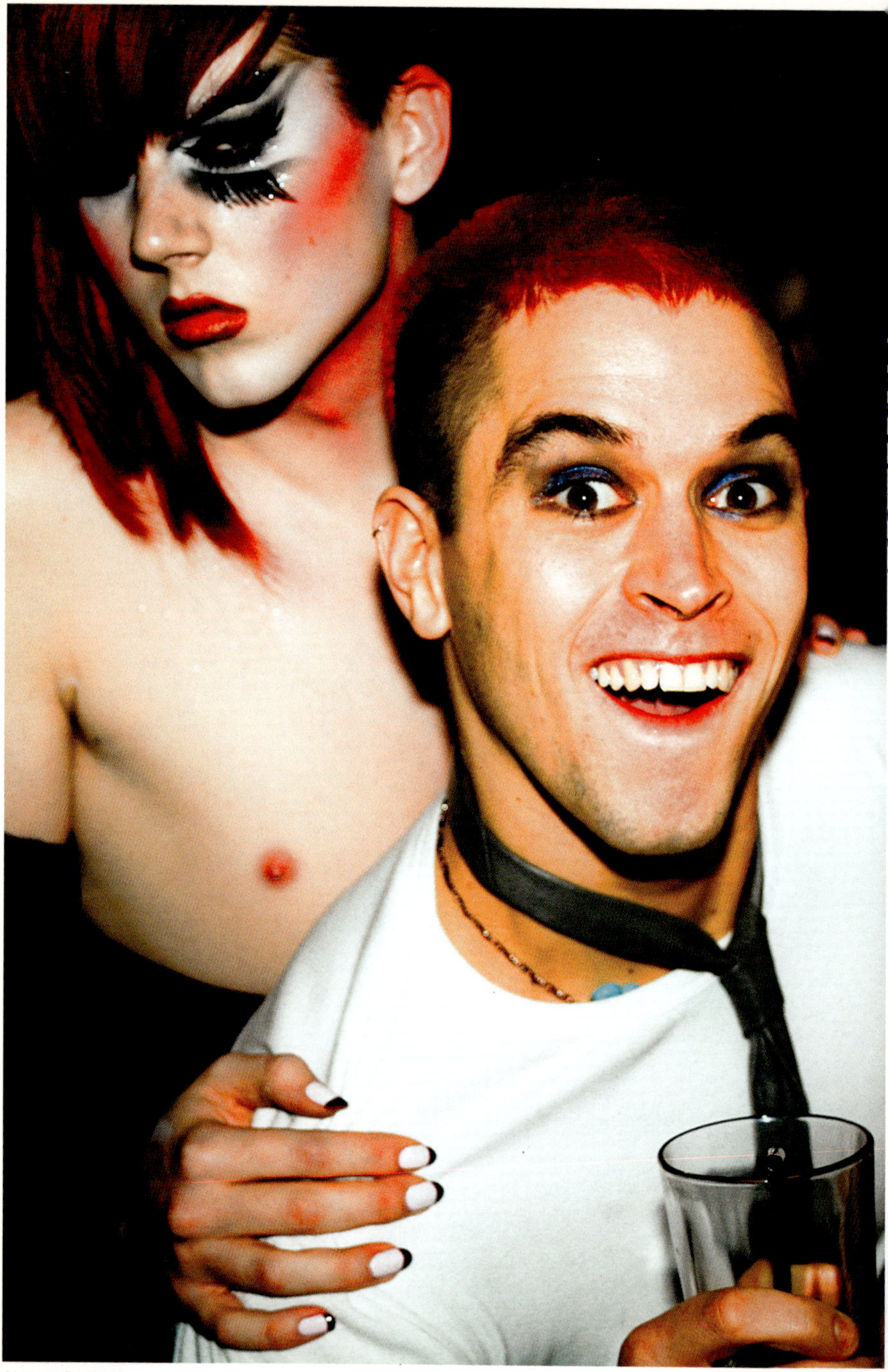

Circus – Oct 2006

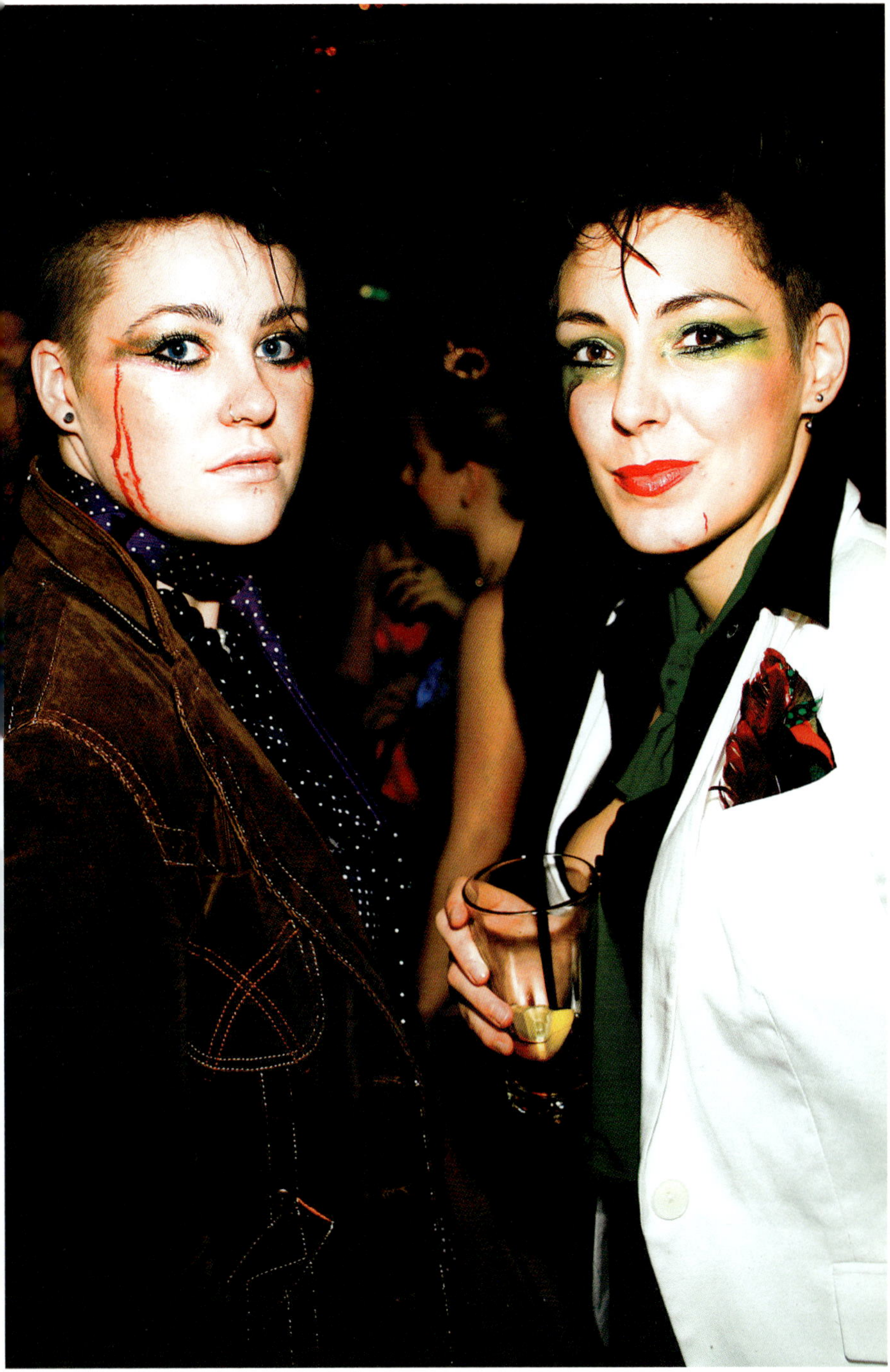

Circus – May 2007

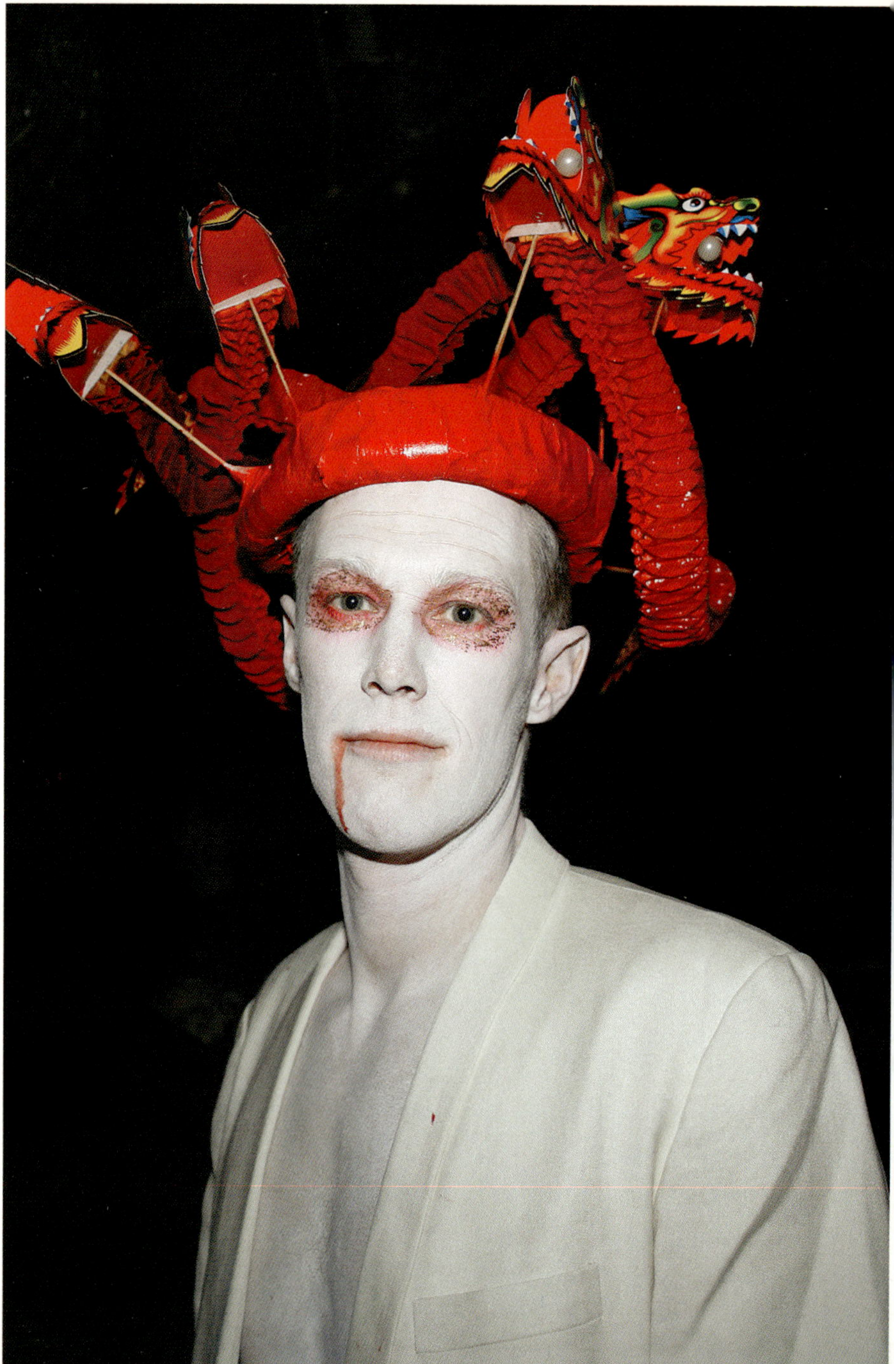

Circus – Oct 2006

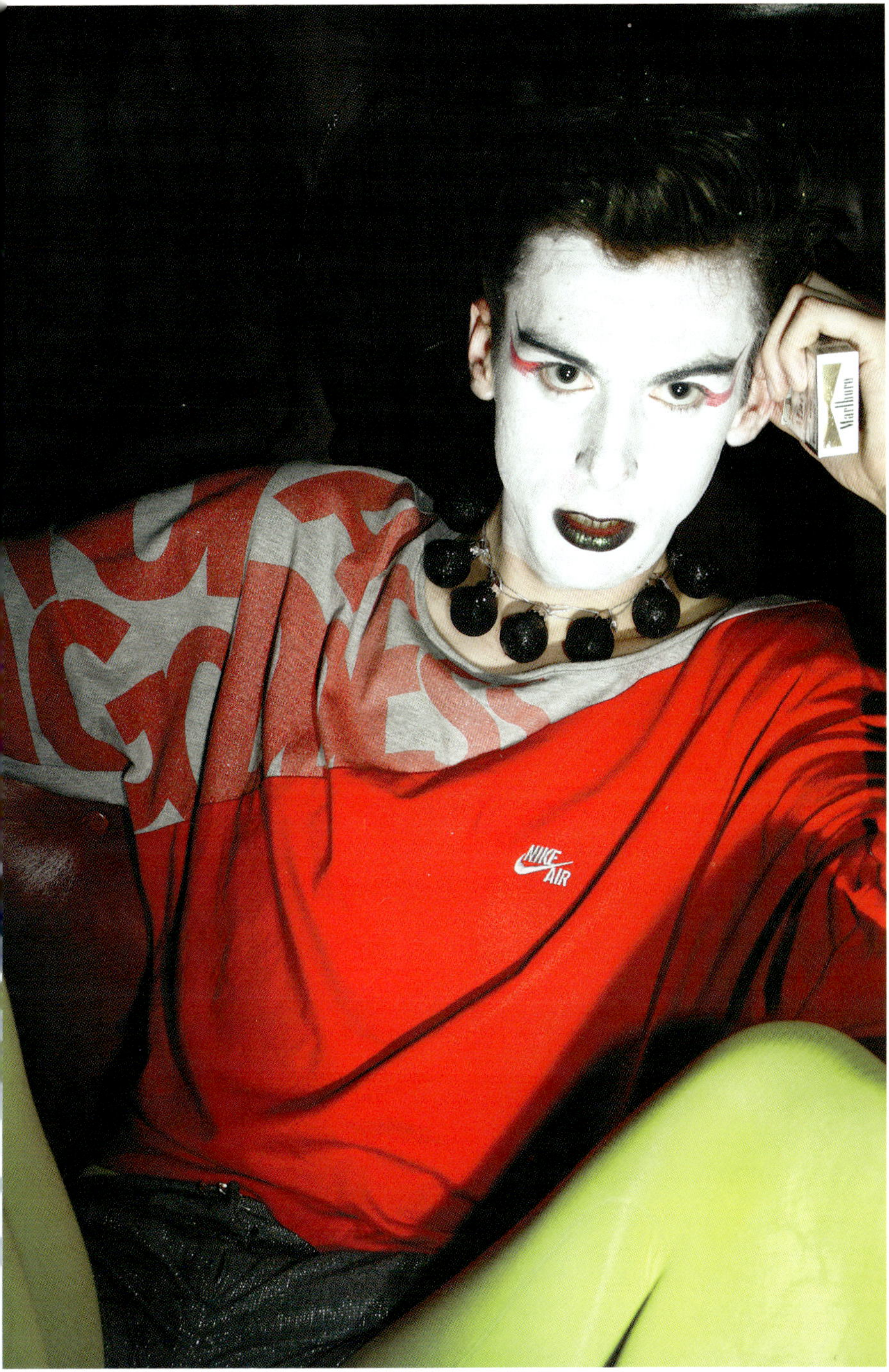

Too2Much – Apr 2007

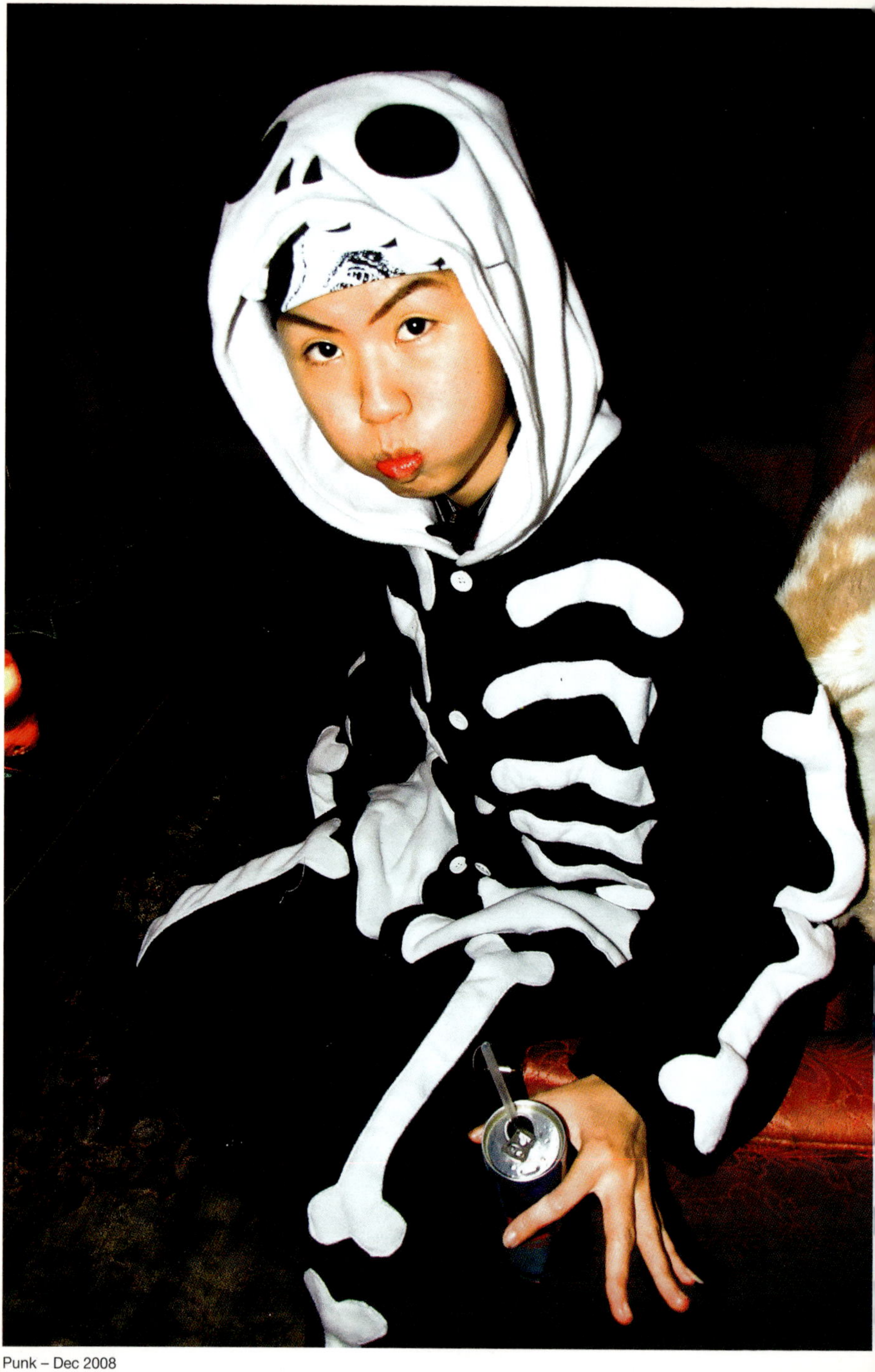

Punk – Dec 2008

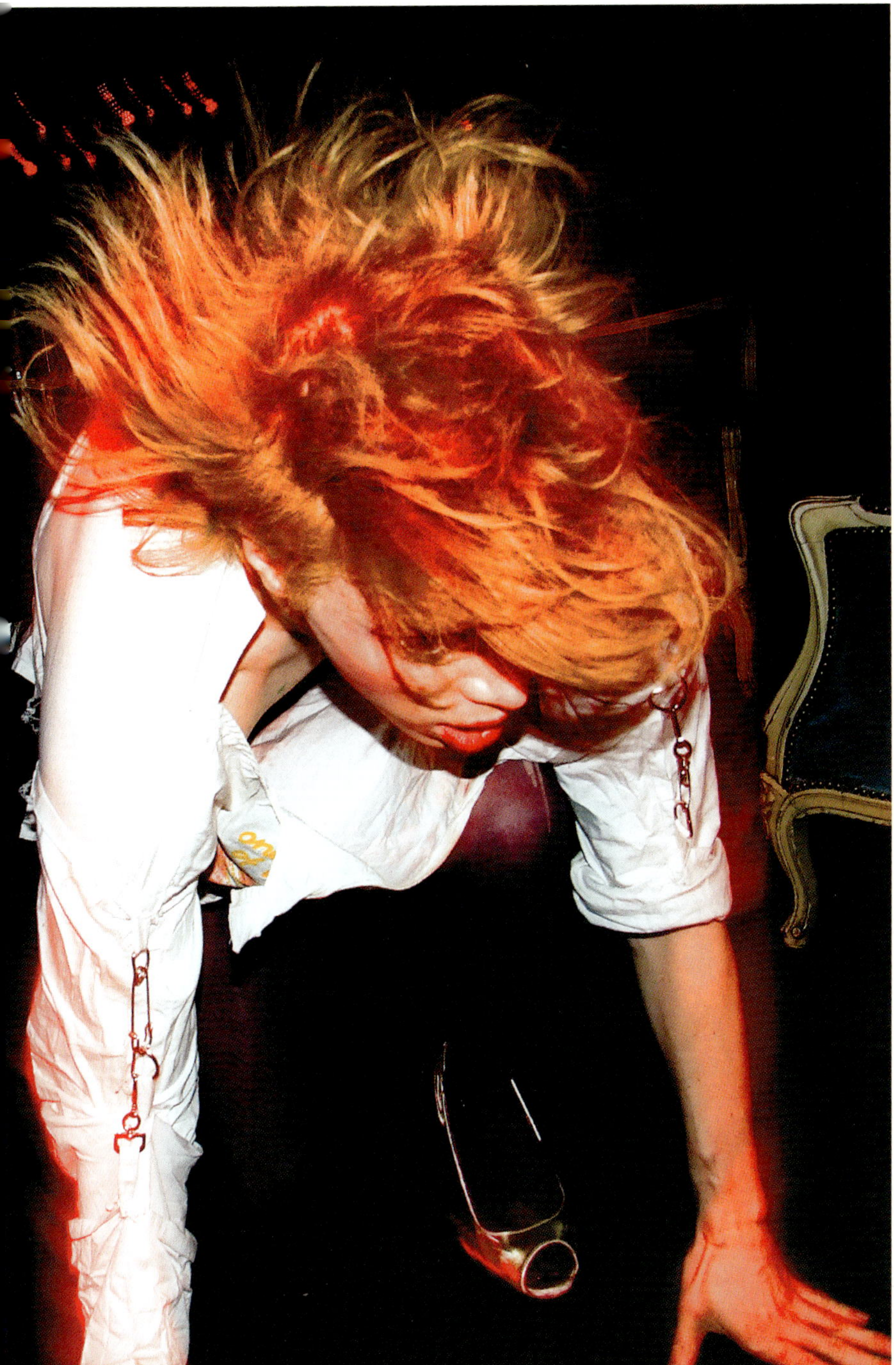

Punk – Jan 2009

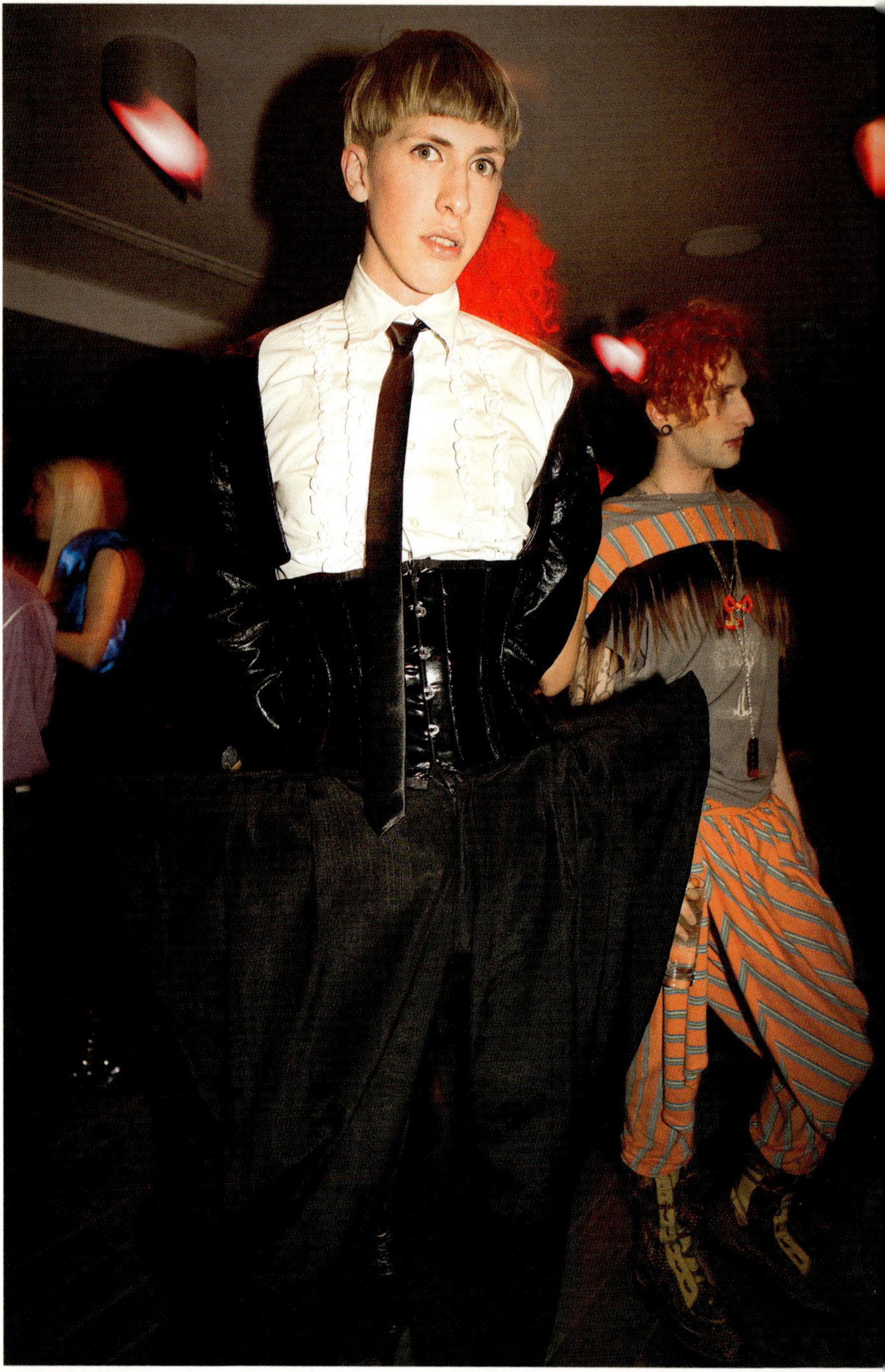

Circus – April 2010

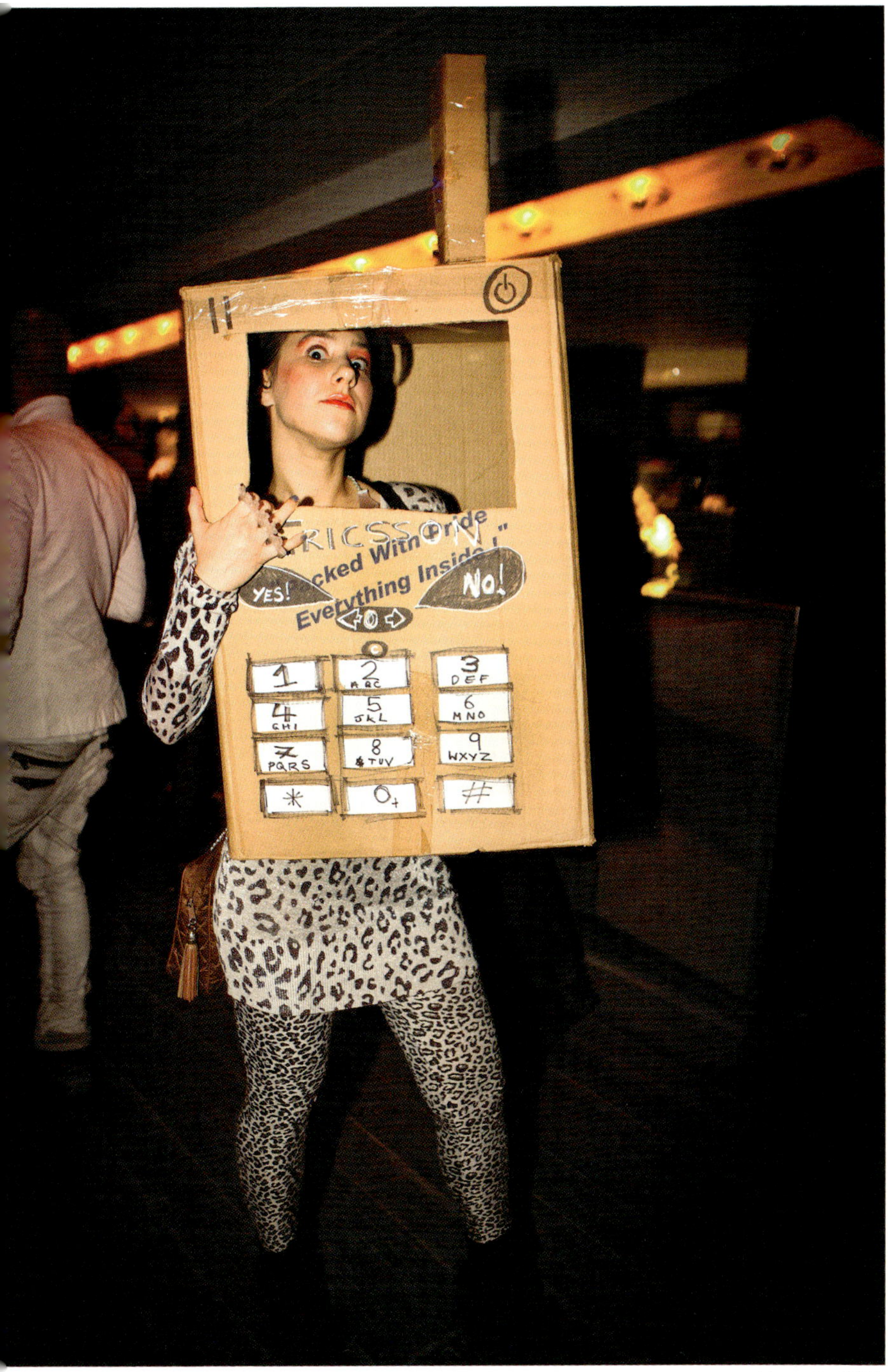

Circus – April 2010

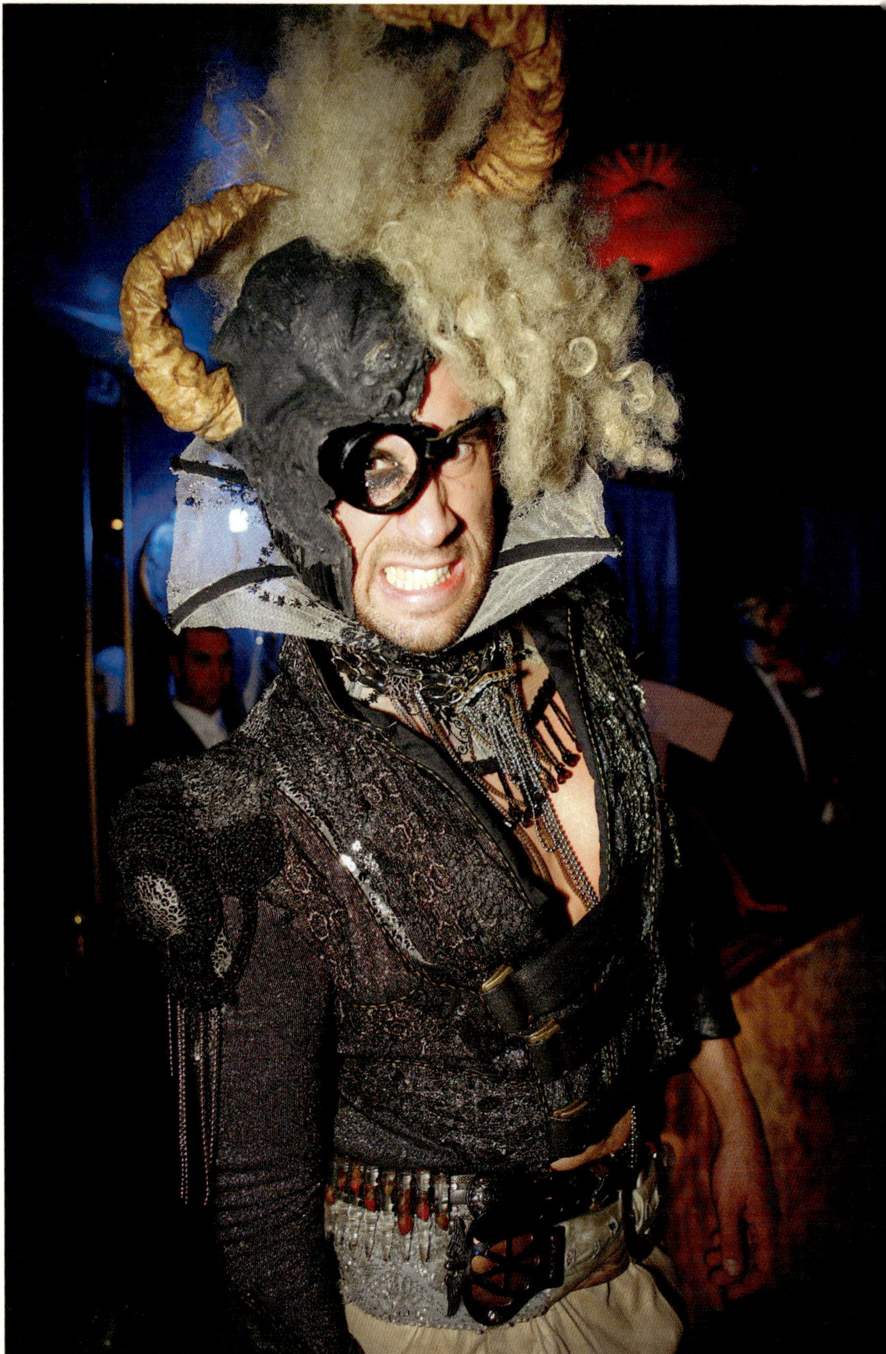

Wig Party@Cafe De Paris – Oct 2010

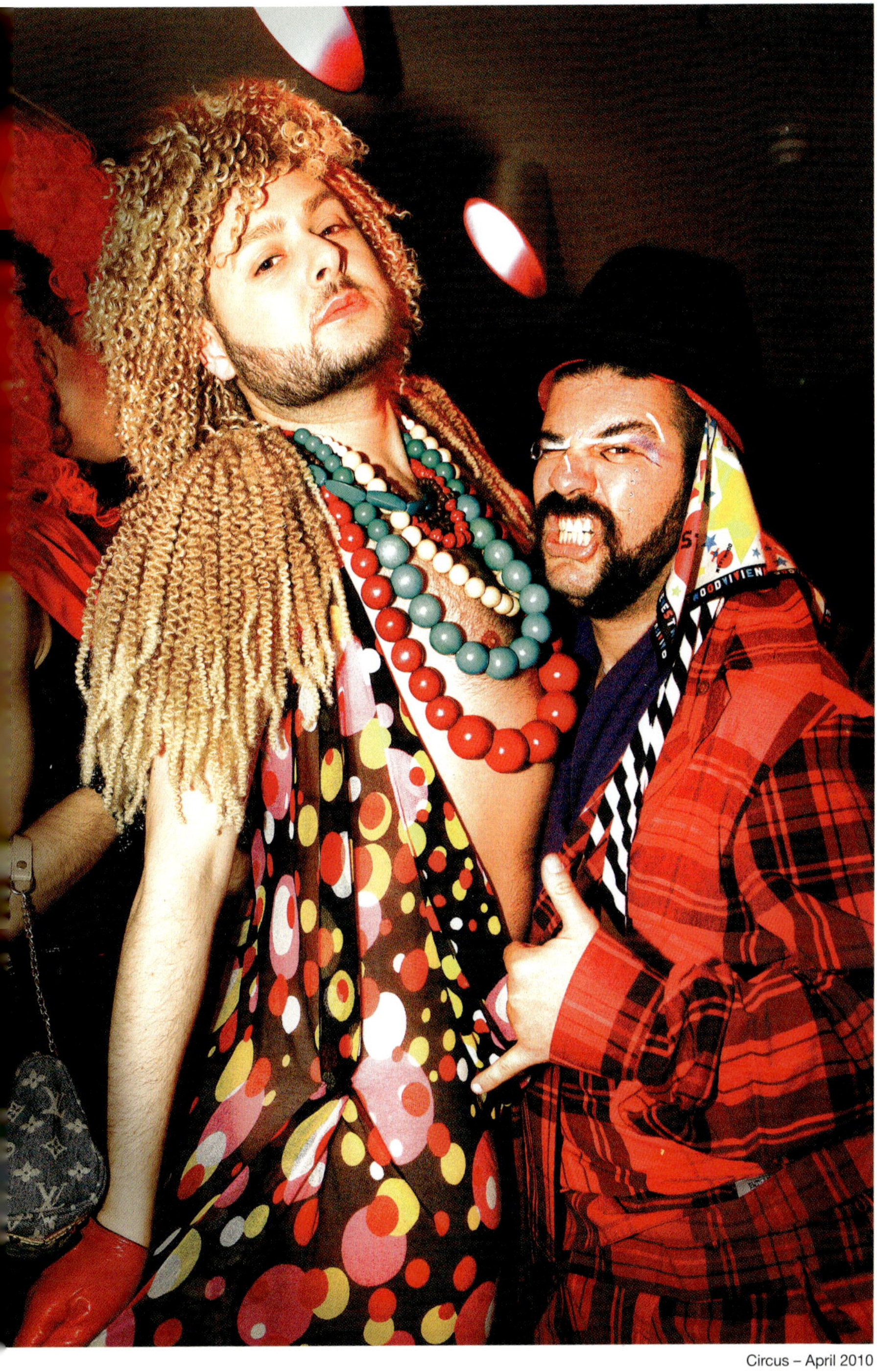

Circus – April 2010

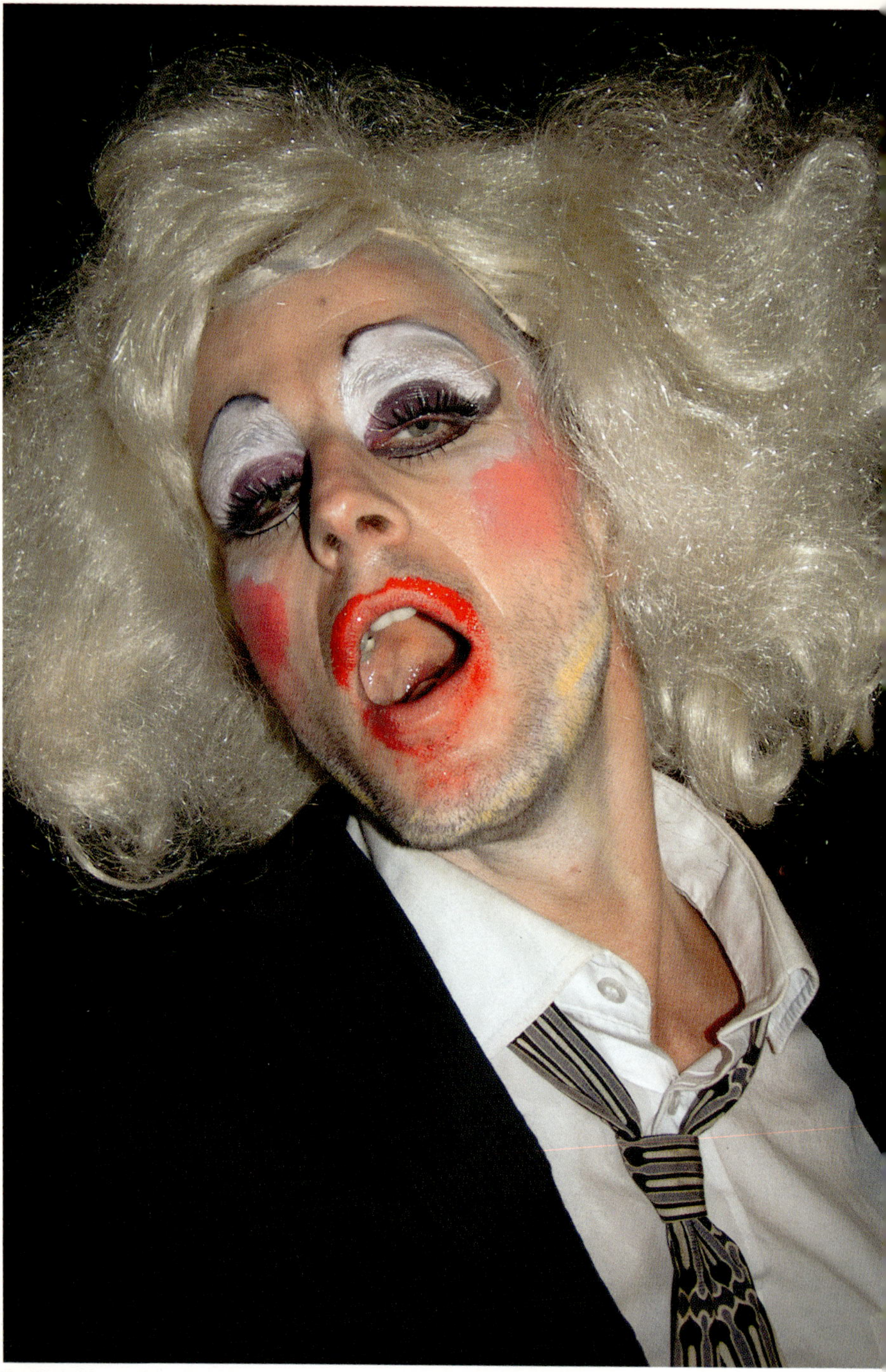

Gay Bingo@SupperClub – April 2010

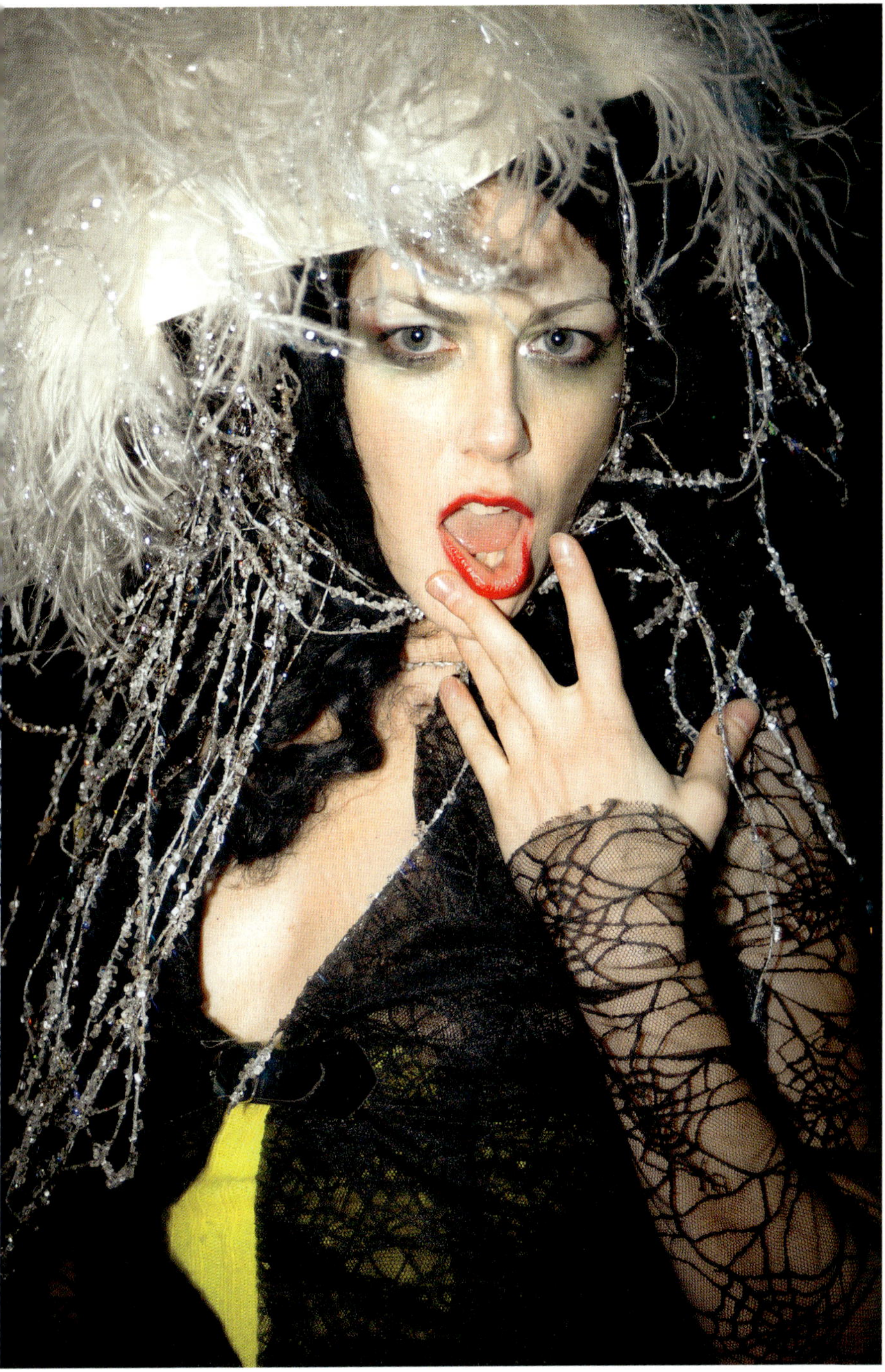

Work@Heaven – June 2008

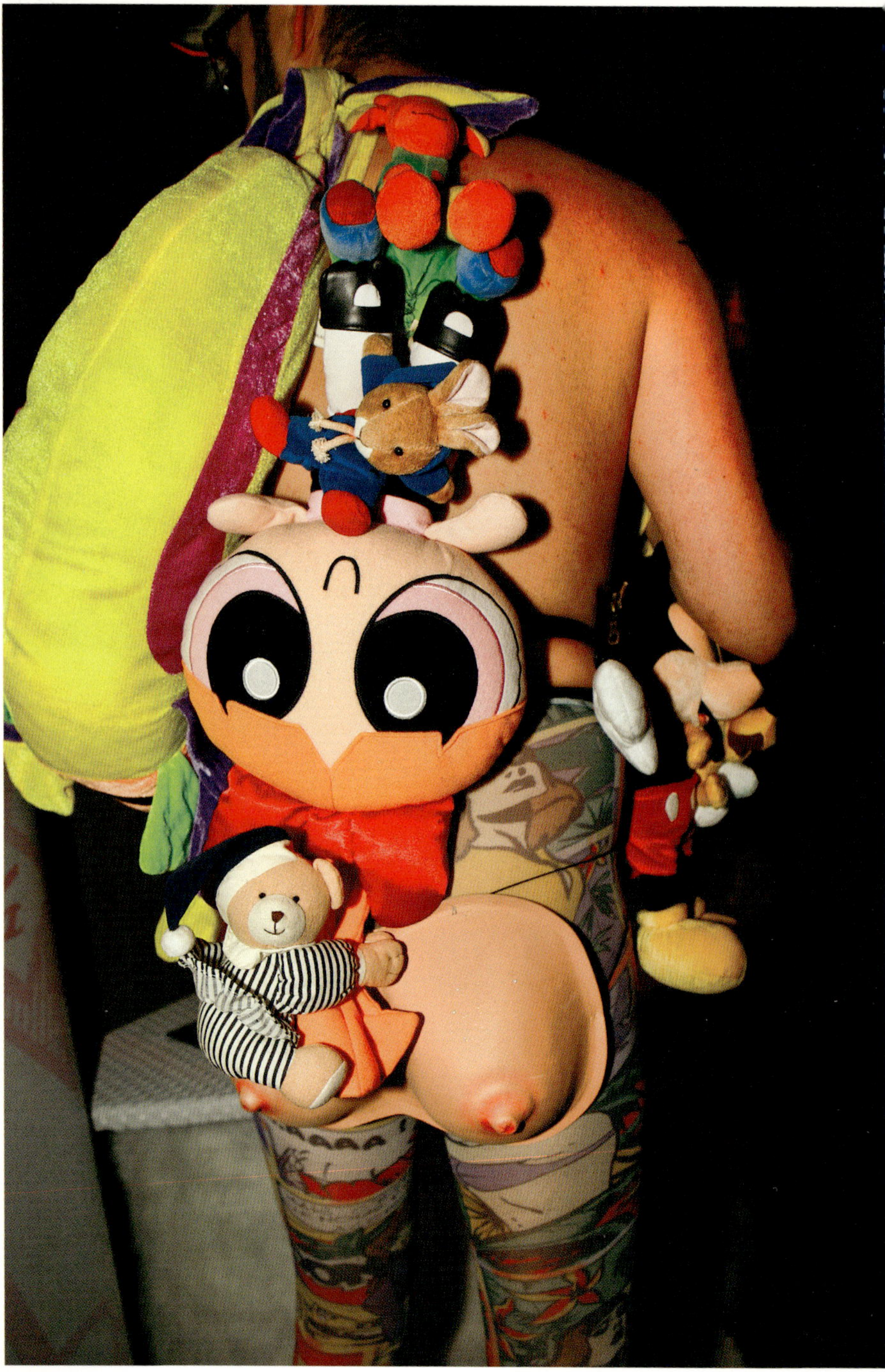

Wig Party@Cafe de Paris – Oct 2010

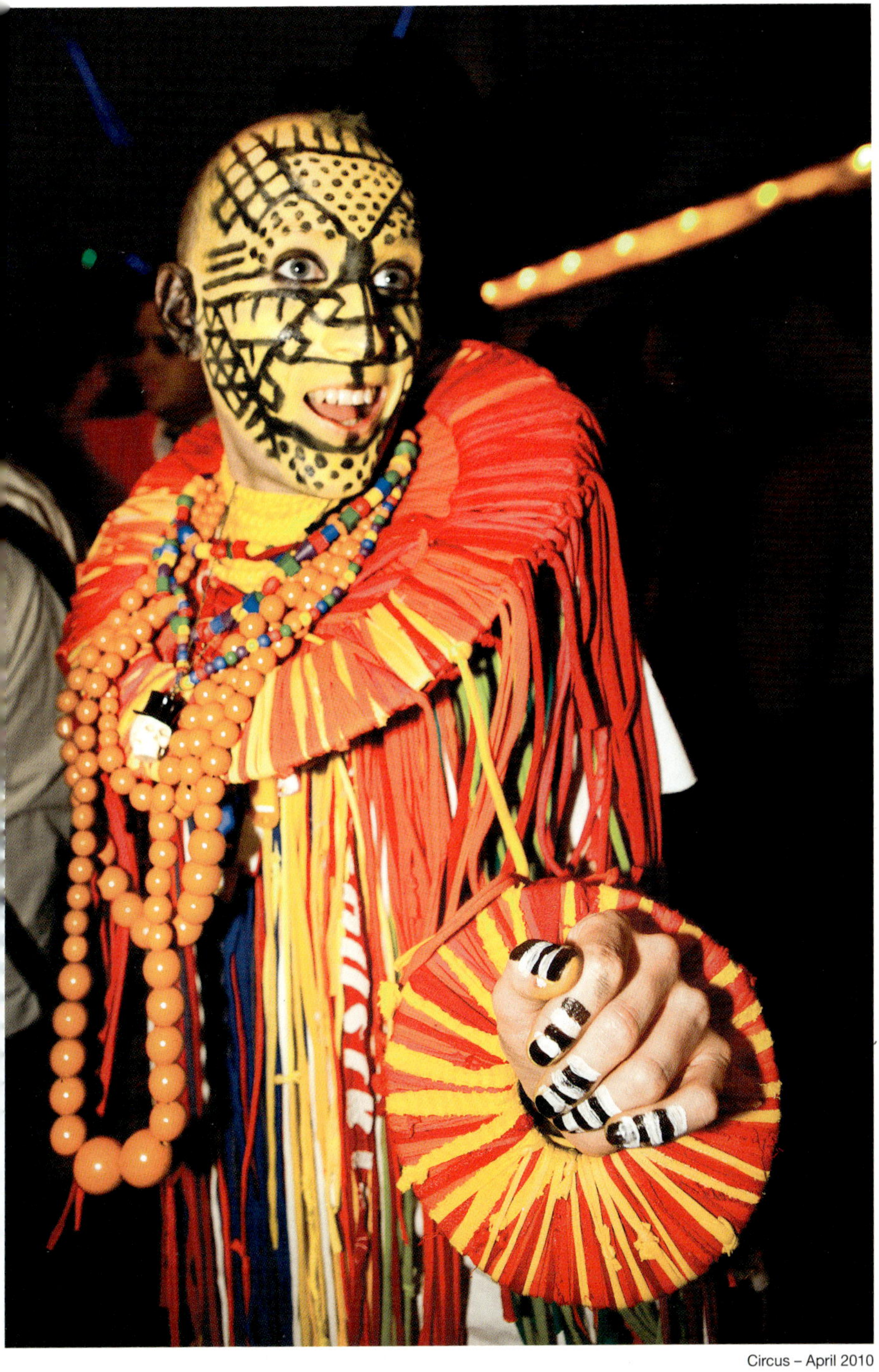

Circus – April 2010

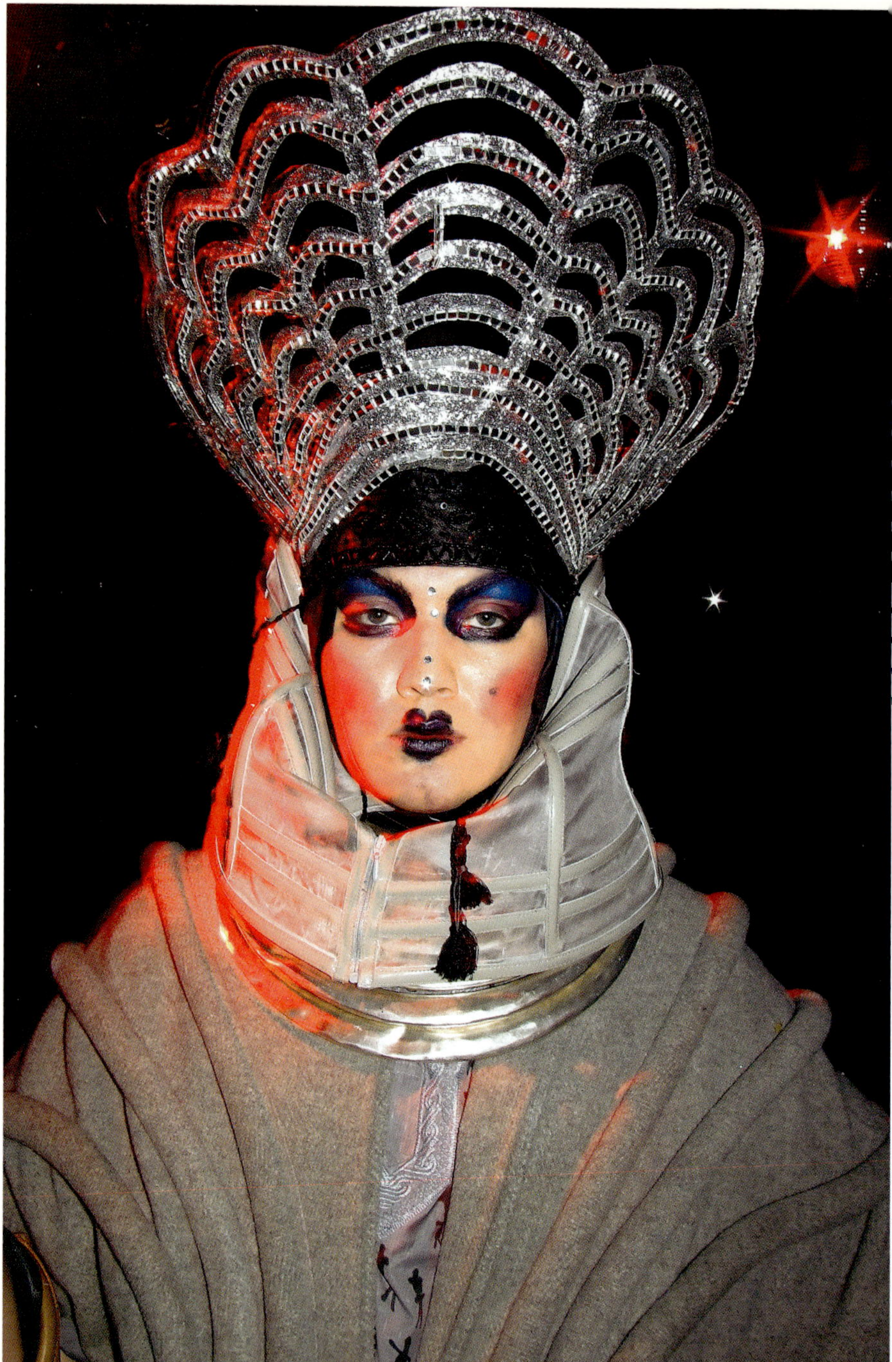

Caligula – Sept 2010

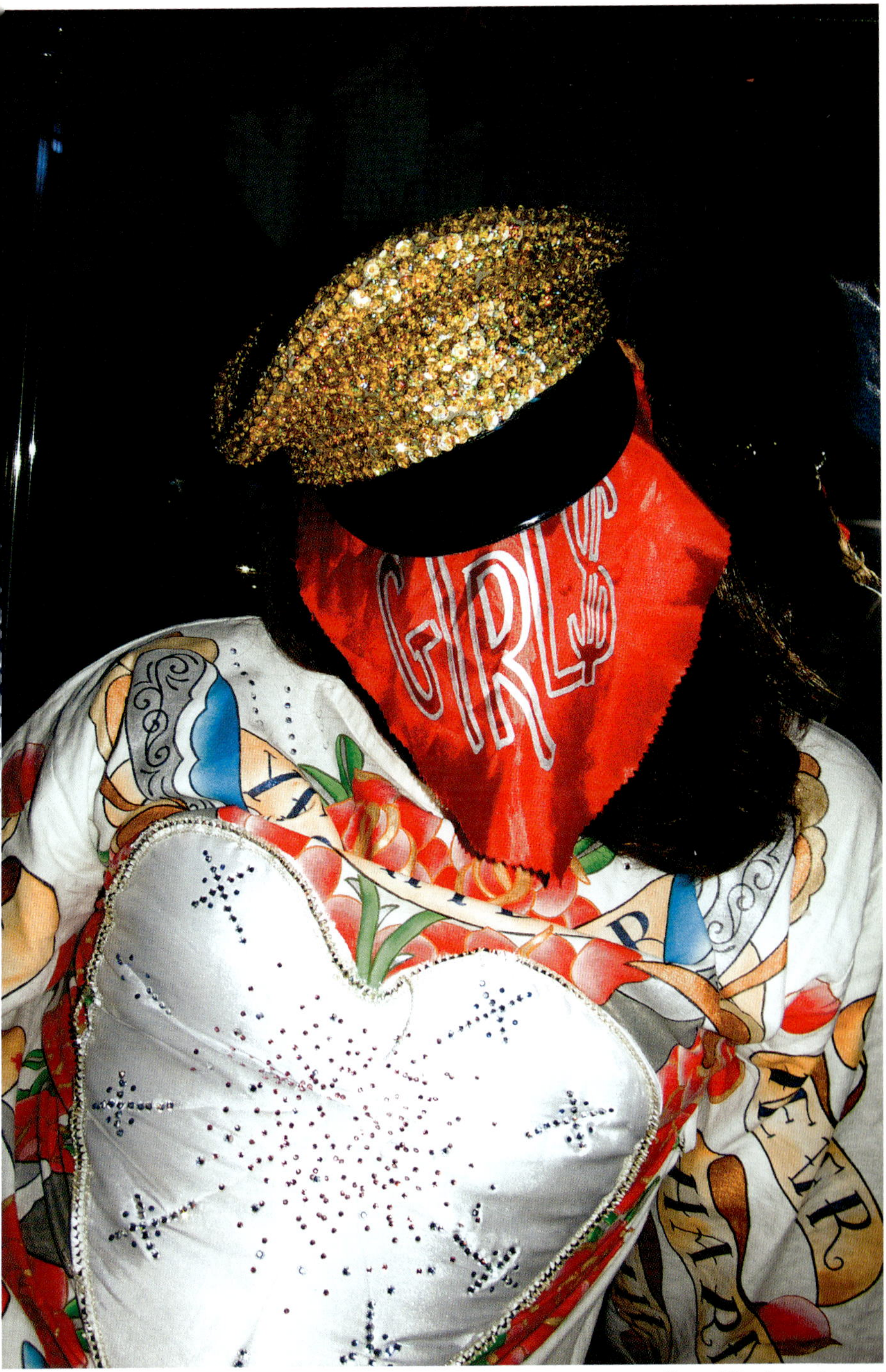

House of Blue Eyes – Sept 2010

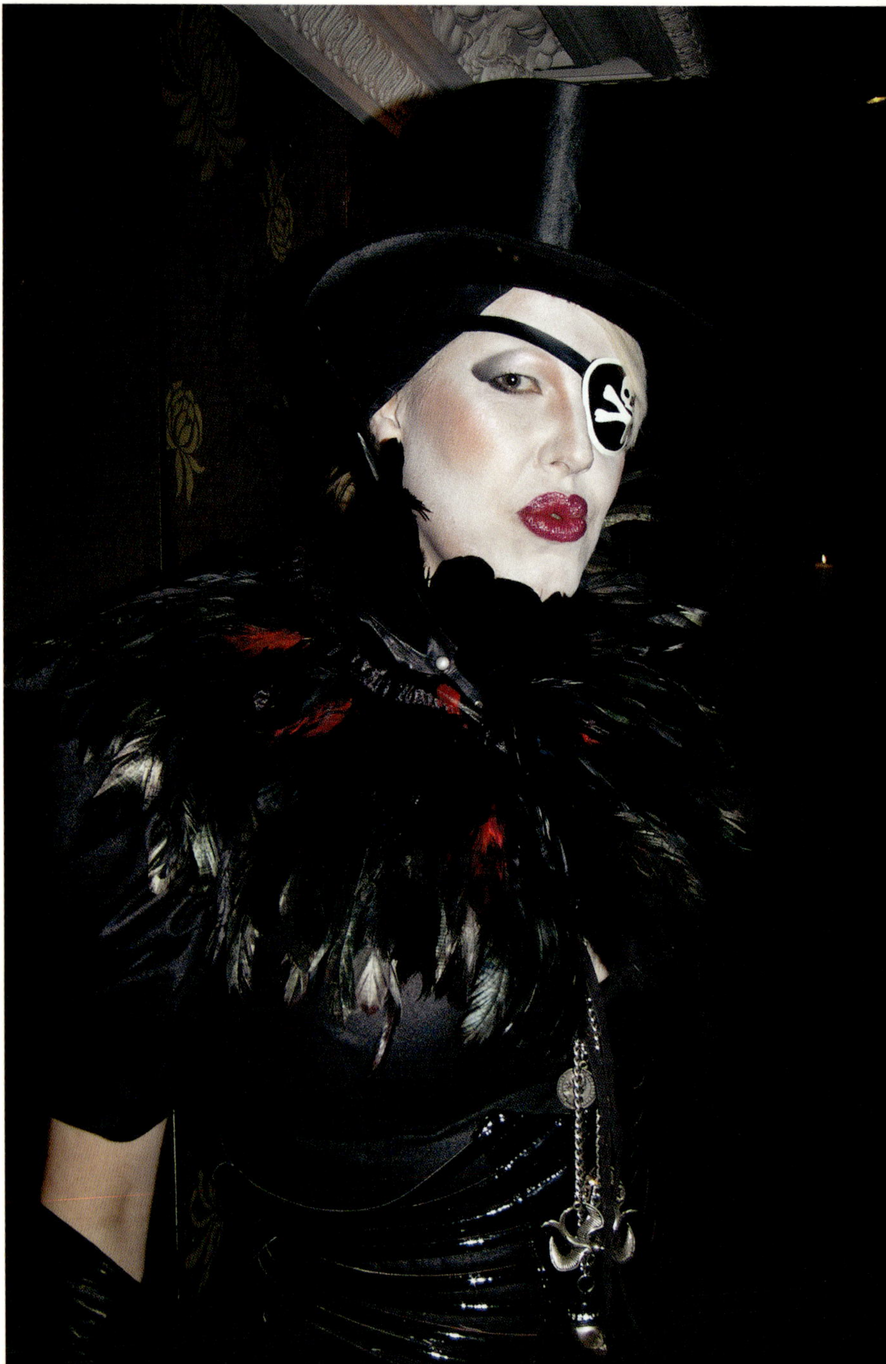

The Face – Oct 2010

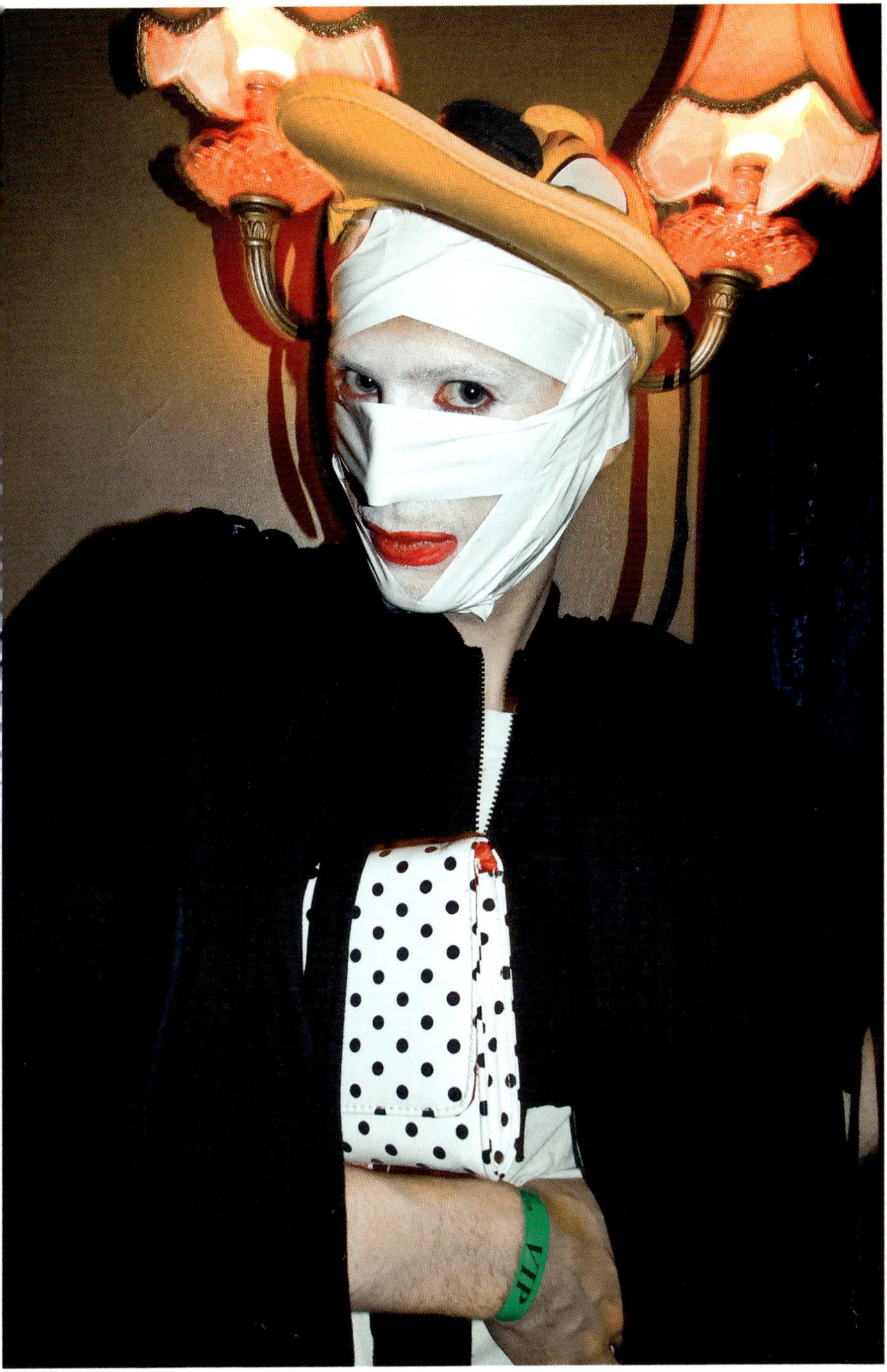

Paradise@Cafe De Paris – Sept 2010

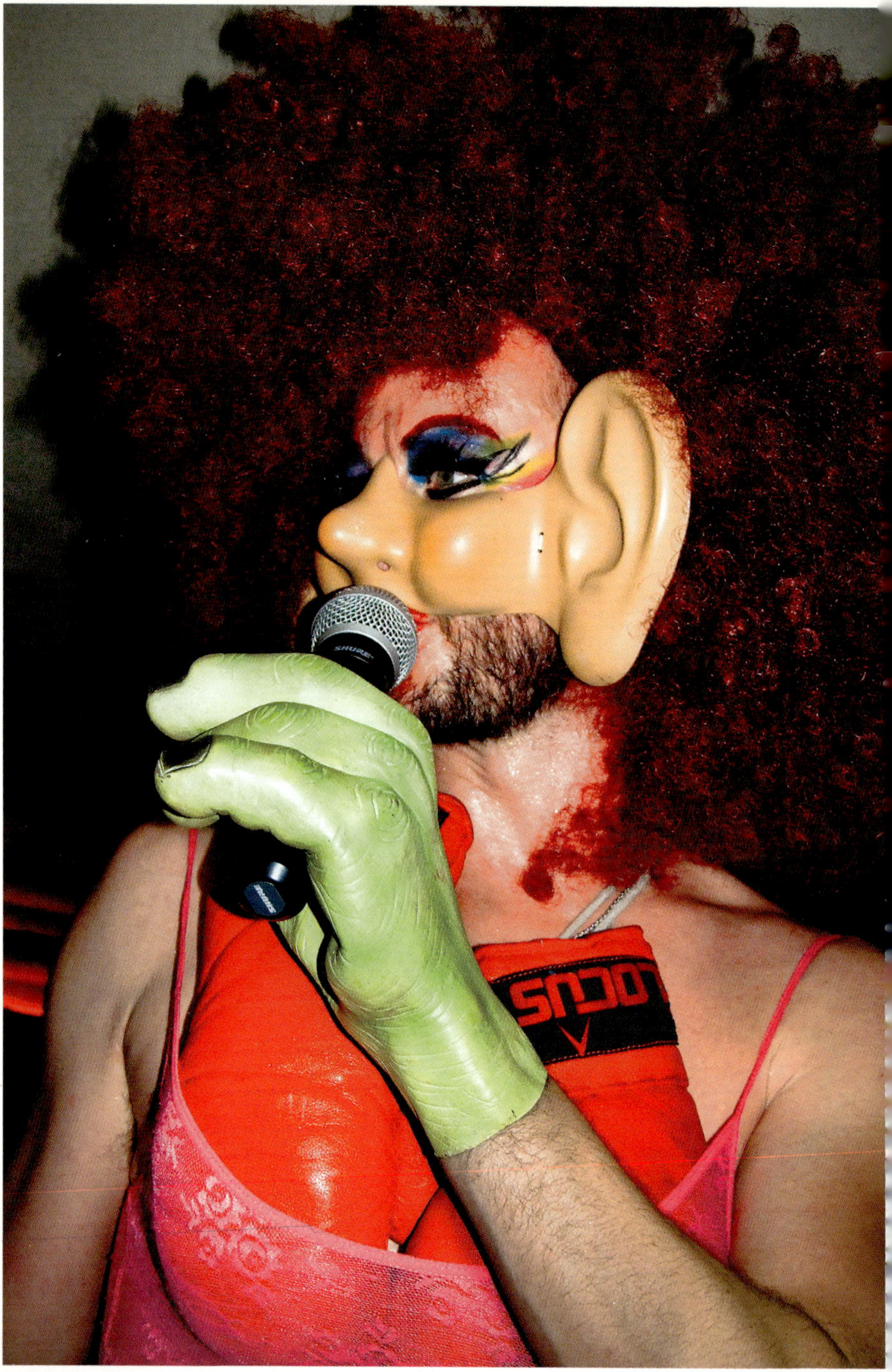

Floridita – Nov 2009

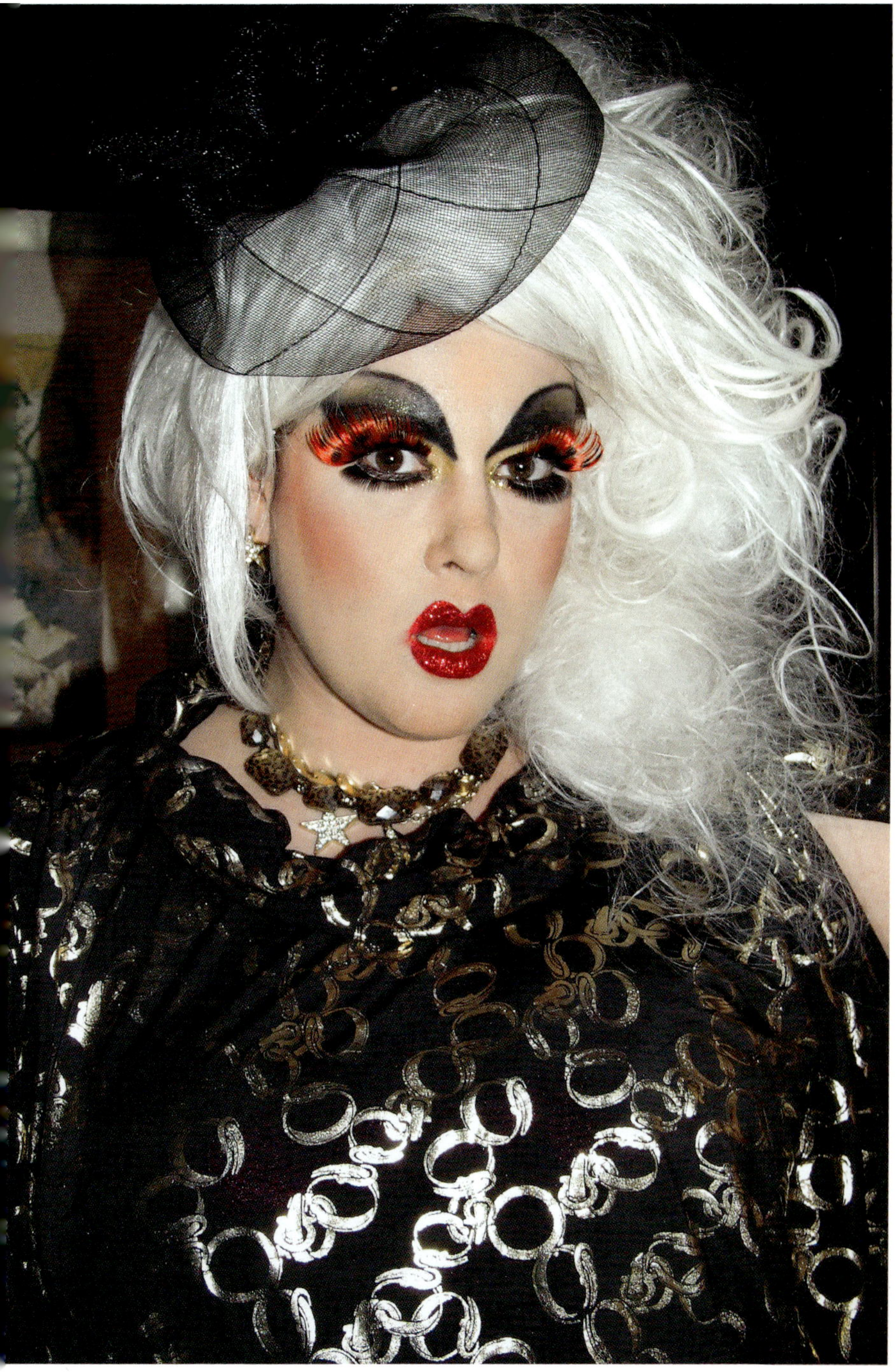

Floridita – Nov 2009

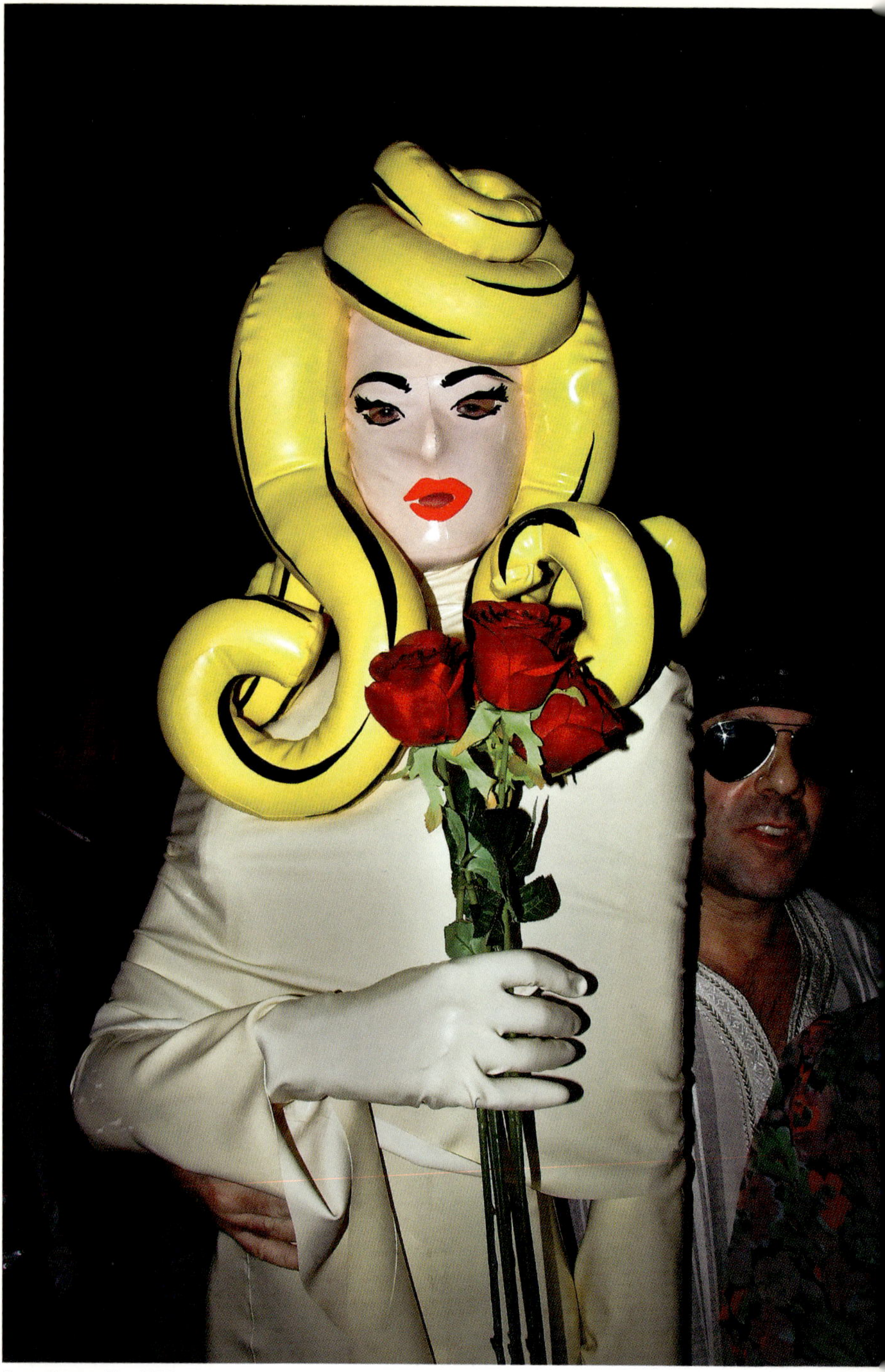

Home House – Nov 2009

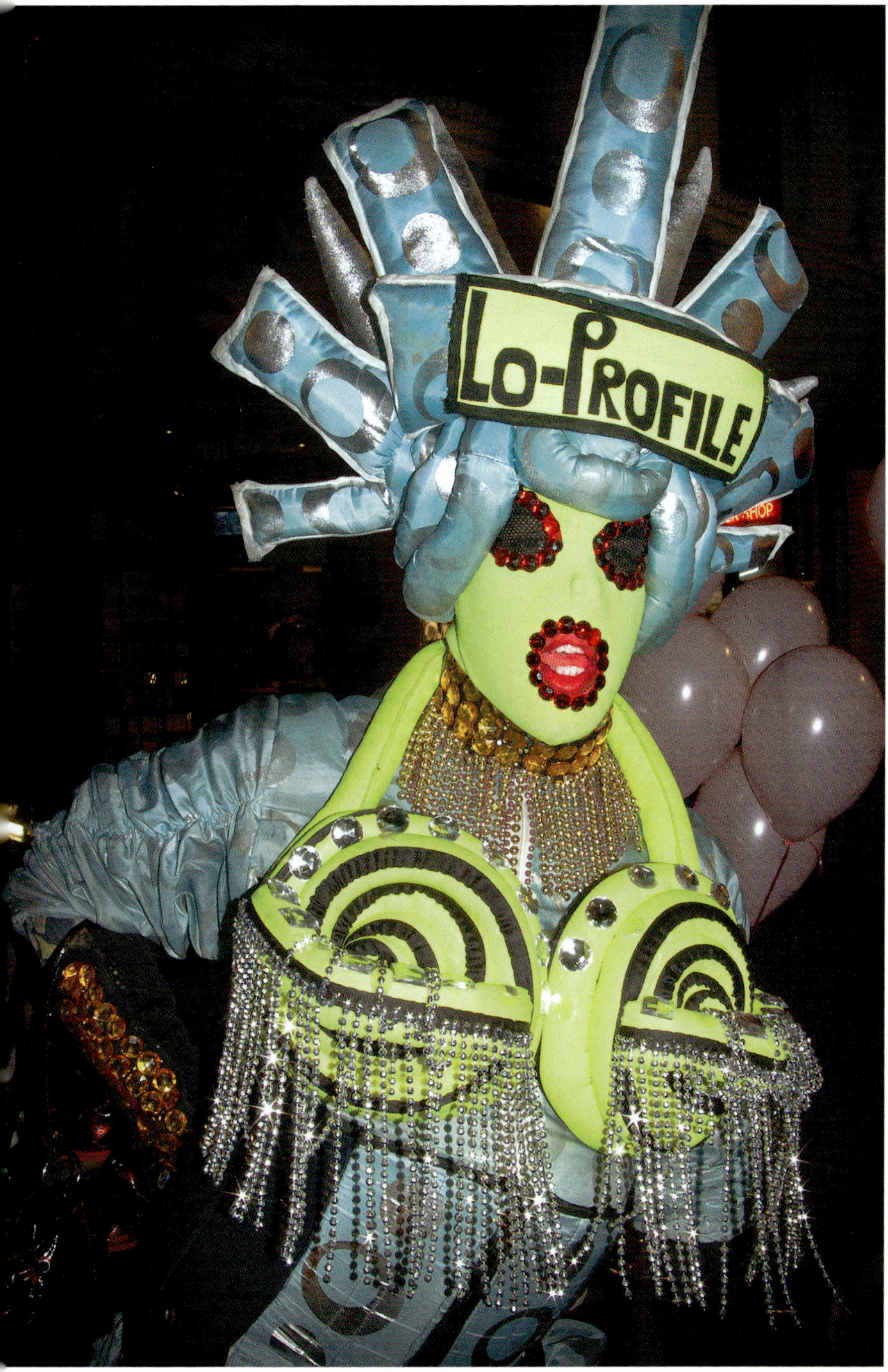

Lo-Profile – Feb 2010

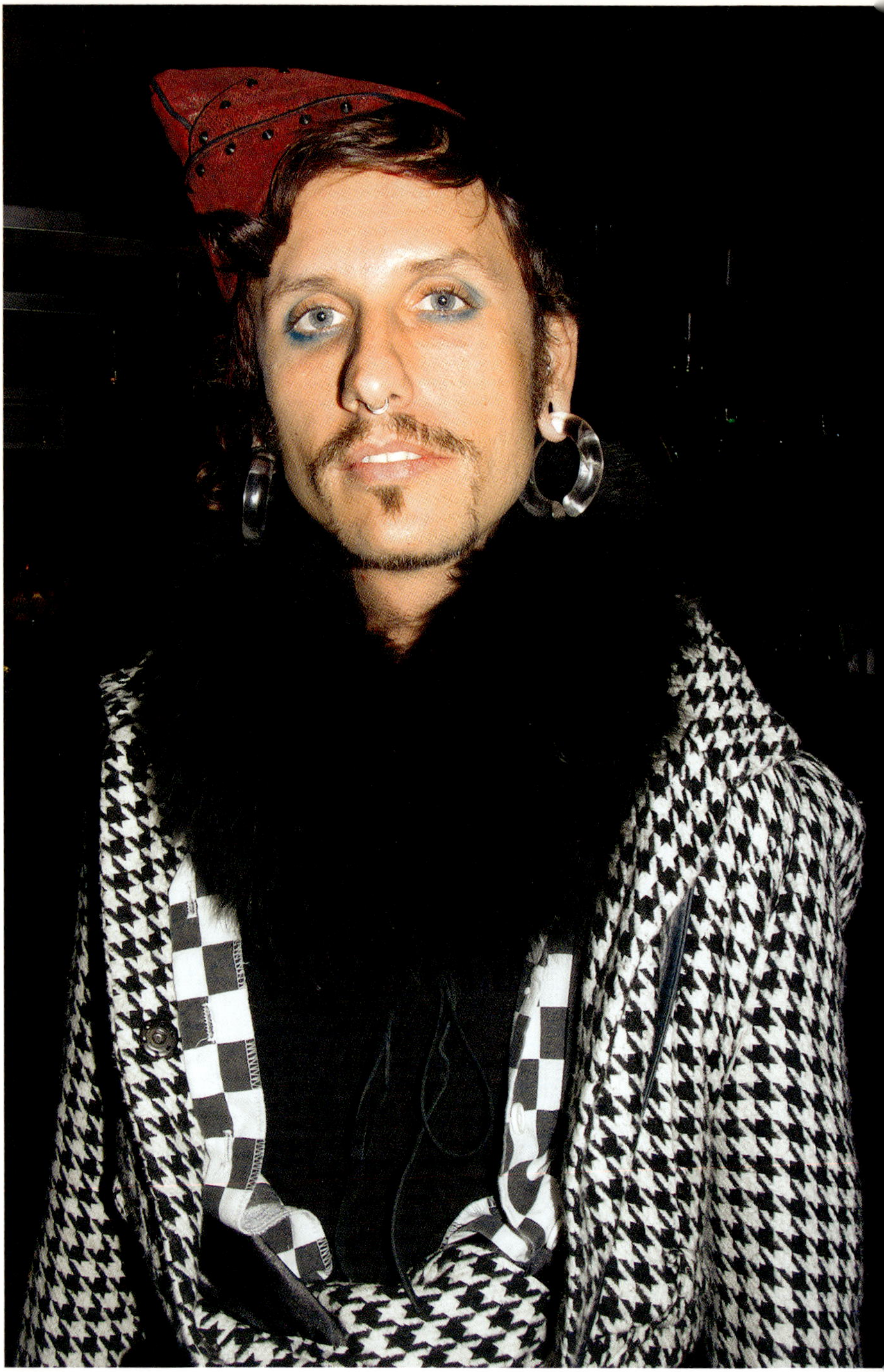

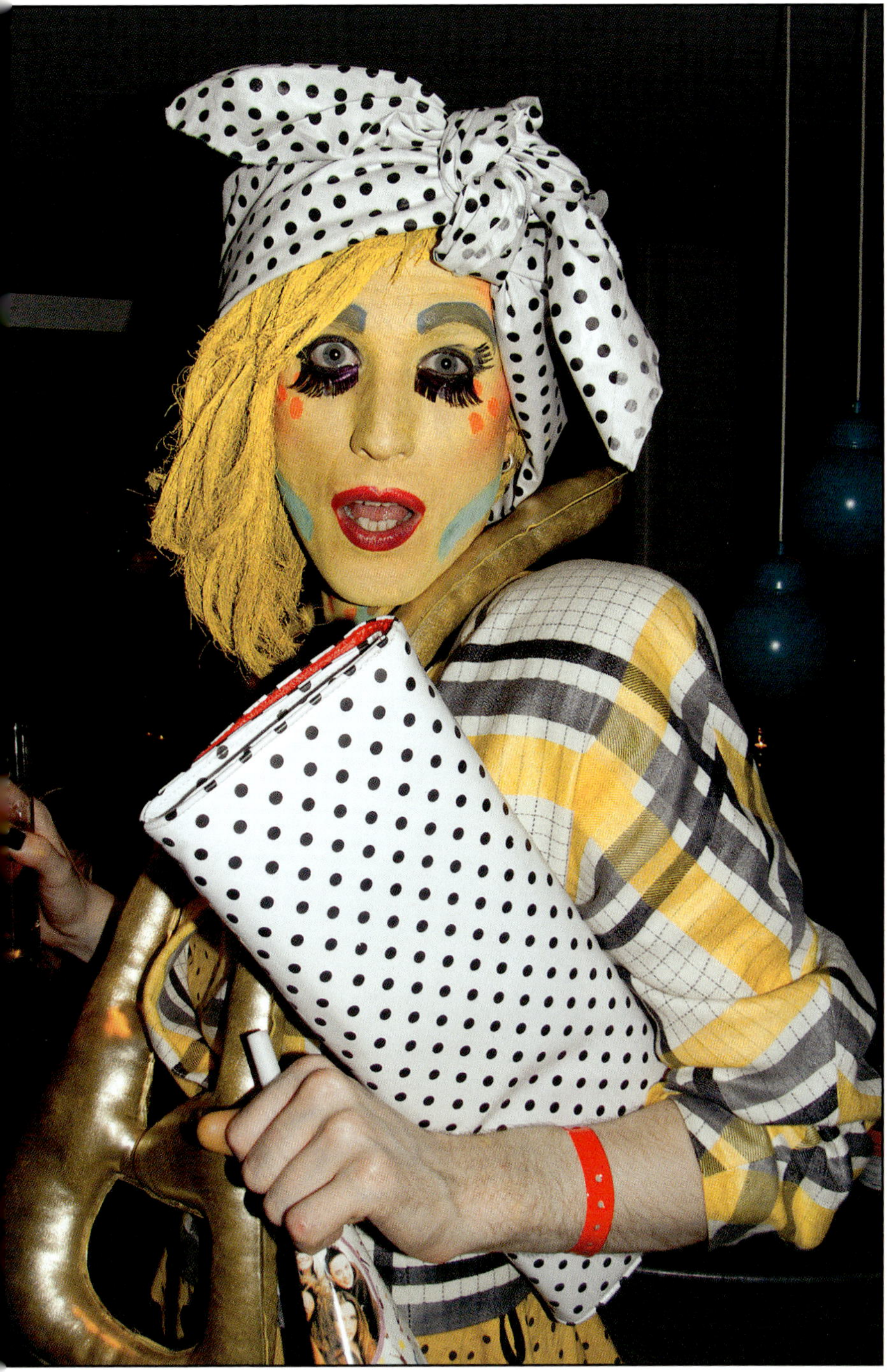

Circus – Oct 2010

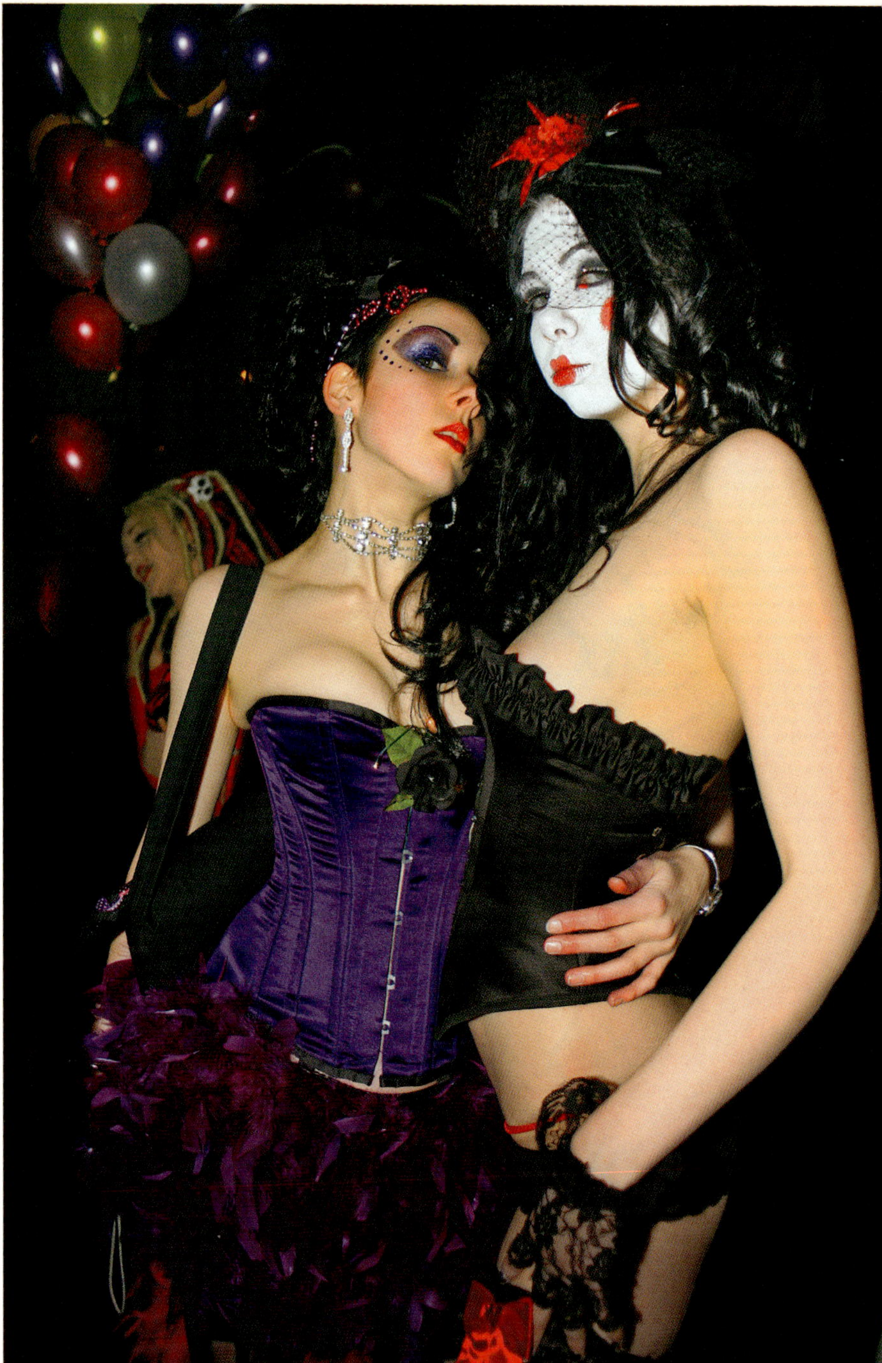

Circus – Sept 2006

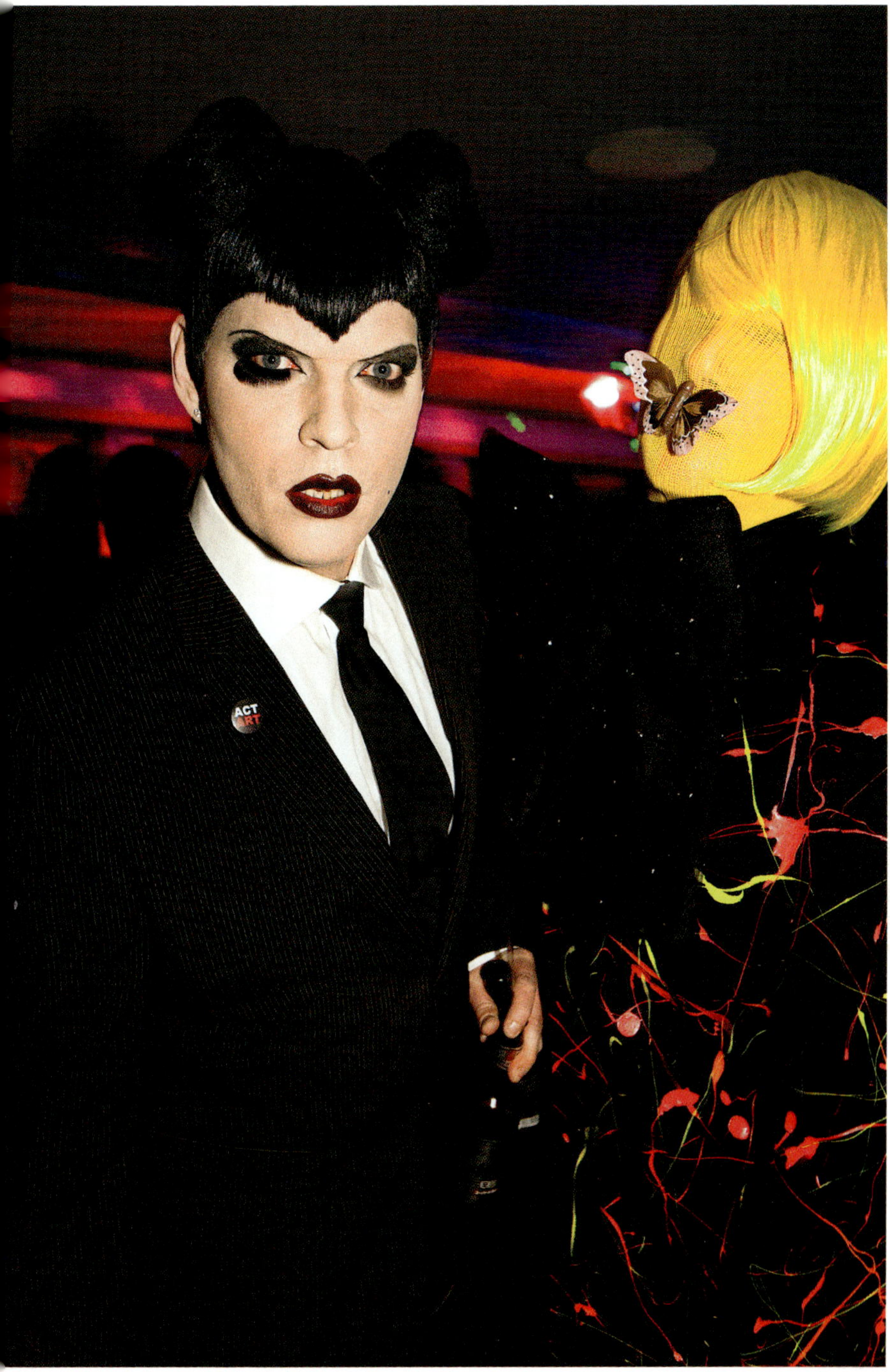

Act Art – June 2010

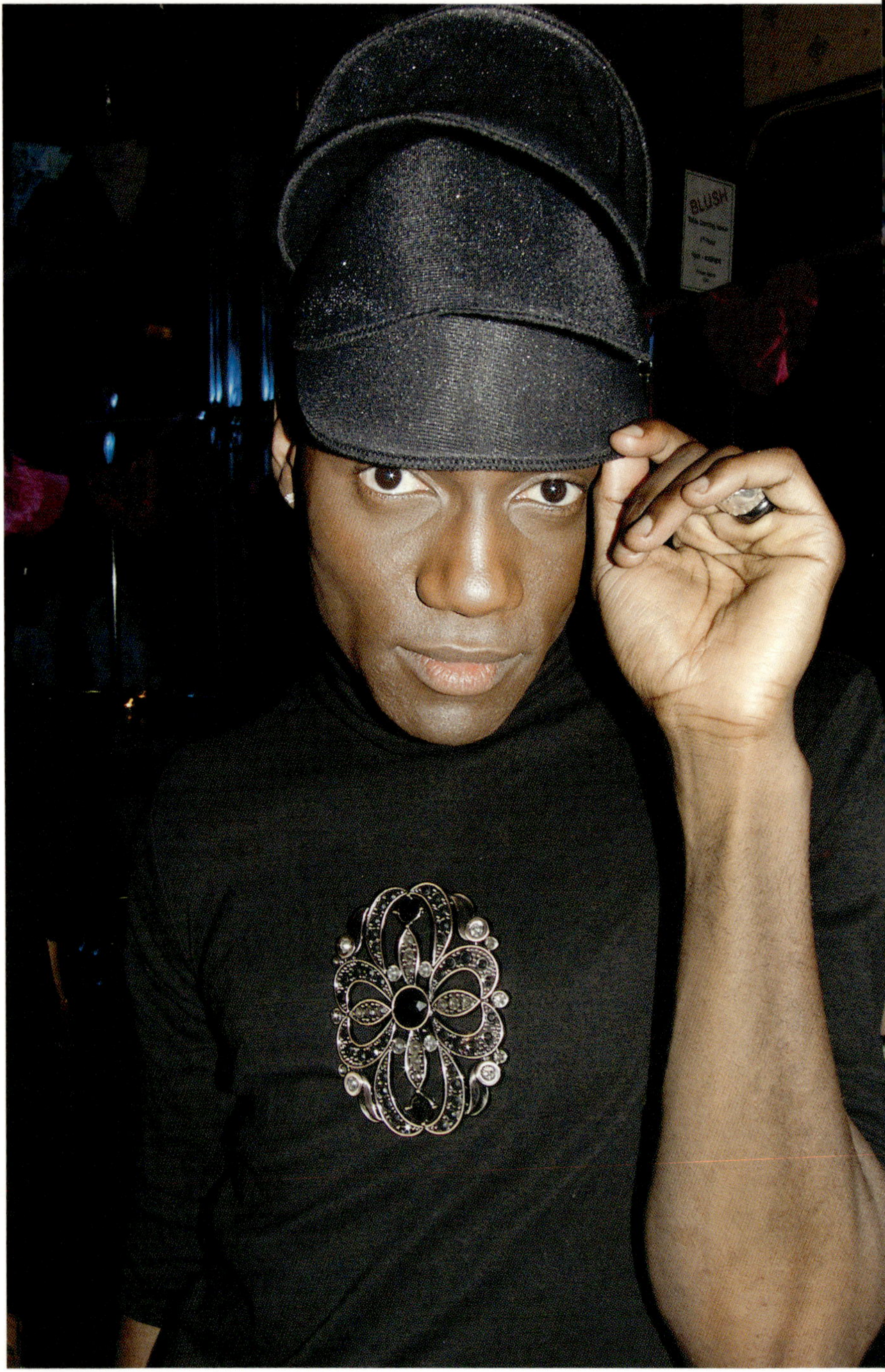

Nag Nag Nag – Oct 2005

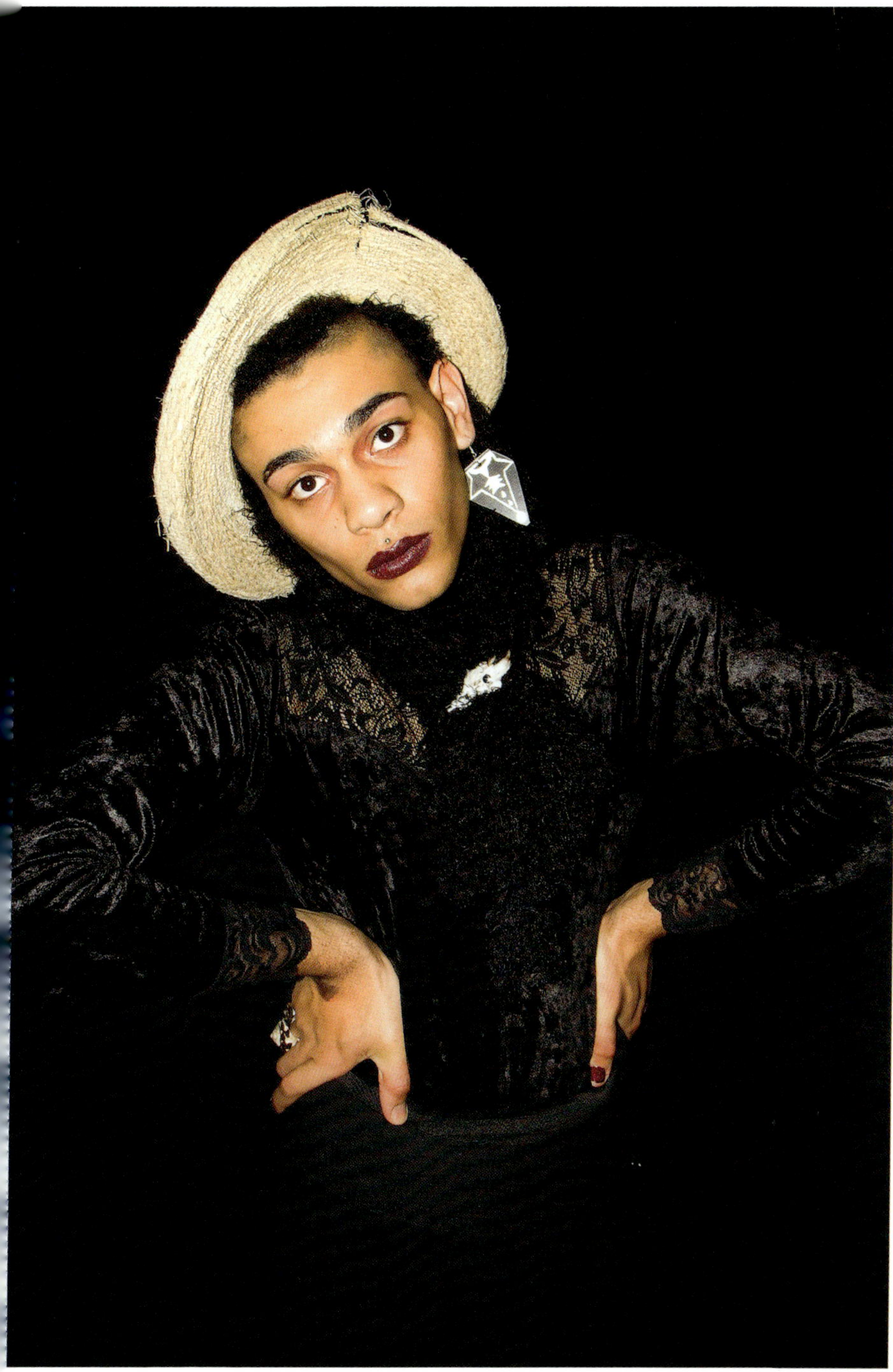

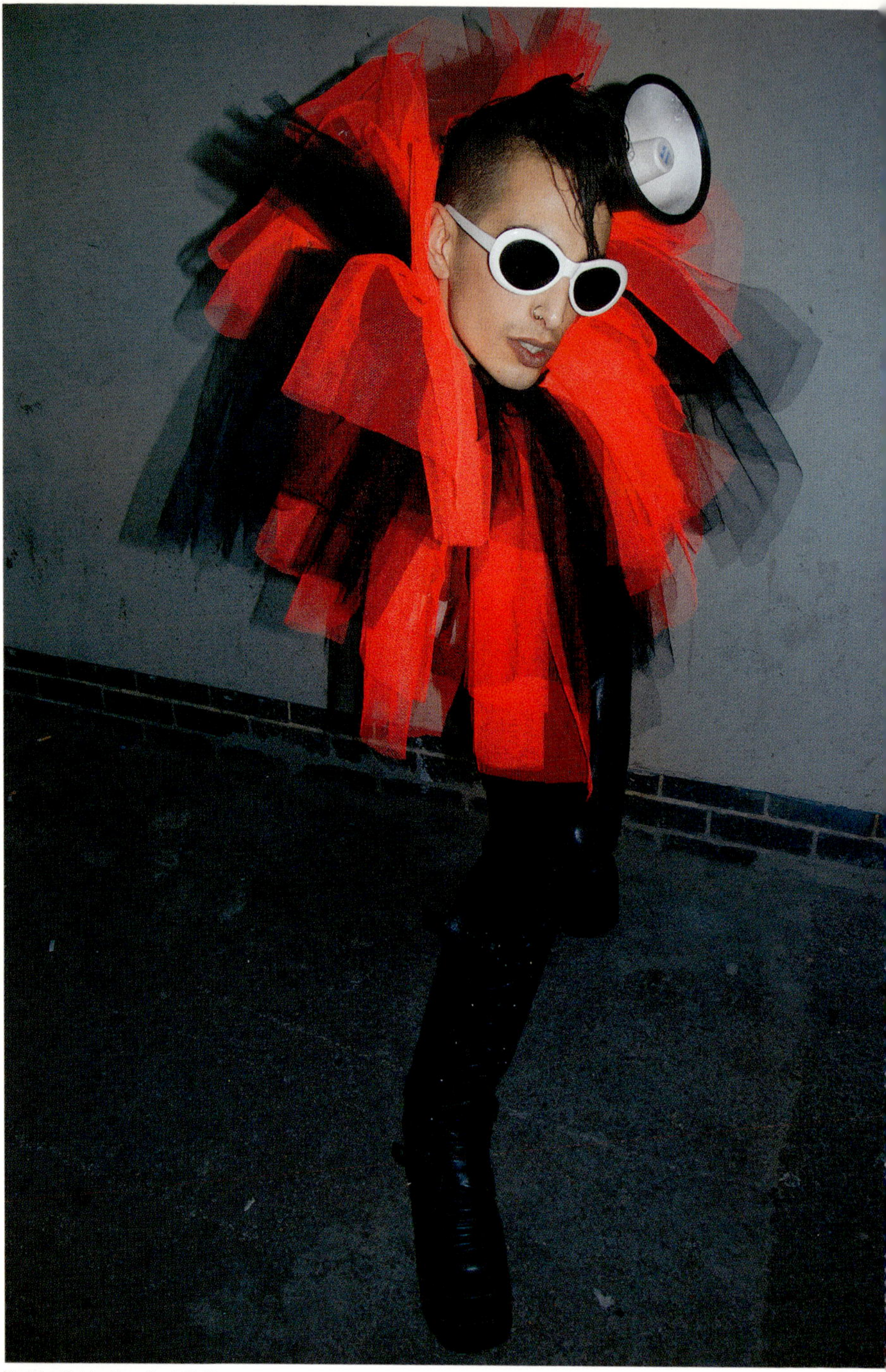

Shabba Dabba Da – Sept 2010

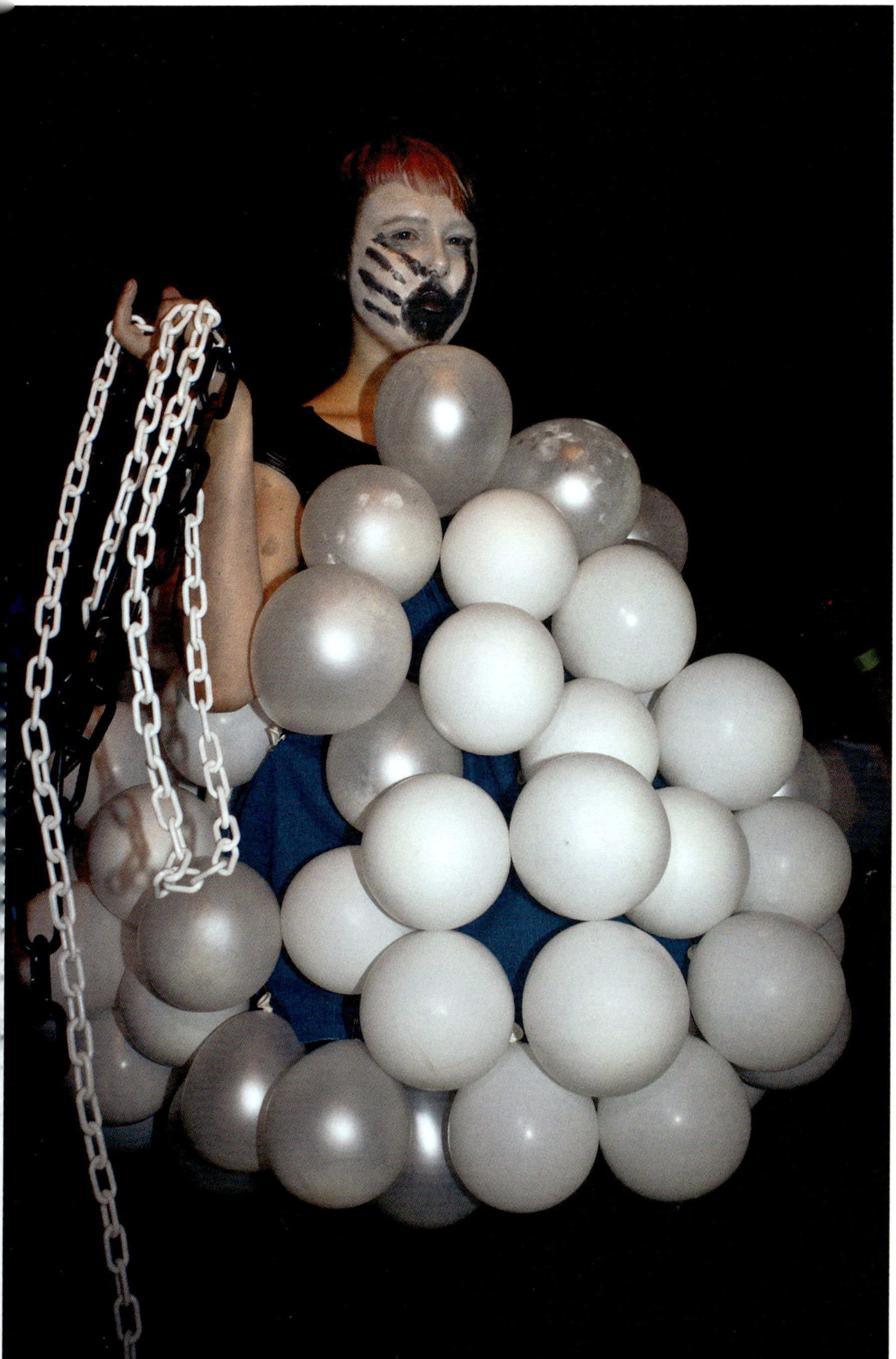

Work@Heaven – Sept 2007

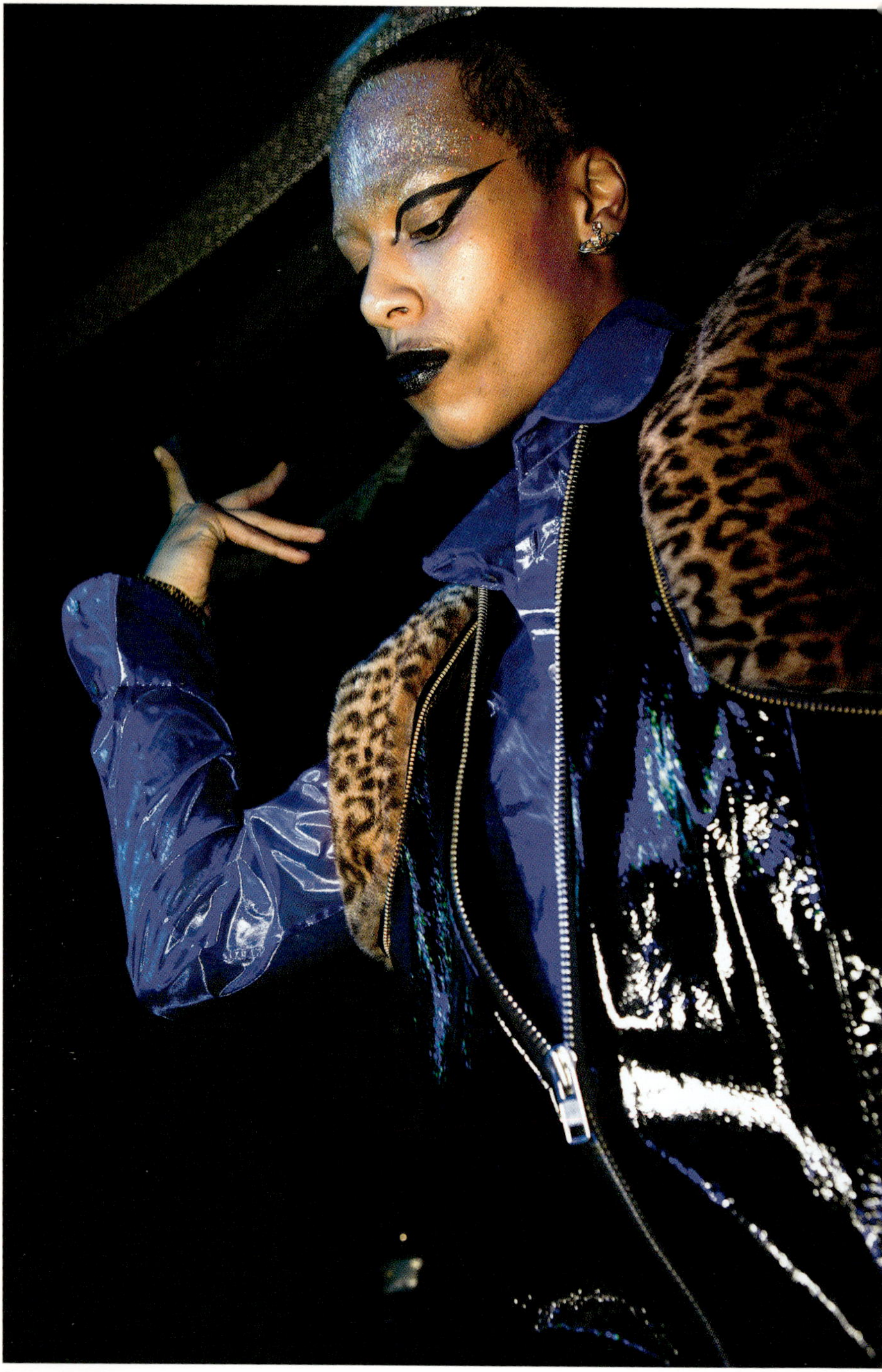

Strutt – June 2007

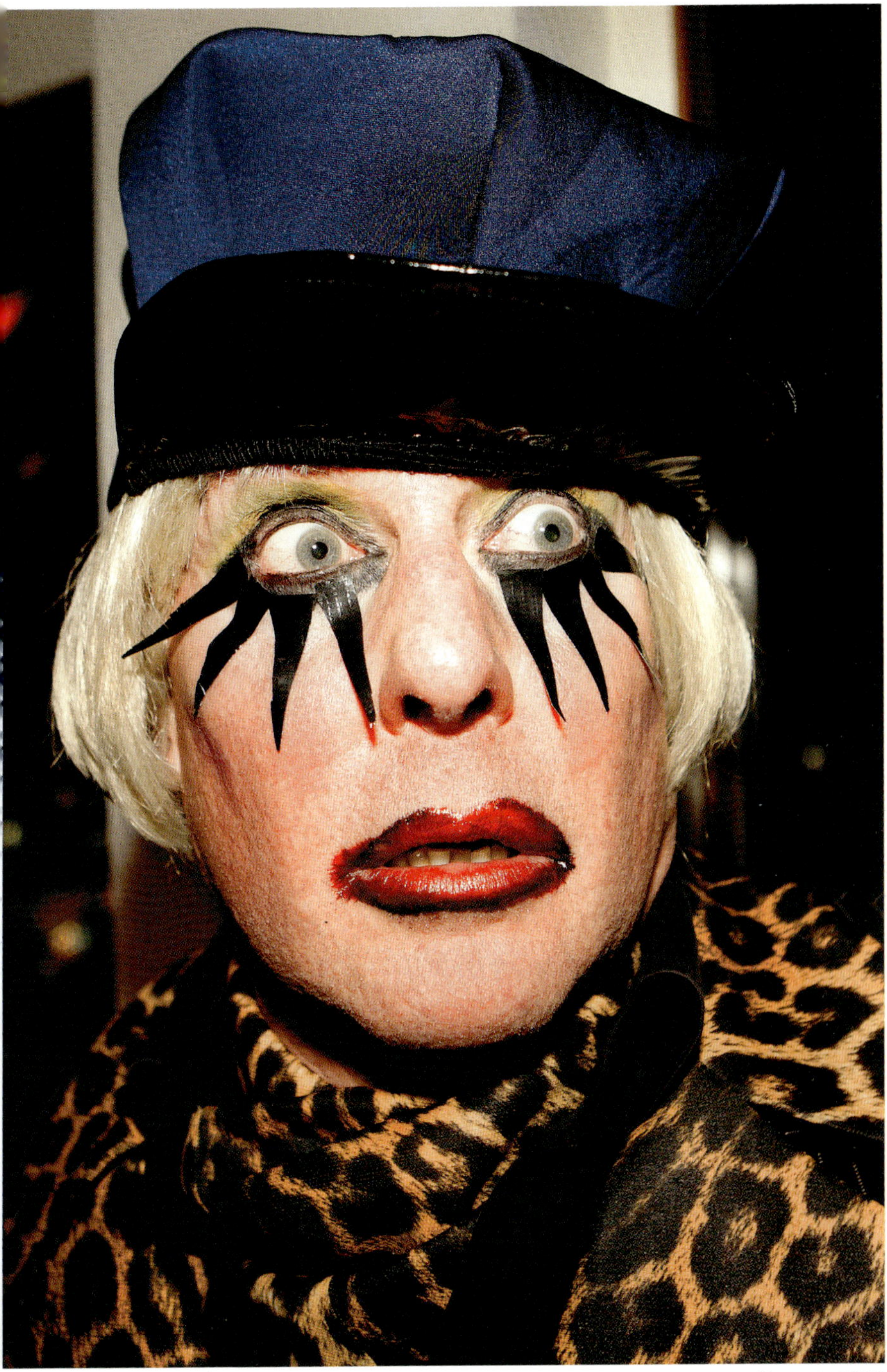

Circus – April 2010

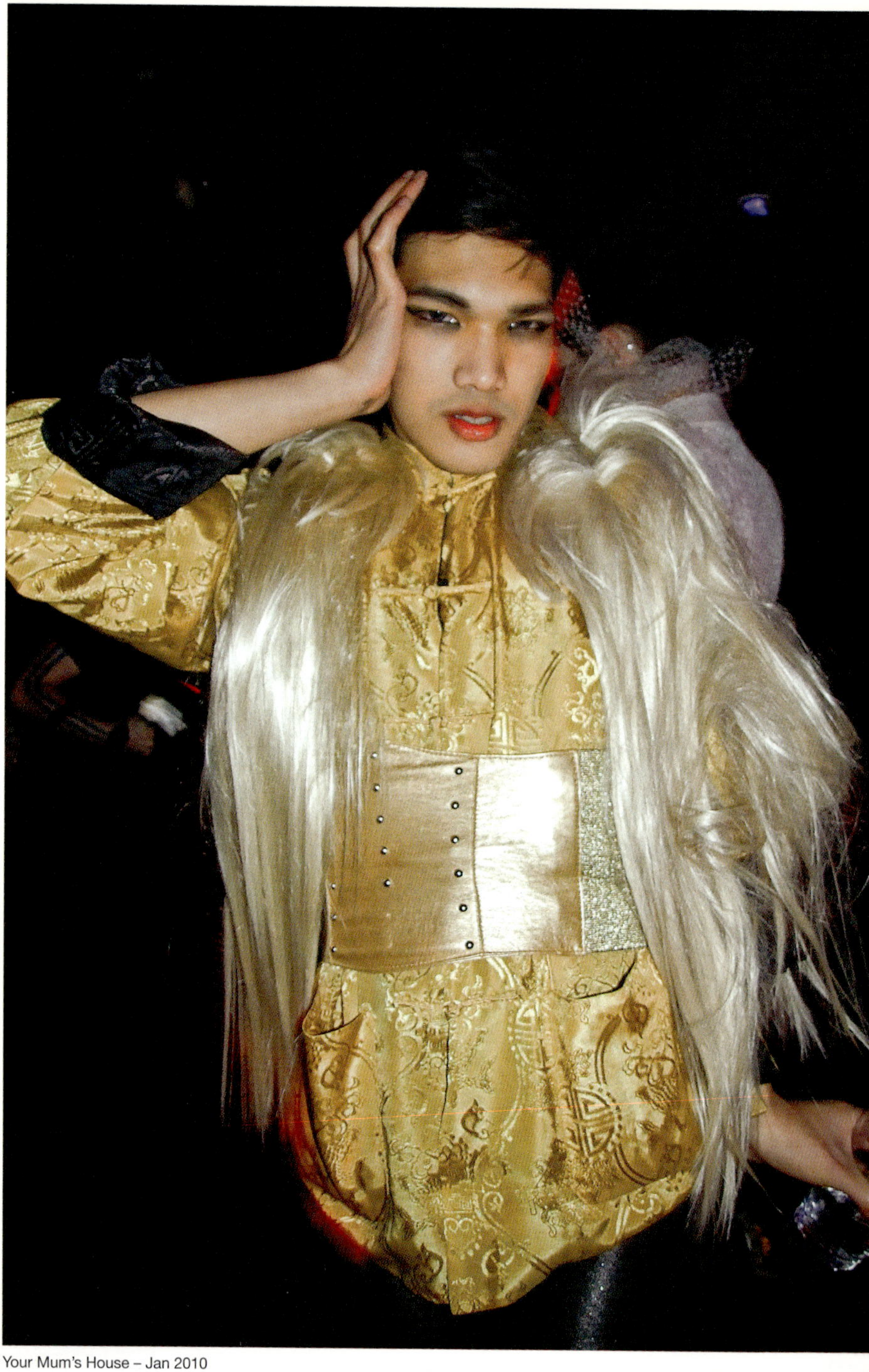

Your Mum's House – Jan 2010

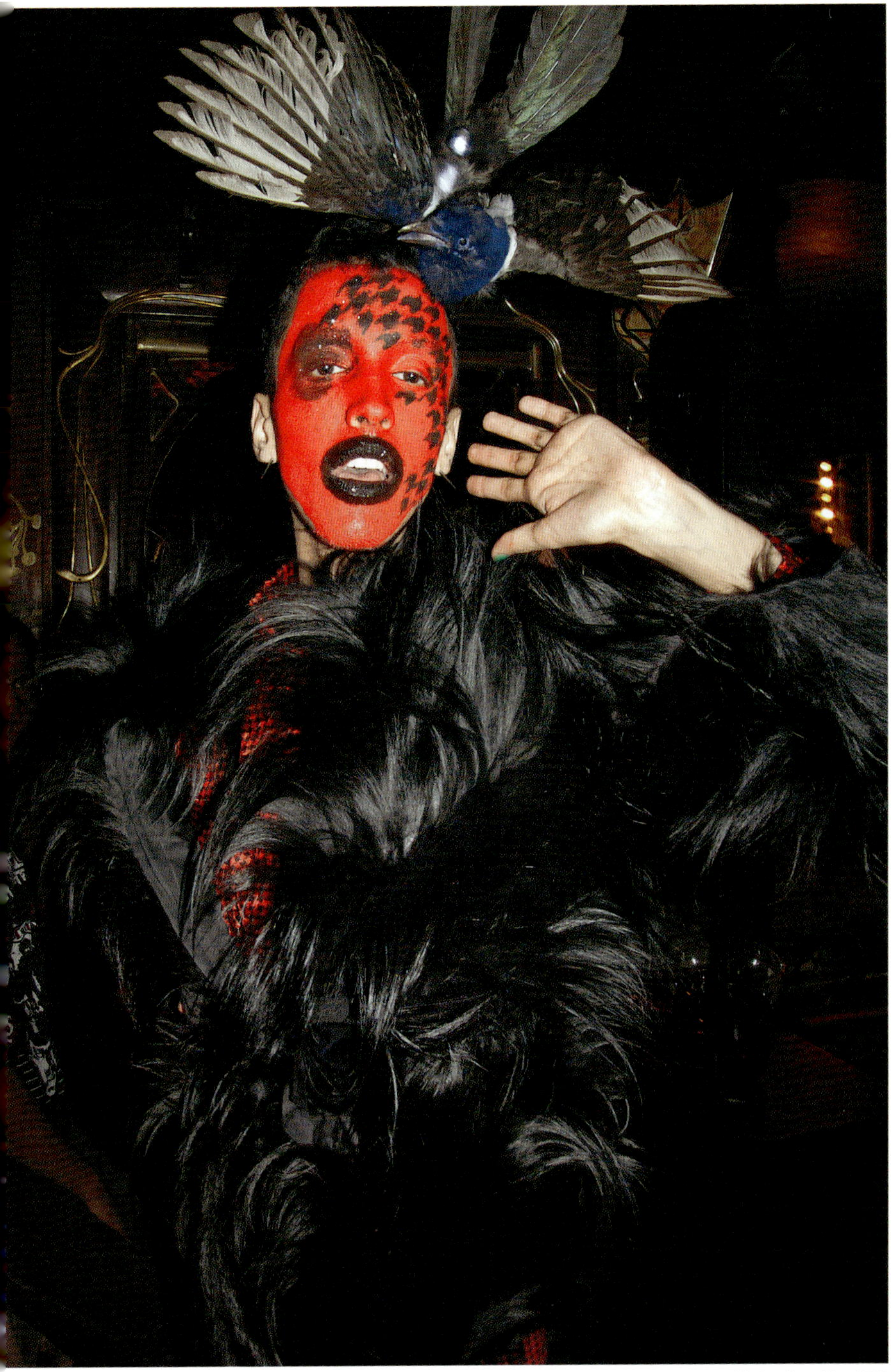

Kashpoint – May 2003

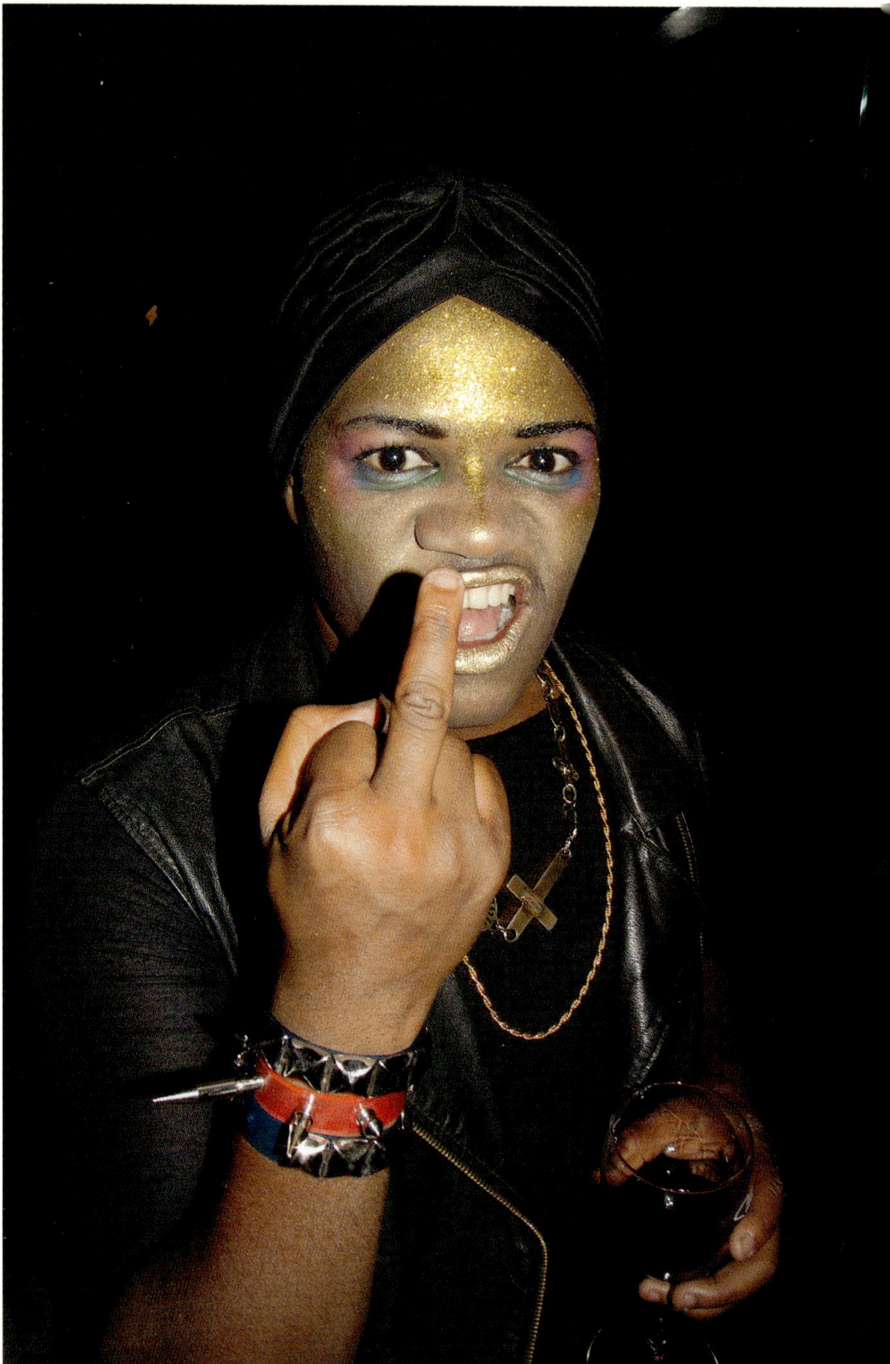

House of Blue Eyes – Sept 2010

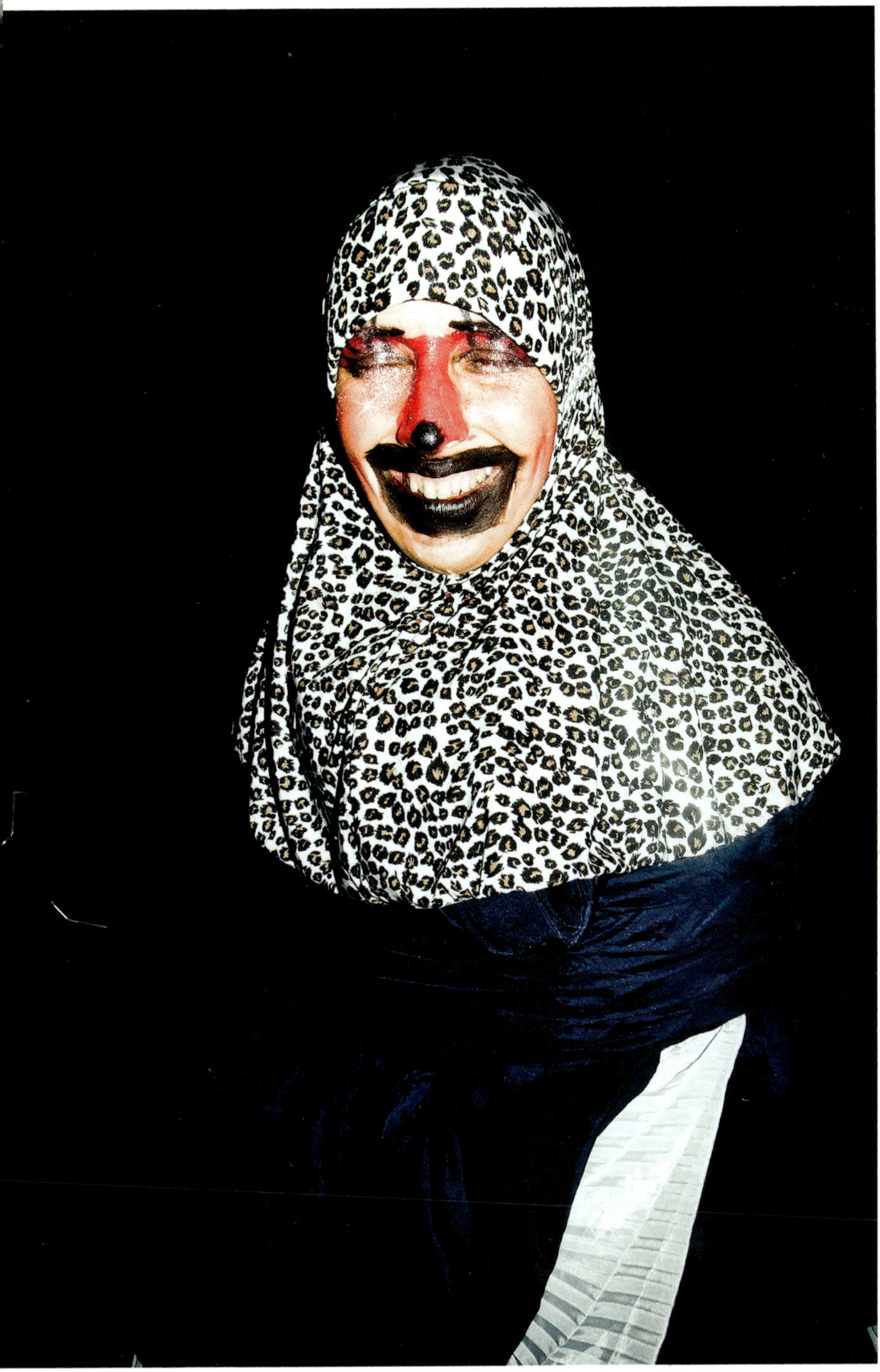

Shabba Dabba Da – Oct 2010

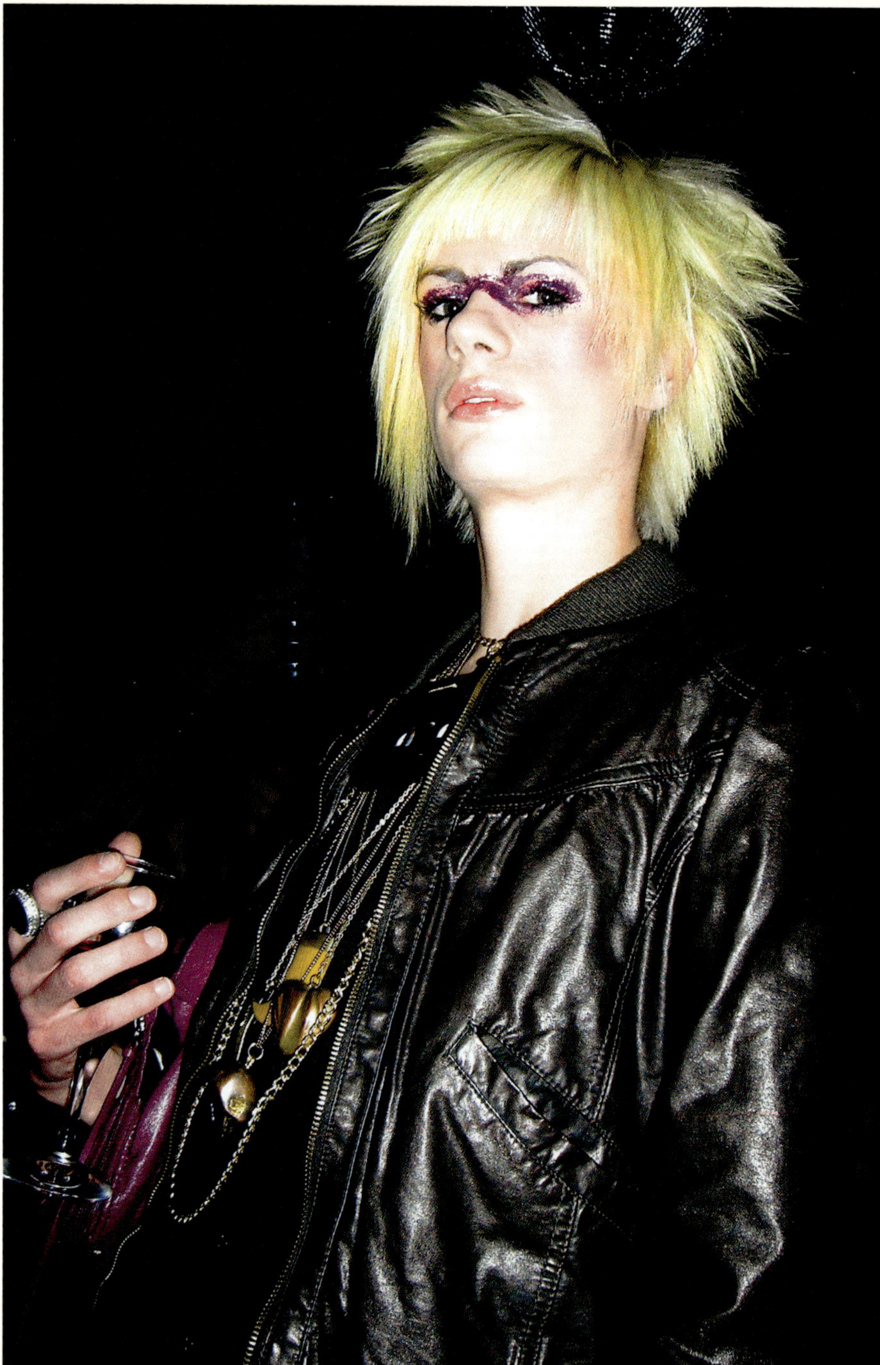

Nag Nag Nag – Feb 2006

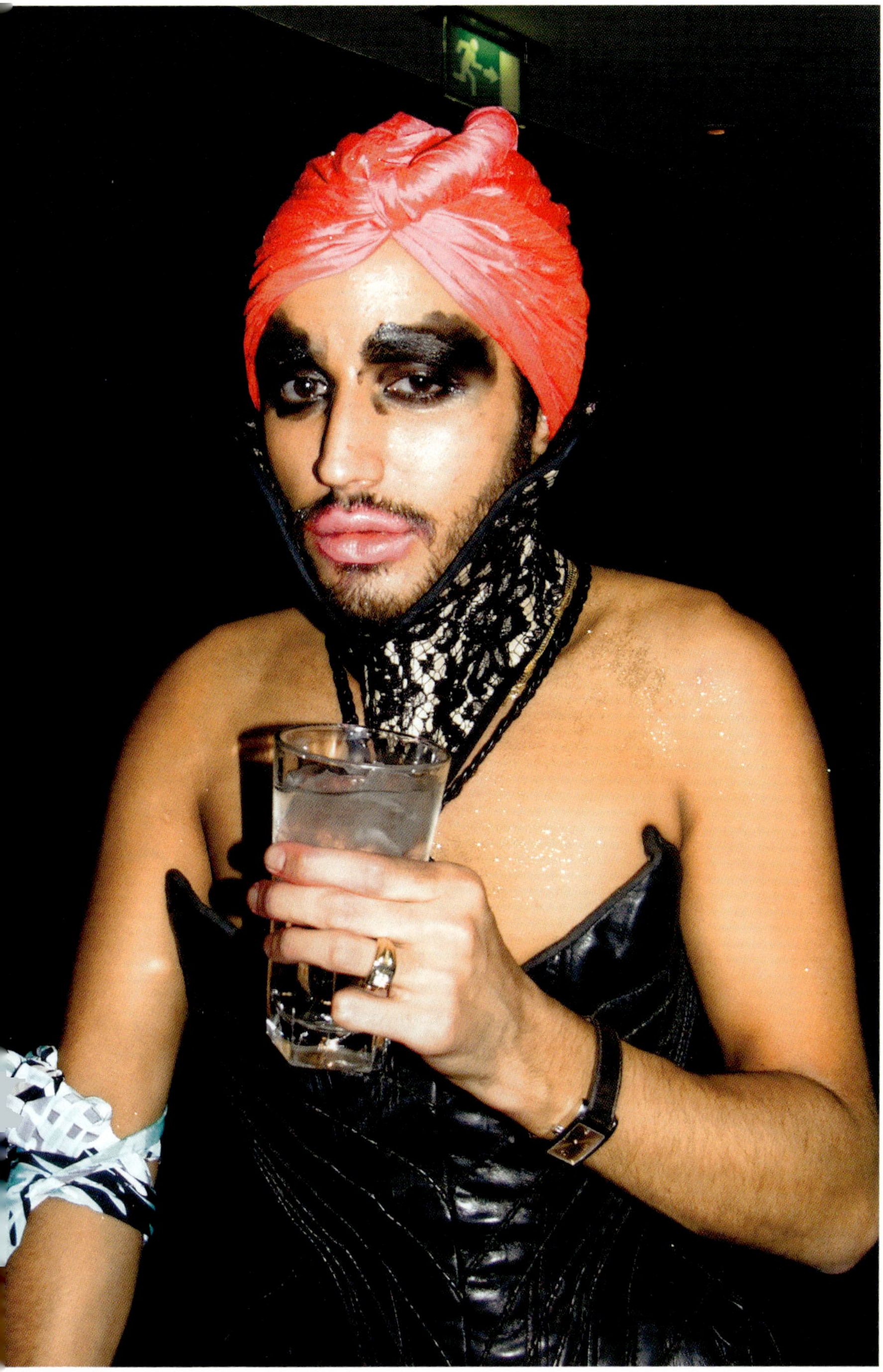

Nag Nag Nag – Feb 2006

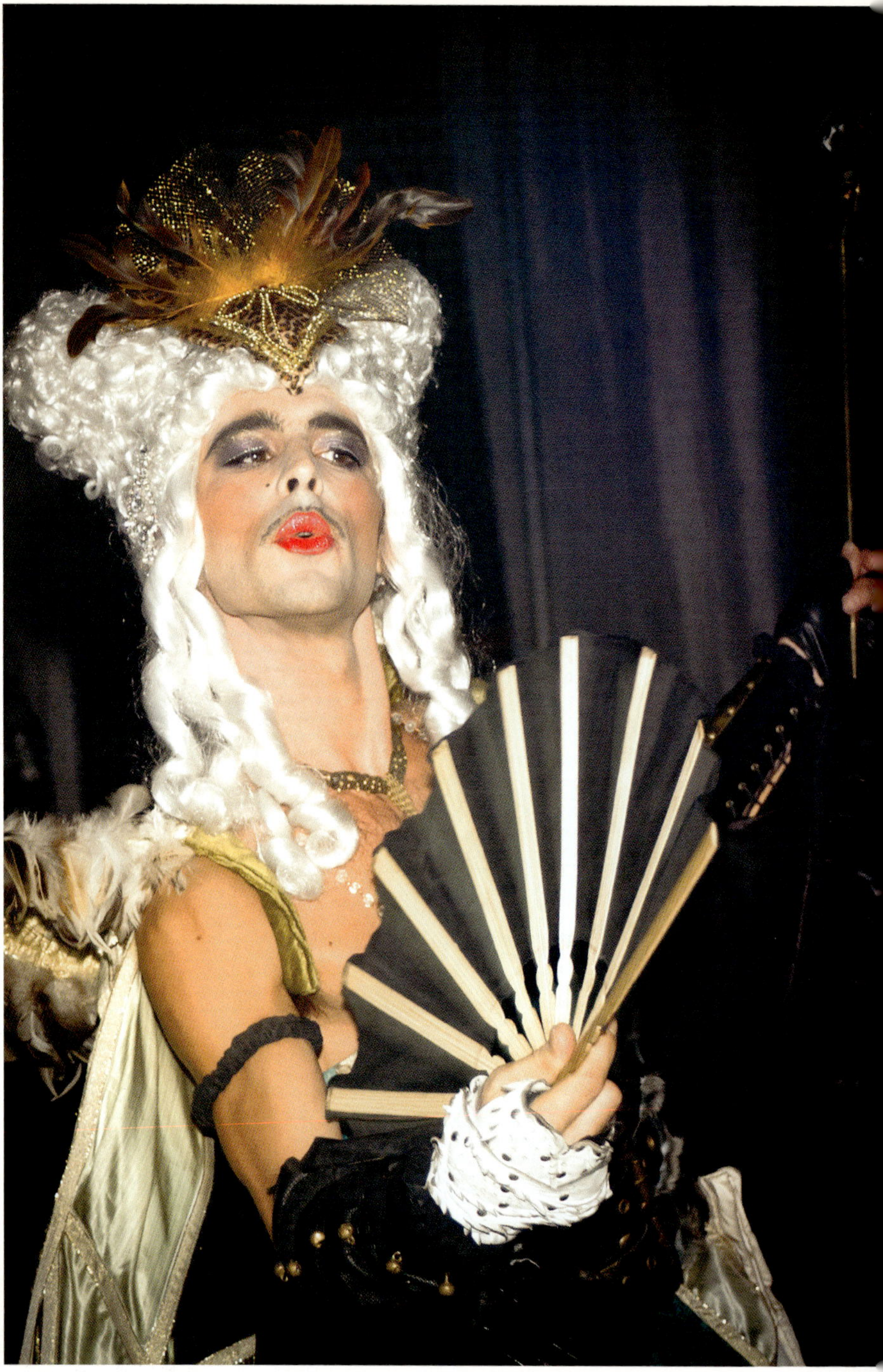

Work@Heaven – June 2008

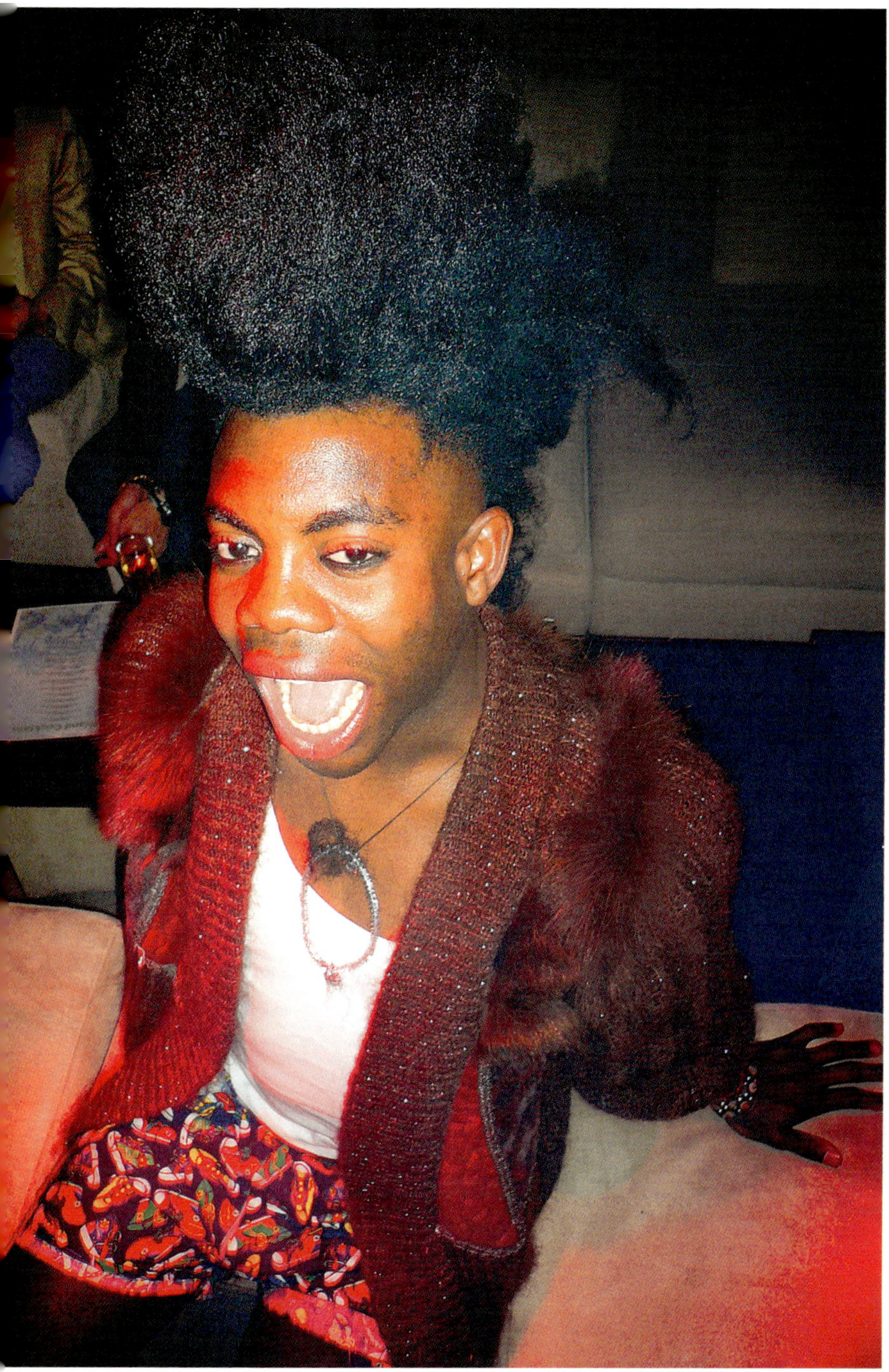

Nag Nag Nag – May 2004

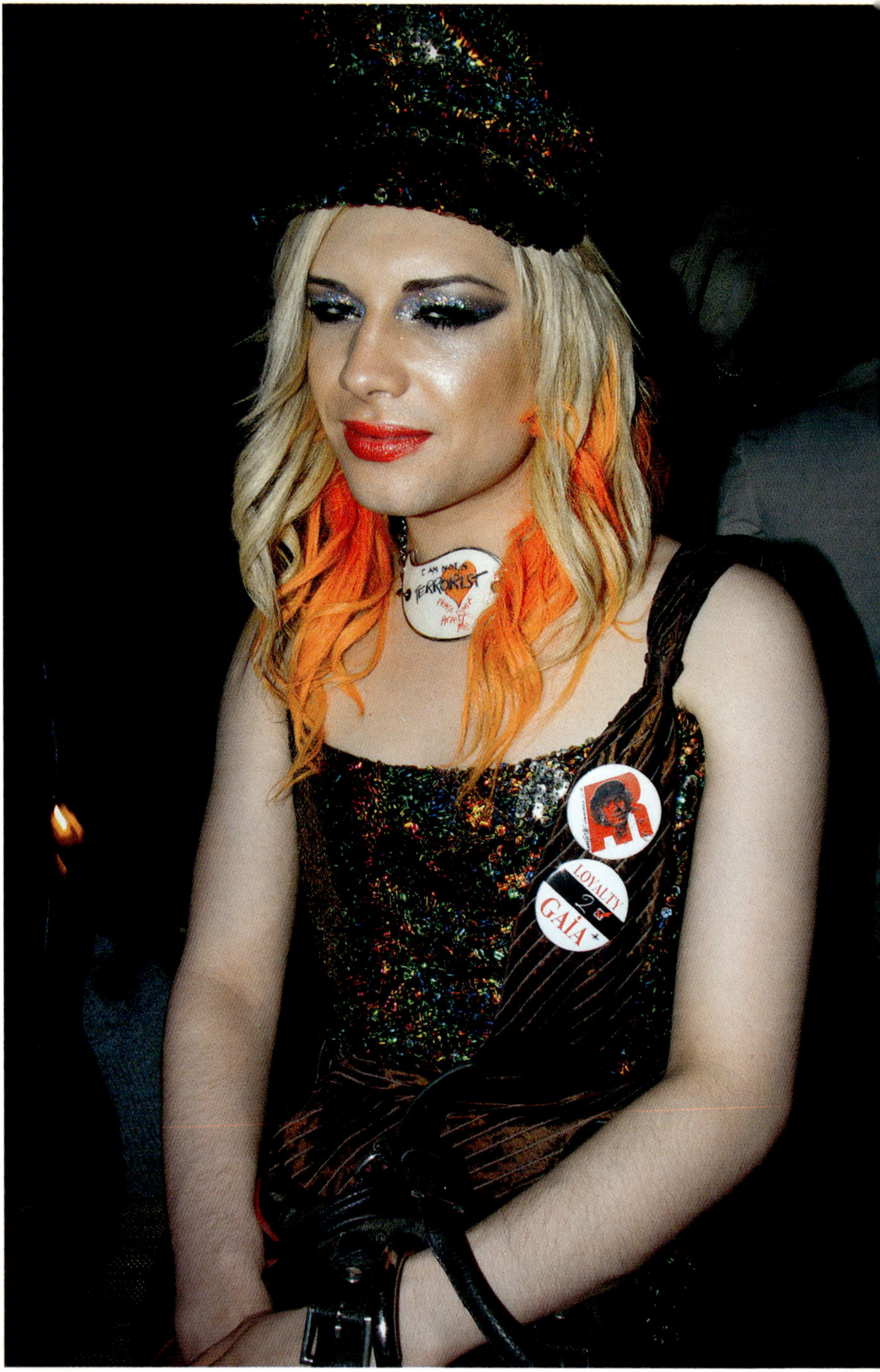

Mayday@Home House – May 2010

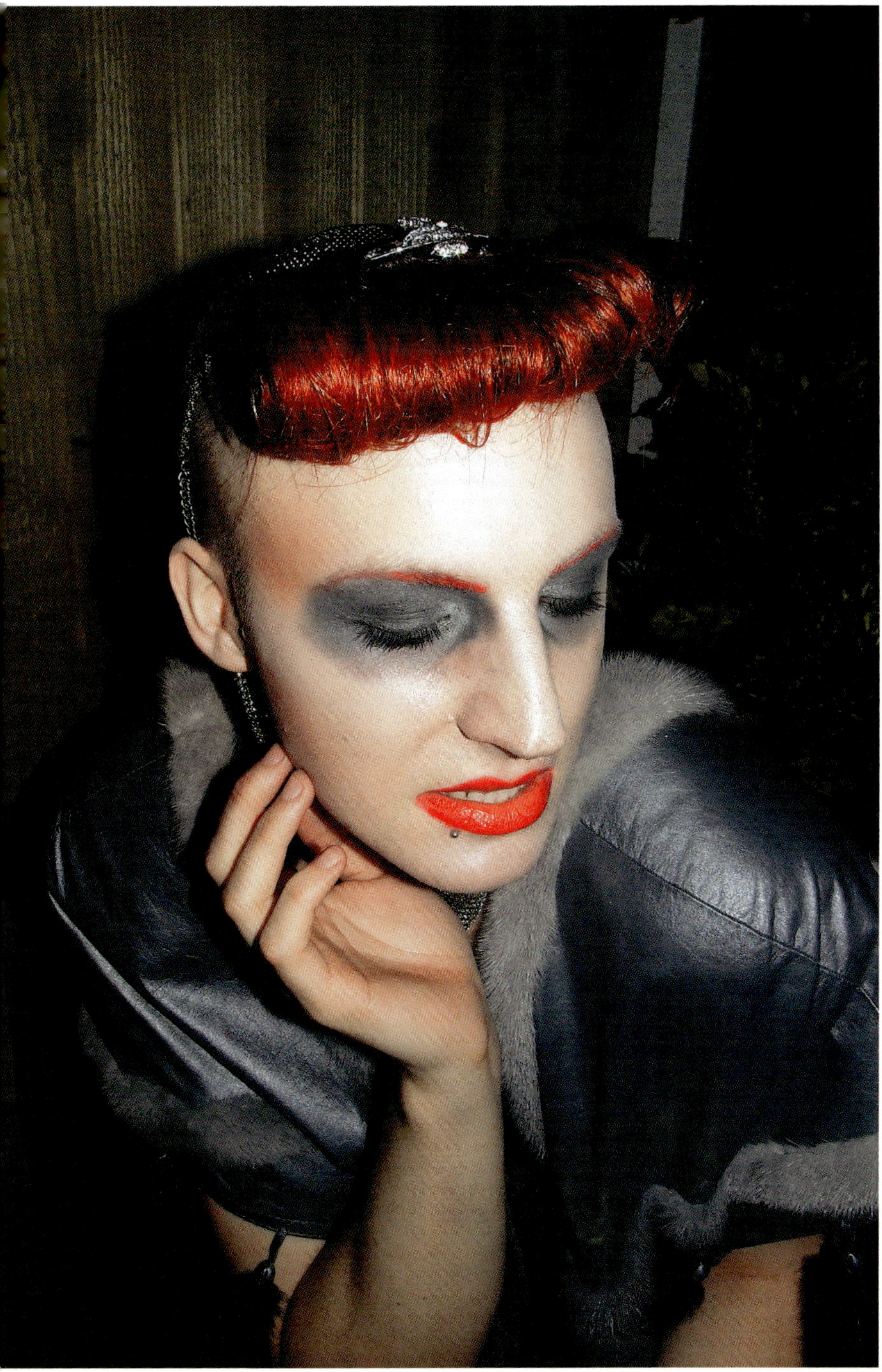

Caligula – Sept 2010

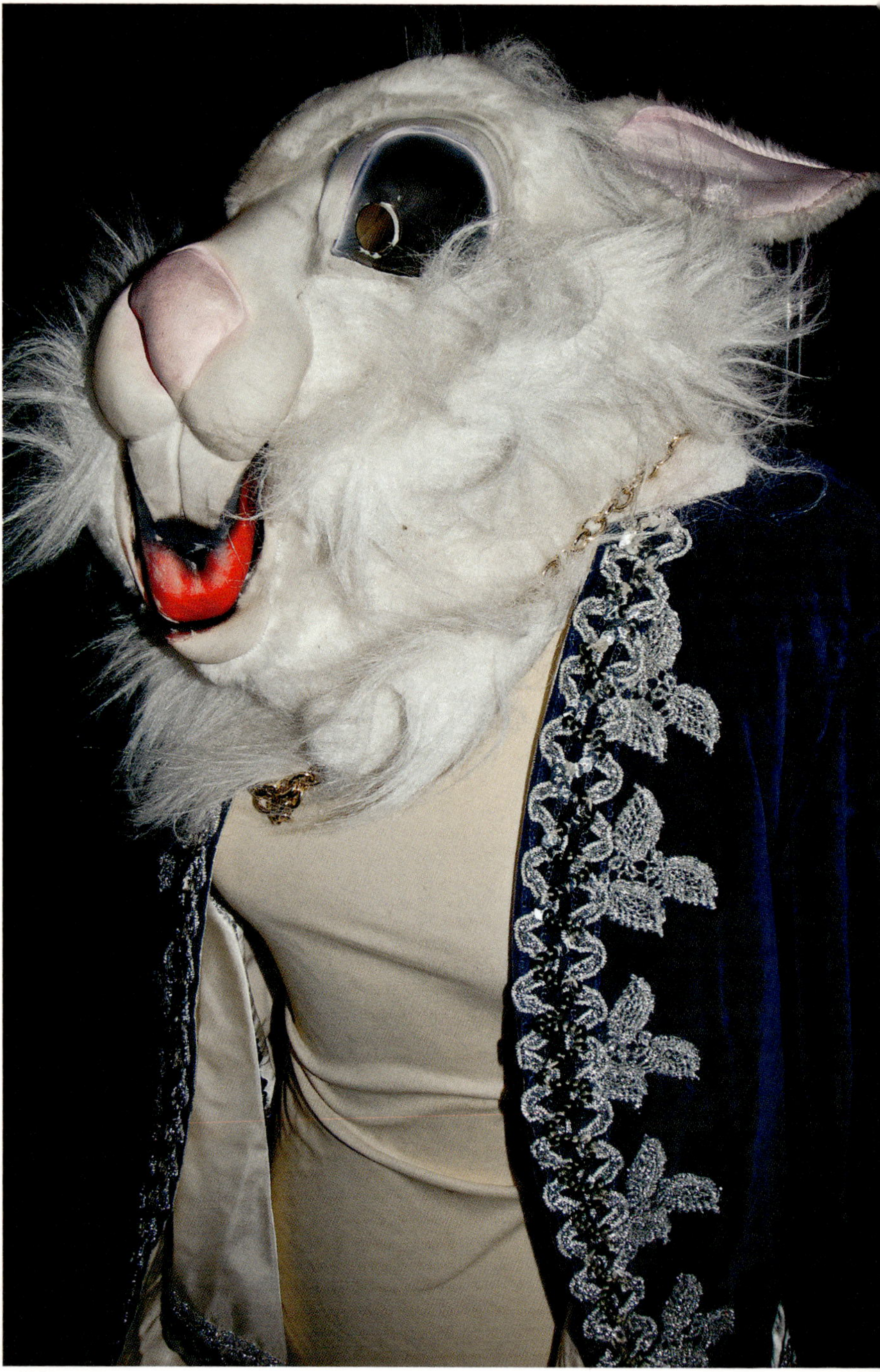

Wearable Art@Egg – Sept 2010

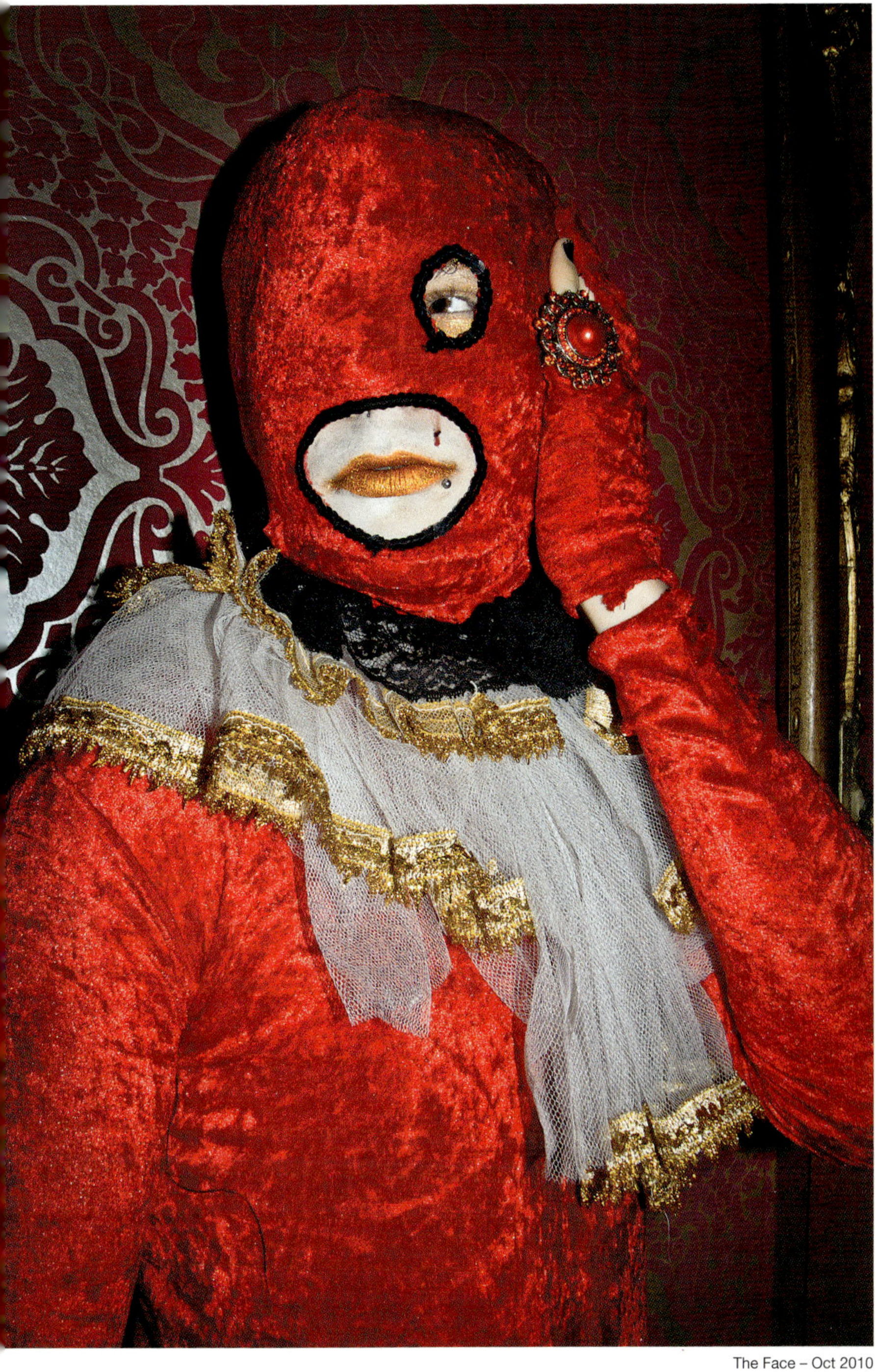

The Face – Oct 2010

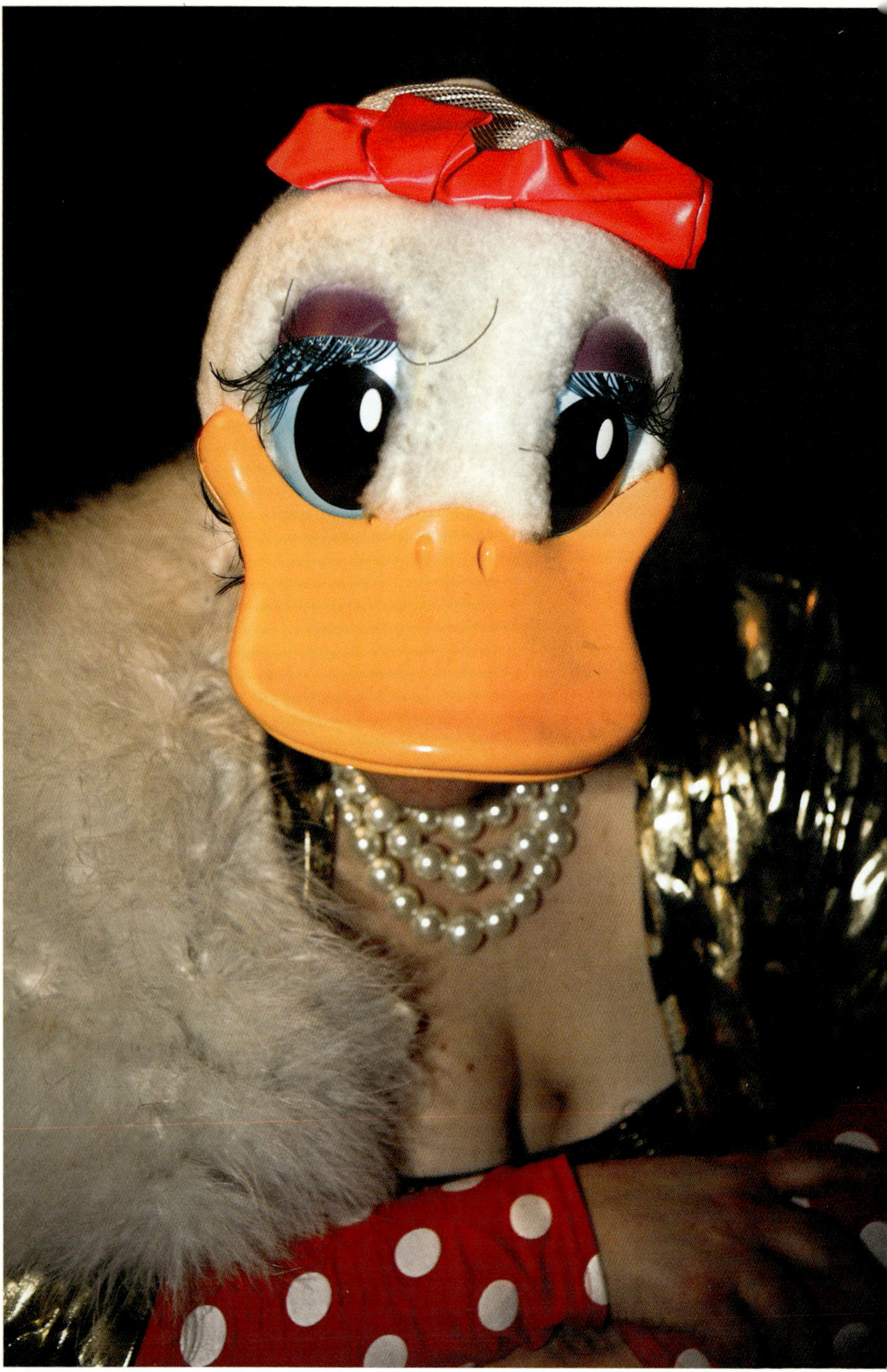

Circus – April 2010

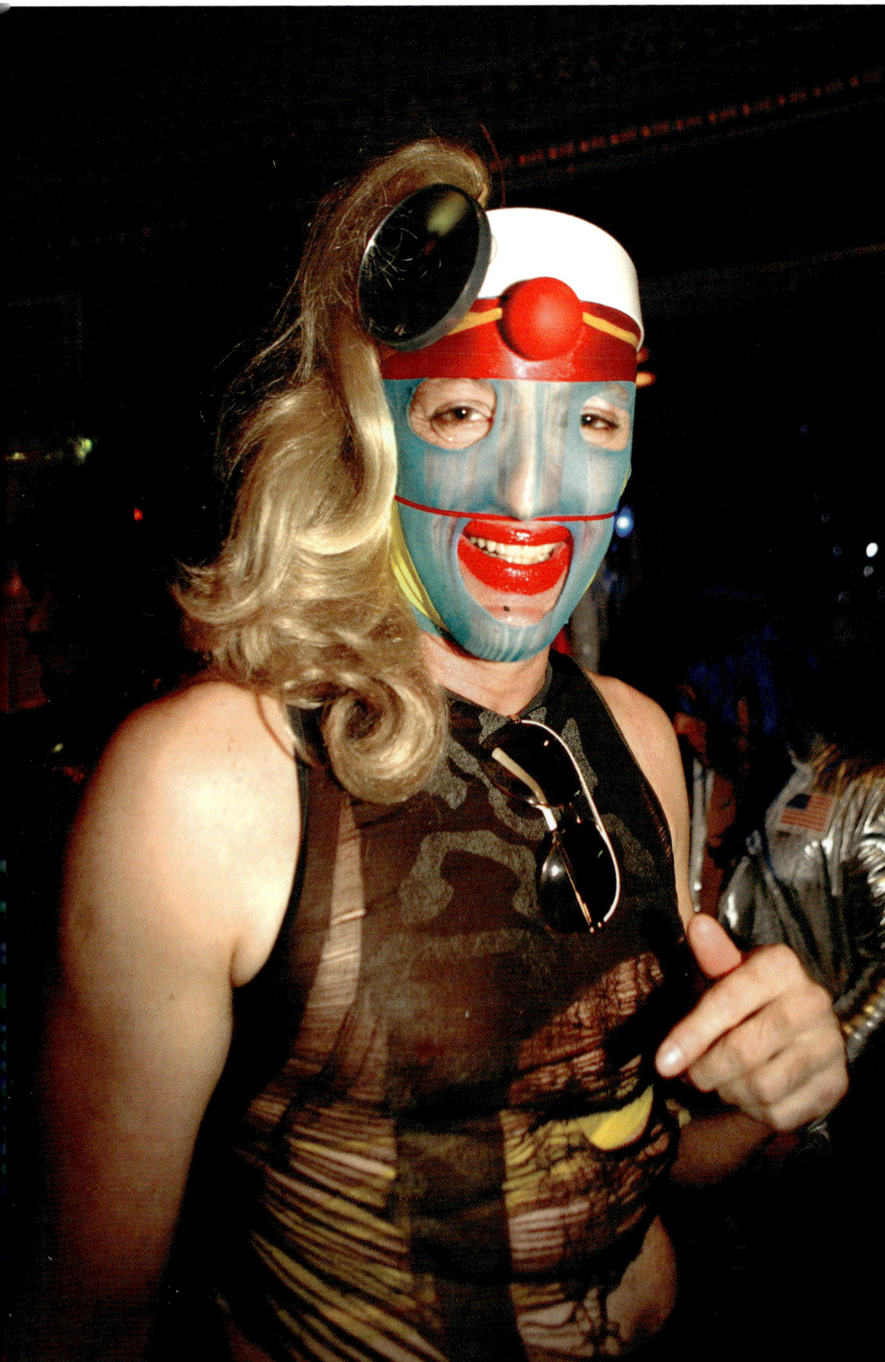

Wig Party@Cafe De Paris – Oct 2010

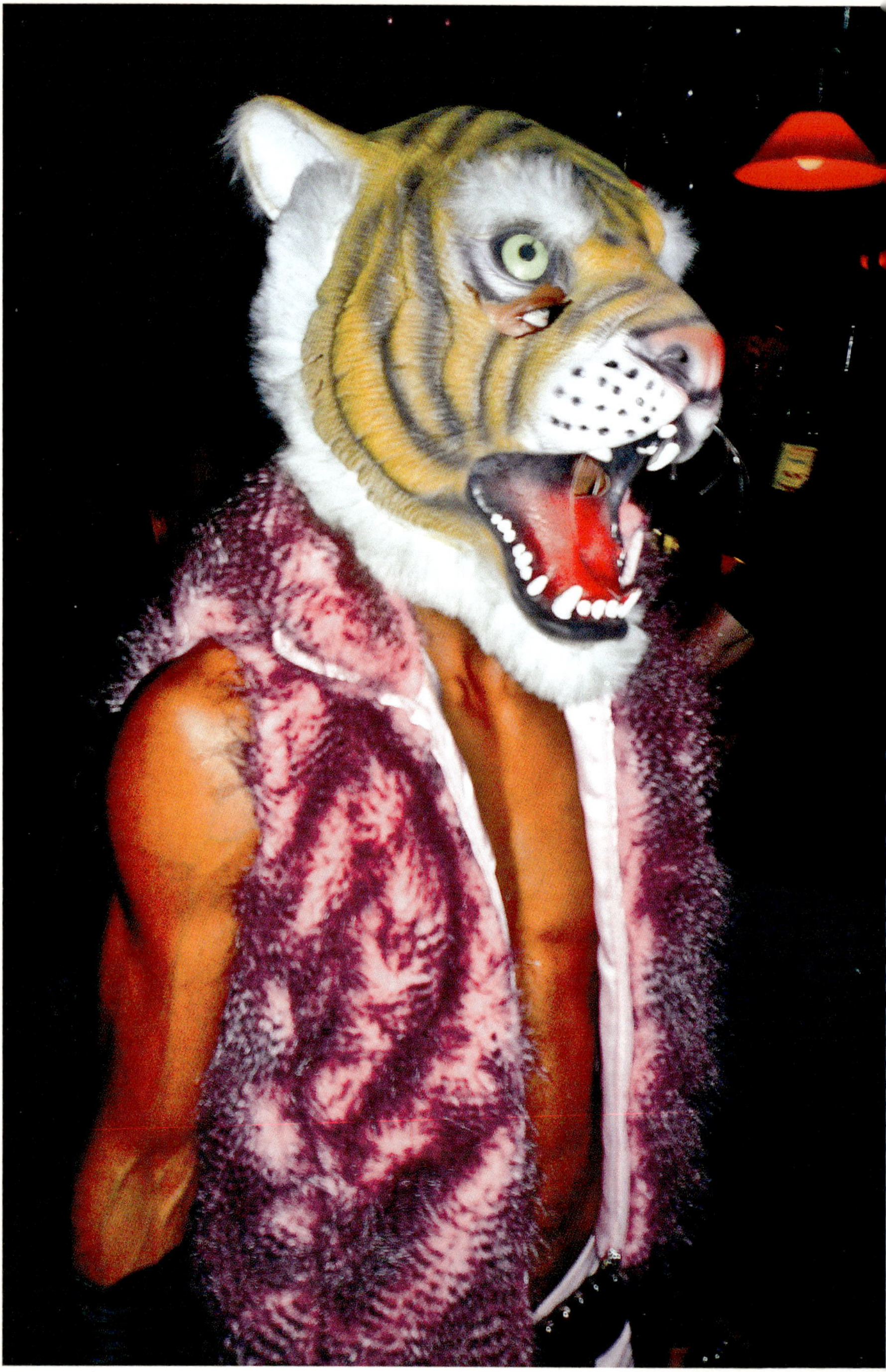

Kashpoint – Apr 2004

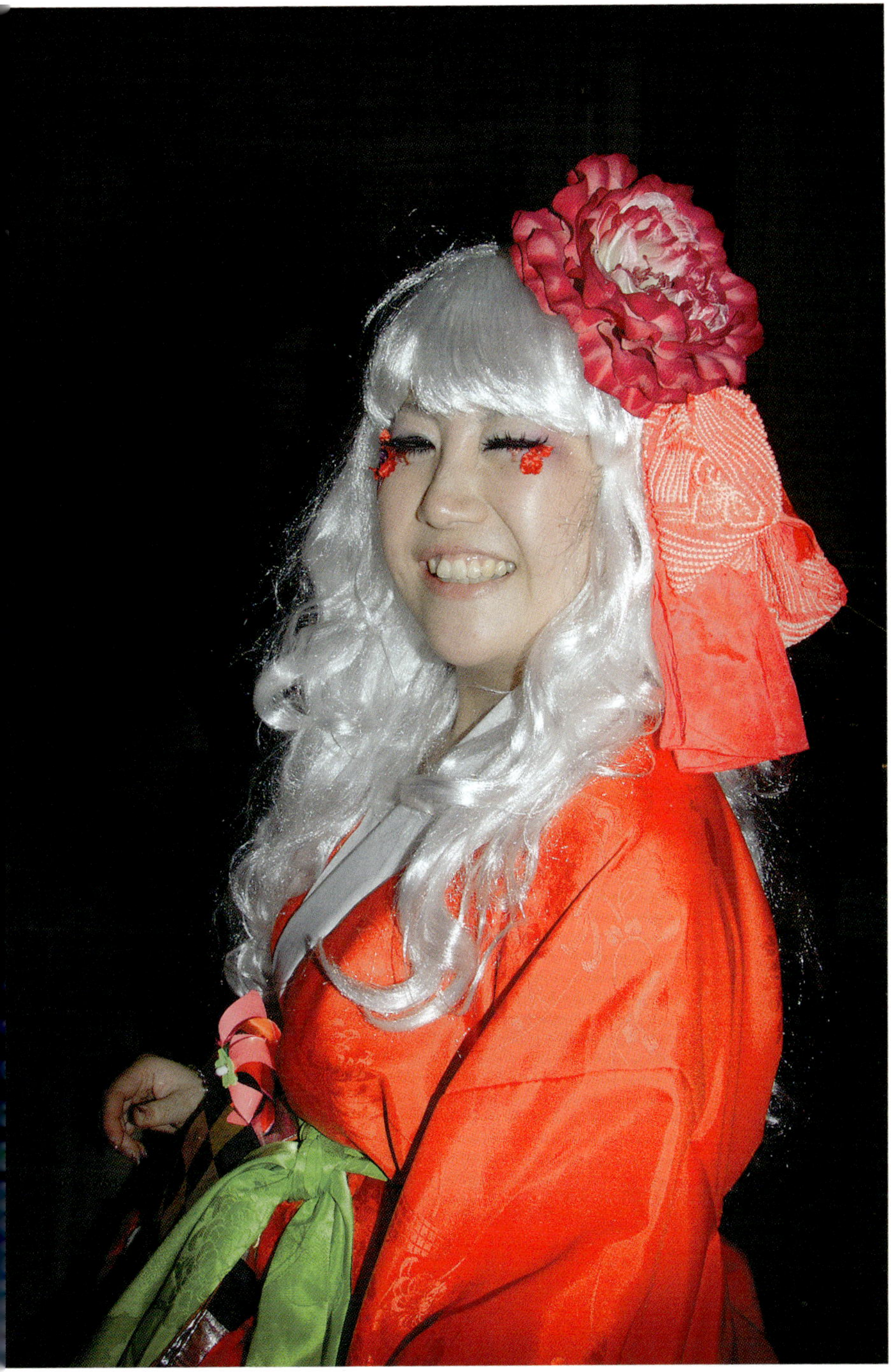

Home House – Nov 2009

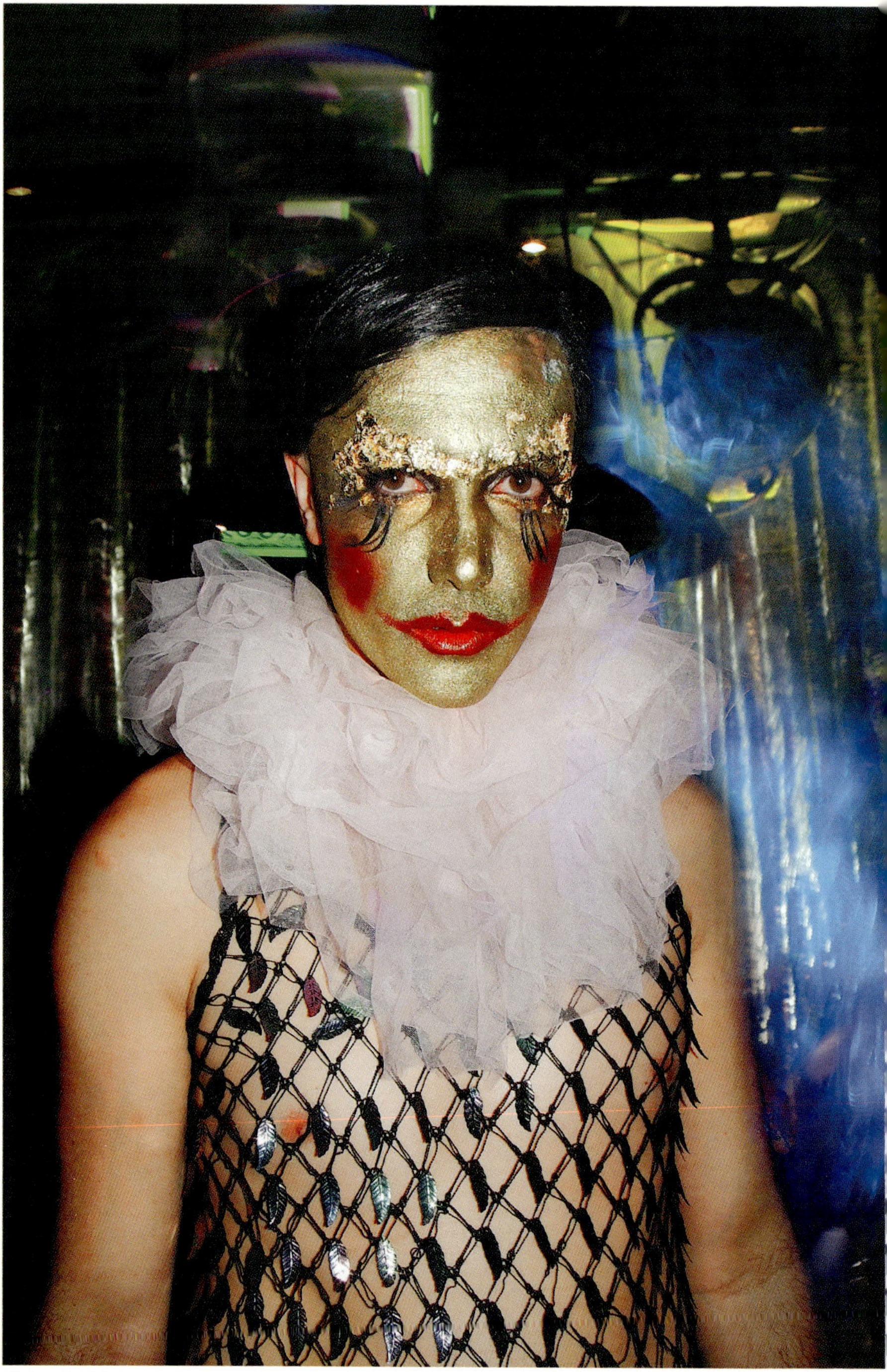

Circus – Oct 2010

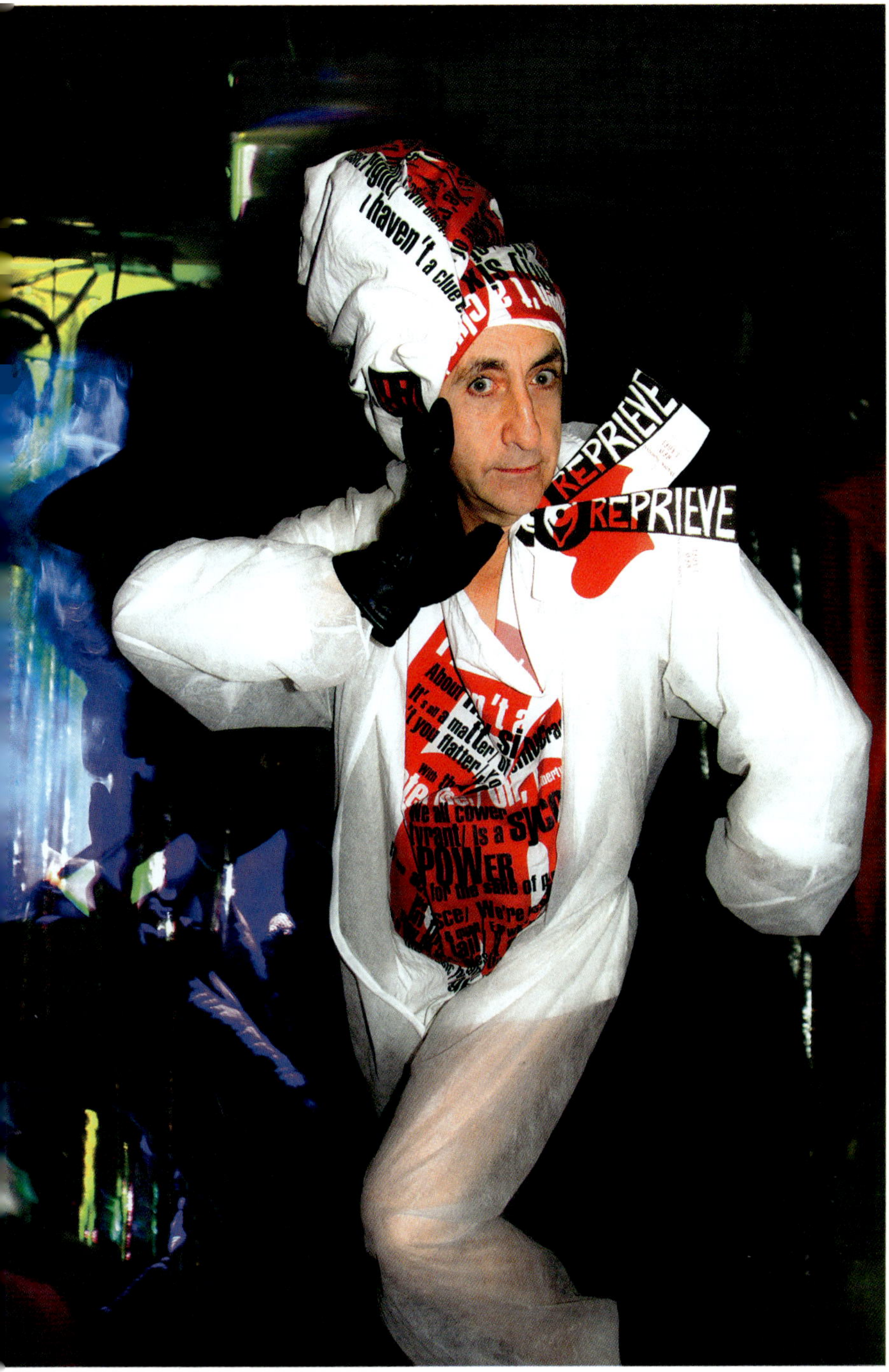

Circus – Oct 2010

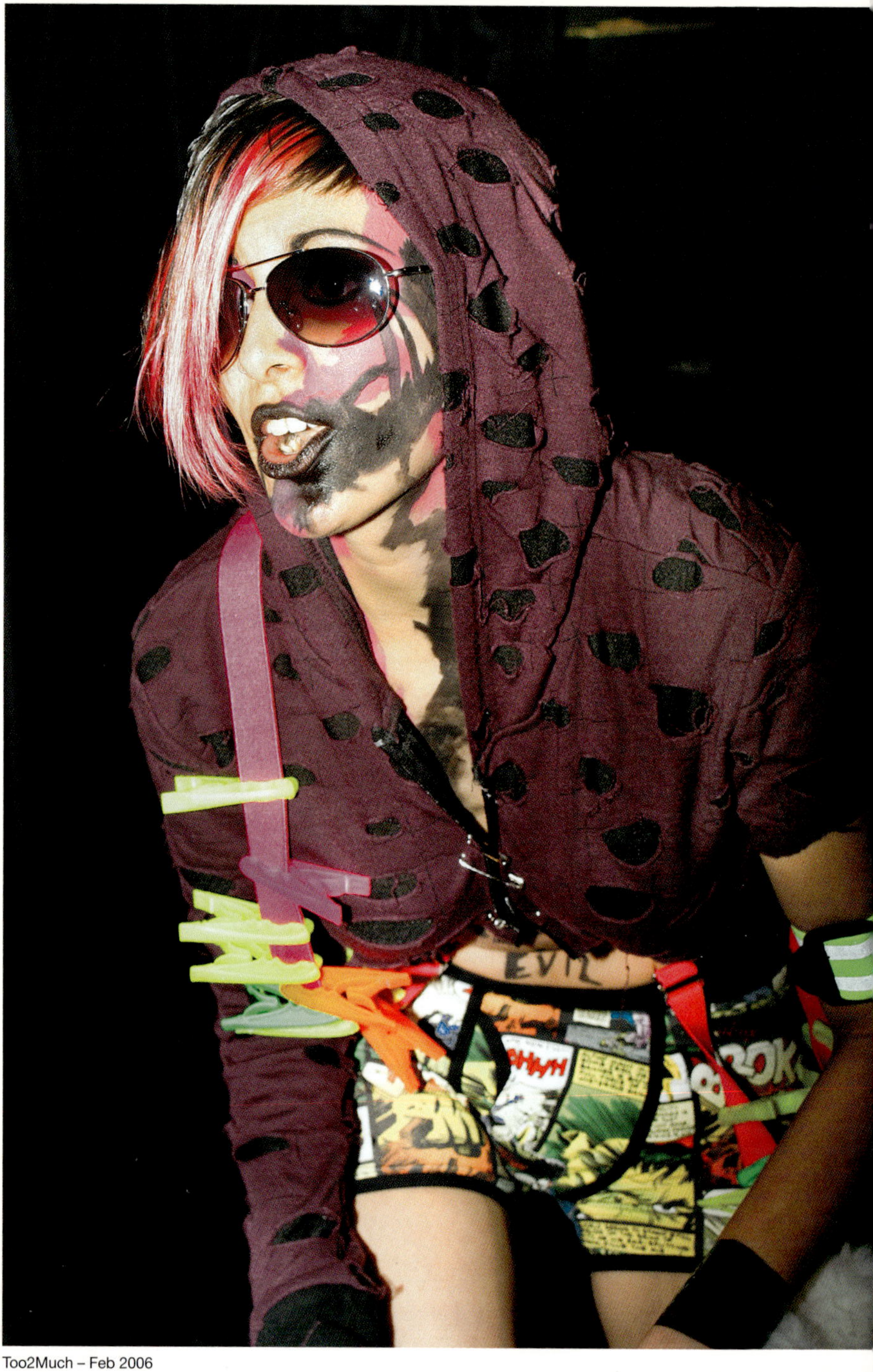

Too2Much – Feb 2006

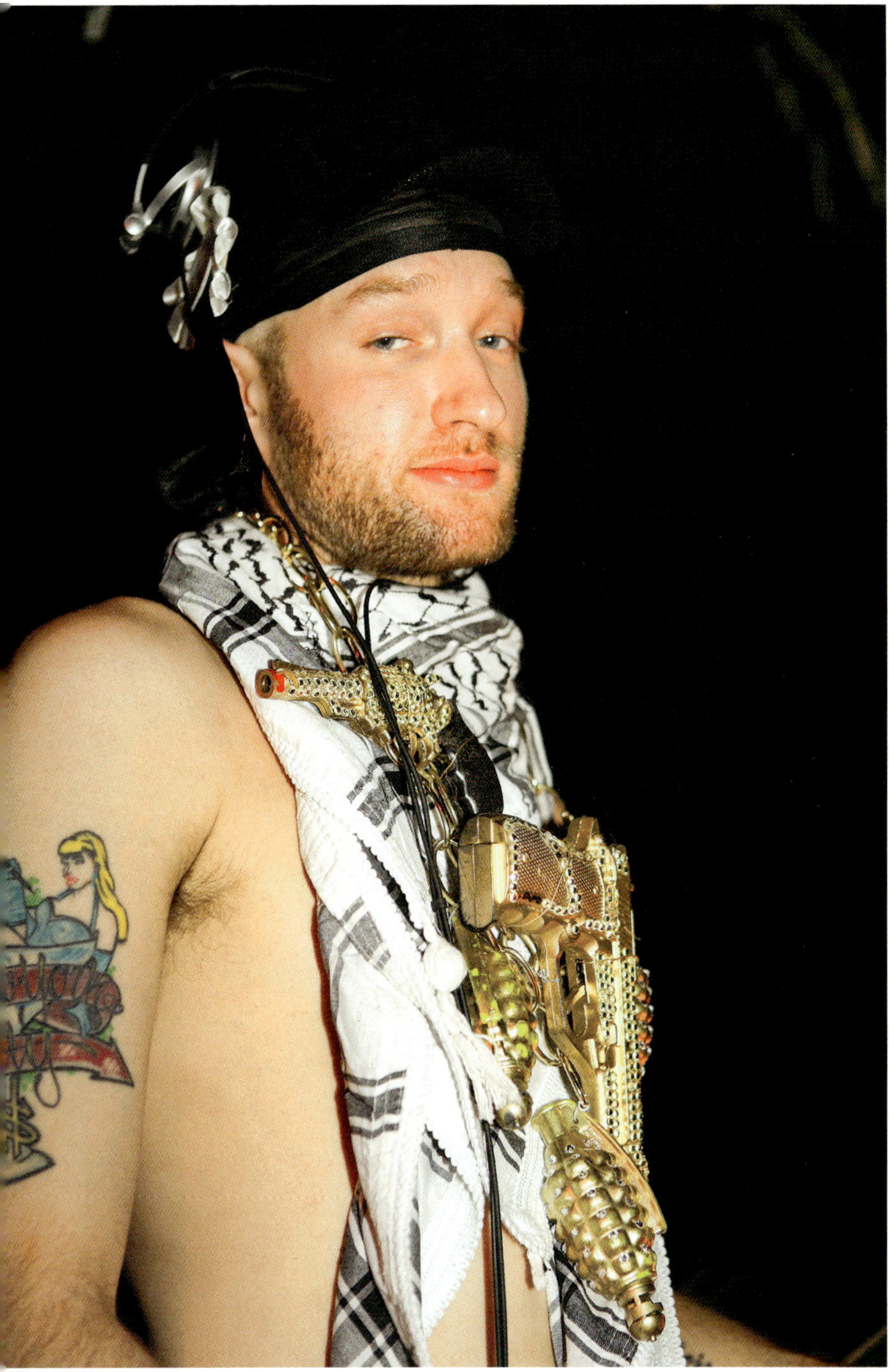

Circus – Feb 2007

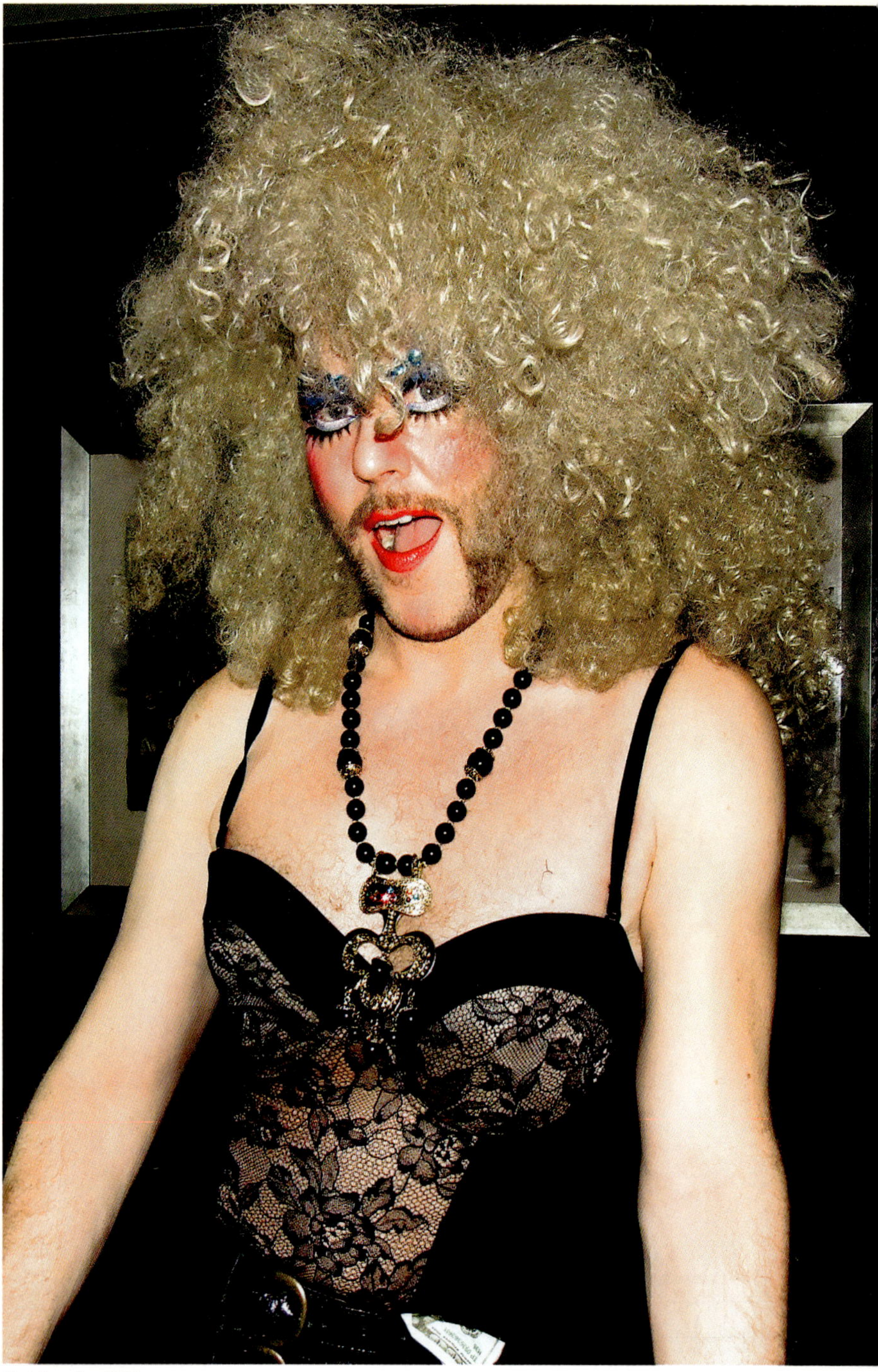

Floridita – Nov 2009

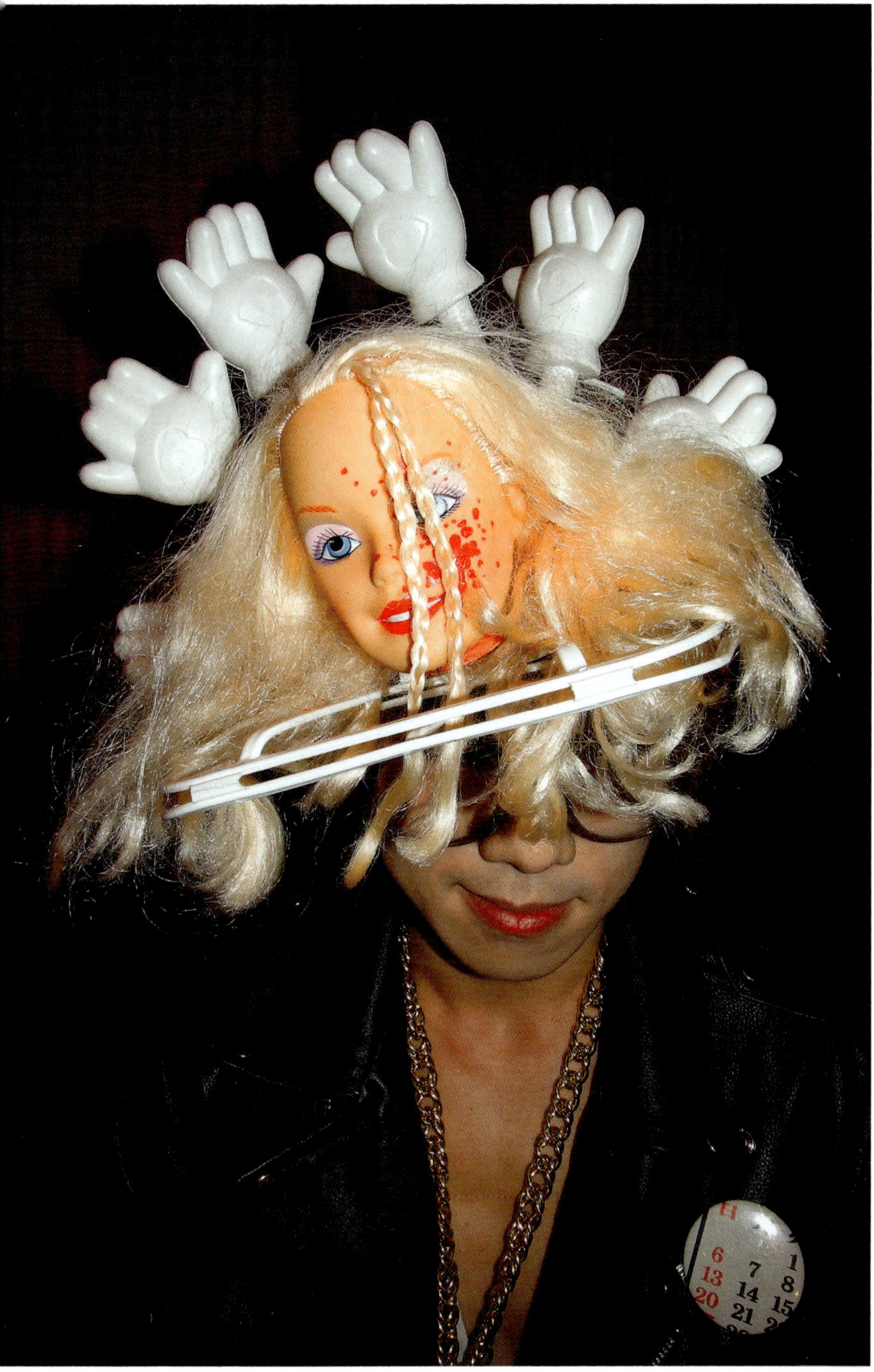

Shabba Dabba Da – Nov 2010

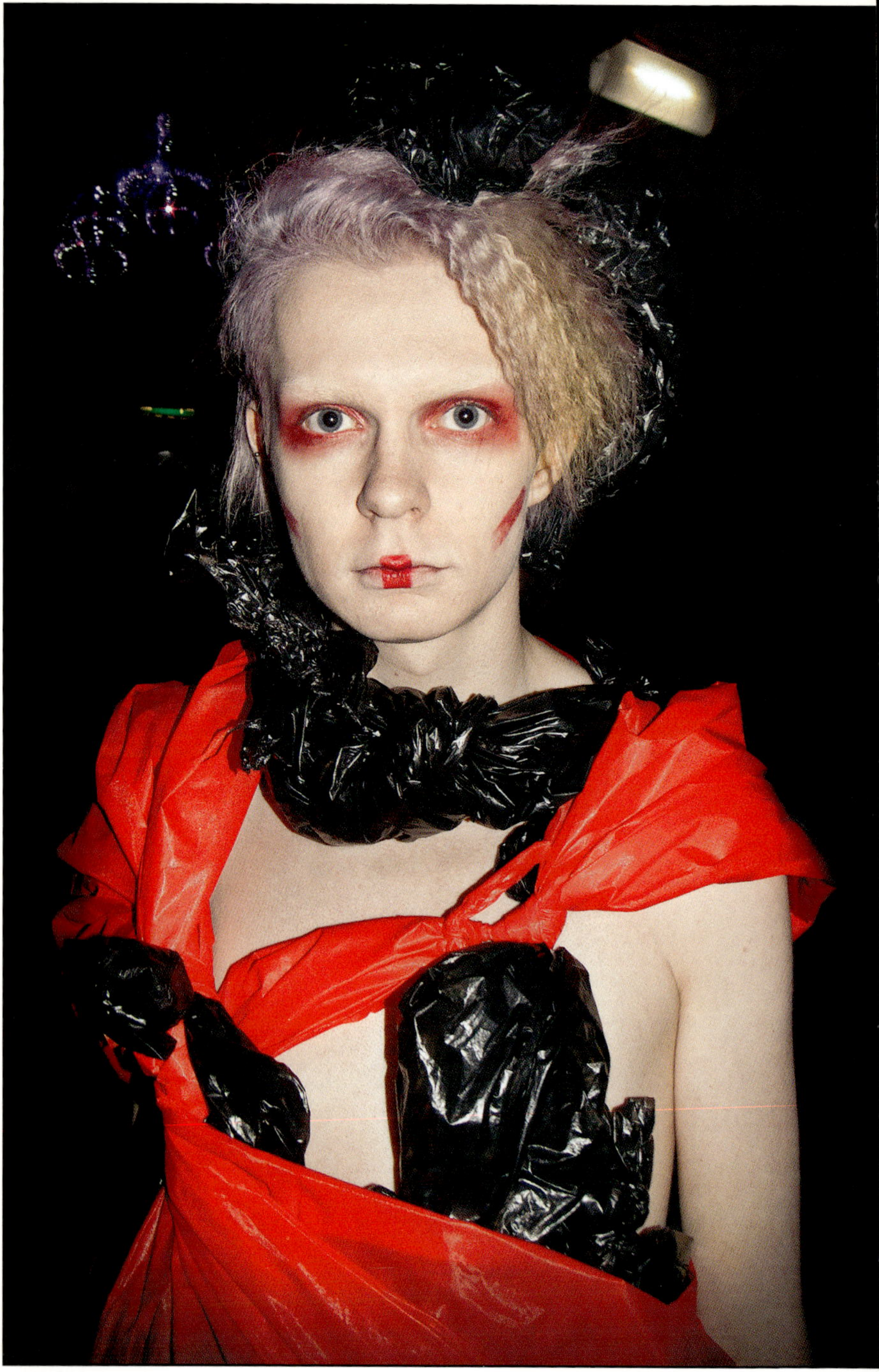

Boombox – July 2007

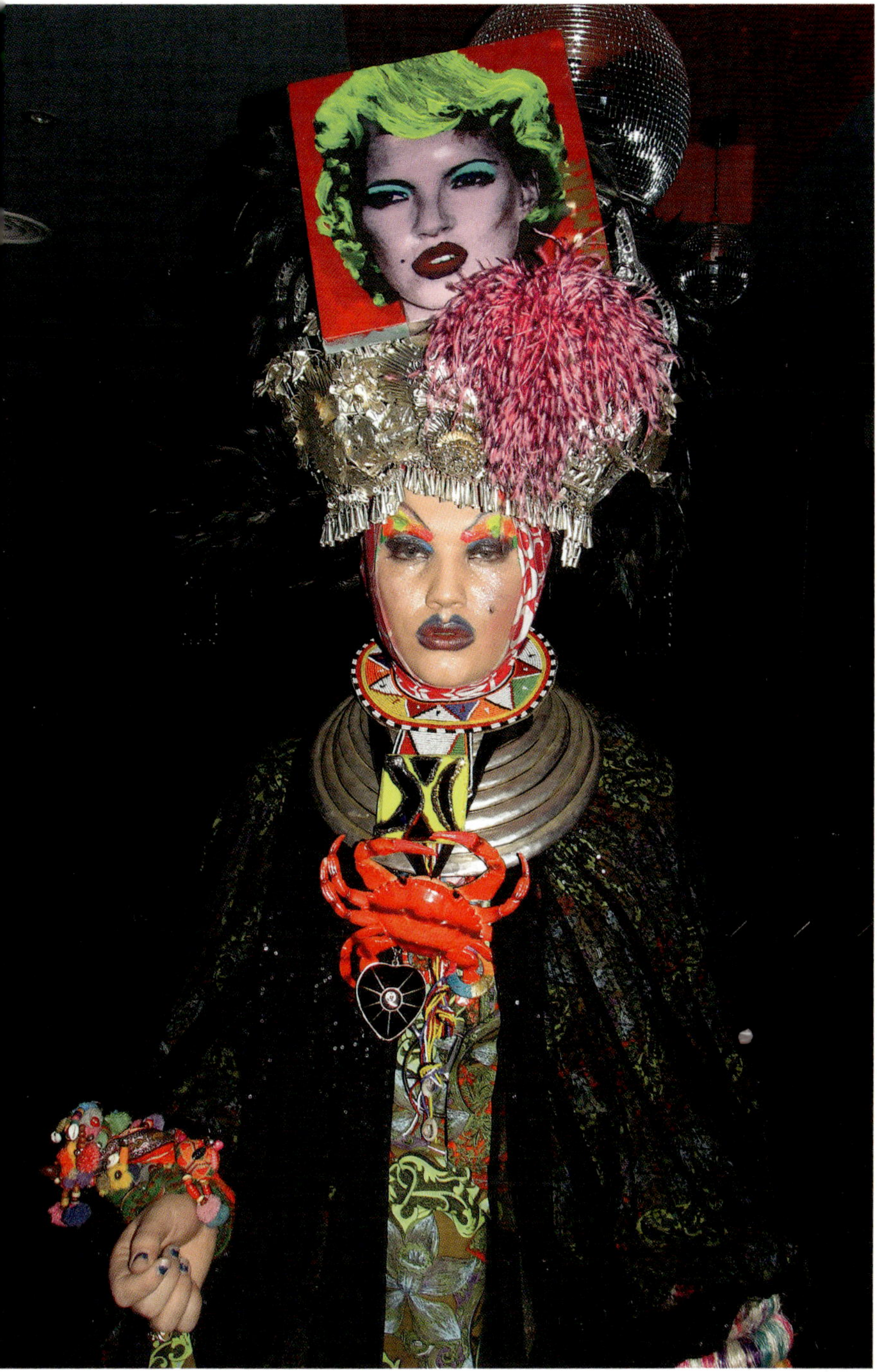

Shabba Dabba Da – Nov 2010

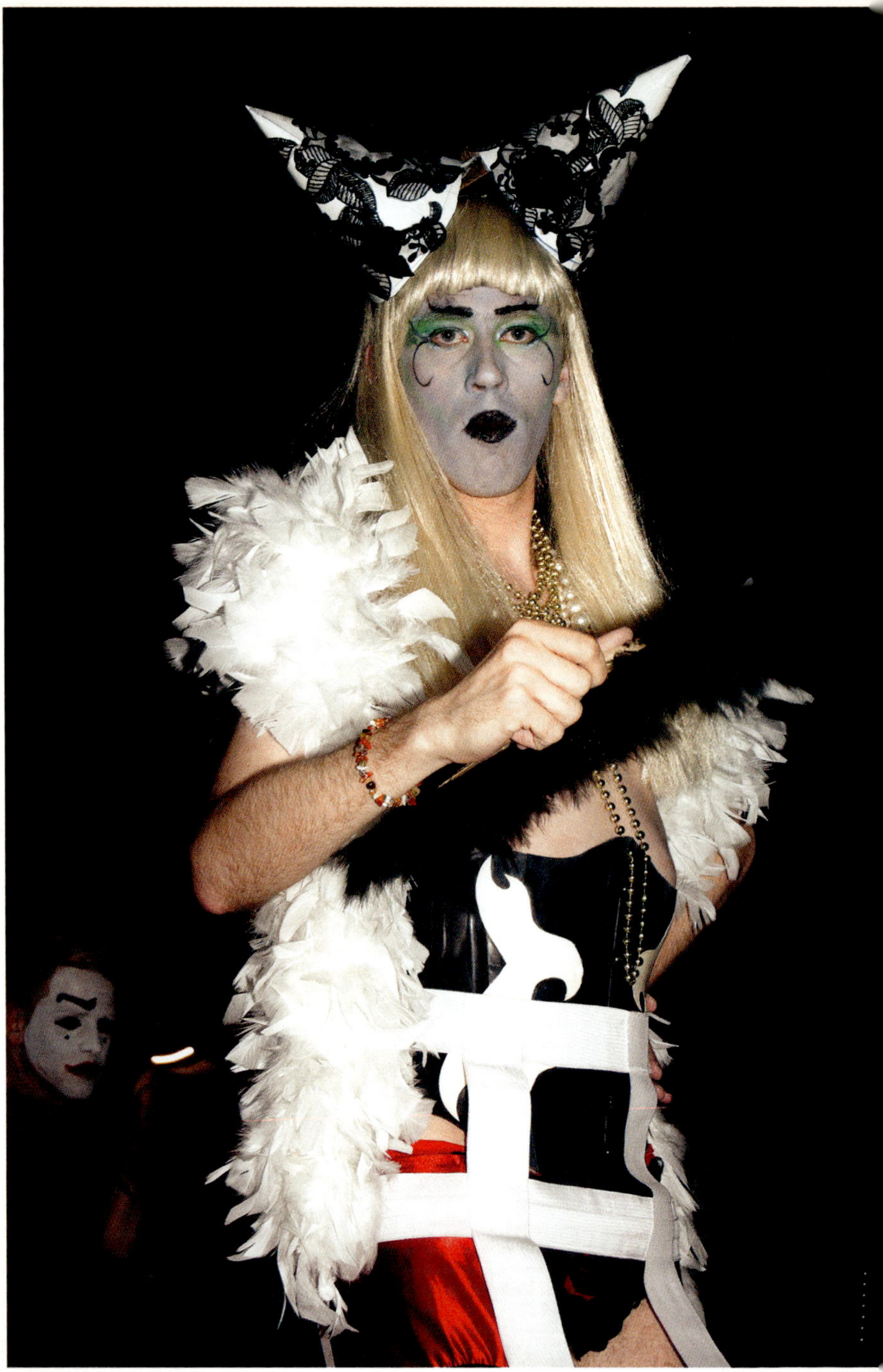

Work@Heaven – June 2007

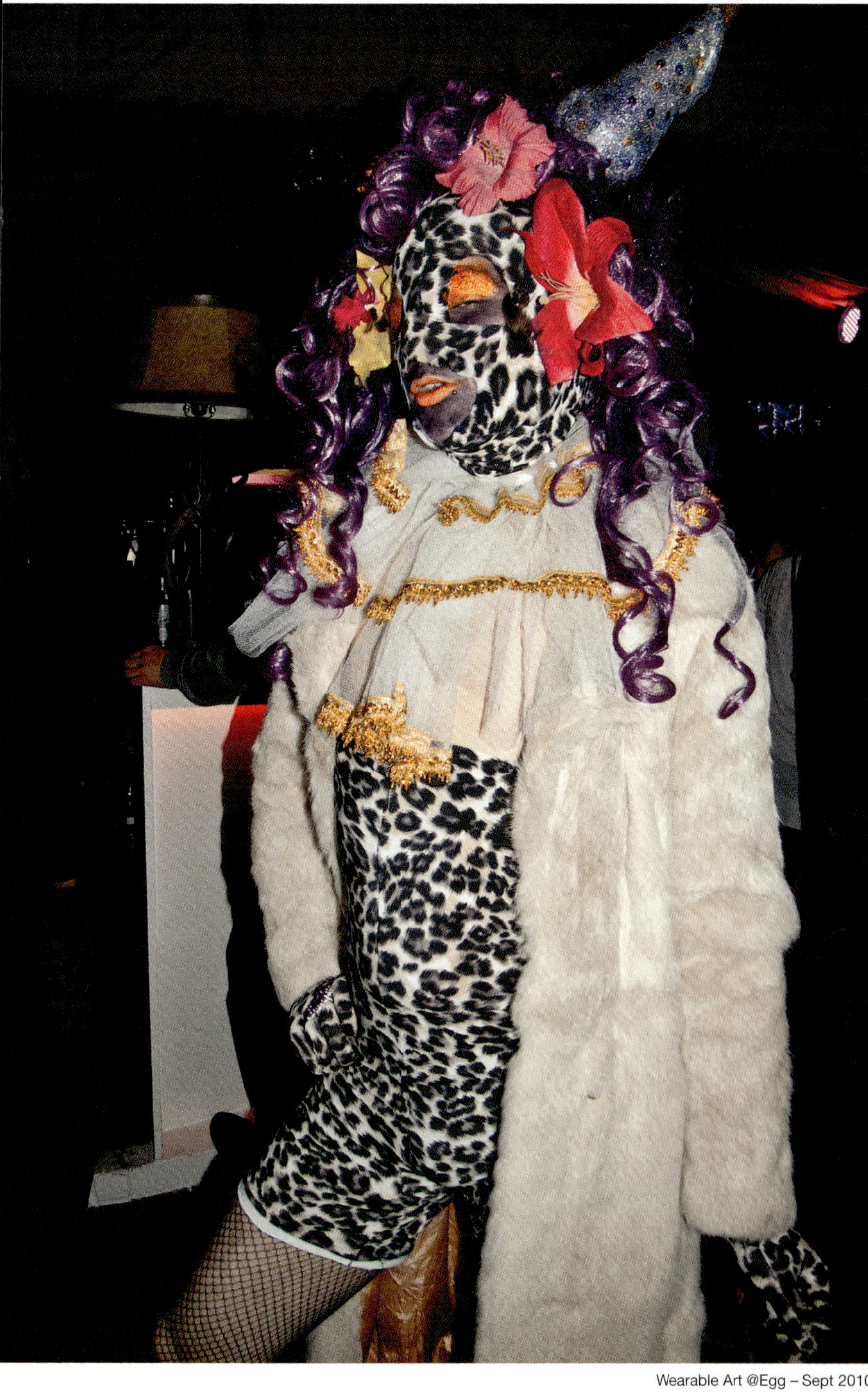

Wearable Art @Egg – Sept 2010

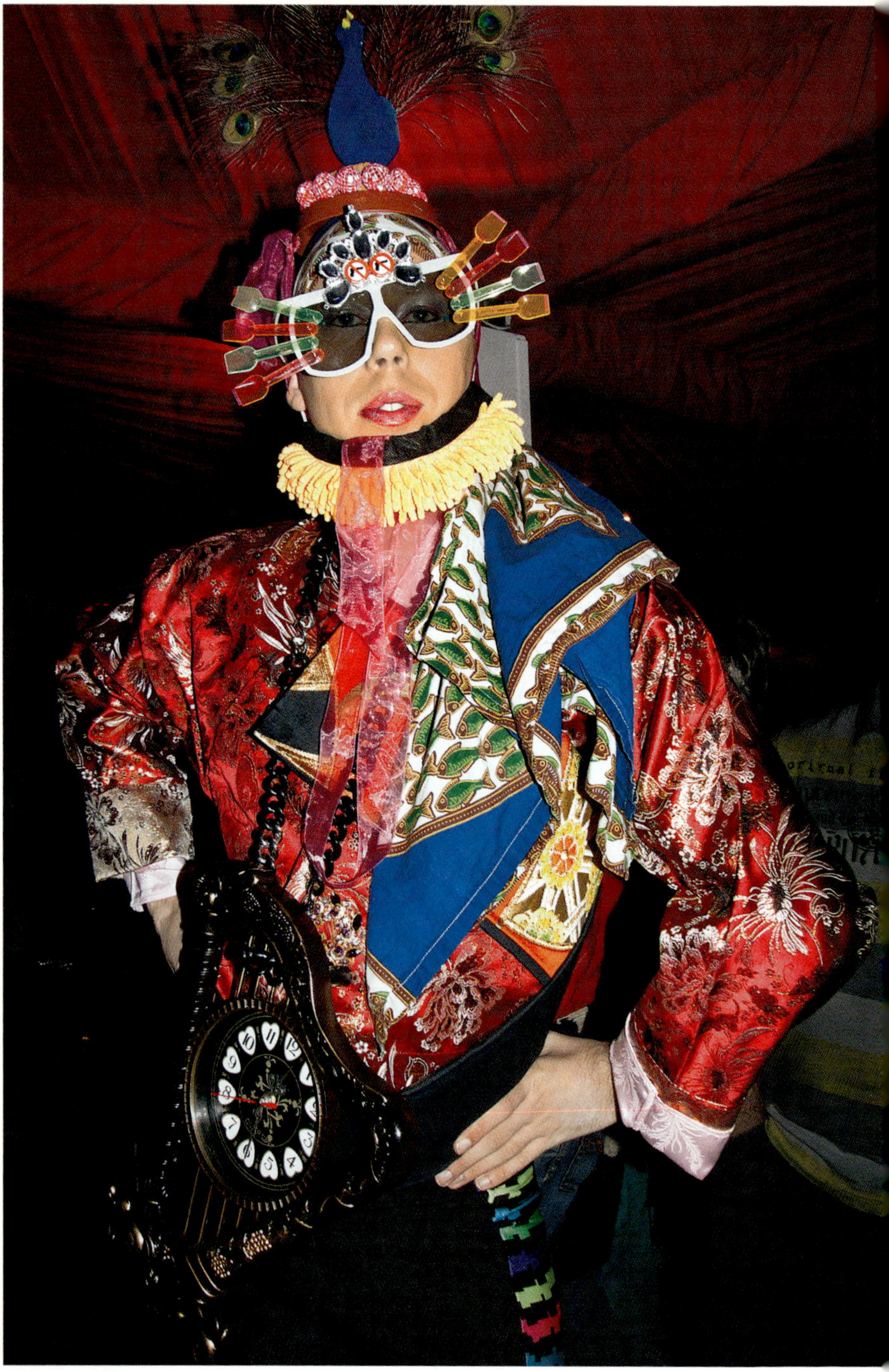

Wearable Art@Egg – Sept 2010

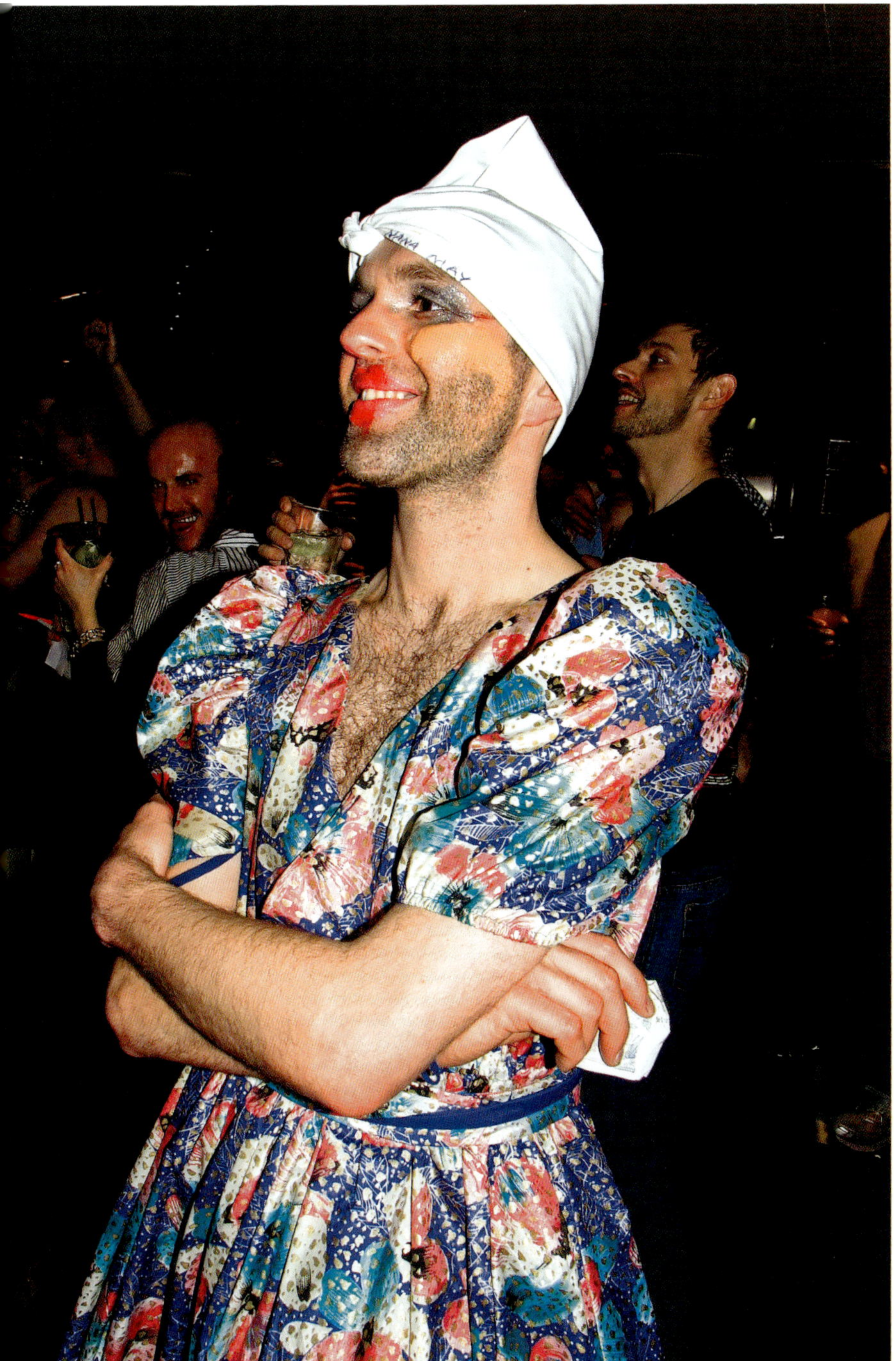

Gay Bingo@Floridita – Nov 2009

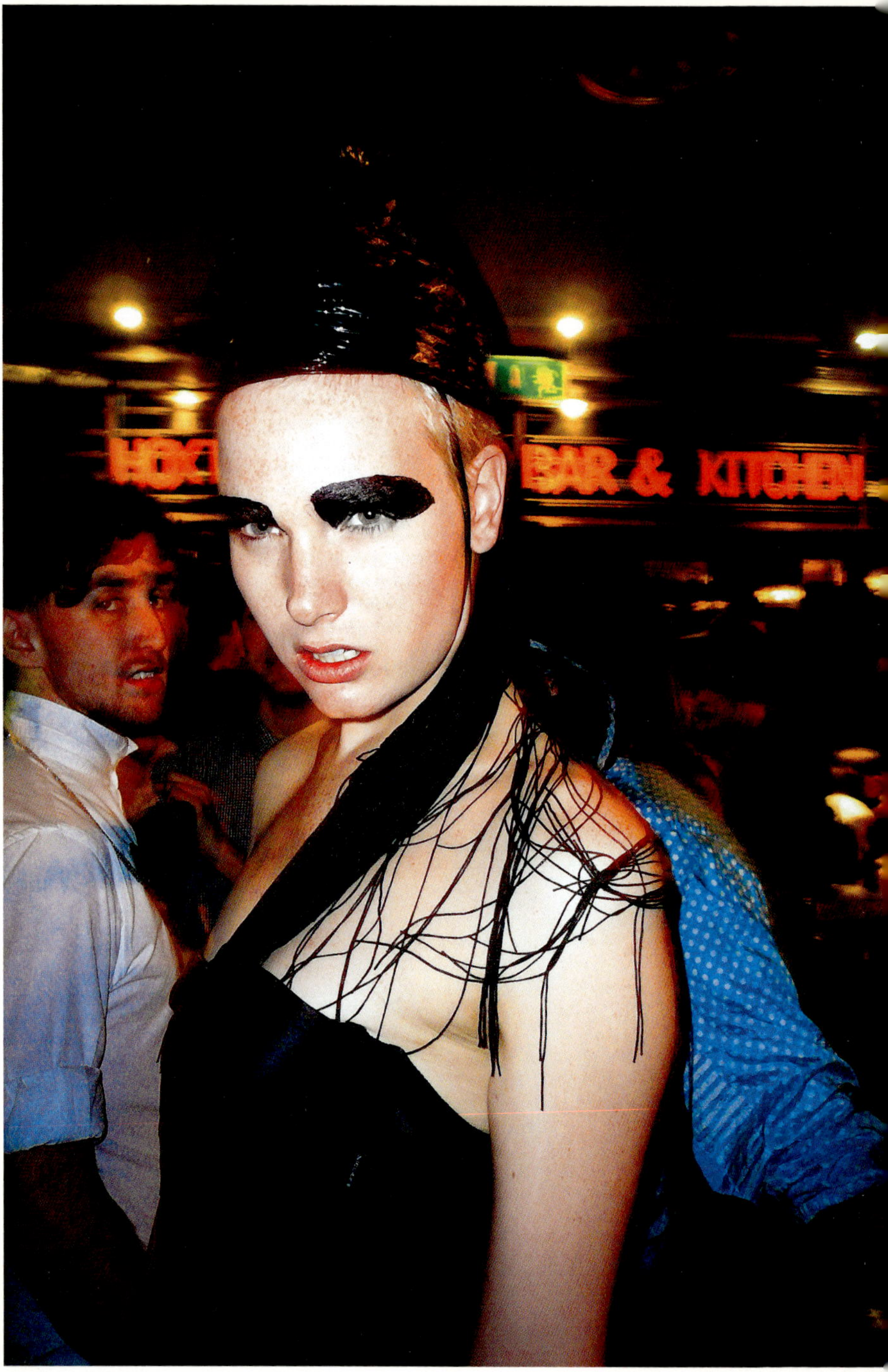

Boombox – Jan 2007

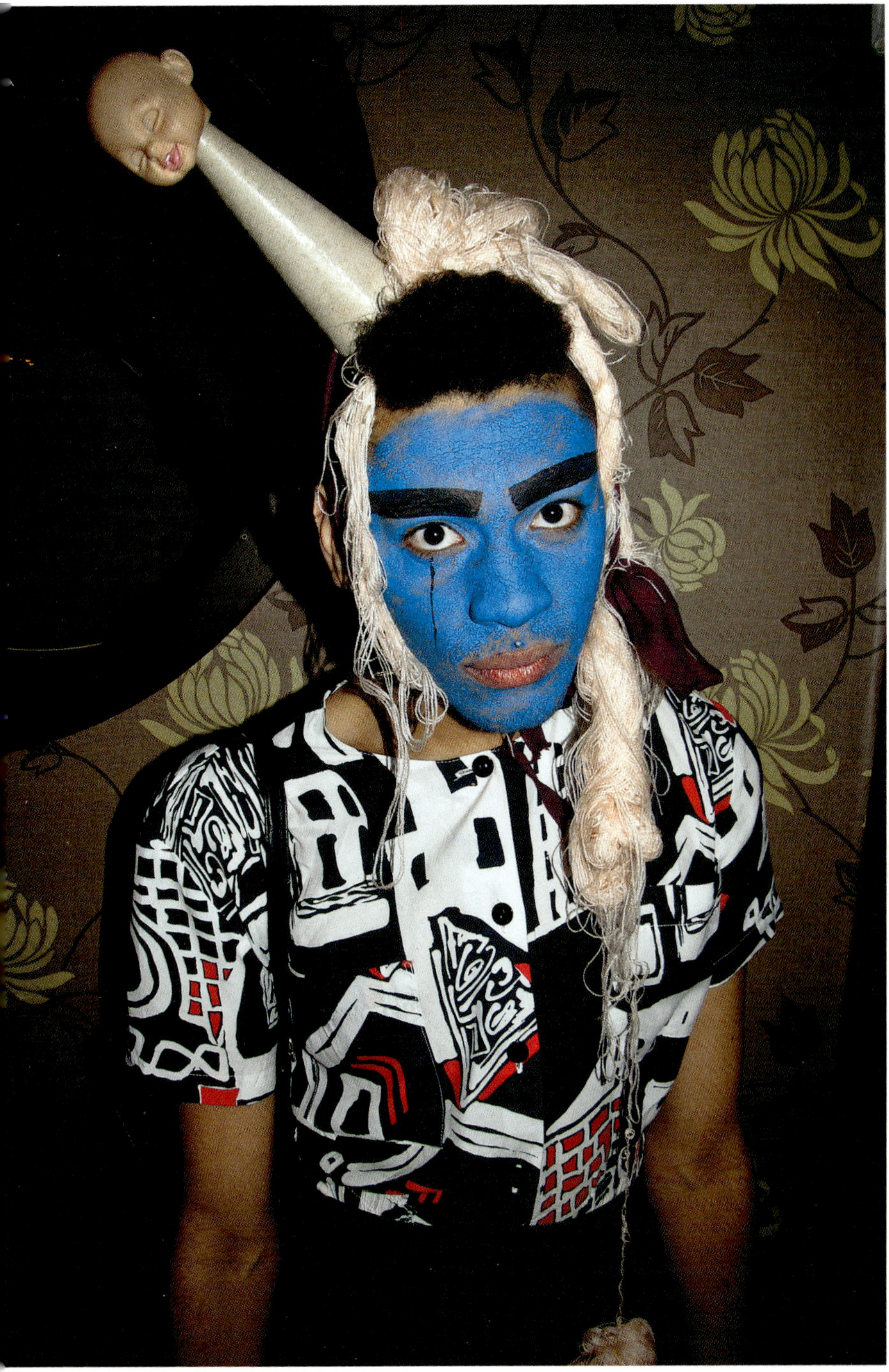

The Face – Oct 2010

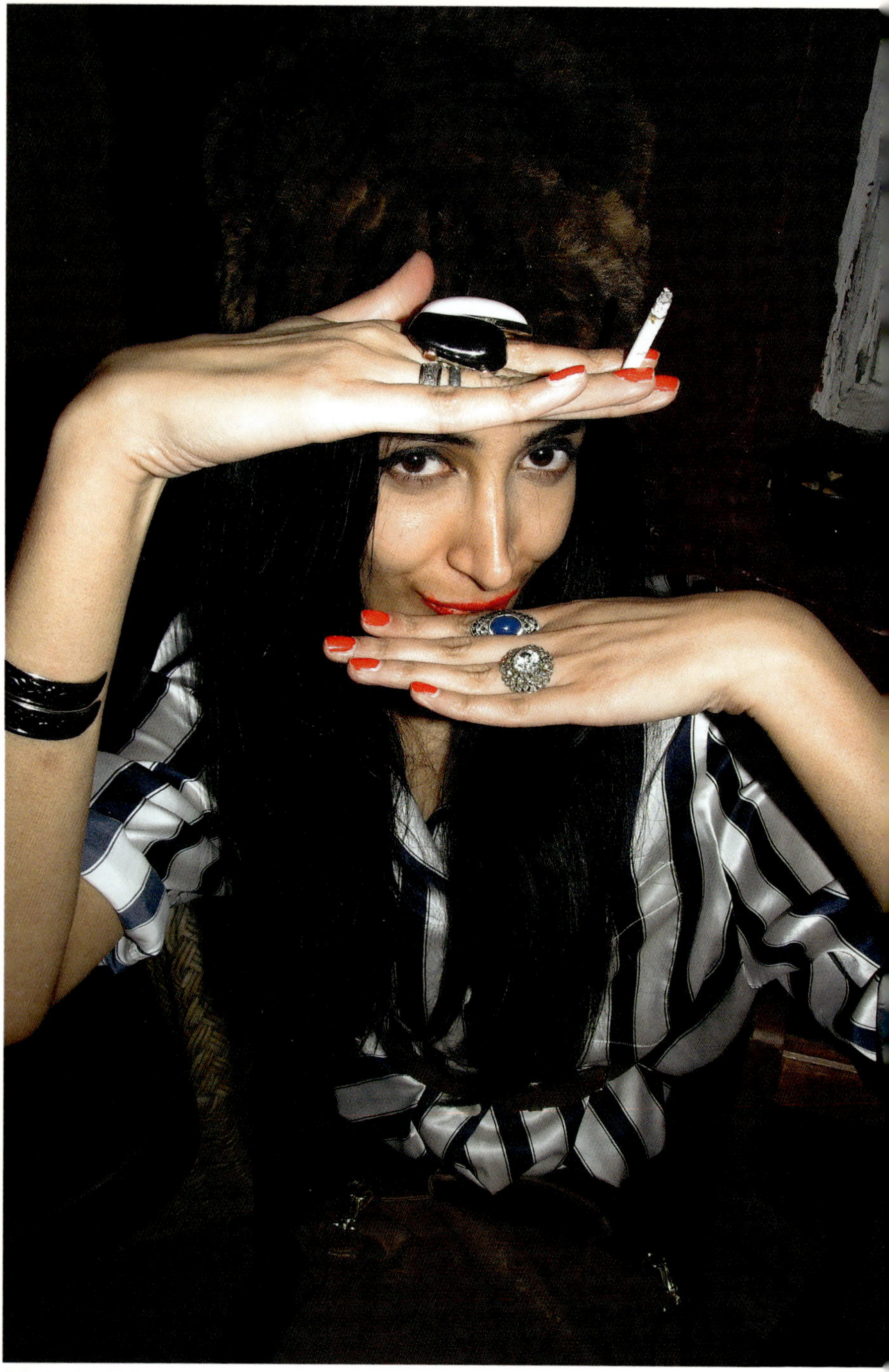

Caligula – Aug 2010

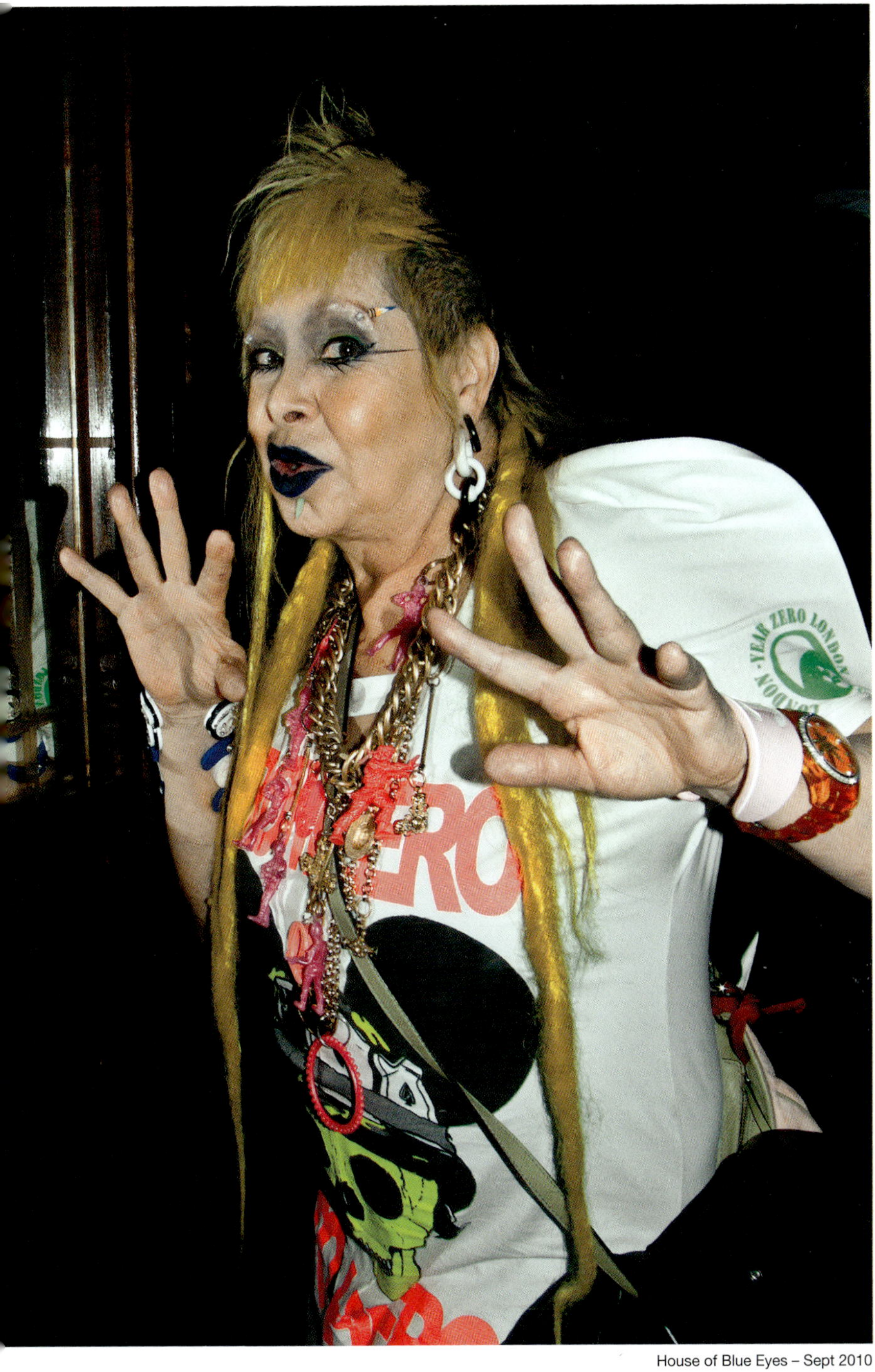

House of Blue Eyes – Sept 2010

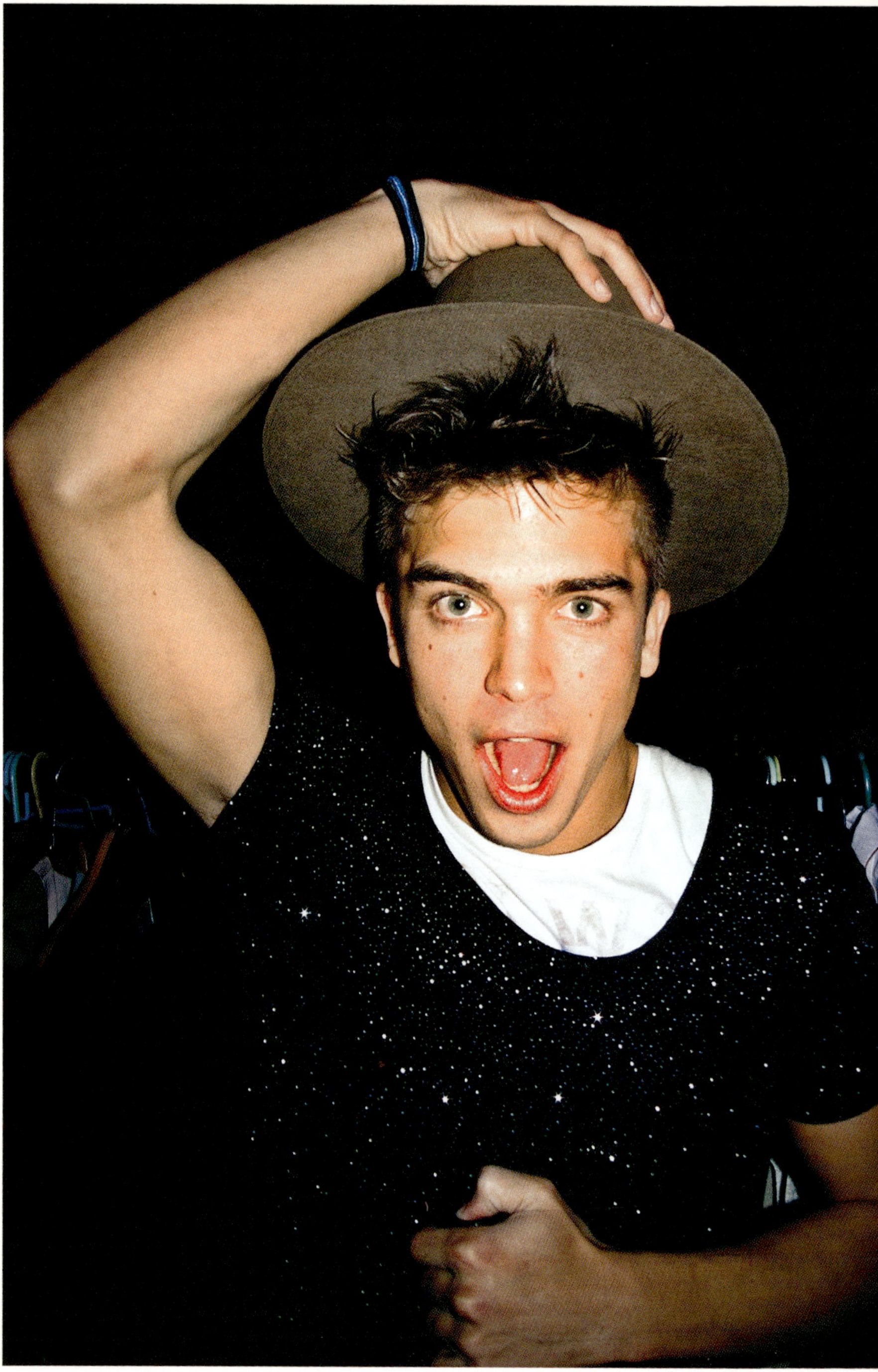

Wearable Art@Egg – Sept 2010

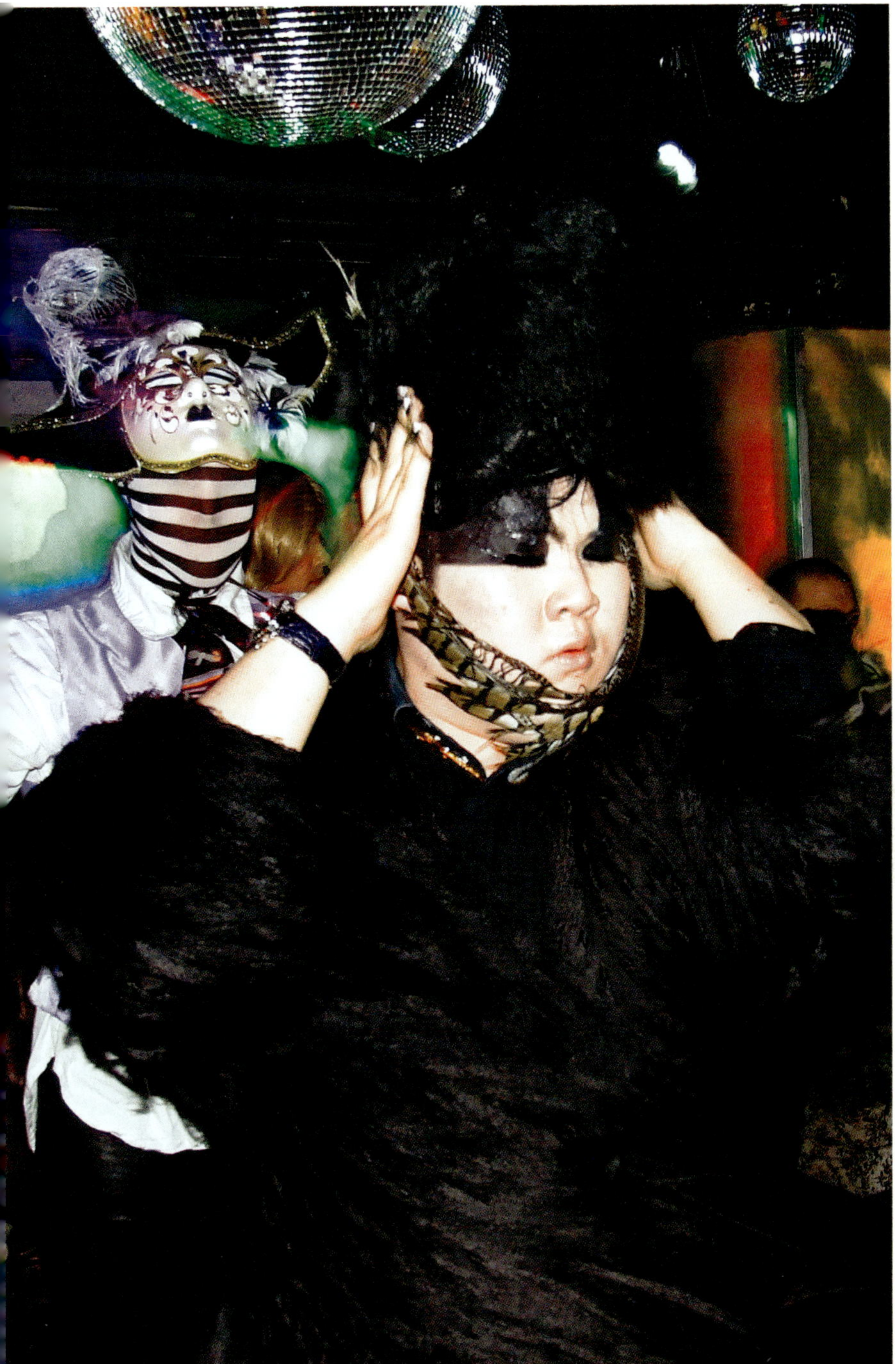

Your Mum's House – Jan 2010

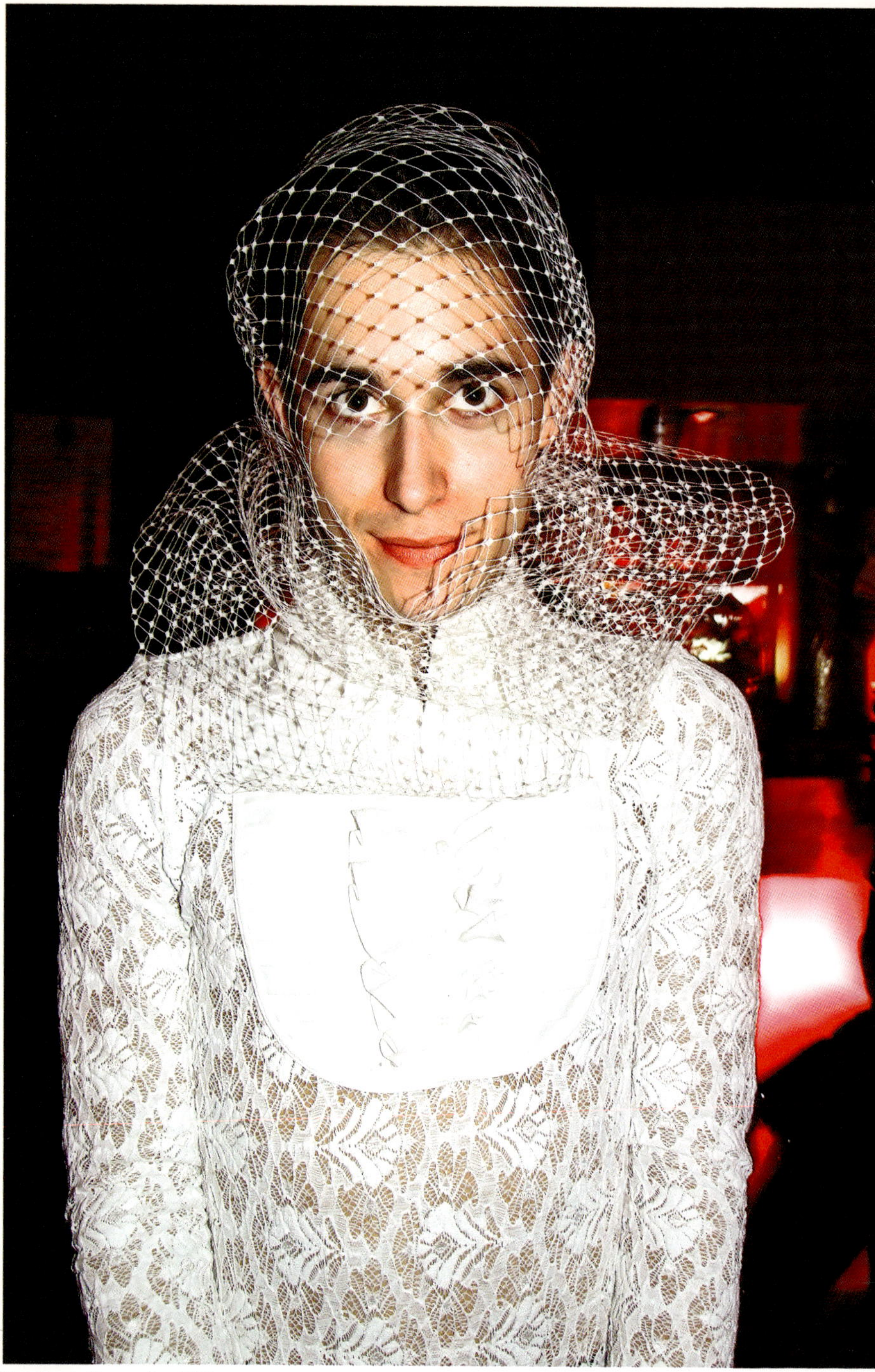

Your Mum's House – Dec 2009

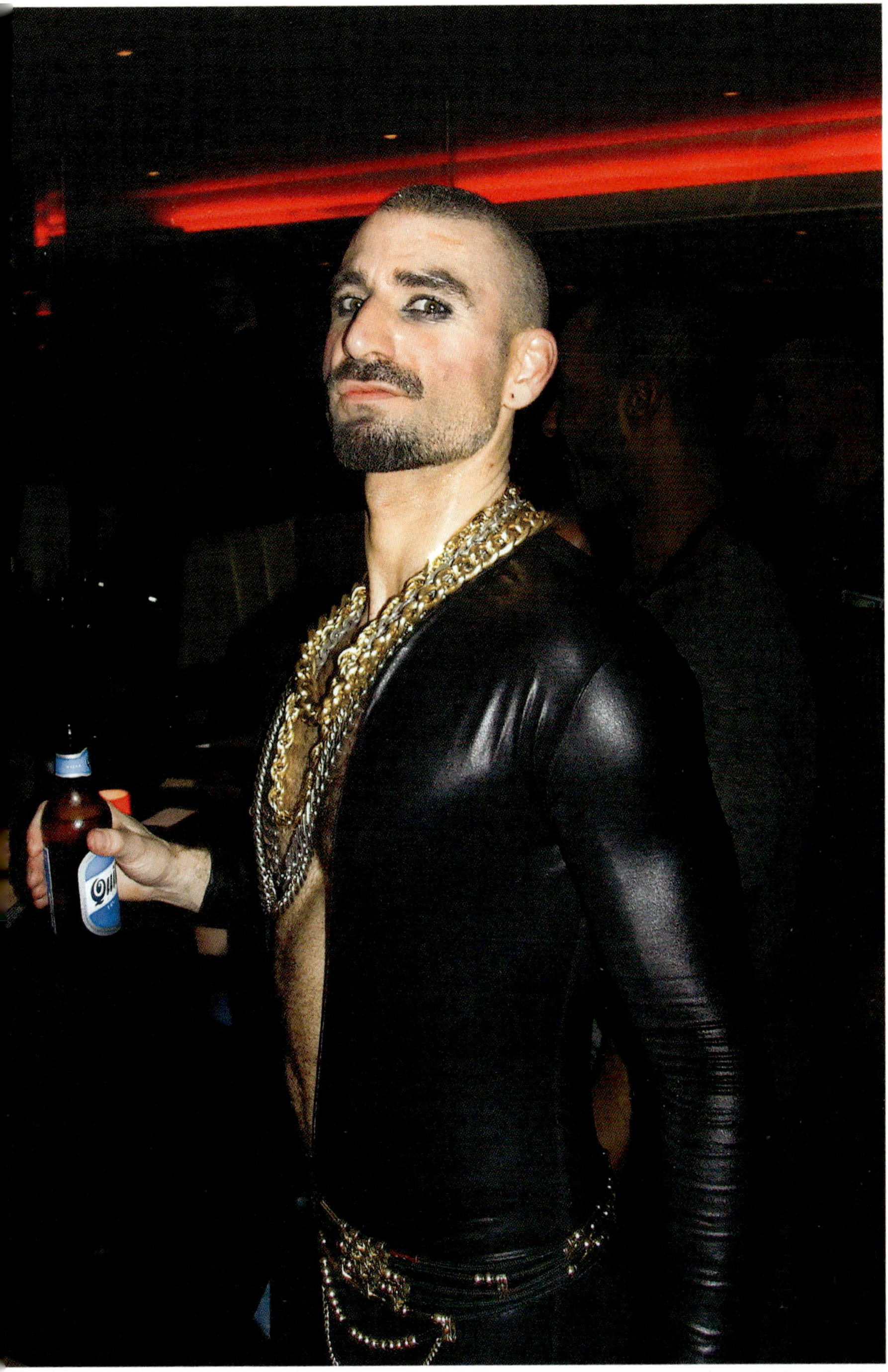

Gay Bingo@Floridita – Nov 2009

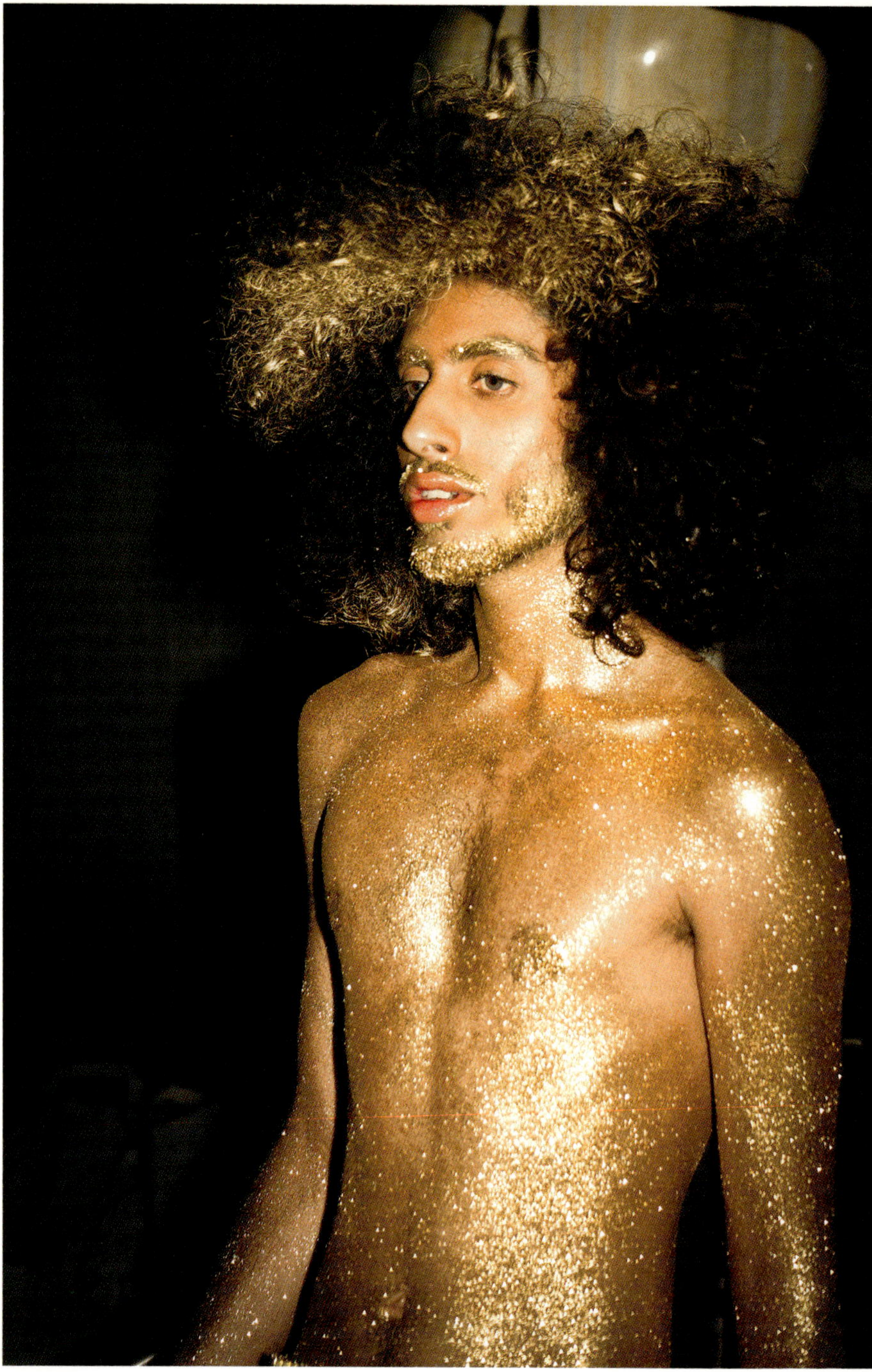

House of Blue Eyes – Sept 2009

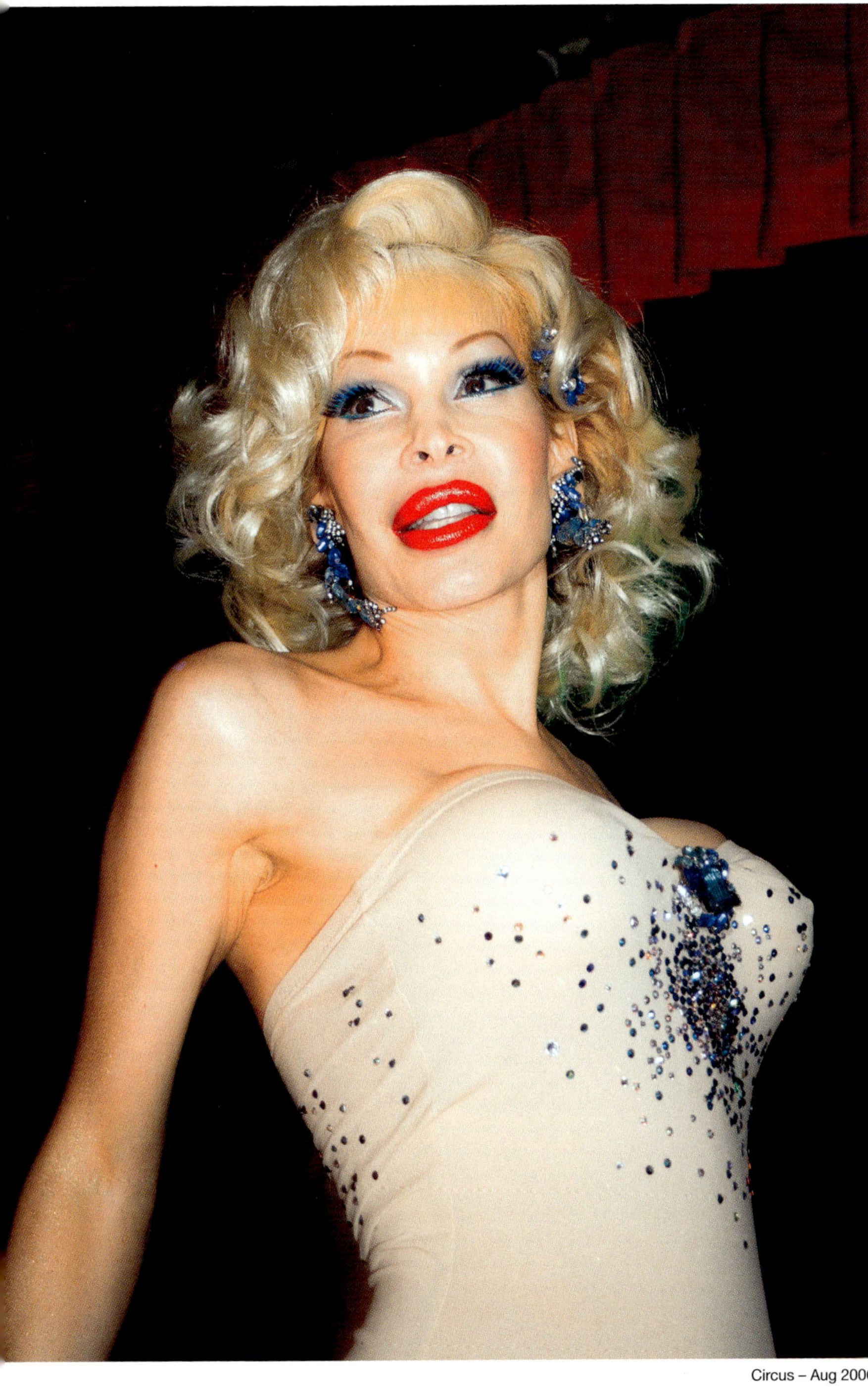

Circus – Aug 2006

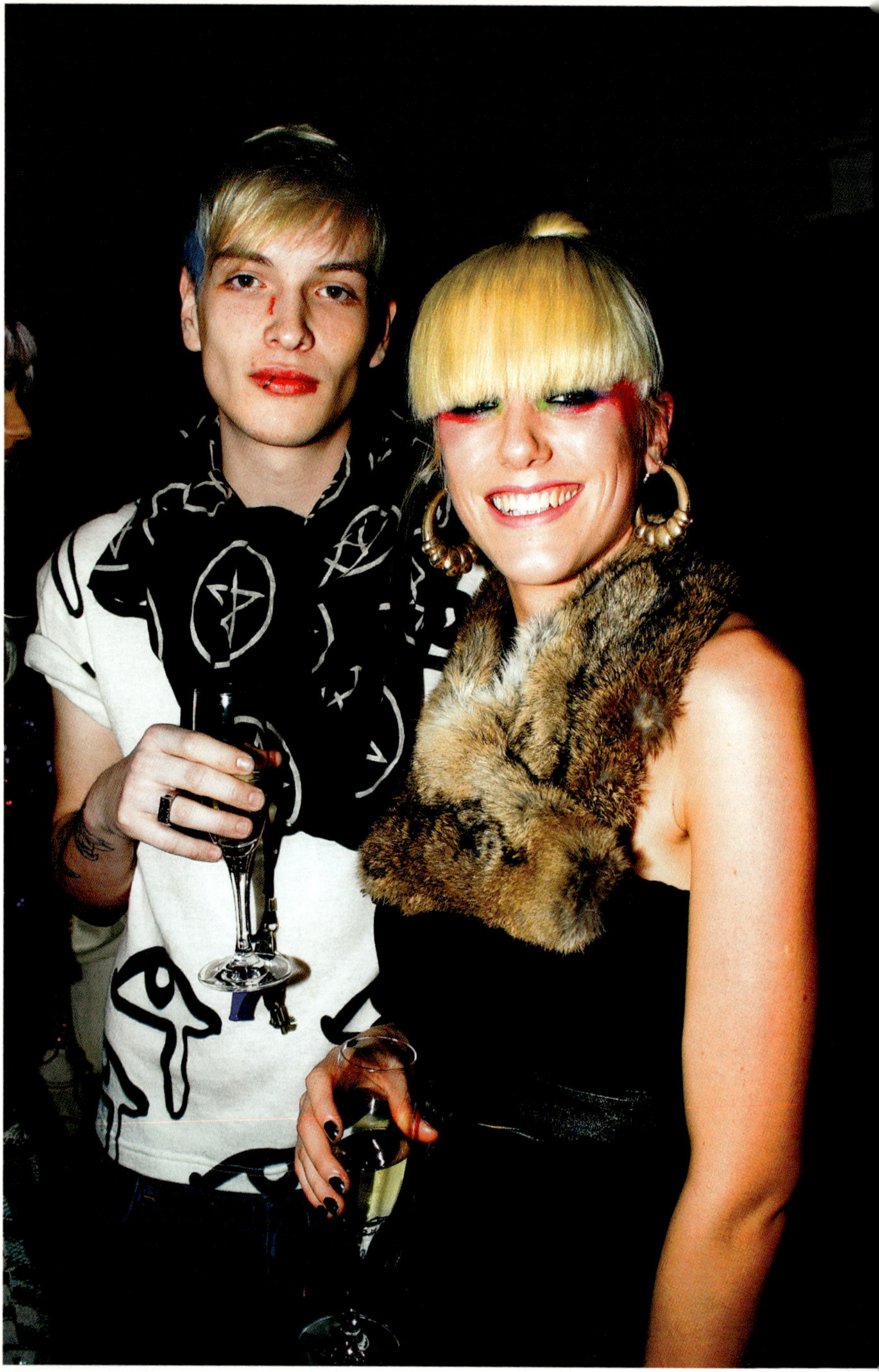

POP party – Sept 2007

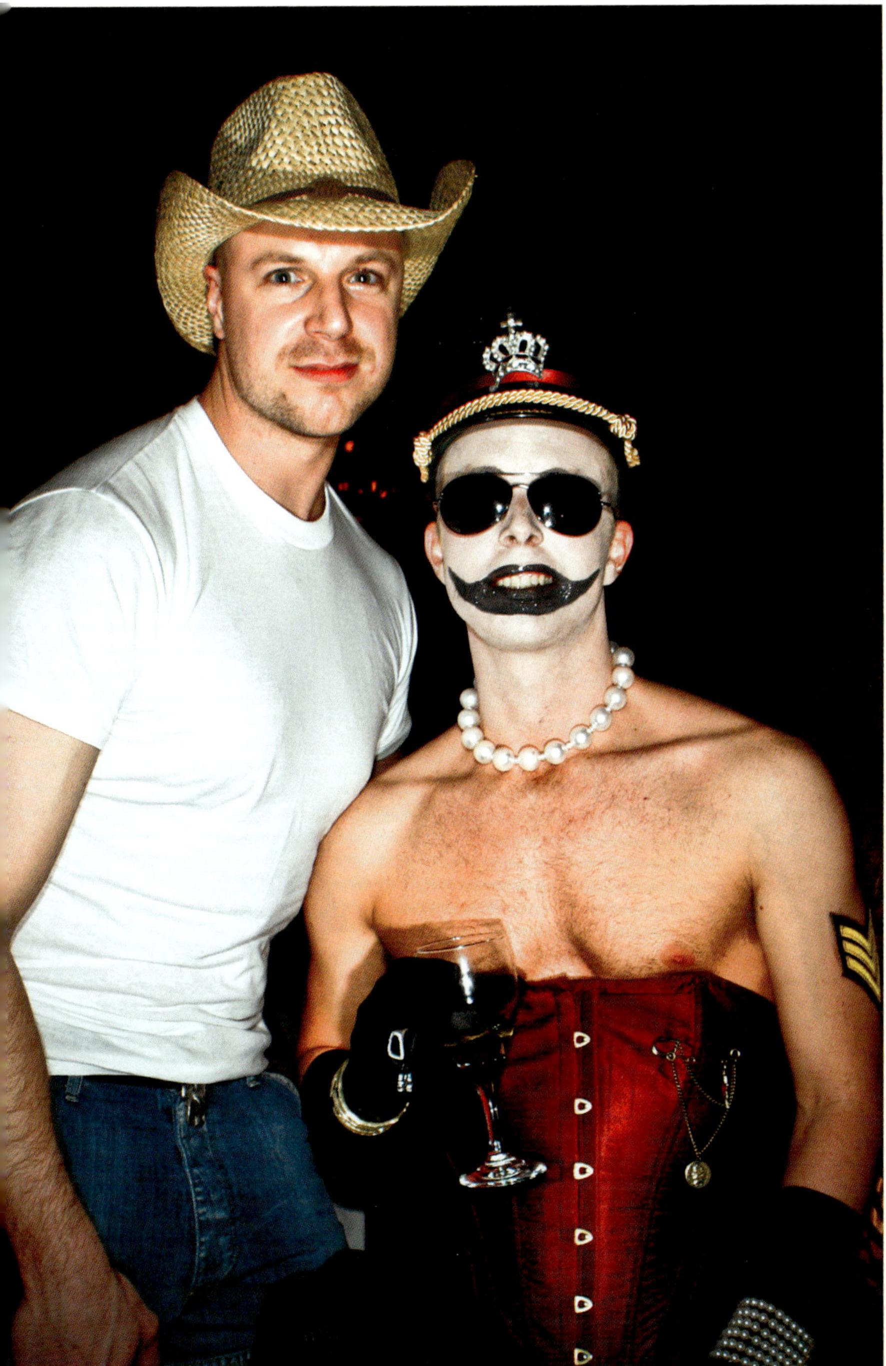

Circus – Oct 2006

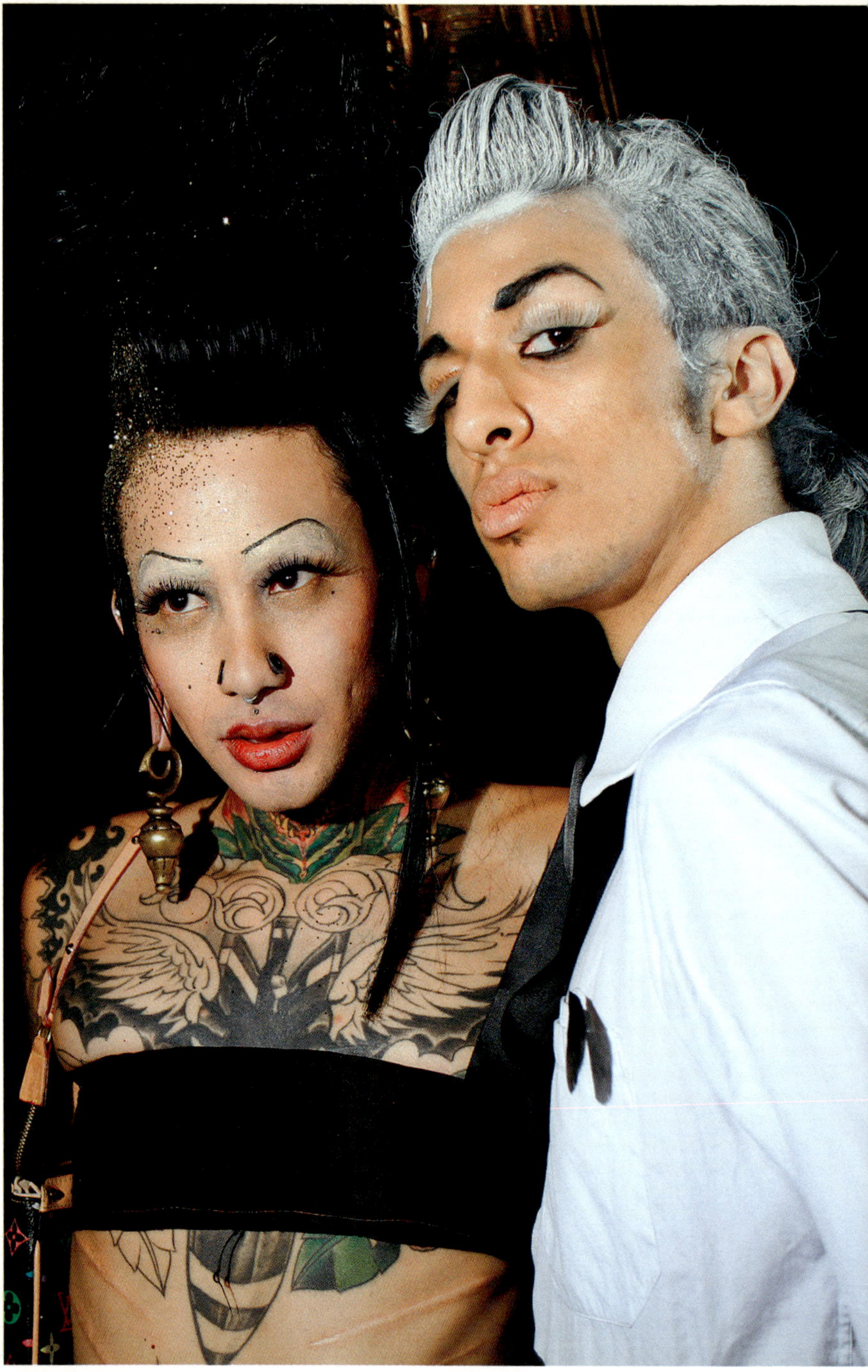

Circus – Nov 2007

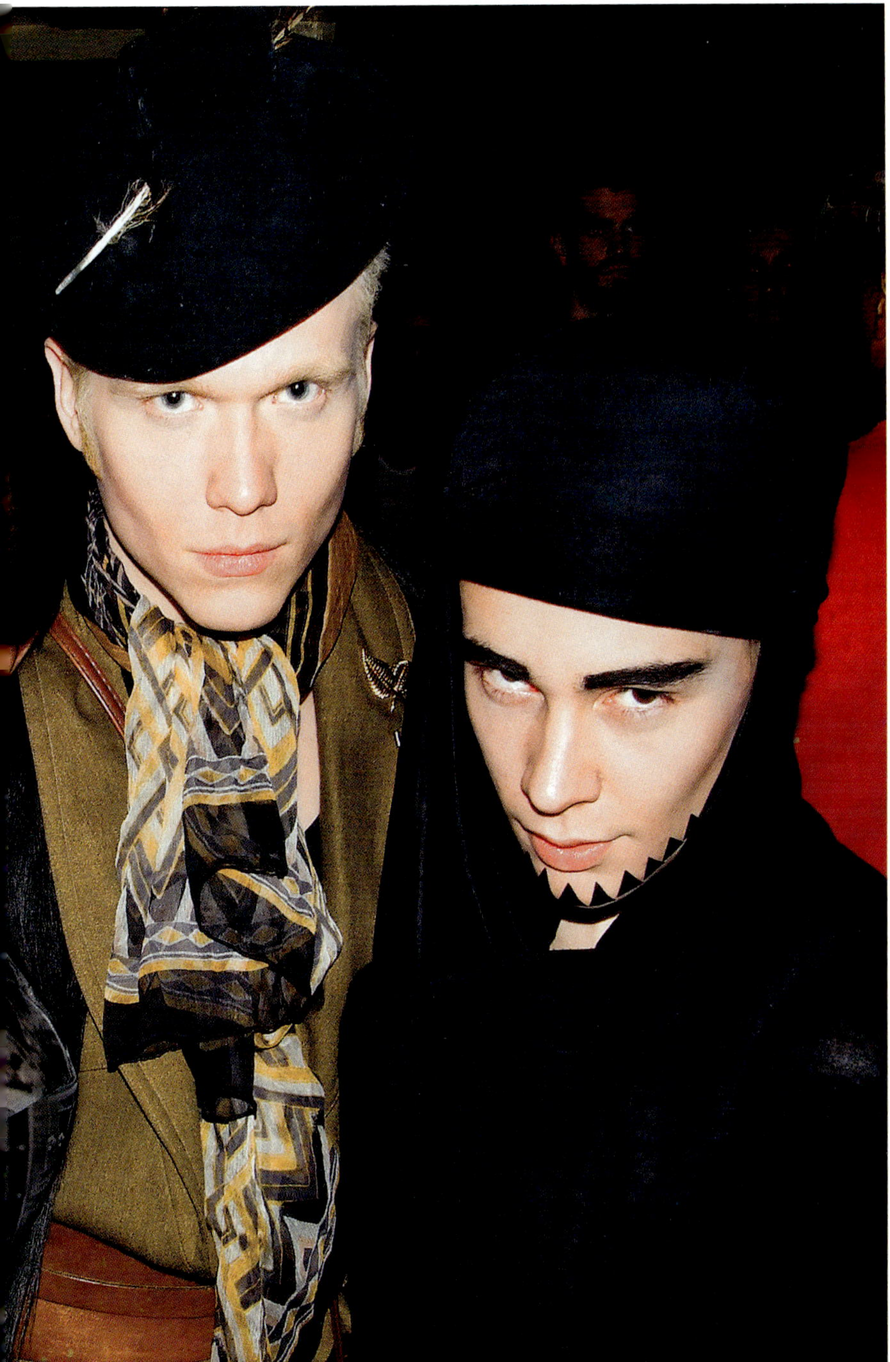

Paradise@Cafe De Paris – Sept 2010

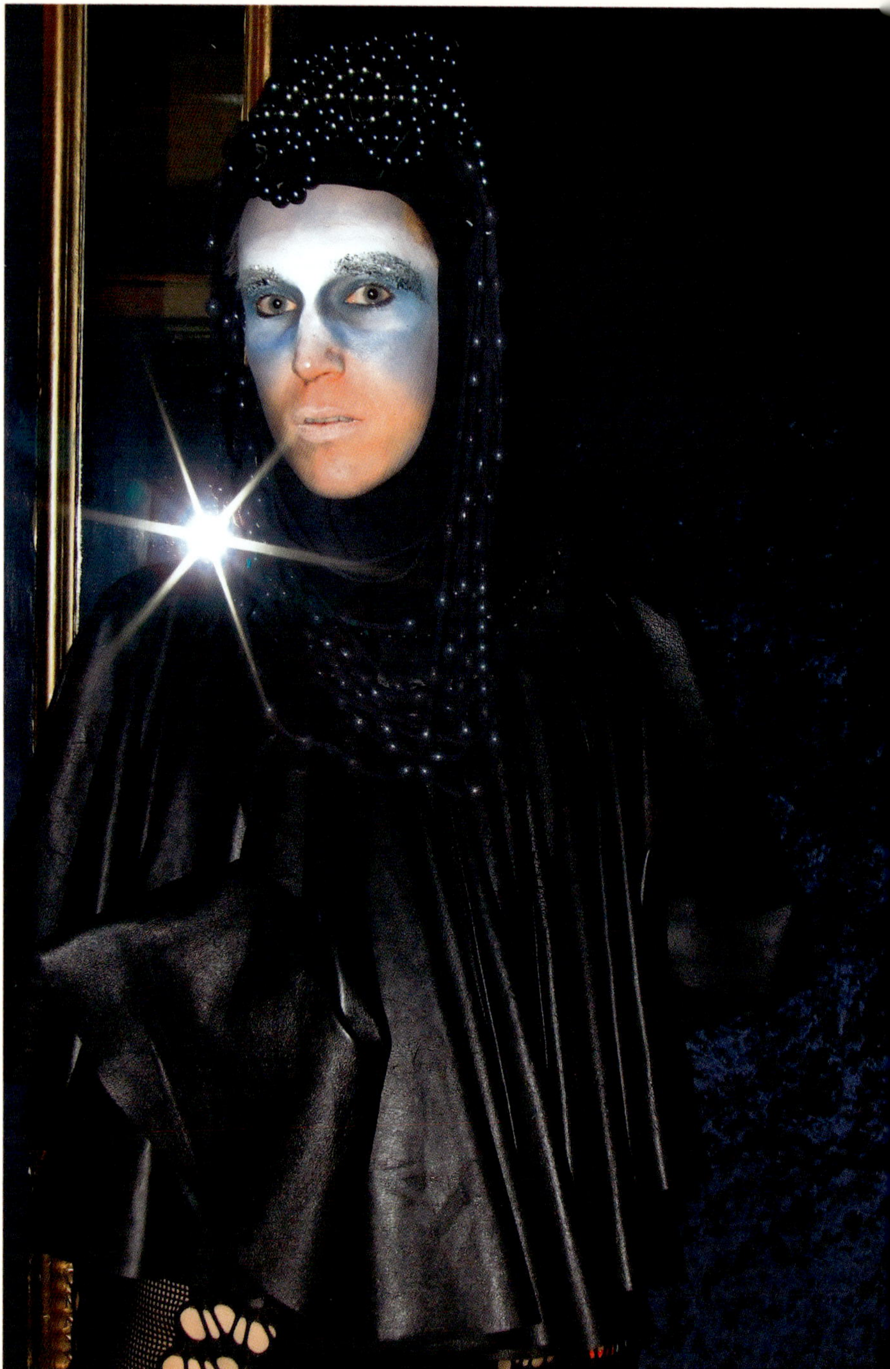

Paradise@Cafe De Paris – Sept 2010

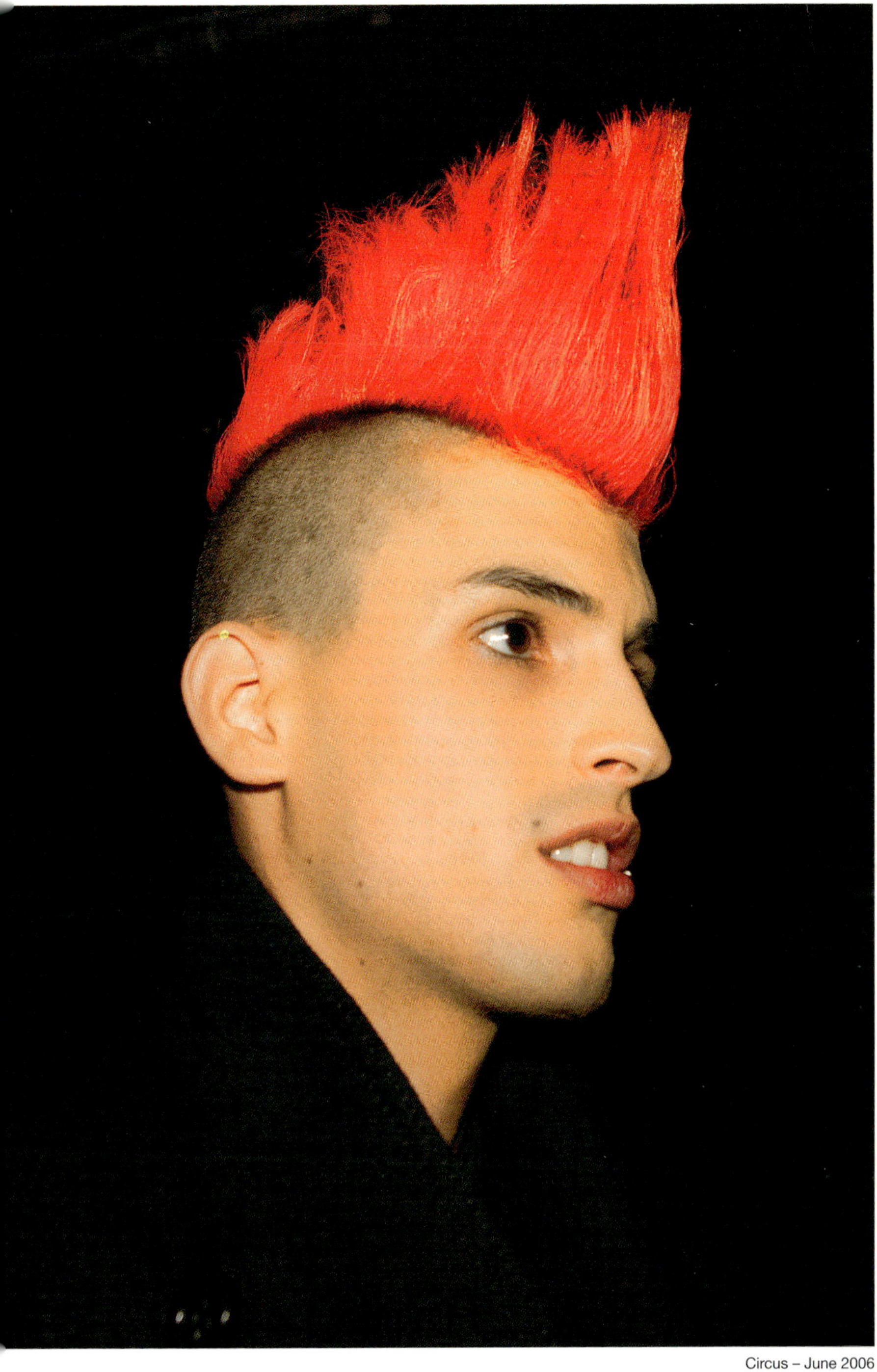

Circus – June 2006

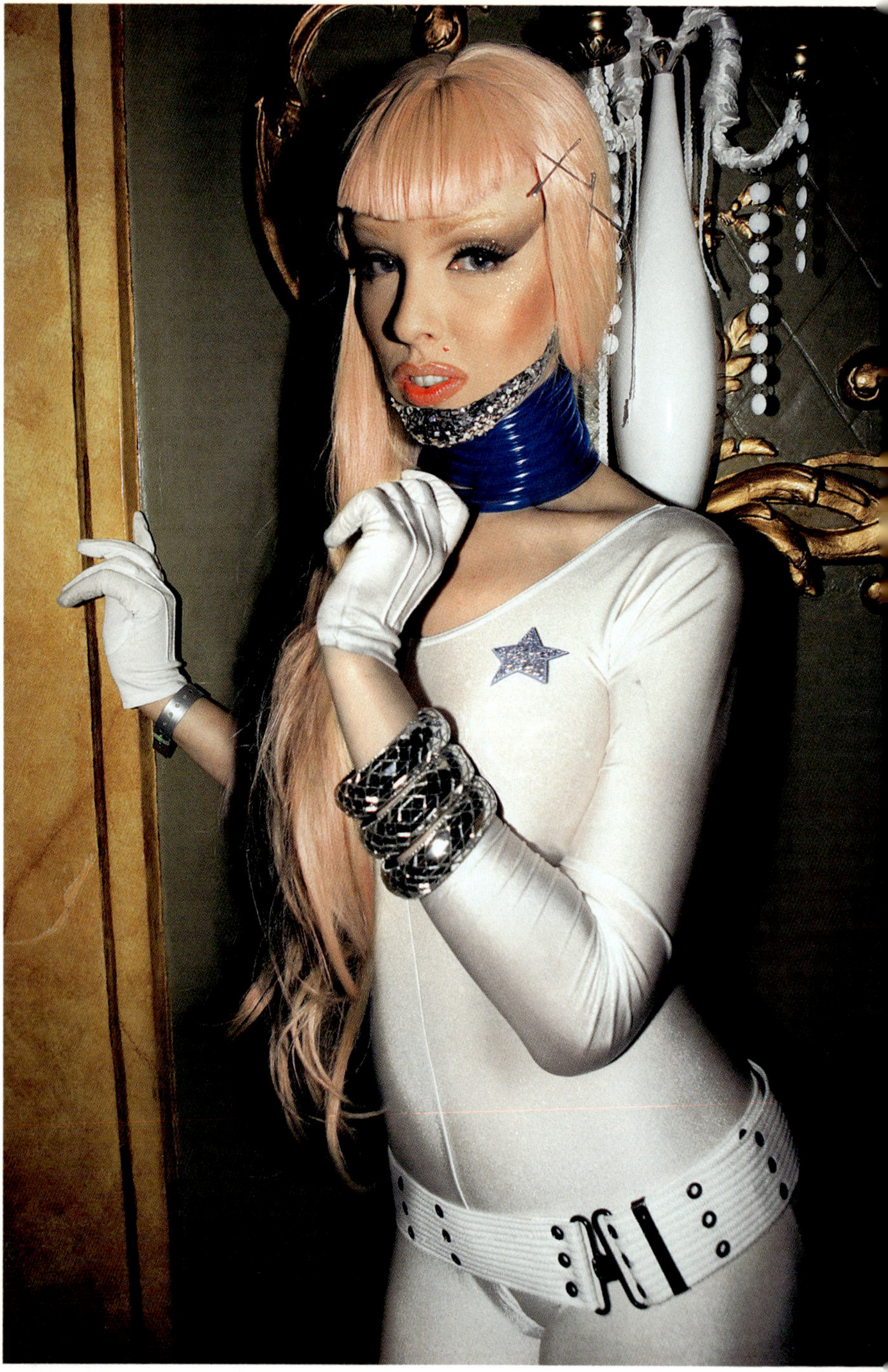

Wig Party@Cafe De Paris – Oct 2010

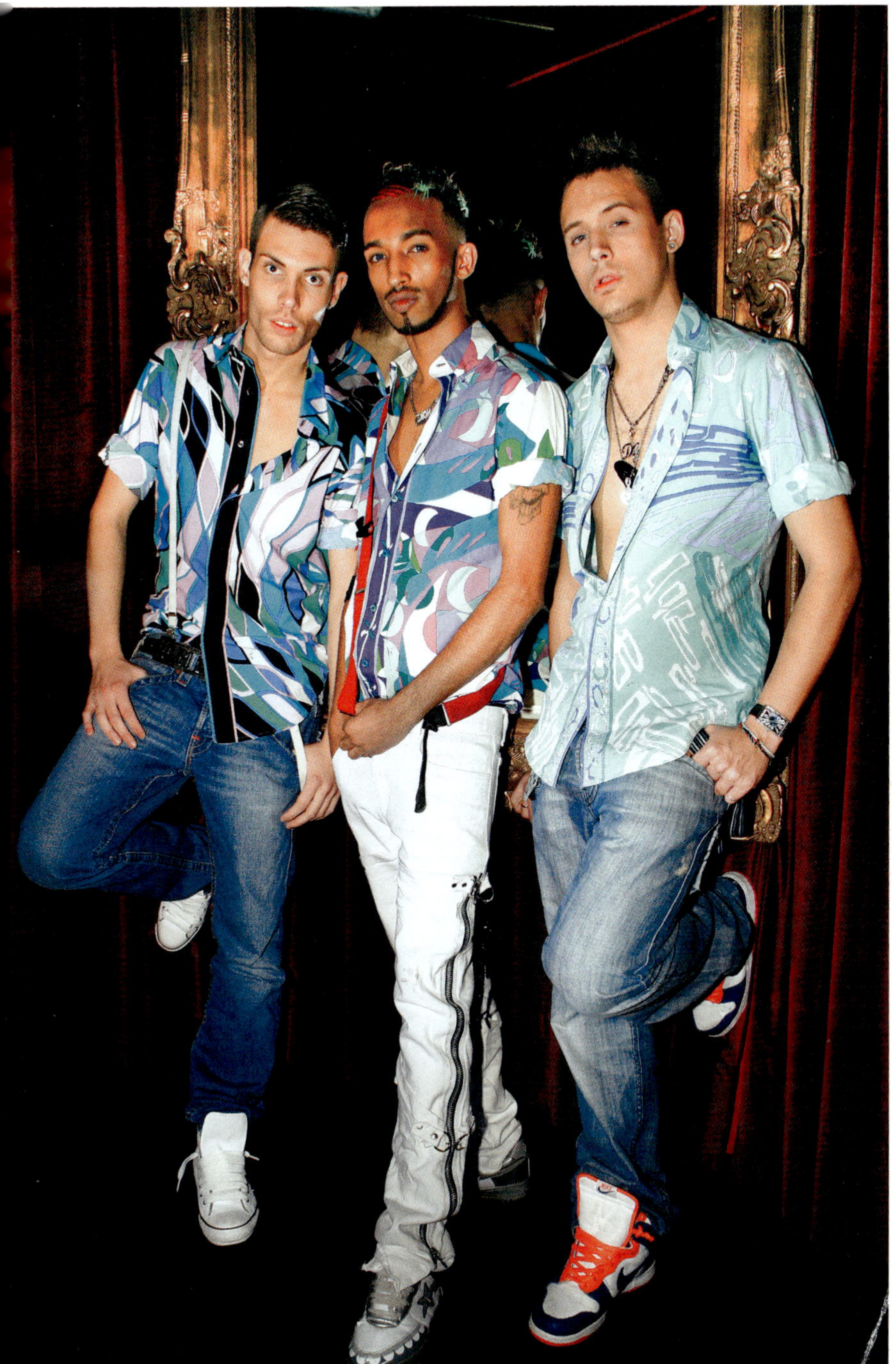

Circus – Feb 2007

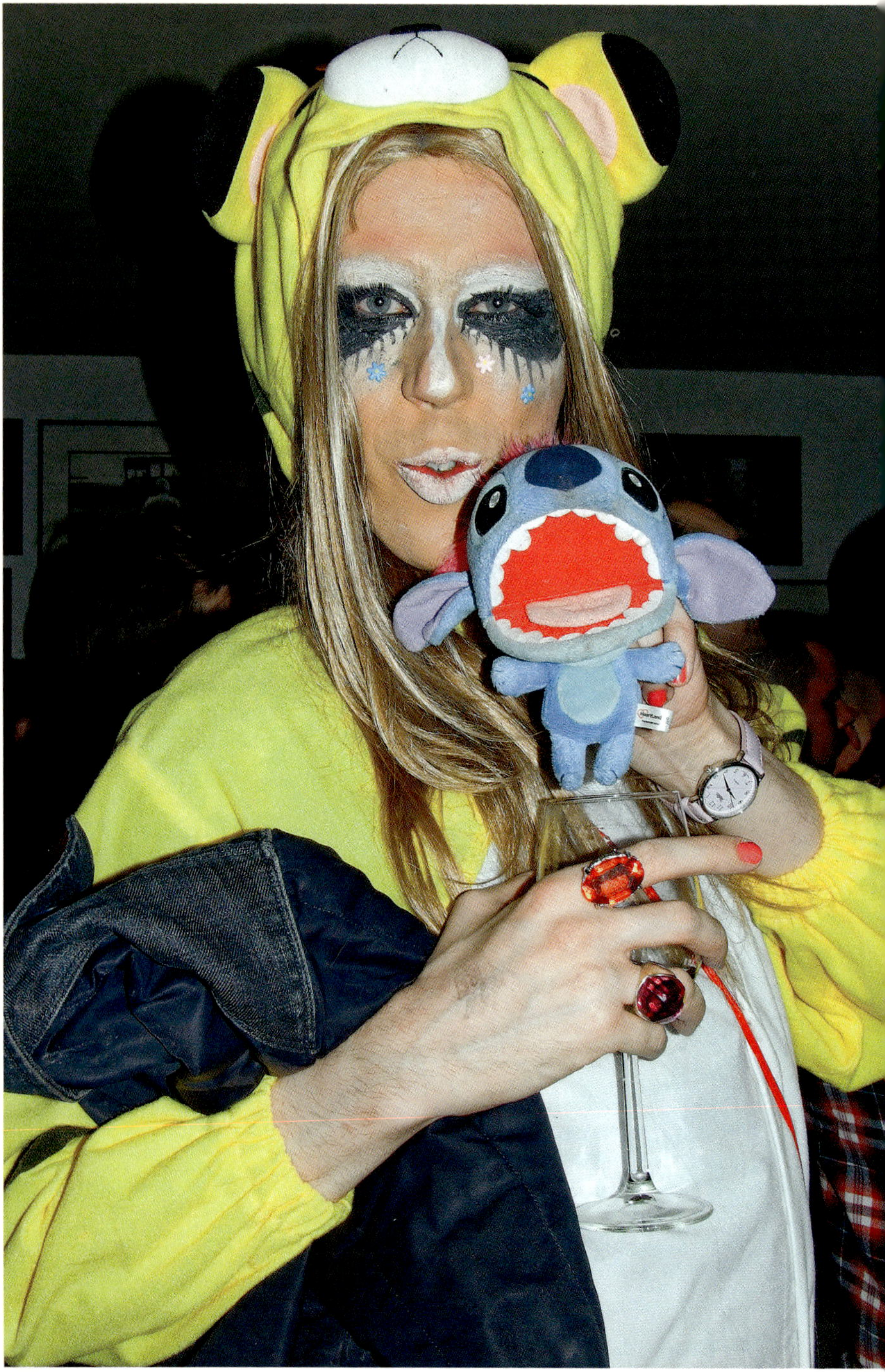

Gay Bingo@Floridita – Dec 2009

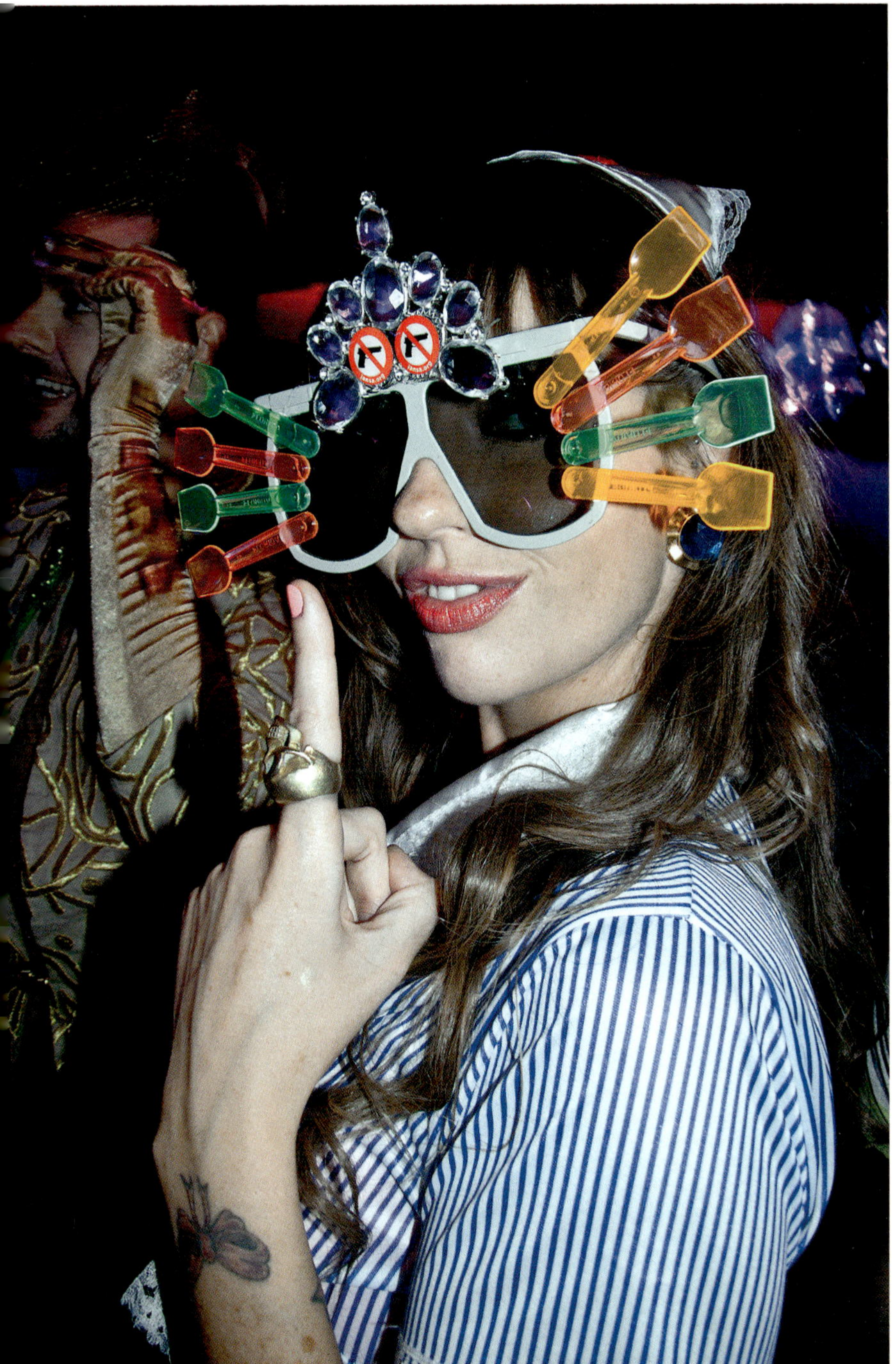

Wearable Art@Egg – Sept 2010

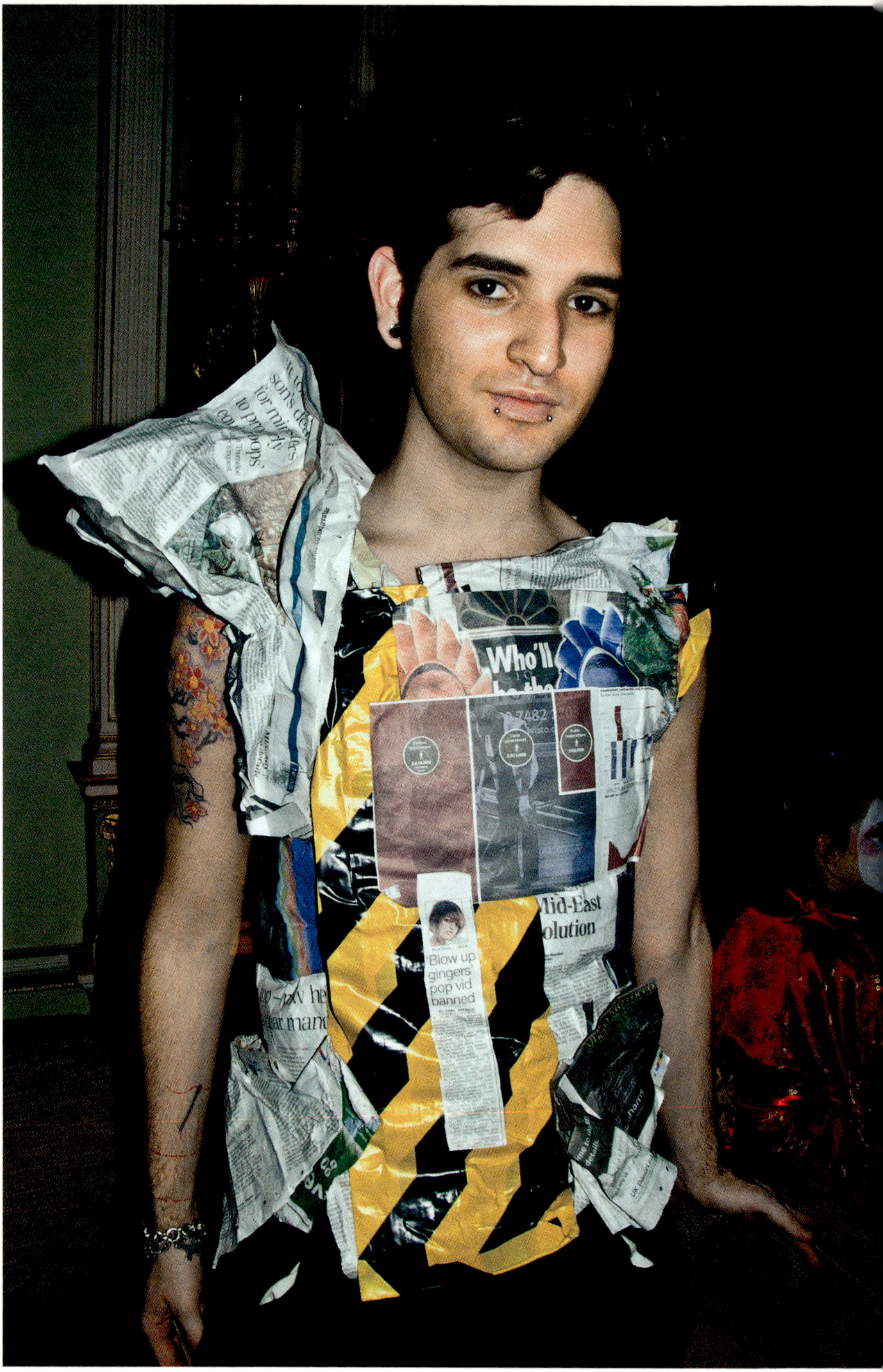

Mayday@Home House – May 2010

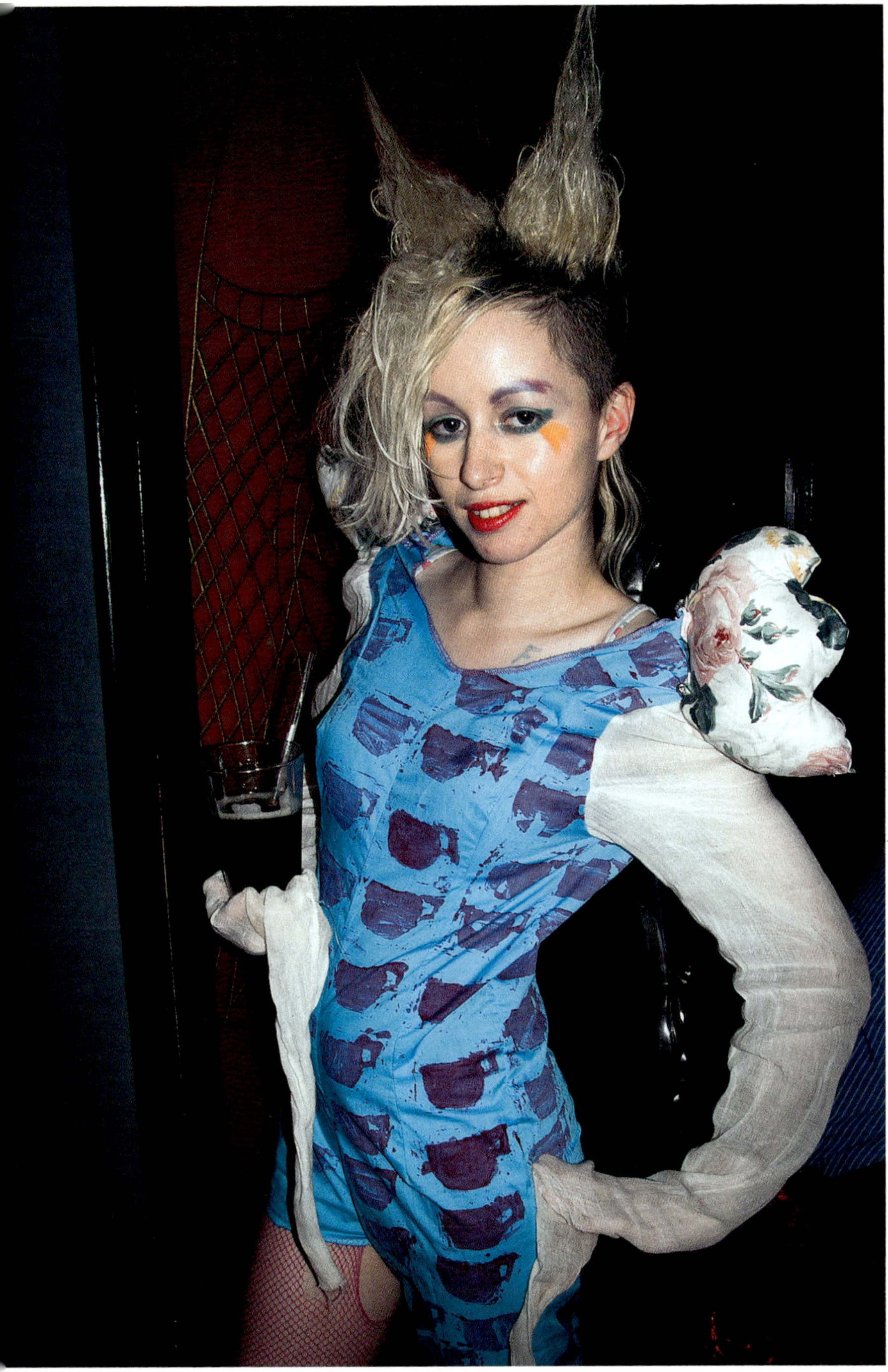

Shabba Dabba Da – Sept 2010

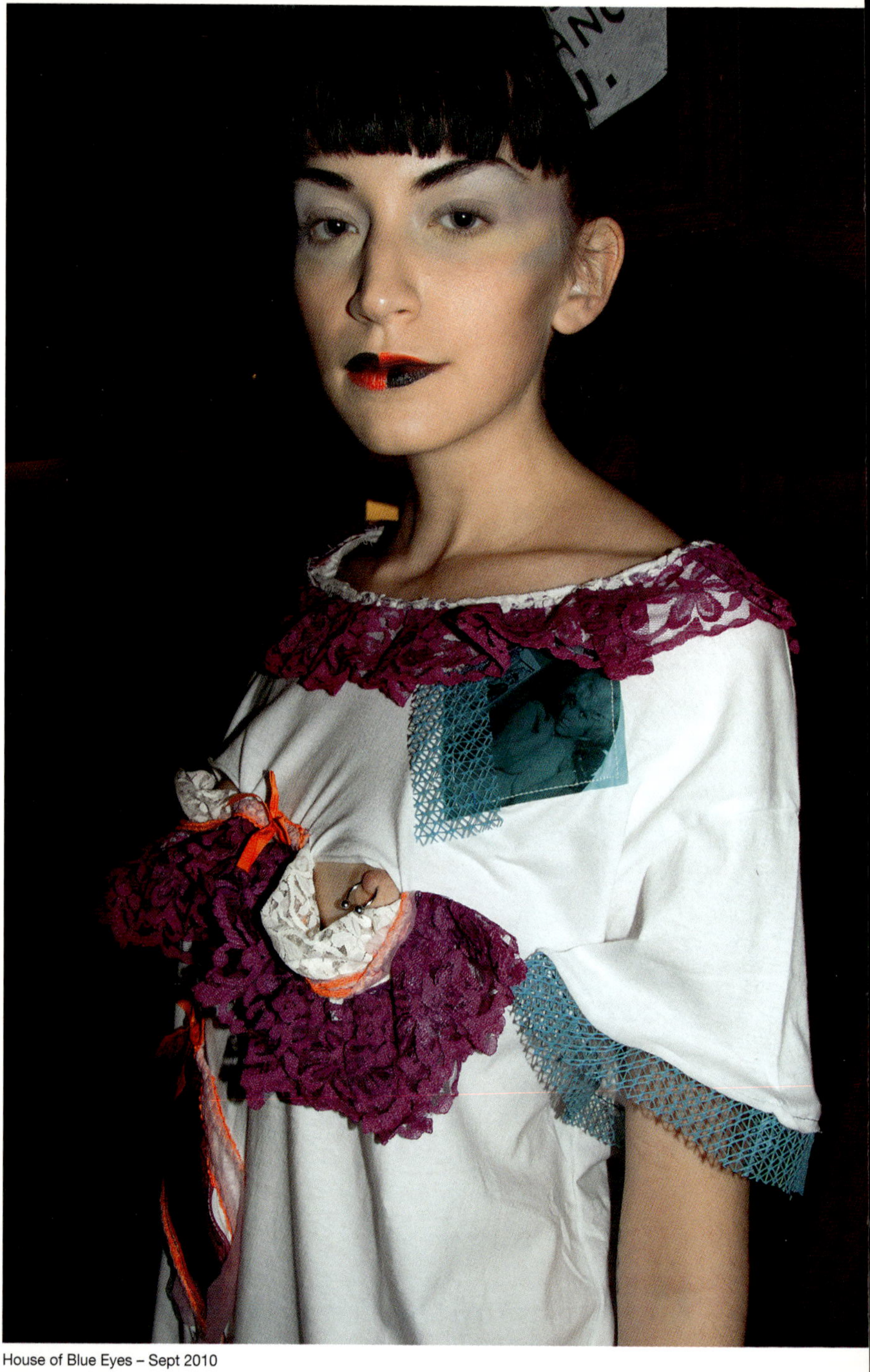

House of Blue Eyes – Sept 2010

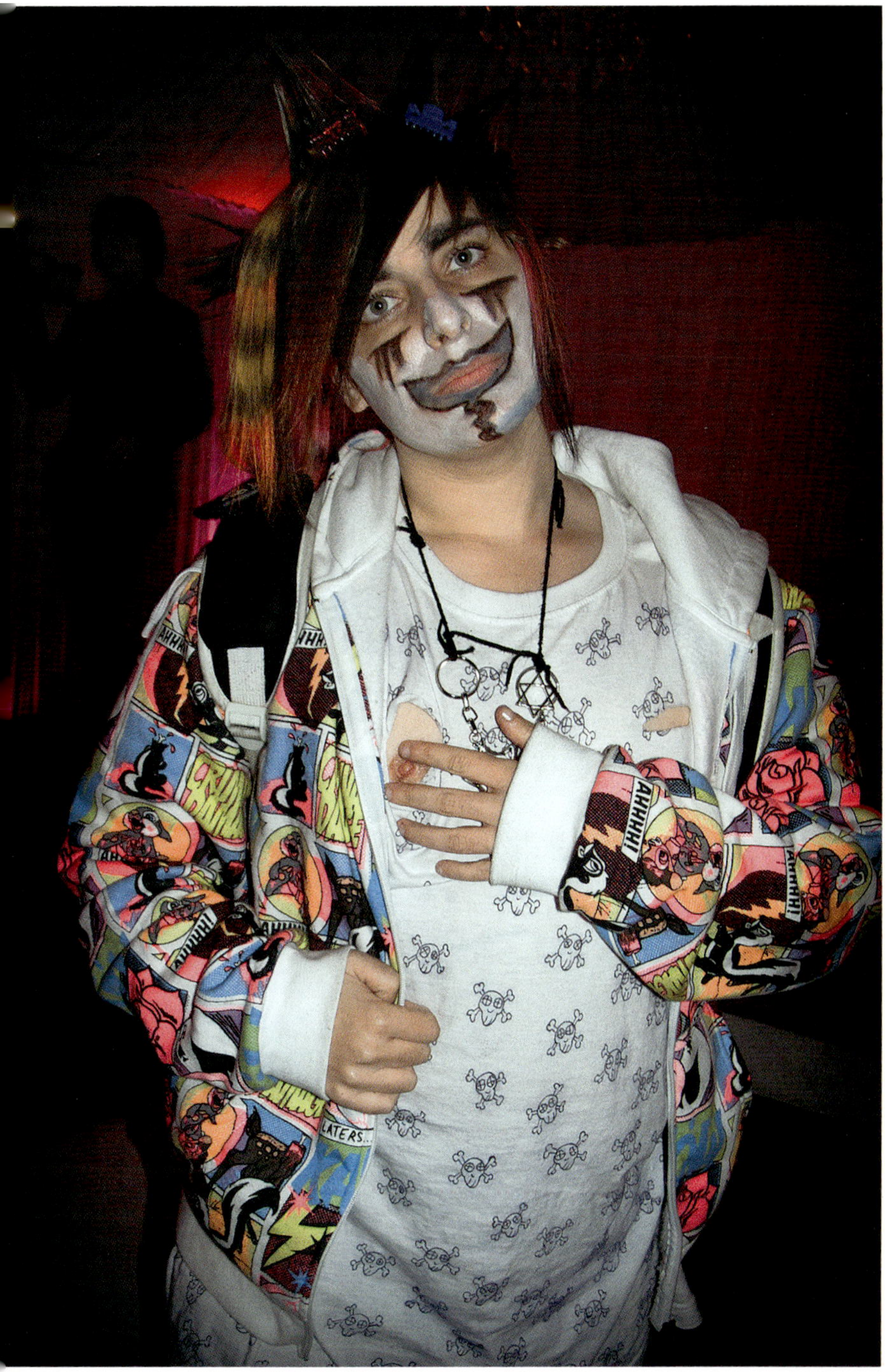

Wearable Art@Egg – Sept 2010

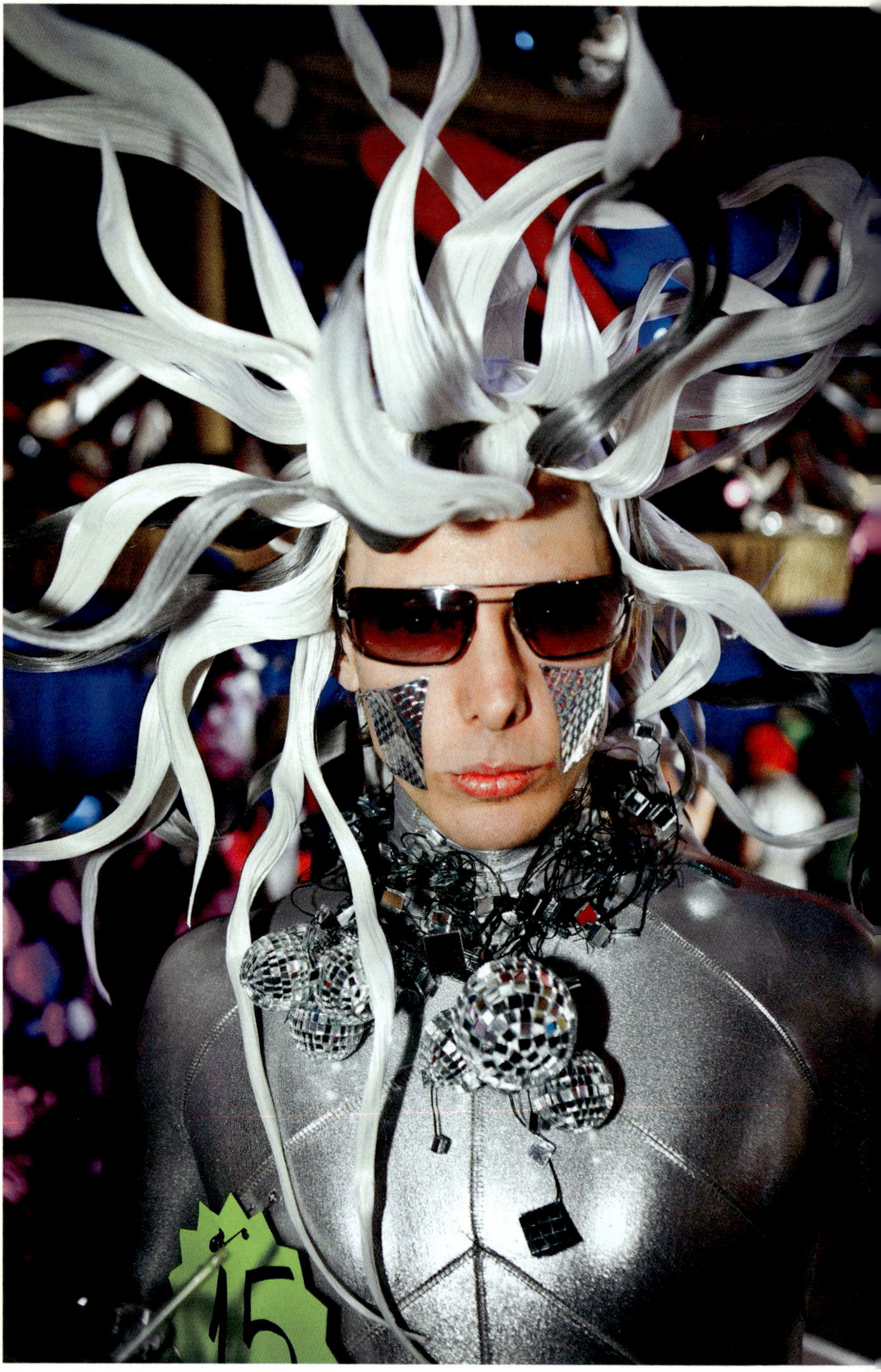

Wig Party@Cafe De Paris – Oct 2010

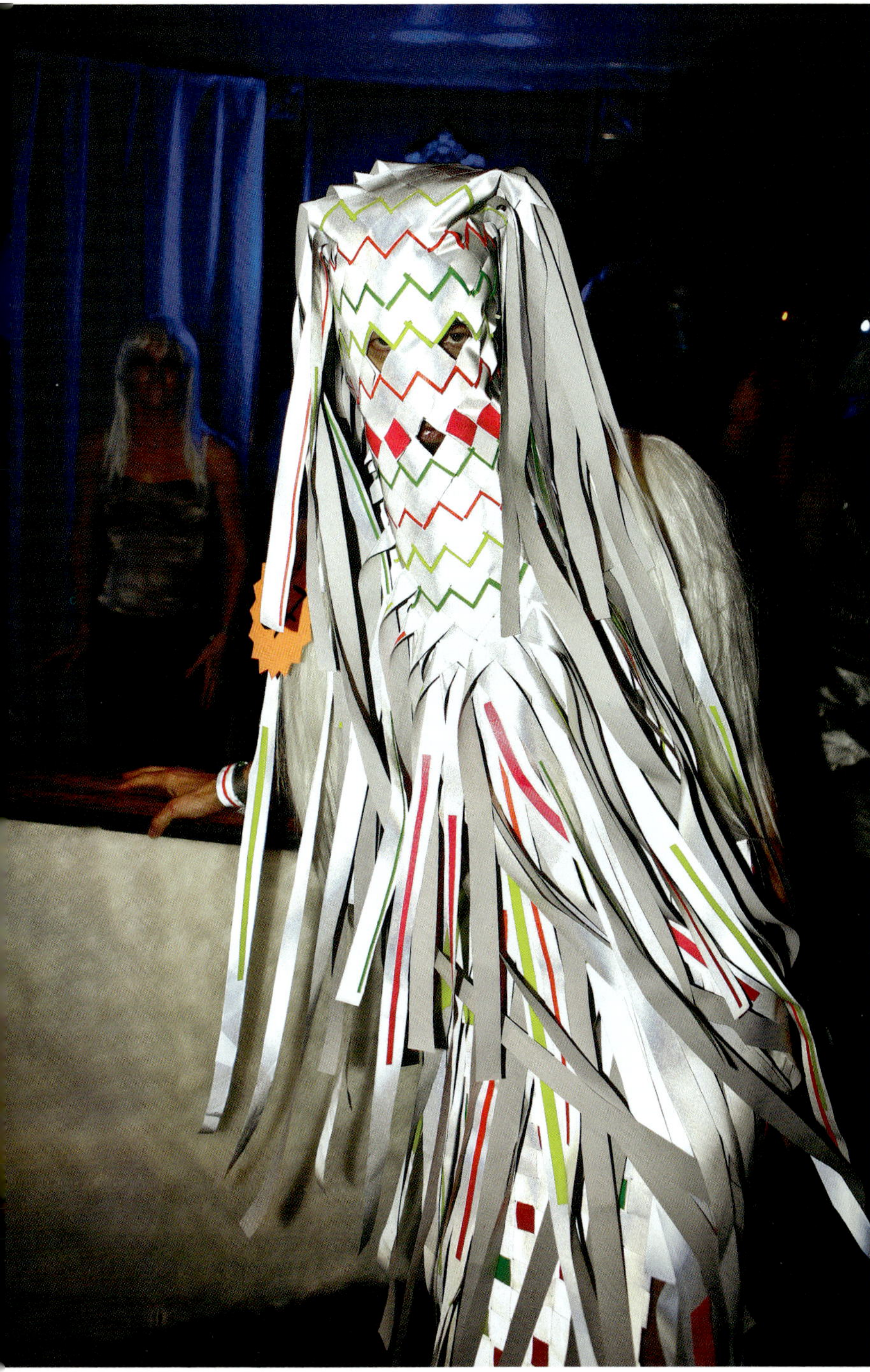

Wig Party@Cafe De Paris – Oct 2010

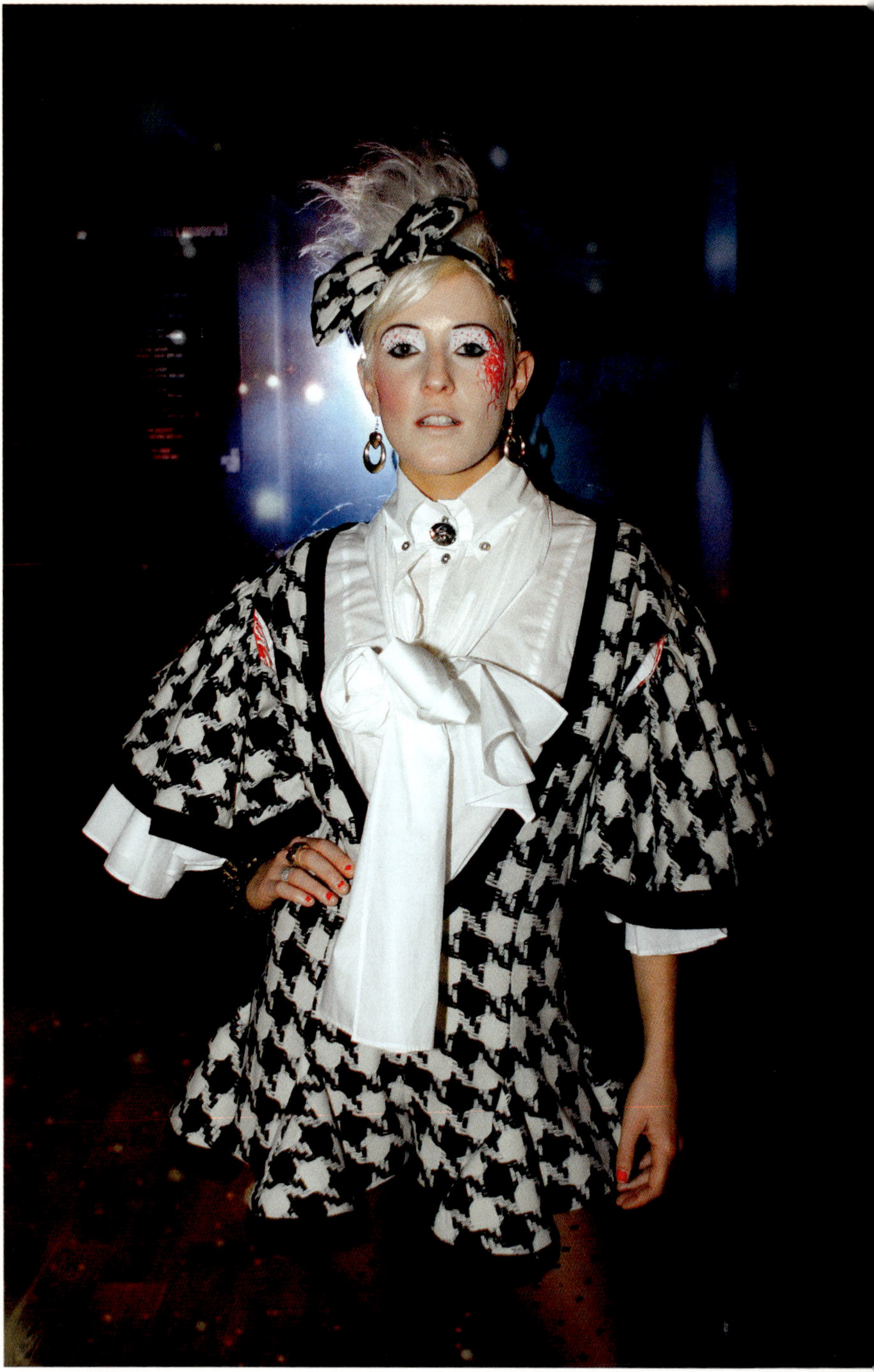

Strutt – Sept 2008

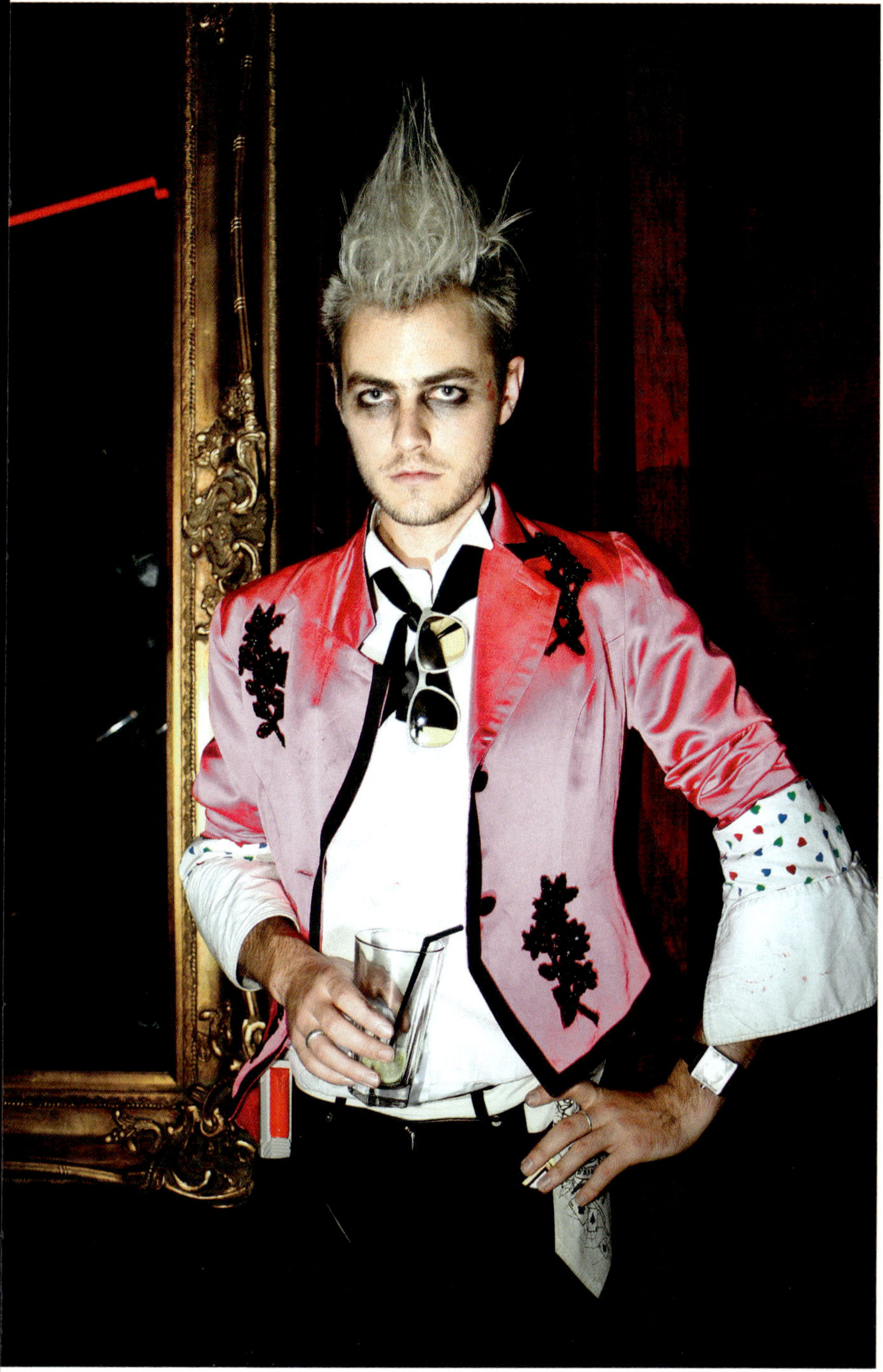

Soho Revue Bar – Feb 2007

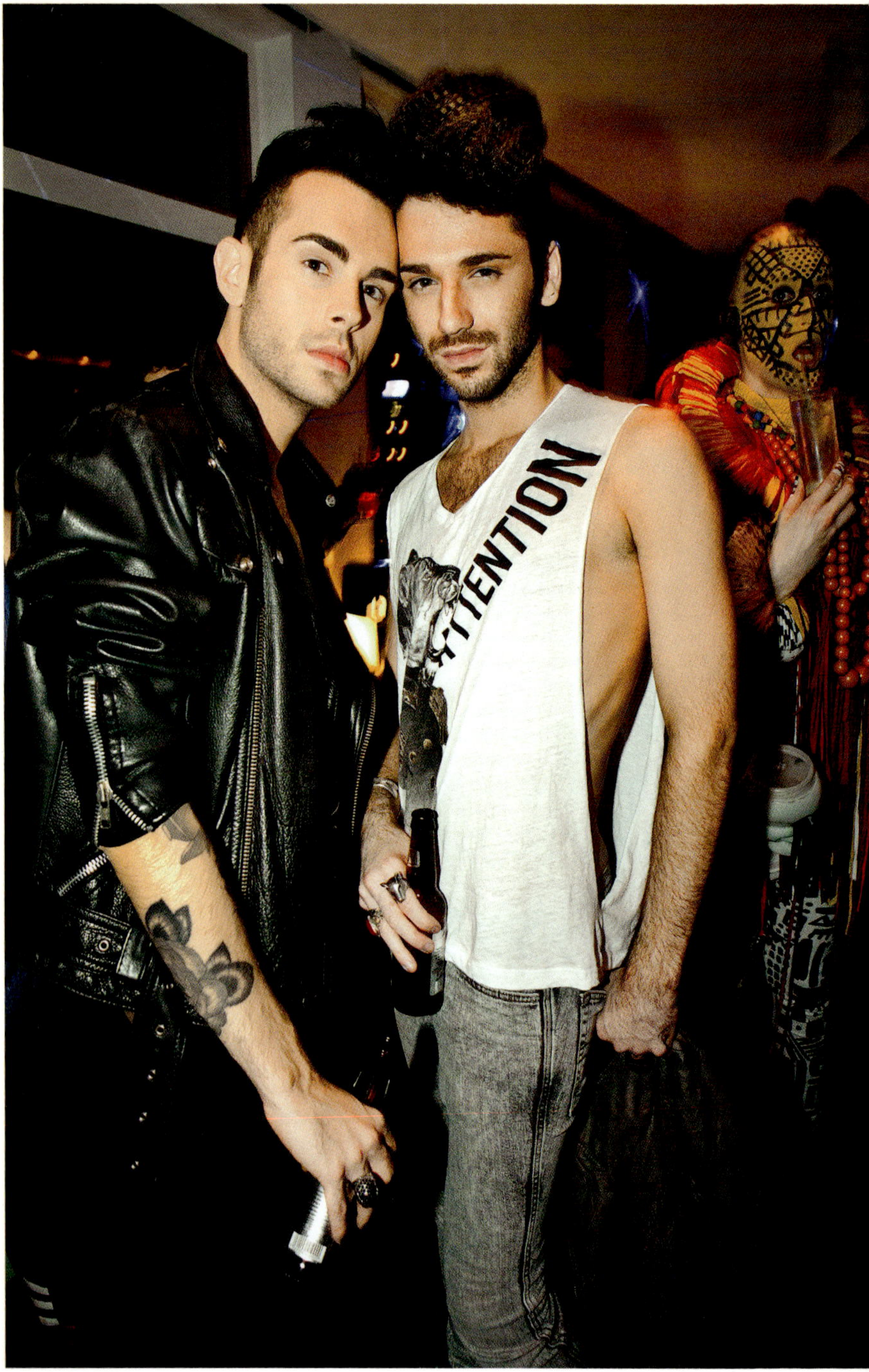
ATTENTION

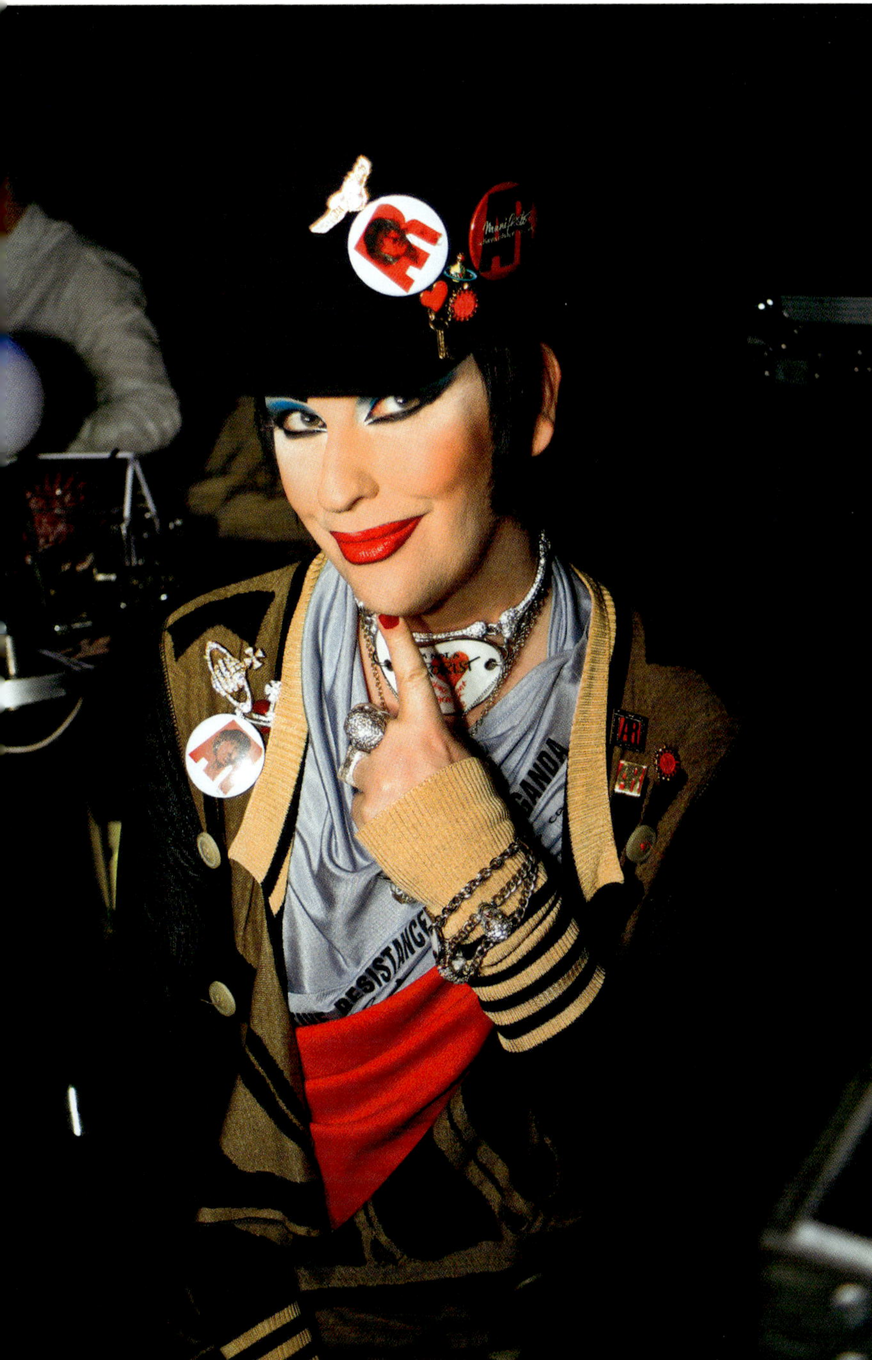

Trannyshack – Feb 2007

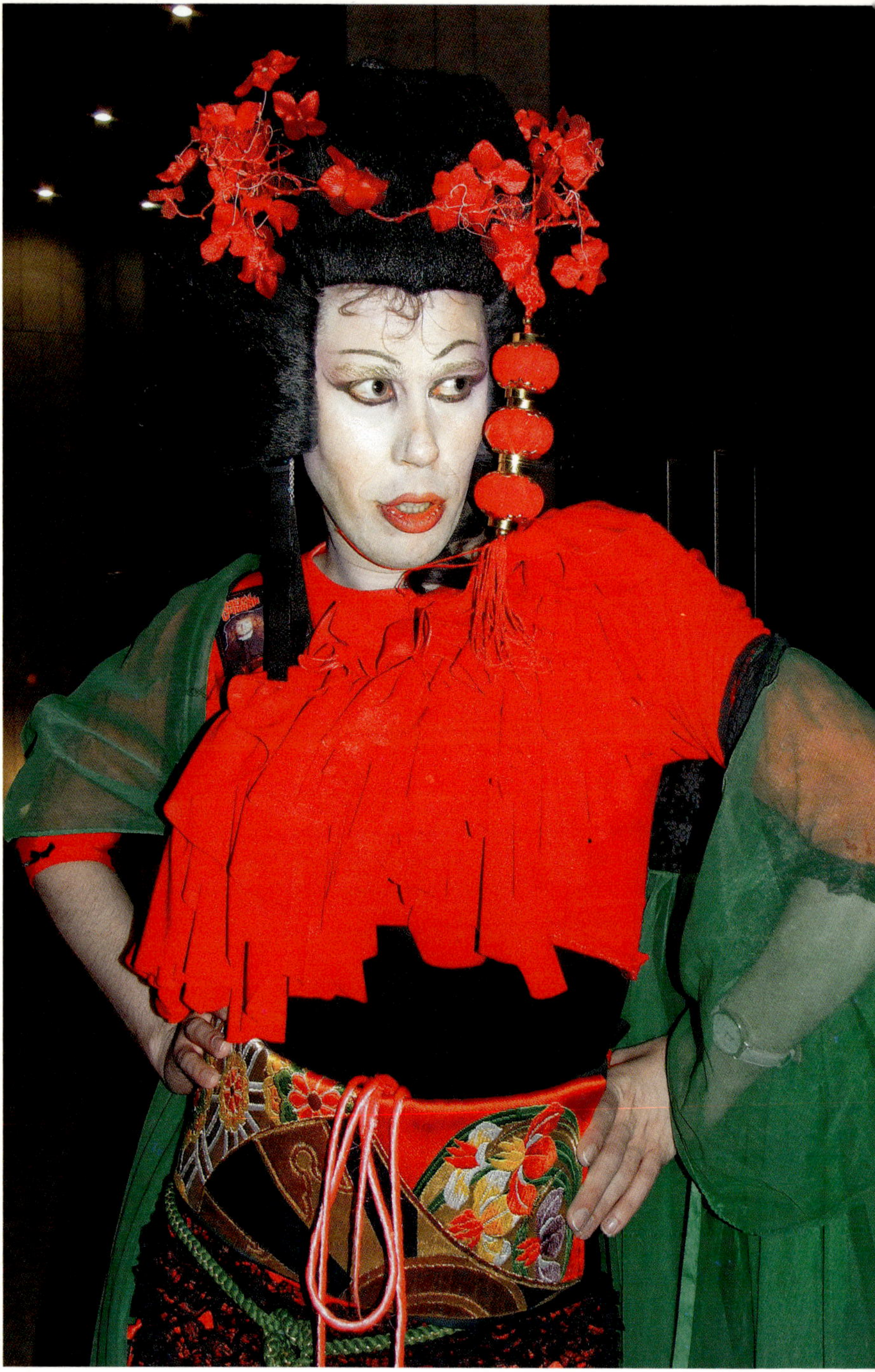

Caligula – Aug 2010

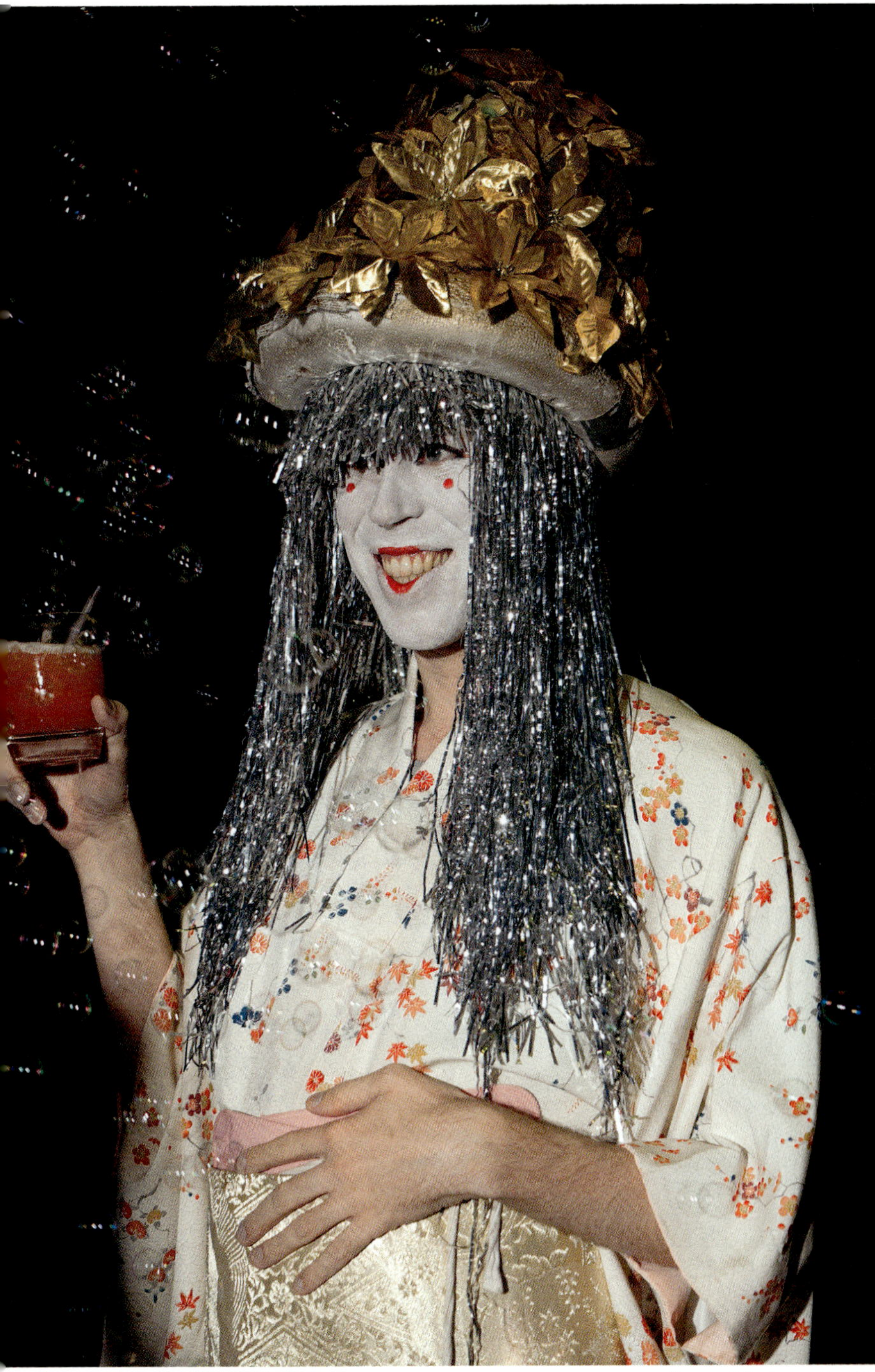

House of Blue Eyes – Jan 2008

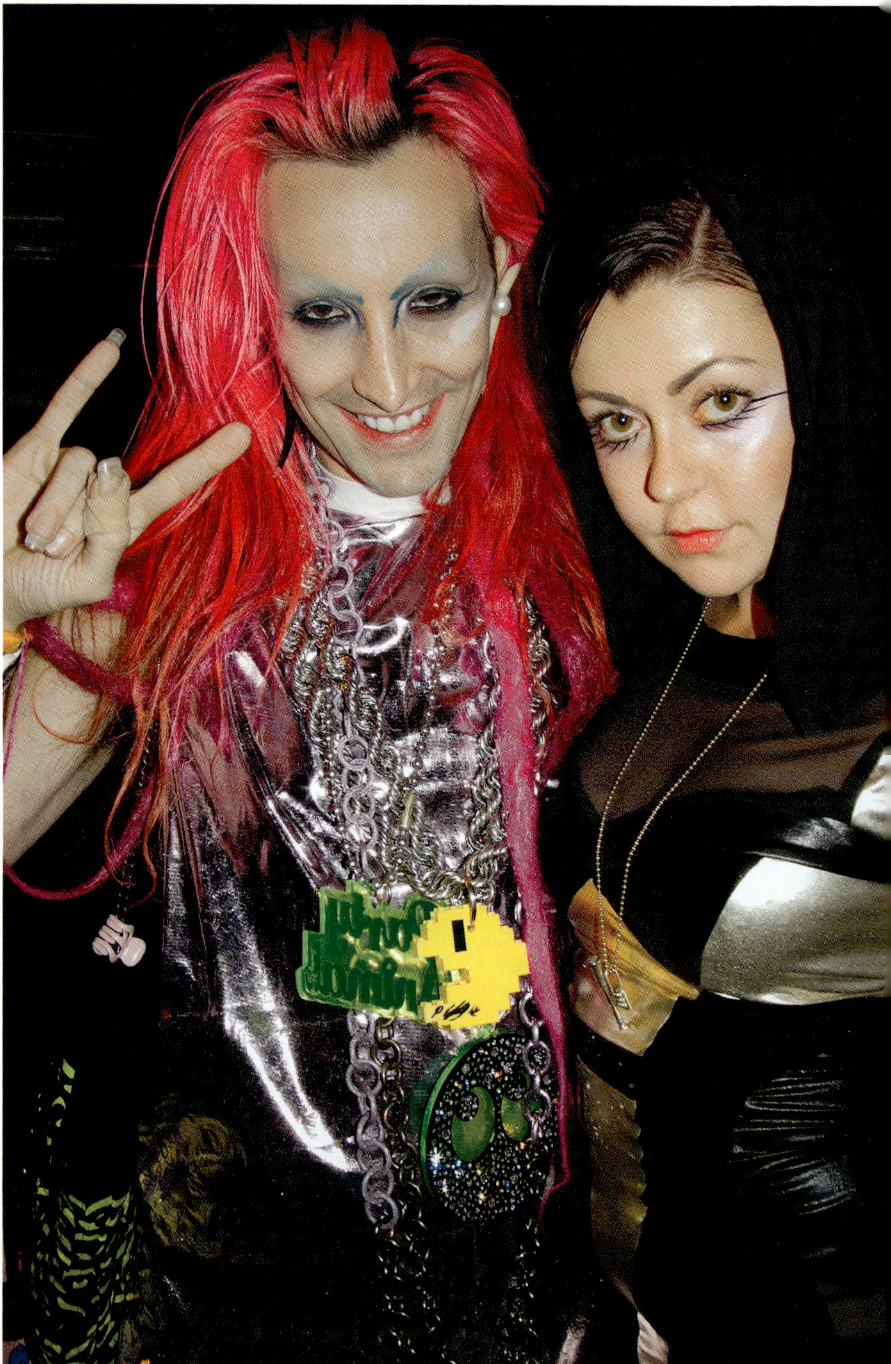

House of Blue Eyes – Sept 2010

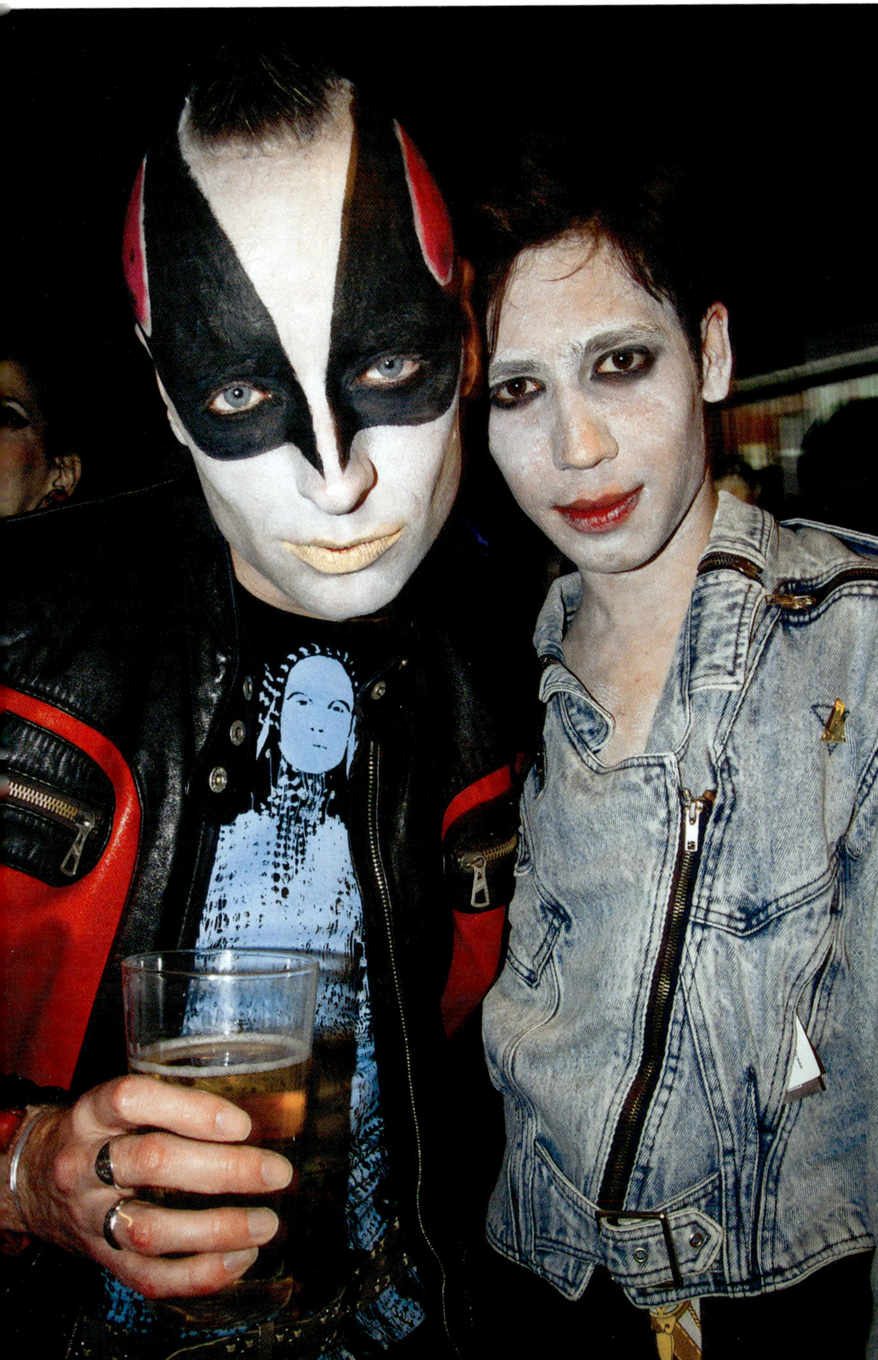

The Face – May 2010

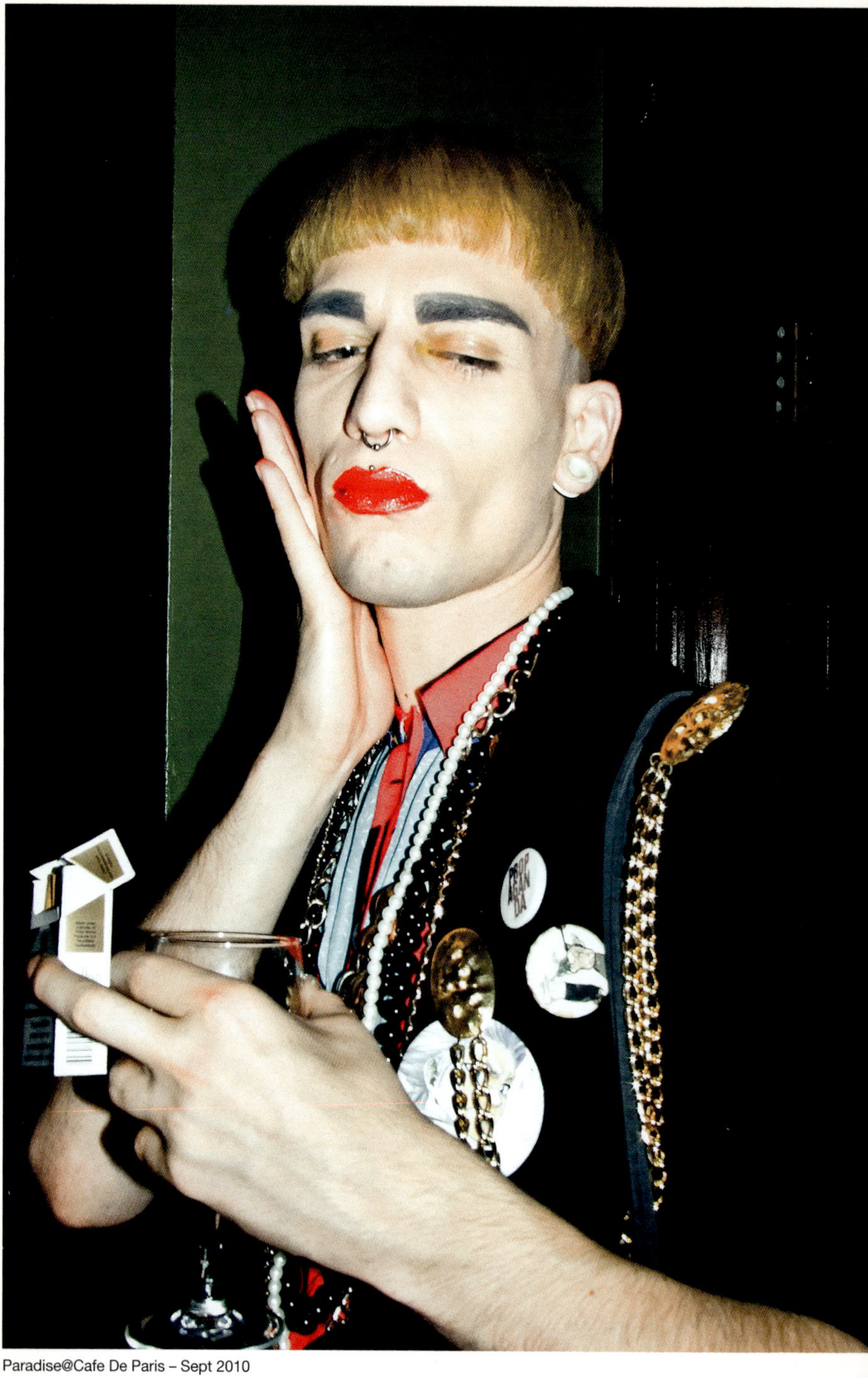

Paradise@Cafe De Paris – Sept 2010

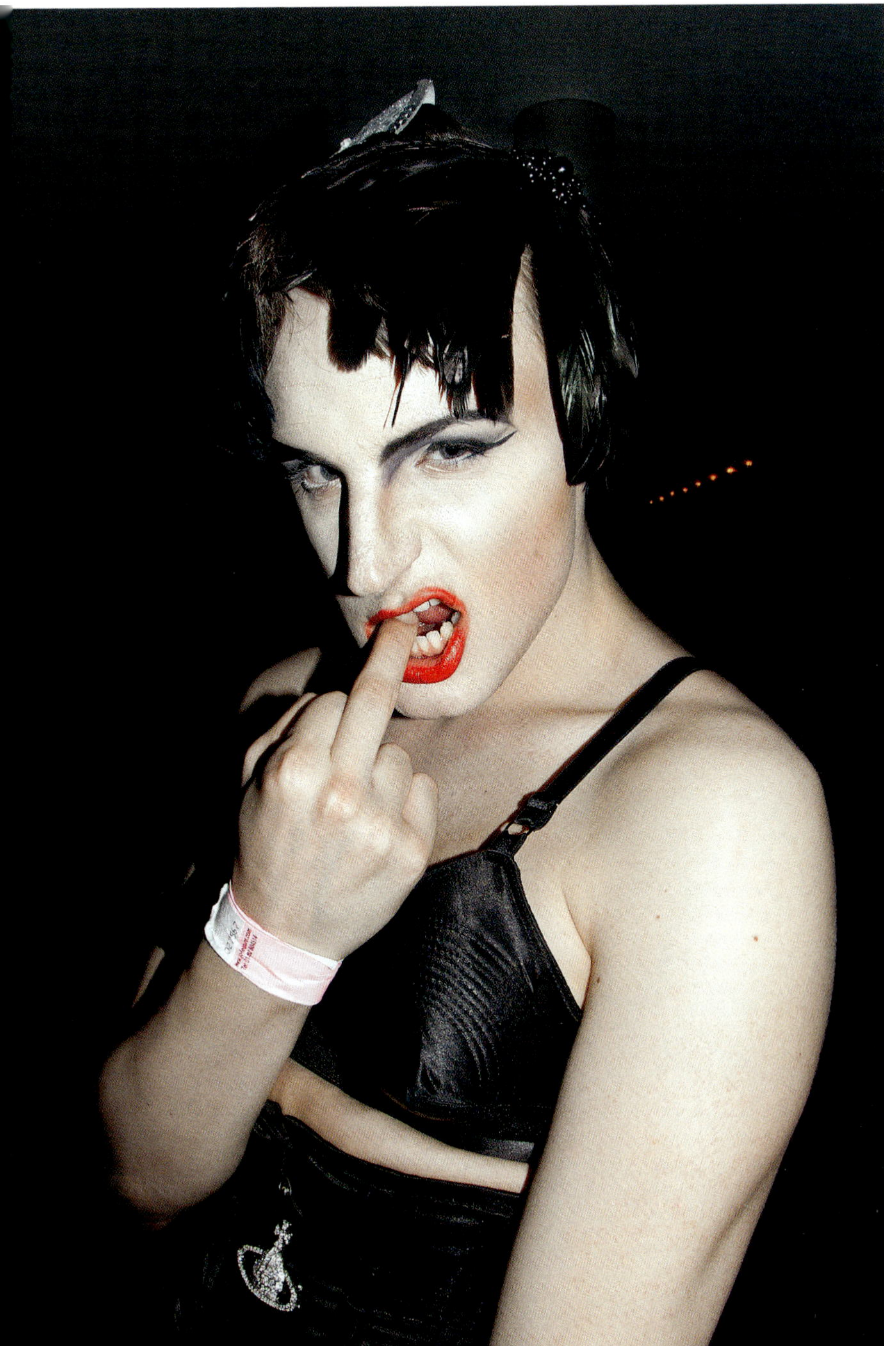

Circus – May 2010

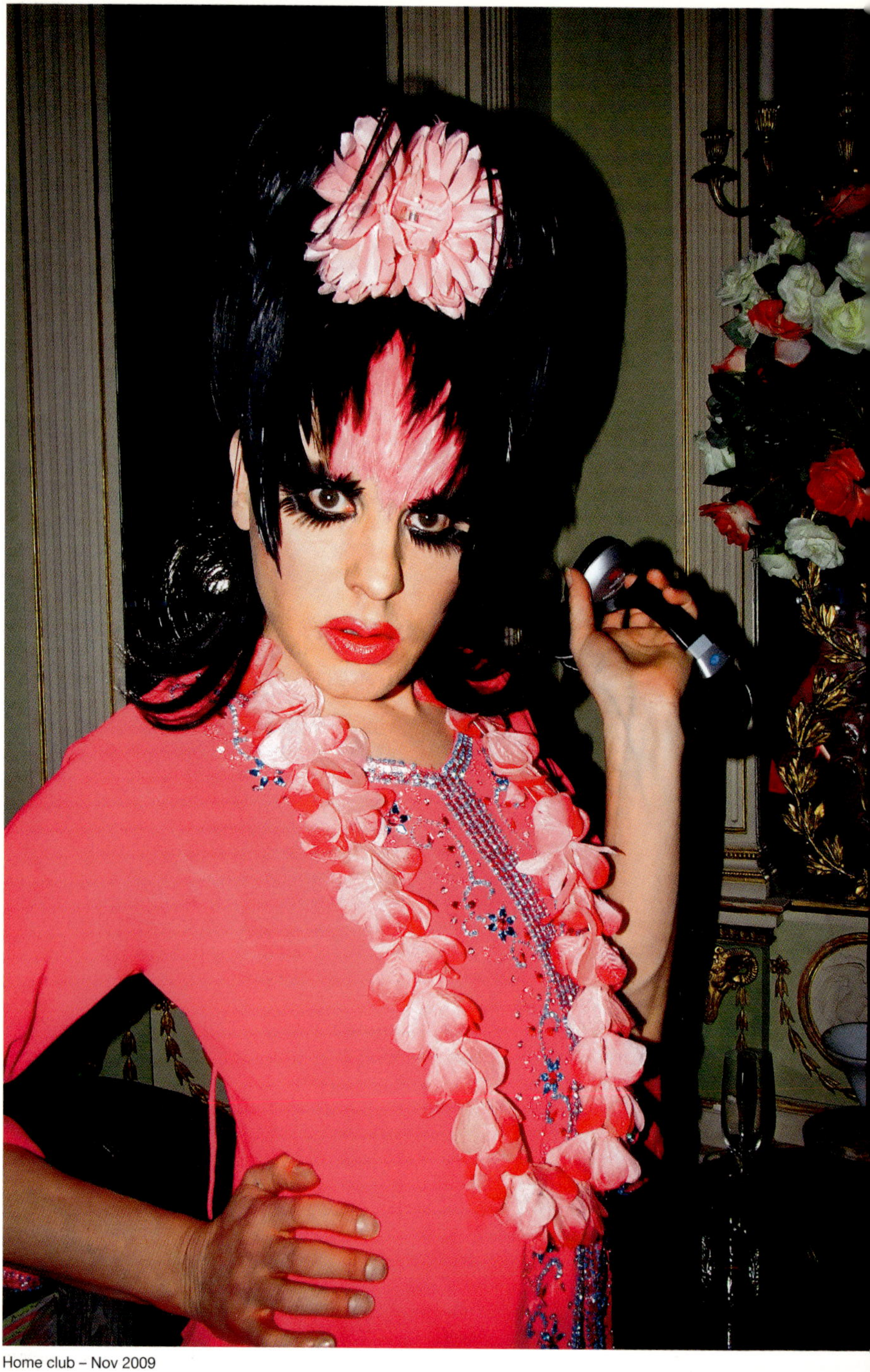

Home club – Nov 2009

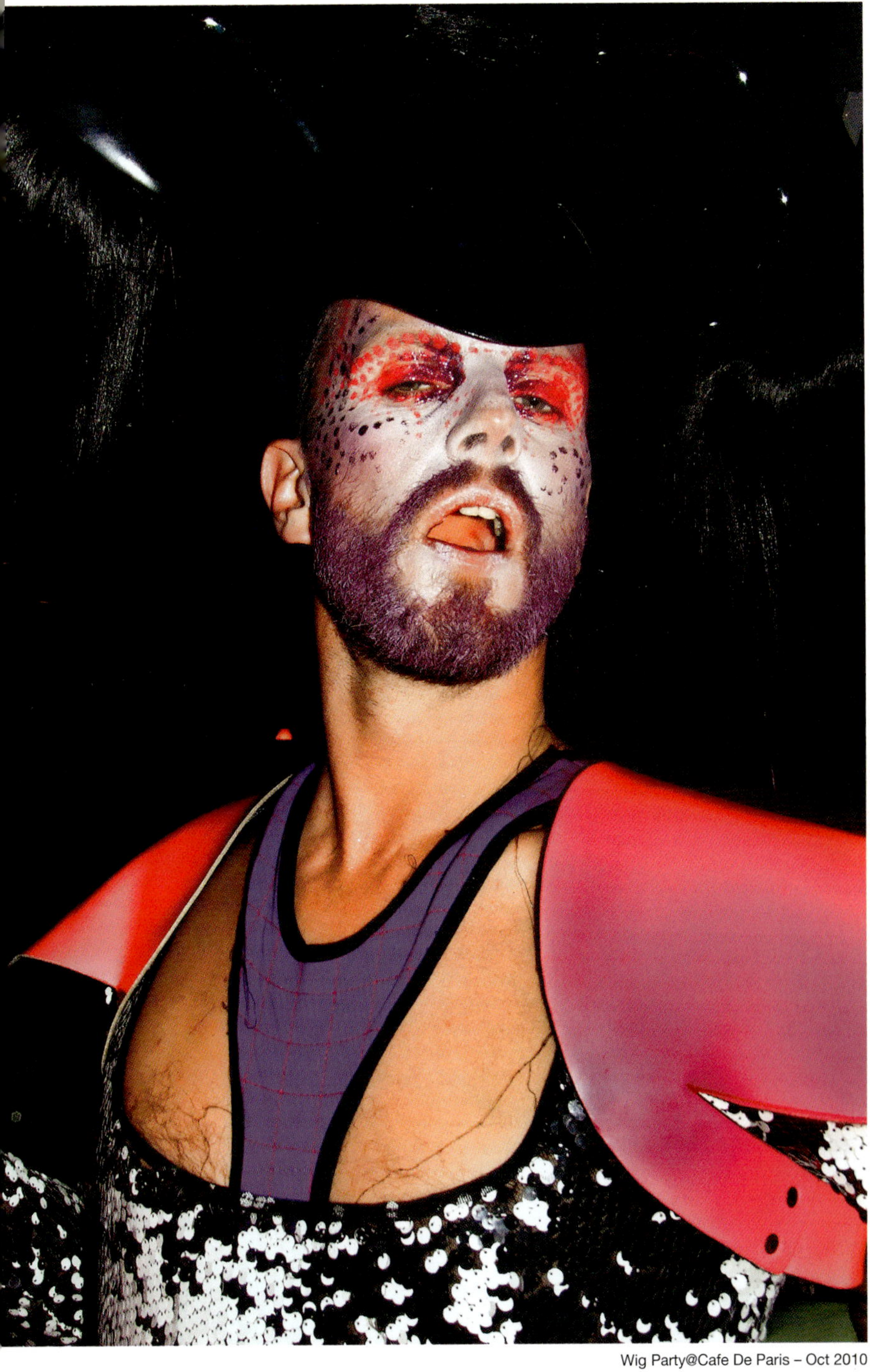

Wig Party@Cafe De Paris – Oct 2010

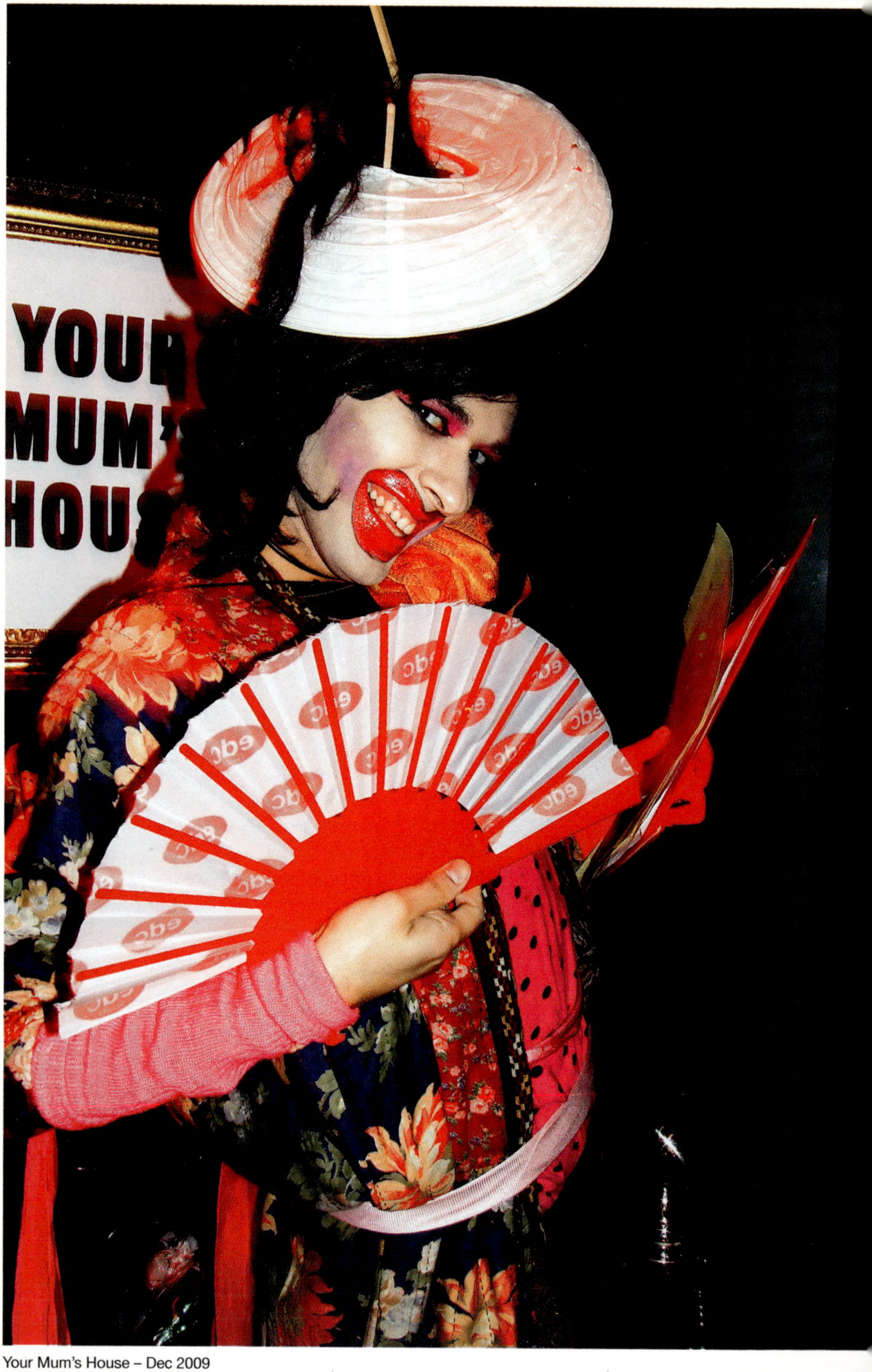

Your Mum's House – Dec 2009

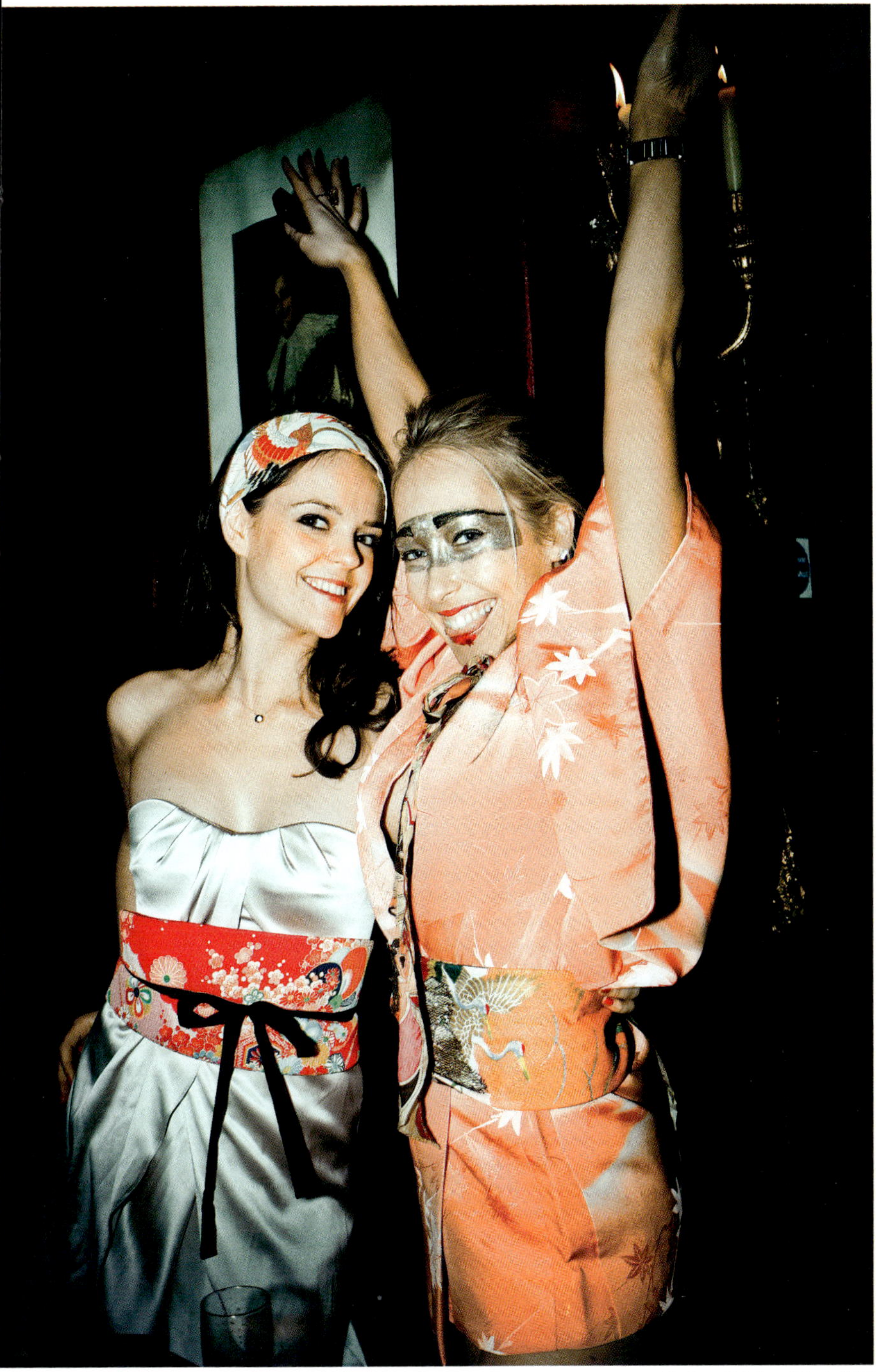

Hedges & Butler – March 2007

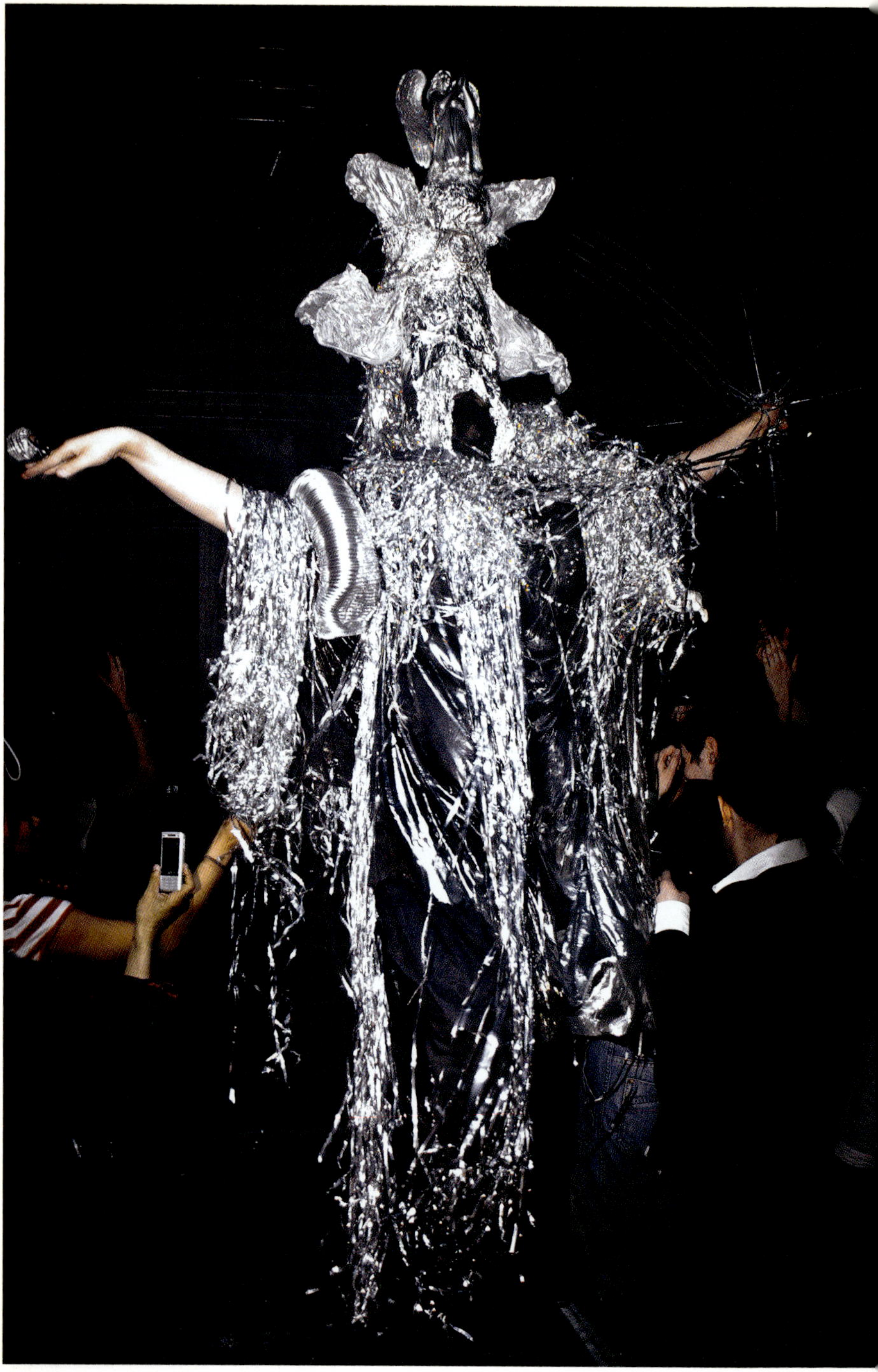

Work@Heaven – June 2007

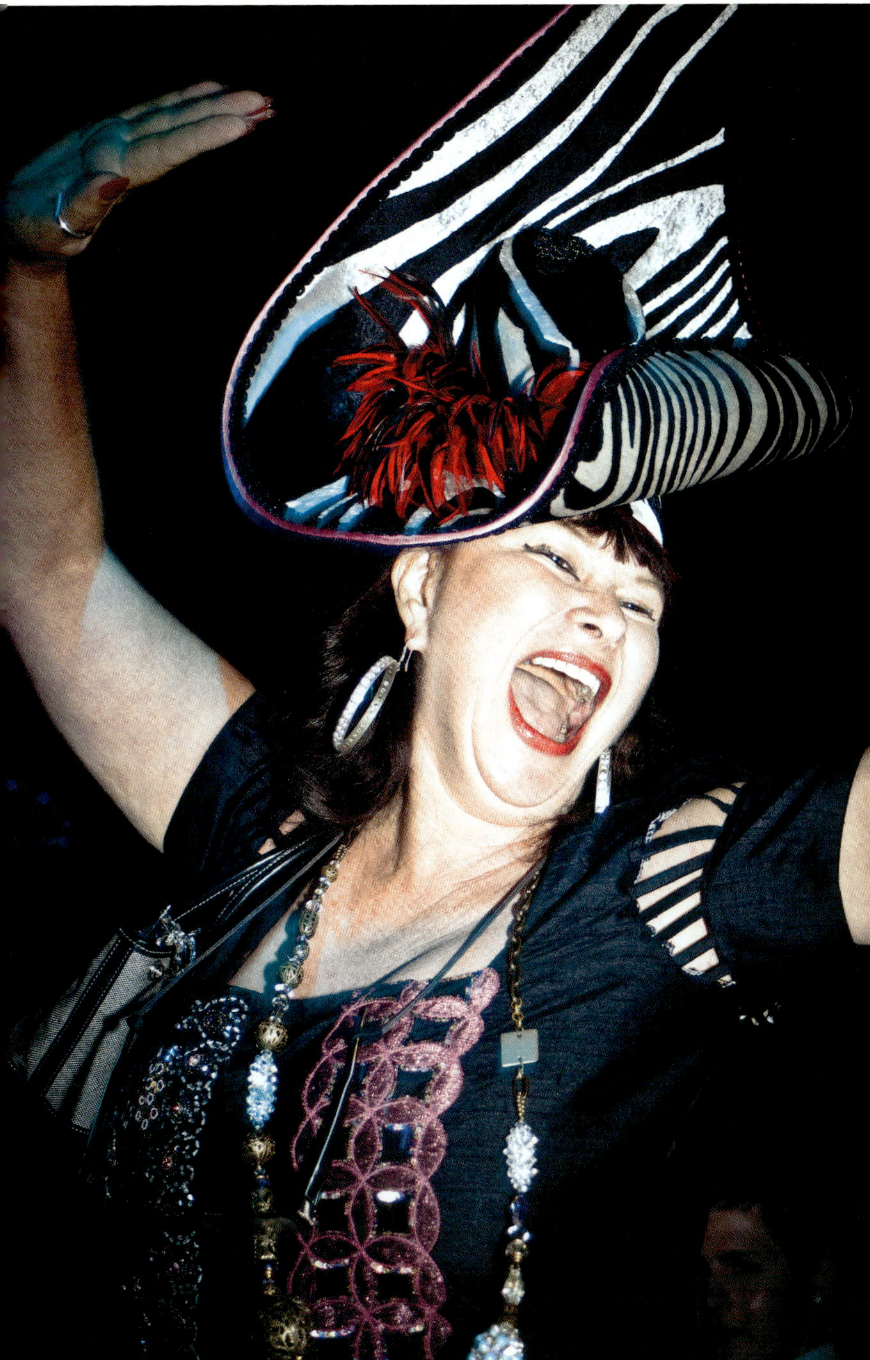

Work@Heaven – June 2007

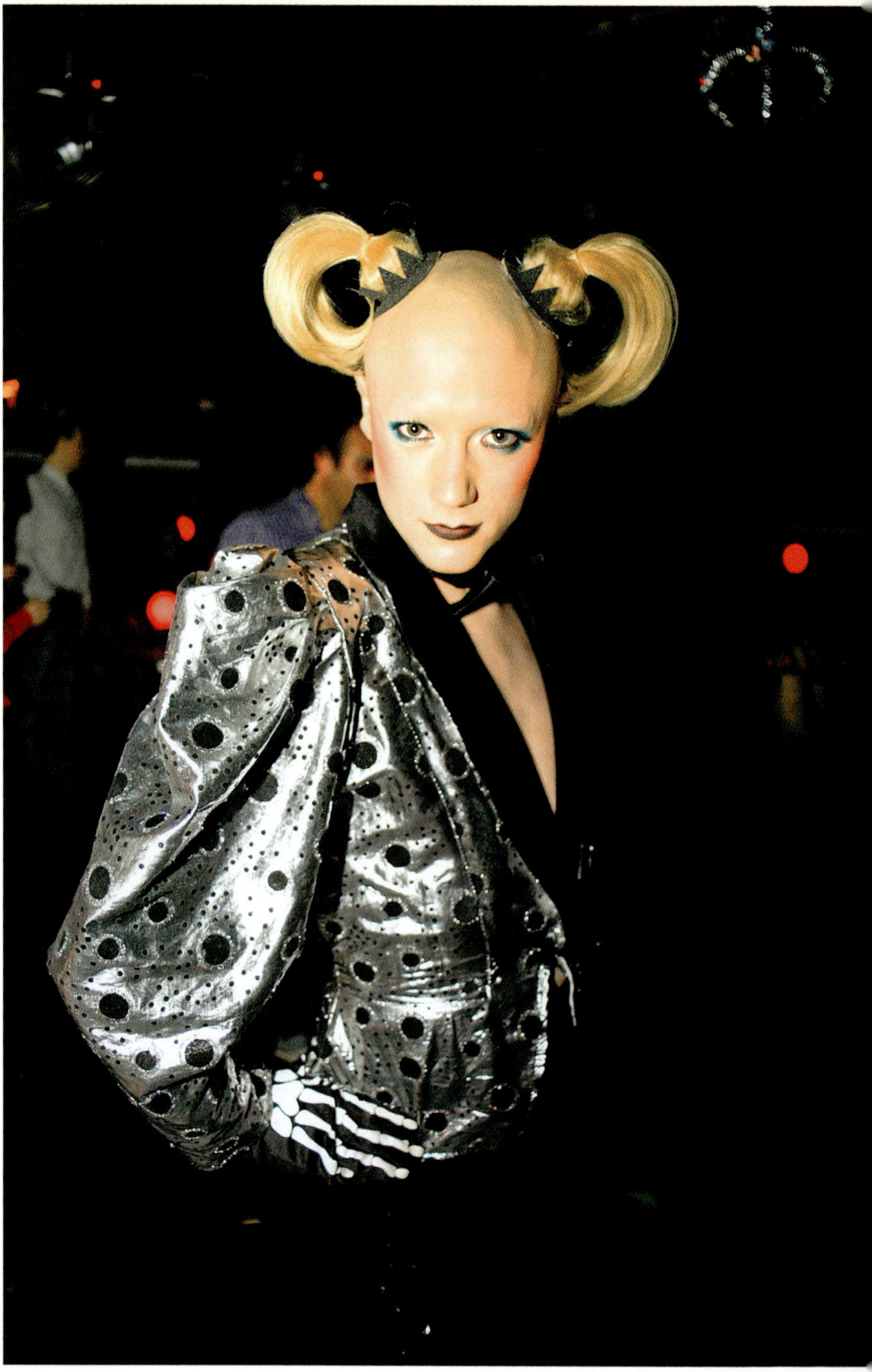

Circus – Oct 2007

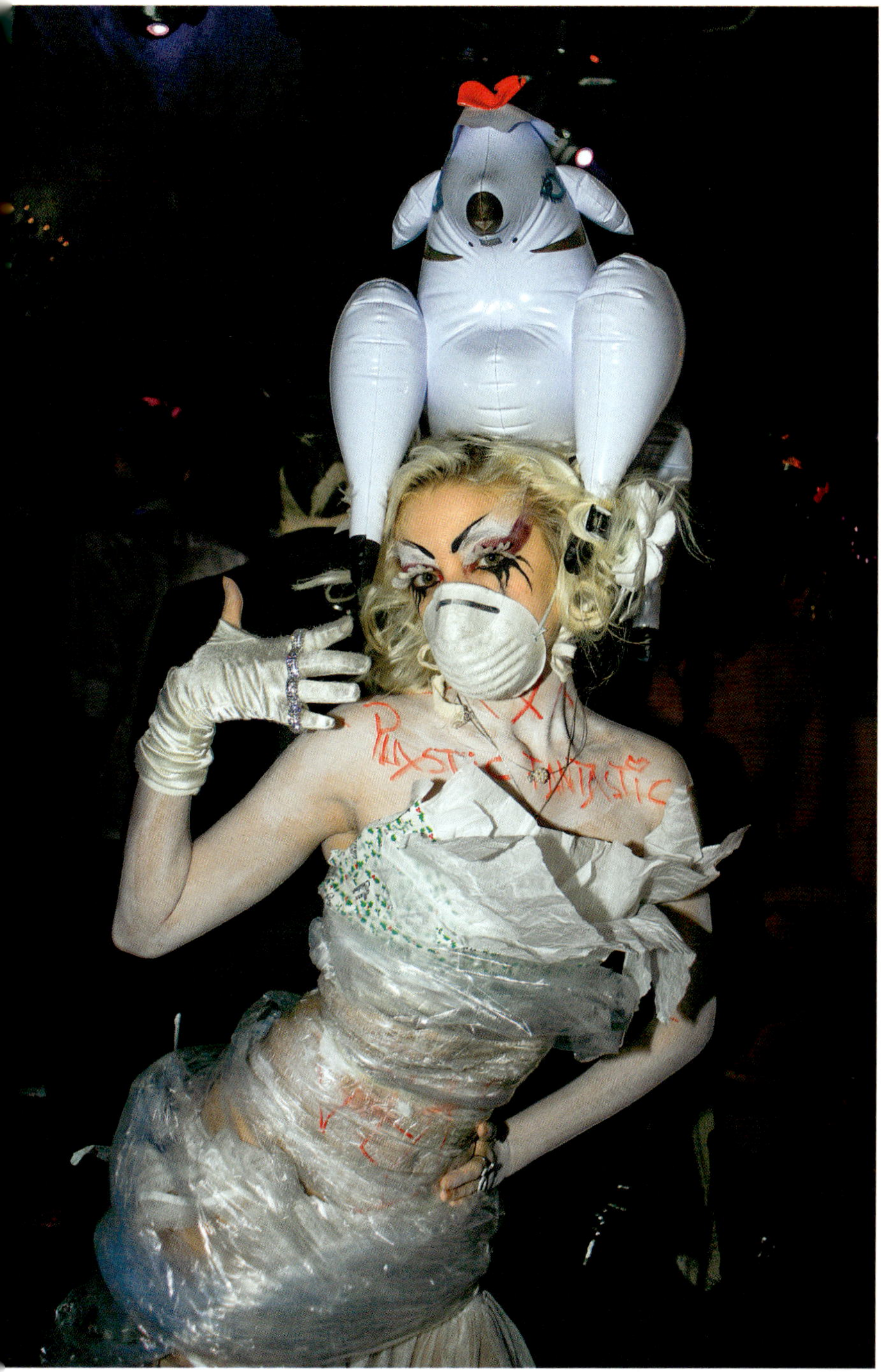

Kashpoint – April 2004

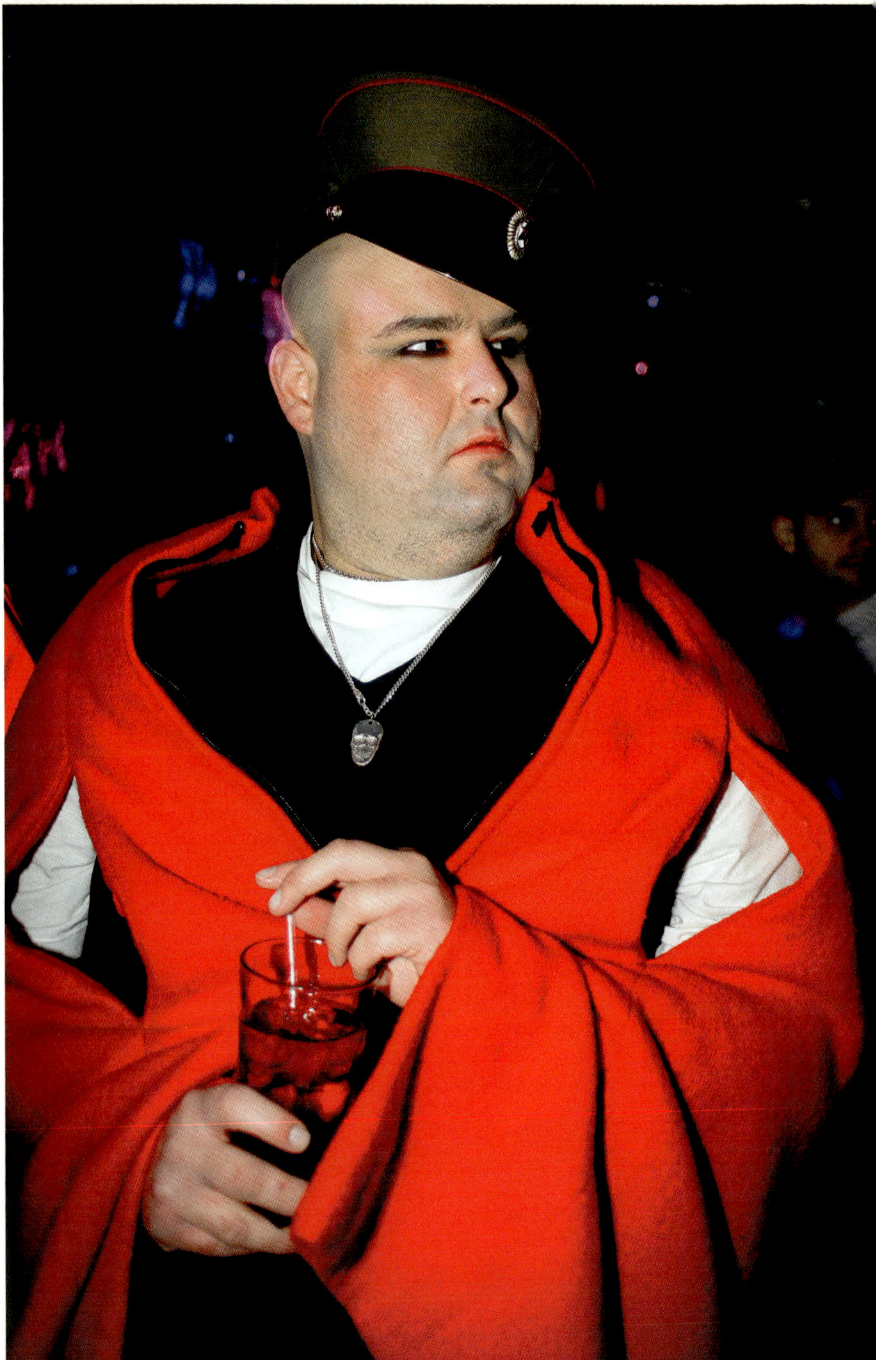

Too2Much – Feb 2006

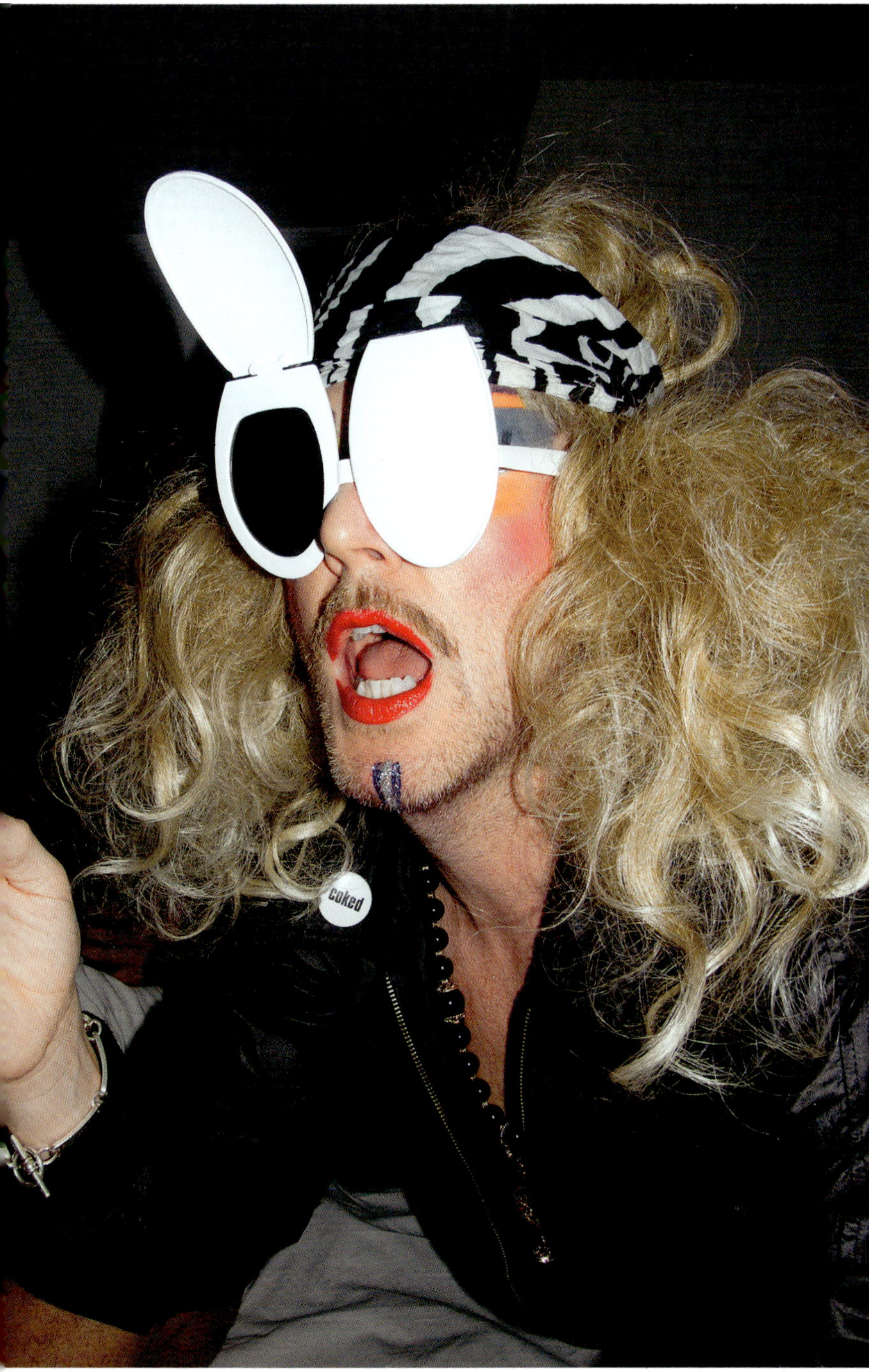

Gay Bingo@SupperClub – April 2010

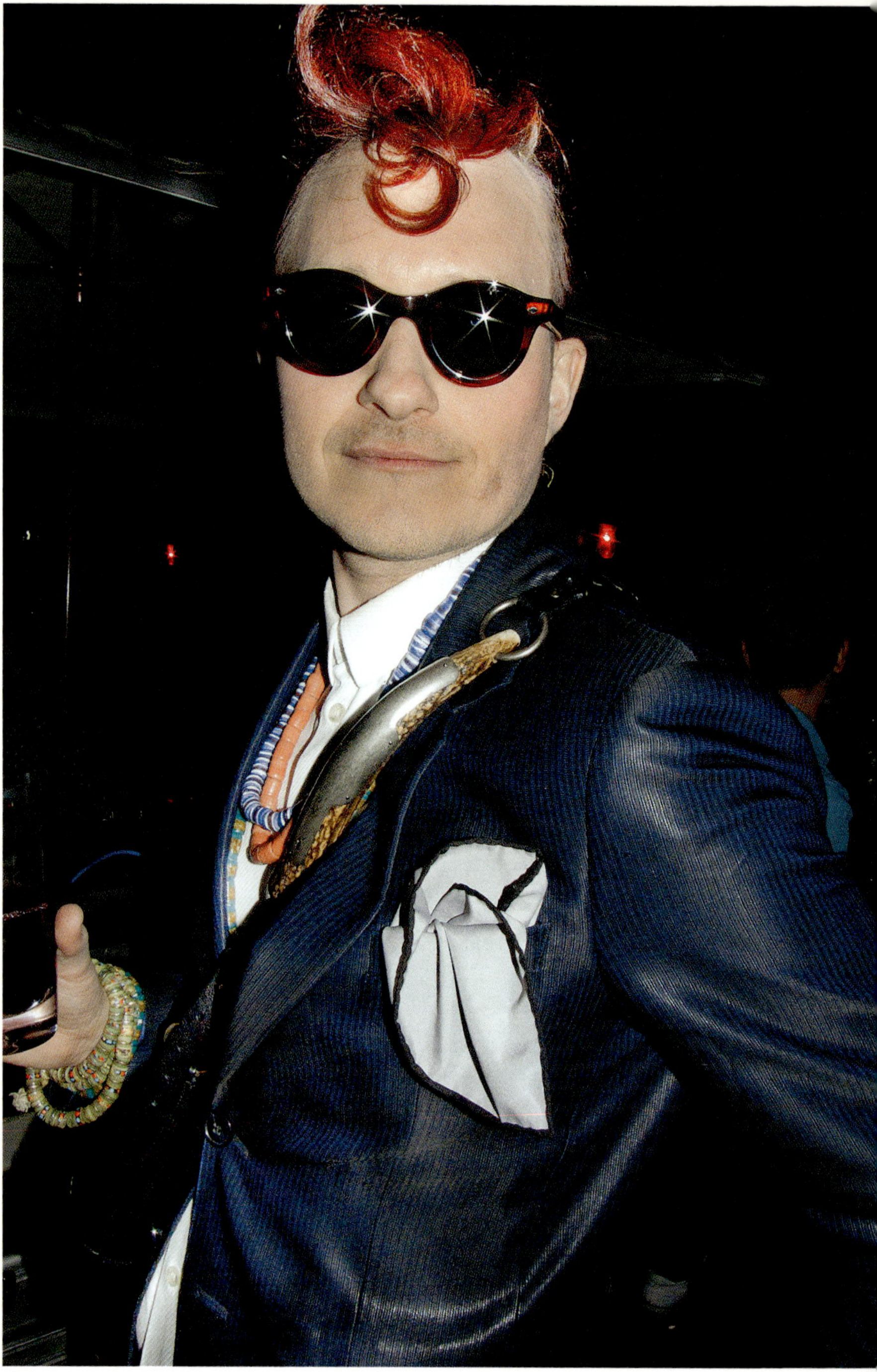

Shoreditch House – May 2009

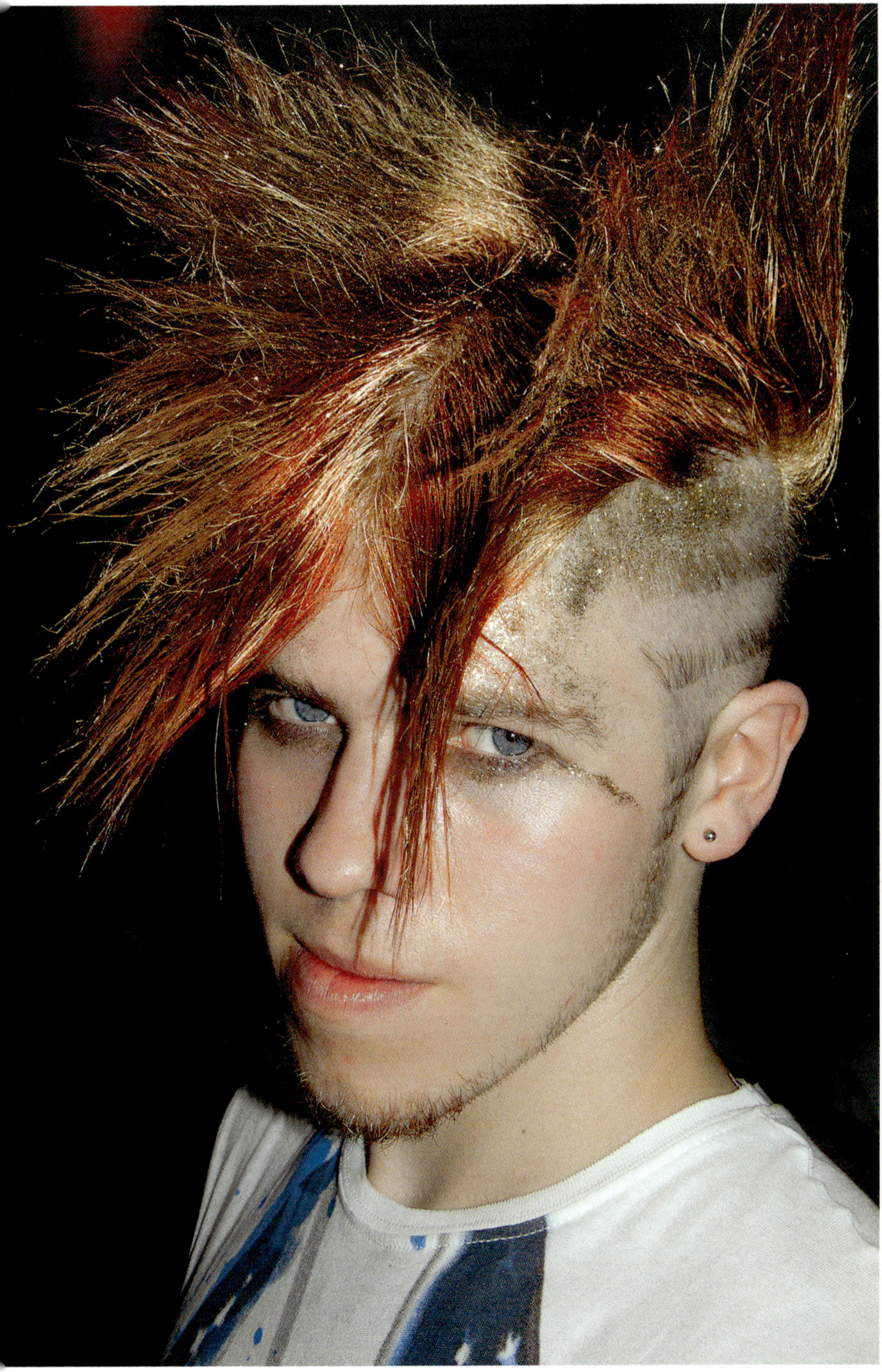

Shoreditch House – Aug 2009

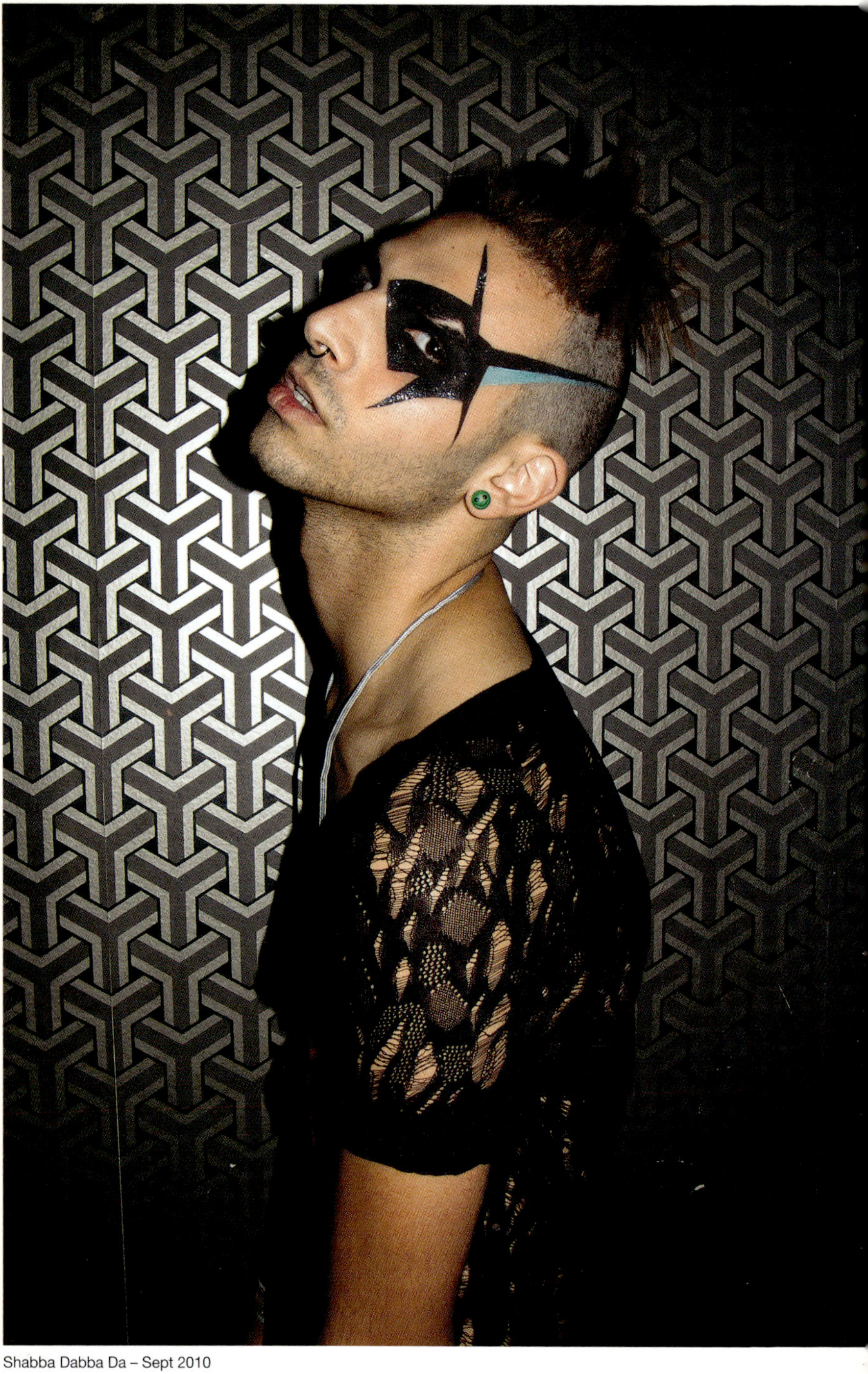

Shabba Dabba Da – Sept 2010

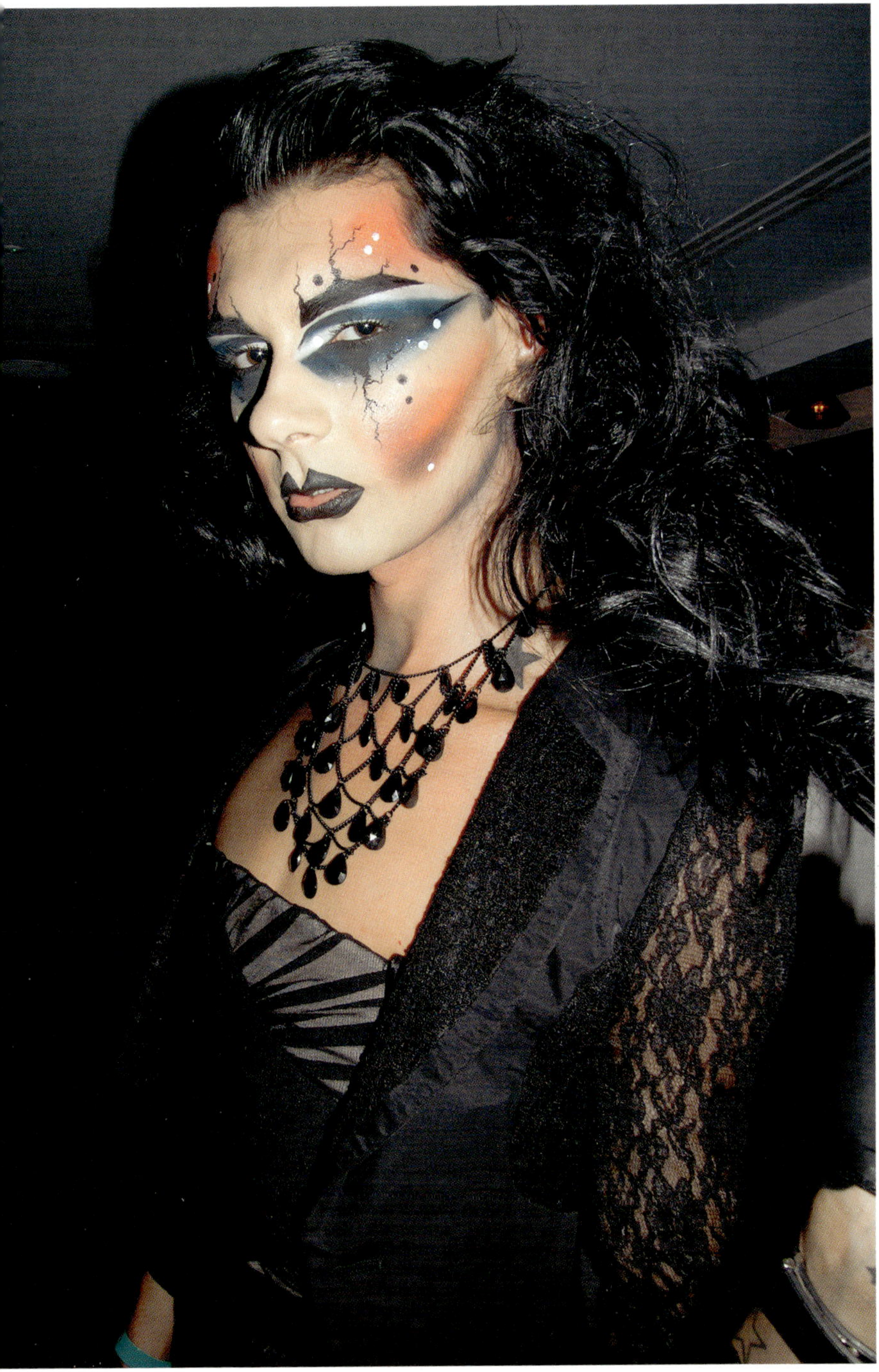

Circus – April 2010

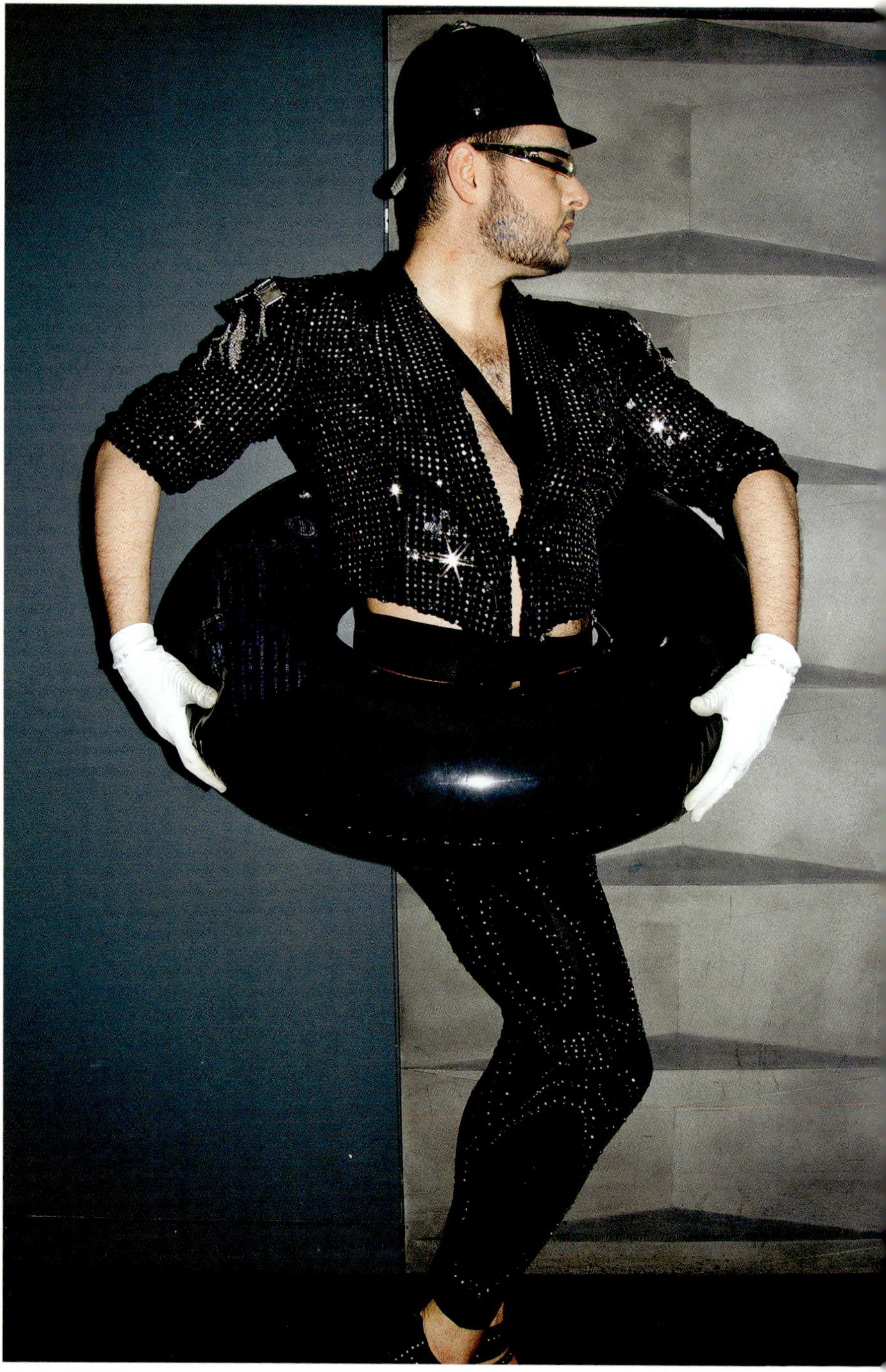

Circus – July 2010

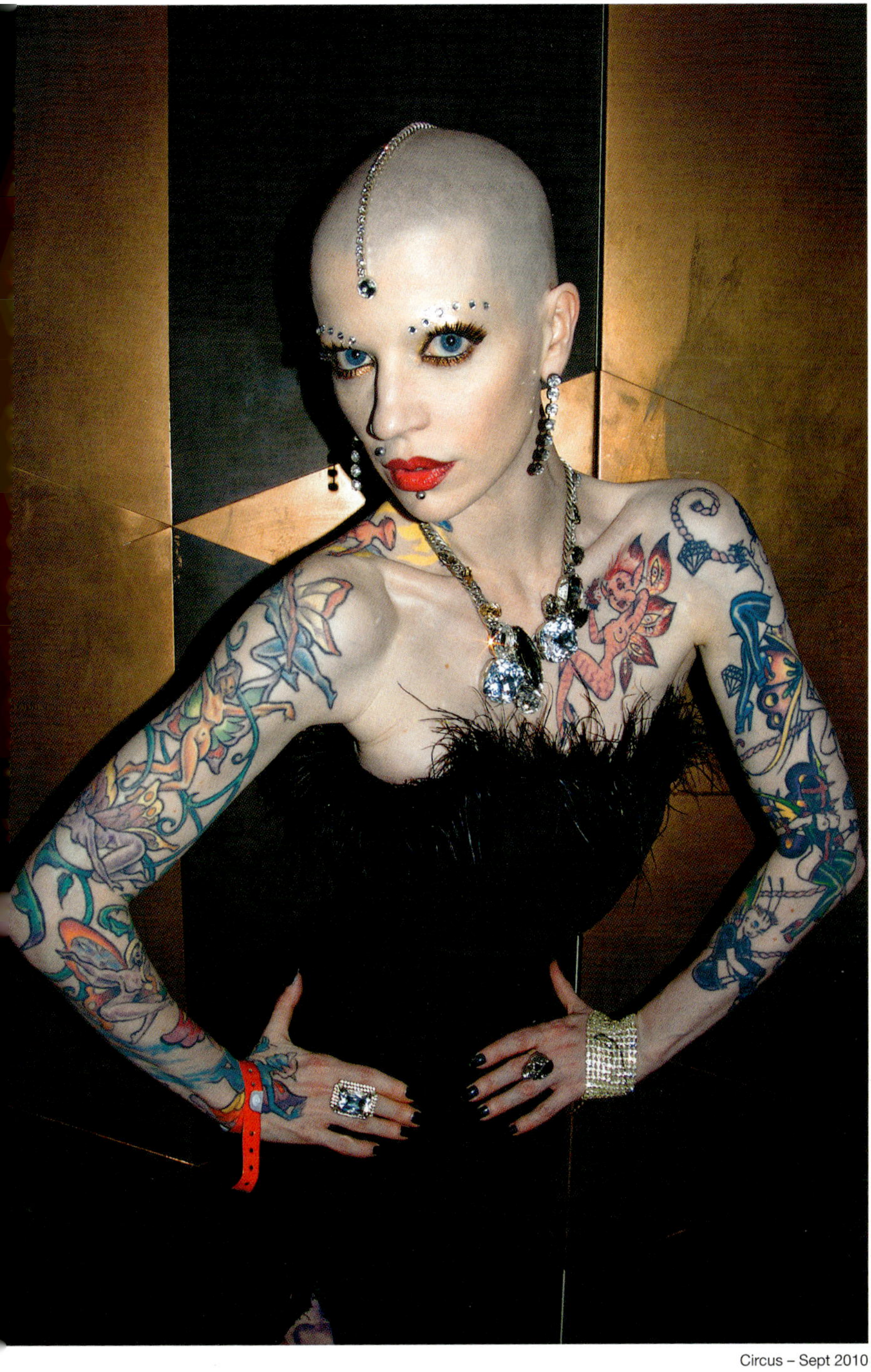

Circus – Sept 2010

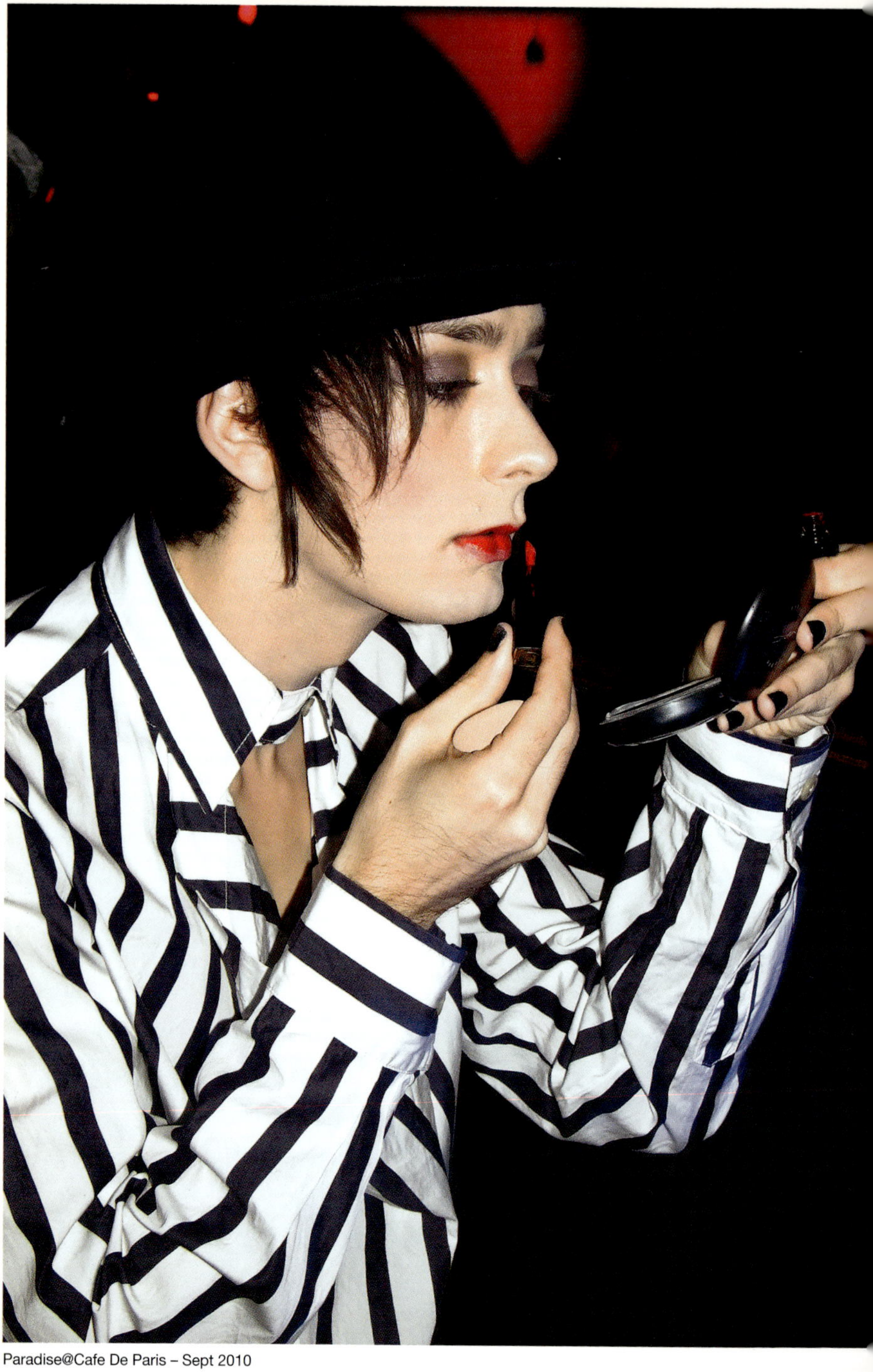

Paradise@Cafe De Paris – Sept 2010

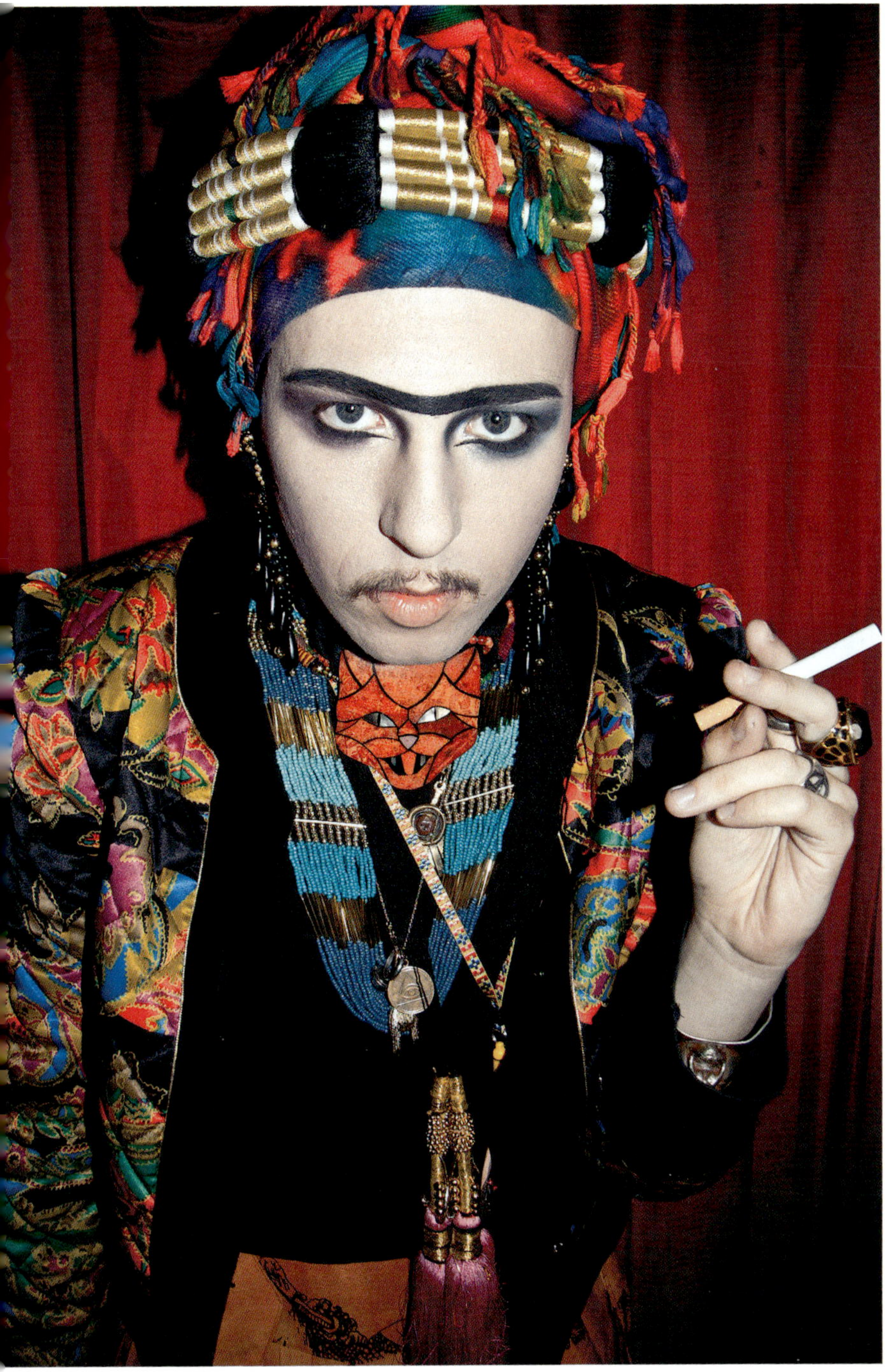

Wearable Art@Egg – Sept 2010

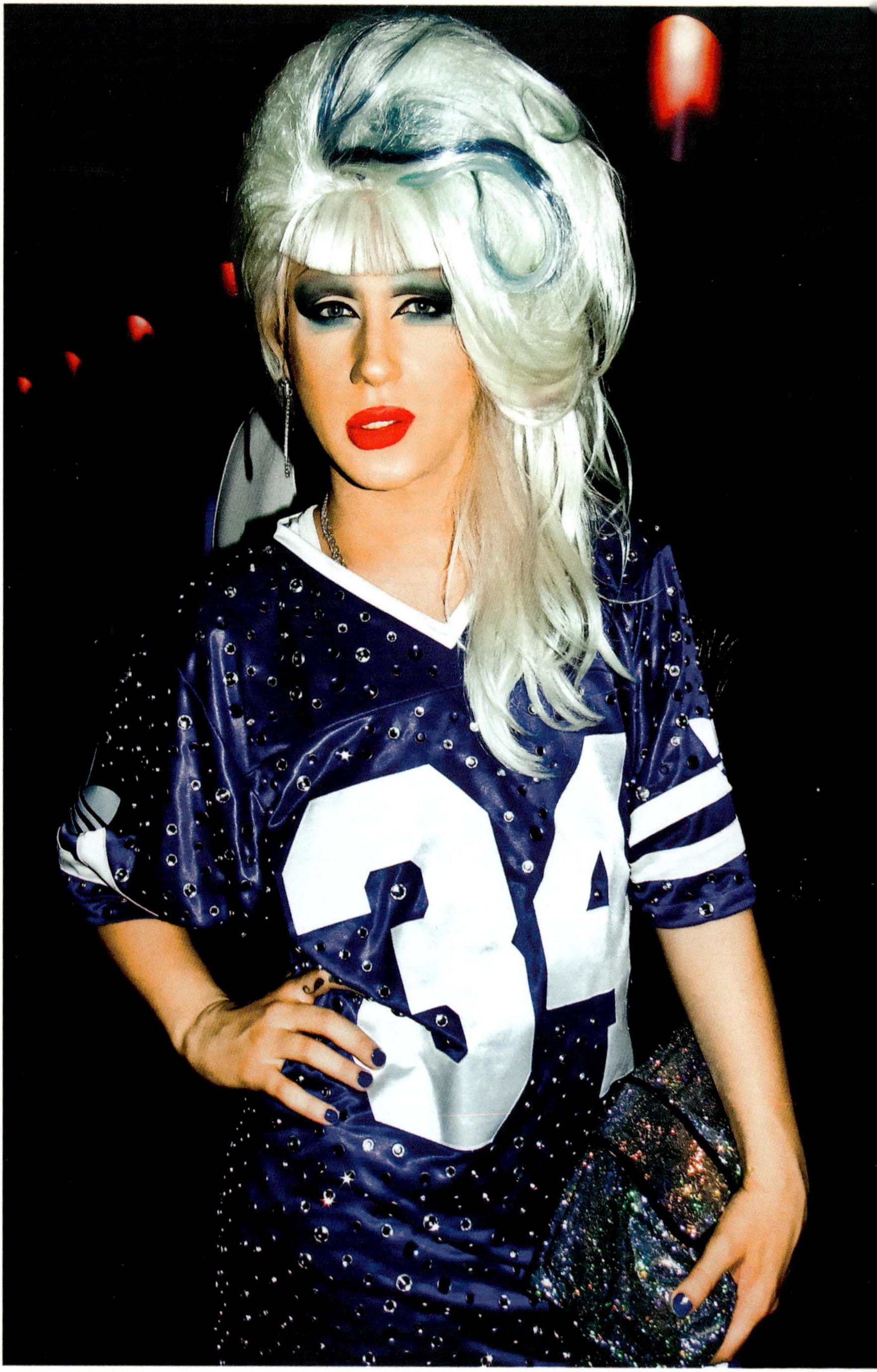

Circus – Sept 2010

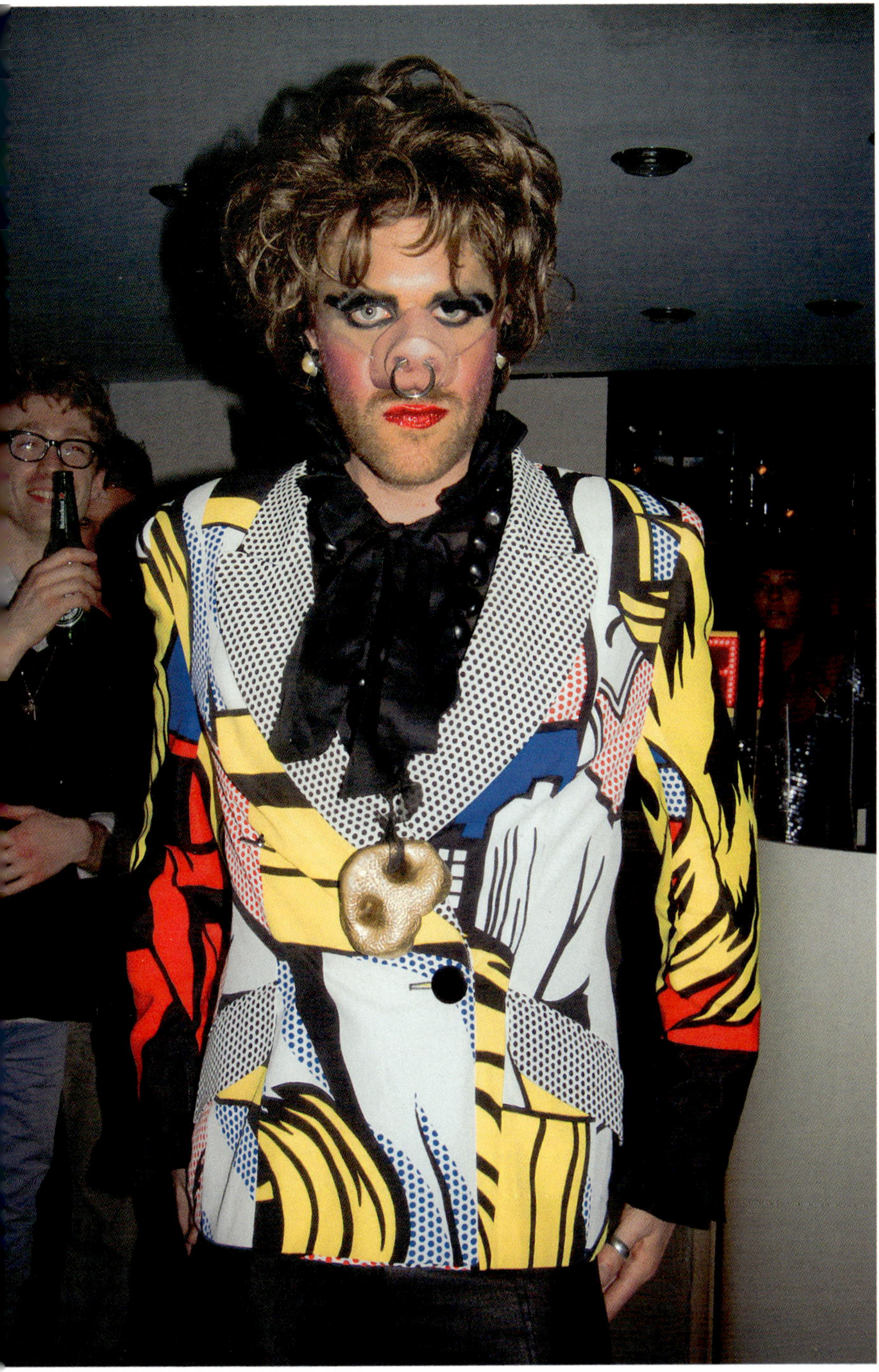

Gay Bingo@SupperClub – April 2010

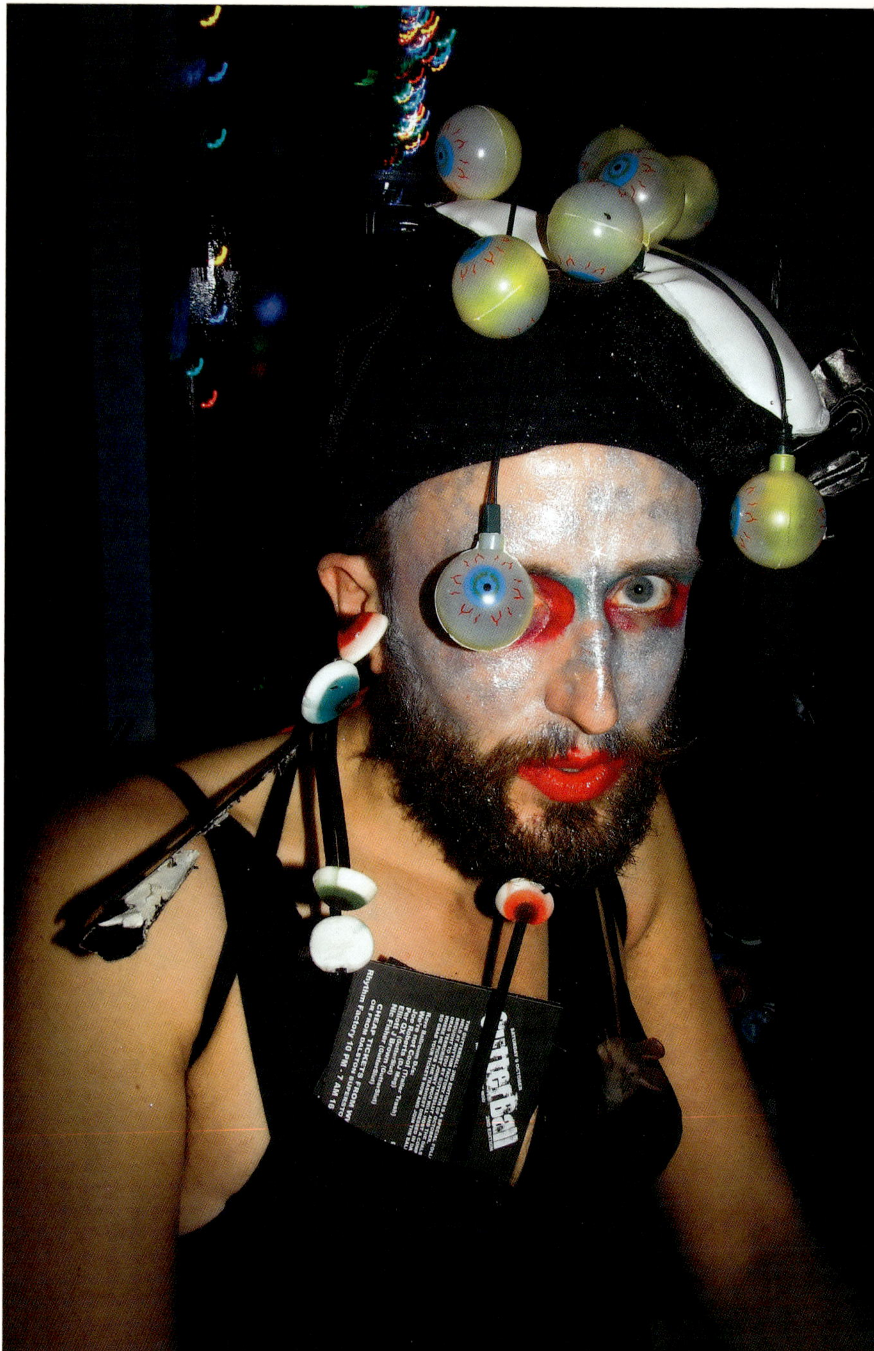

GutterBall – Sept 2010

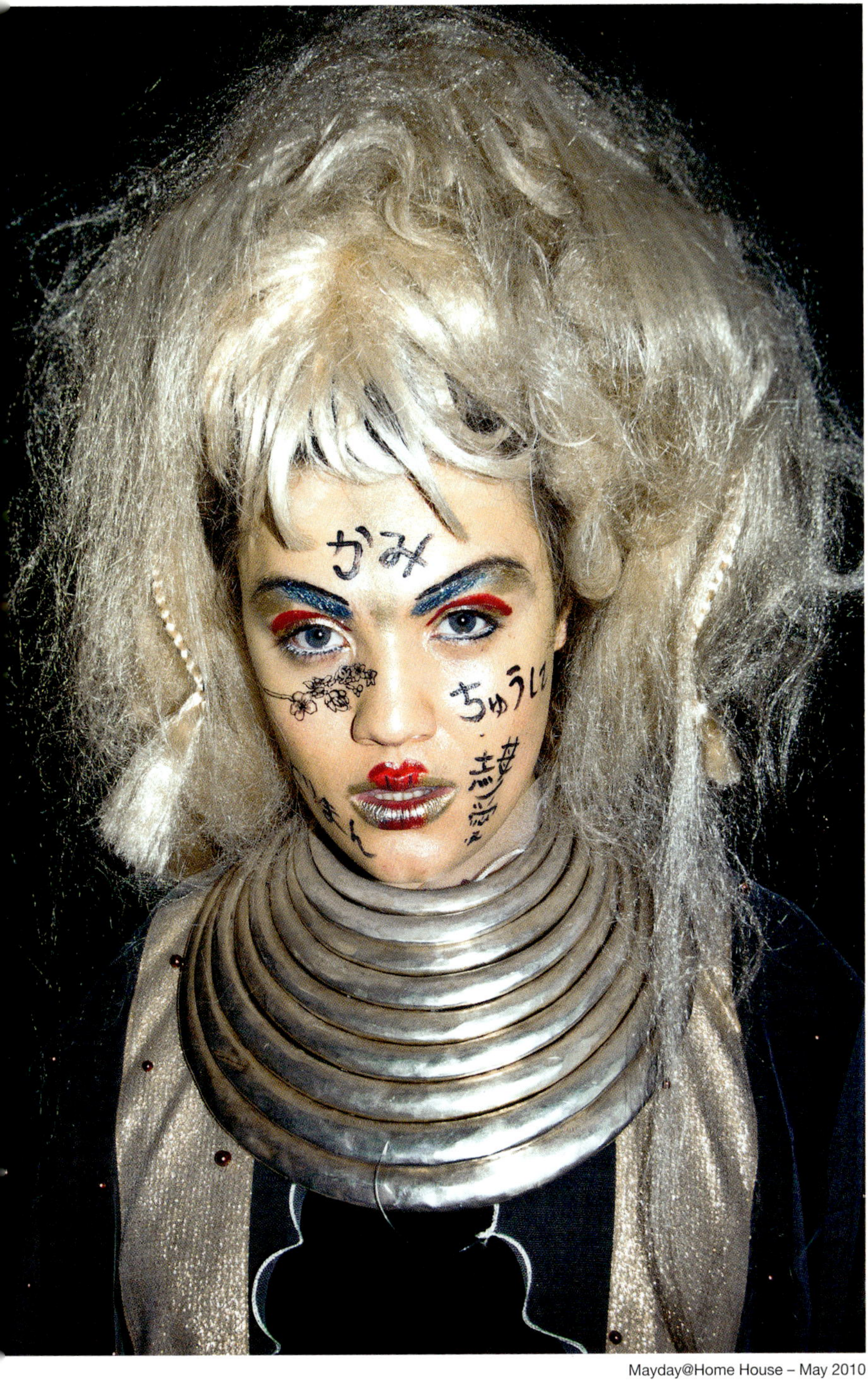

Mayday@Home House – May 2010

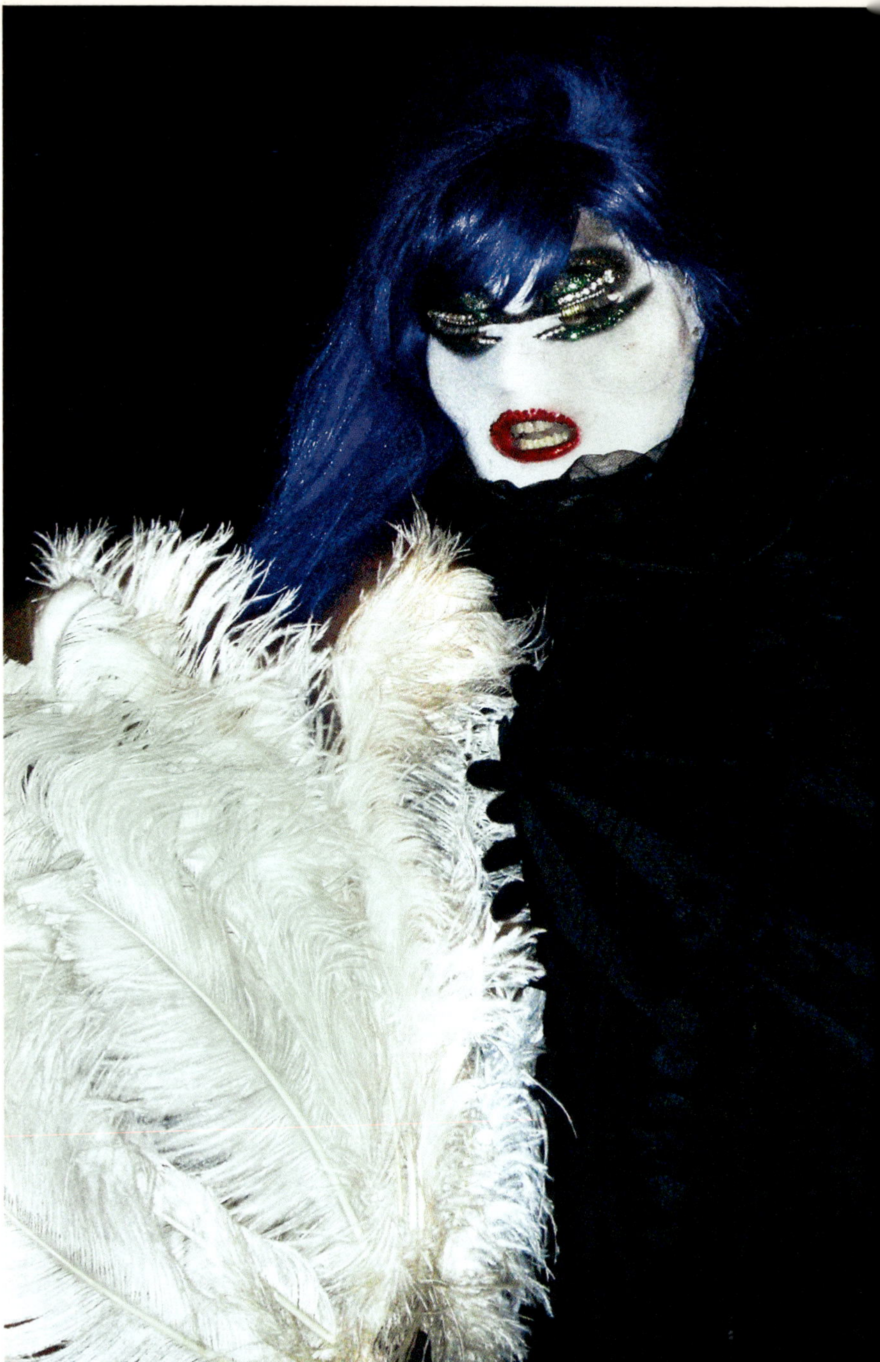

Nag Nag Nag – July 2003

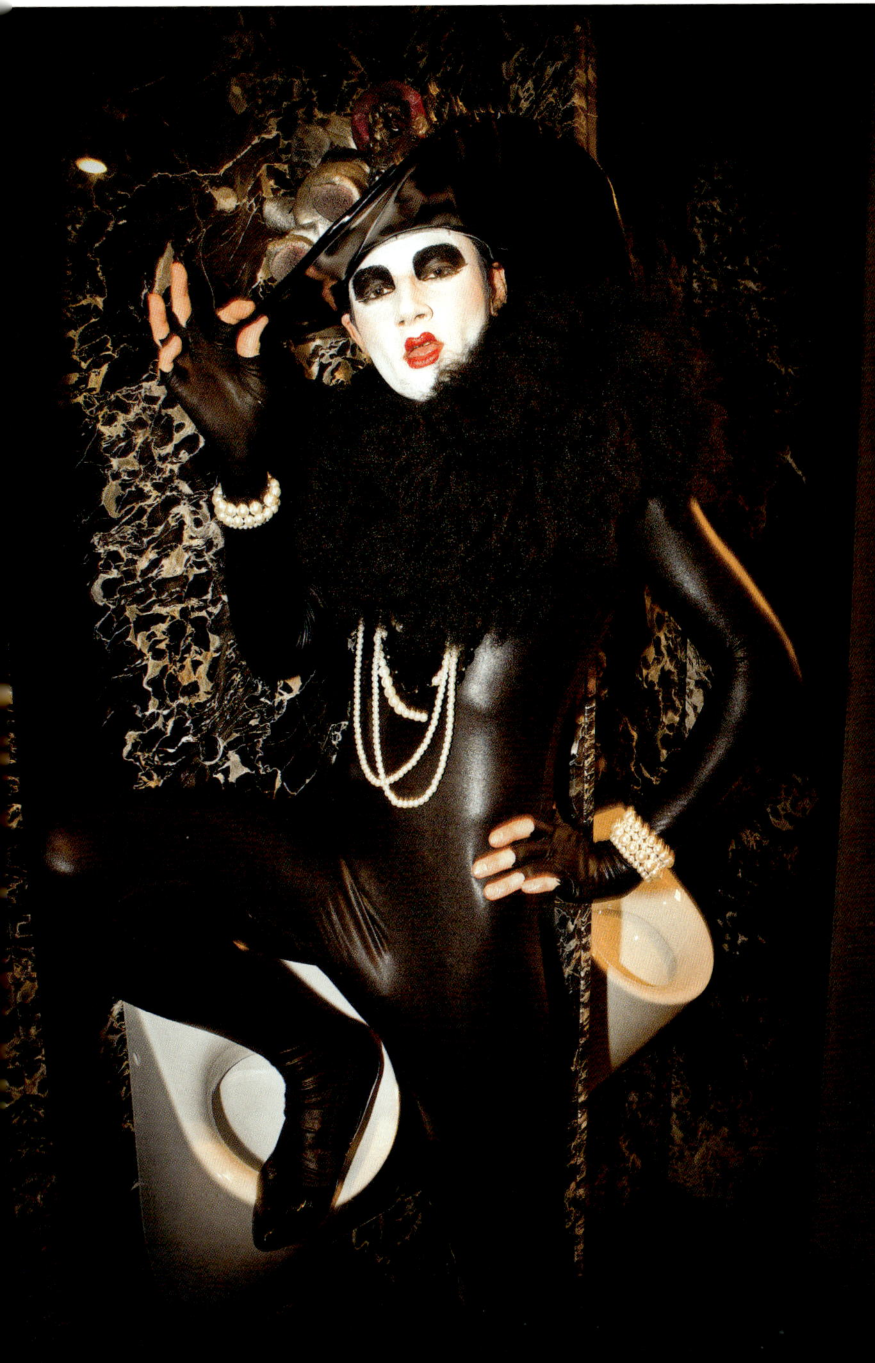

Circus – April 2010

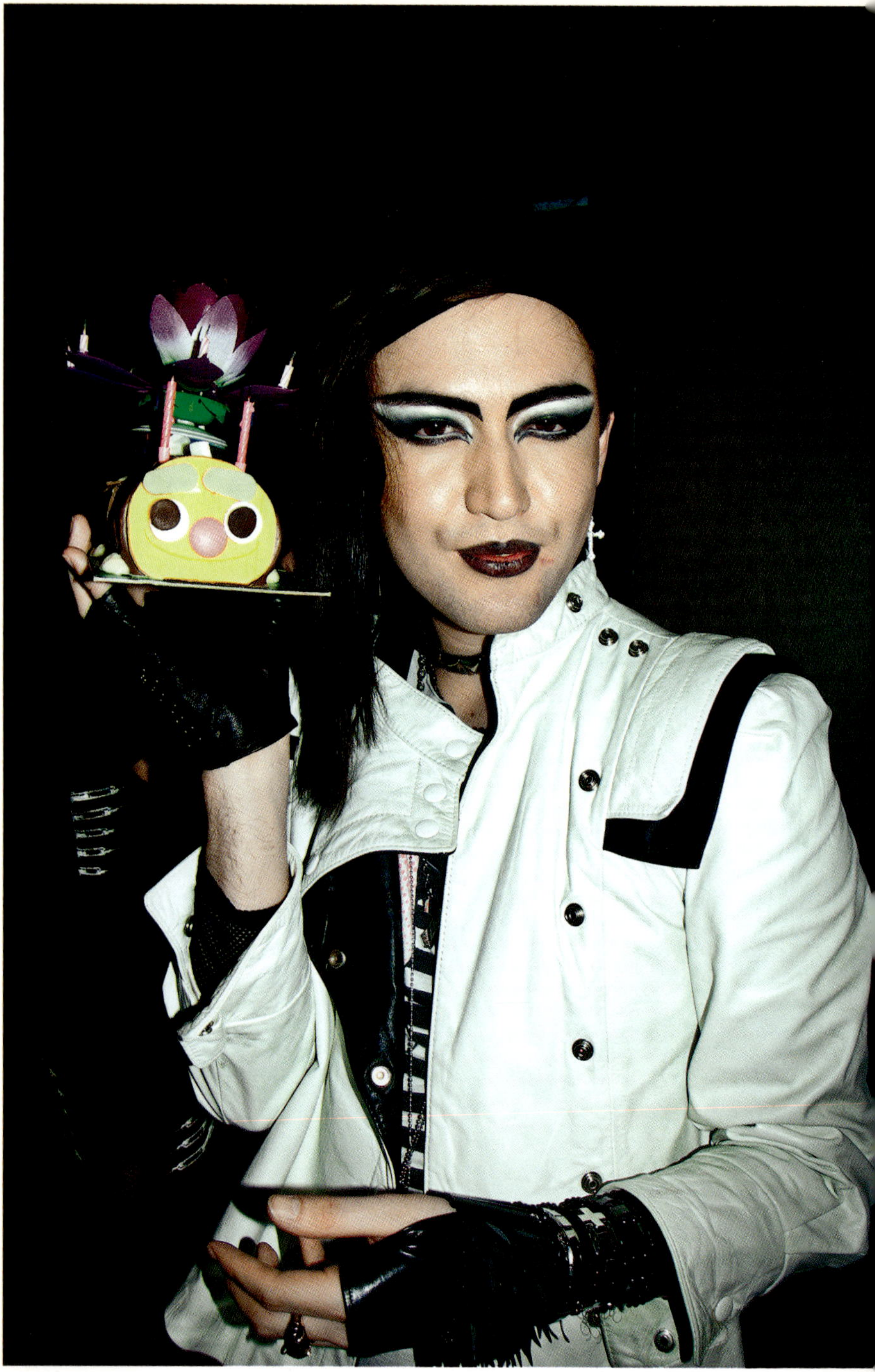

The Face – Oct 2010

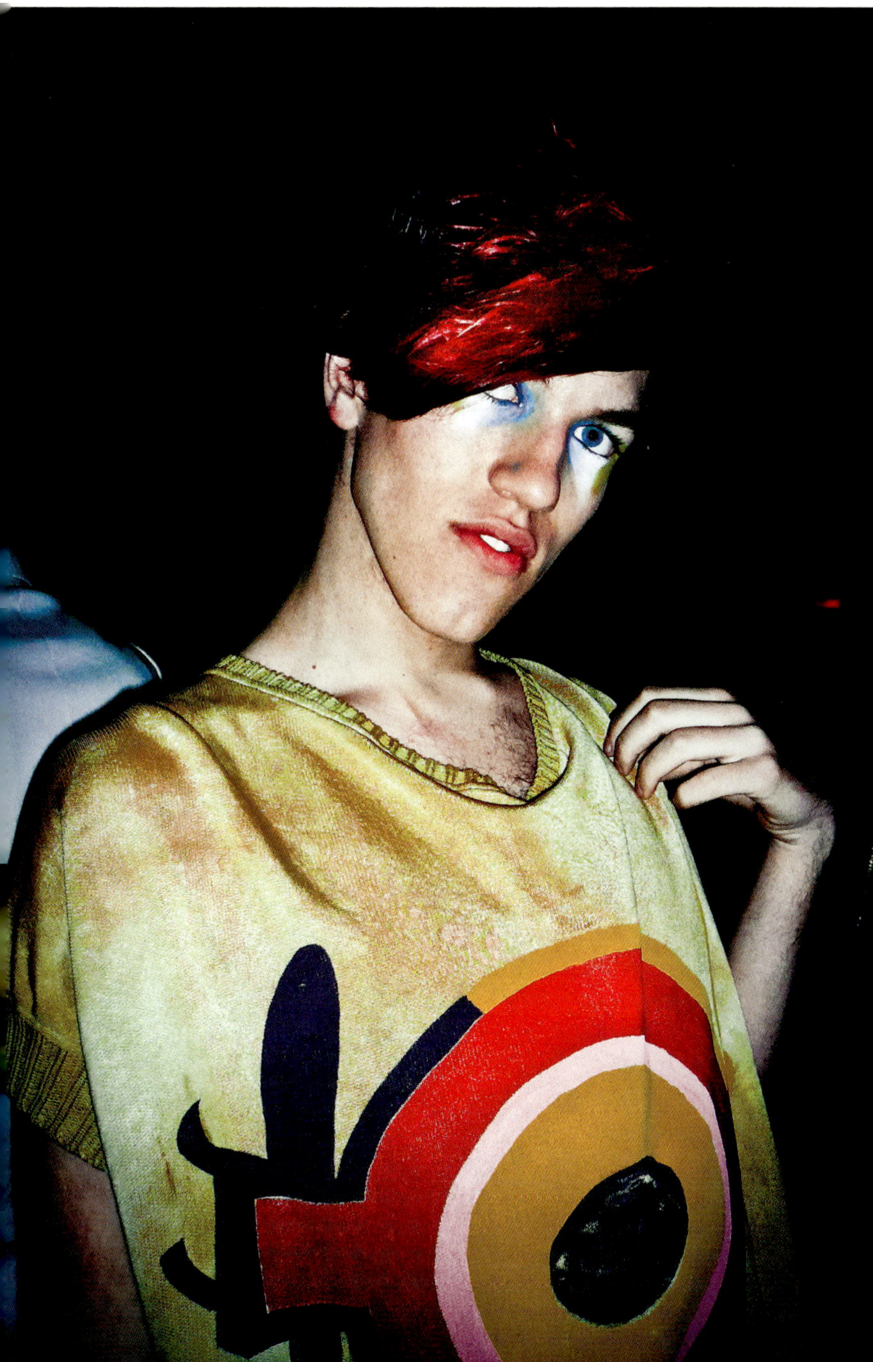

Boombox – July 2007

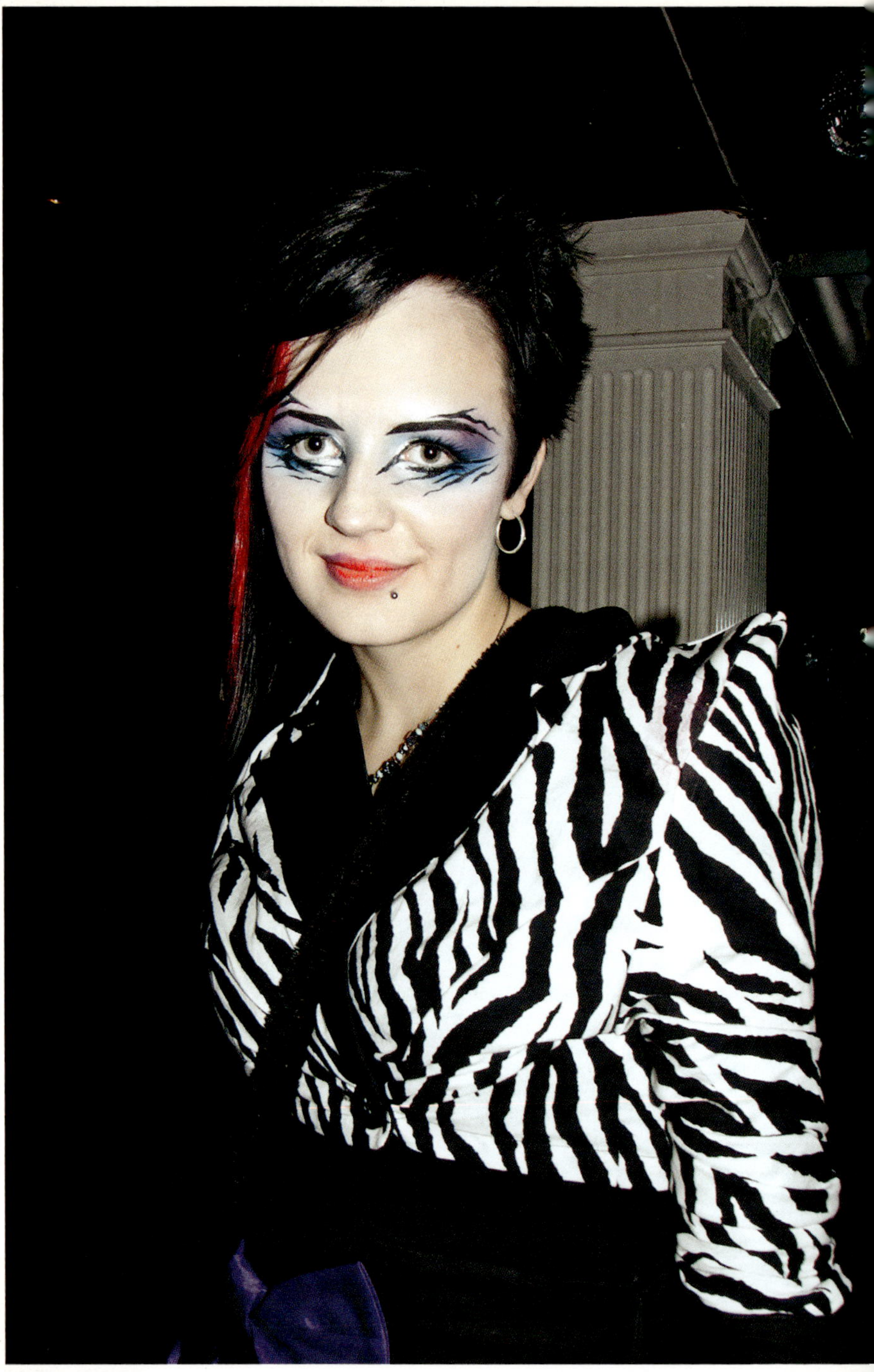

The Face – Oct 2010

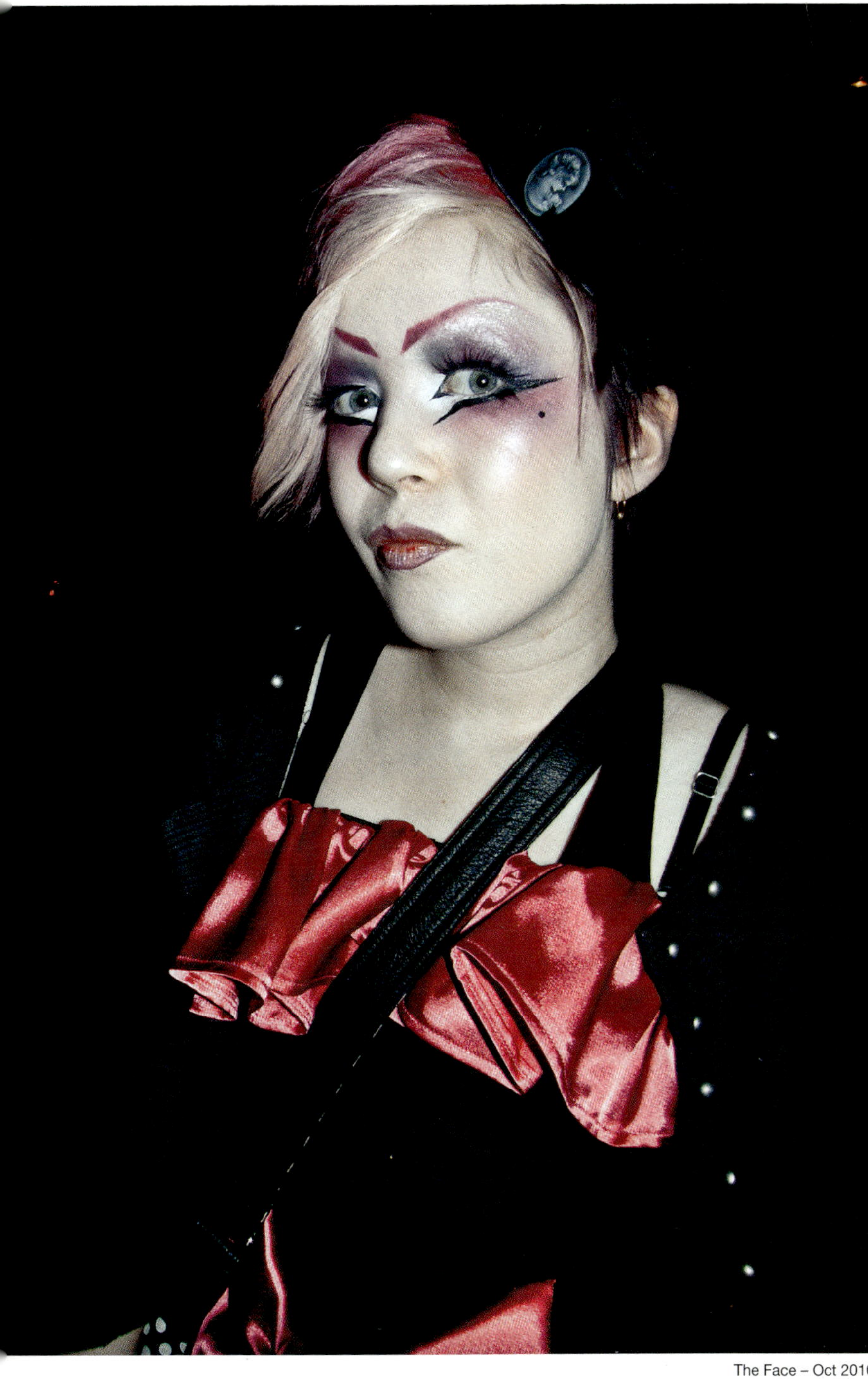

The Face – Oct 2010

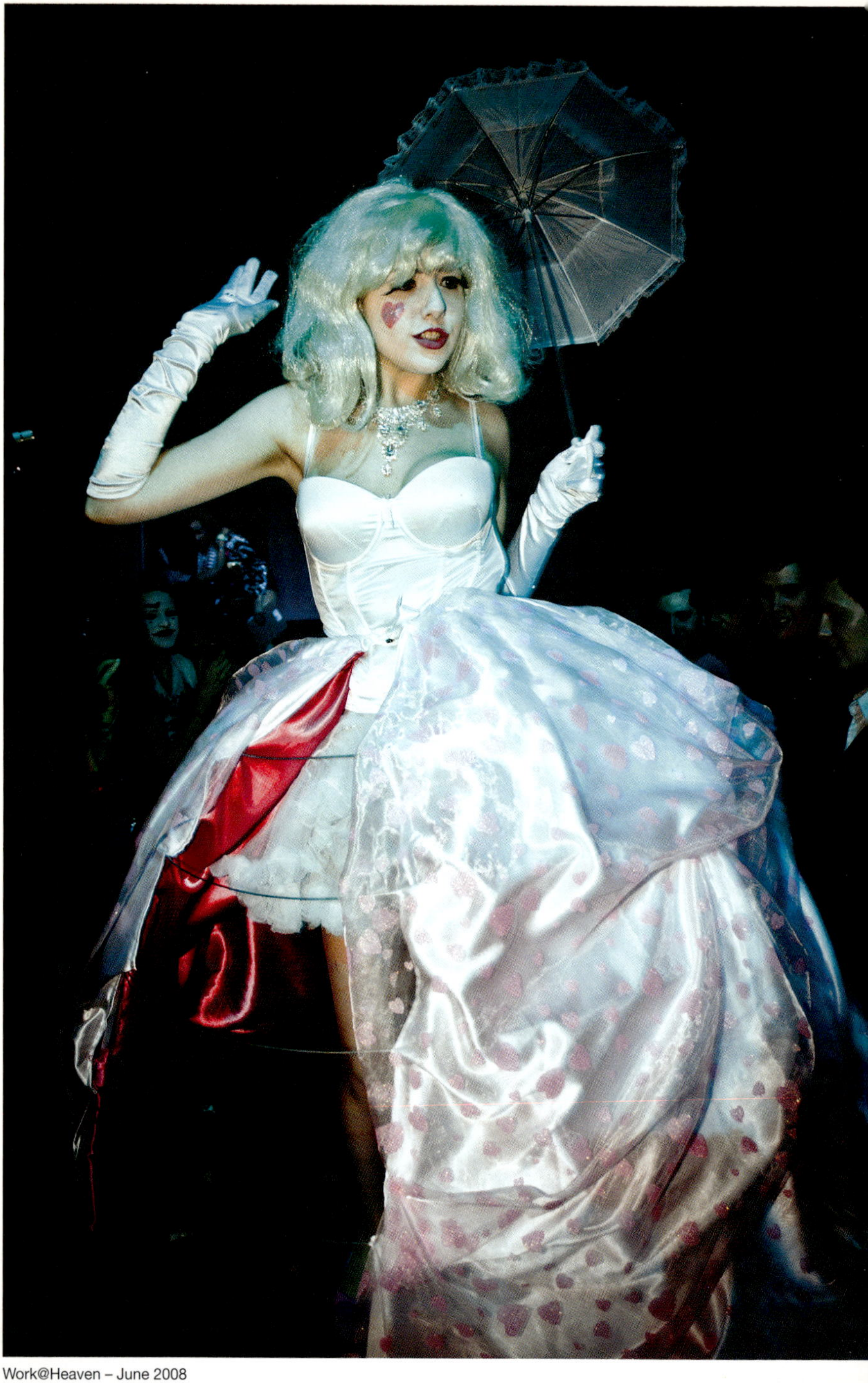

Work@Heaven – June 2008

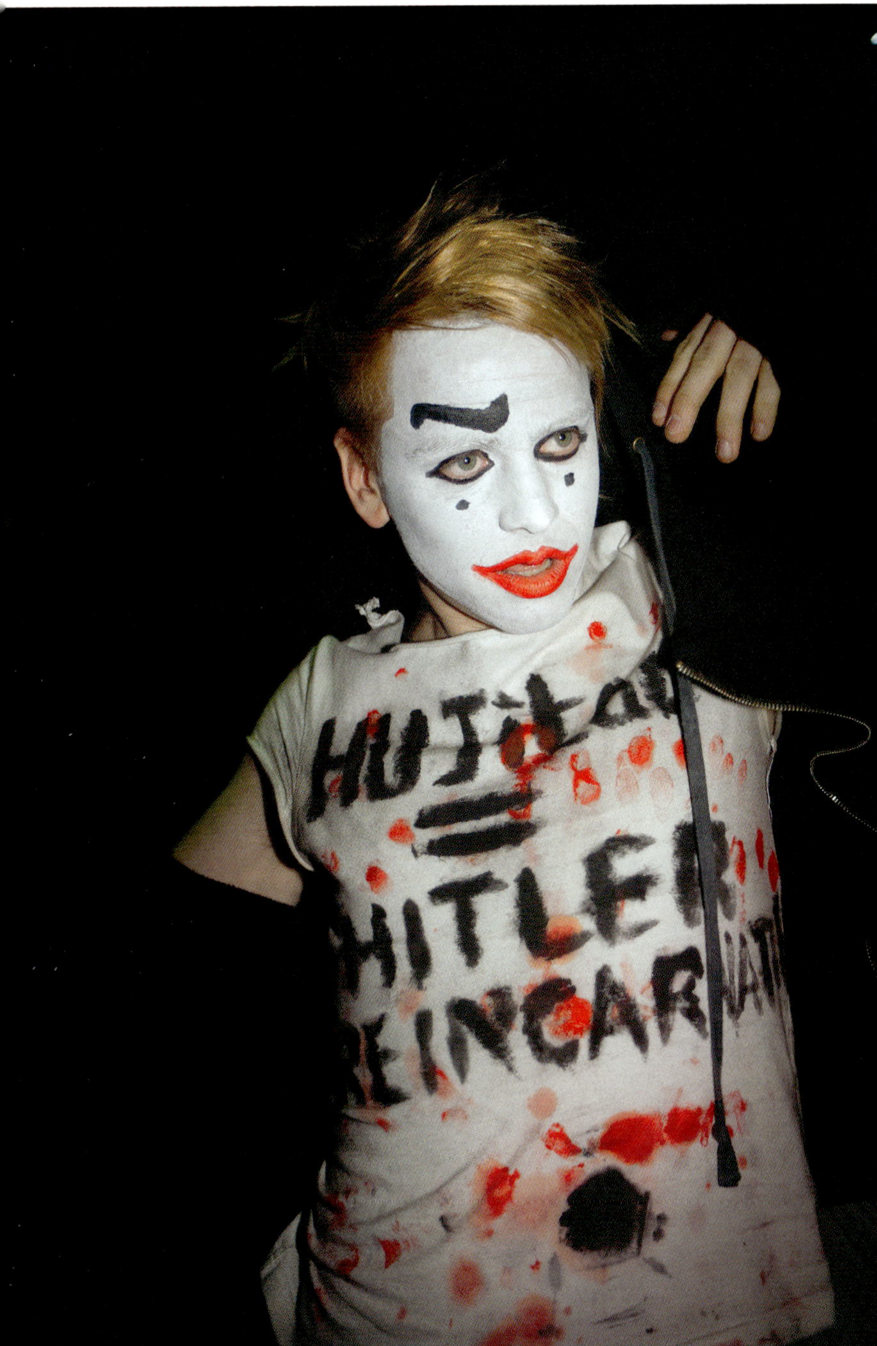

Work@Heaven – June 2008

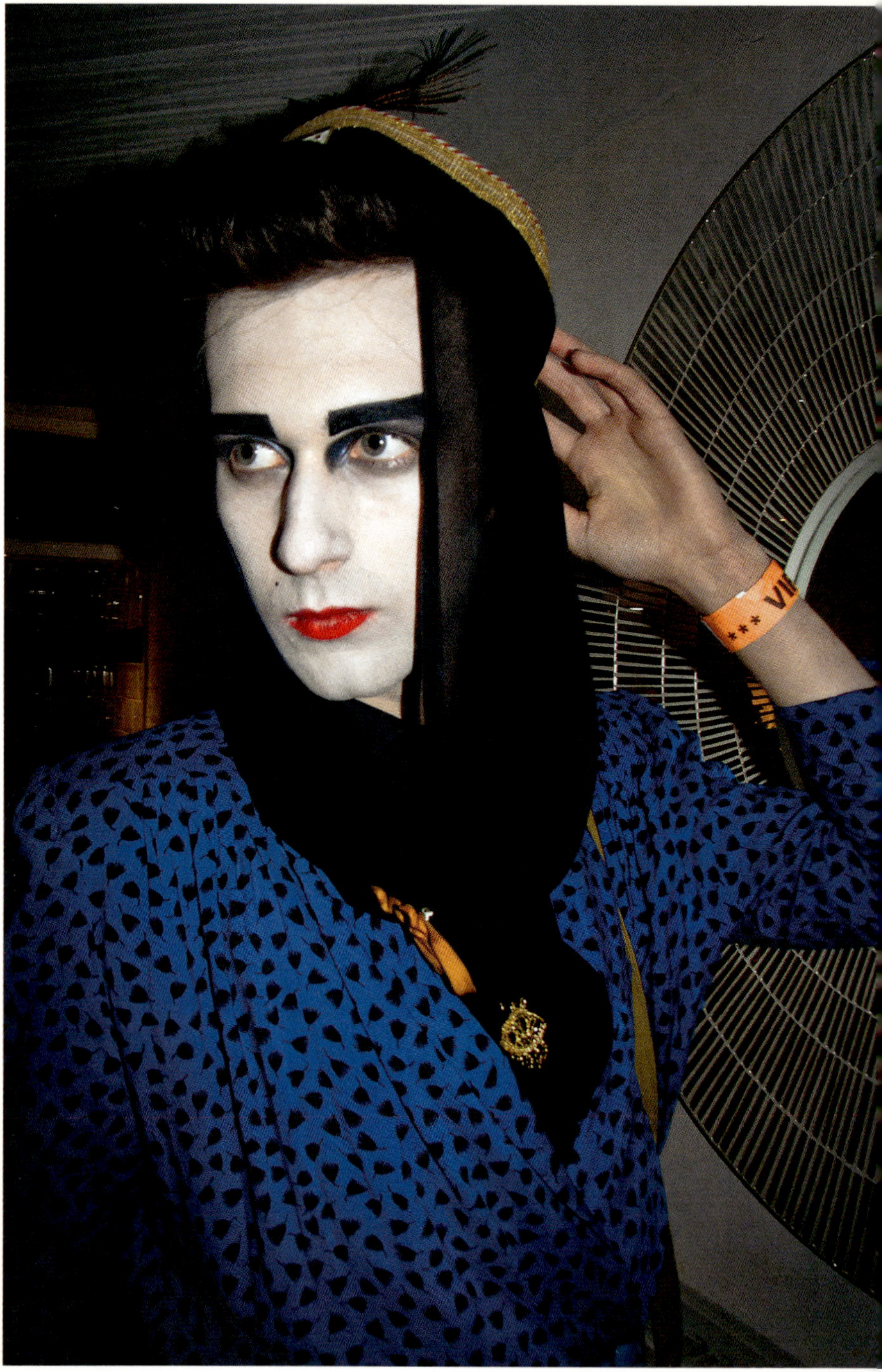

Wearable Art@Egg – Sept 2010

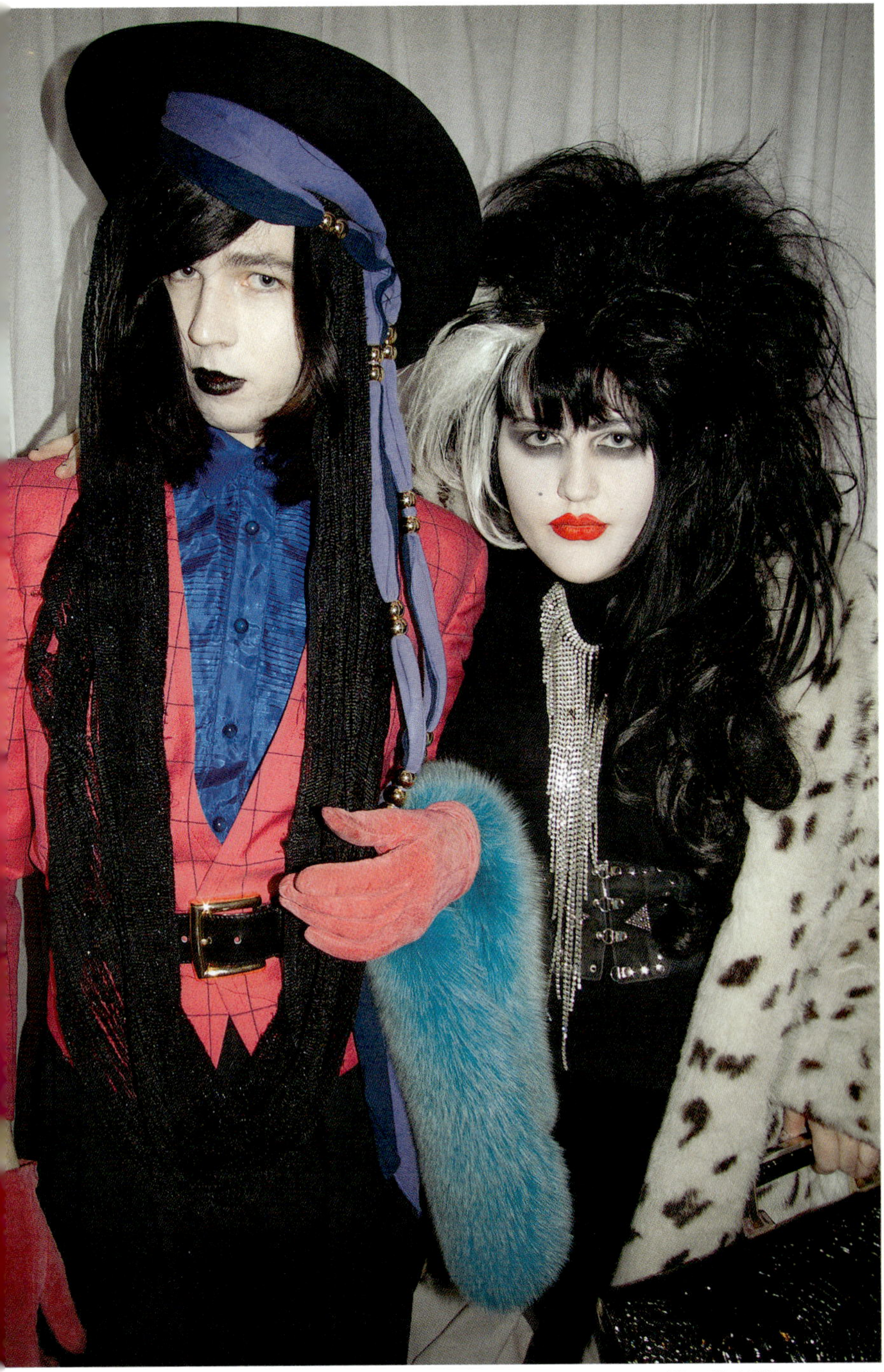

Wearable Art@Egg – Sept 2010

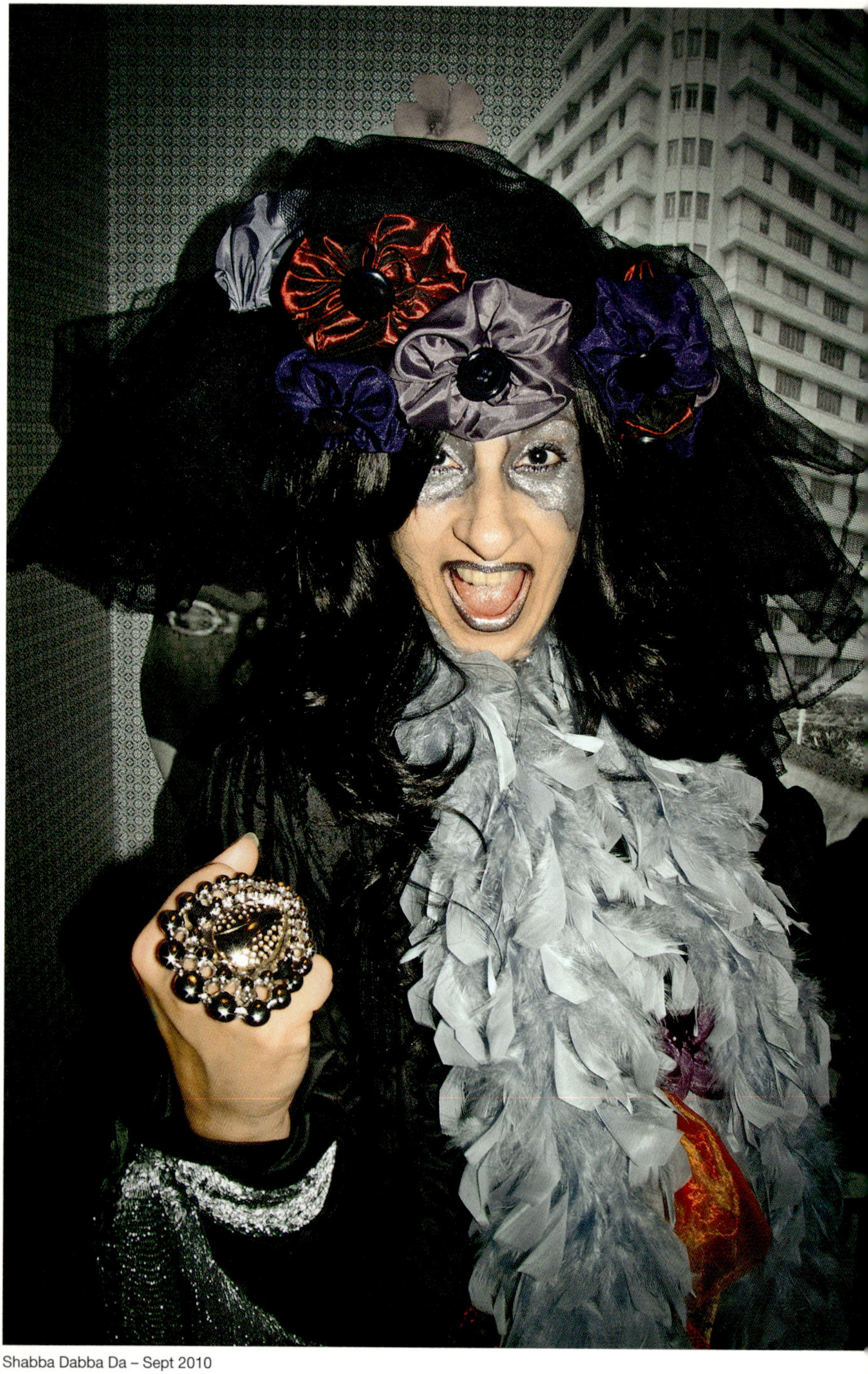

Shabba Dabba Da – Sept 2010

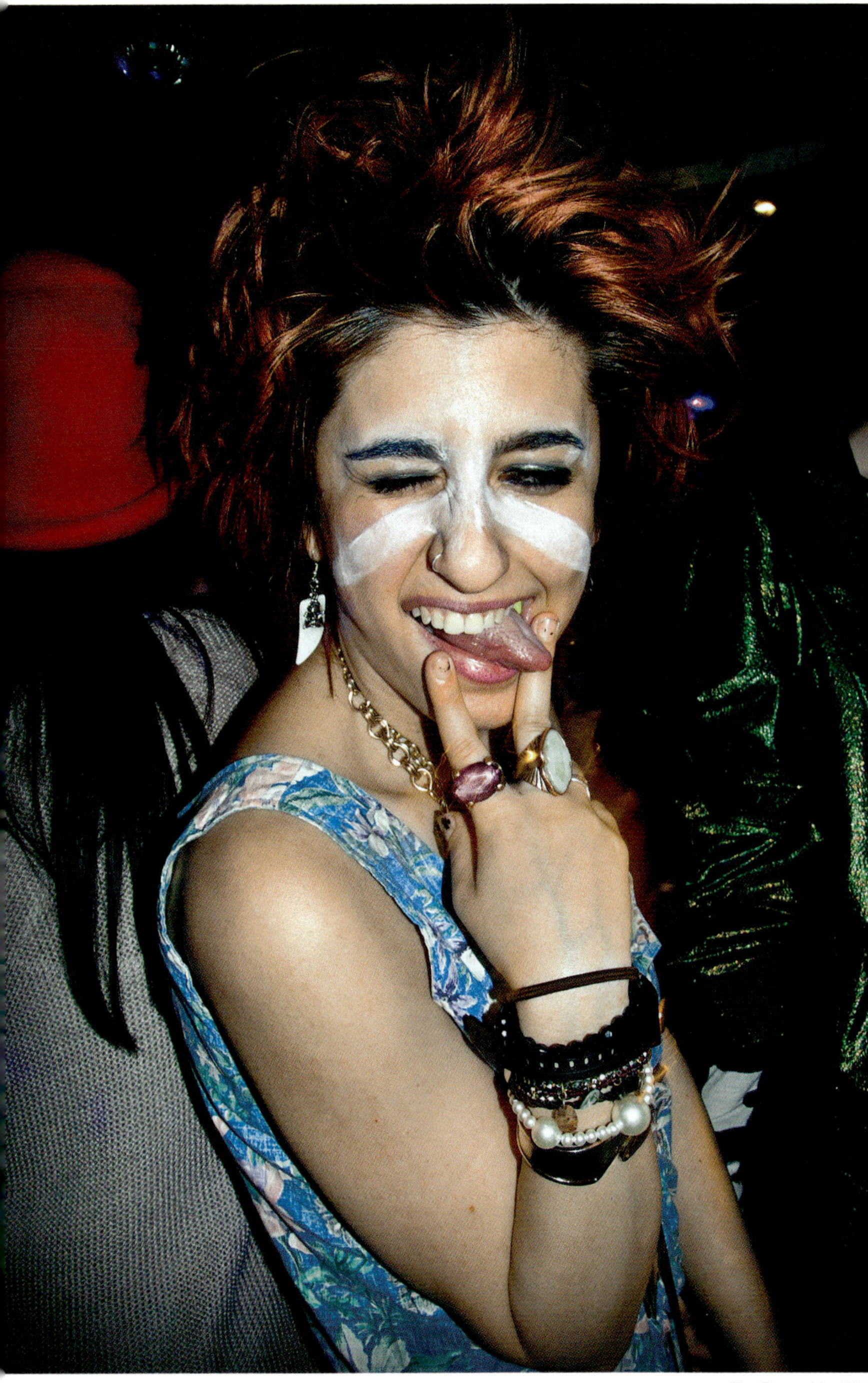

The Face – May 2010

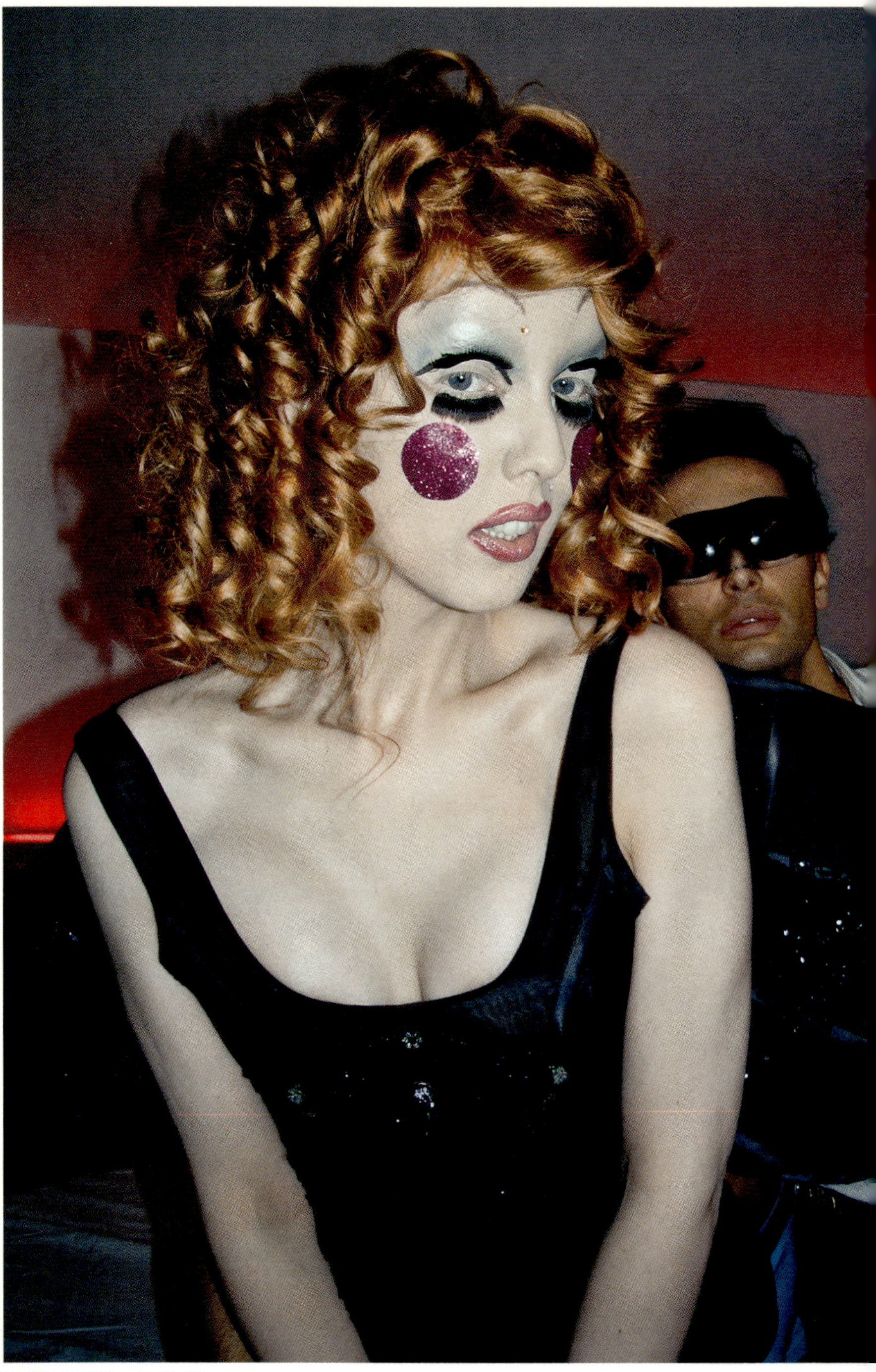

Toy@SupperClub – May 2010

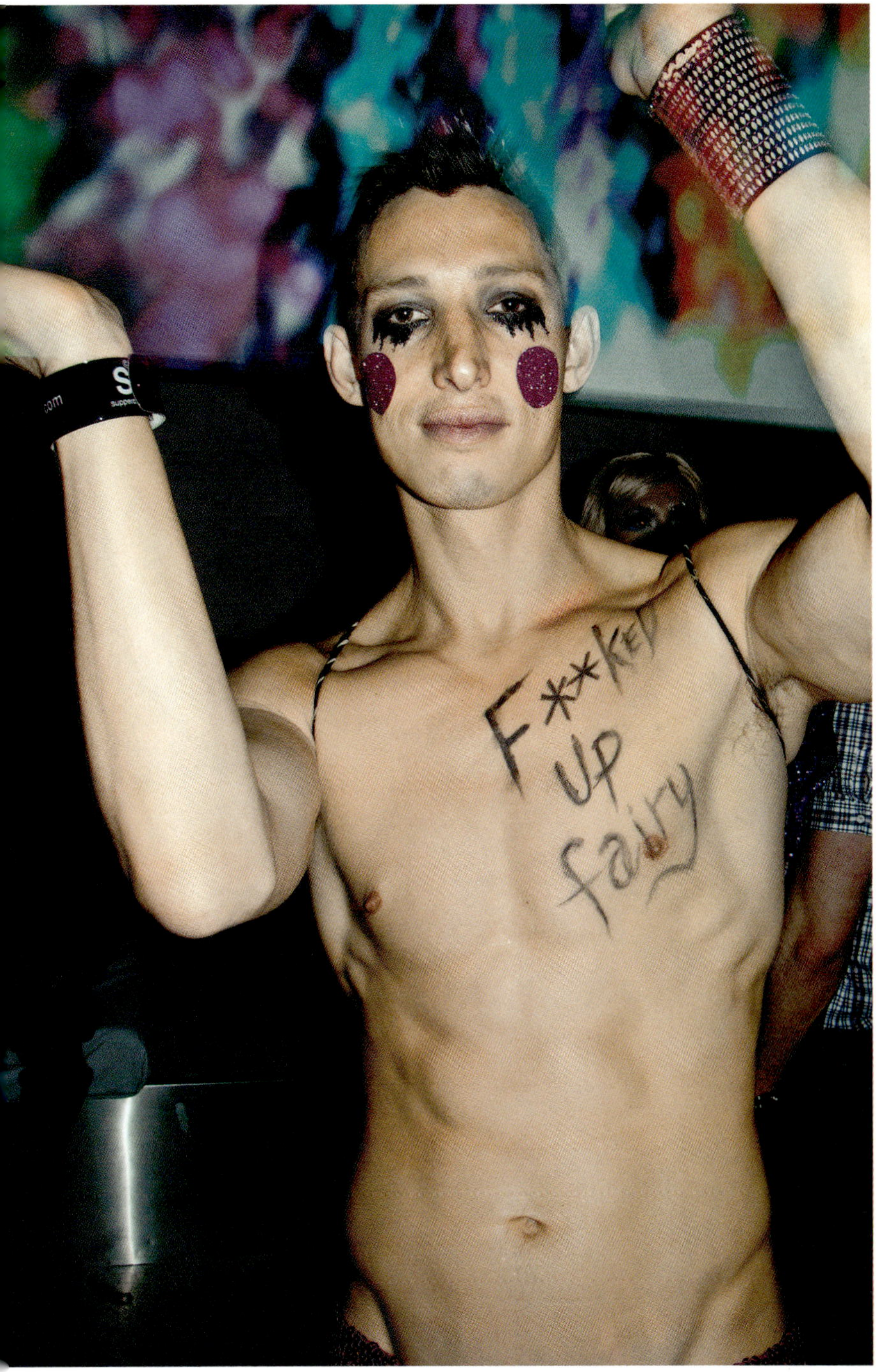

Toy@SupperClub – May 2010

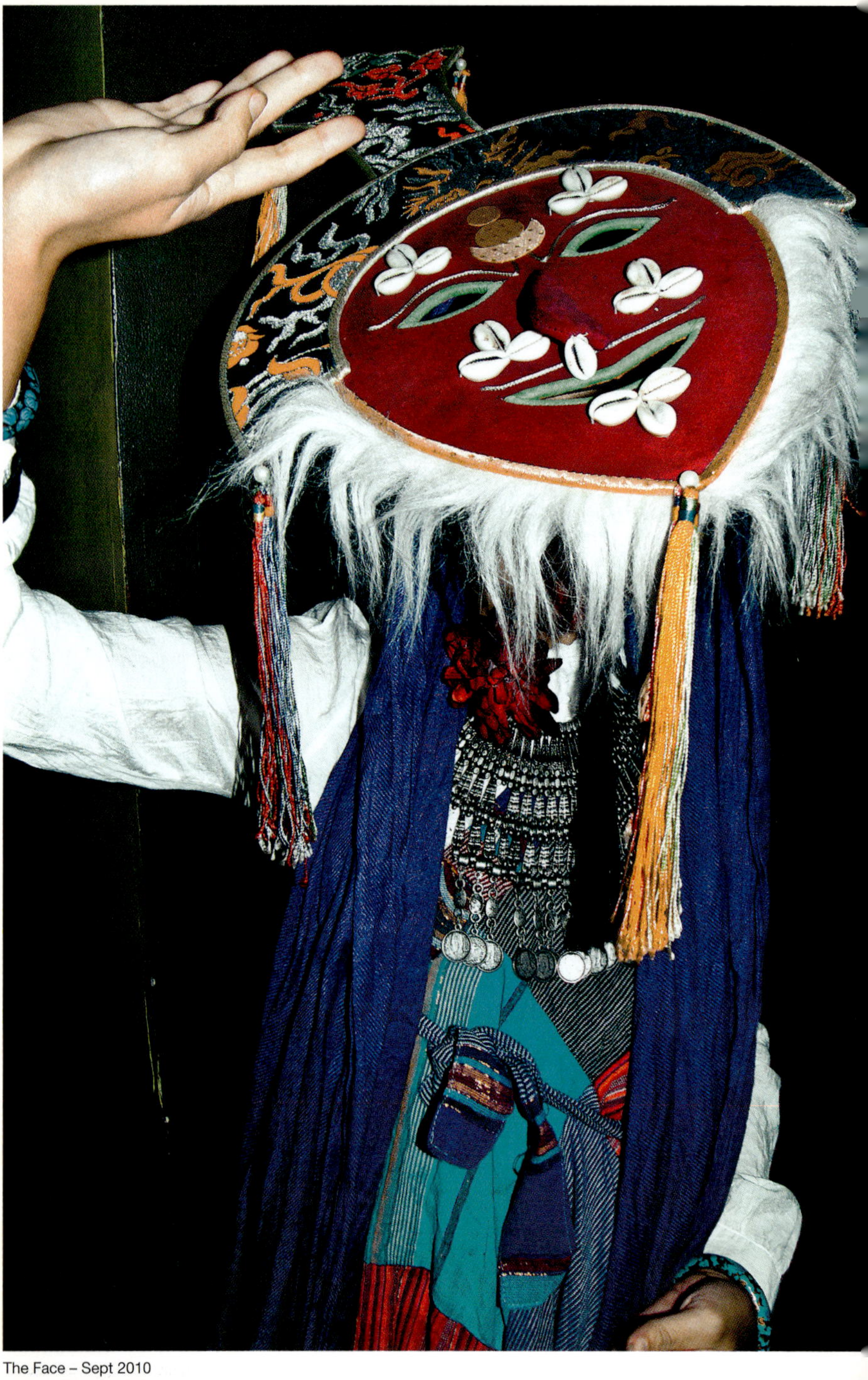

The Face – Sept 2010

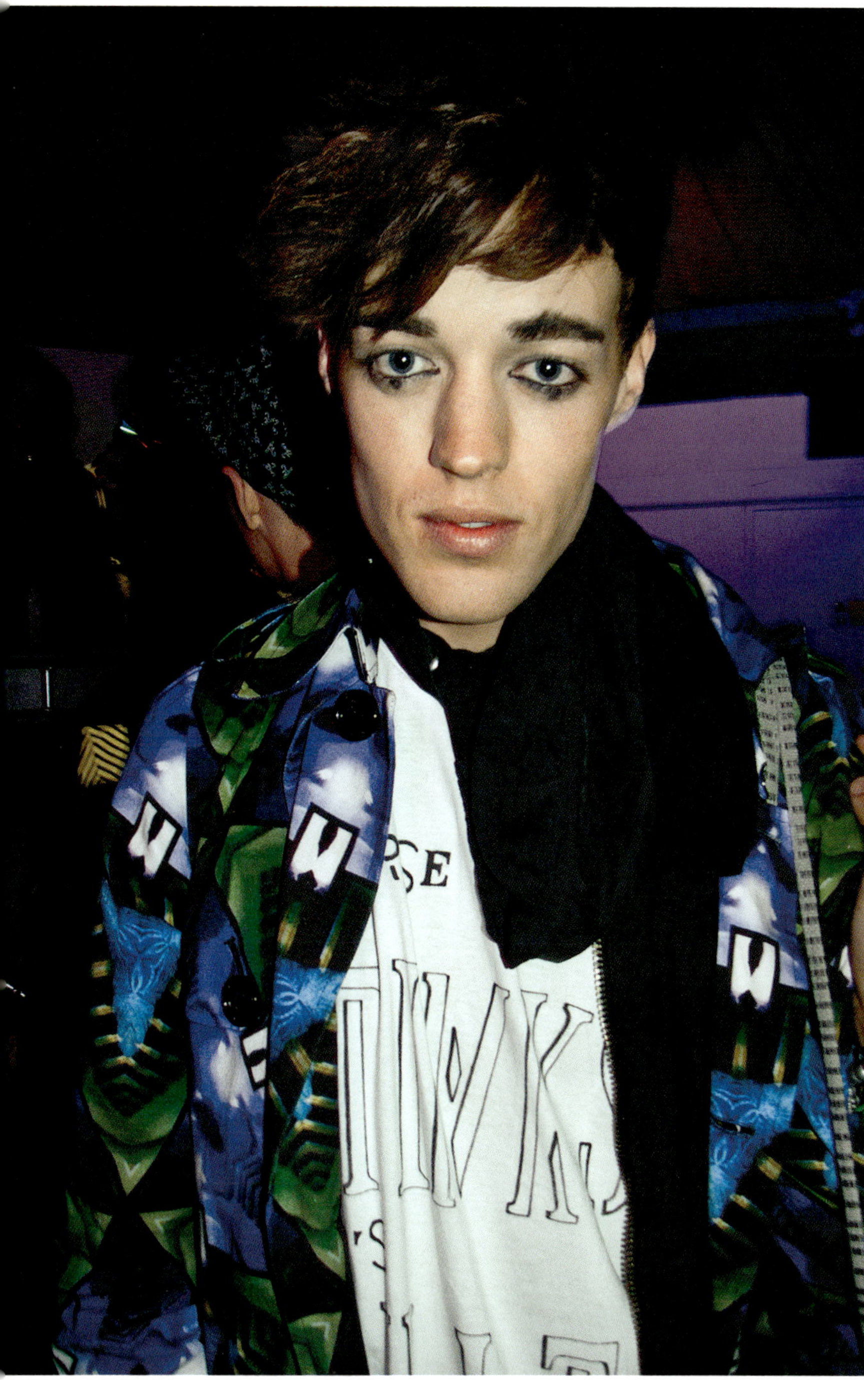

Wearable Art@Egg – Sept 2010

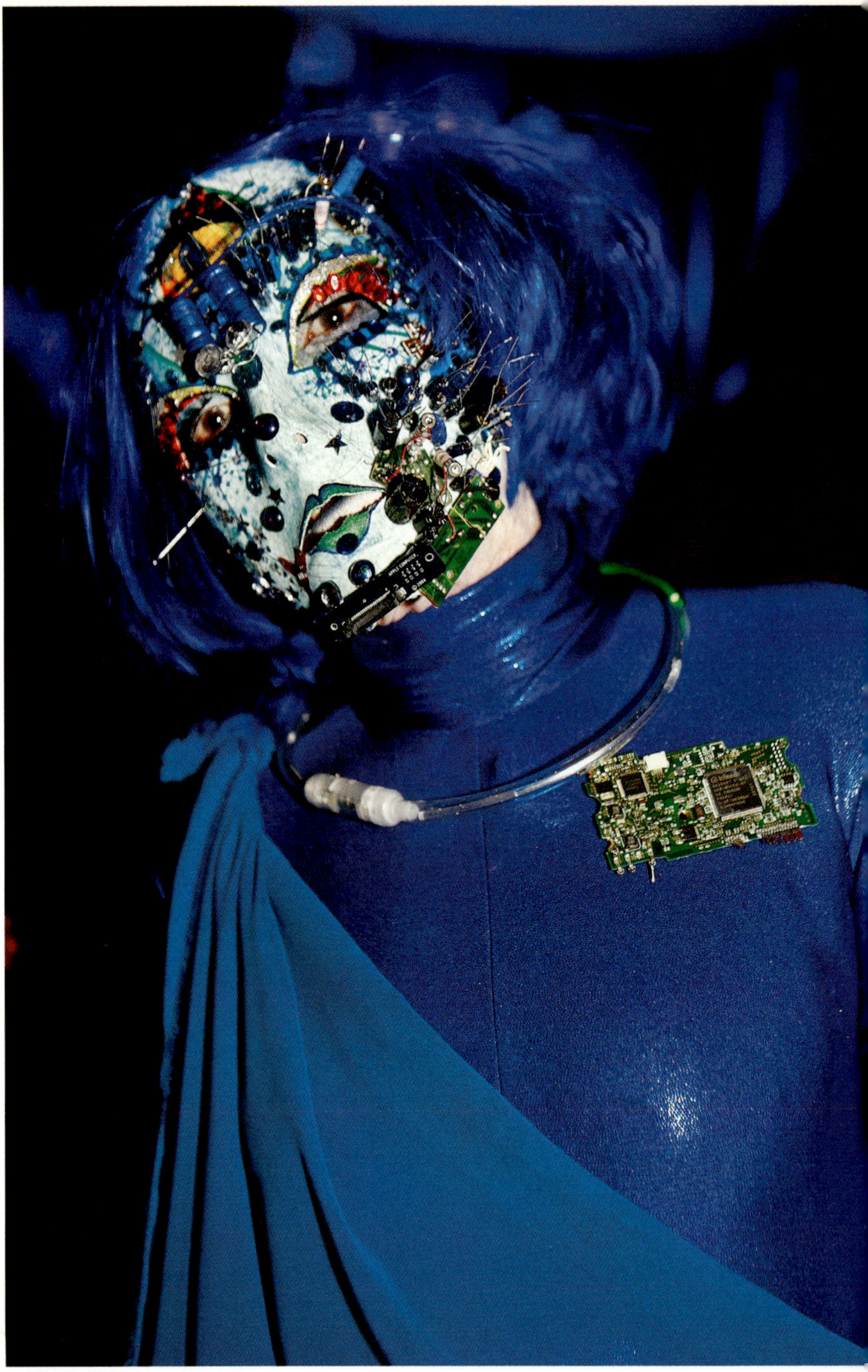

Wig Party@Cafe De Paris – Oct 2010

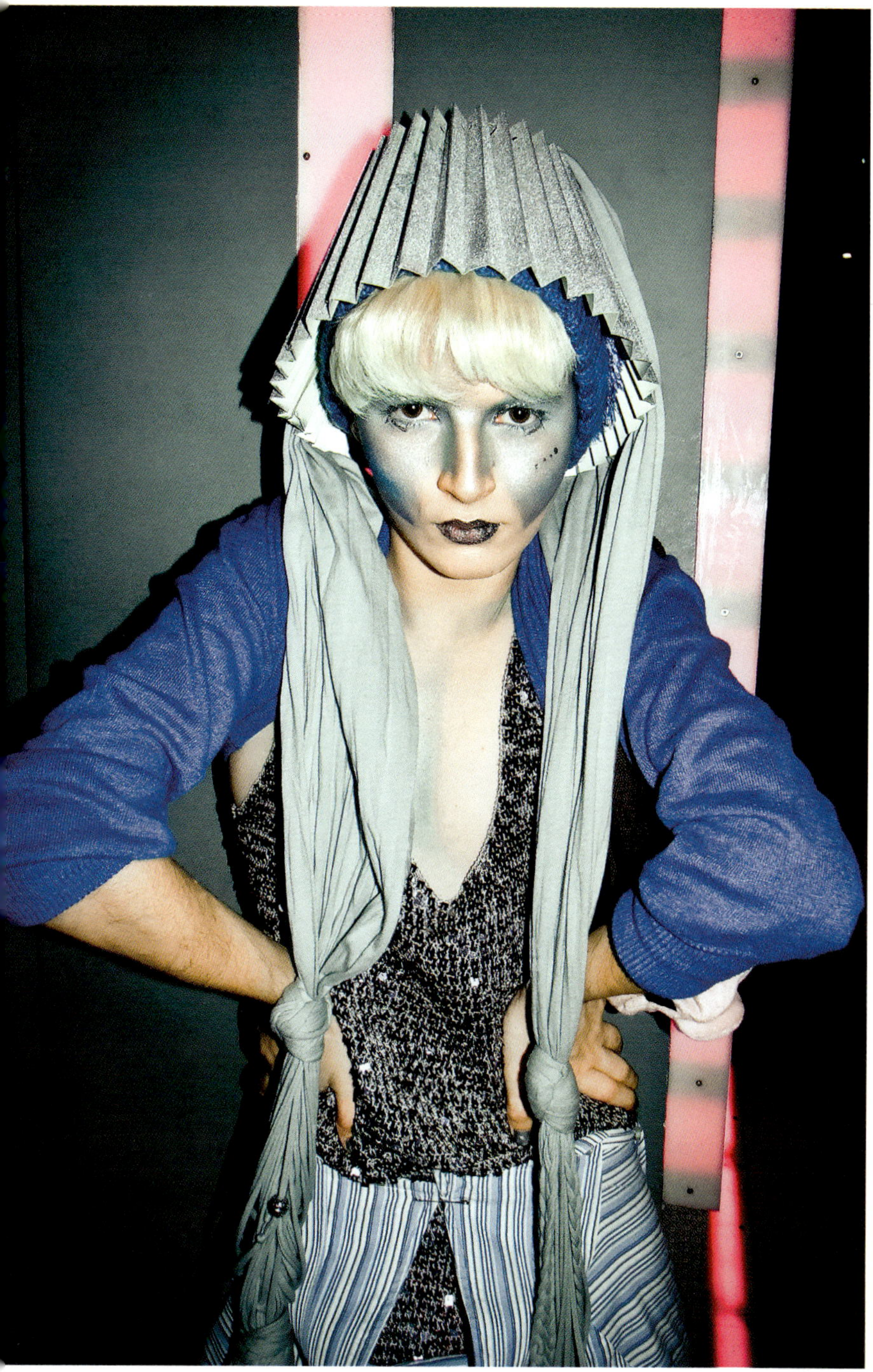

Shabba Dabba Da – Oct 2010

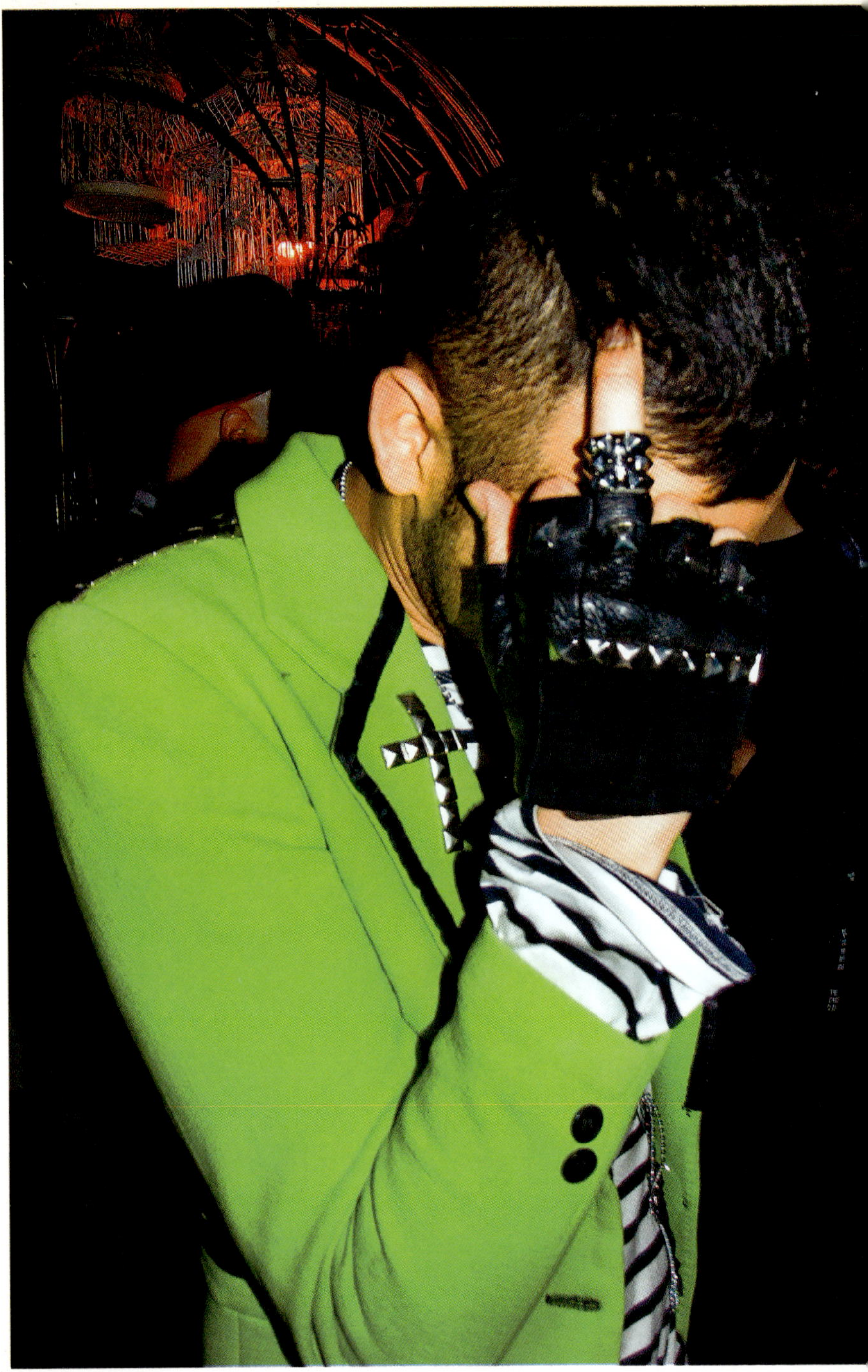

Caligula – Aug 2010

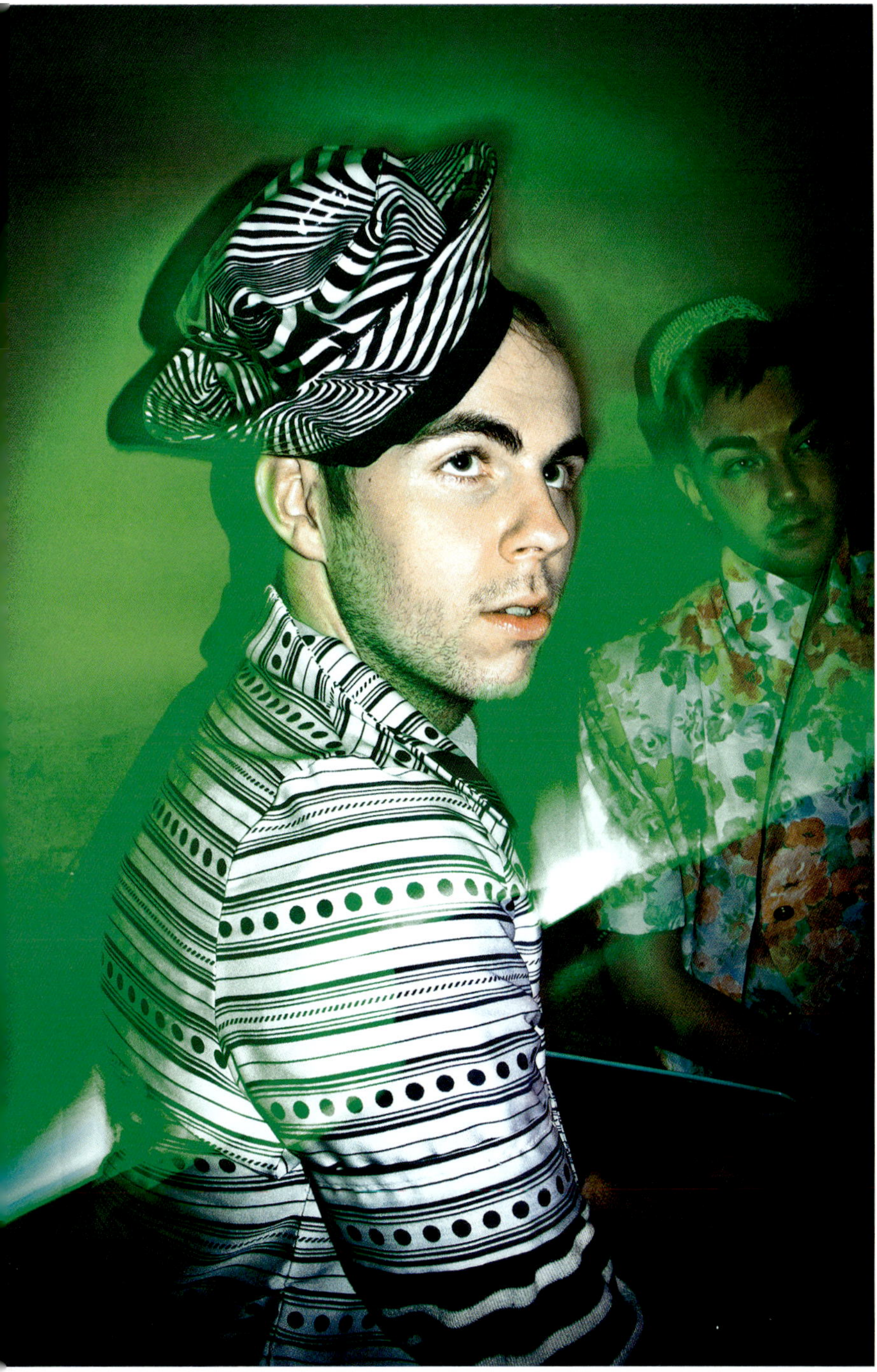

The Face – Sept 2010

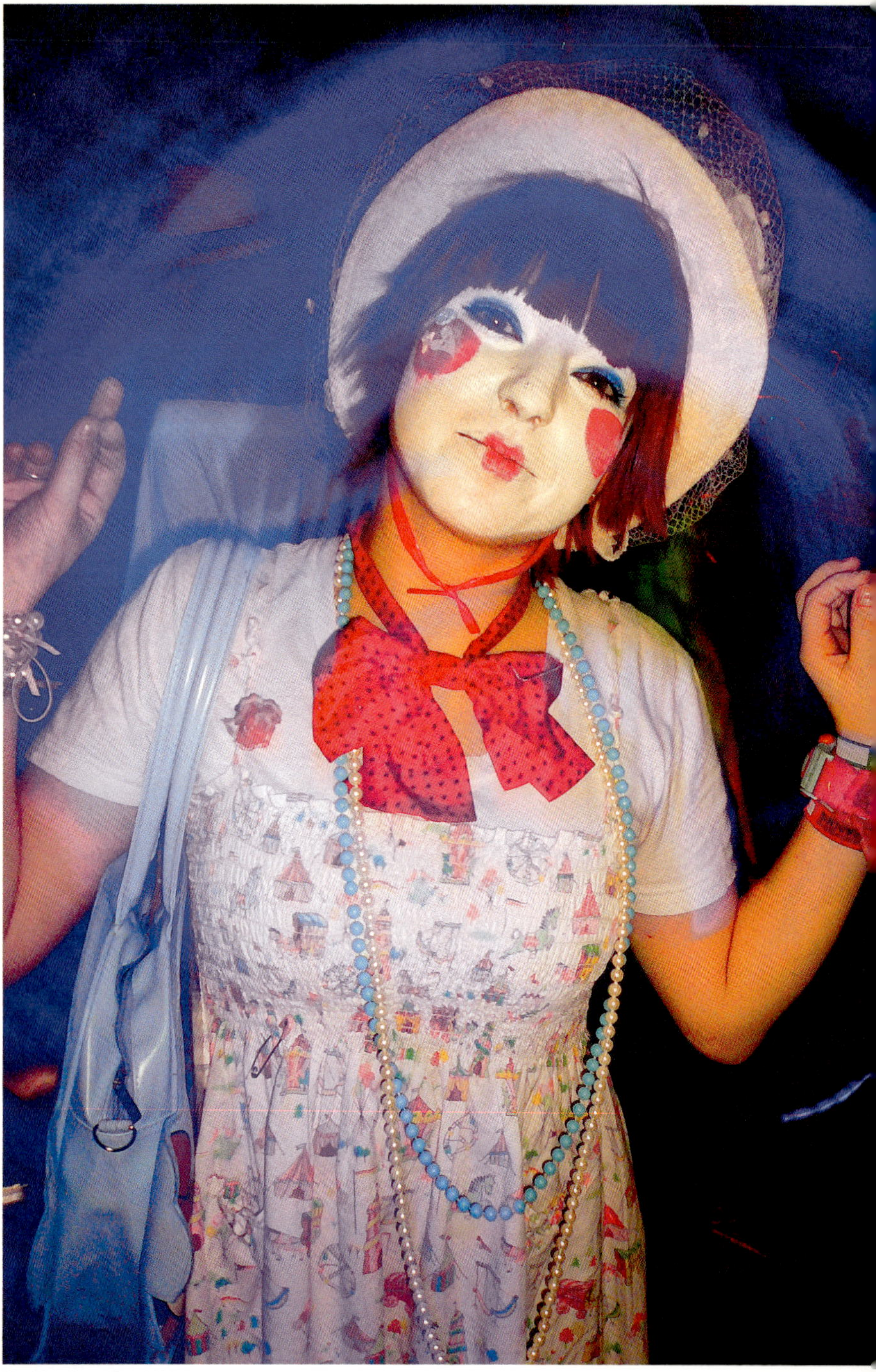

Nag Nag Nag – Dec 2002

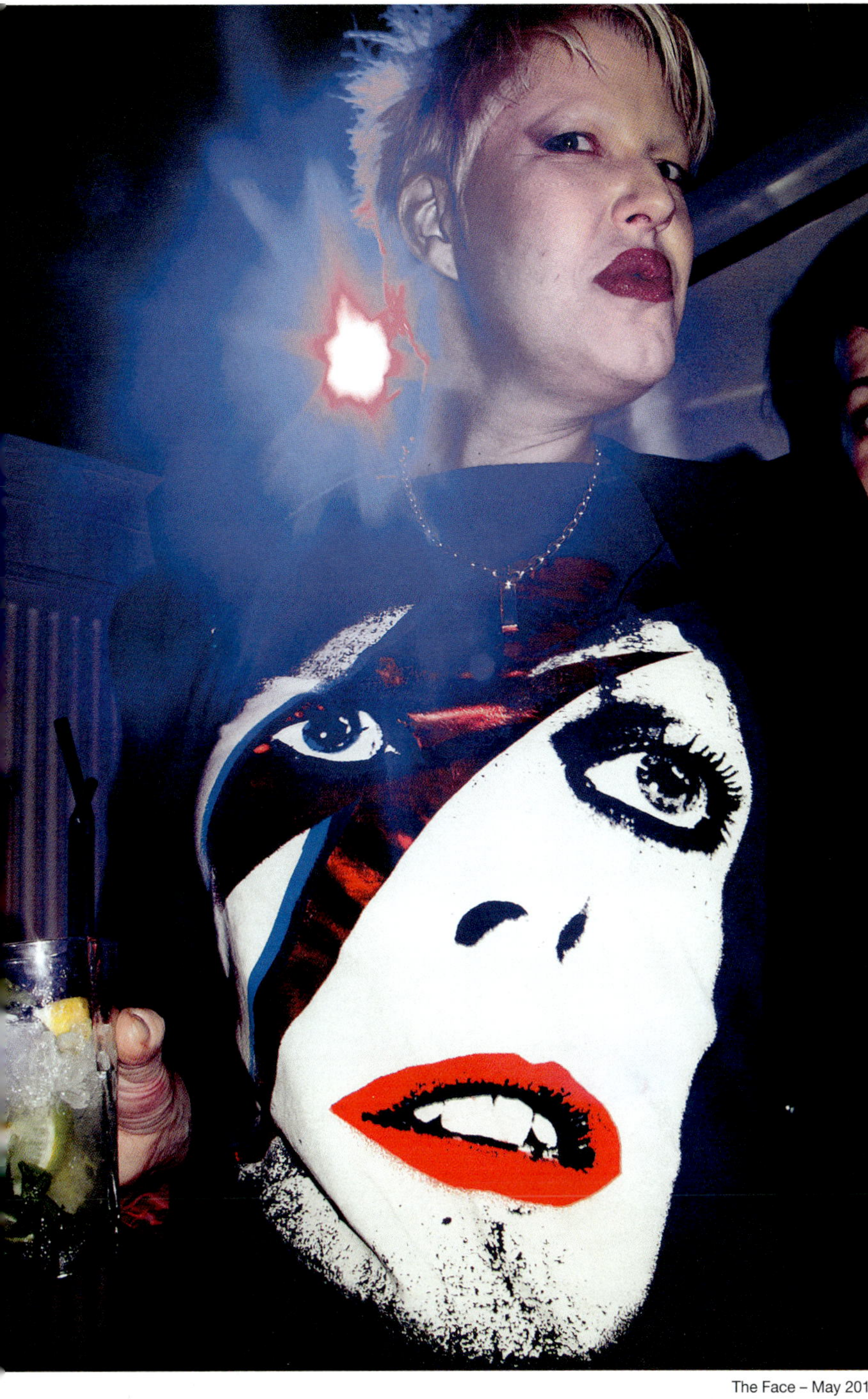

The Face – May 2010

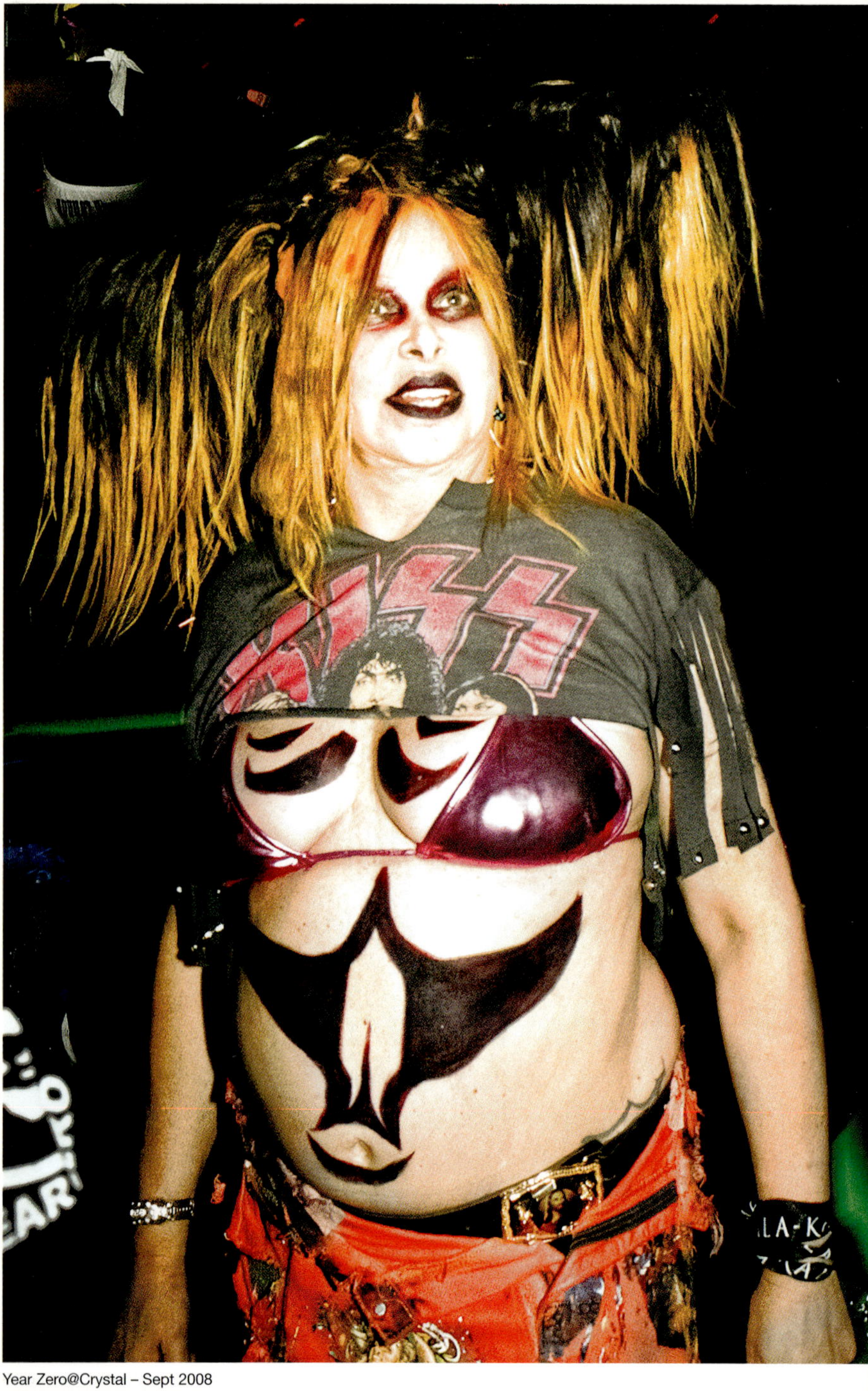

Year Zero@Crystal – Sept 2008

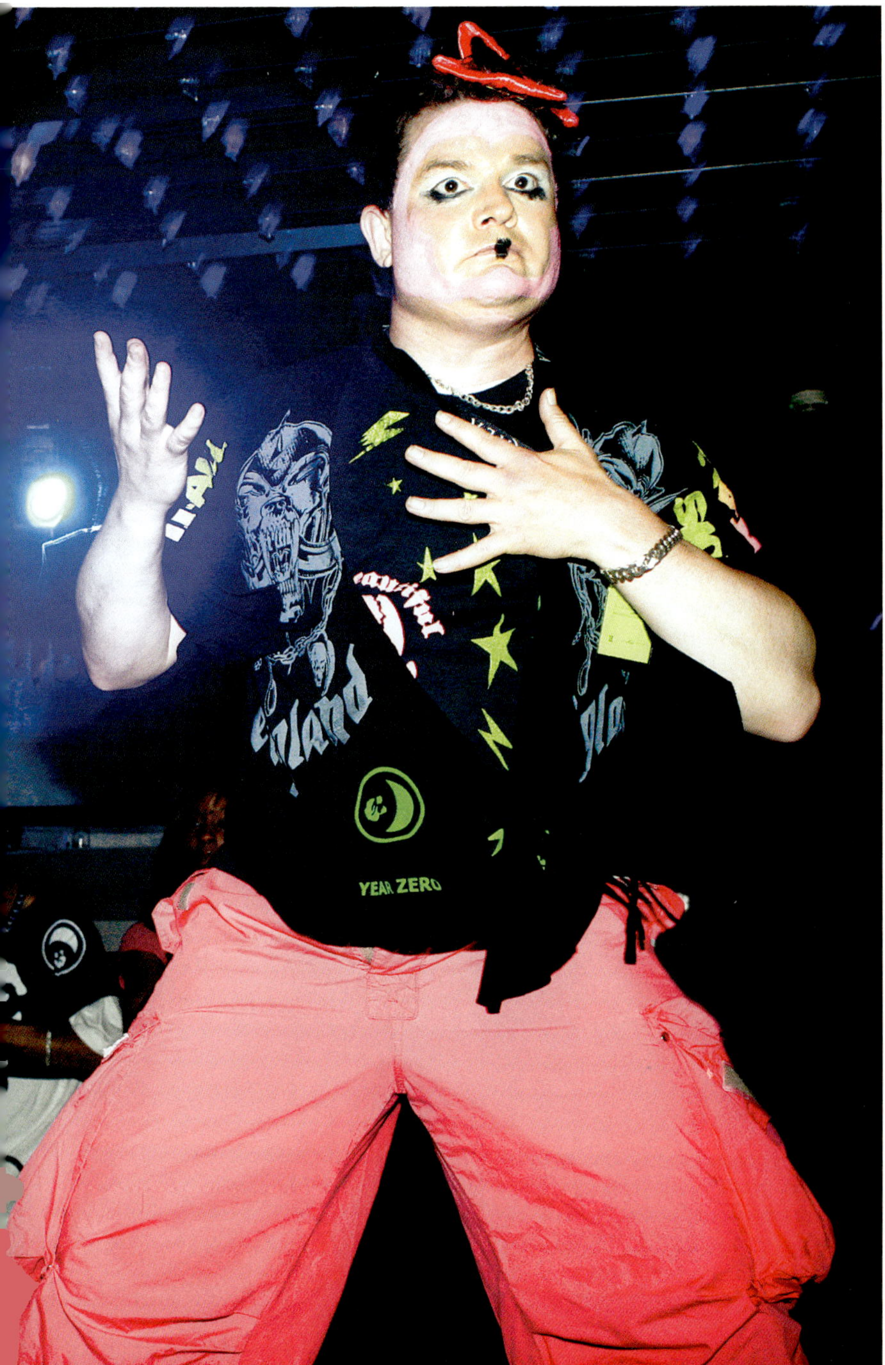

Year Zero@Crystal – Sept 2008

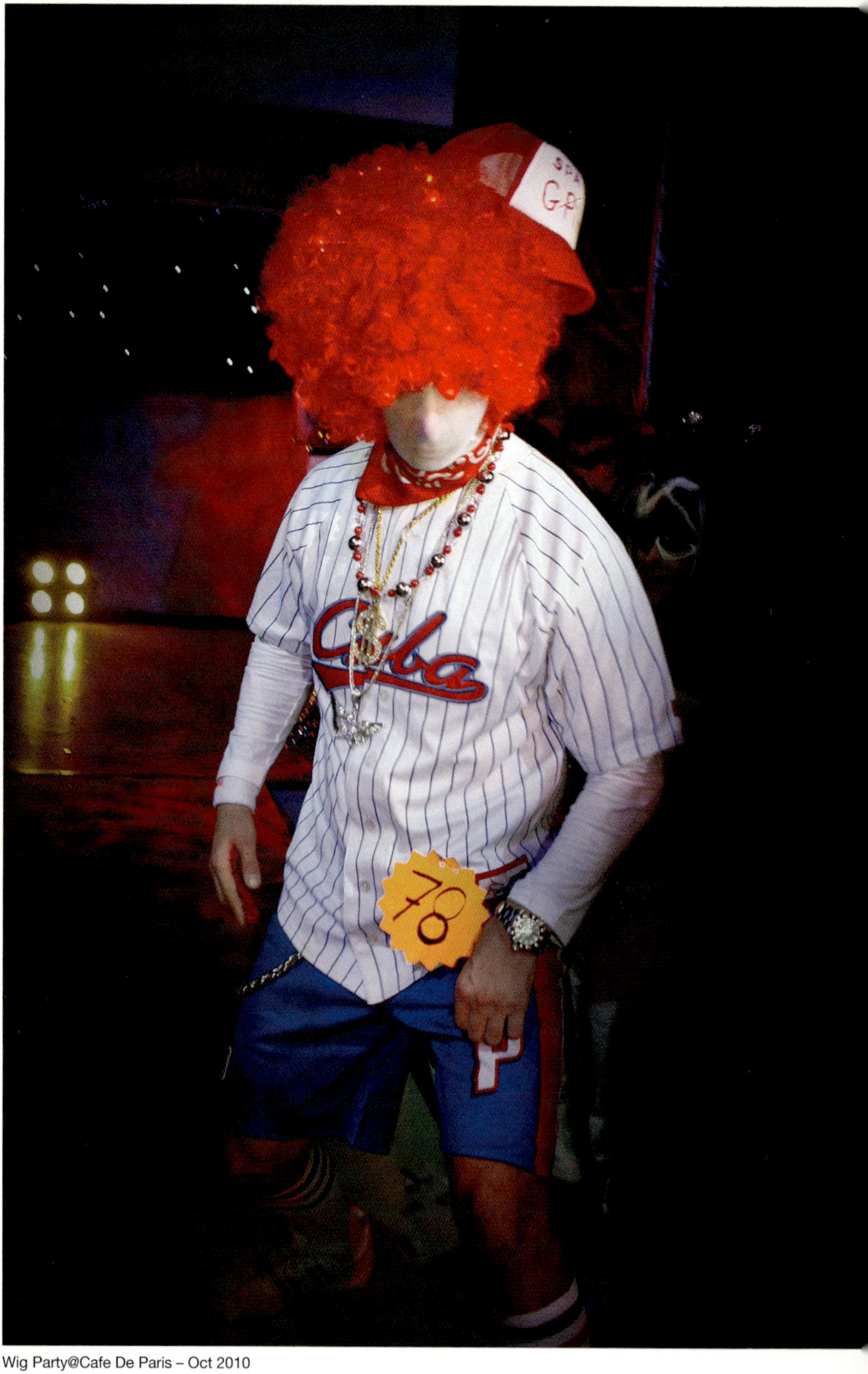

Wig Party@Cafe De Paris – Oct 2010

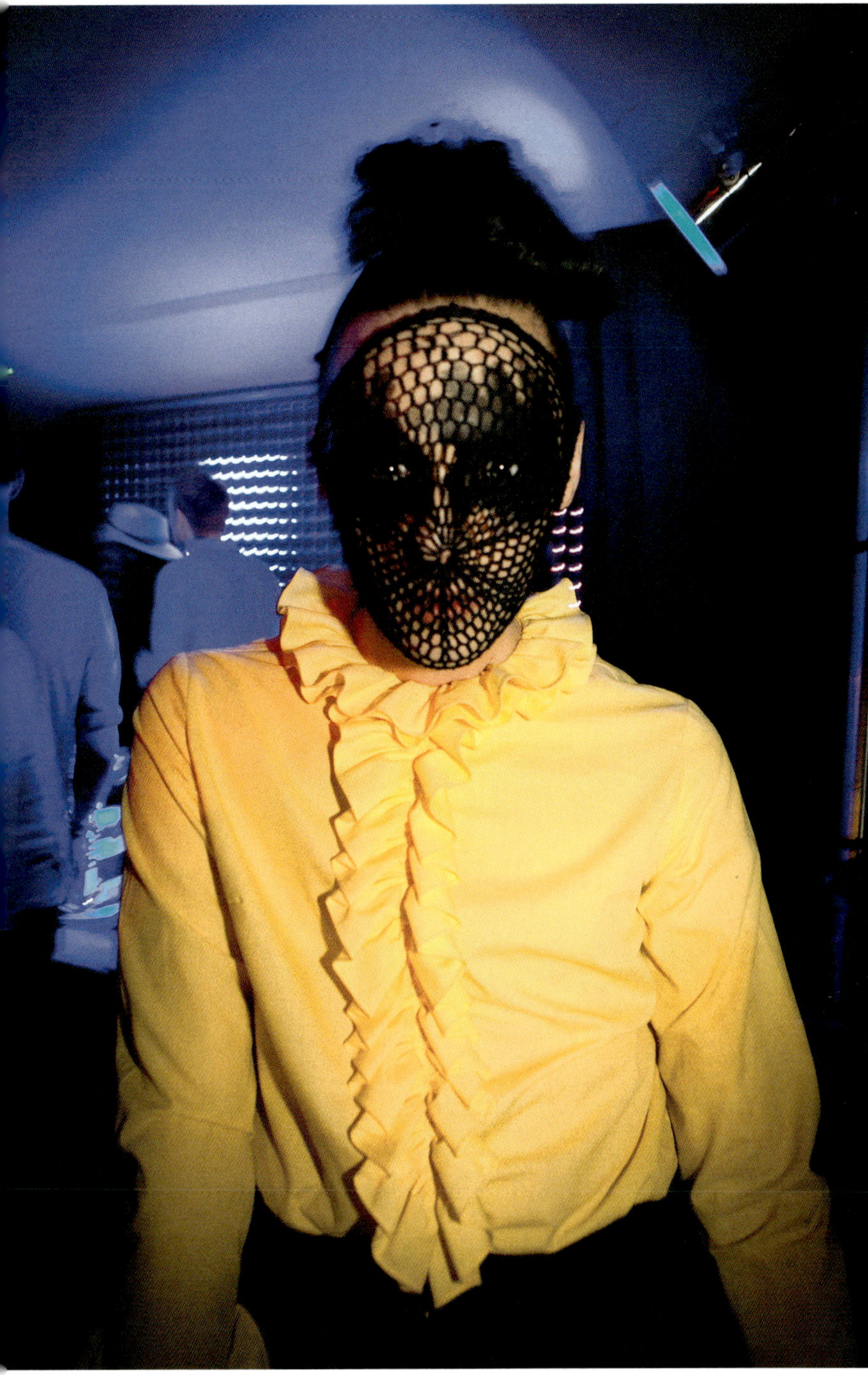

Circus – April 2010

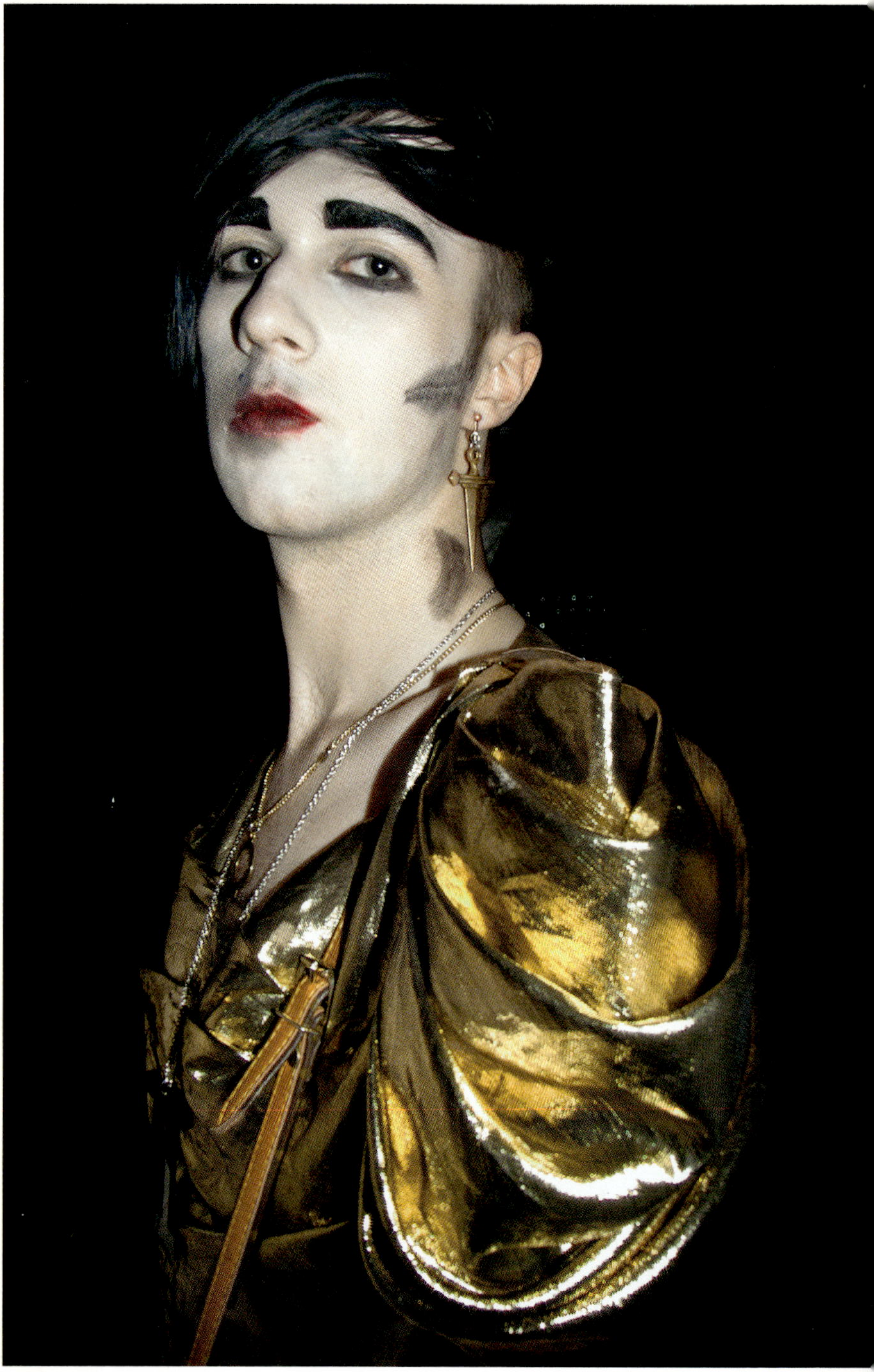

The Face – May 2010

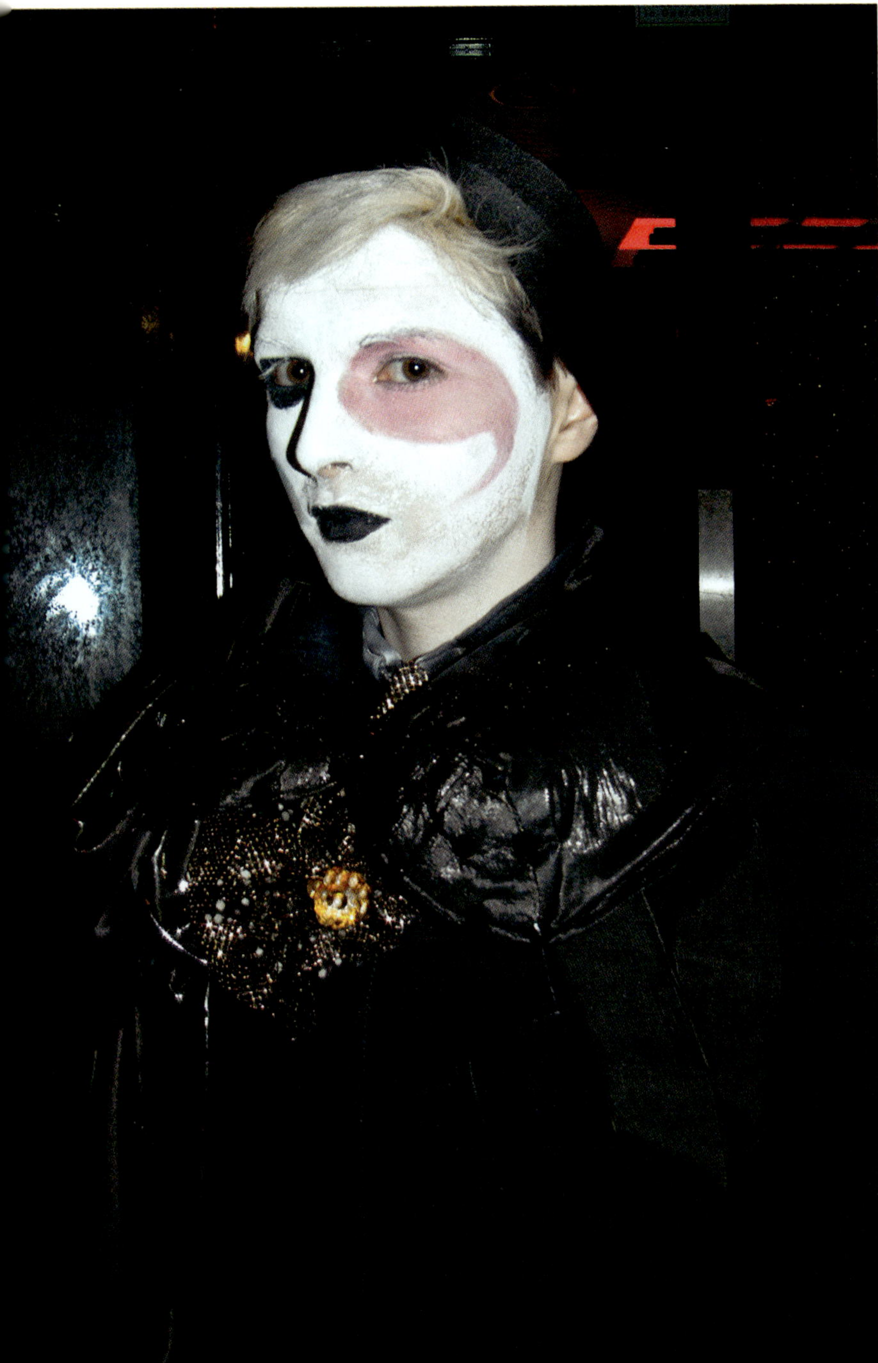

Shabba Dabba Da – Aug 2010

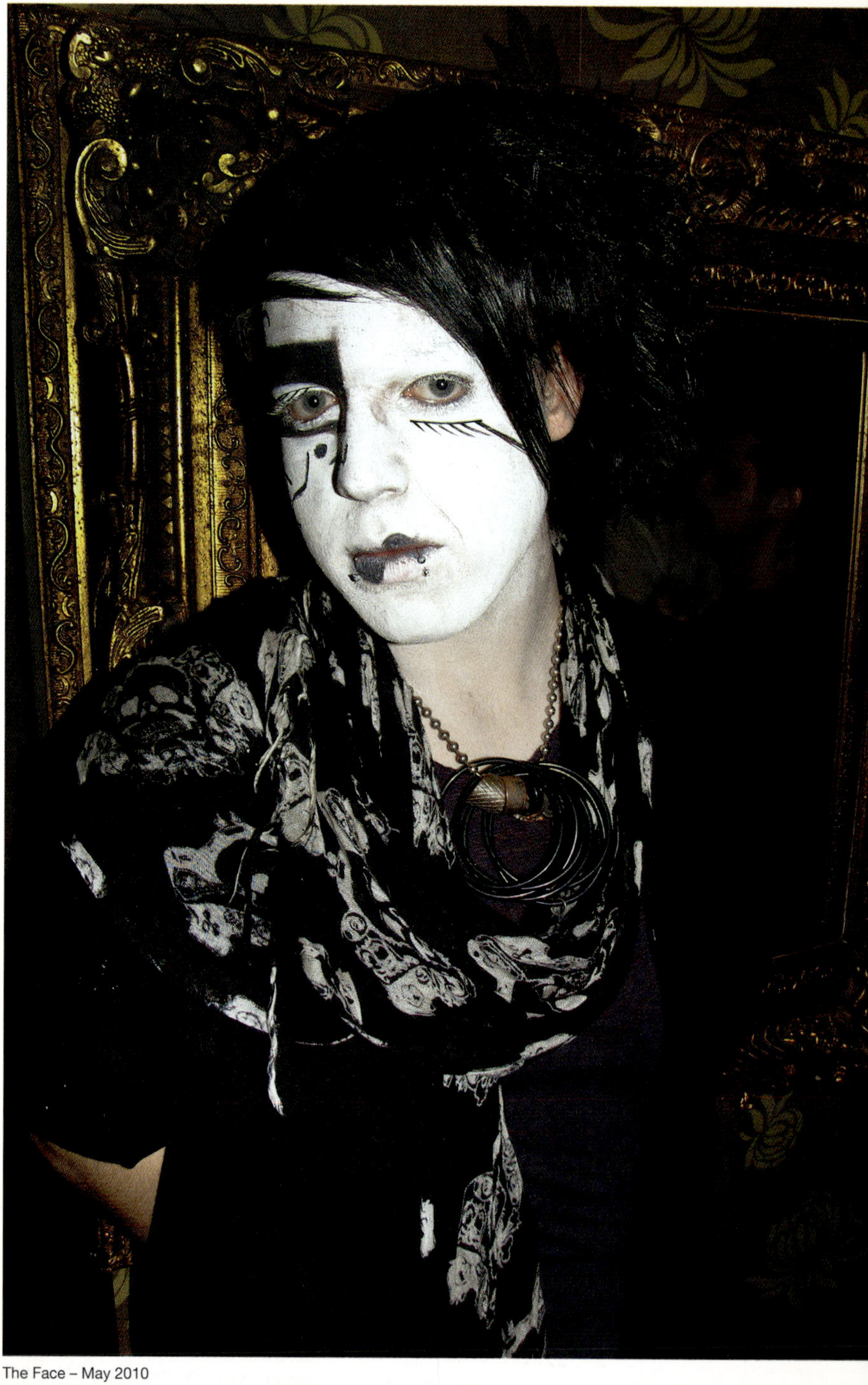

The Face – May 2010

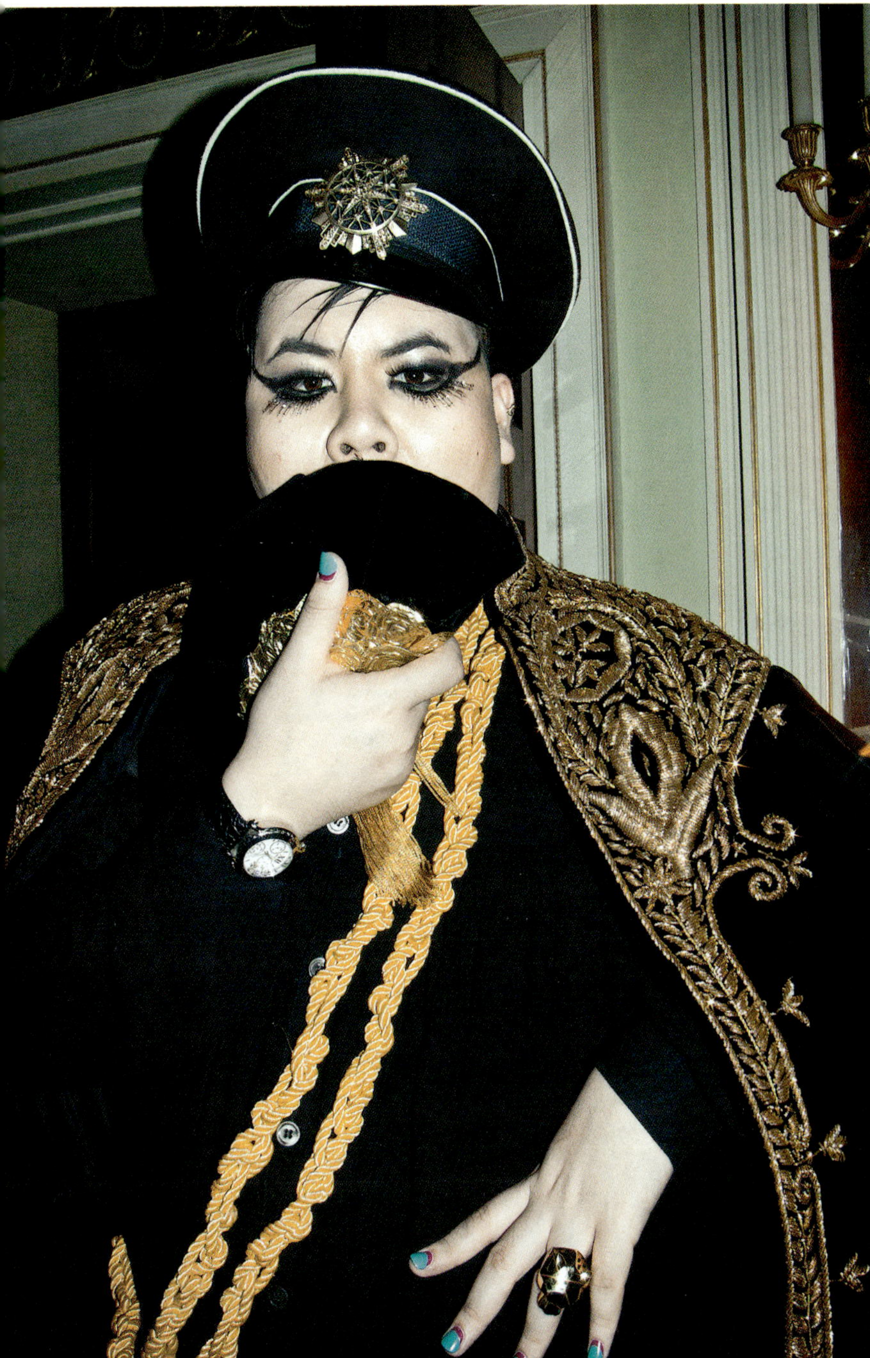

Home House – May 2009

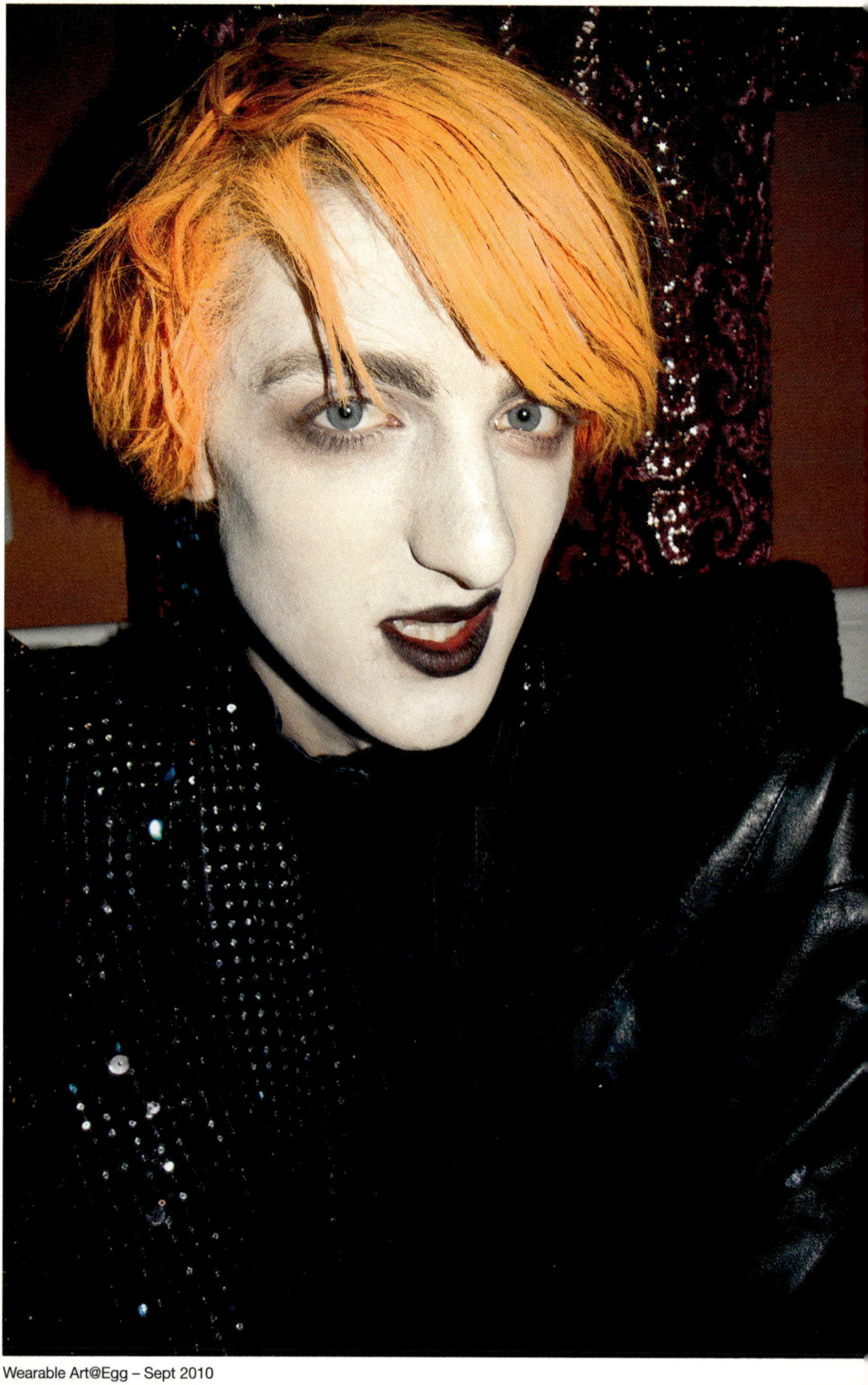

Wearable Art@Egg – Sept 2010

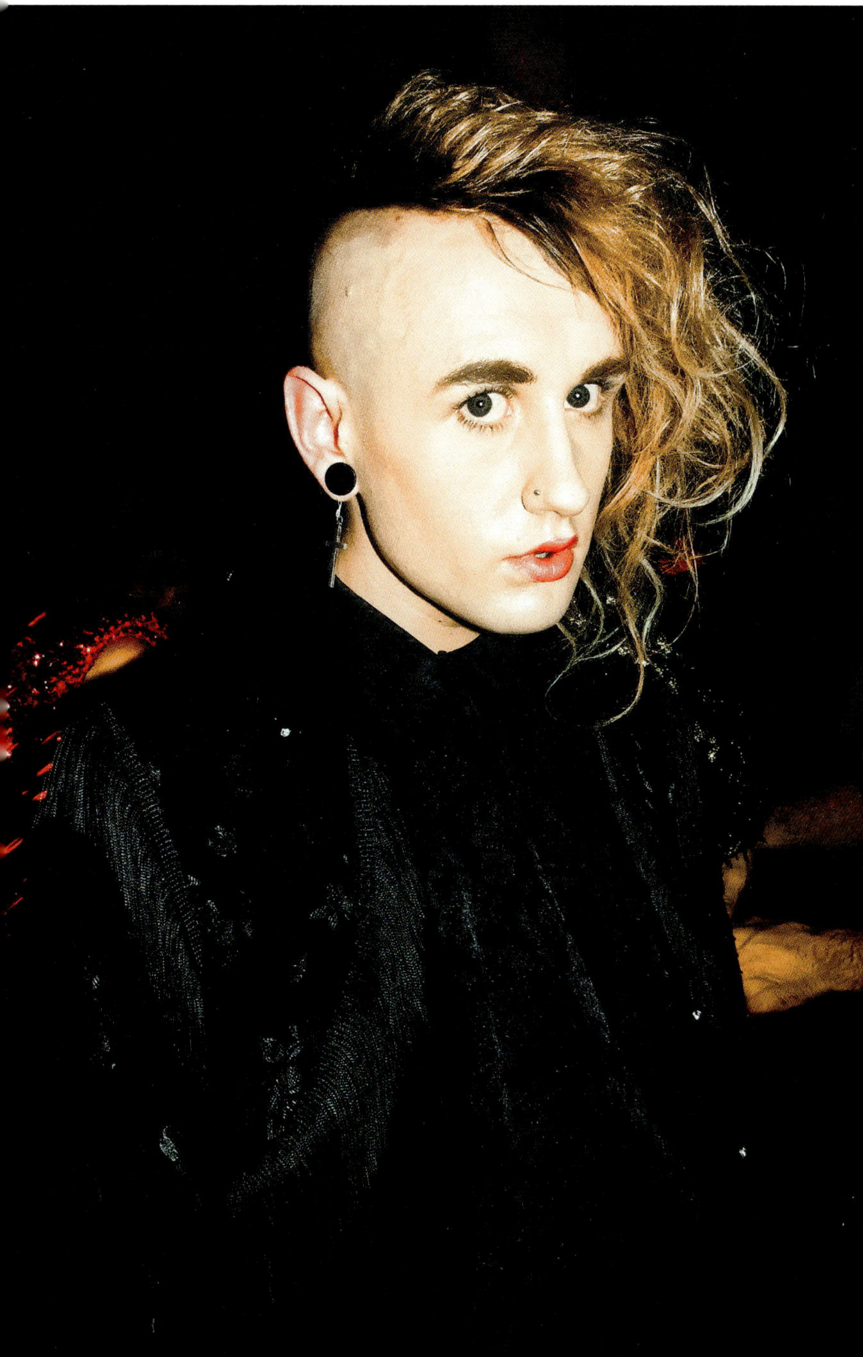

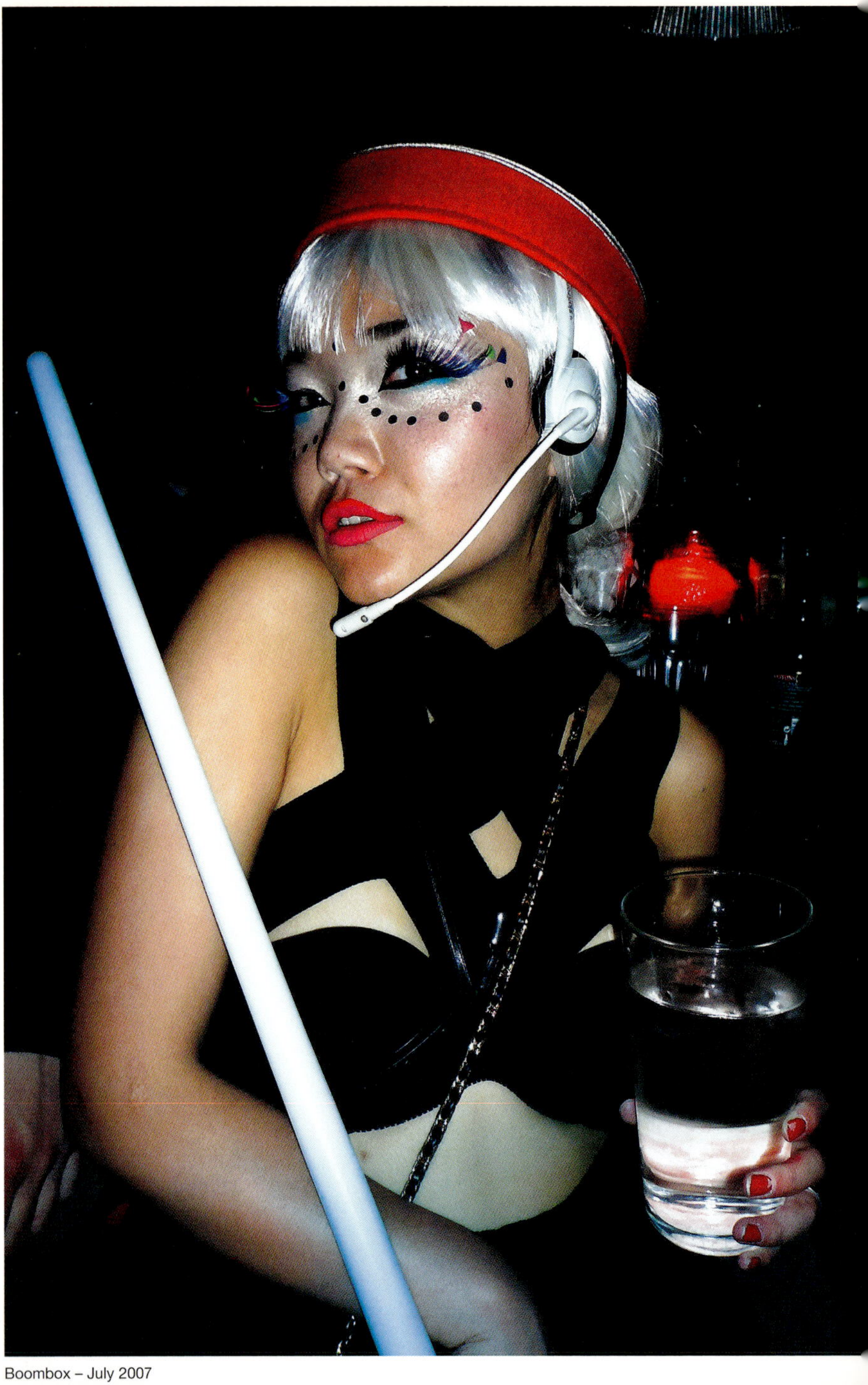

Boombox – July 2007

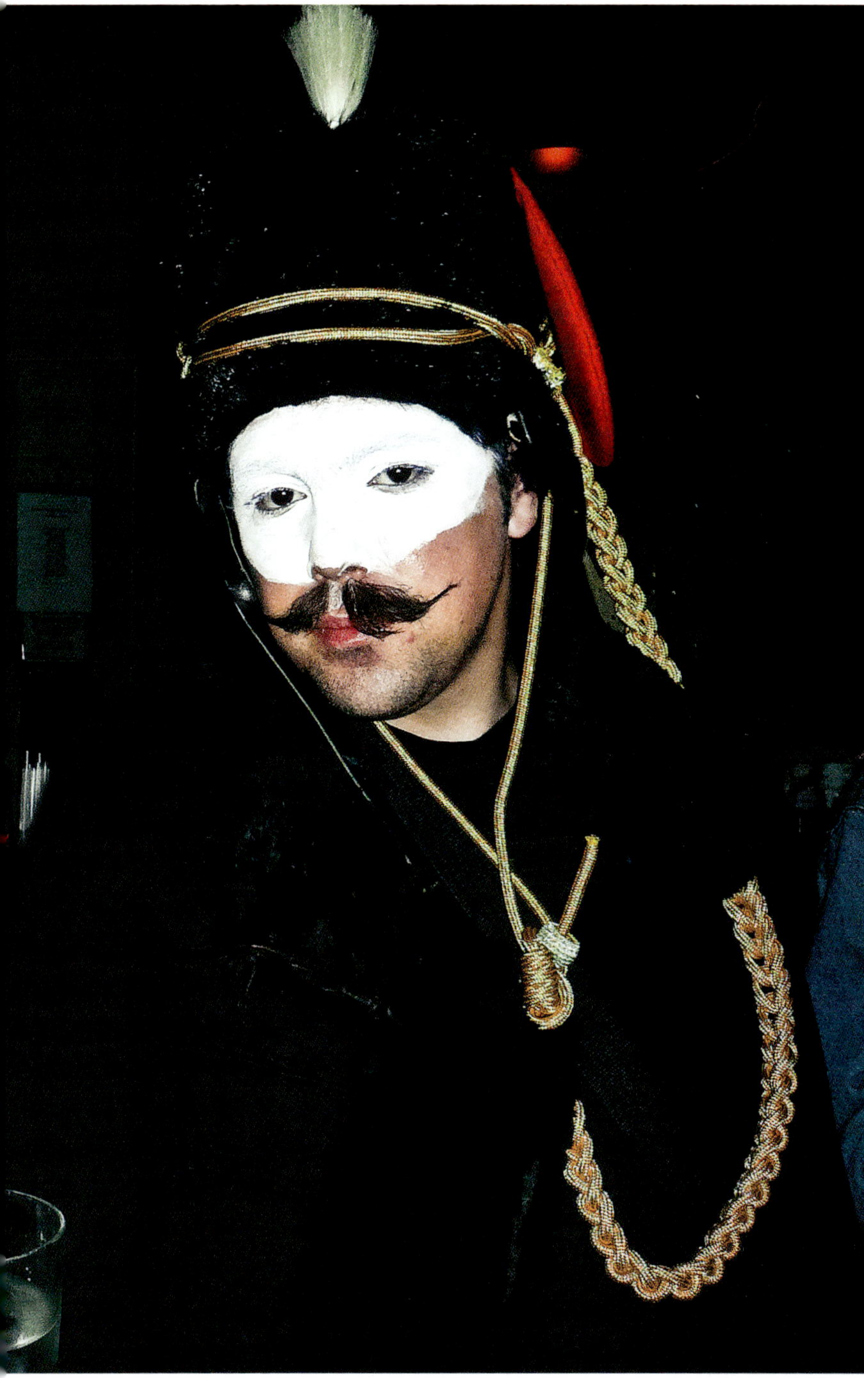

Boombox – July 2007

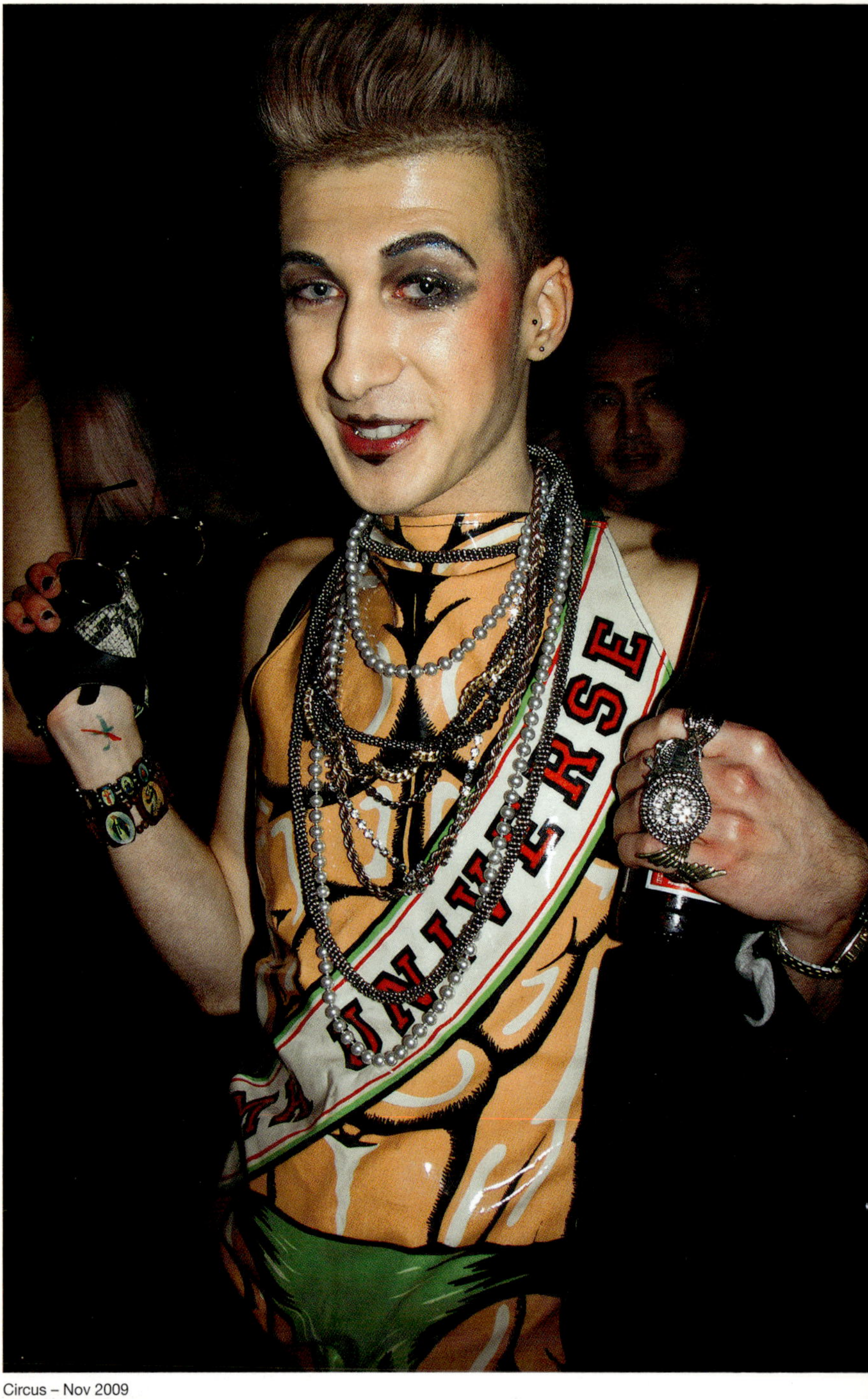

Circus – Nov 2009

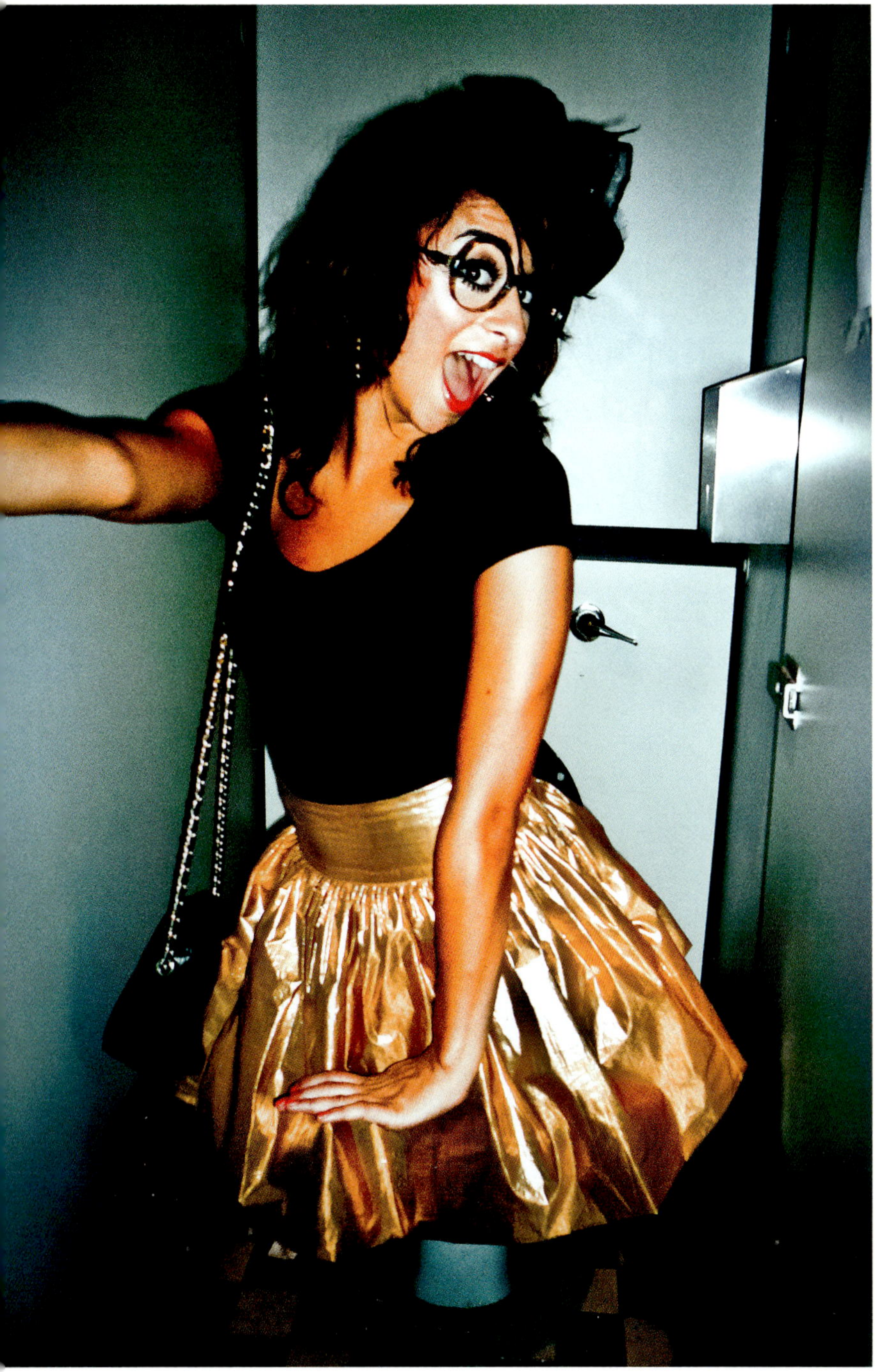

Boombox – Dec 2006

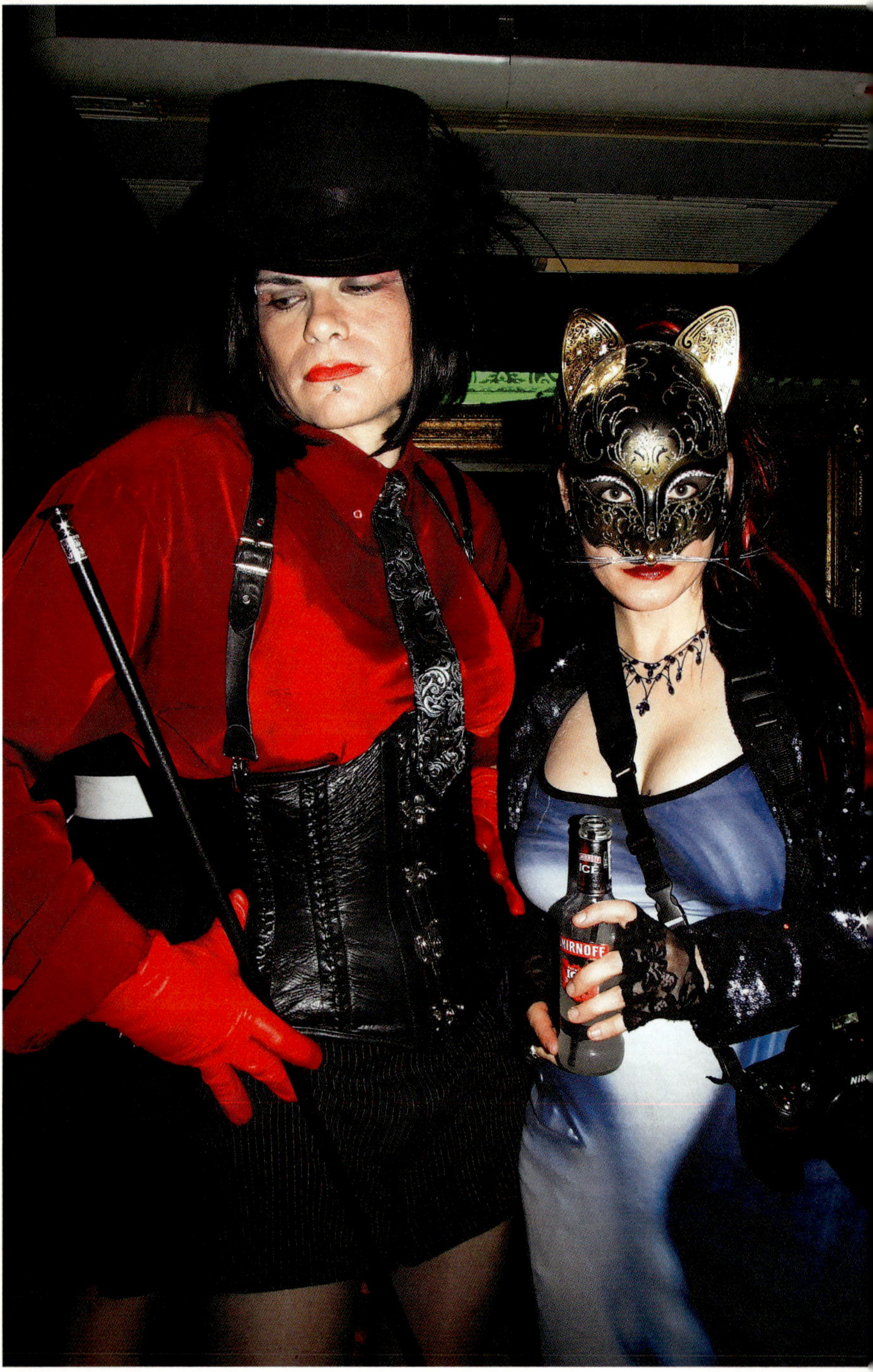

The Face – Sept 2010

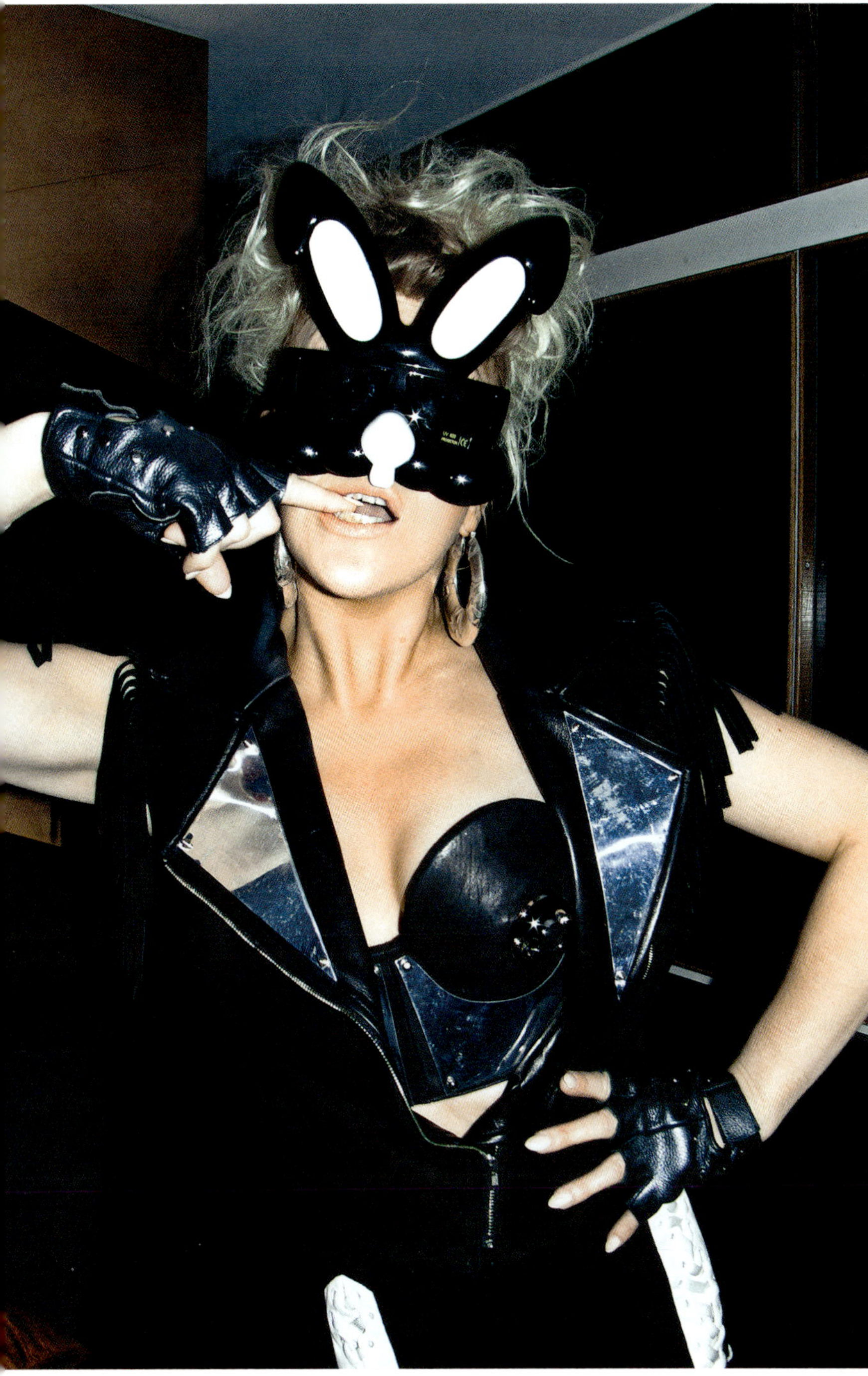

Circus – Sept 2010

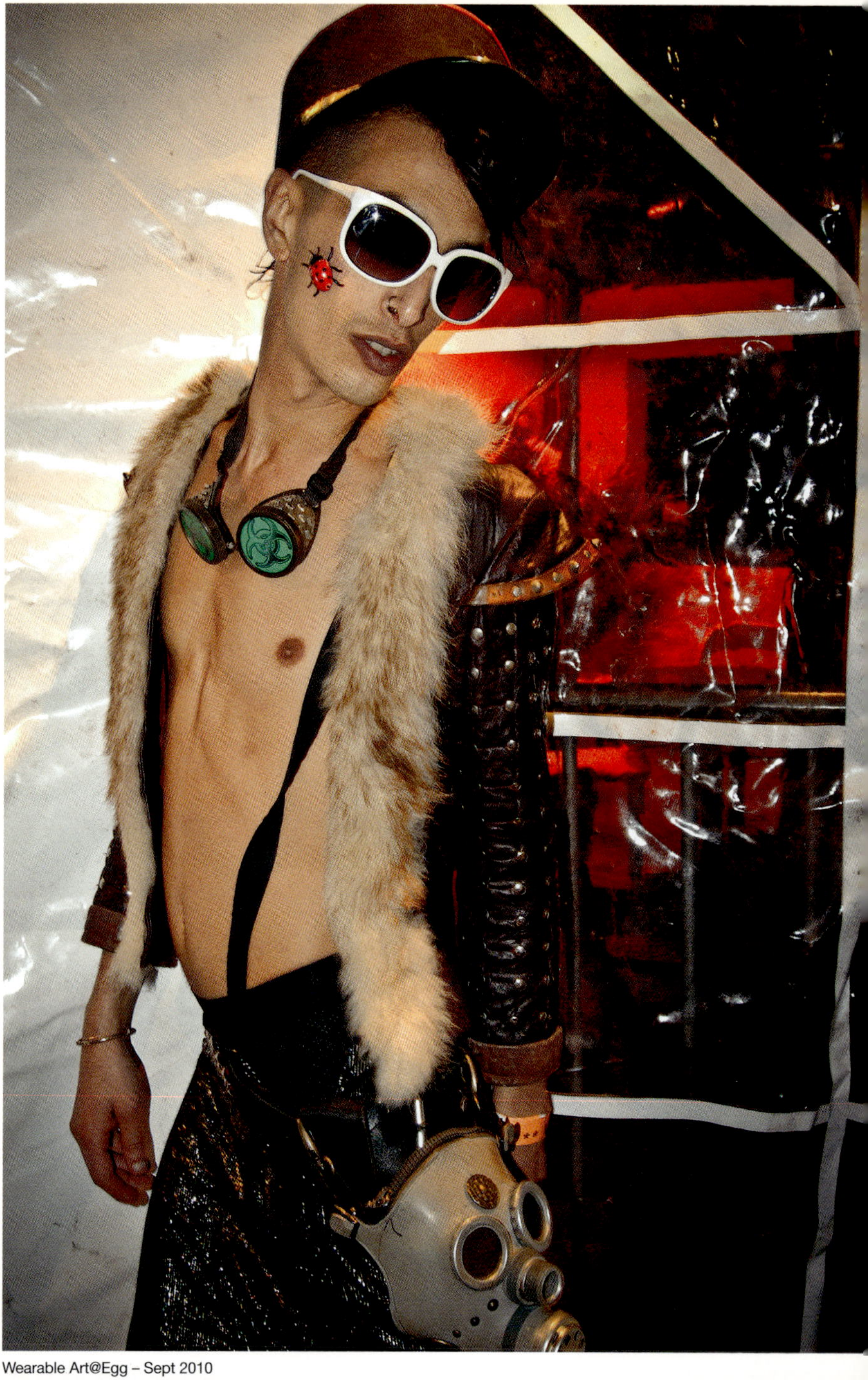

Wearable Art@Egg – Sept 2010

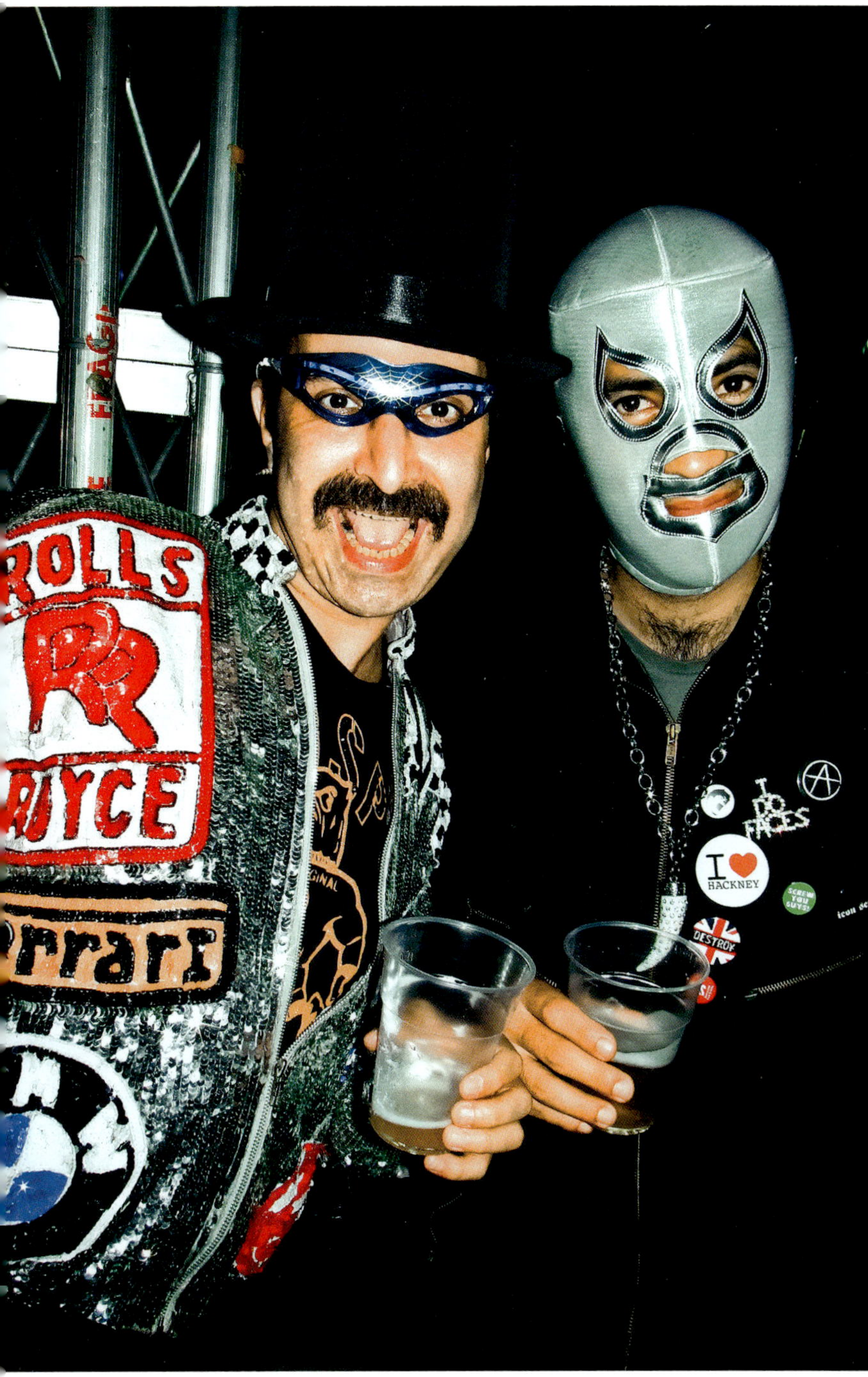
ROLLS
I DO FACES
I ♥ HACKNEY
DESTROY

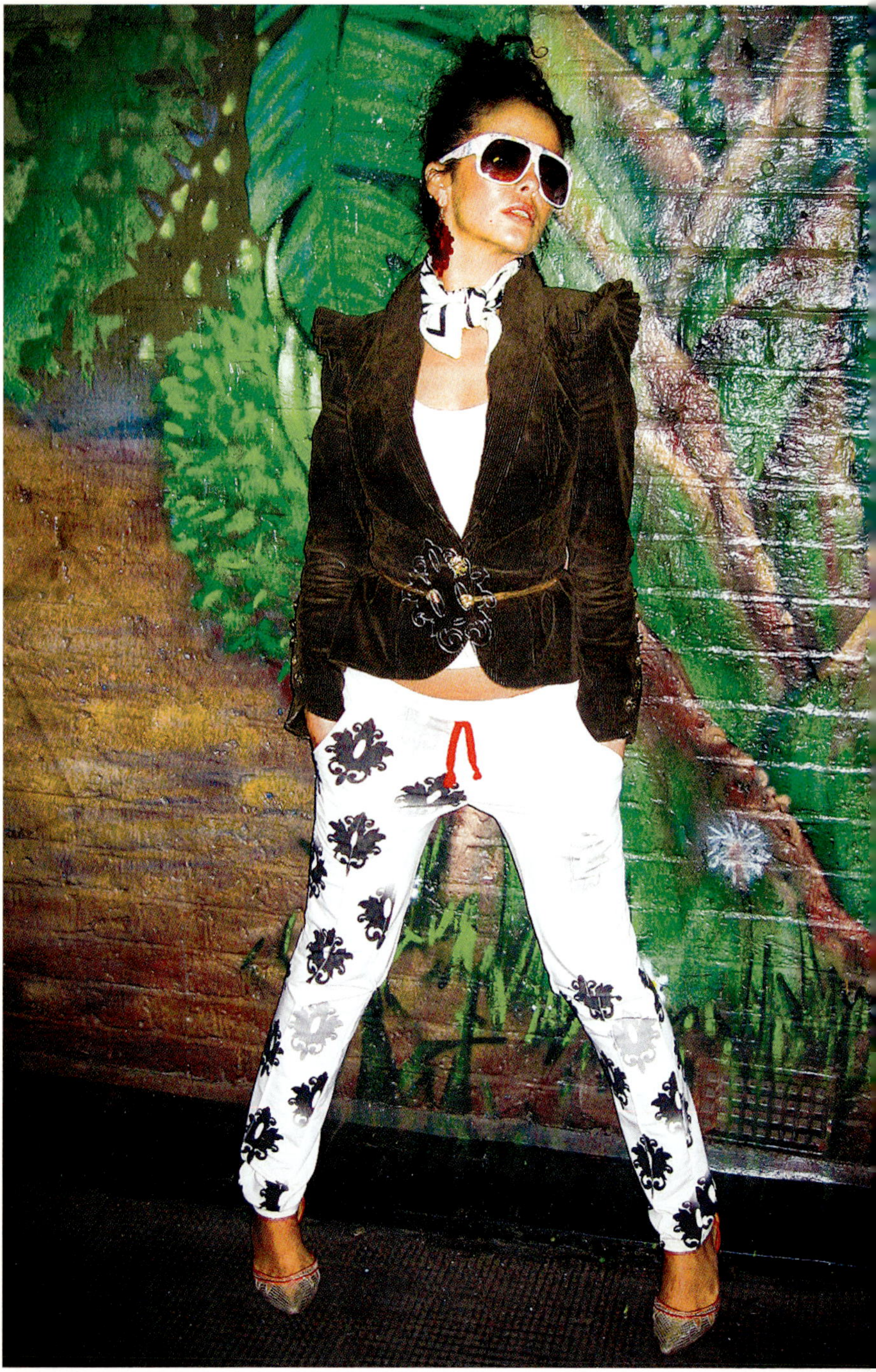

Nag Nag Nag – Aug 2005

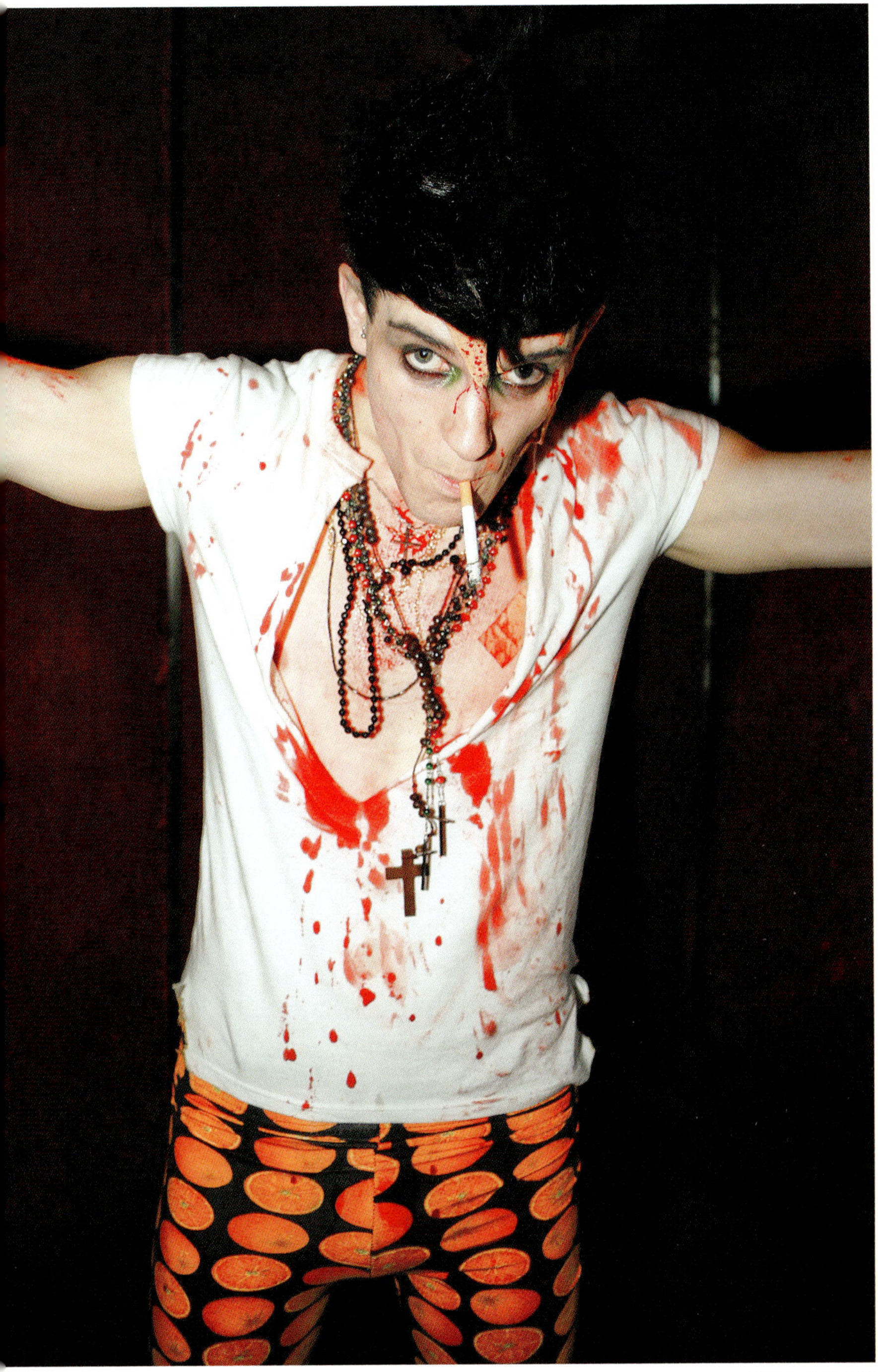

Circus – Nov 2008

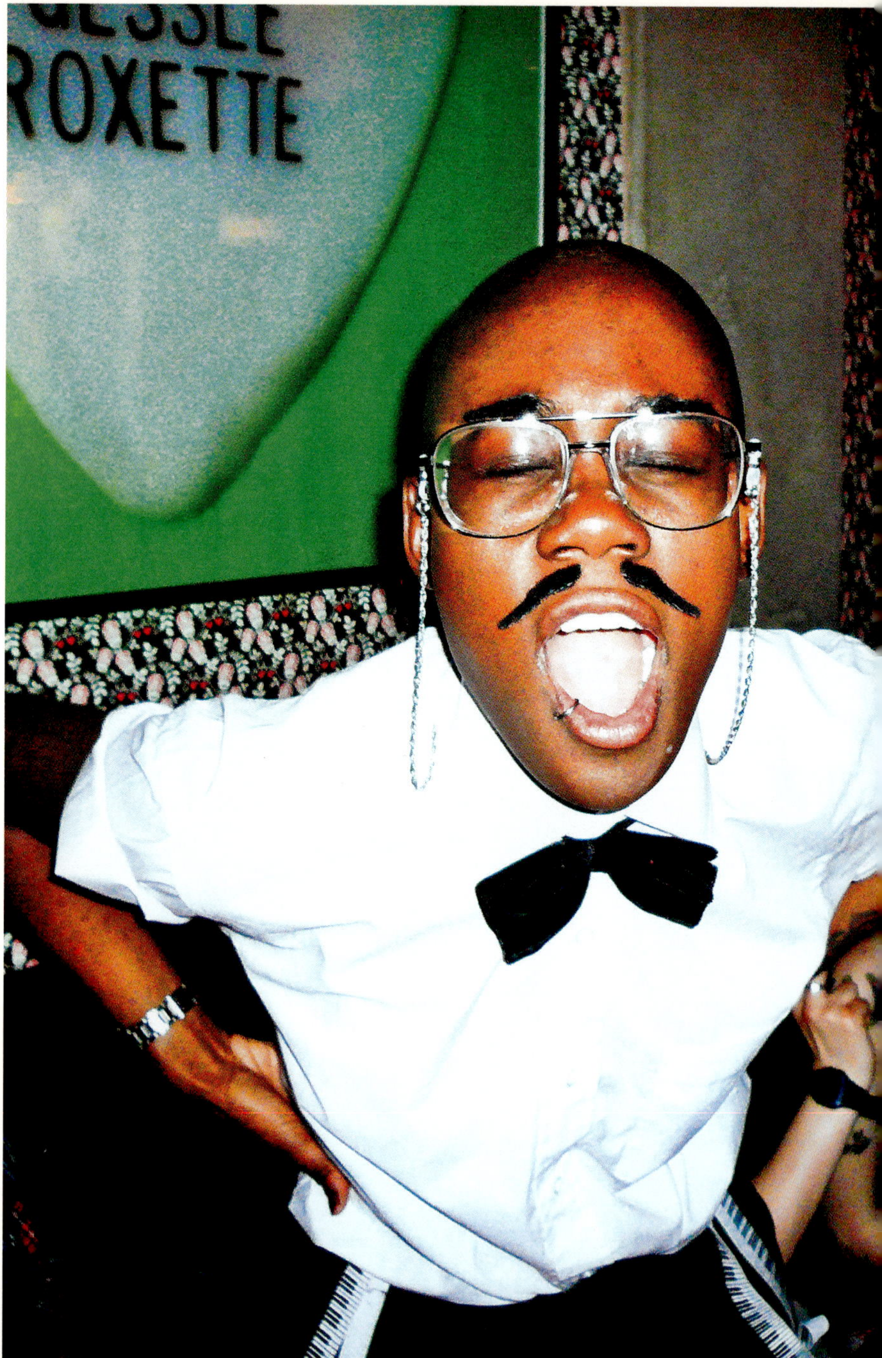

Boombox – Oct 2007

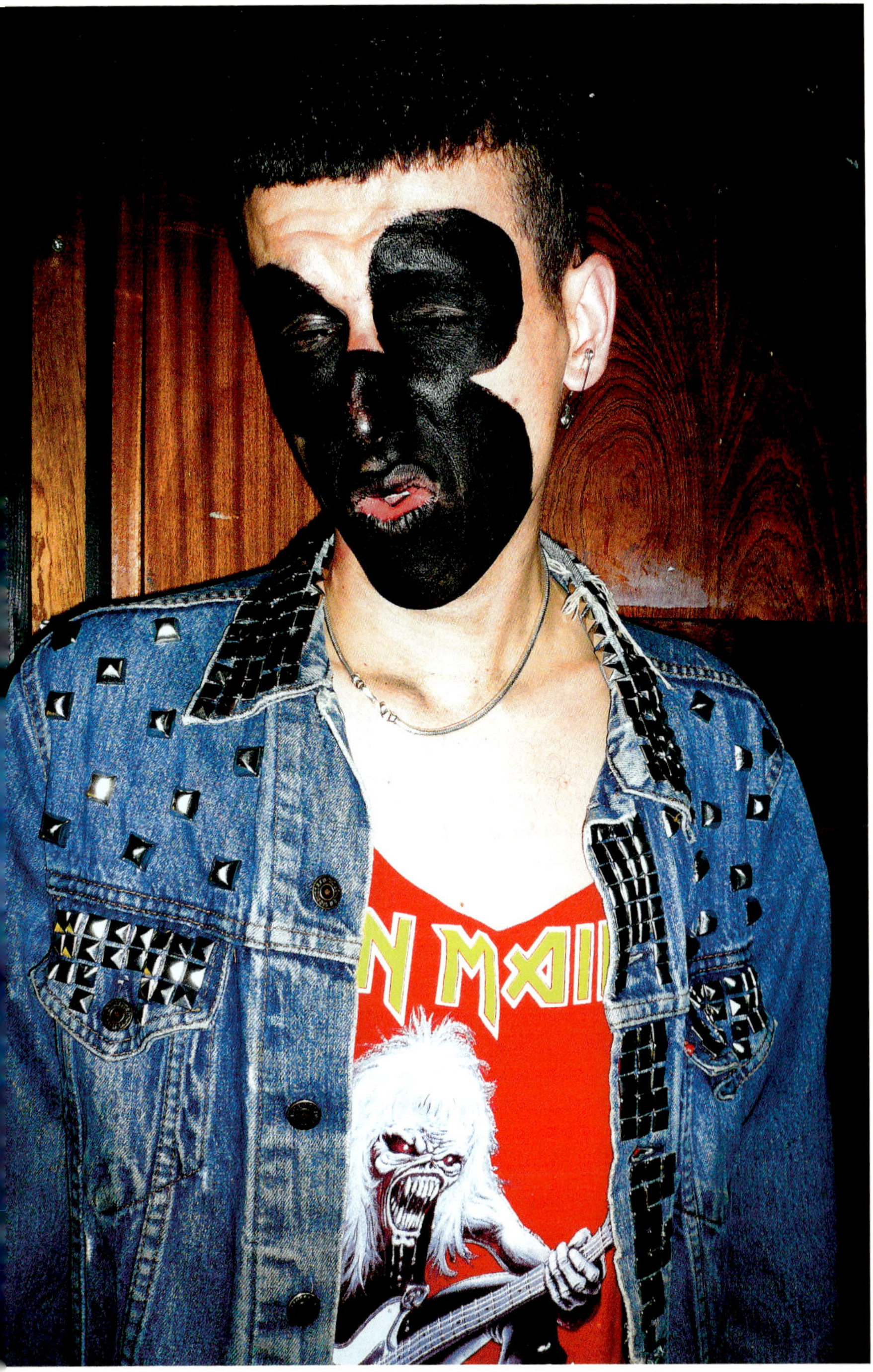

Boombox – June 2007

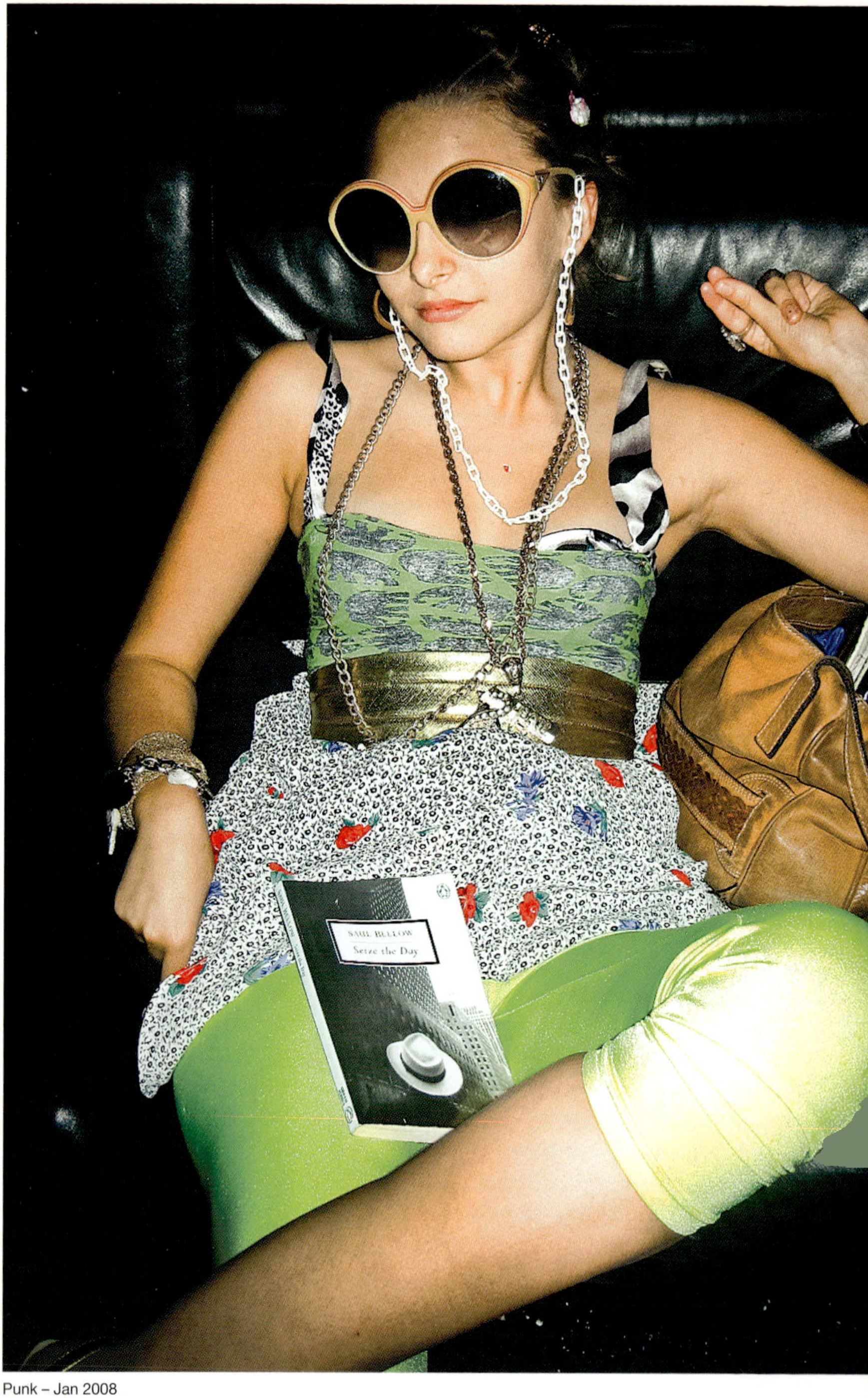

Punk – Jan 2008

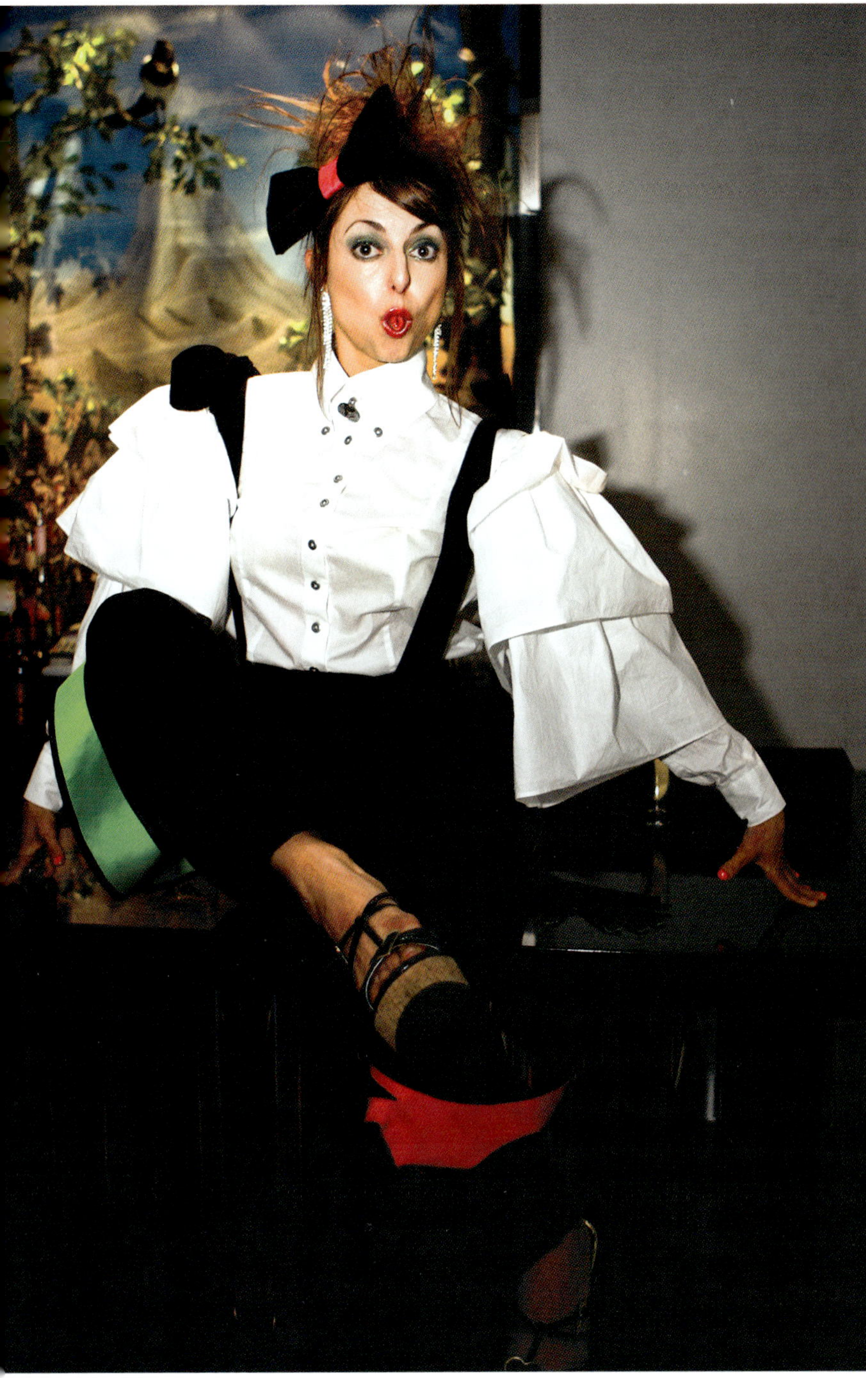

Strutt – Sept 2008

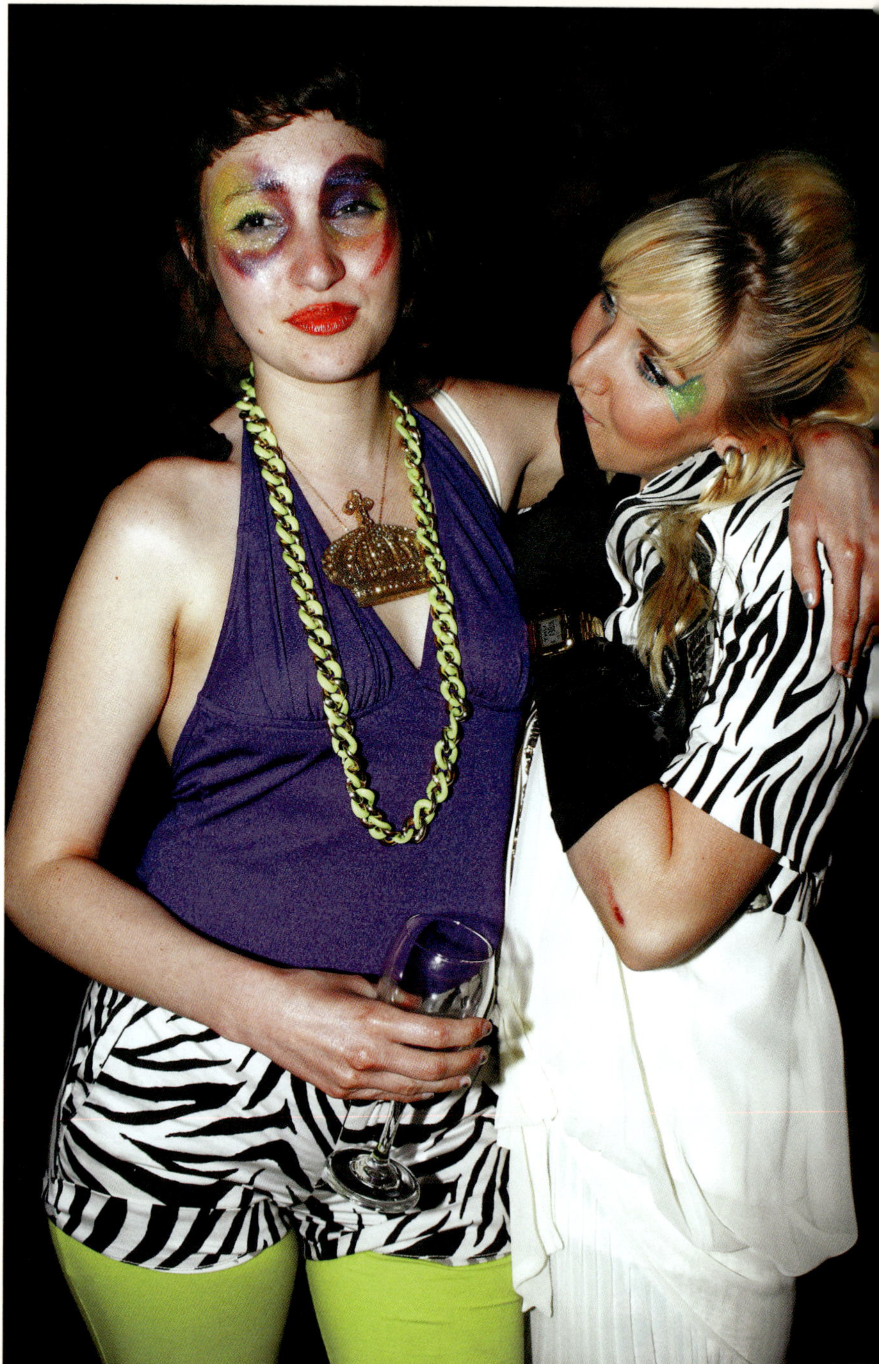

Too2Much – Aug 2004

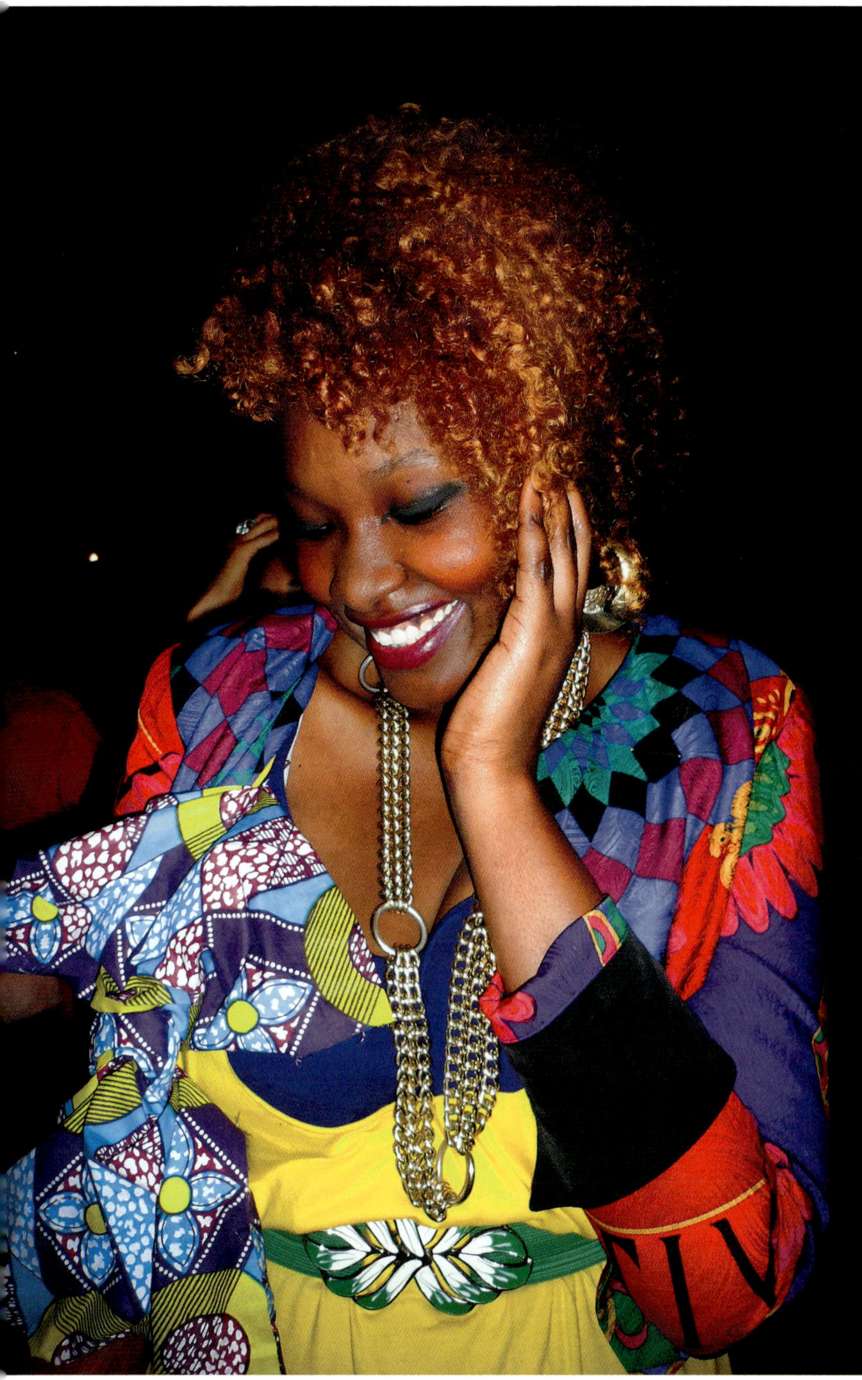

Boombox – Jan 2007

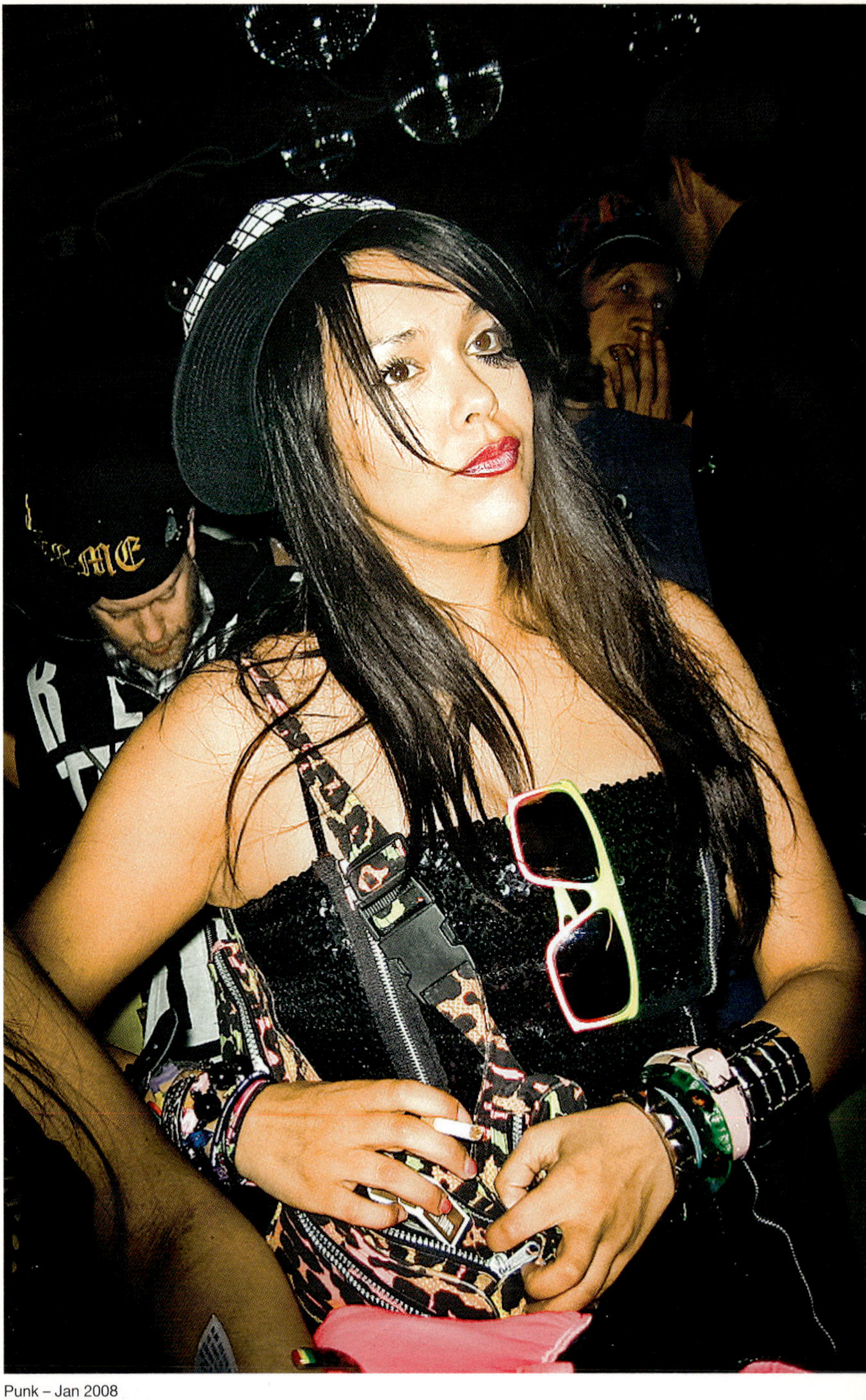

Punk – Jan 2008

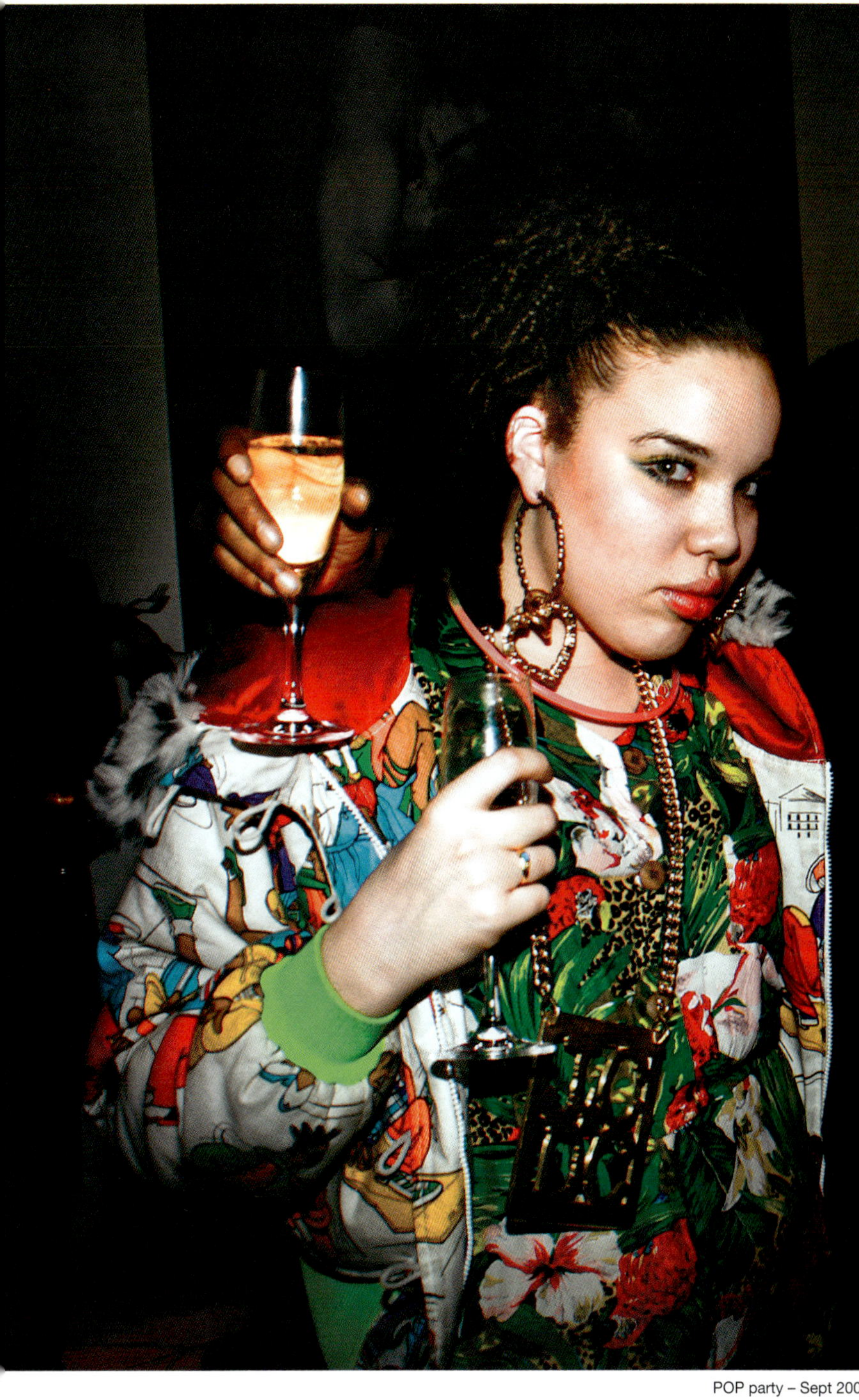

POP party – Sept 2007

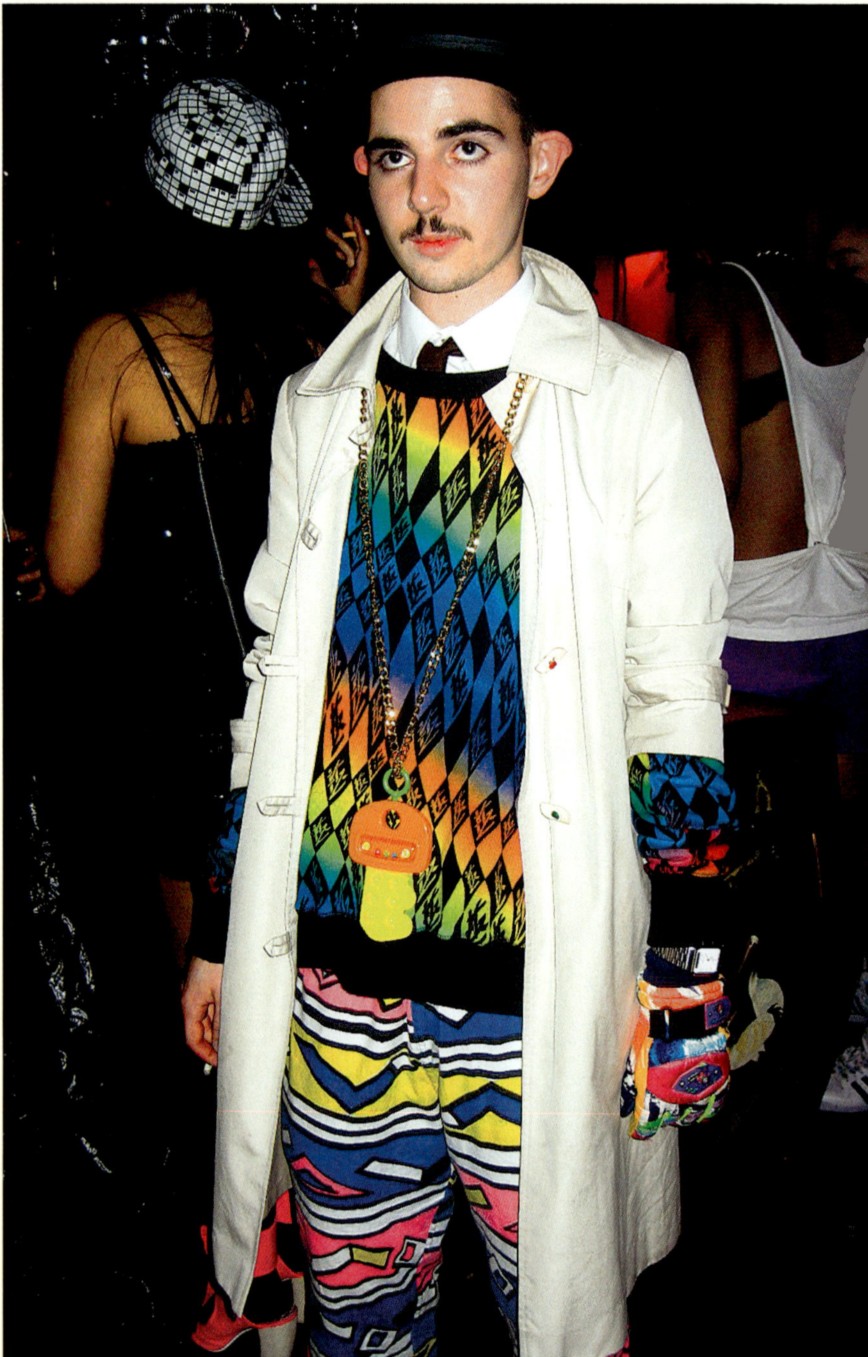

Punk – Jan 2007

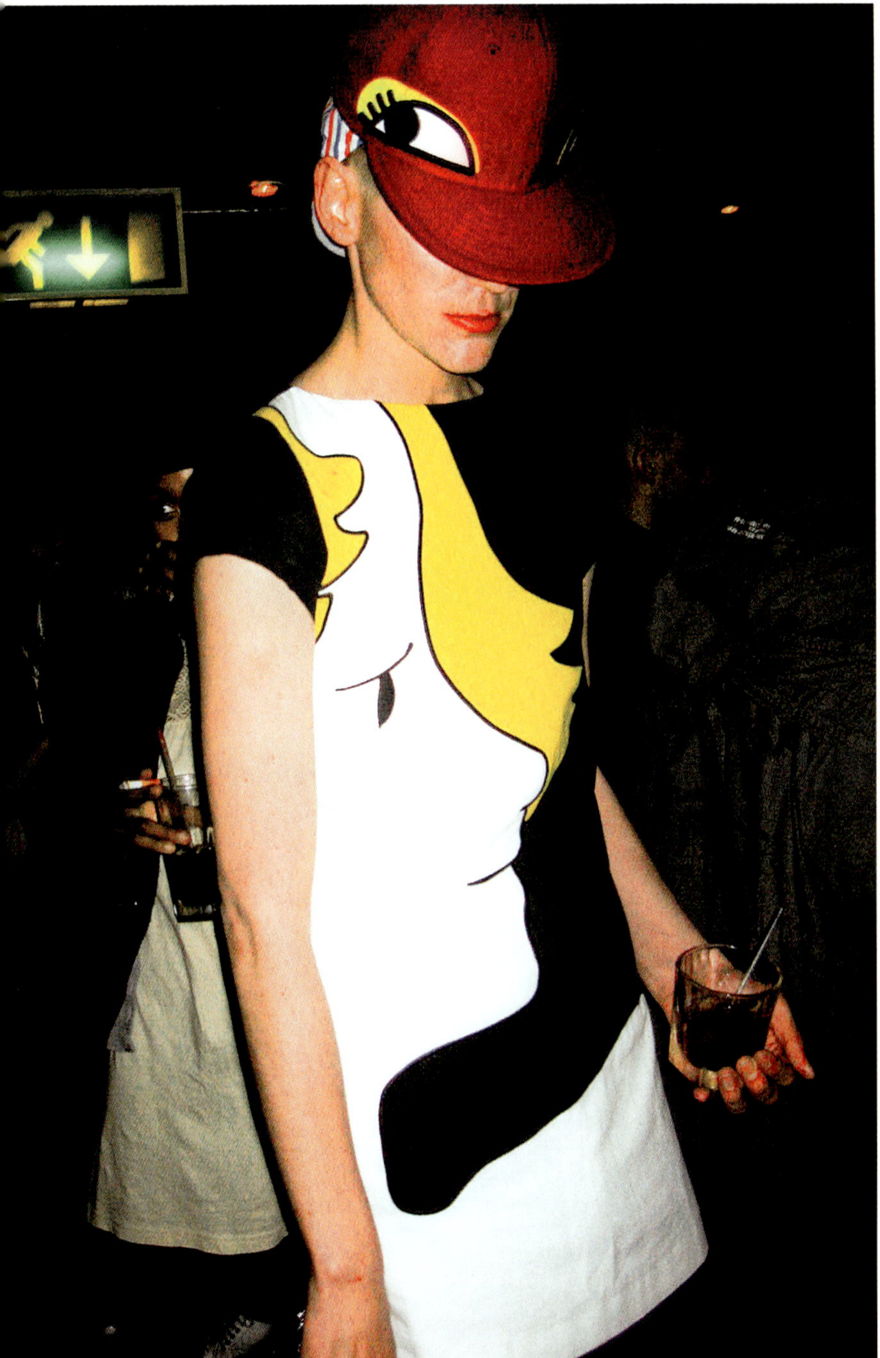

Punk – Jan 2007

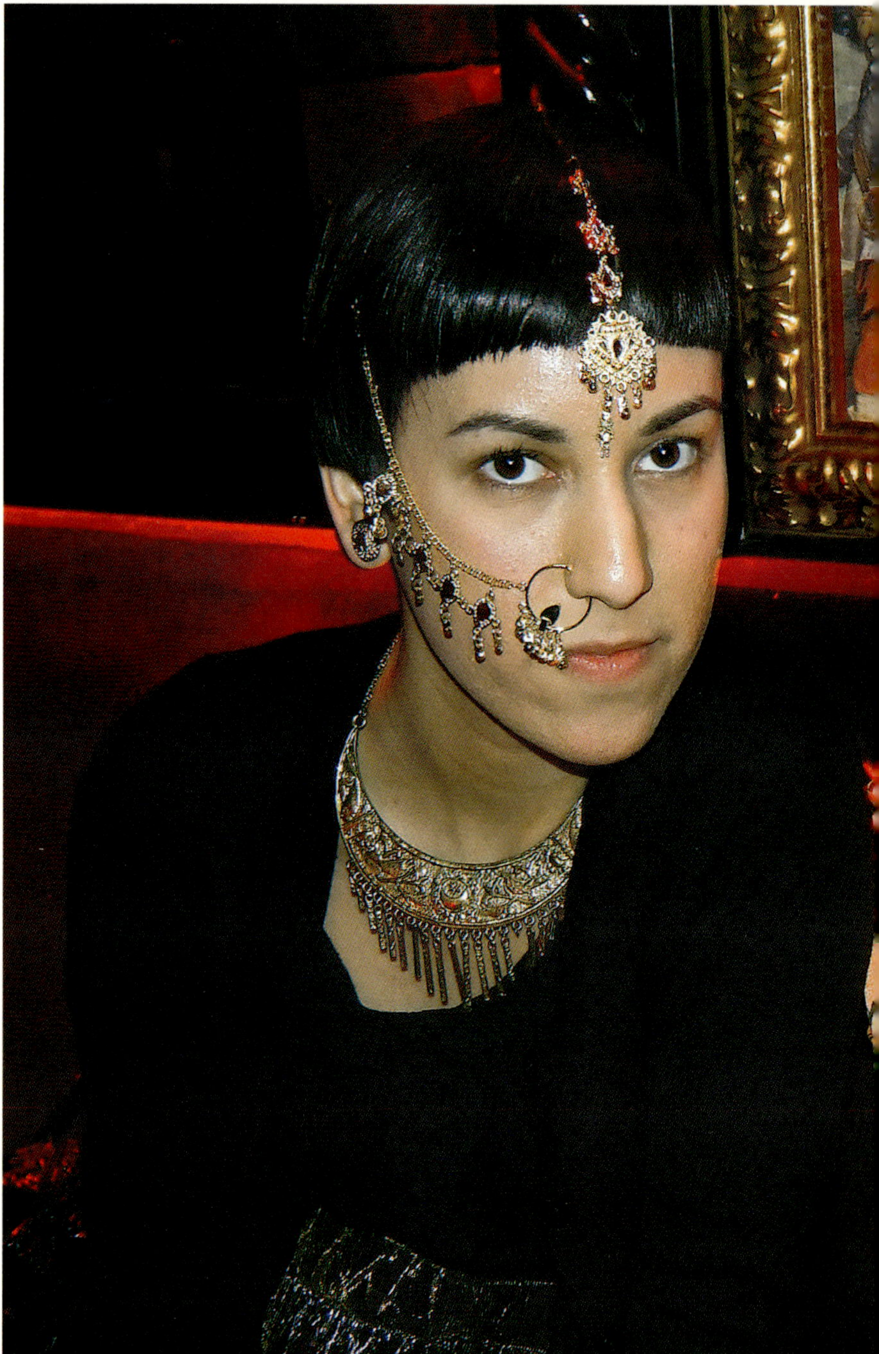

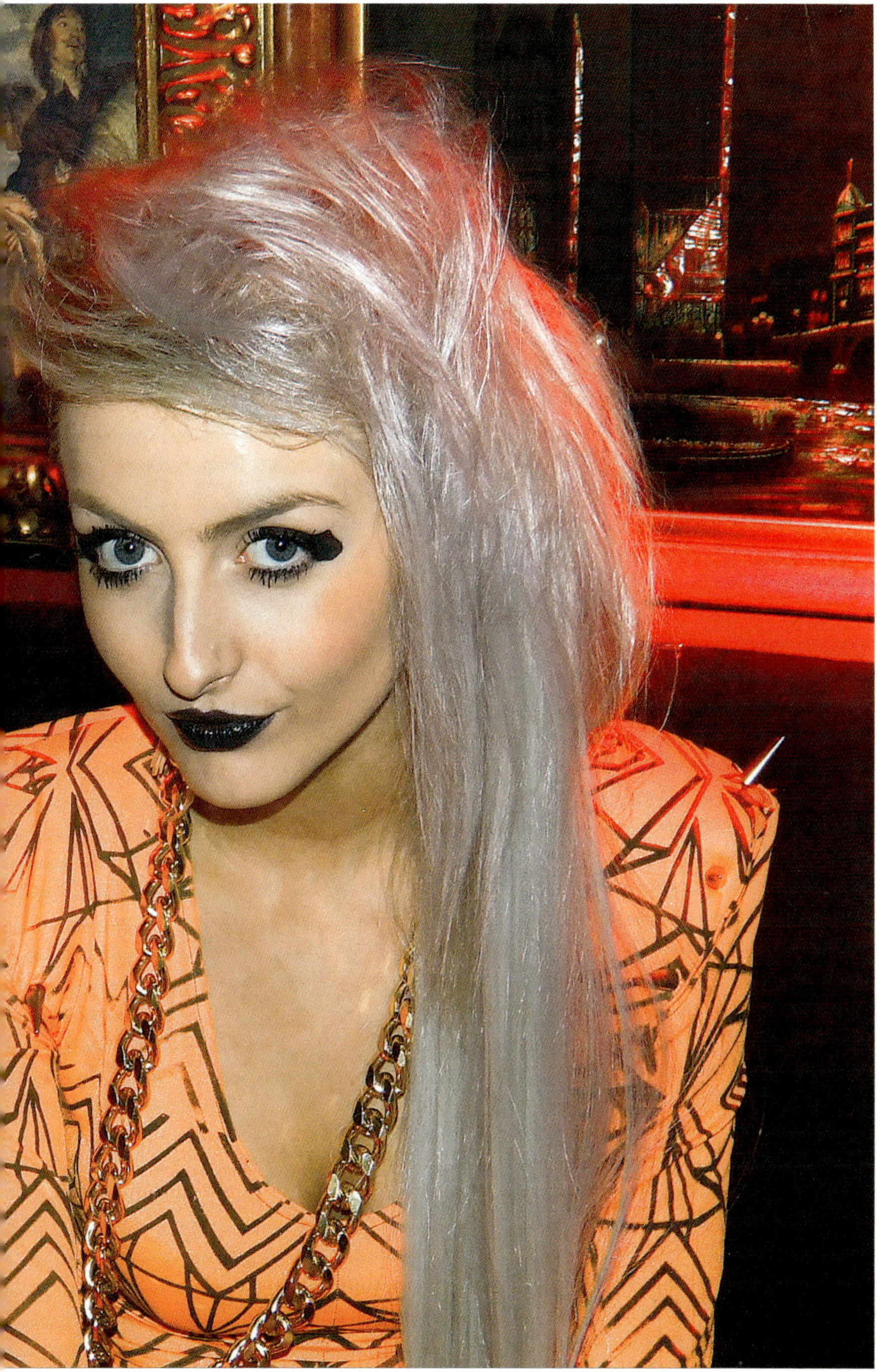

Punk – Jan 2010

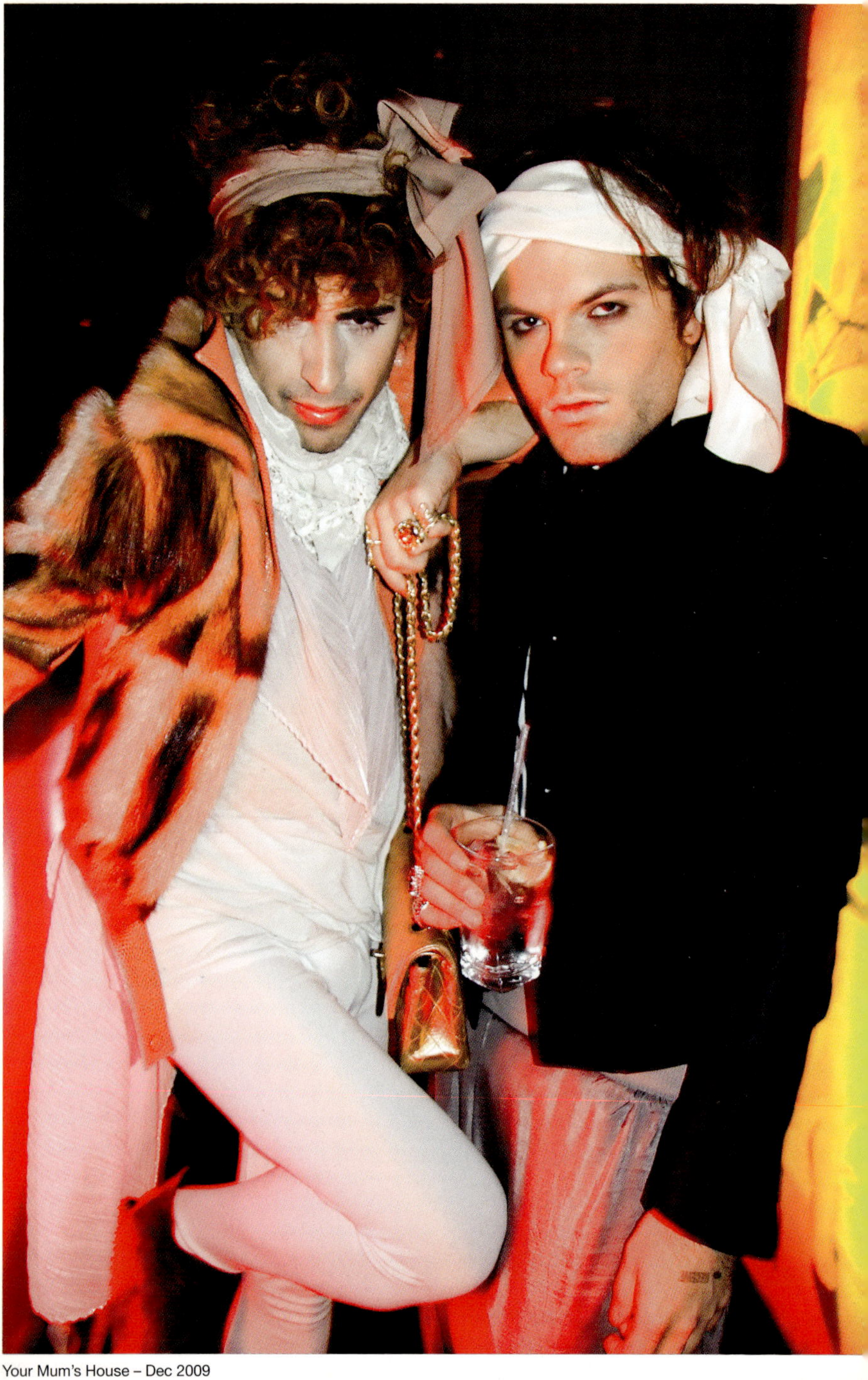

Your Mum's House – Dec 2009

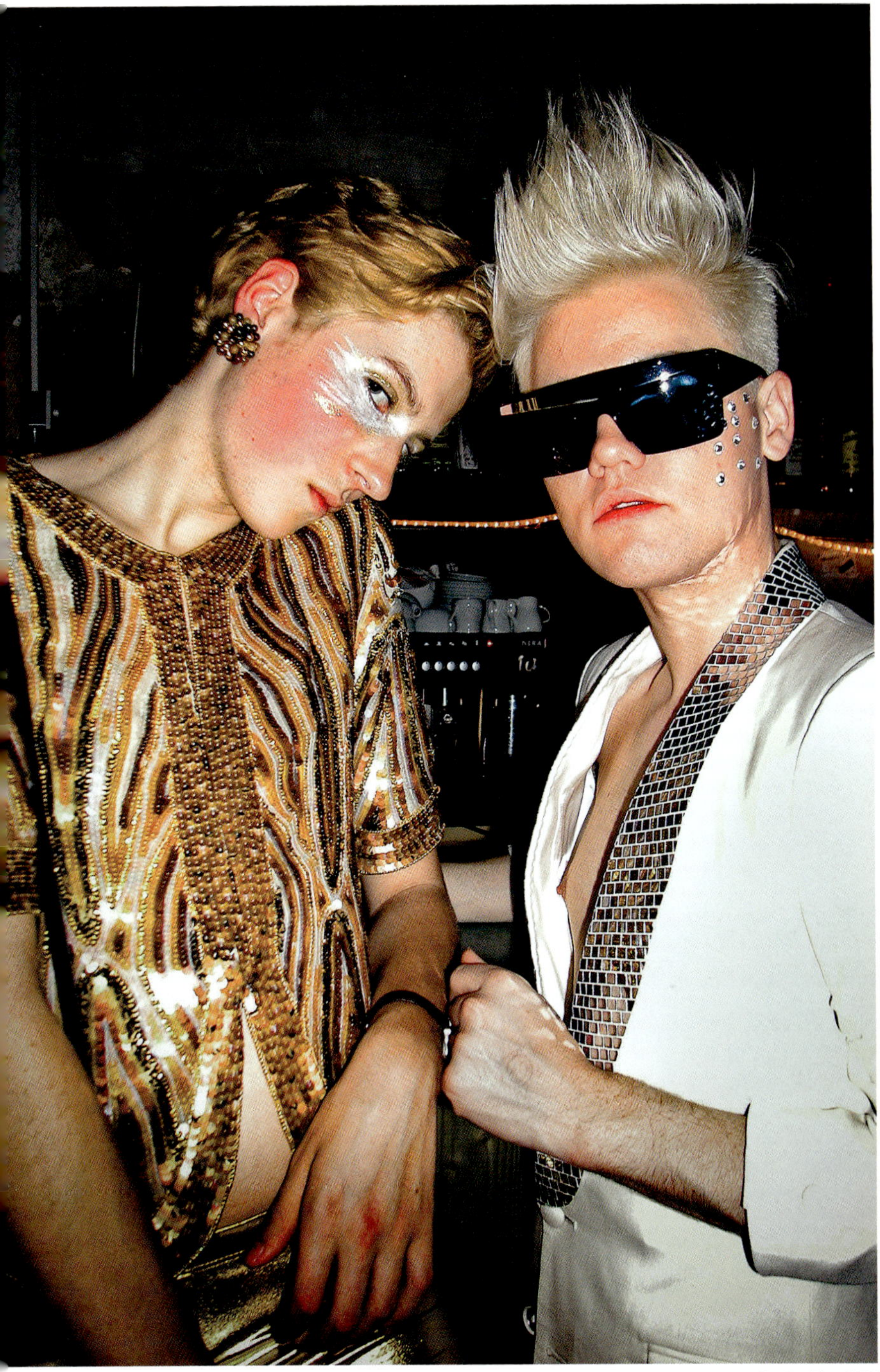

Strutt – Nov 2008

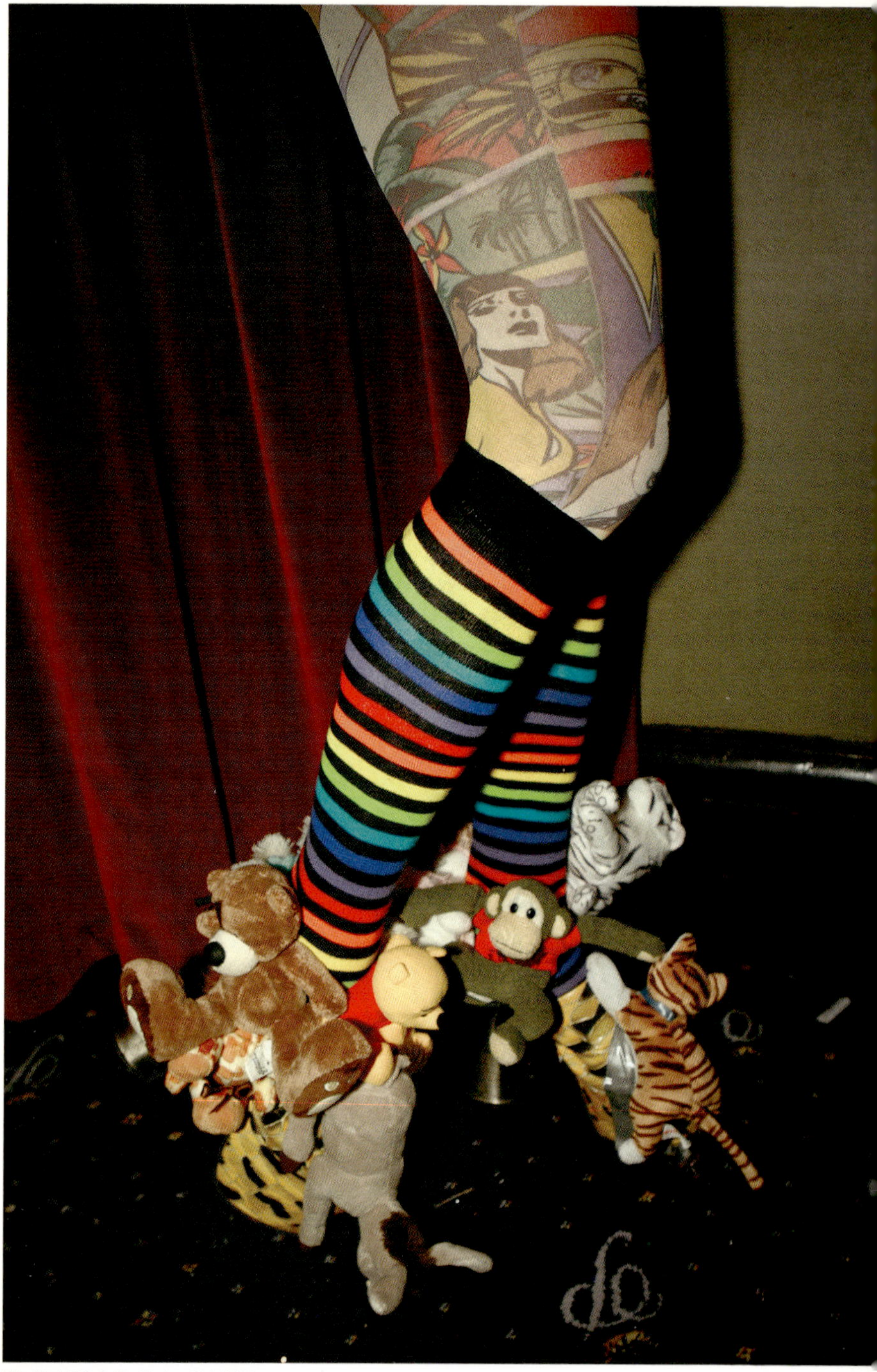

Wig Party@Cafe De Paris – Oct 2009

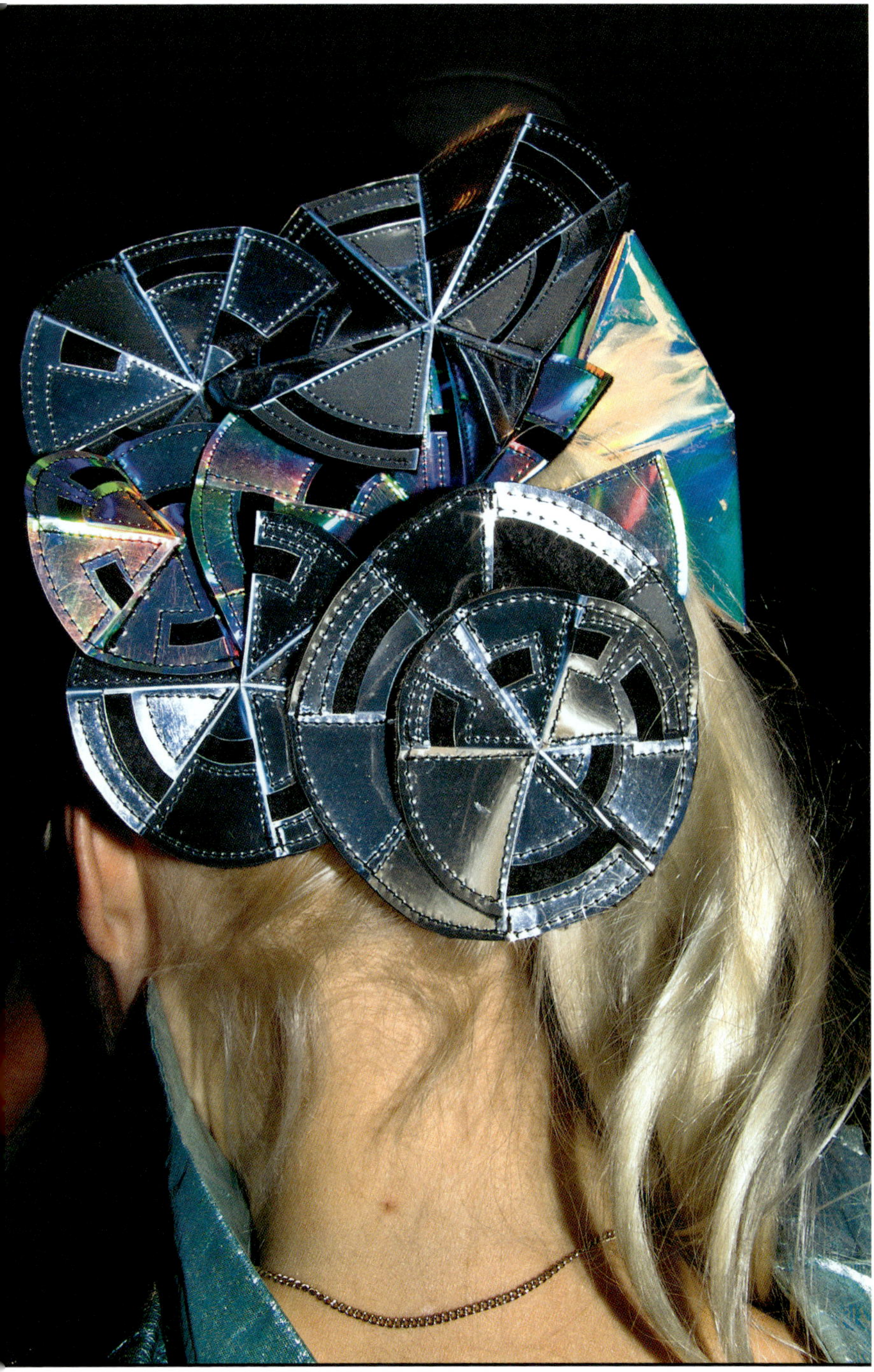

Circus – Oct 2010

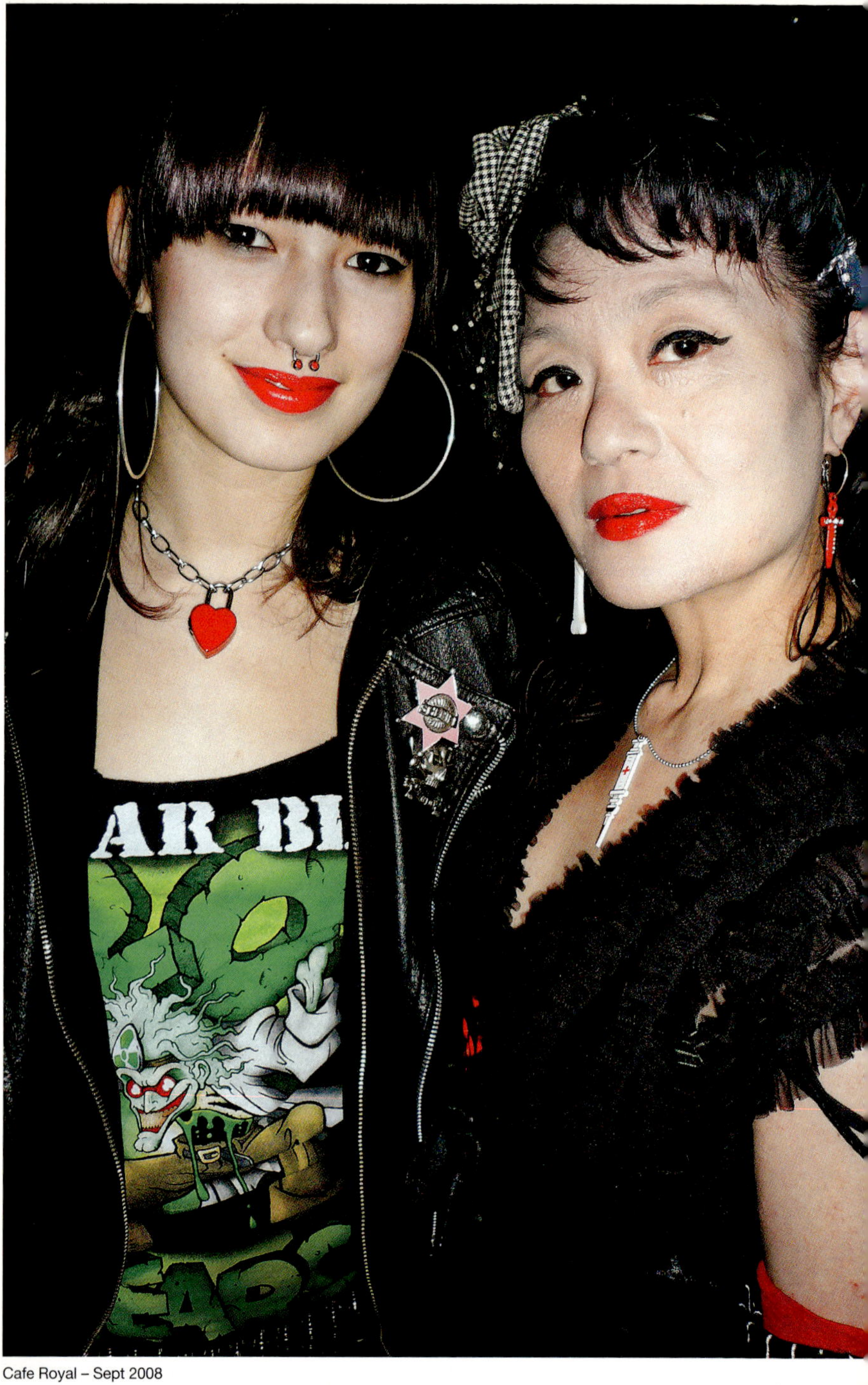

Cafe Royal – Sept 2008

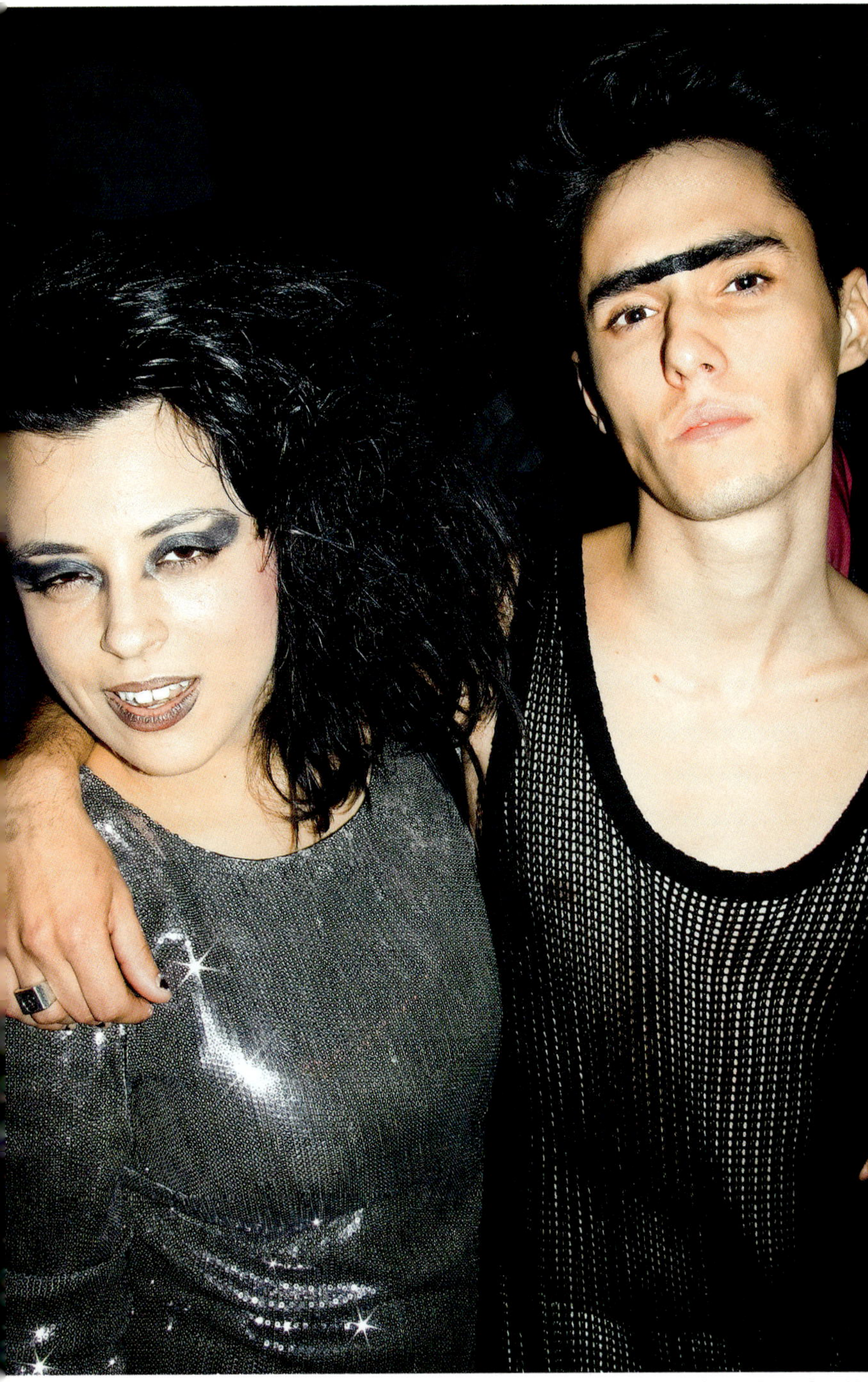

Paradise@Cafe De Paris – Sept 2010

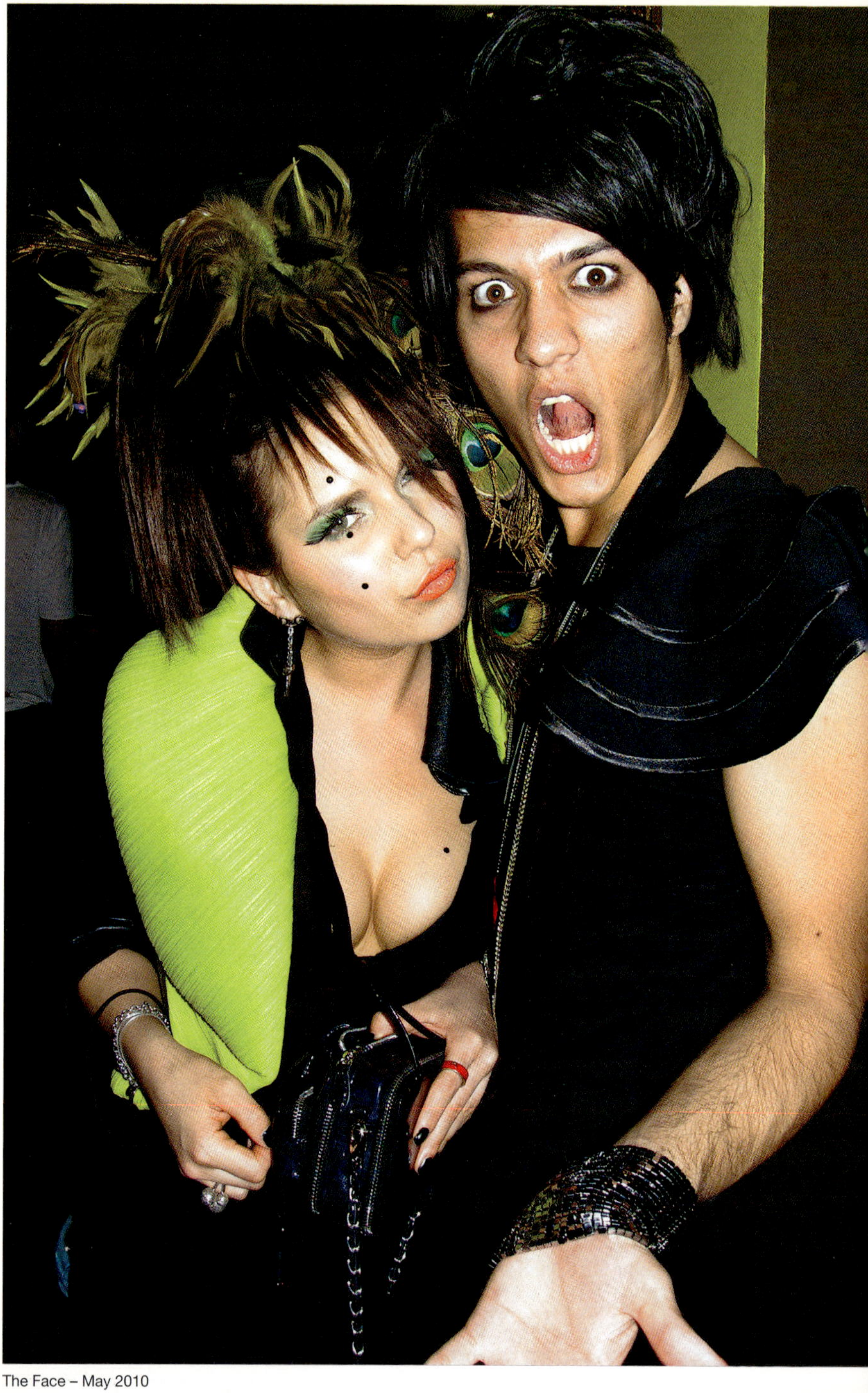

The Face – May 2010

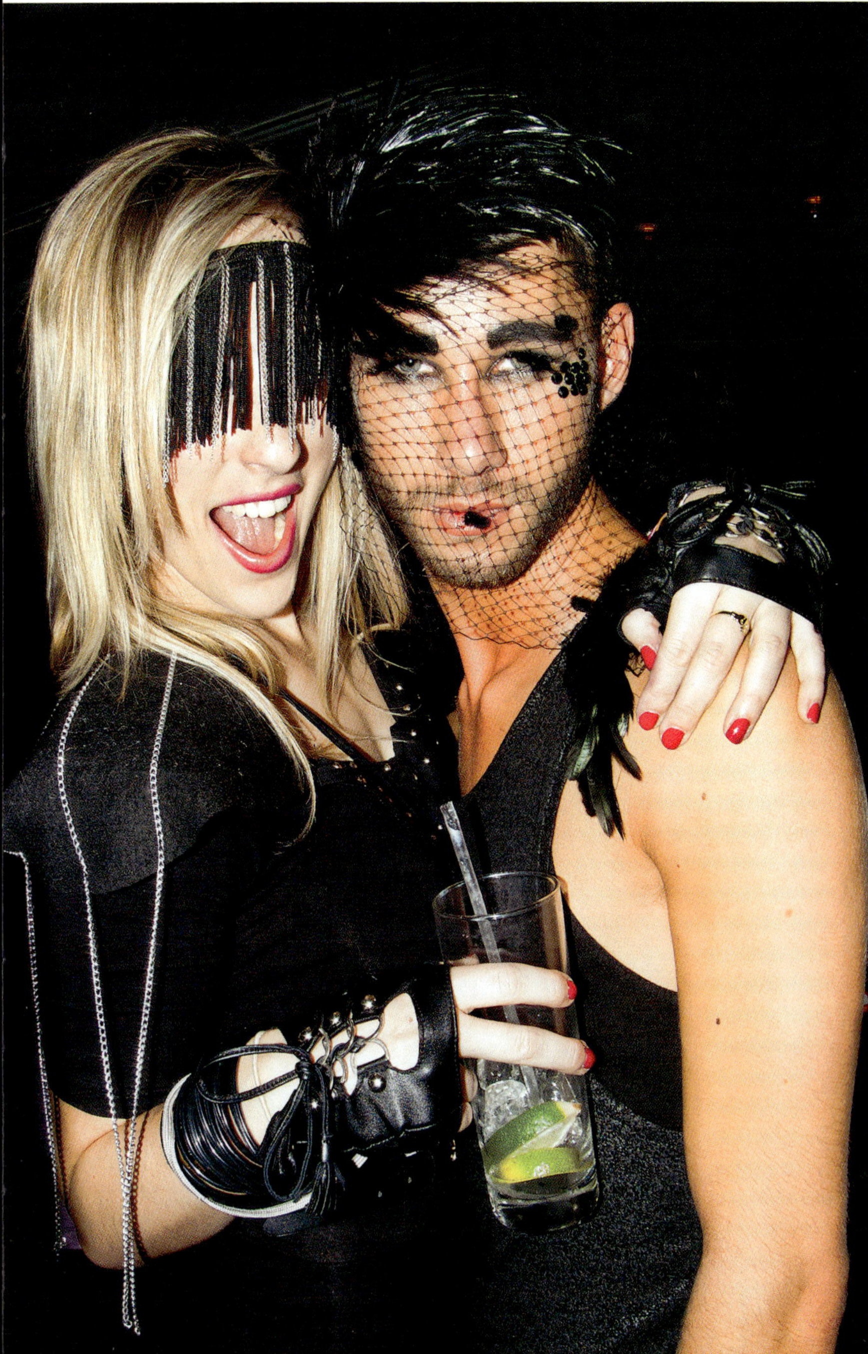

Circus – Sept 2010

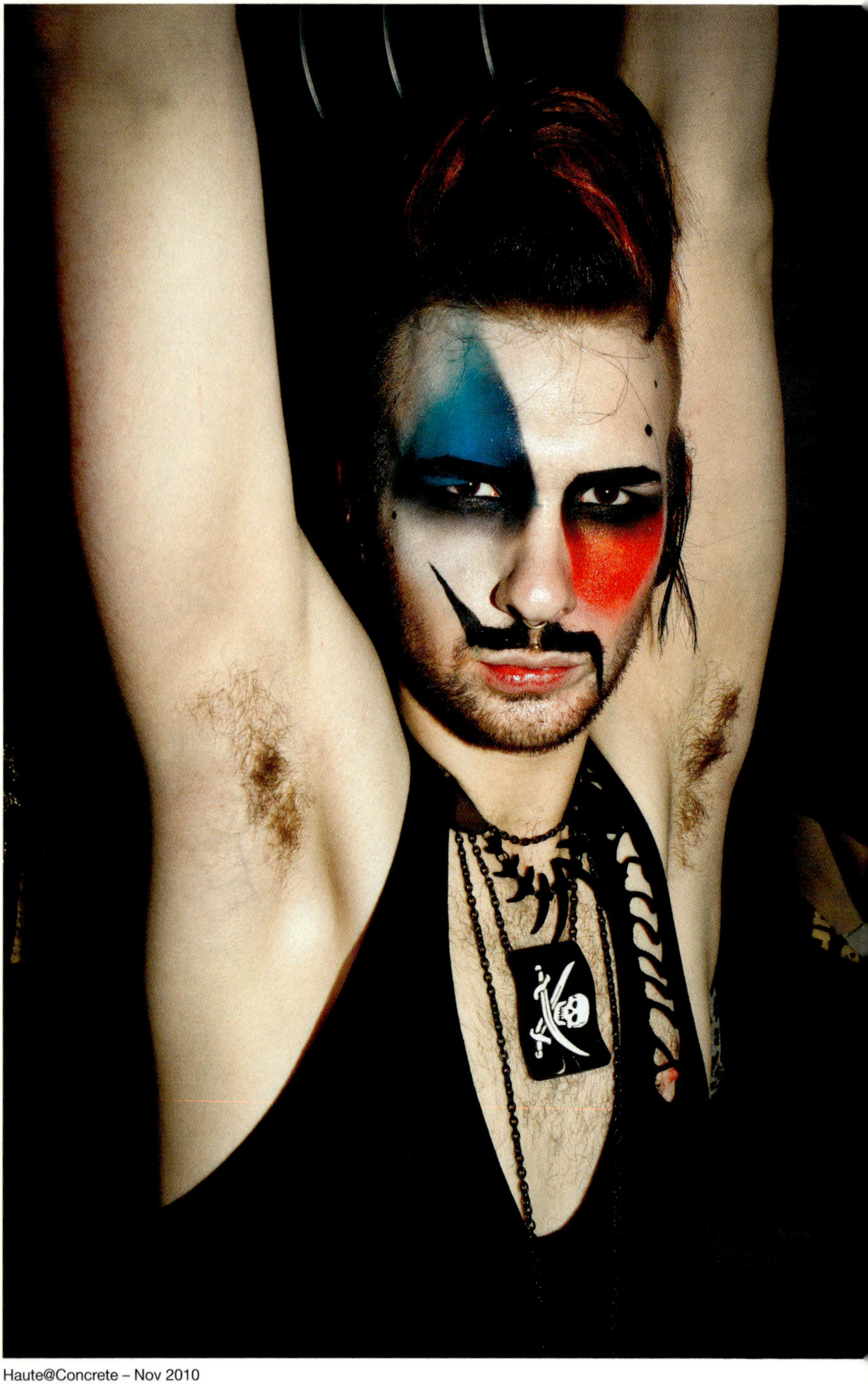

Haute@Concrete – Nov 2010

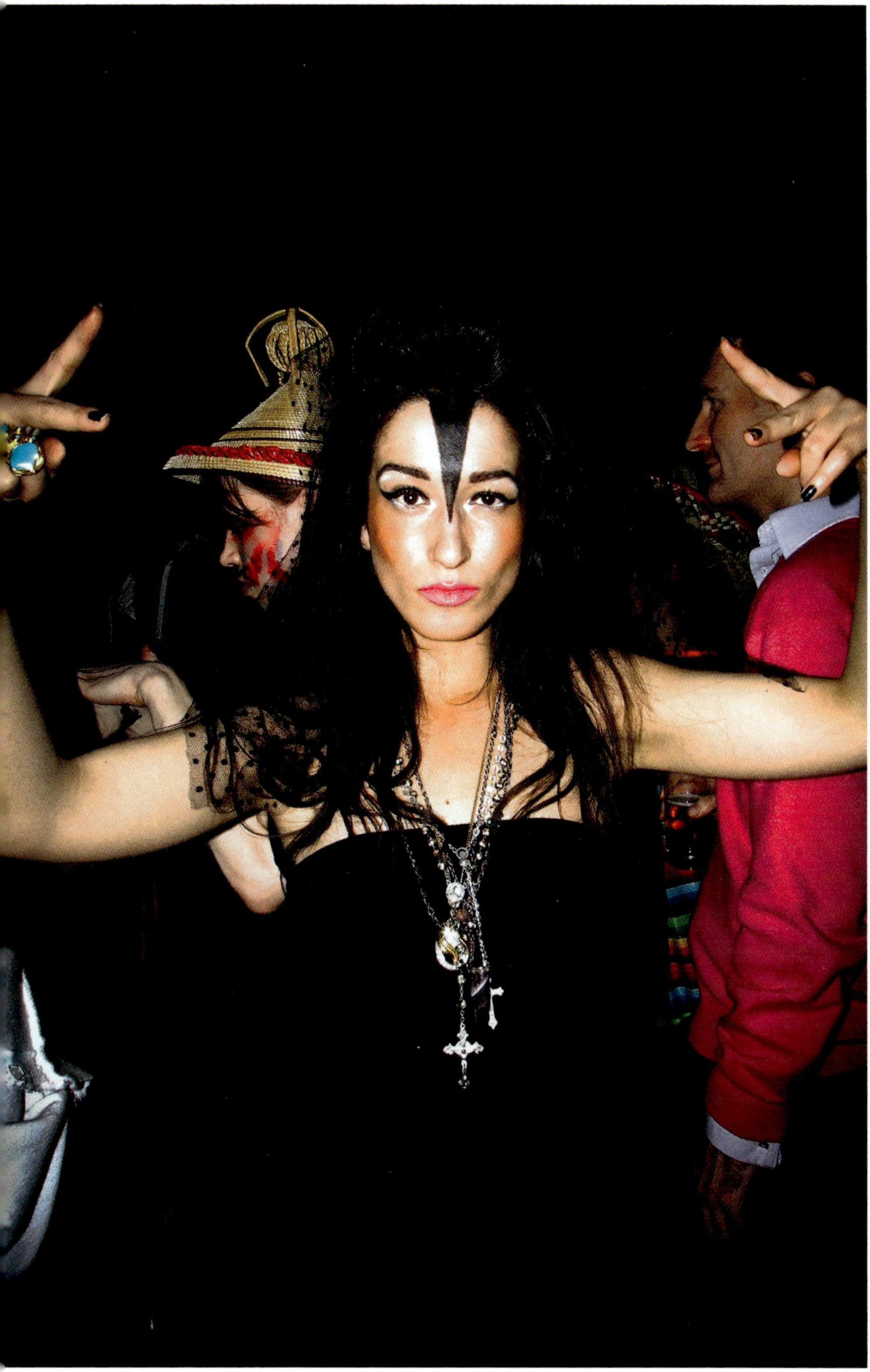

Home House – Jan 2010

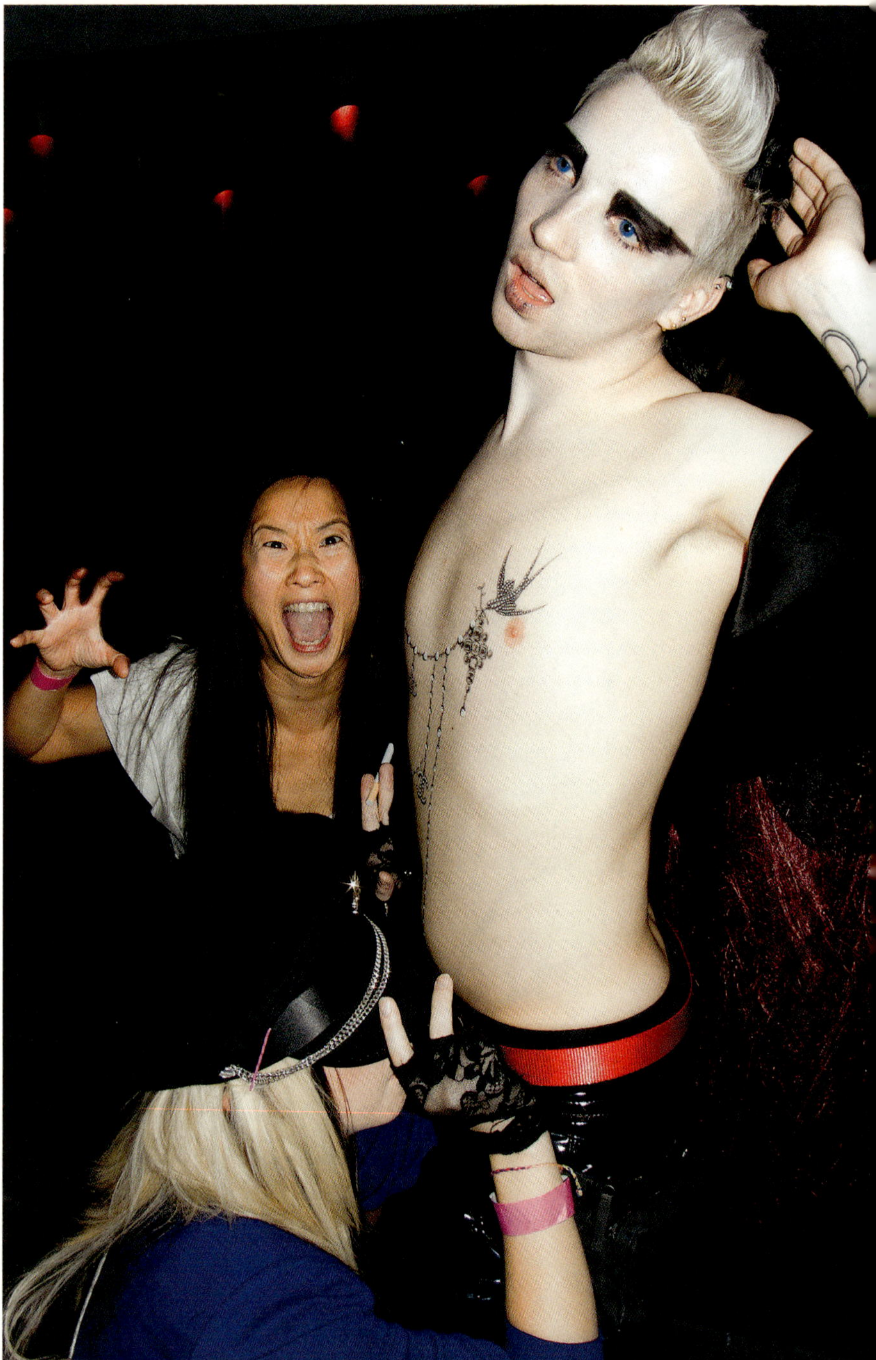

Circus – Sept 2010

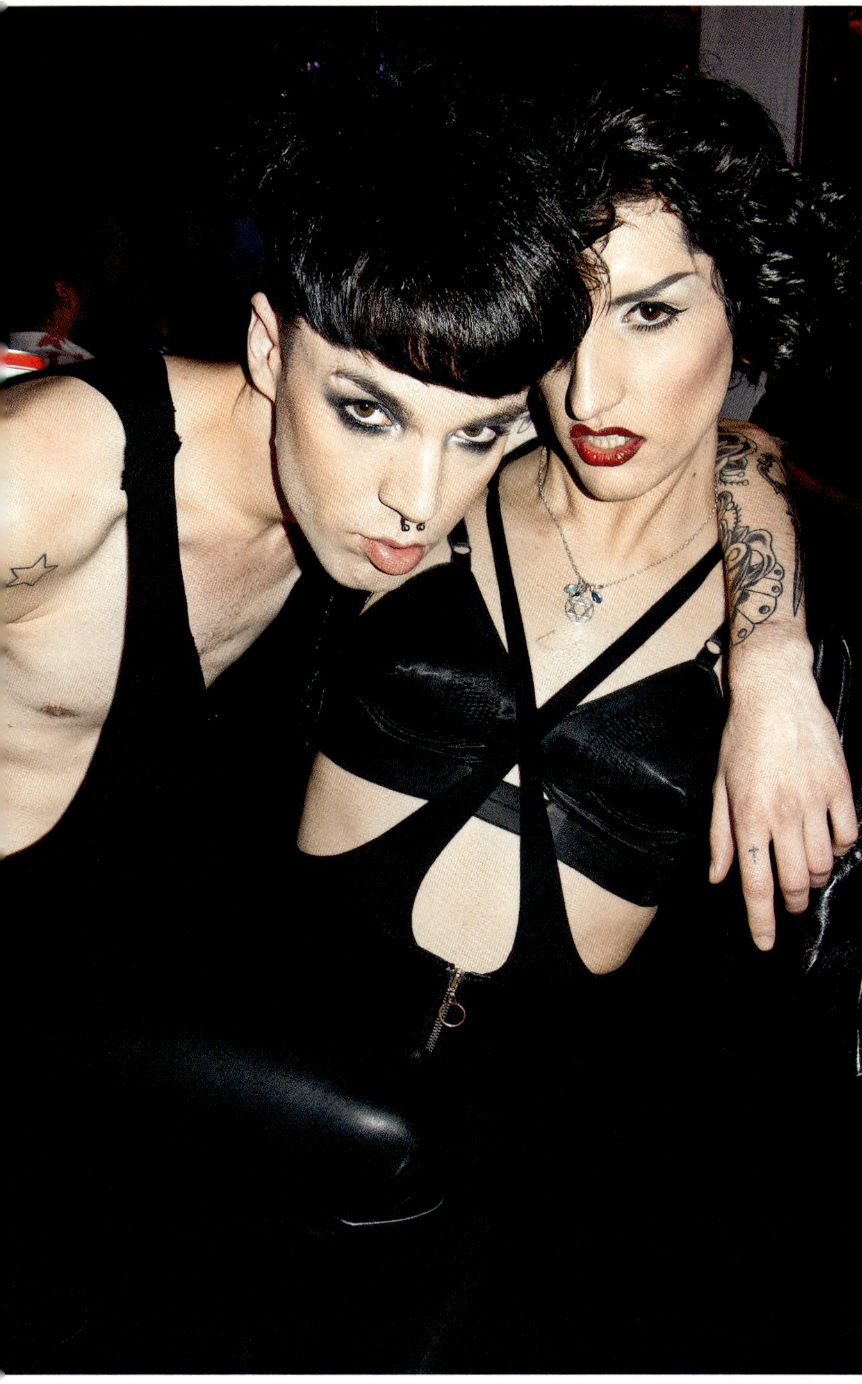

Wearable Art@Egg – Sept 2010

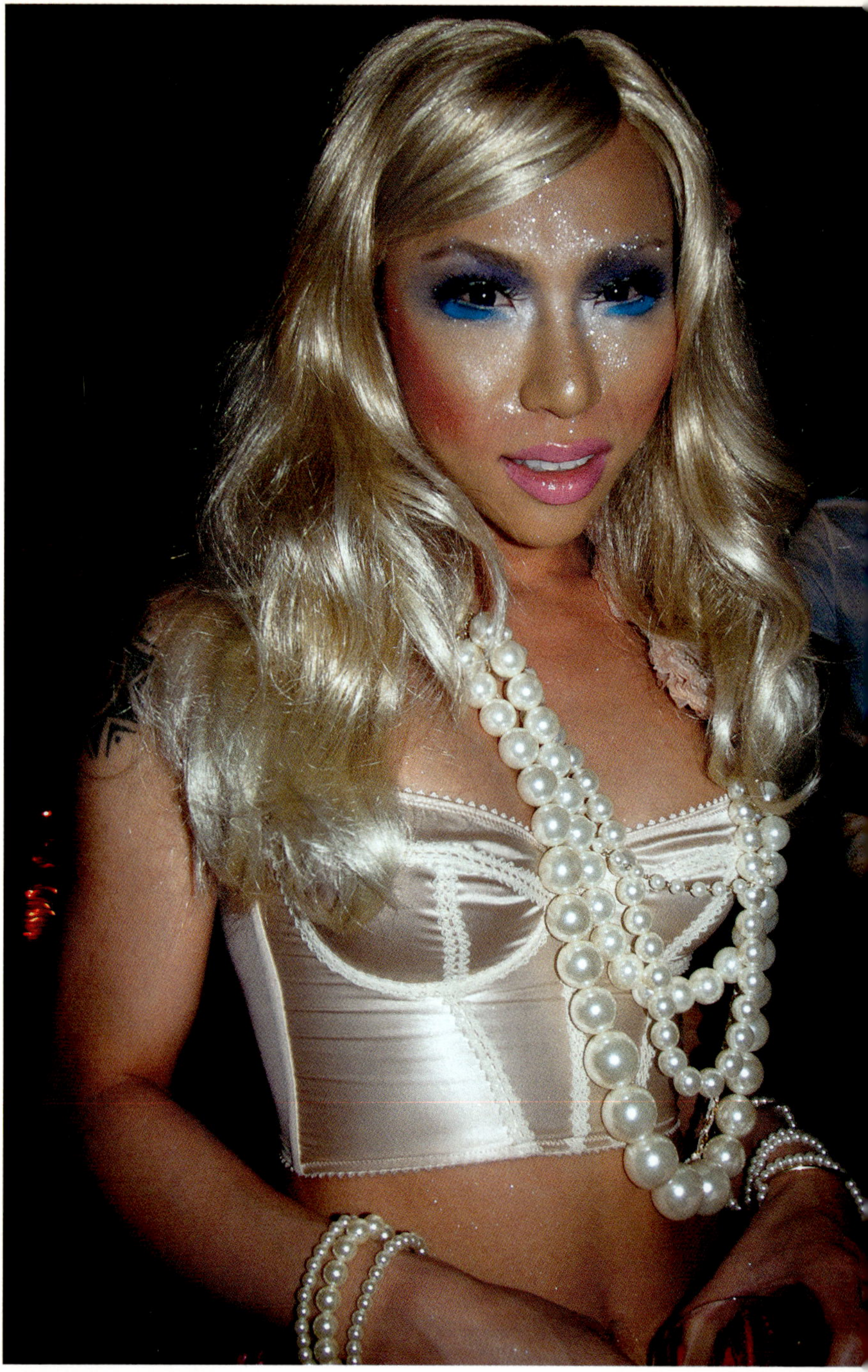

Toy@SupperClub – May 2010

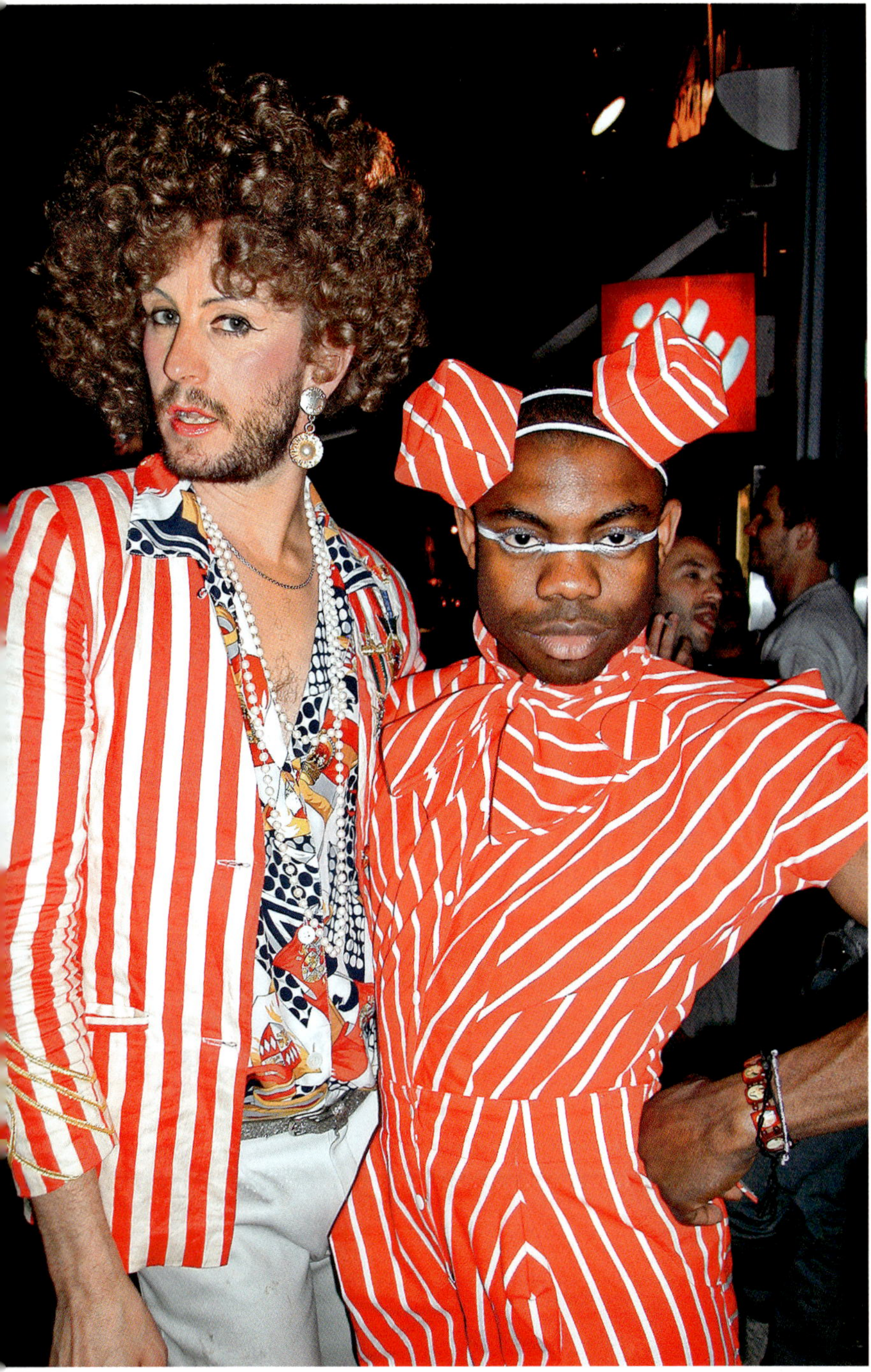

Strutt – May 2008

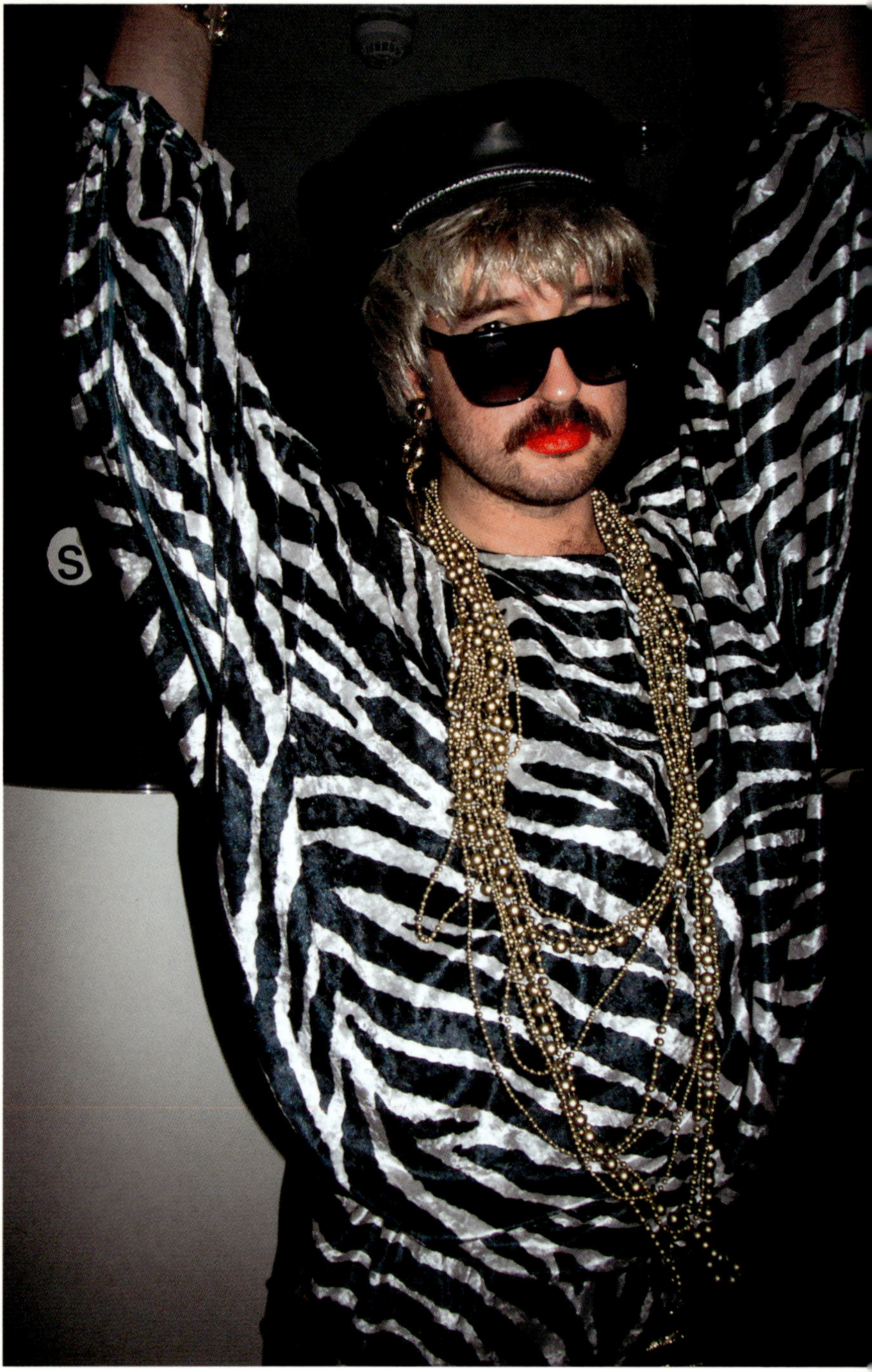

SupperClub – April 2010

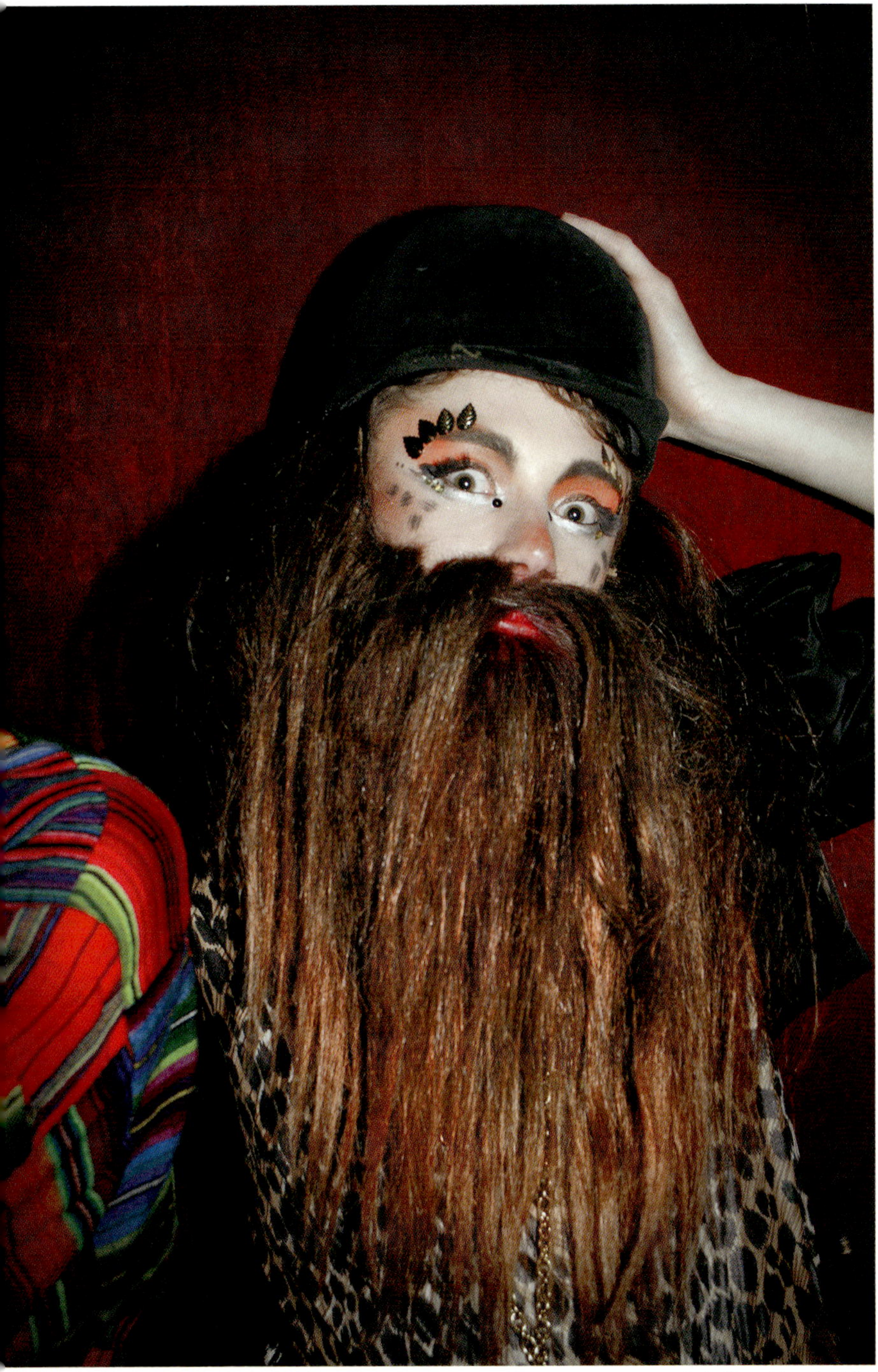

Soho Revue Bar – Jan 2008

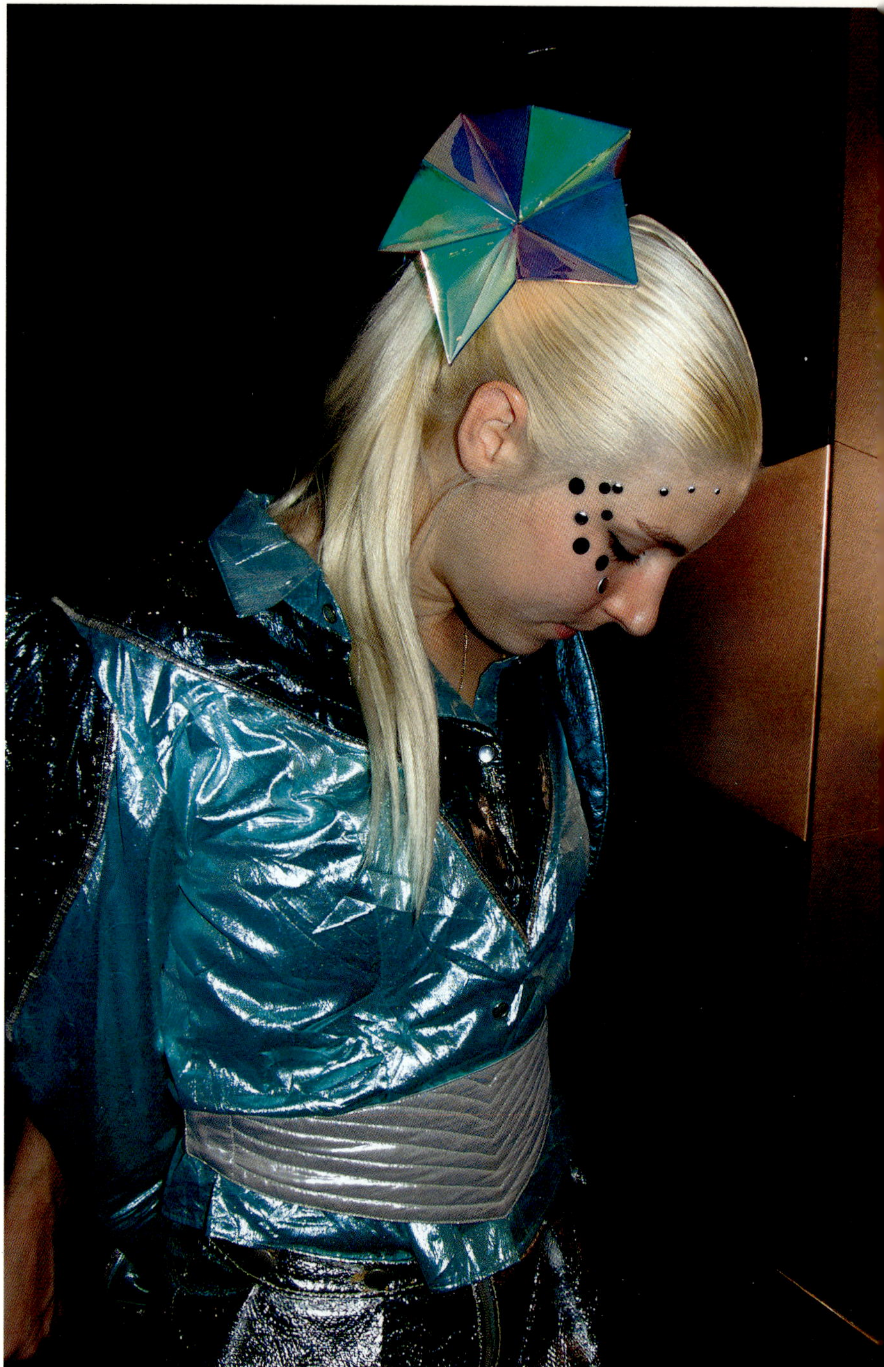

Circus – Sept 2010

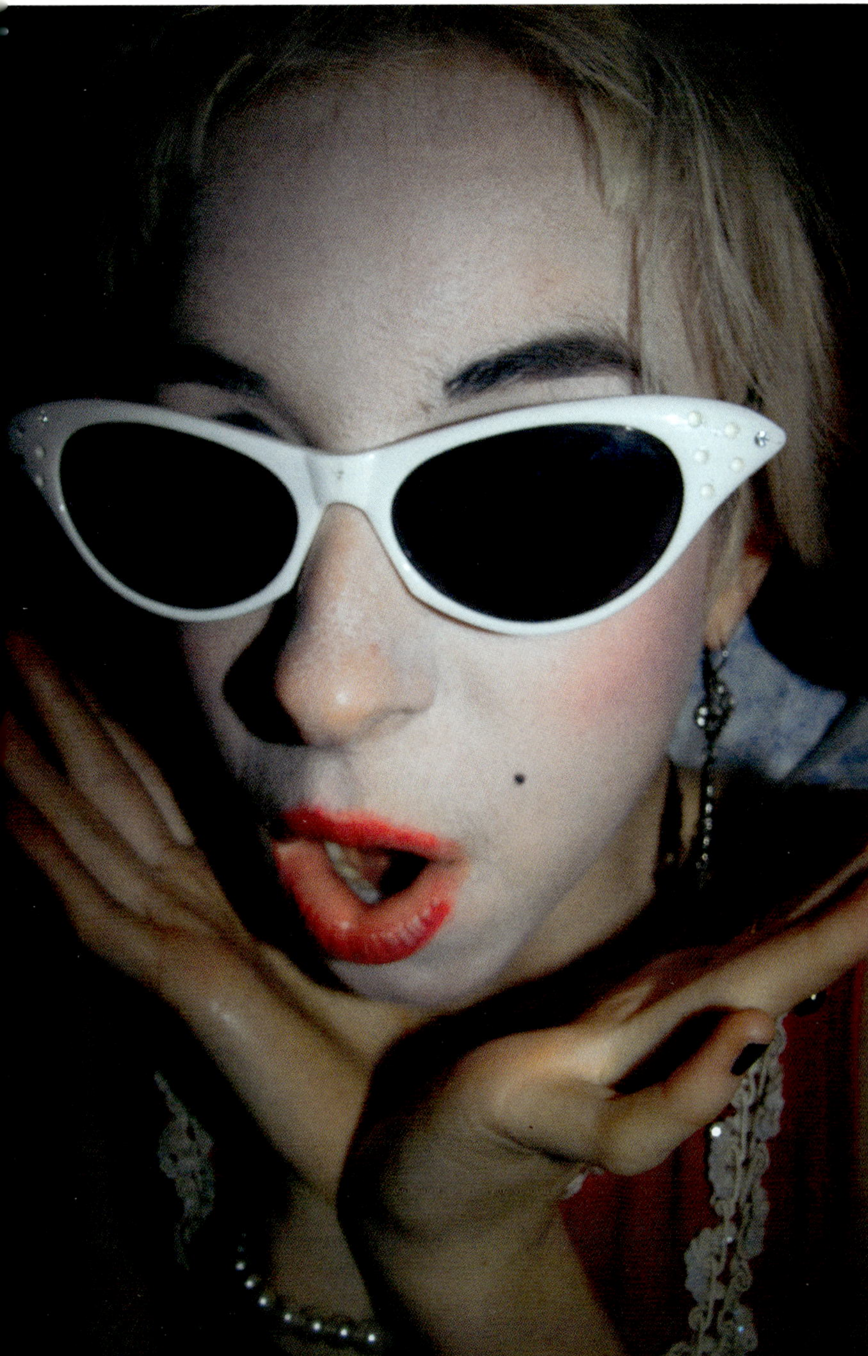

The Face – May 2010

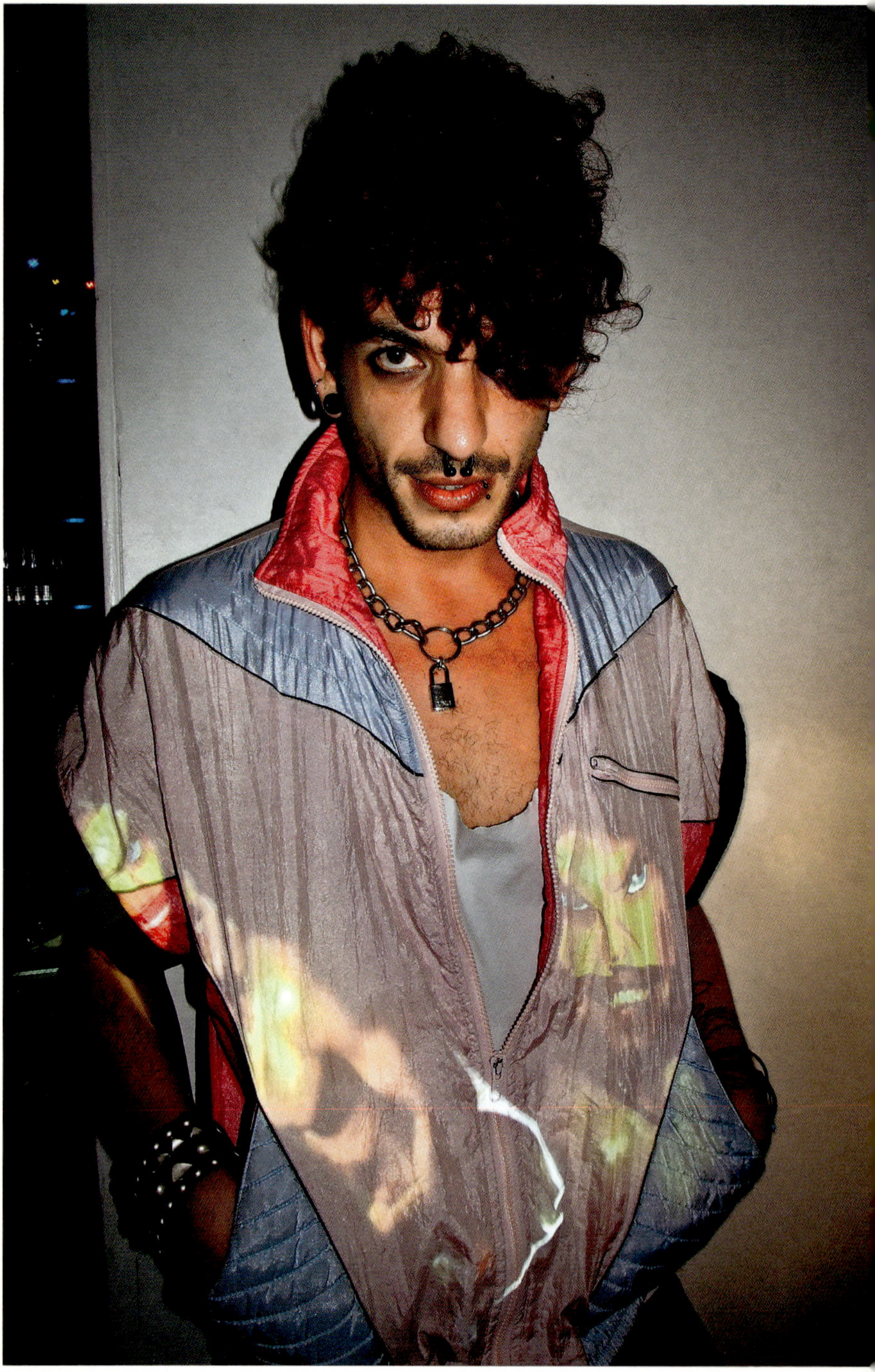

GutterBall – Sept 2010

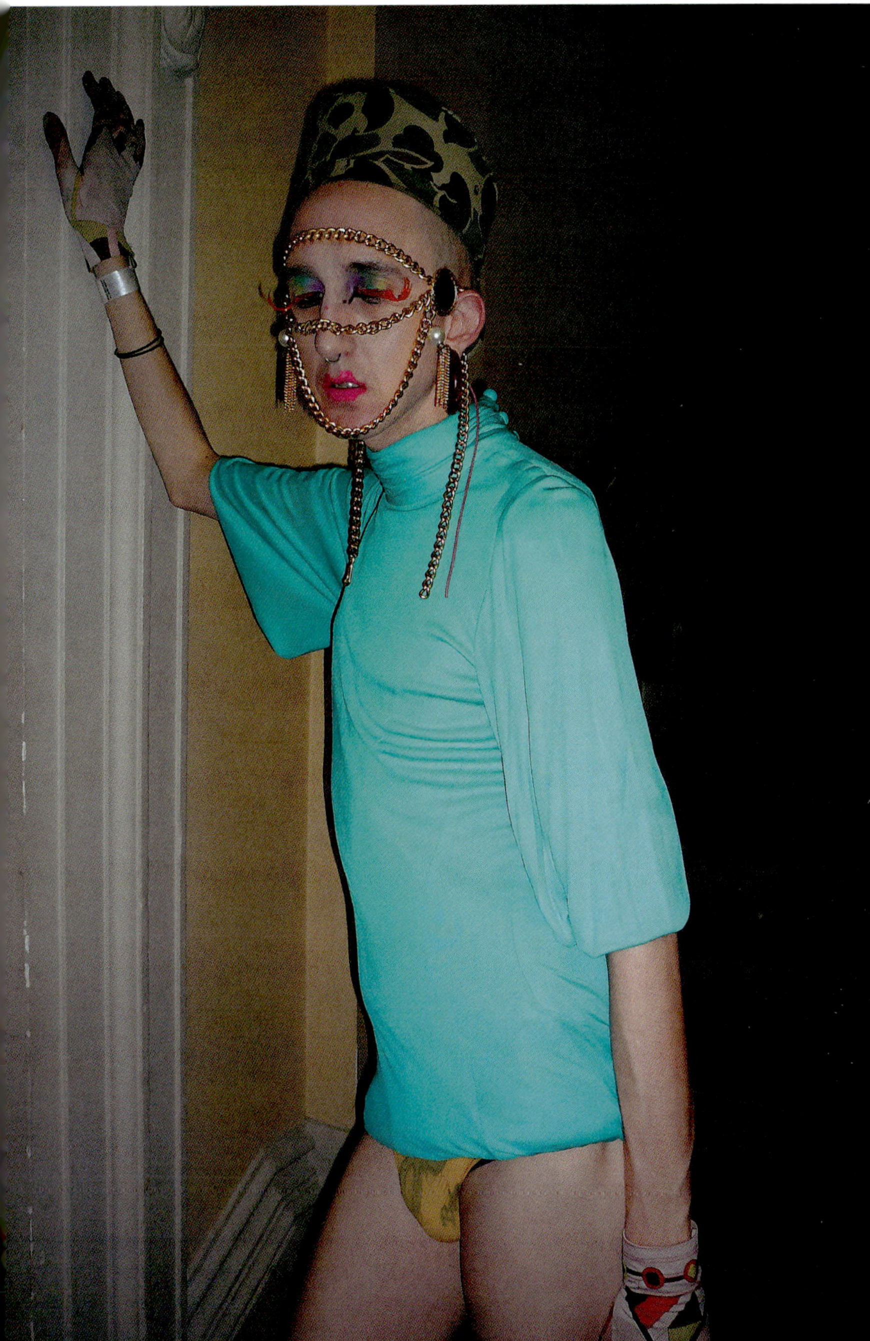

Voguing Ball – July 2007

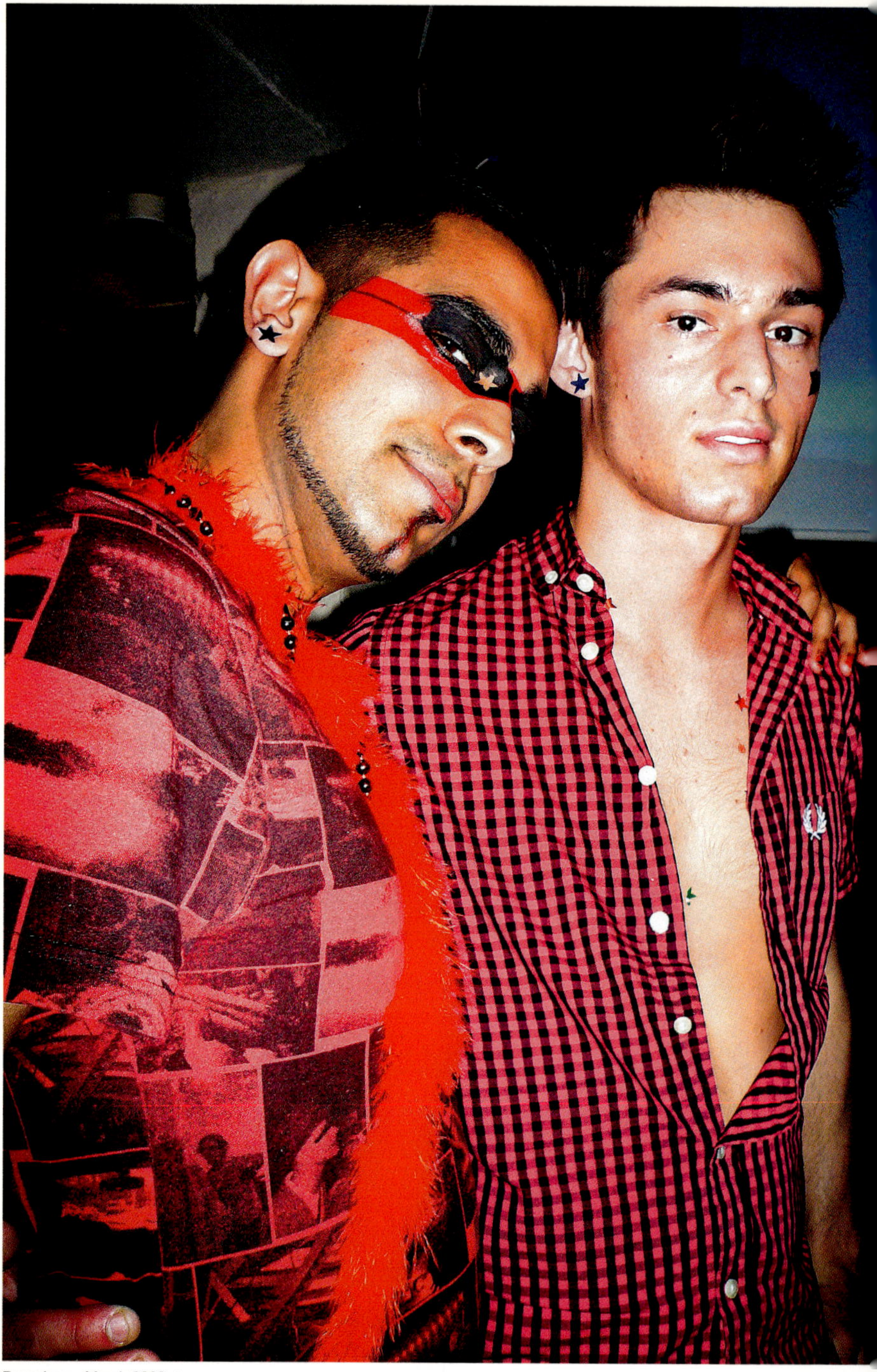

Boombox – March 2008

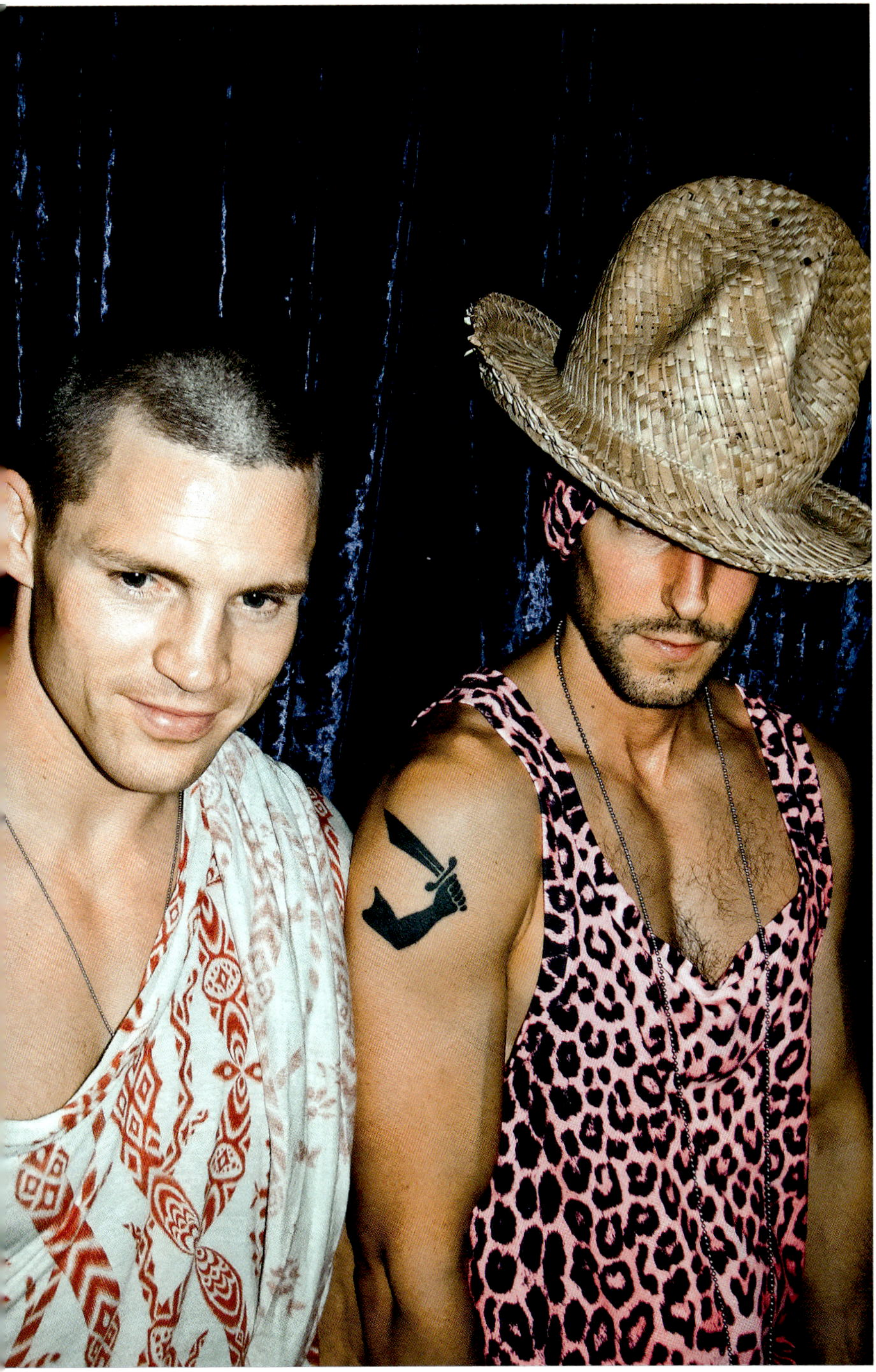

Paradise@Cafe De Paris – Sept 2010

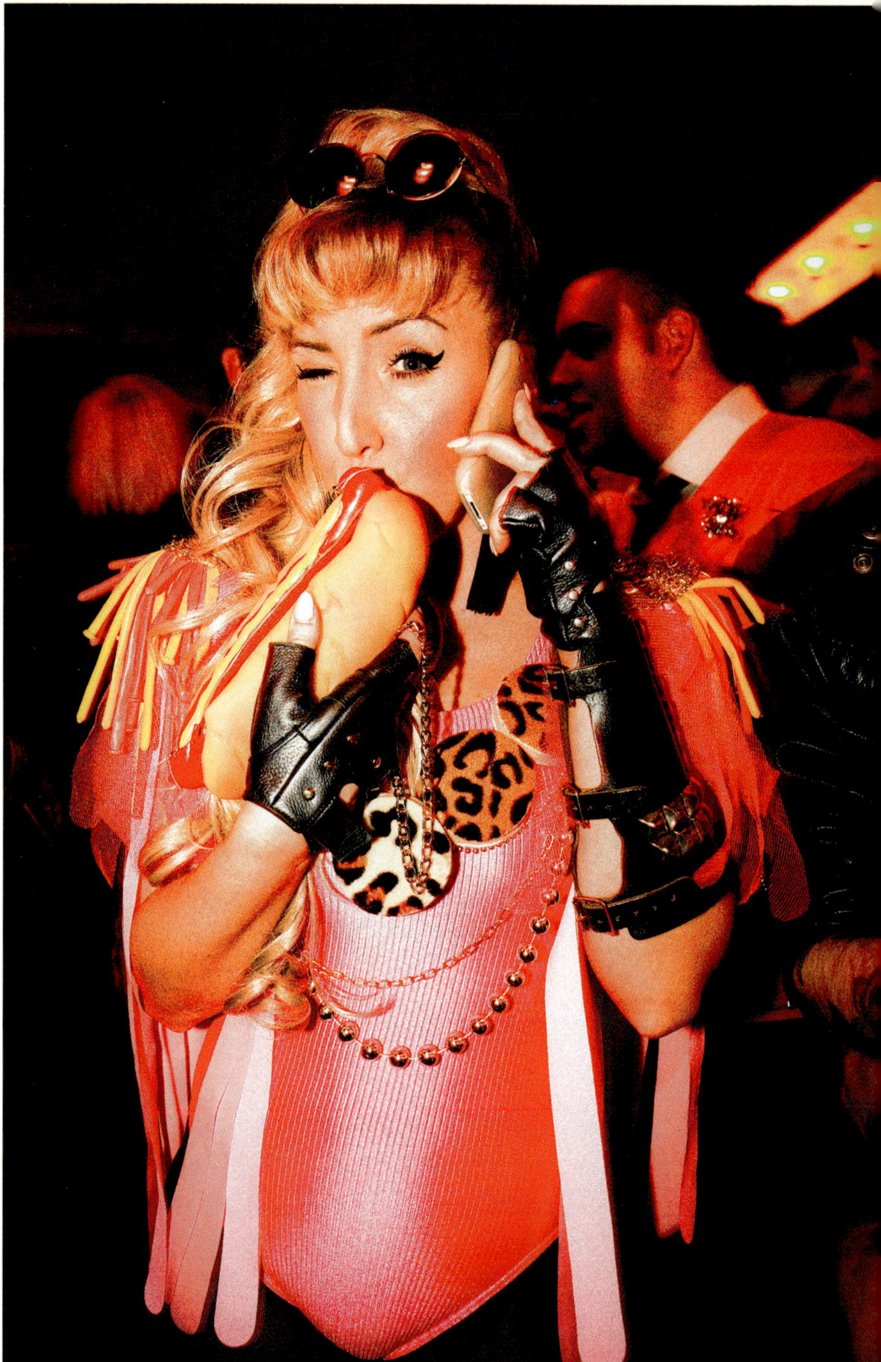

Circus – April 2010

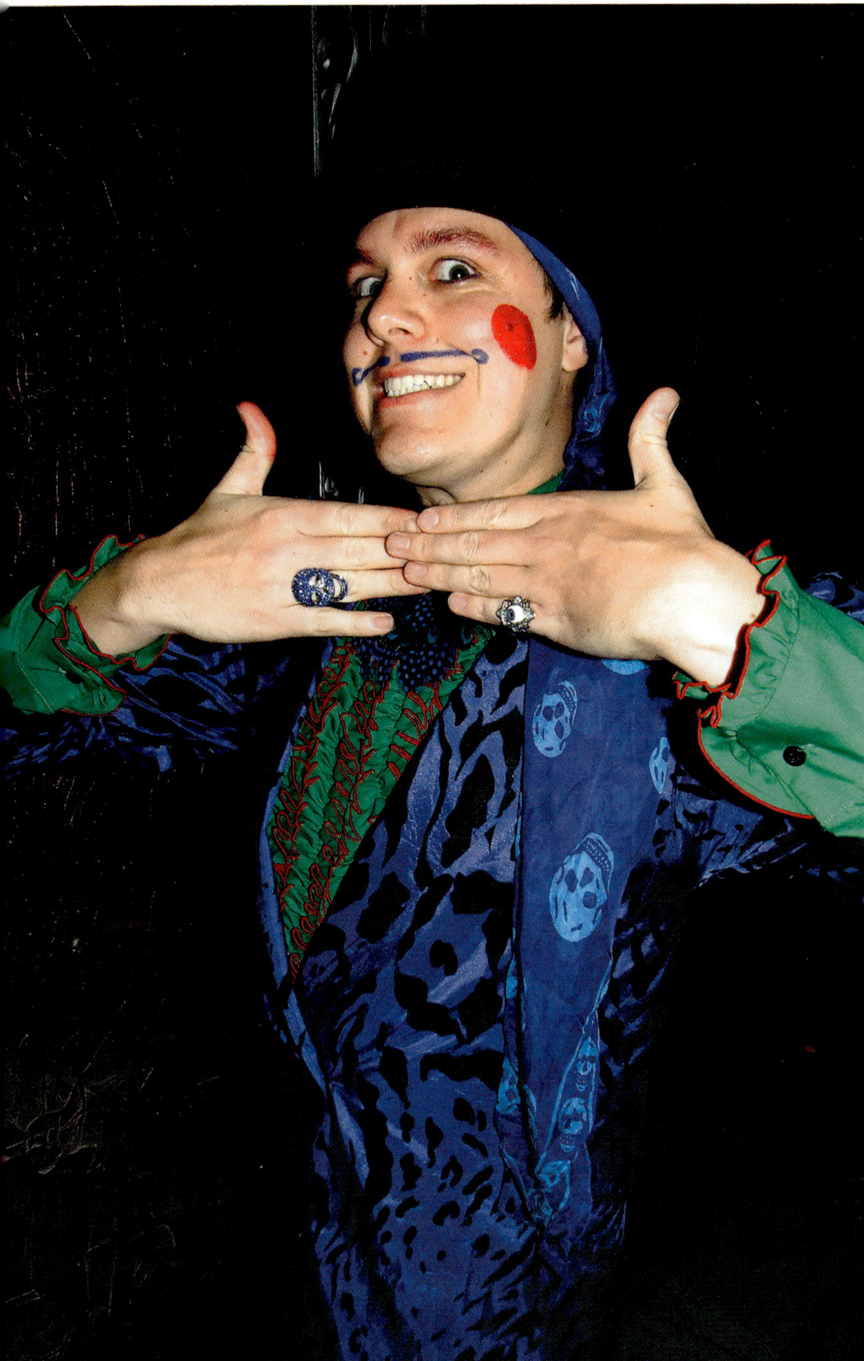

Shabba Dabba Da – Oct 2010

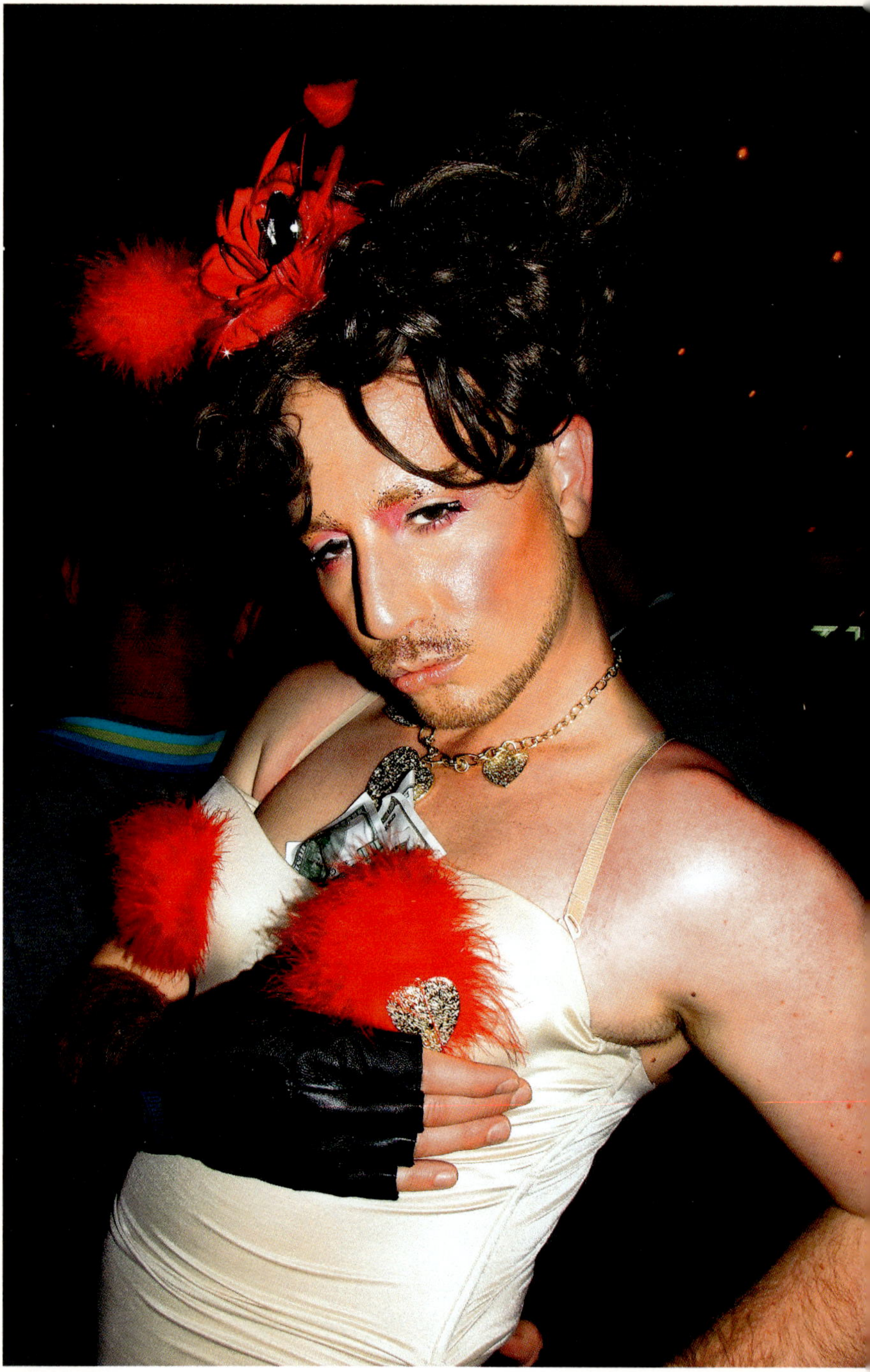

GayBingo@Floridita – Oct 2009

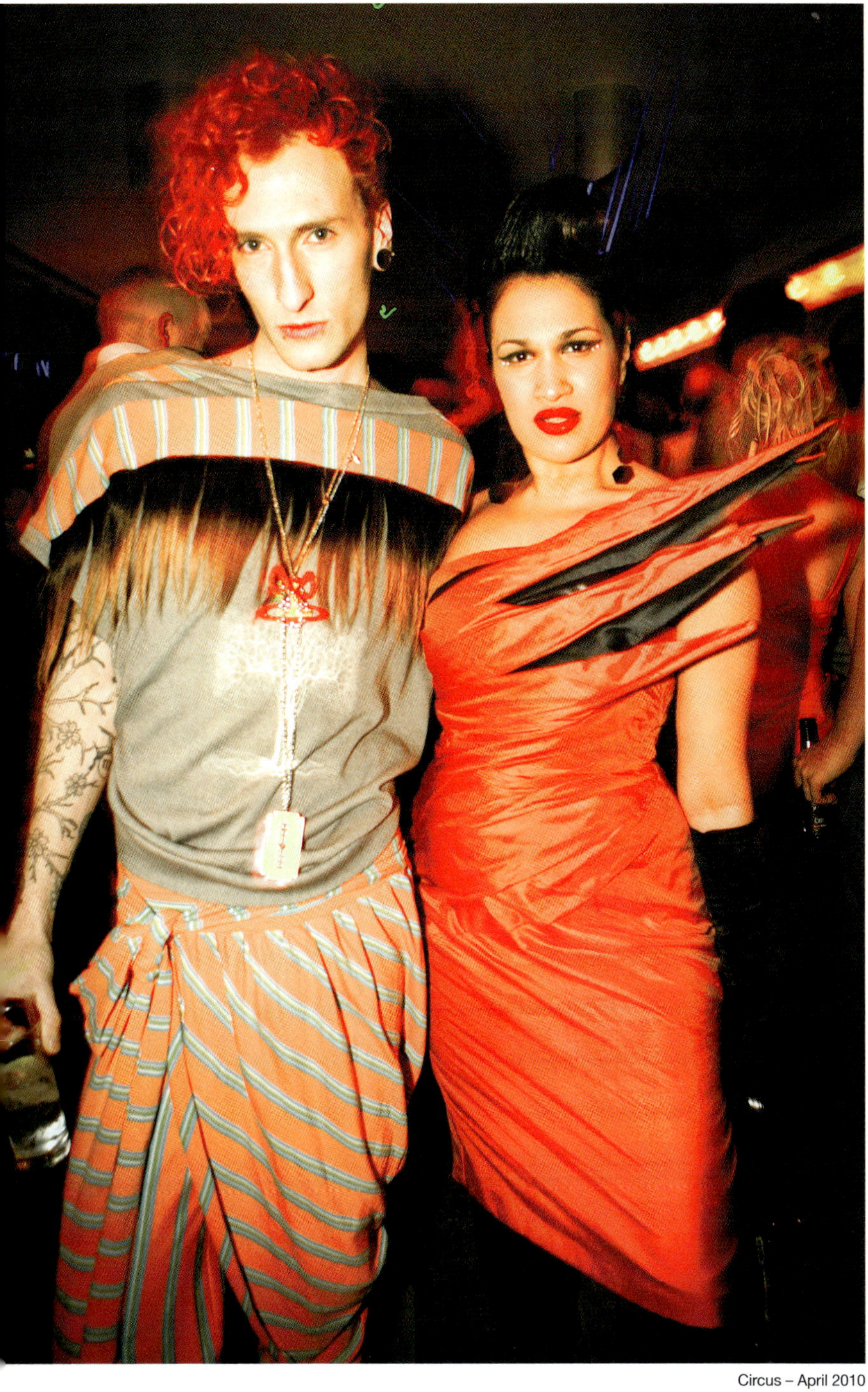

Circus – April 2010

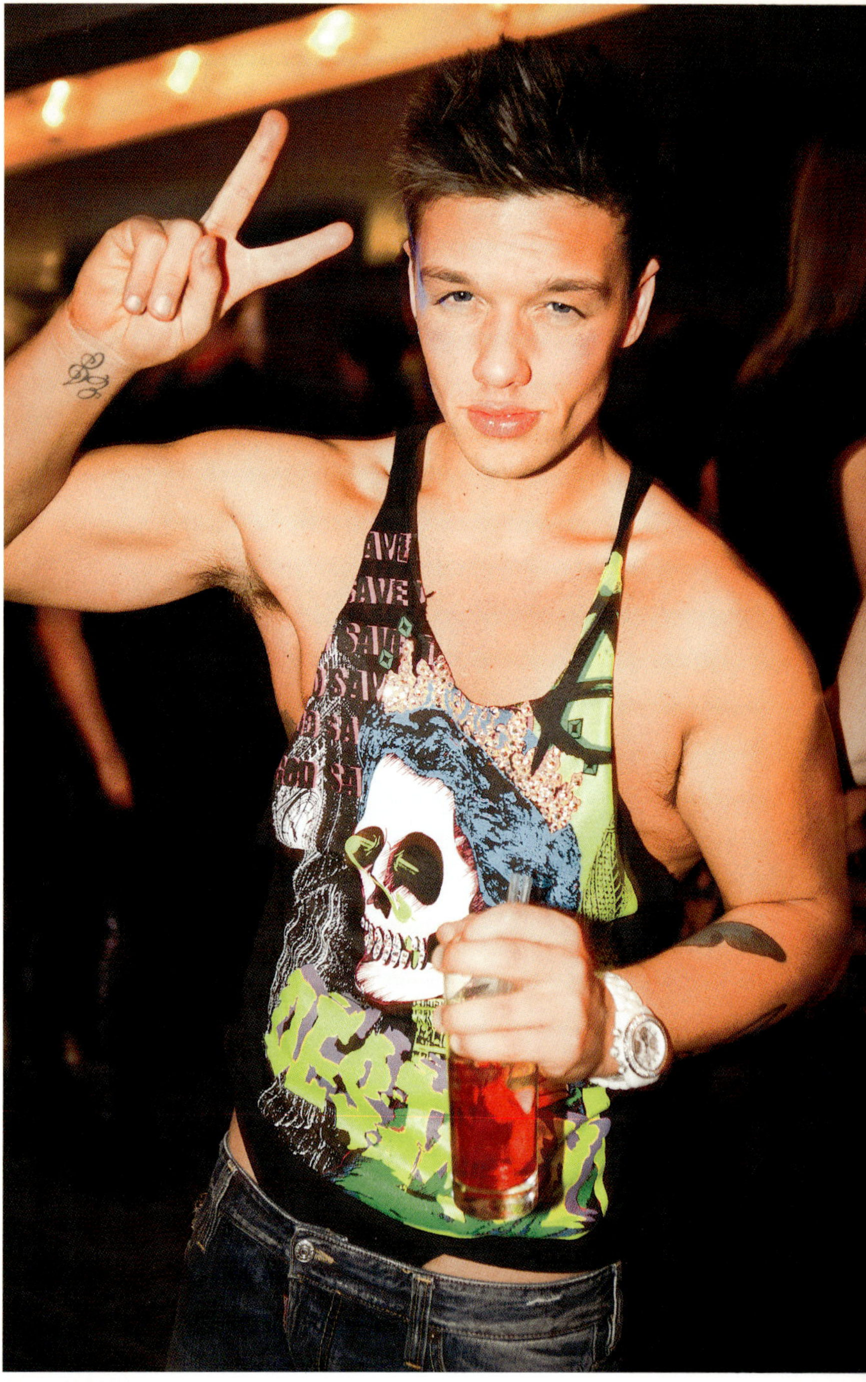

Circus – April 2010

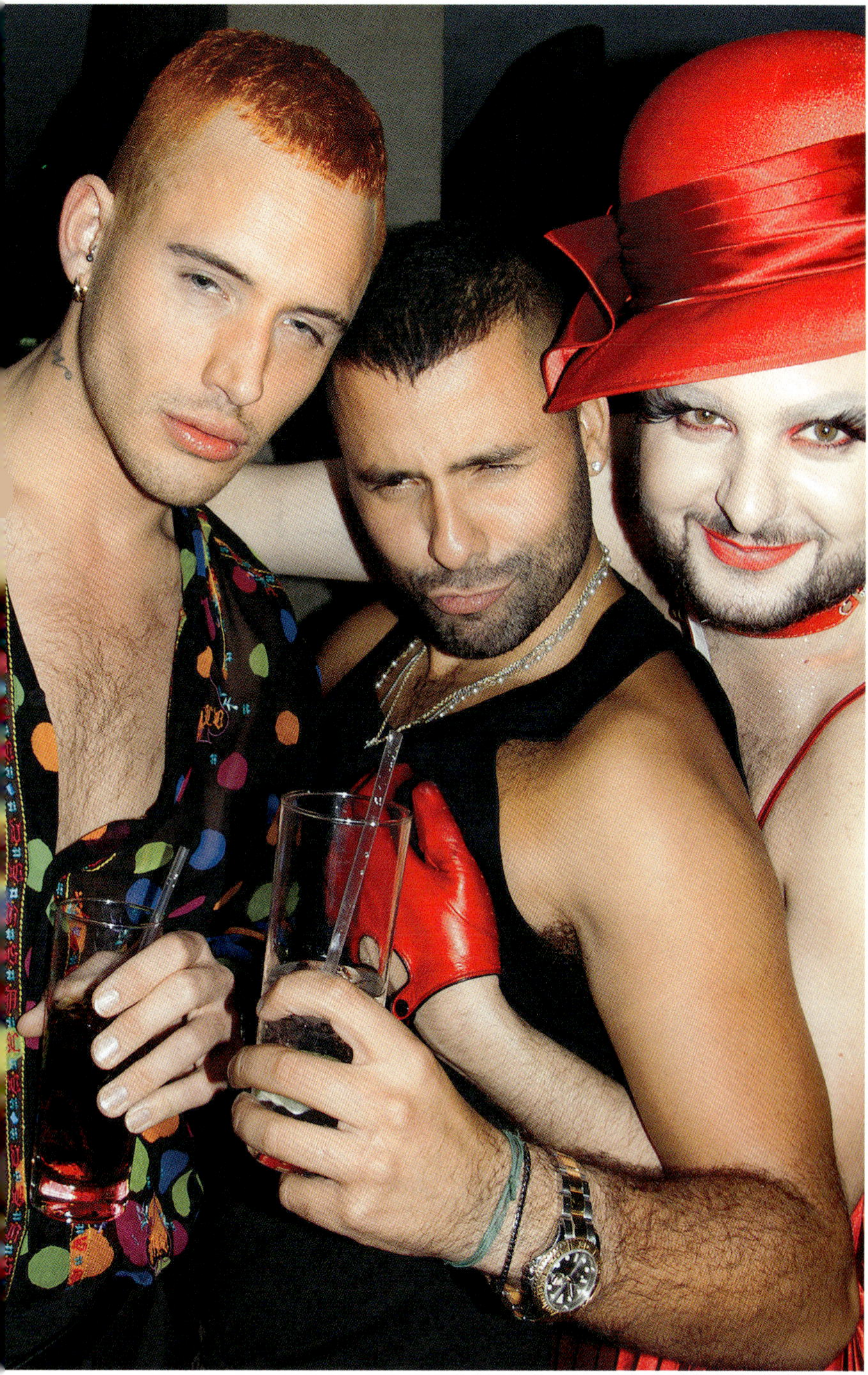

Circus – Sept 2010

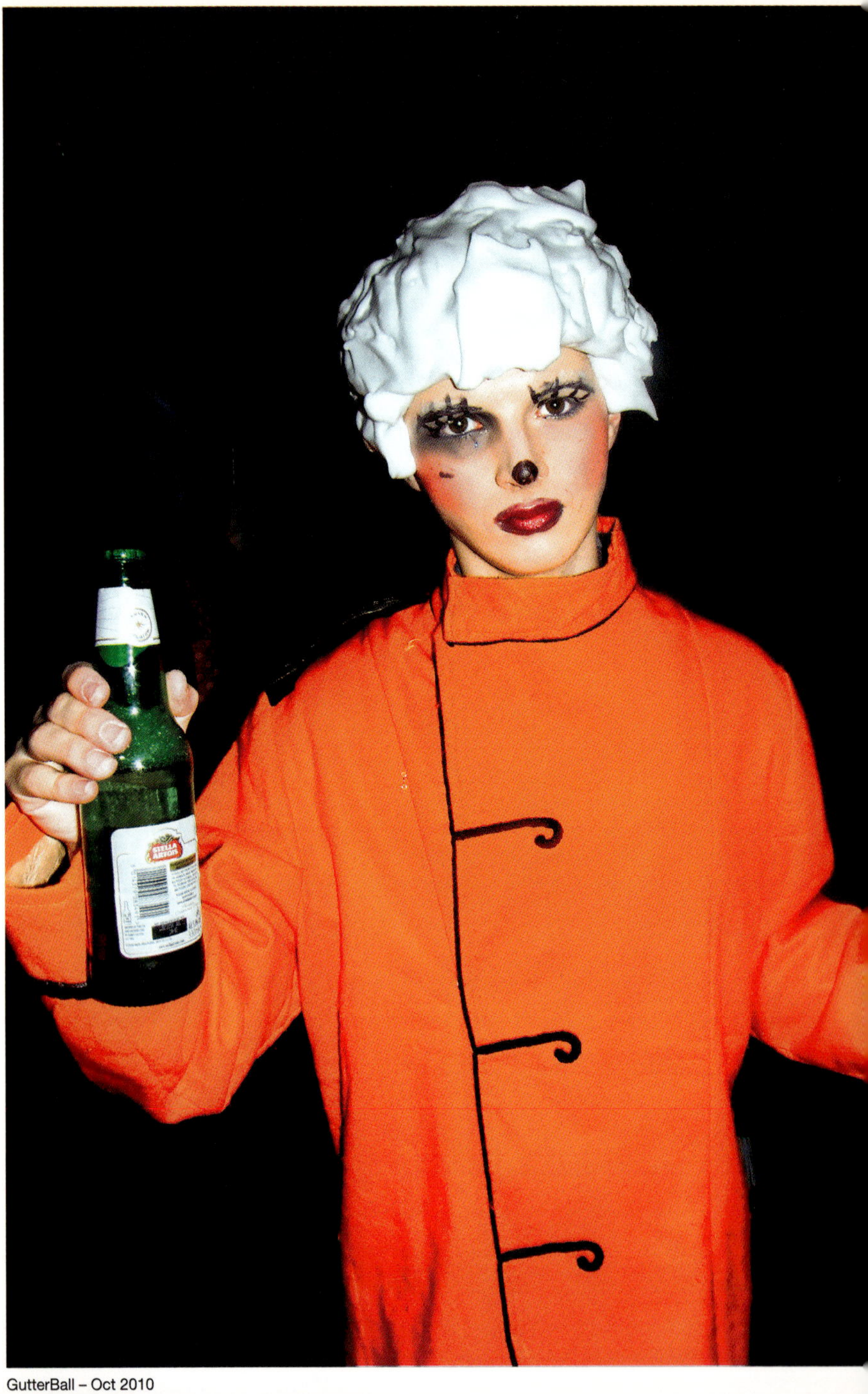

GutterBall – Oct 2010

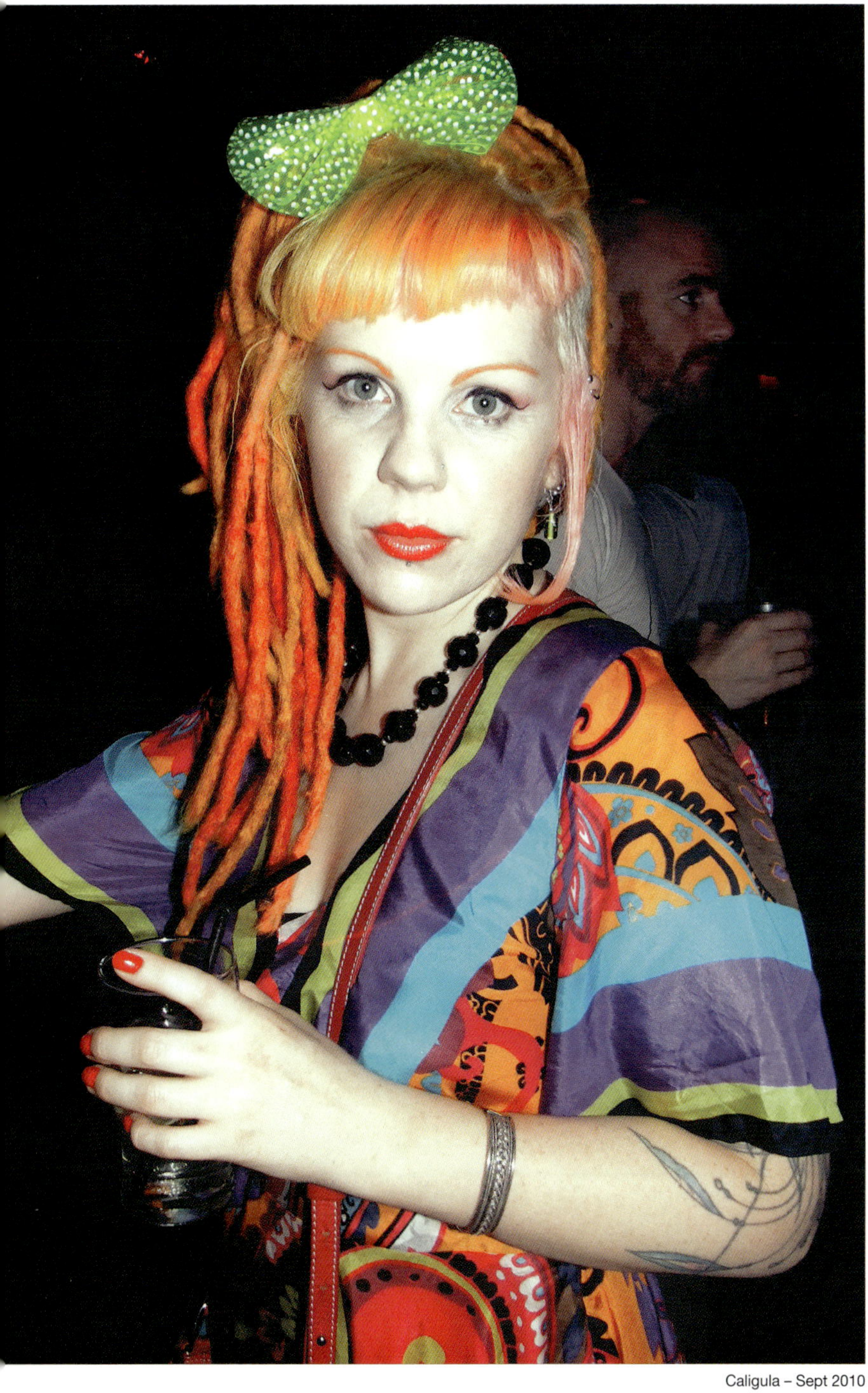

Caligula – Sept 2010

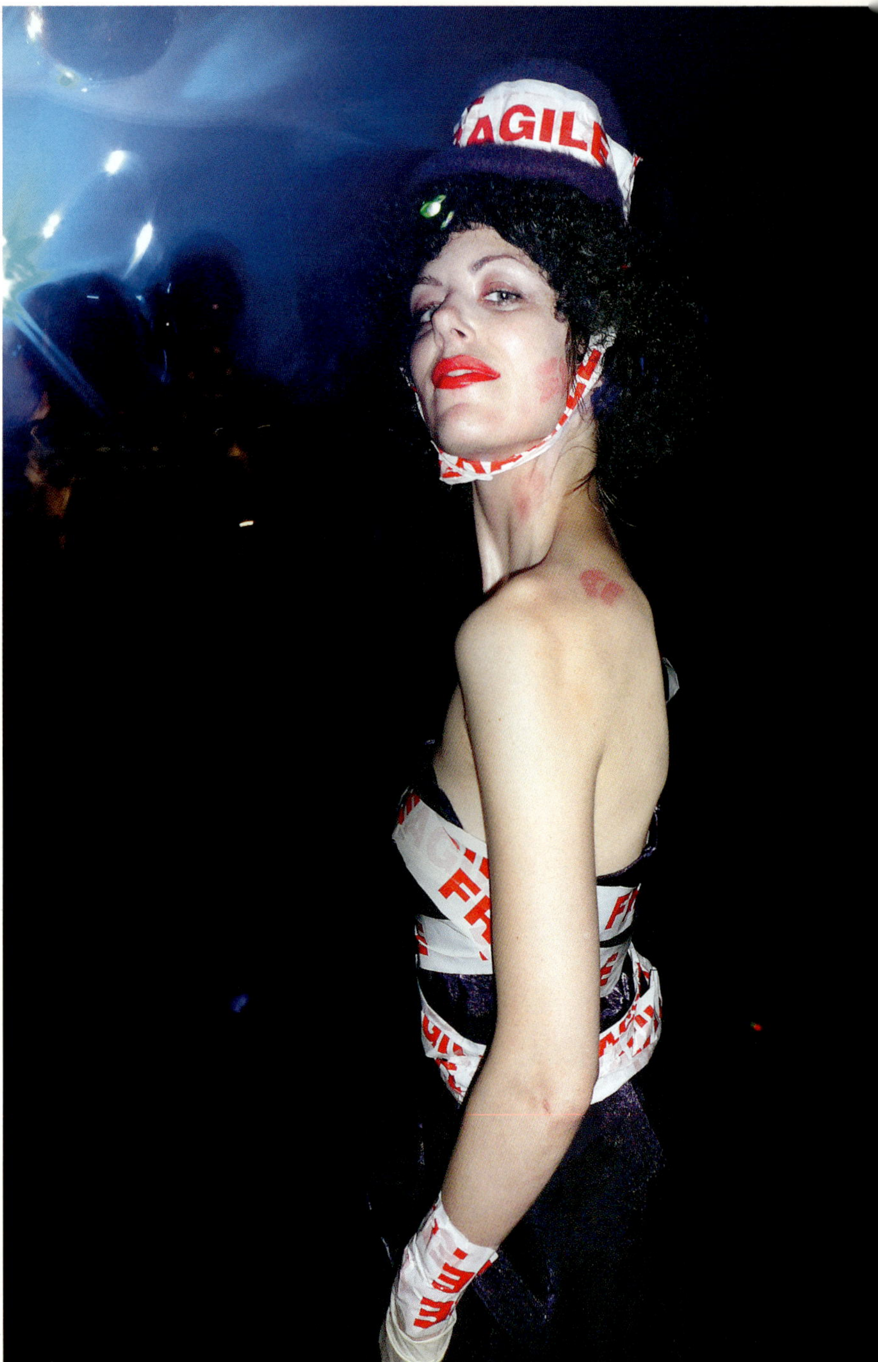

BoomBox – March 2007

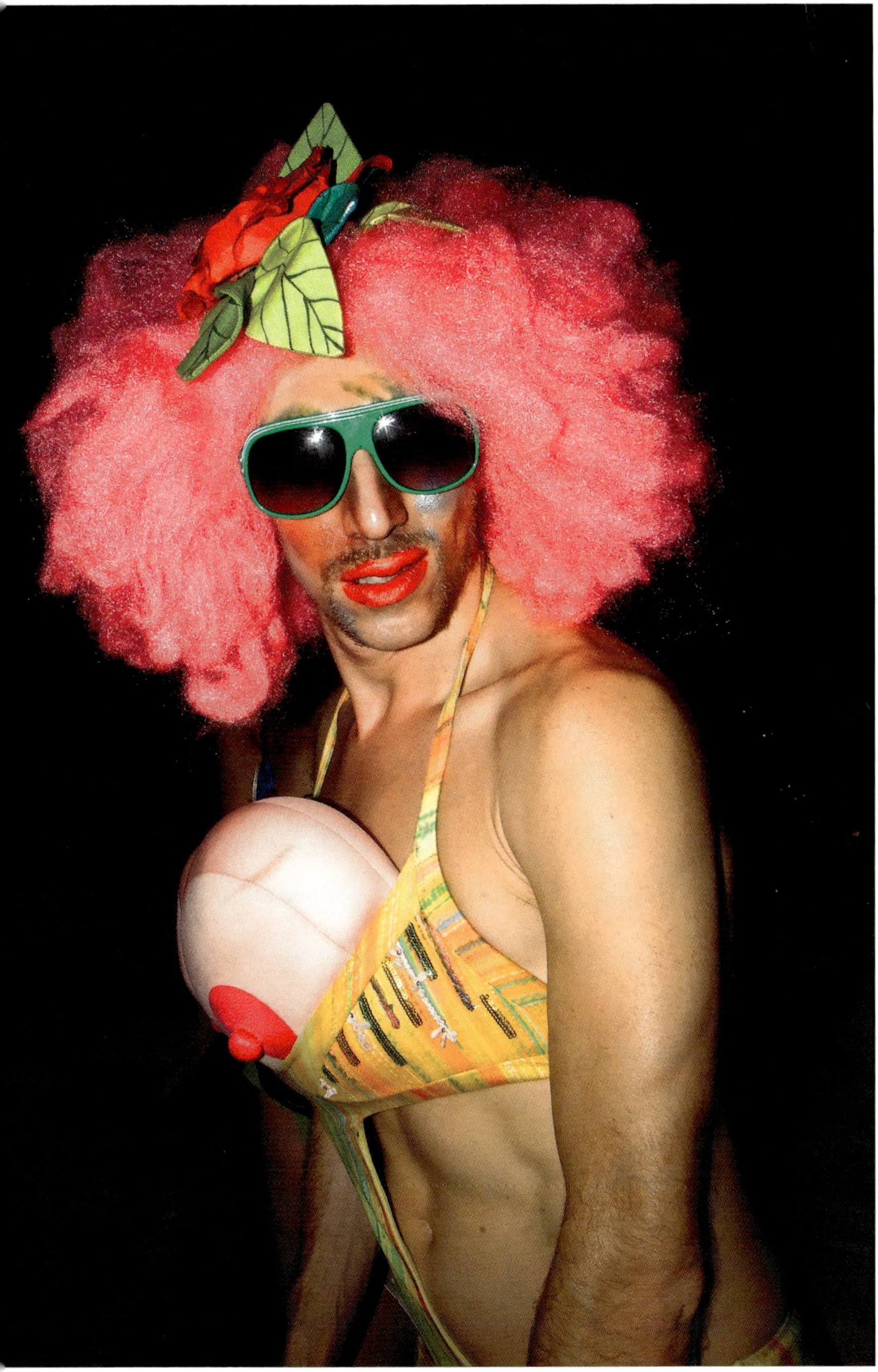
GutterBall – Oct 2010

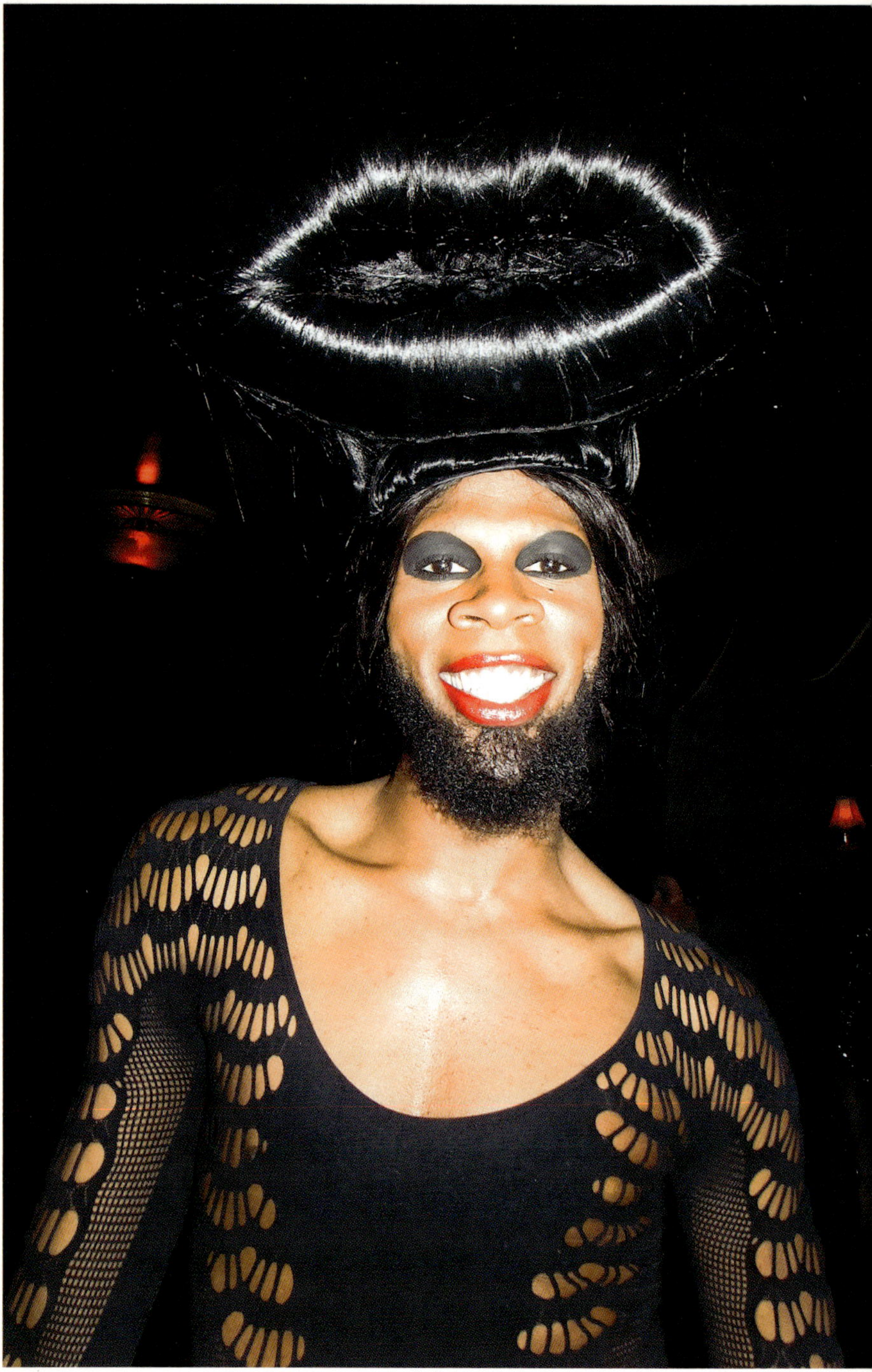

Paradise@Cafe De Paris – Sept 2010

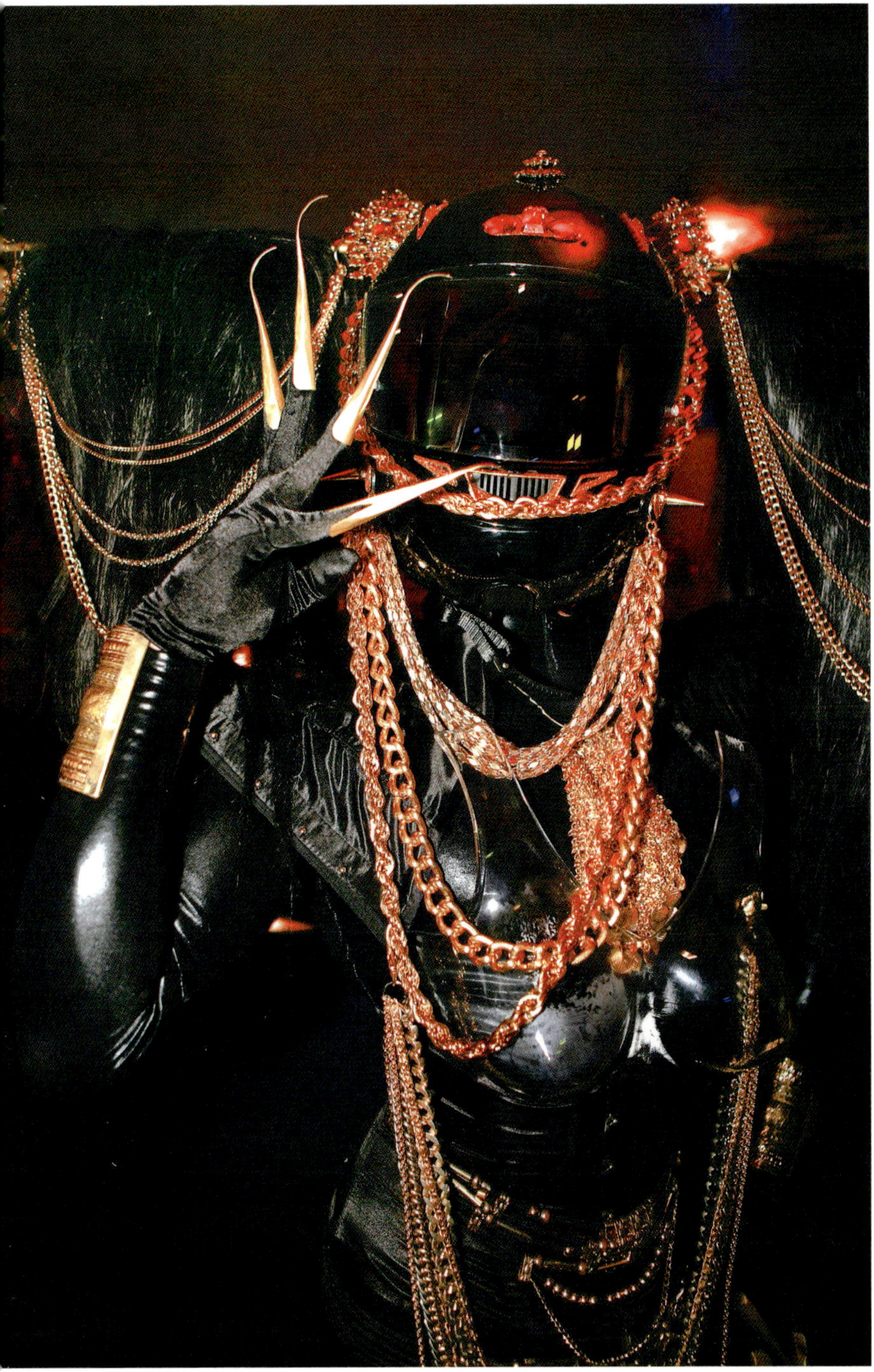

Circus – July 2007

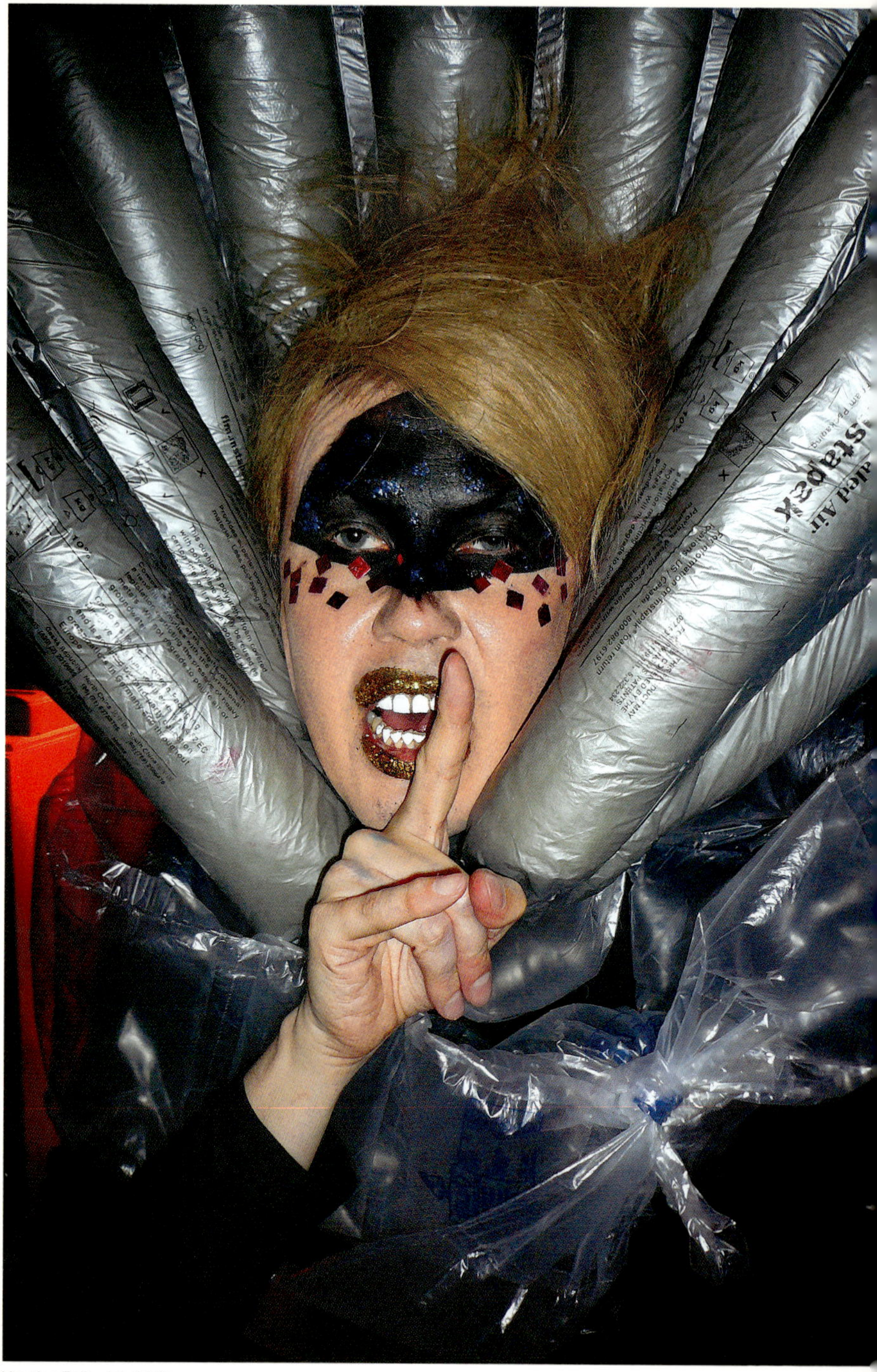

Voguing Ball – July 2007

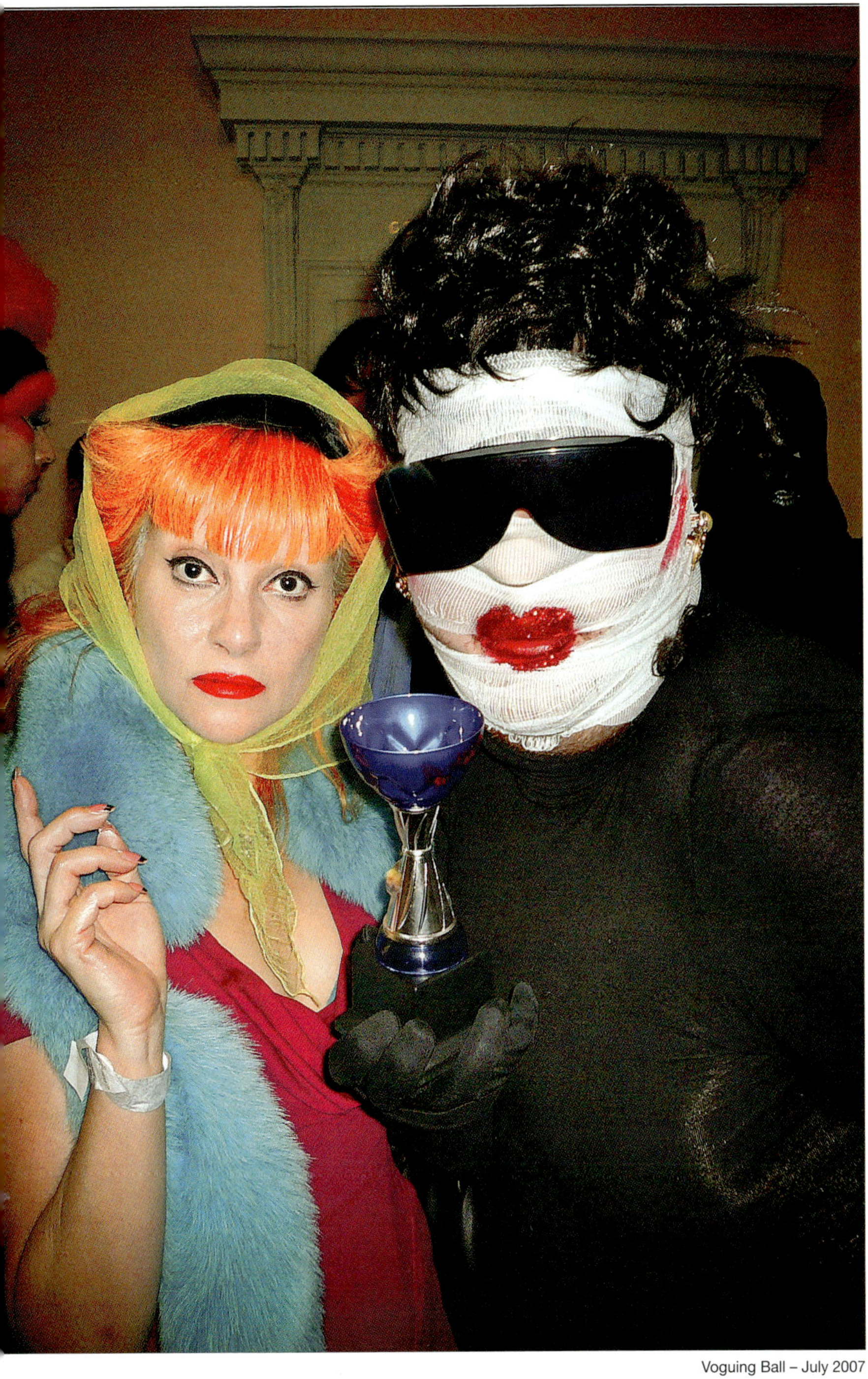

Voguing Ball – July 2007

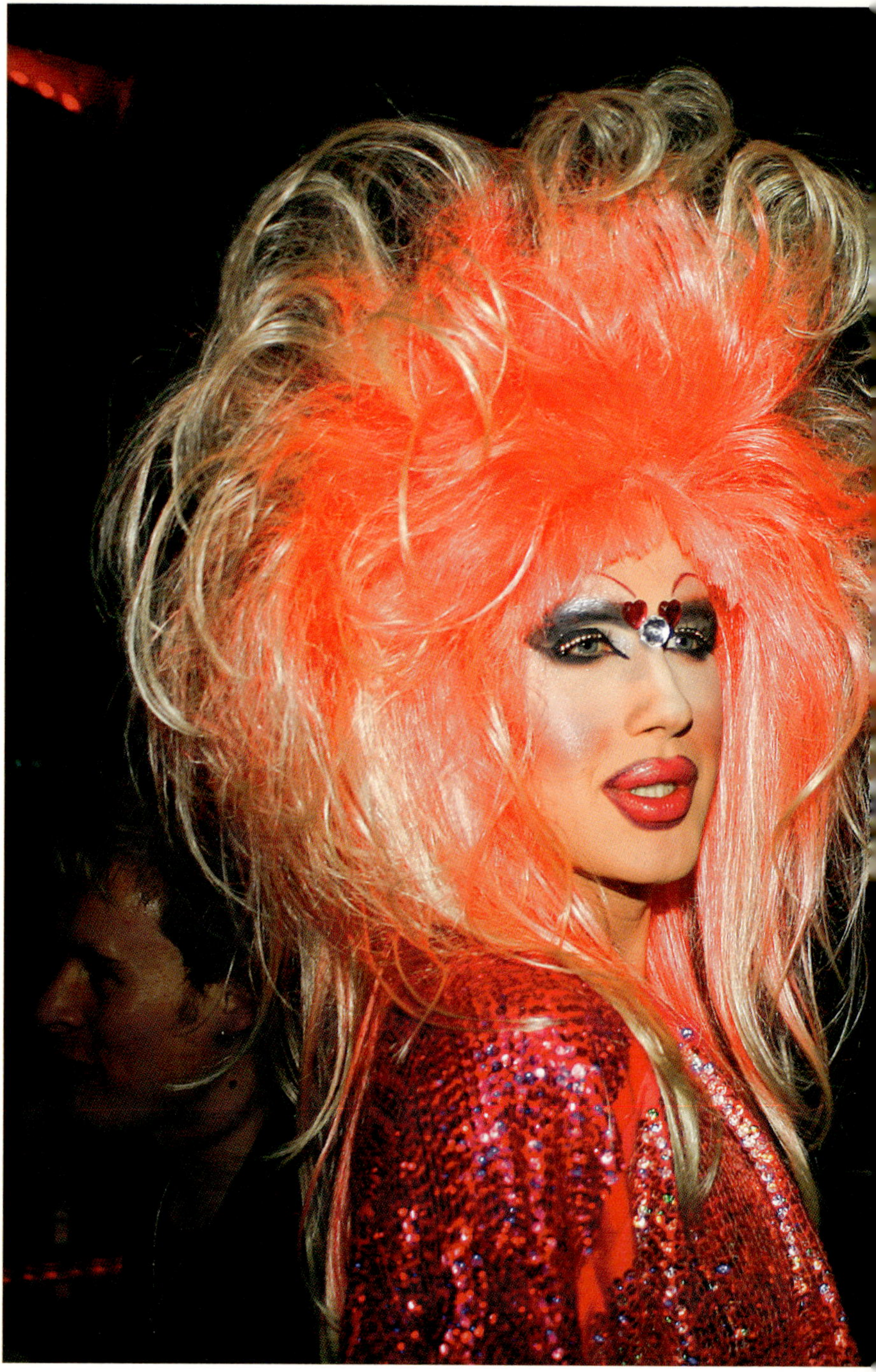

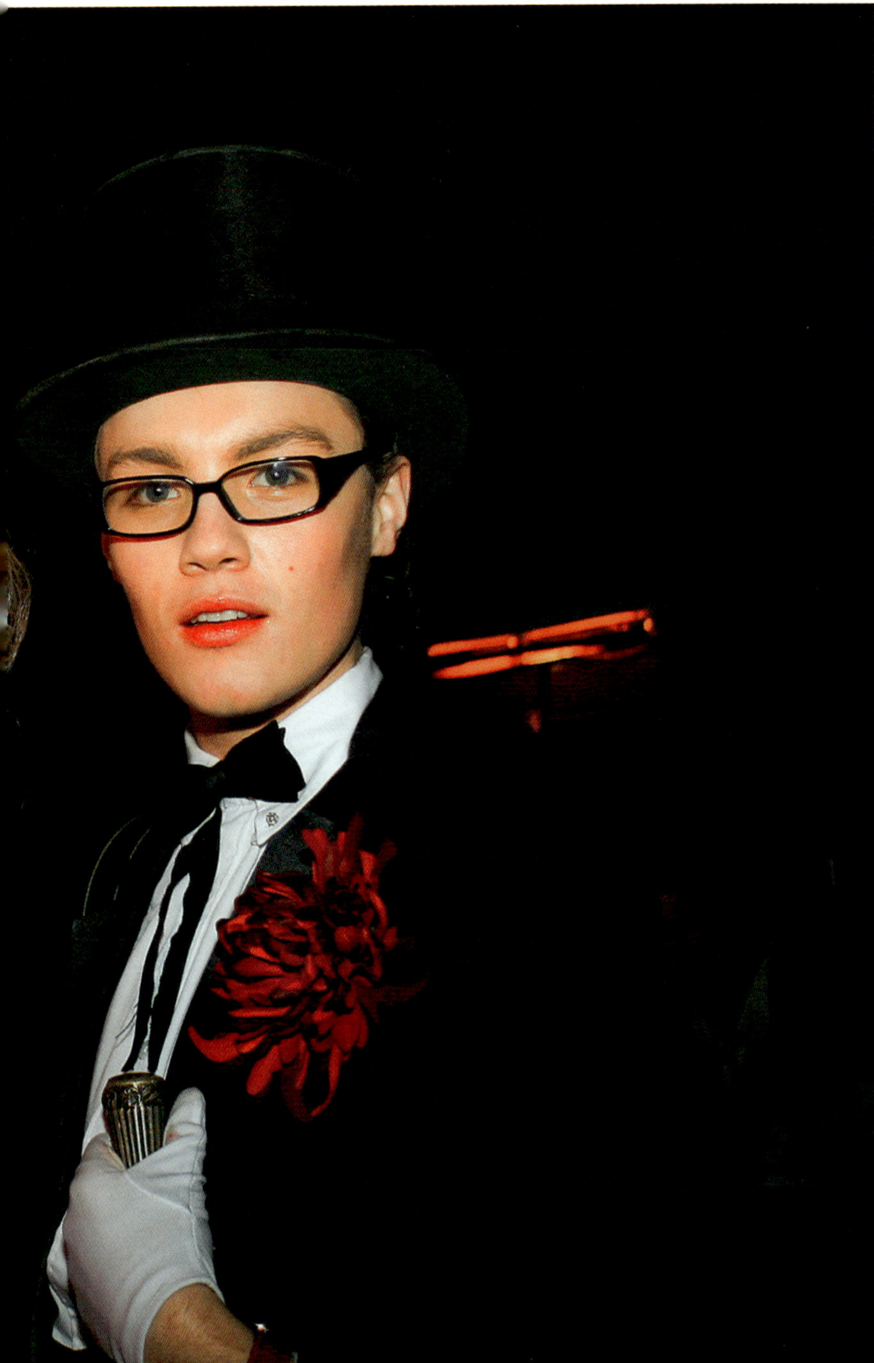

Too2Much – 2006

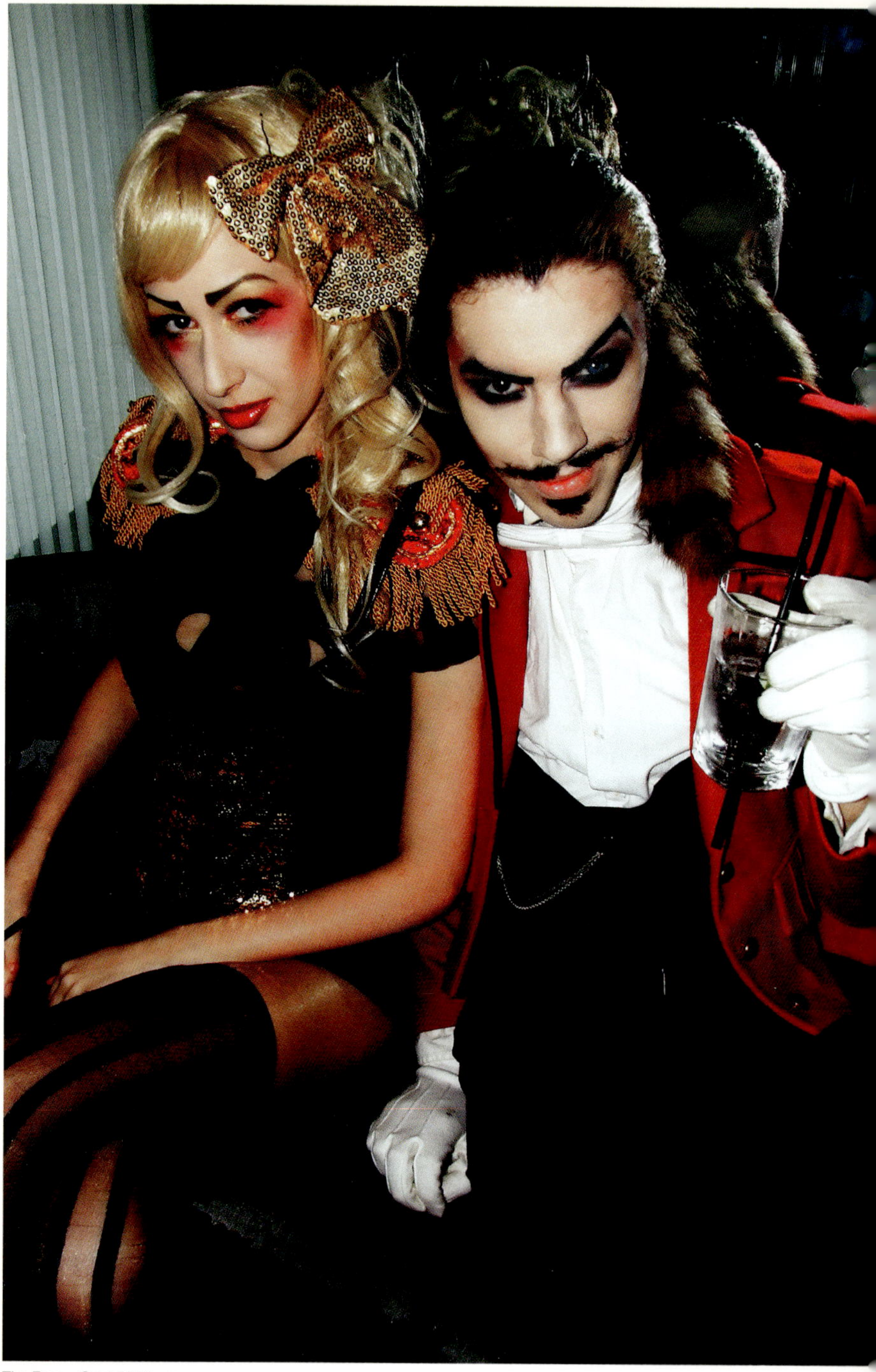

The Face – Sept 2010

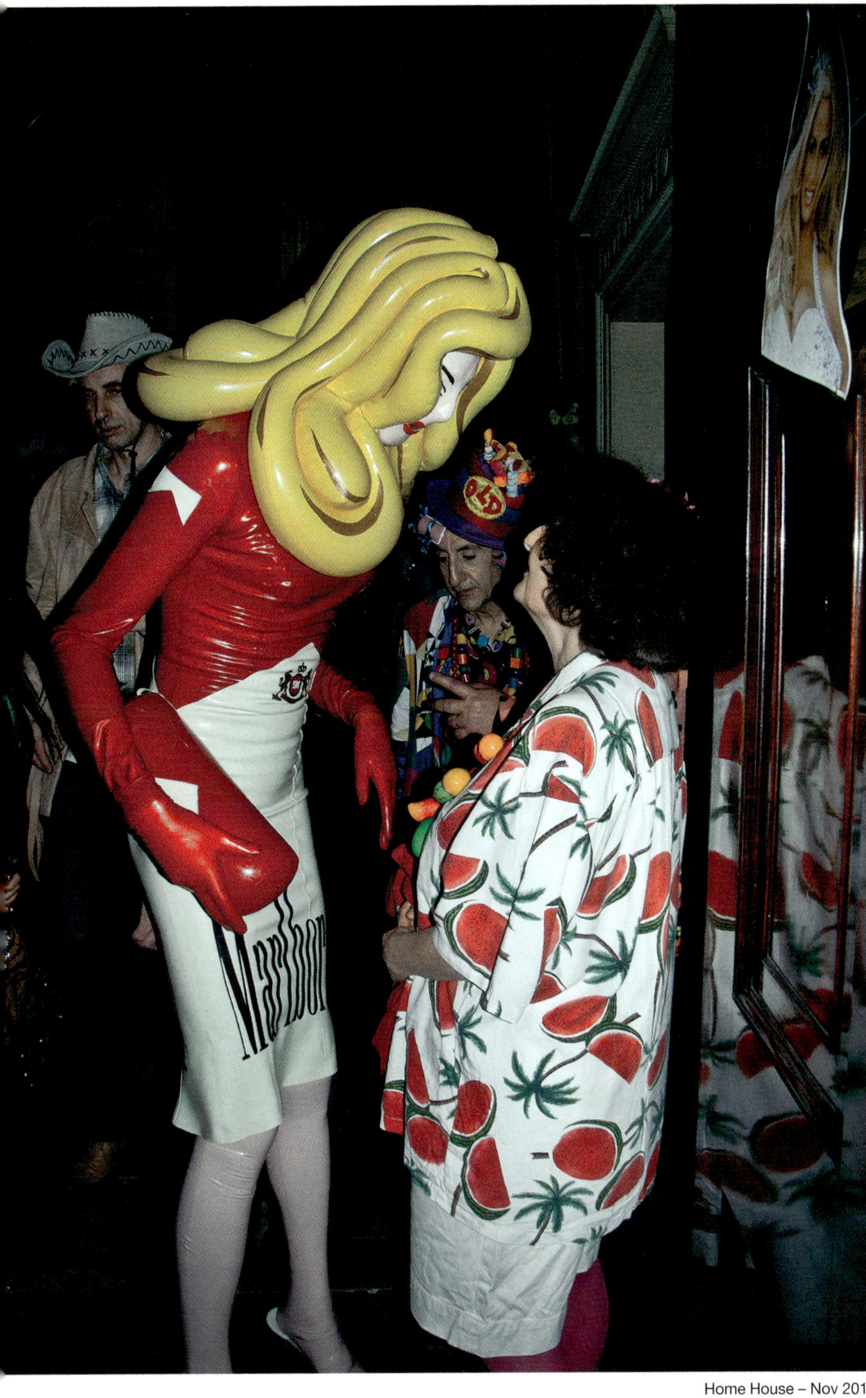

Home House – Nov 2010

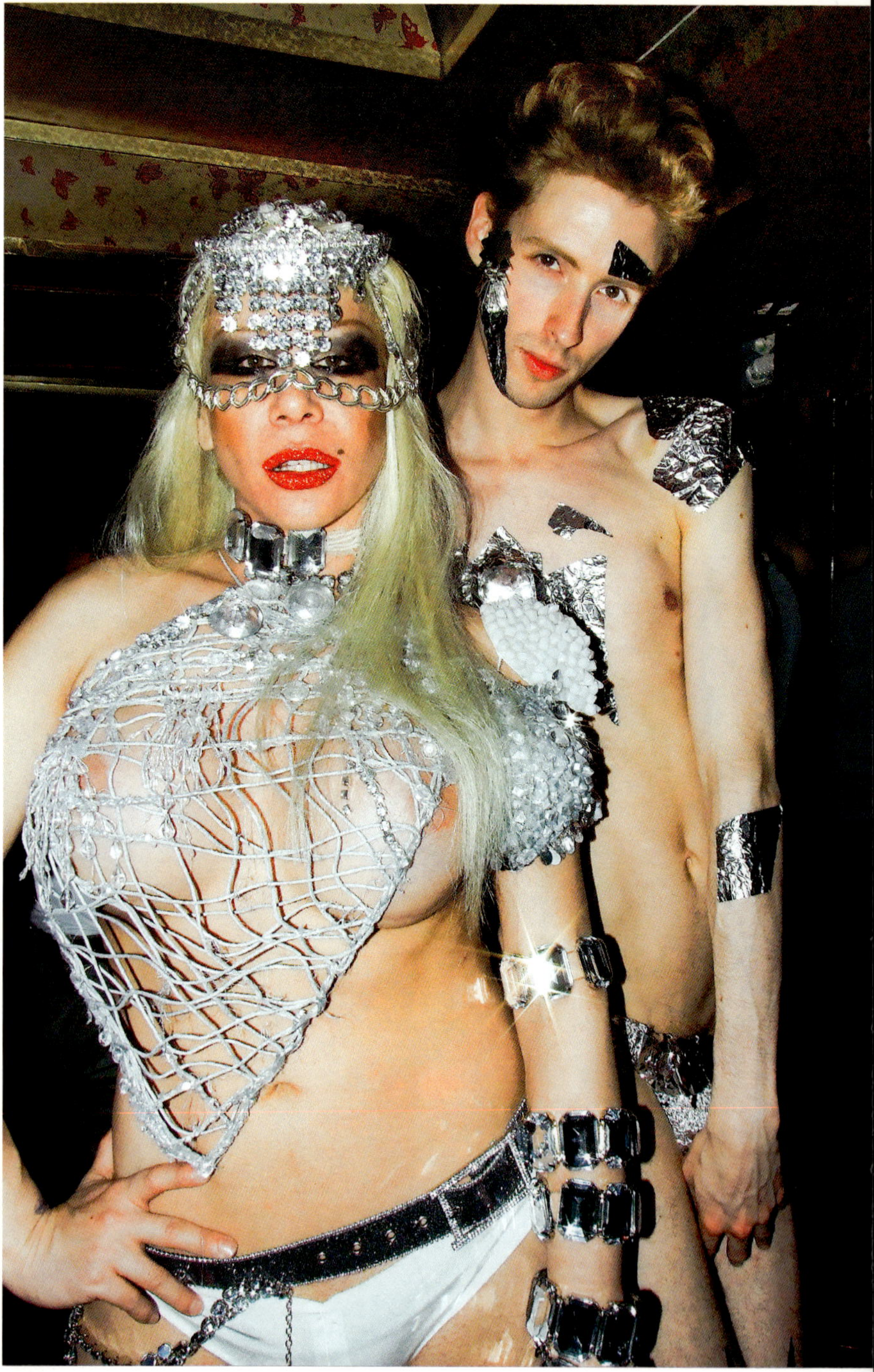

Madame Jojo's – Feb 2010

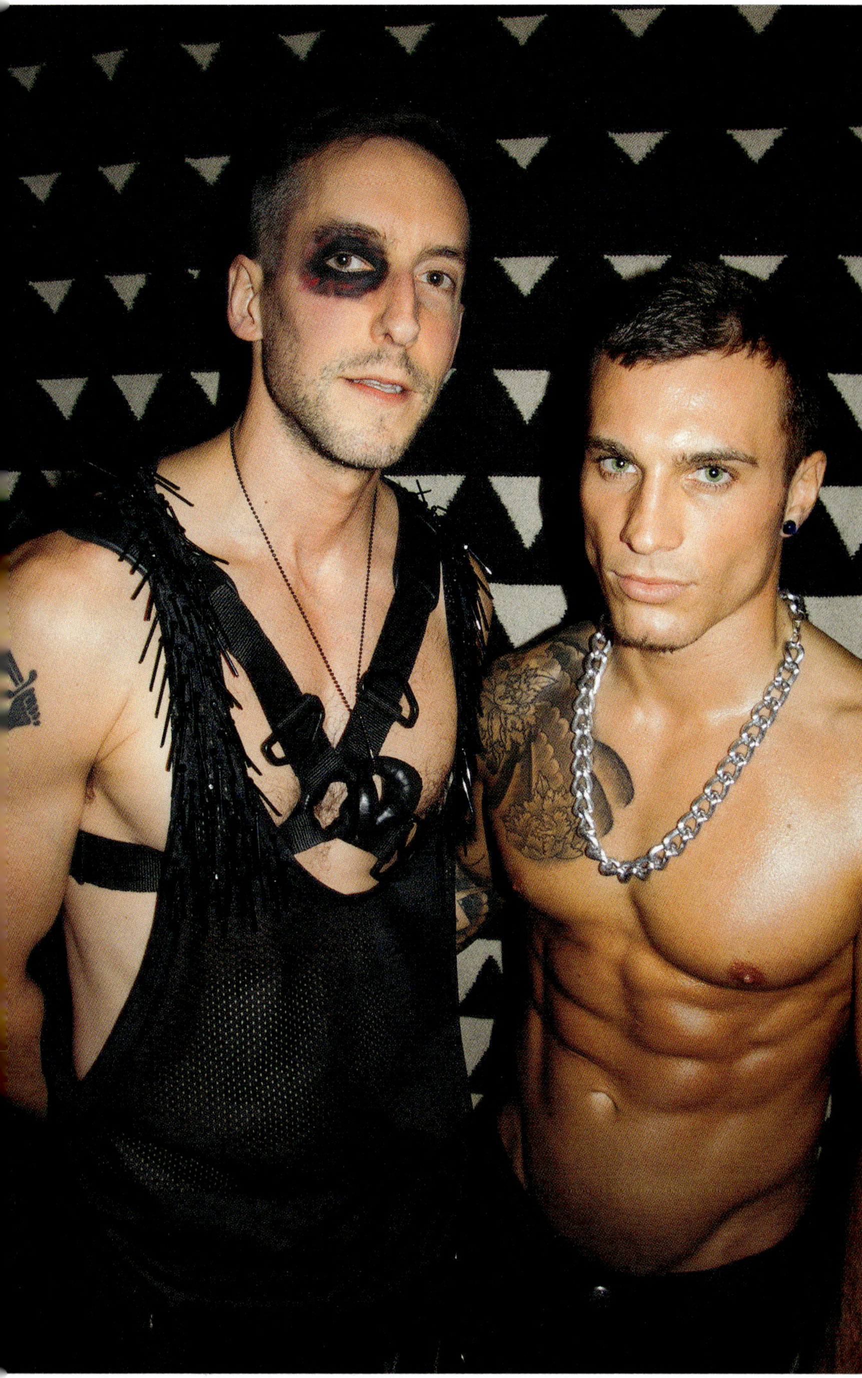

Paramount – Sept 2010

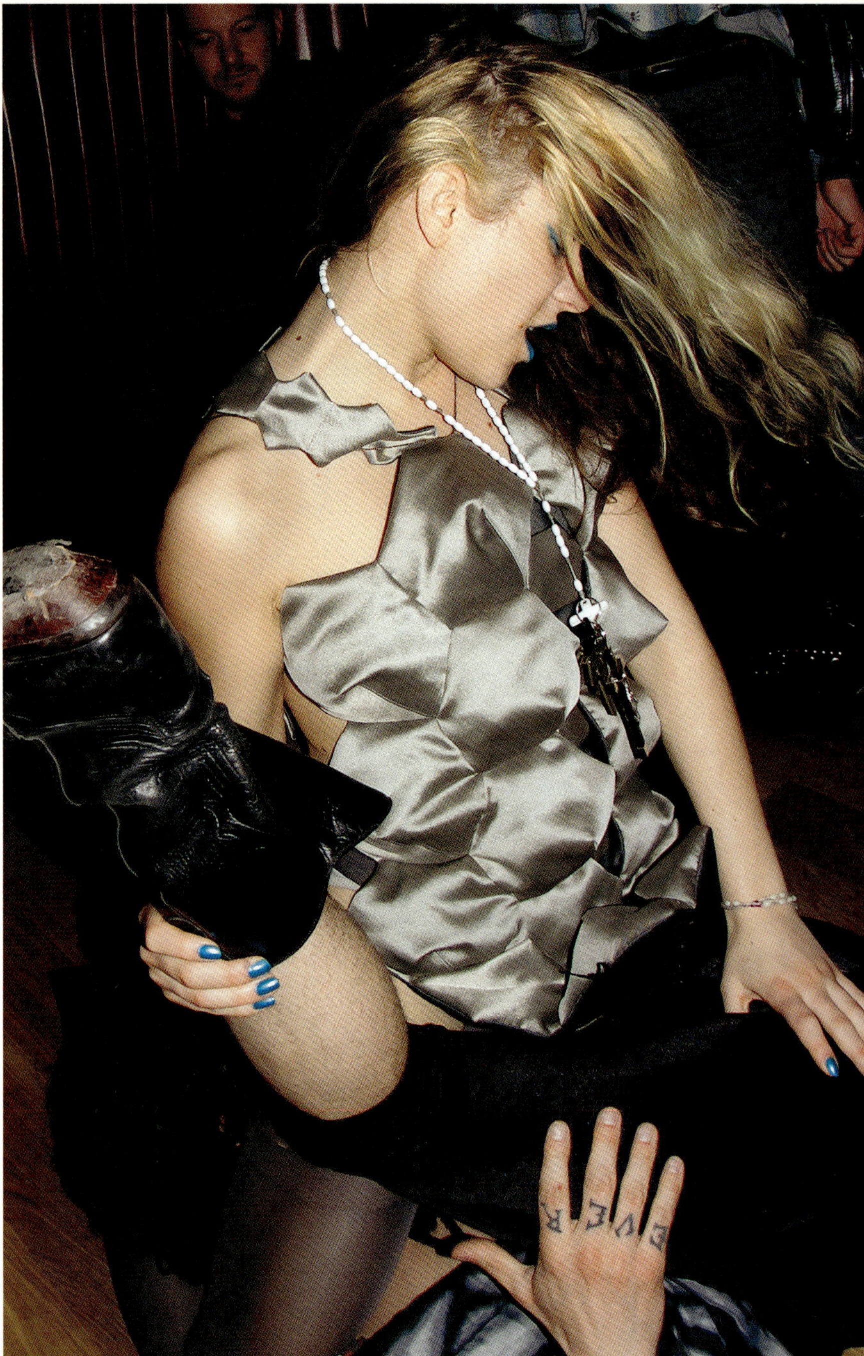

MetBar – April 2010

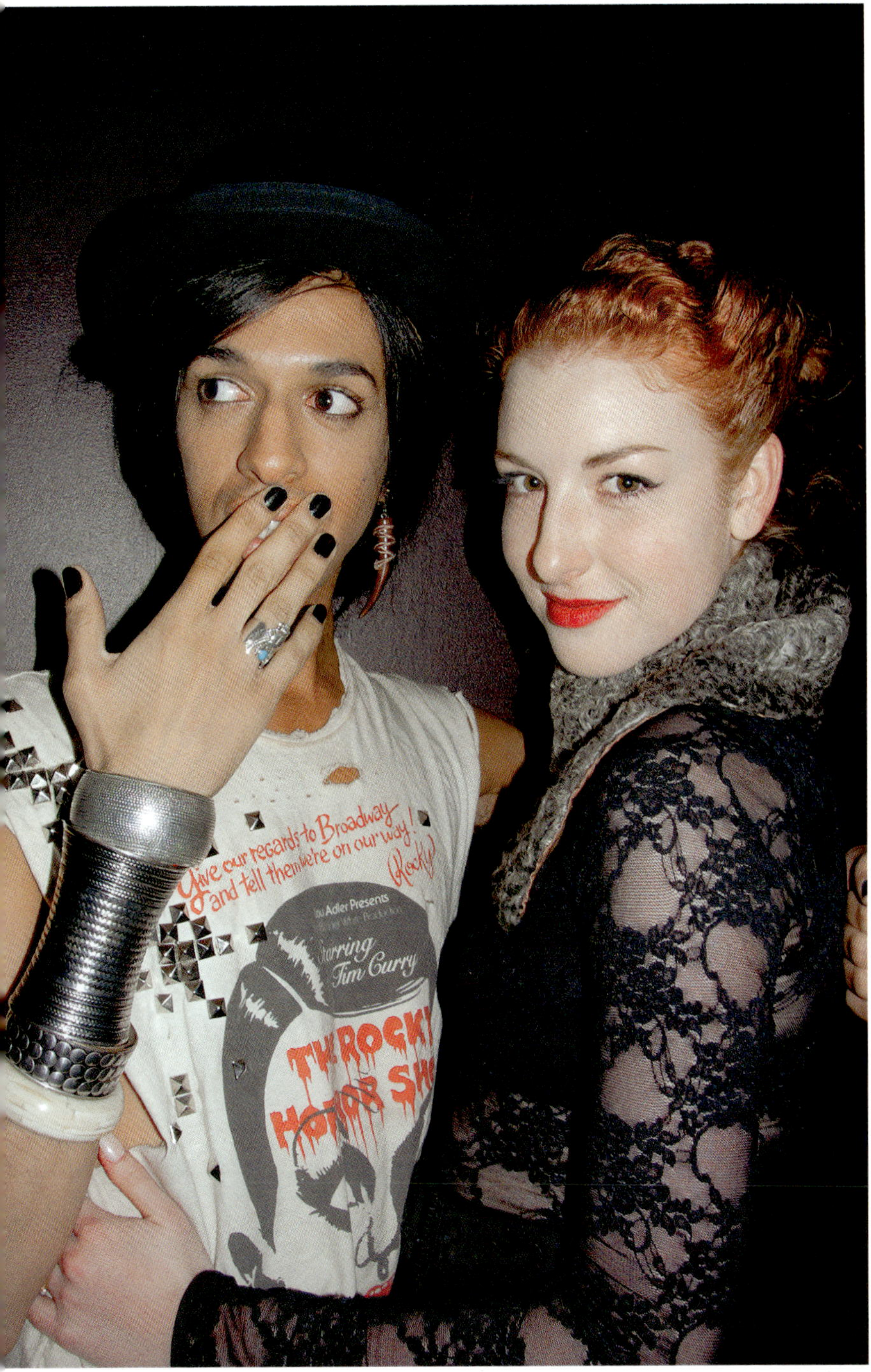

Paramount – Oct 2009

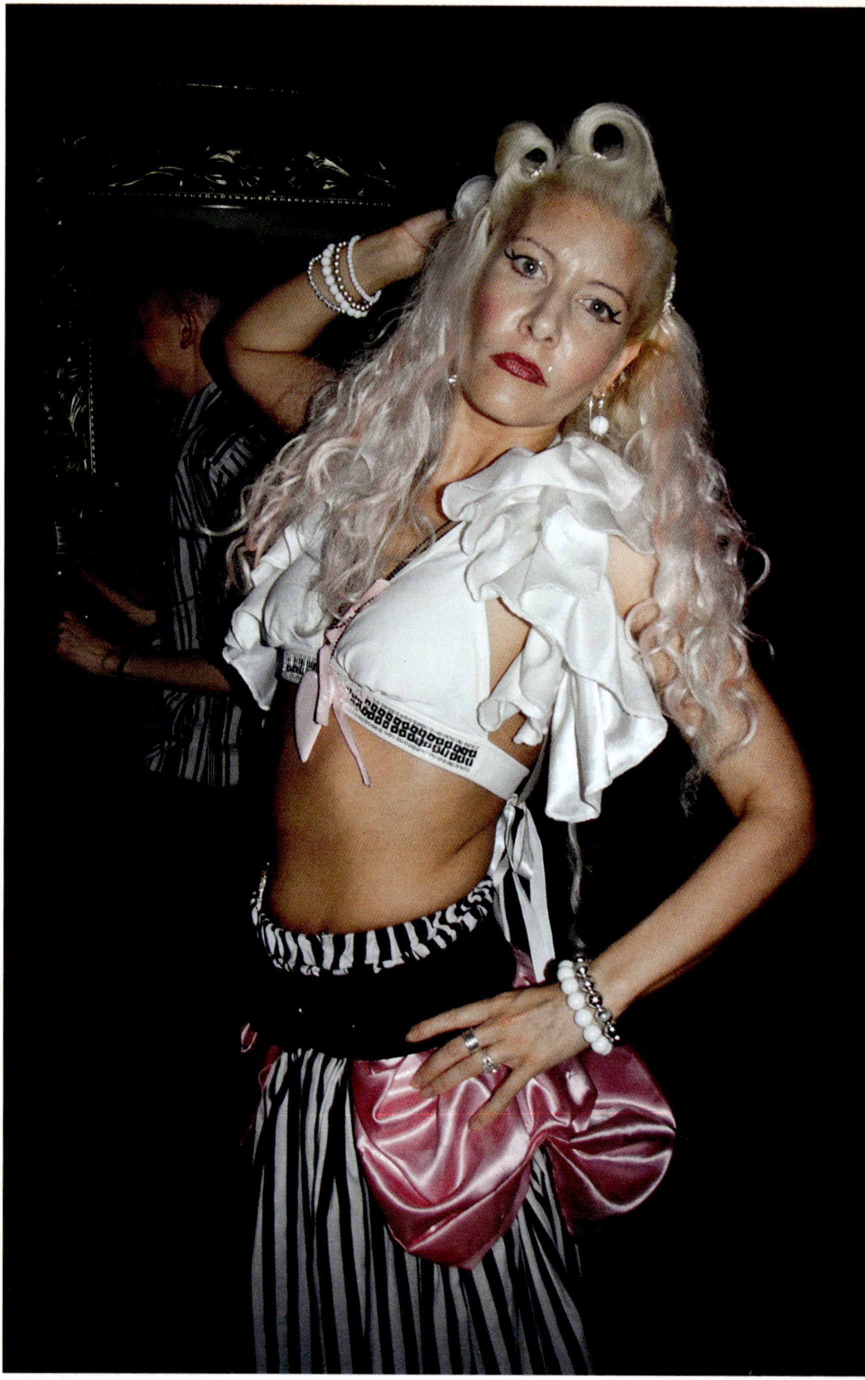

Shabba Dabba Da – Sept 2010

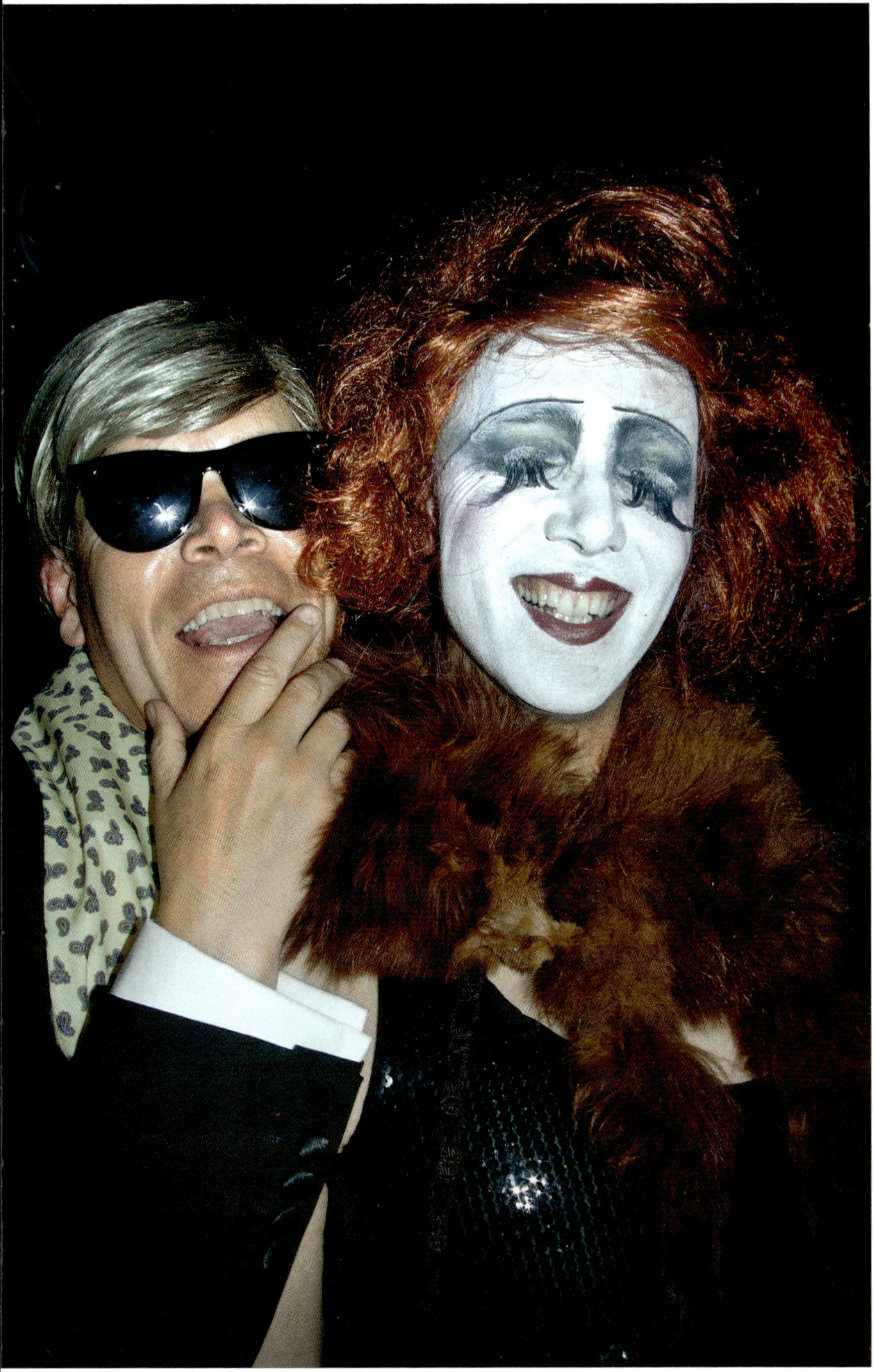

The Face – Oct 2010

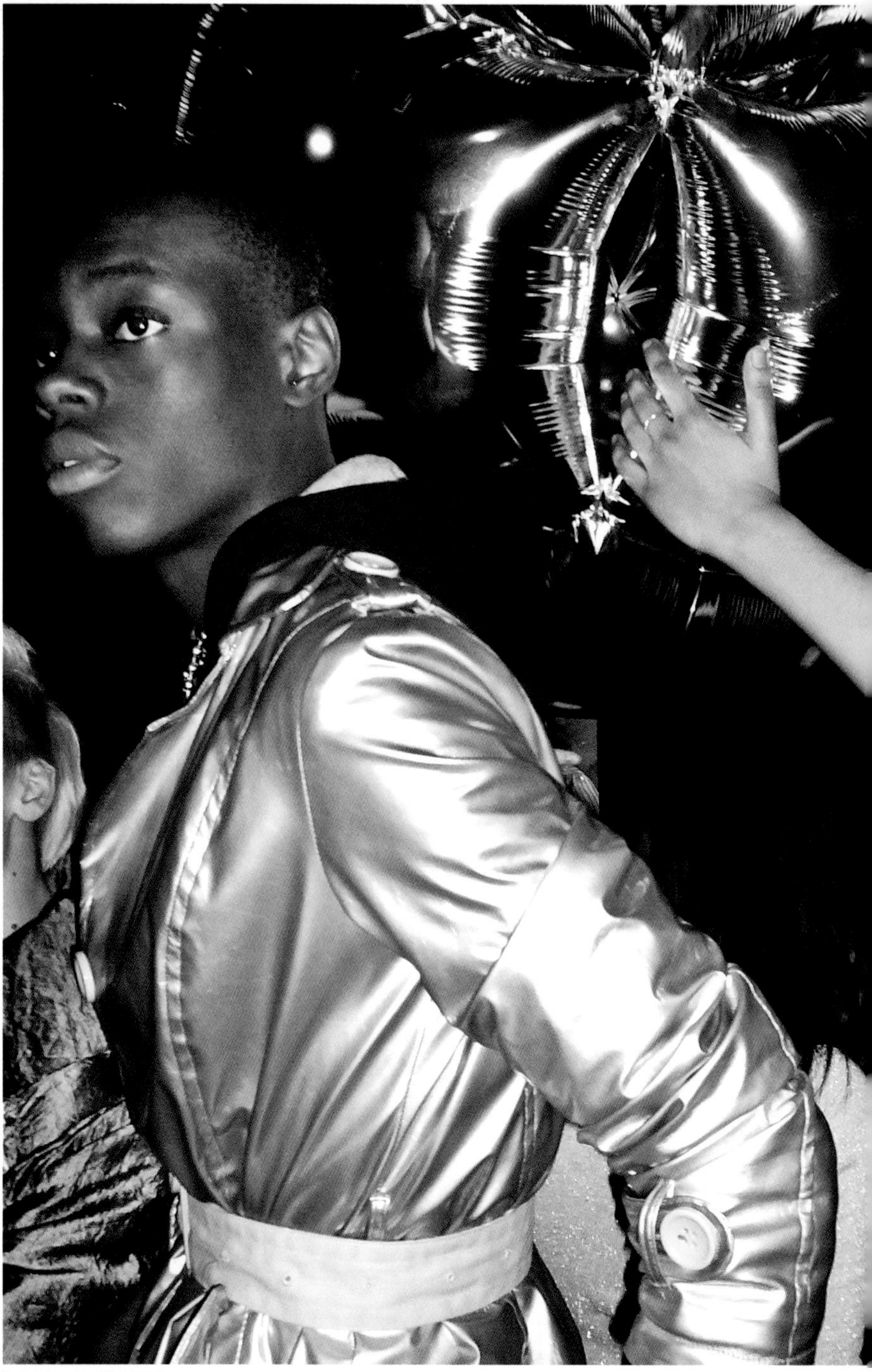

Bungalow 8 – May 2008

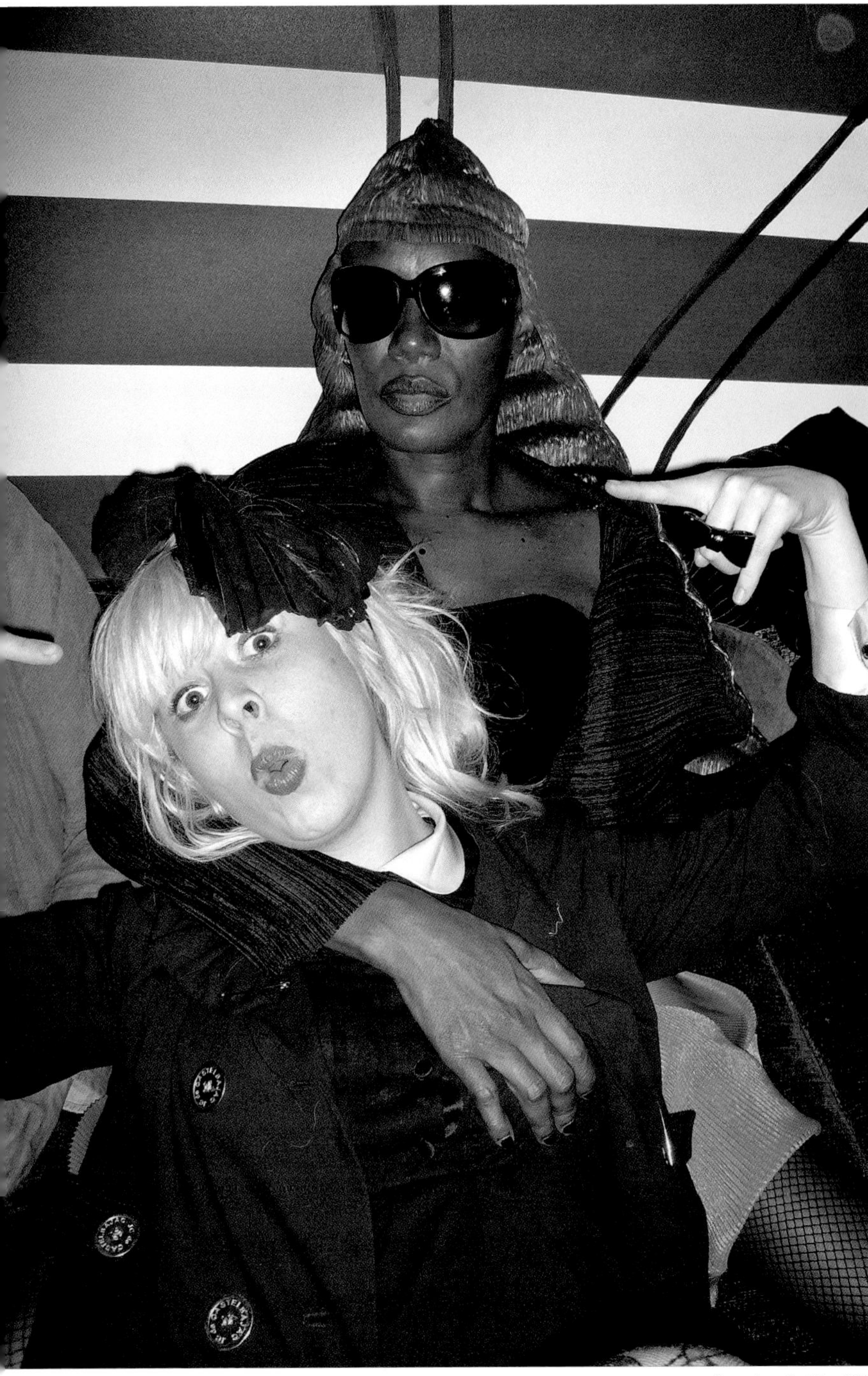

Bungalow 8 – May 2008

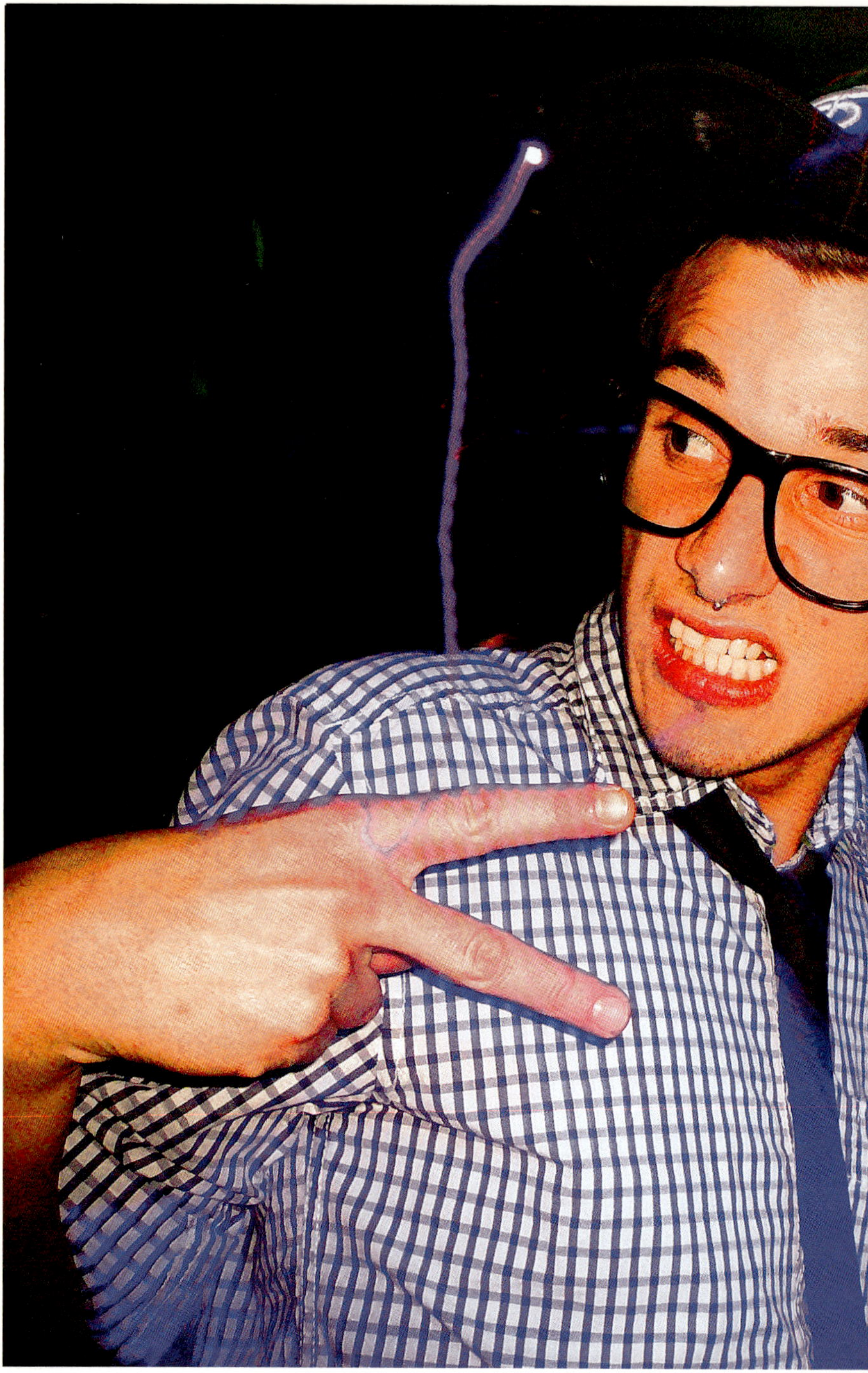

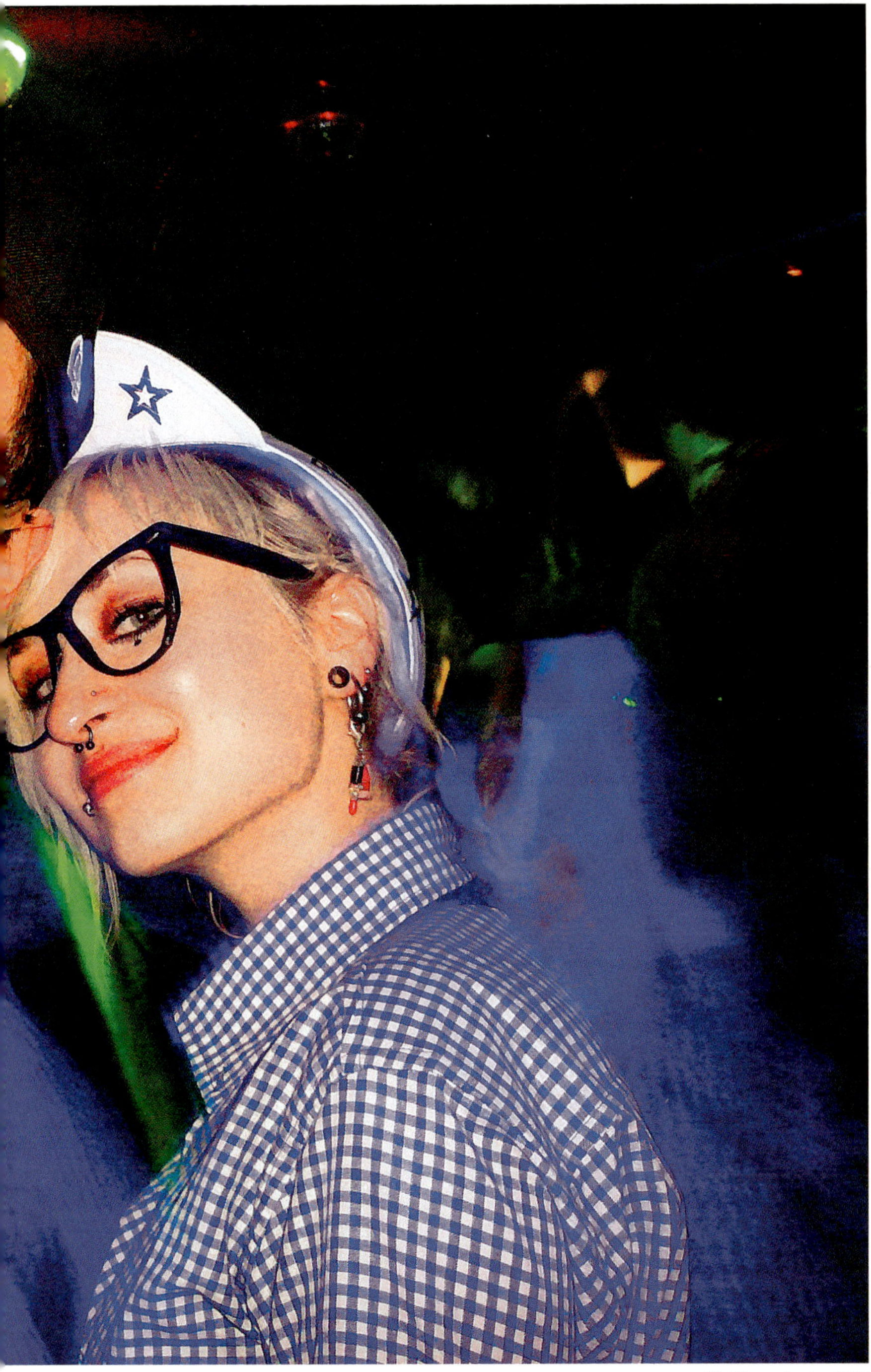

Wet Yourself – Jan 2007

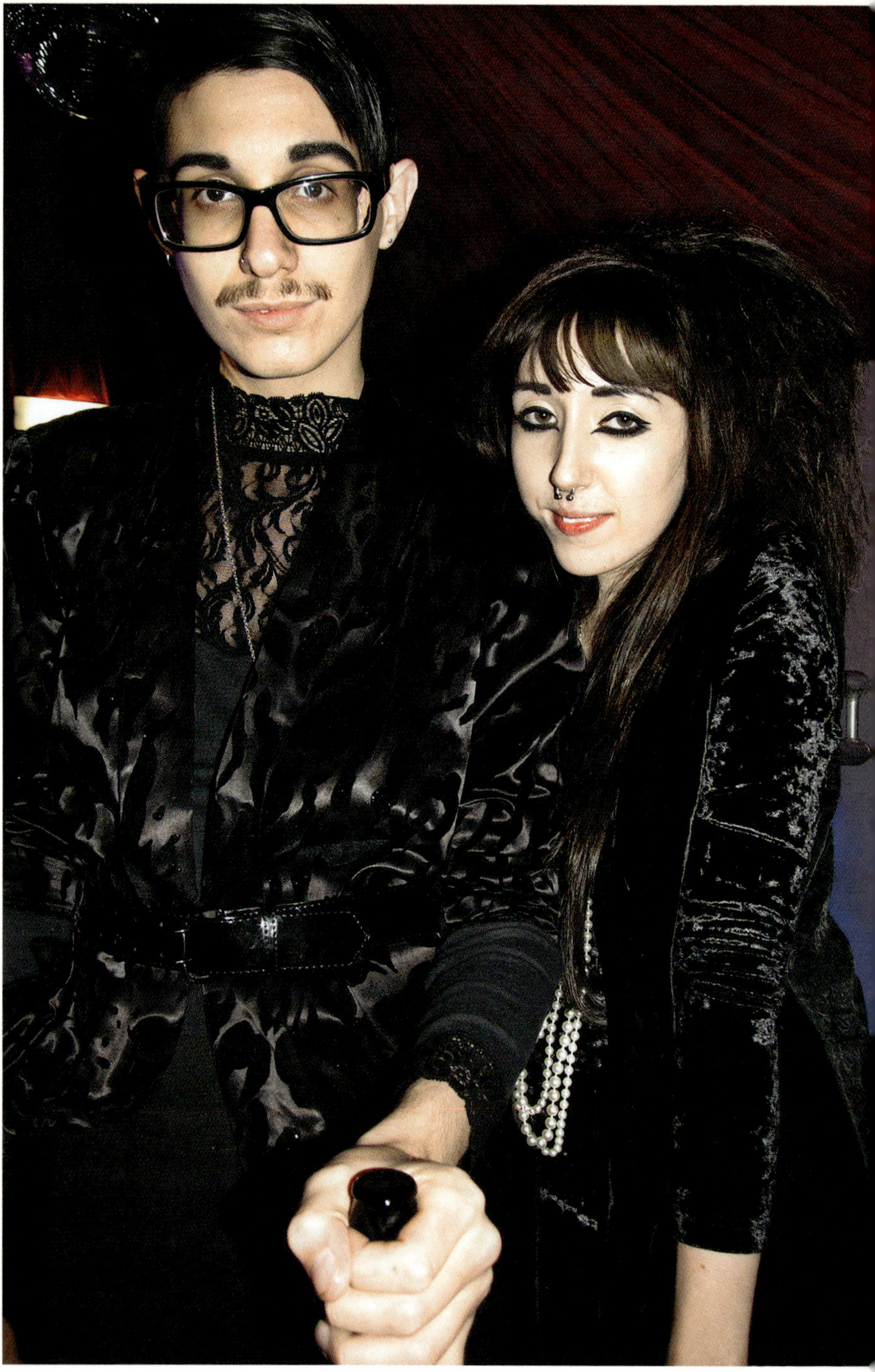

Wearable Art@Egg – Sept 2010

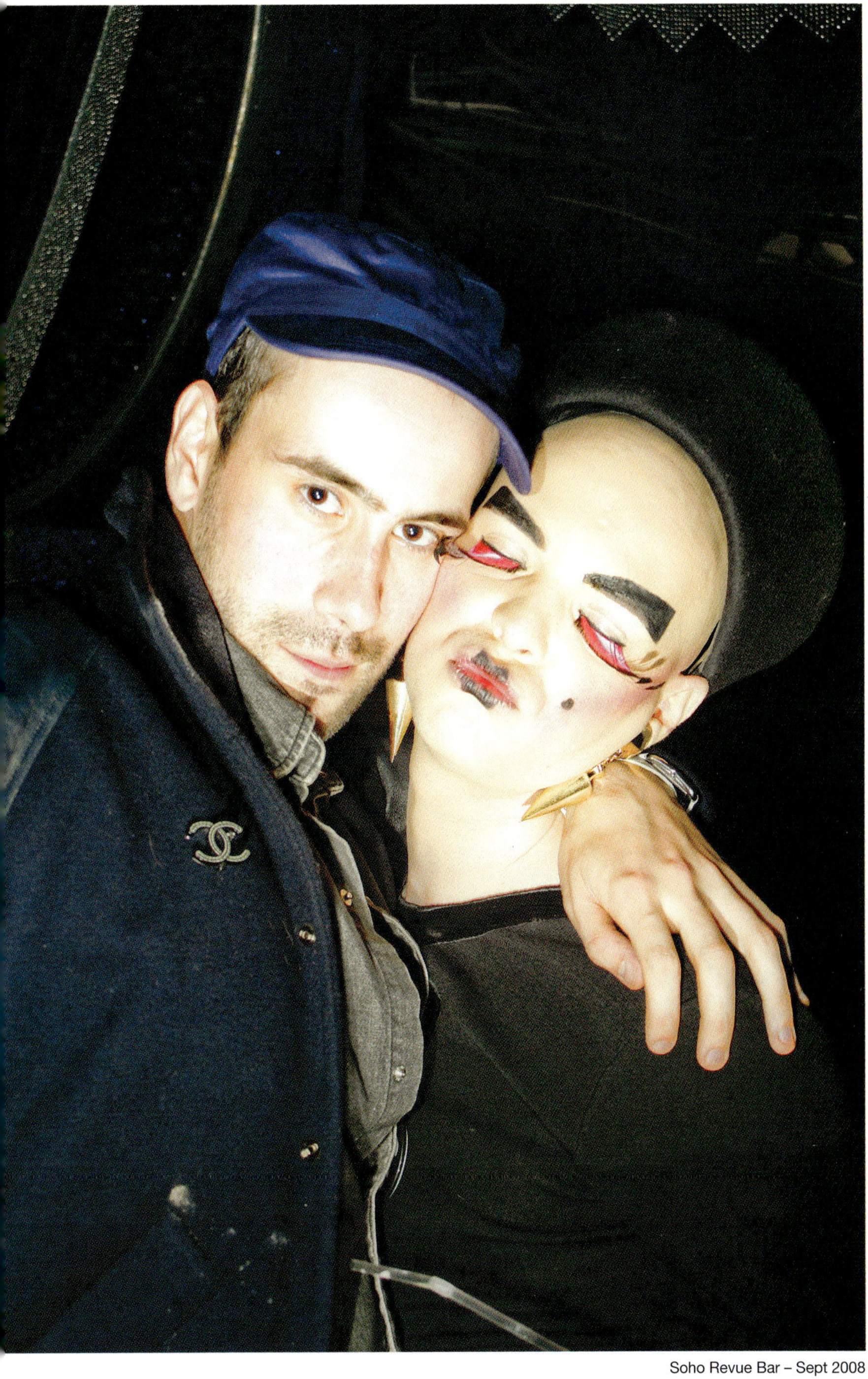

Soho Revue Bar – Sept 2008

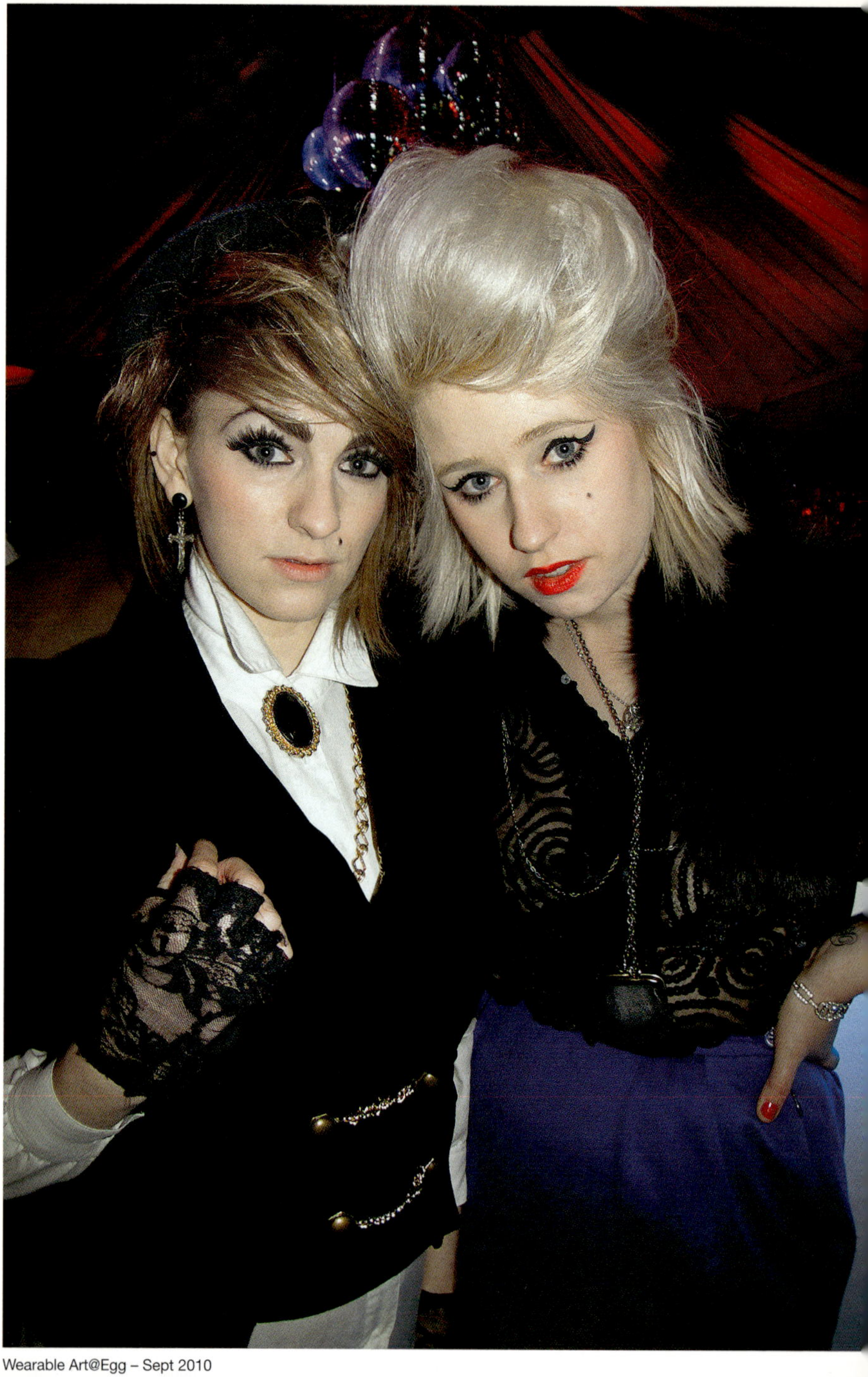

Wearable Art@Egg – Sept 2010

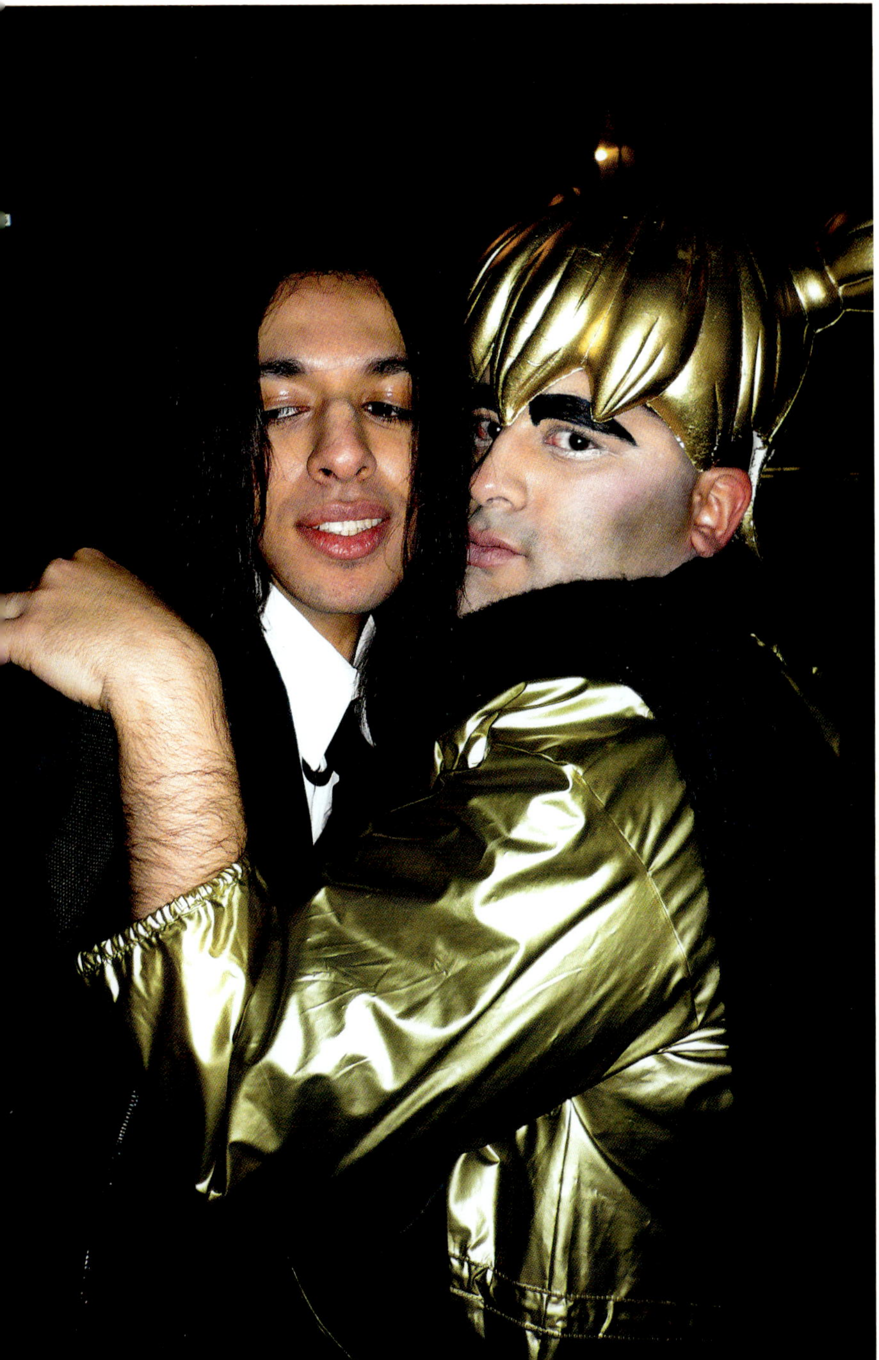

Kashpoint – Sept 2006

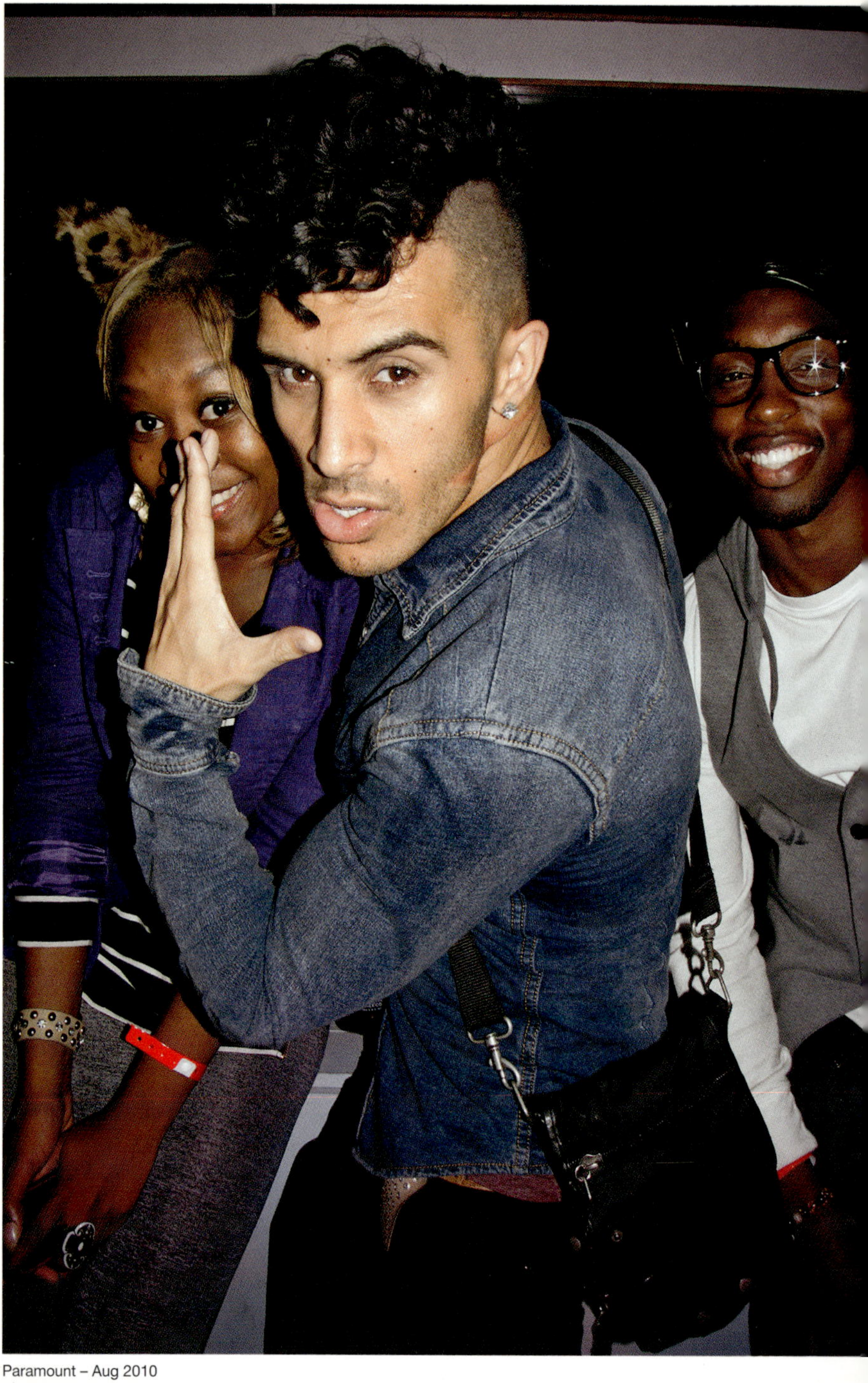

Paramount – Aug 2010

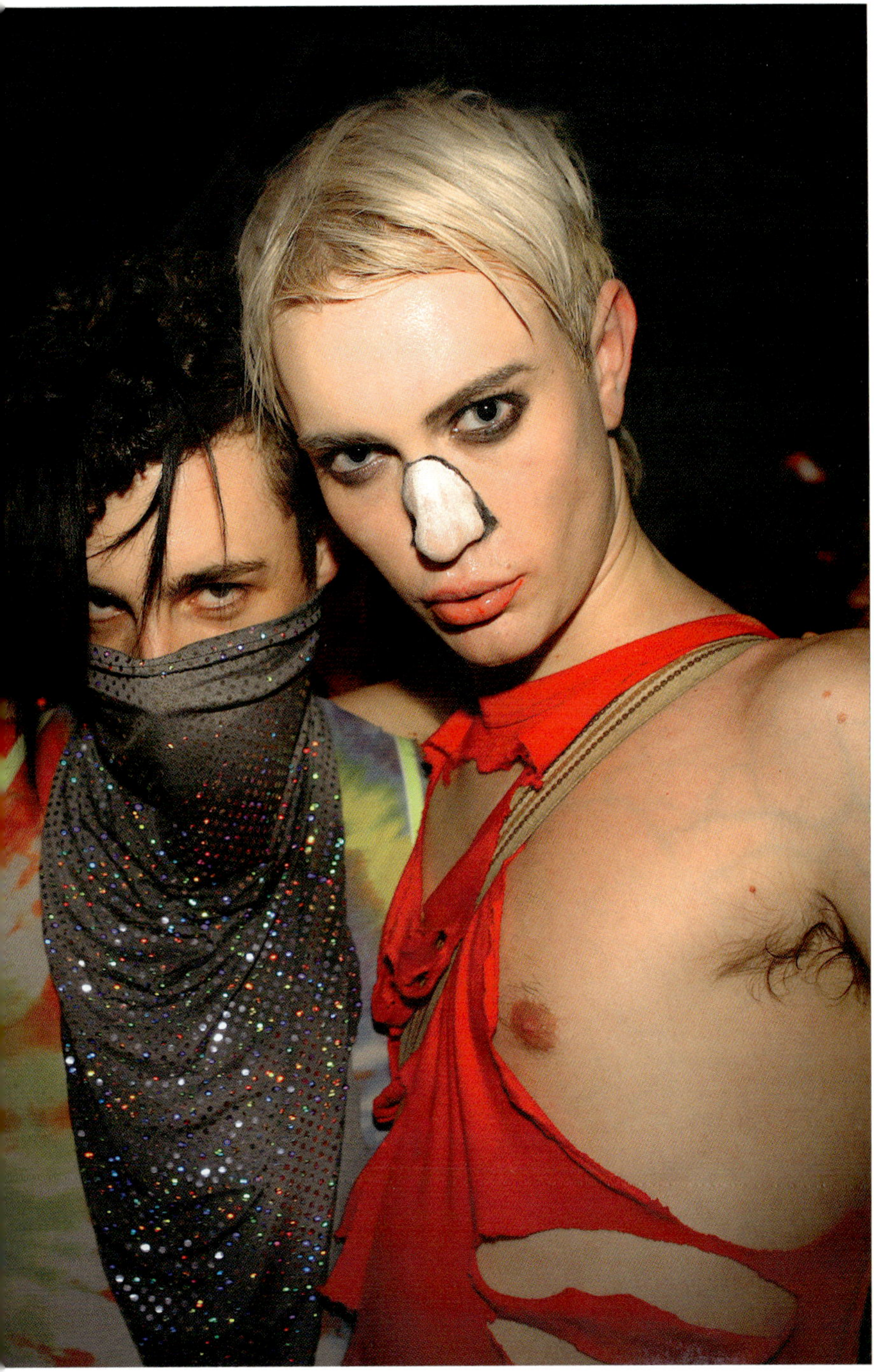

Circus – Nov 2006

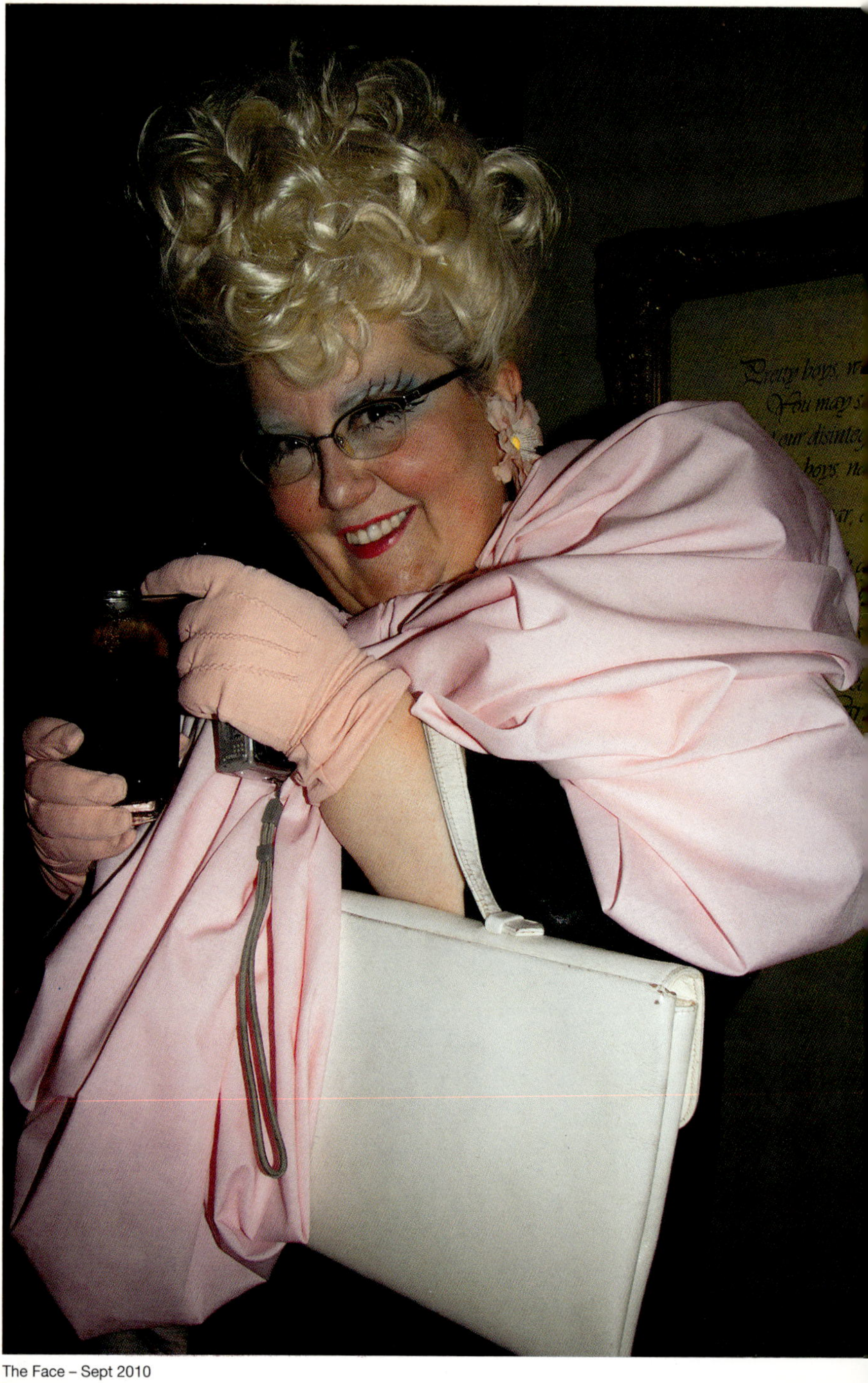

The Face – Sept 2010

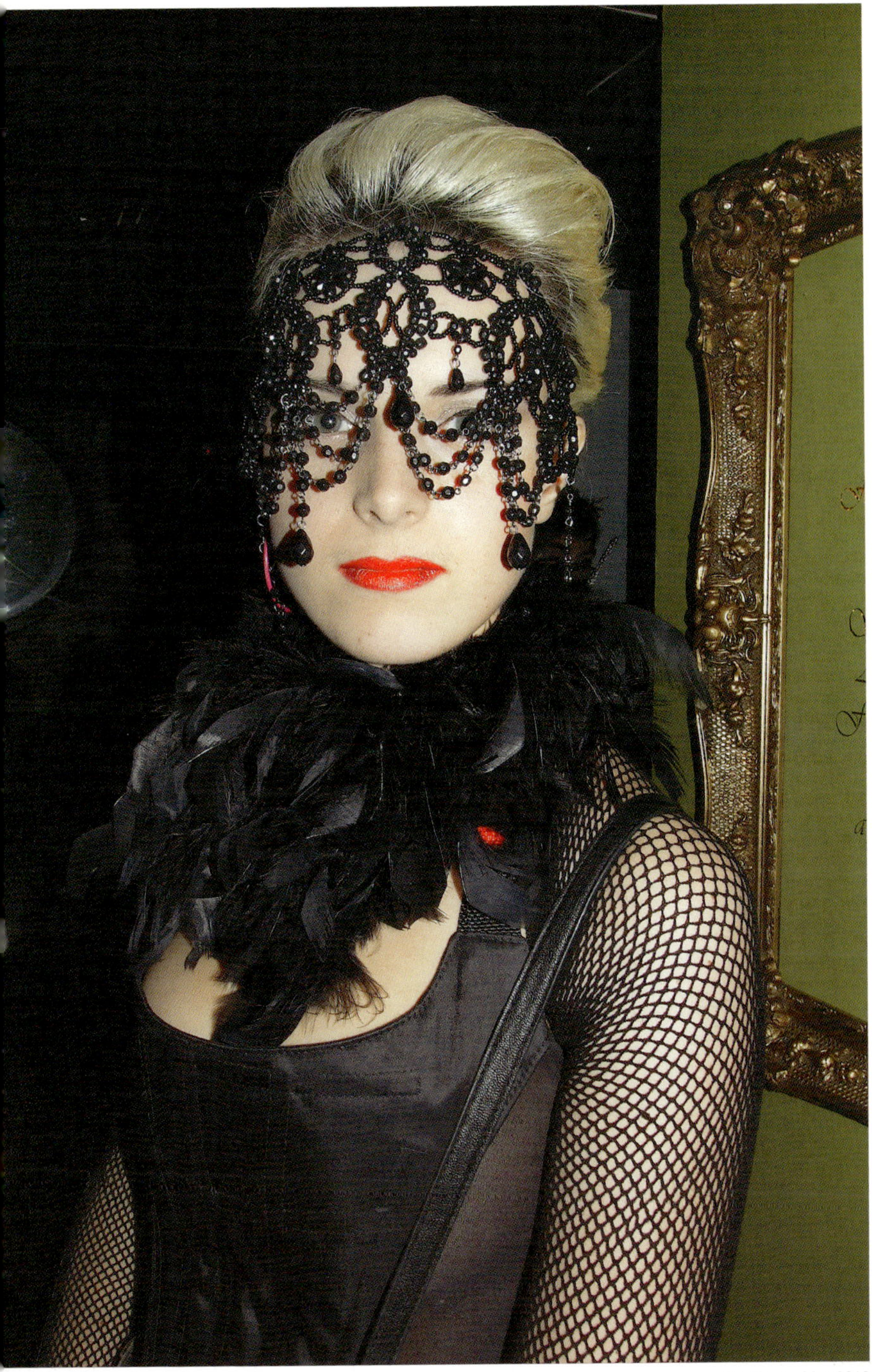

The Face – May 2010

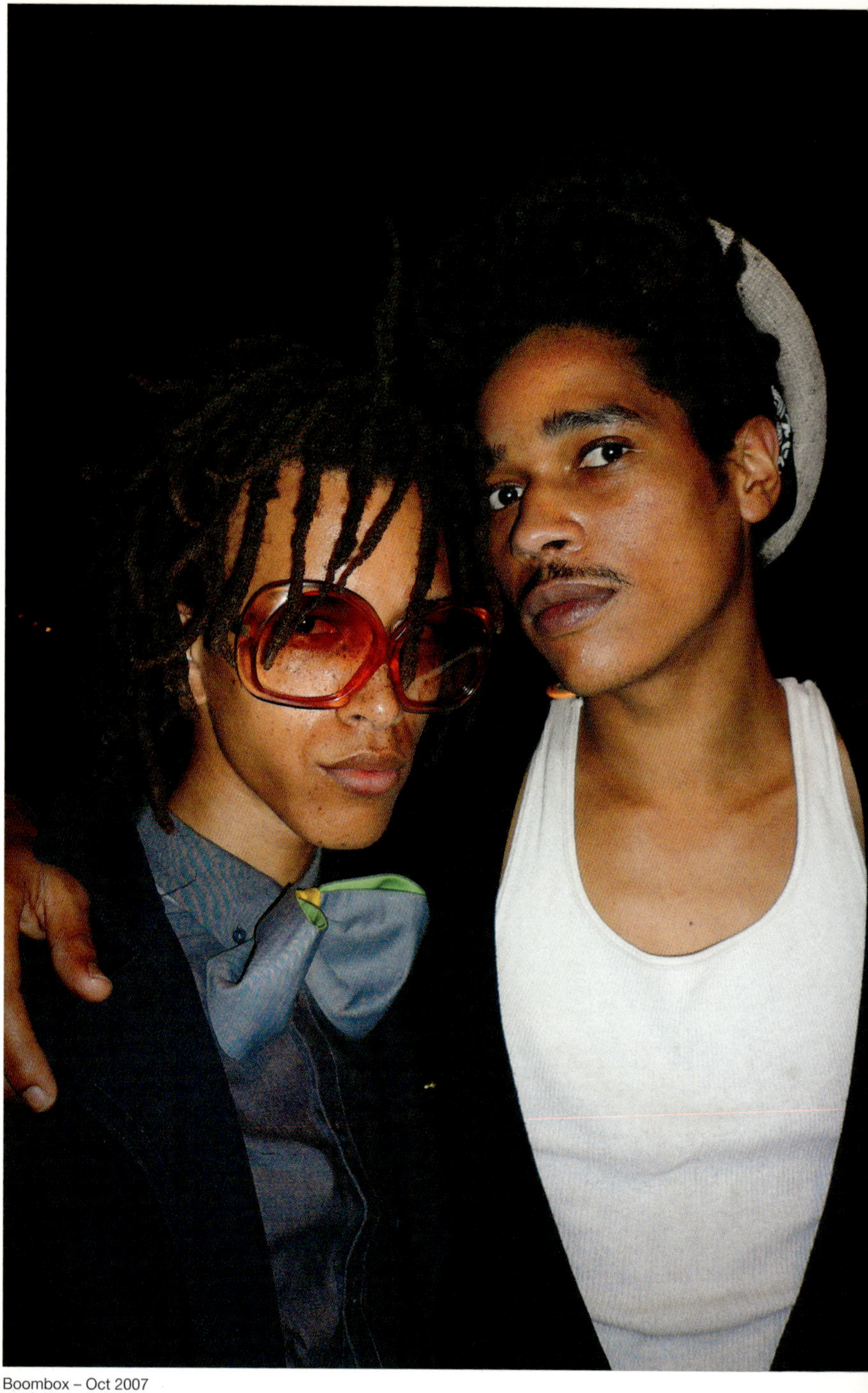

Boombox – Oct 2007

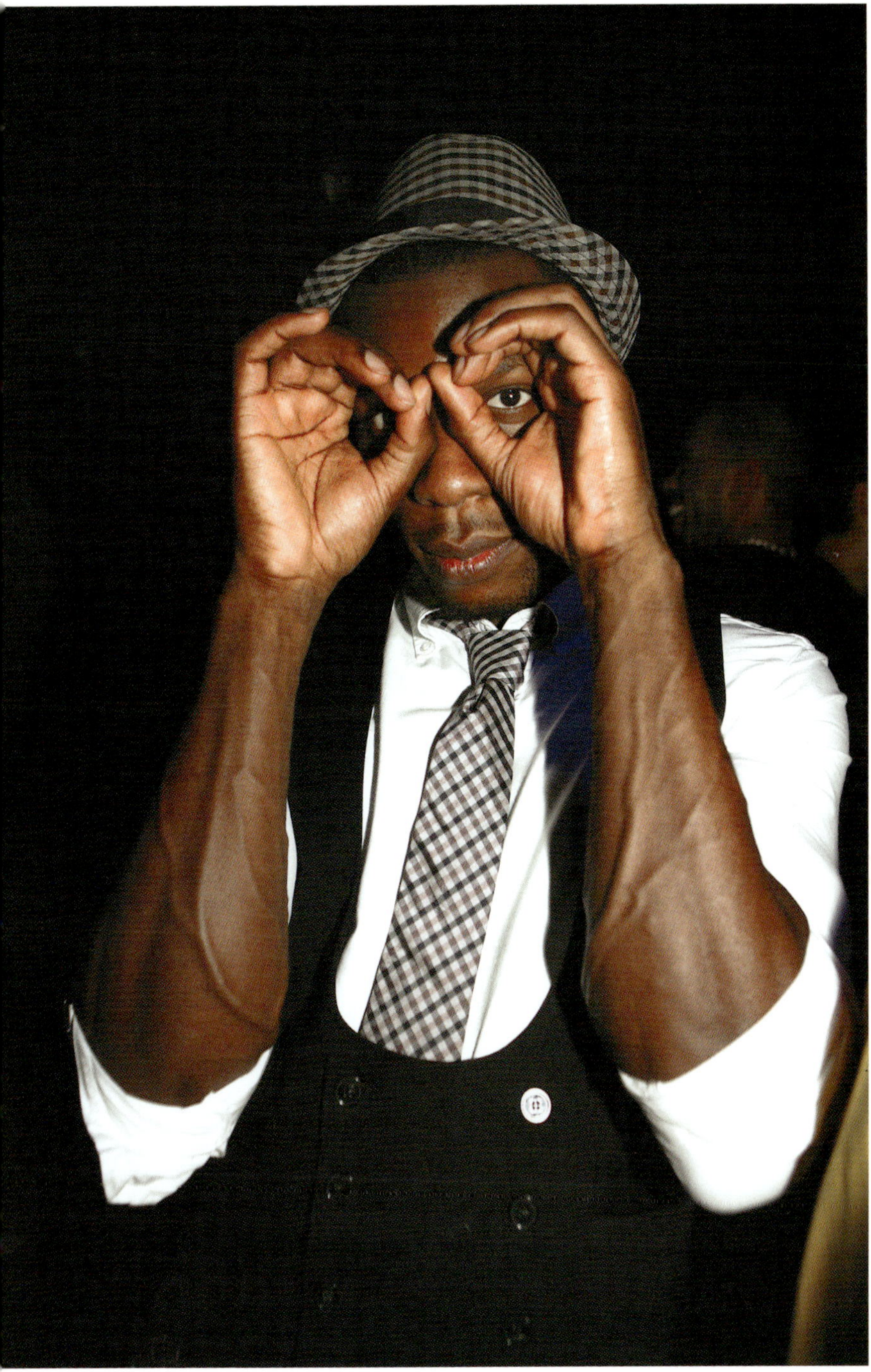

Boombox – May 2007

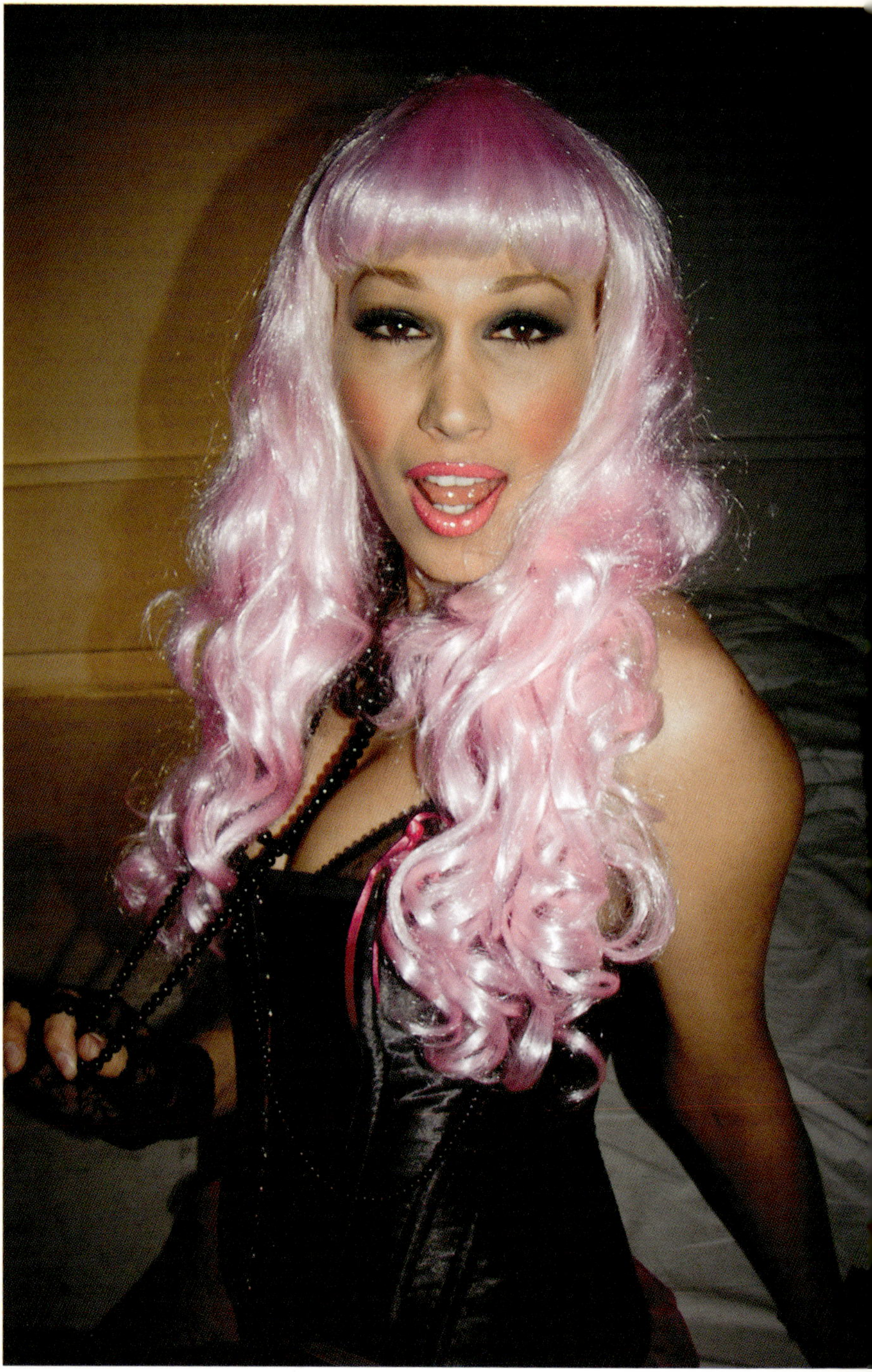

Toy@SupperClub – May 2010

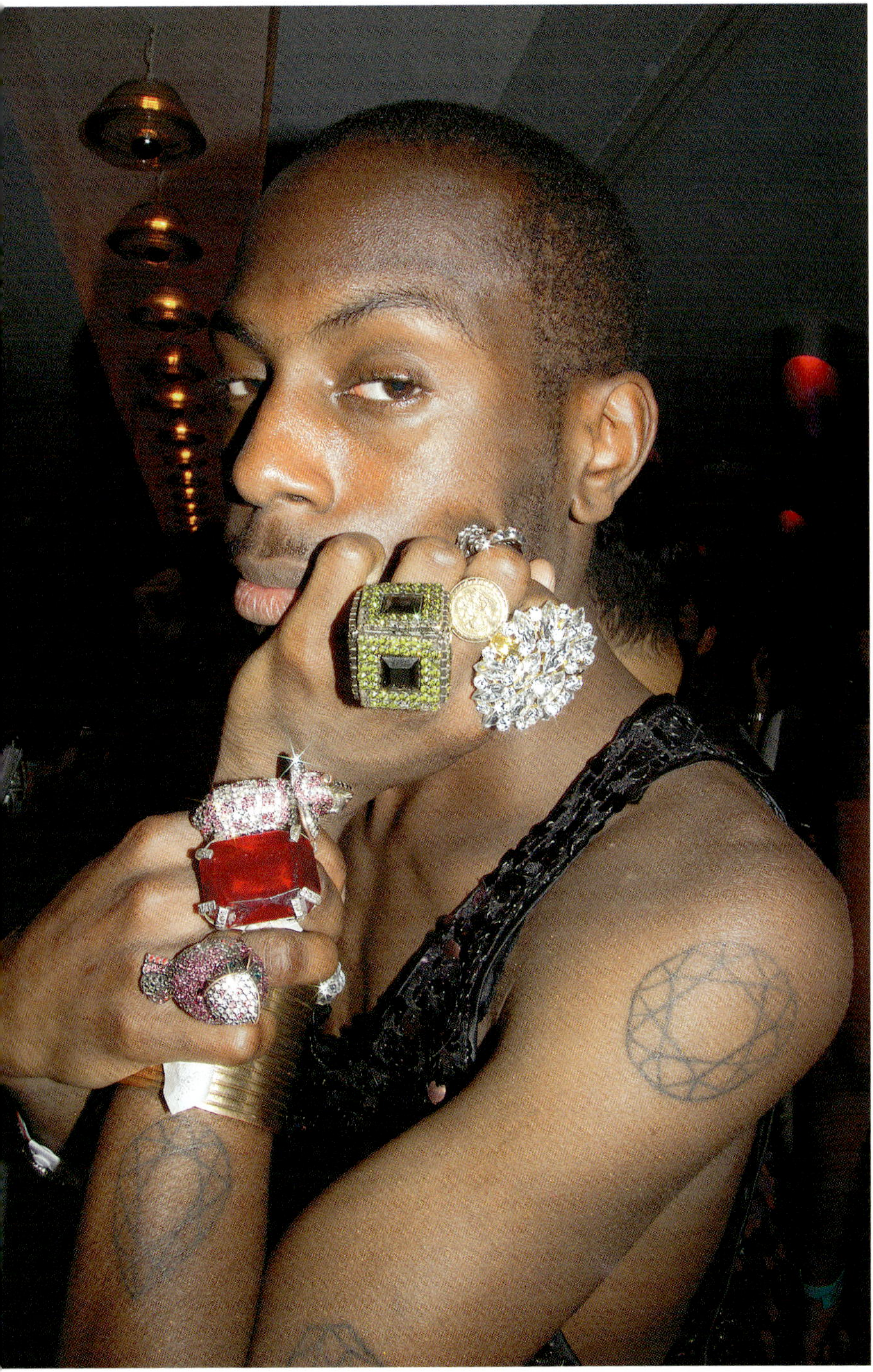

Paramount – Sept 2010

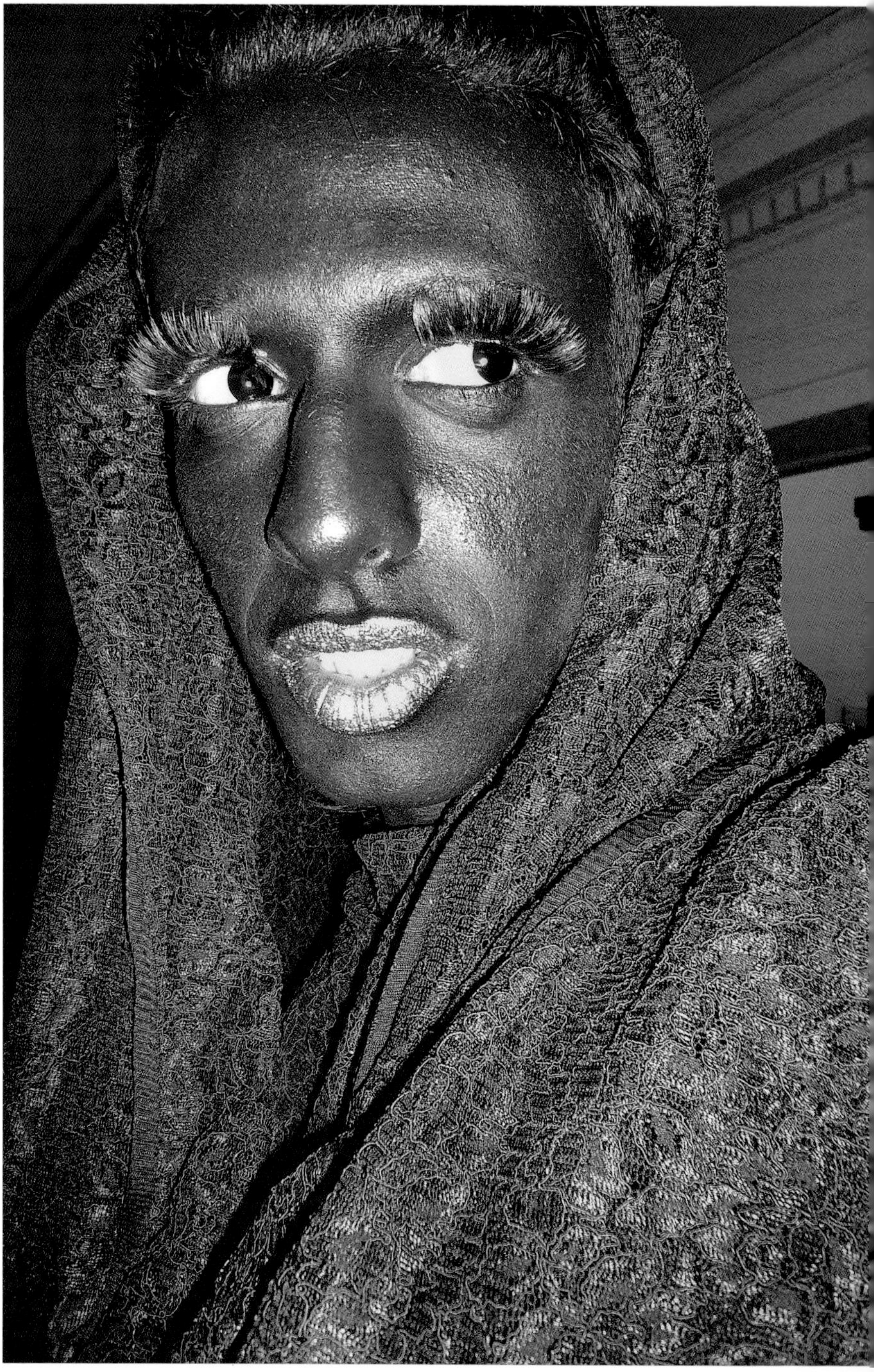

Voguing Ball – July 2007

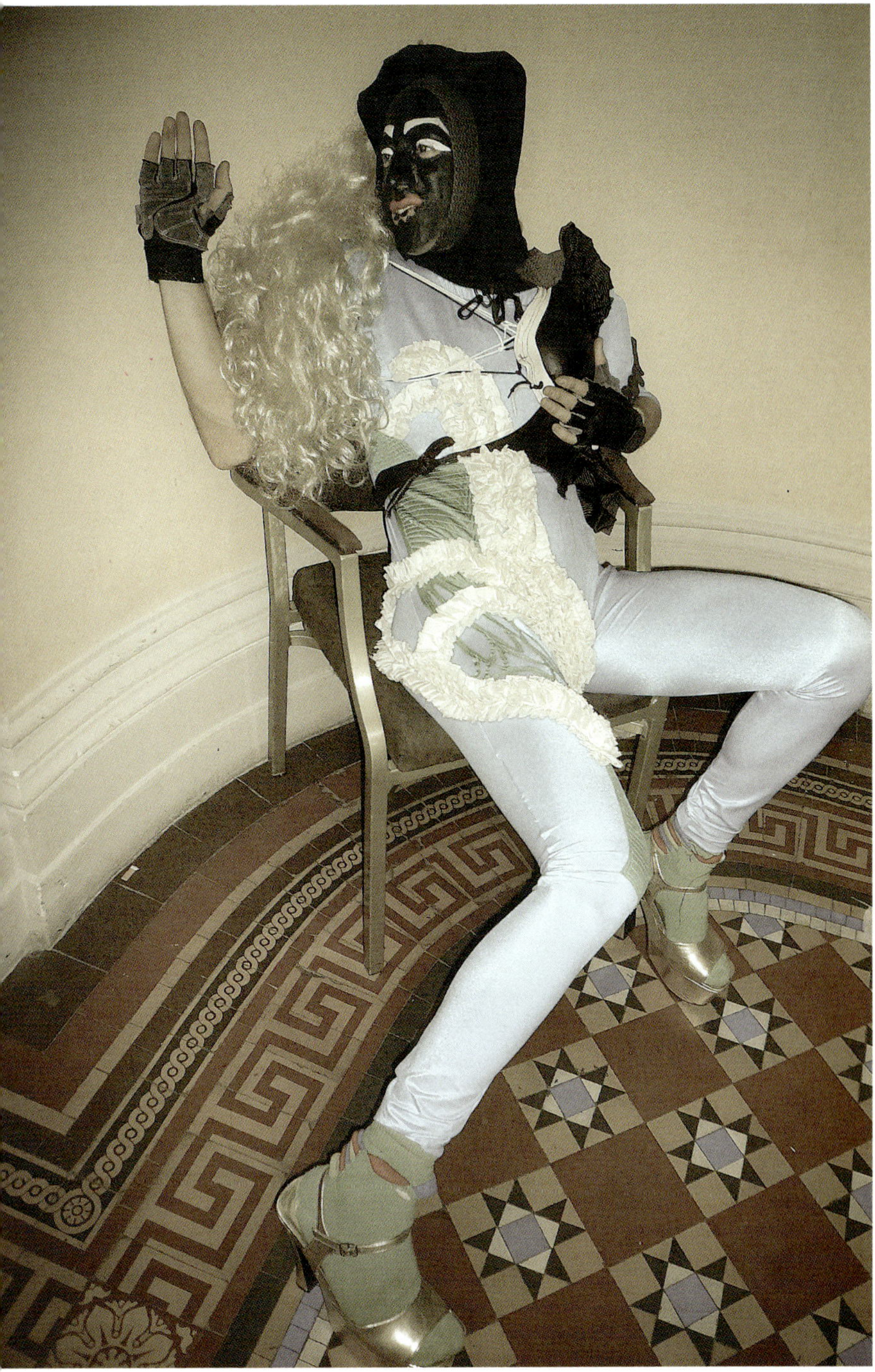

Voguing Ball – July 2007

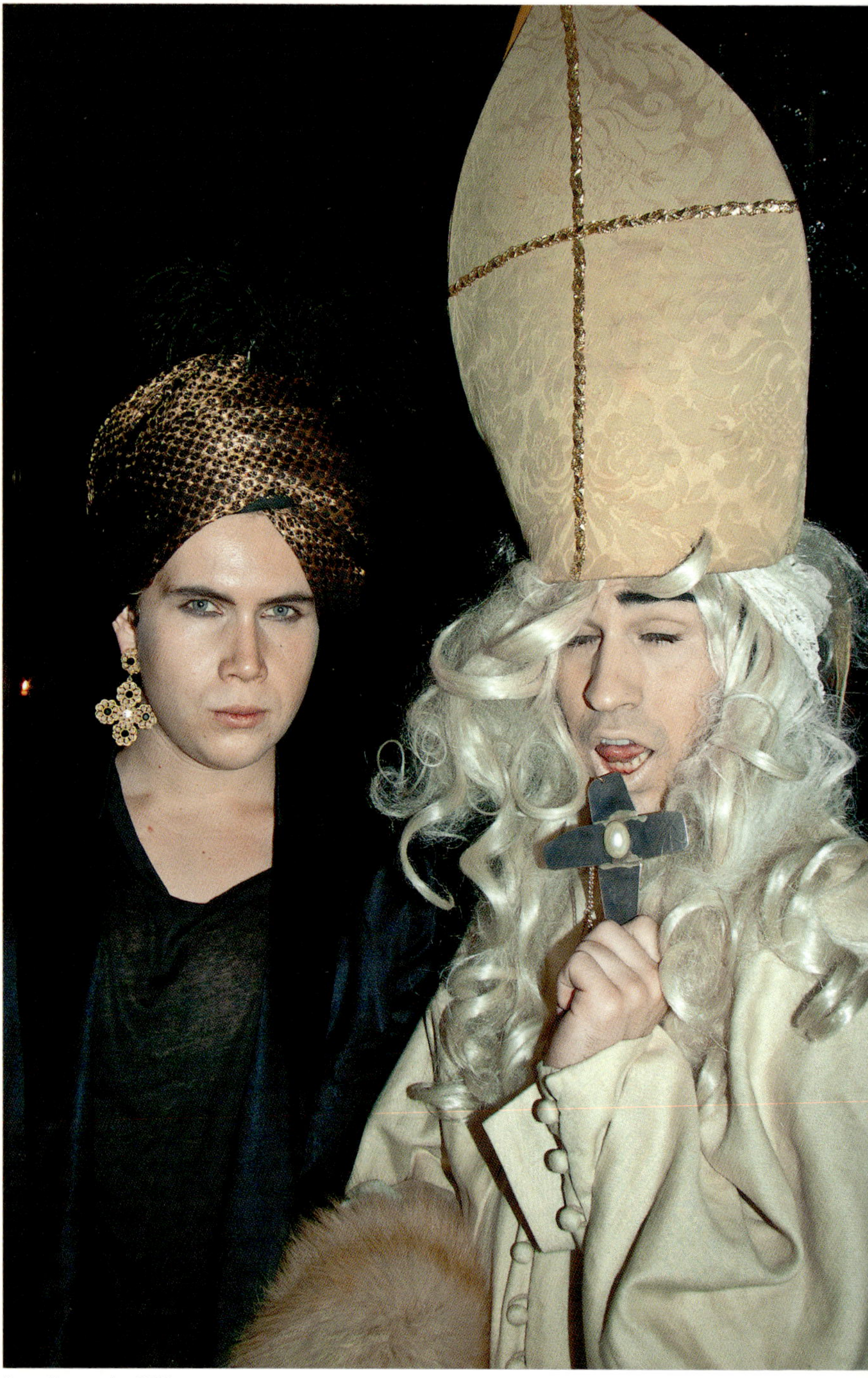

Home House – Jan 2010

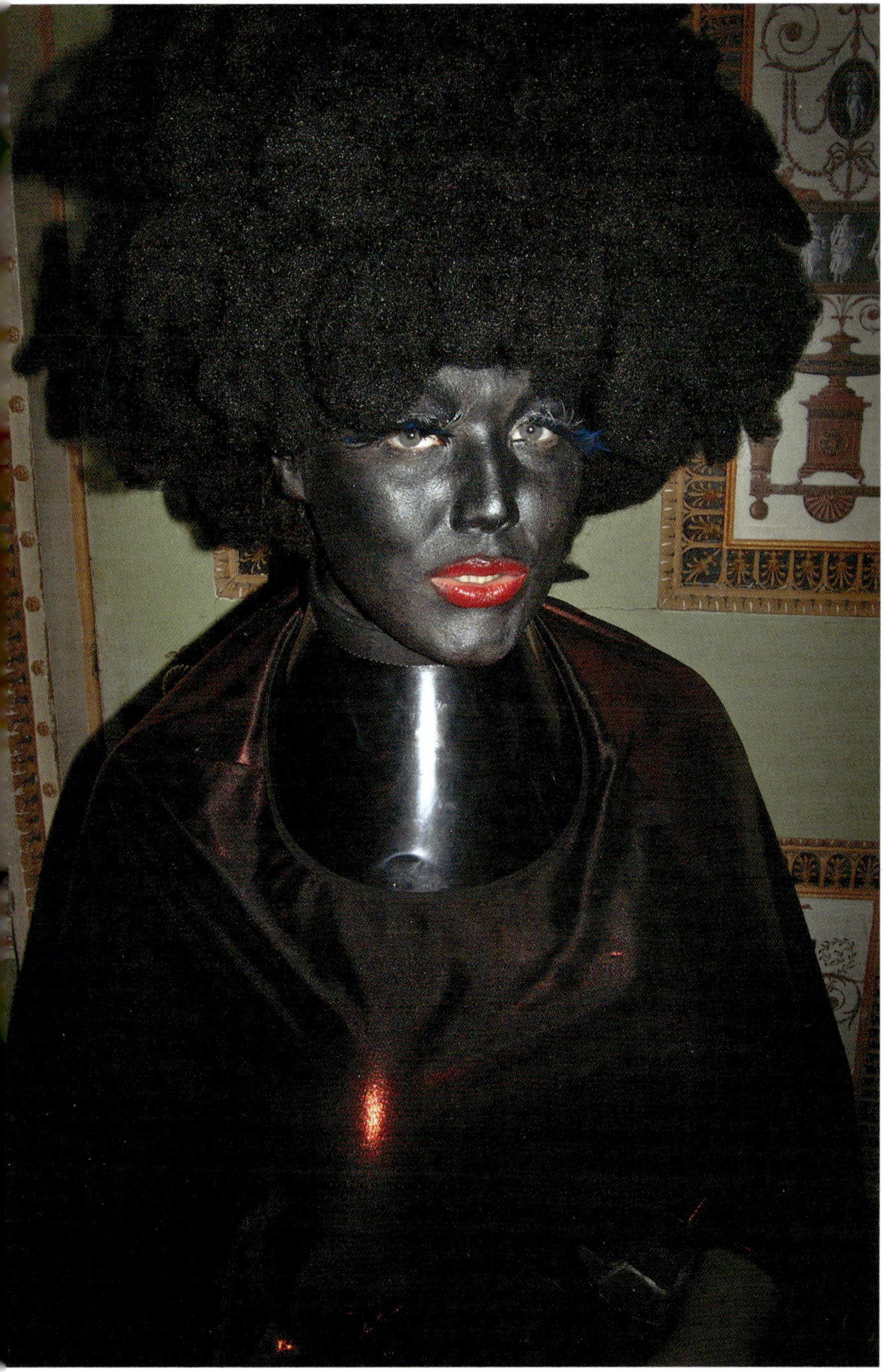

Home House – Nov 2010

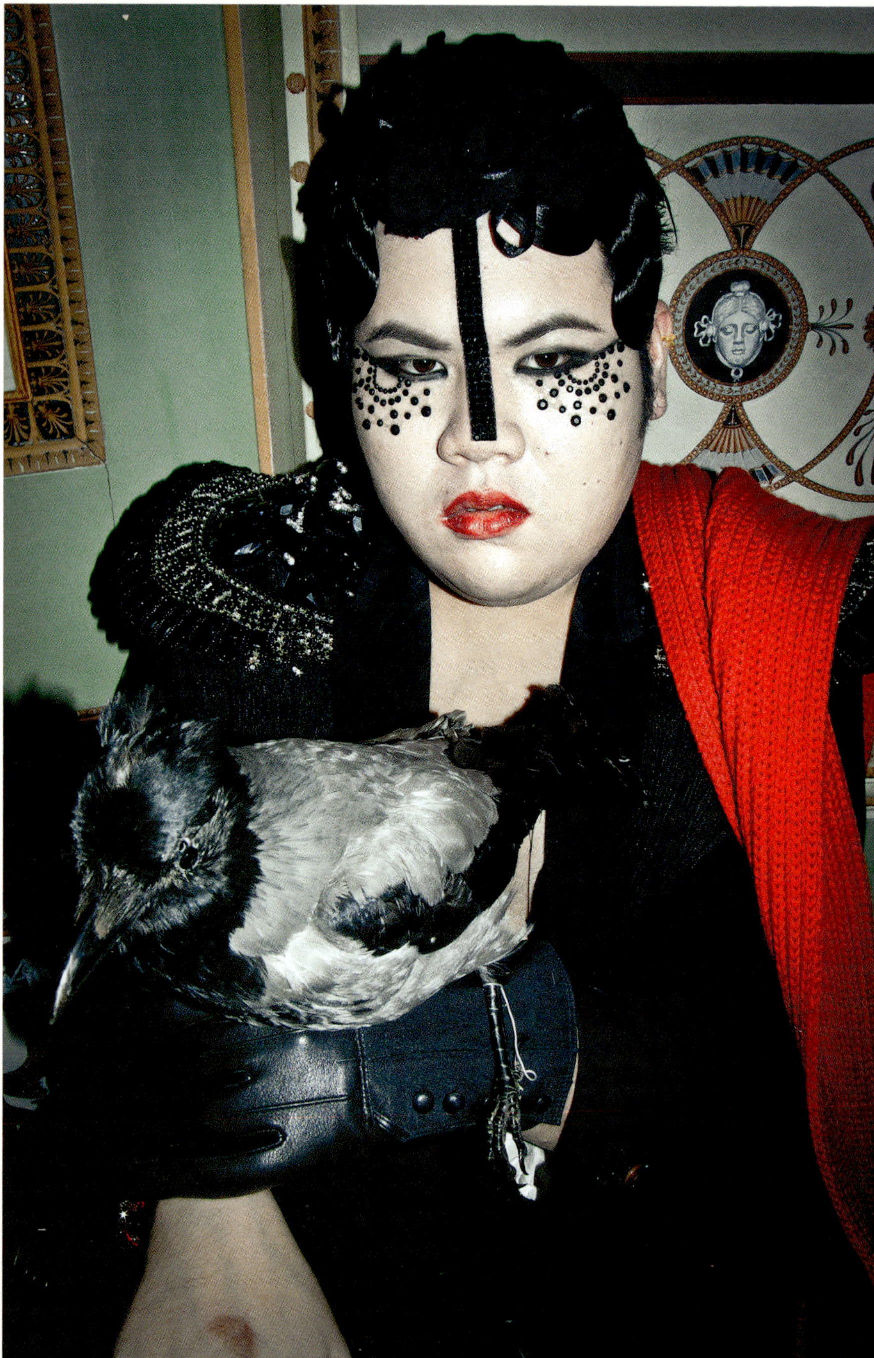

Home House – Nov 2010

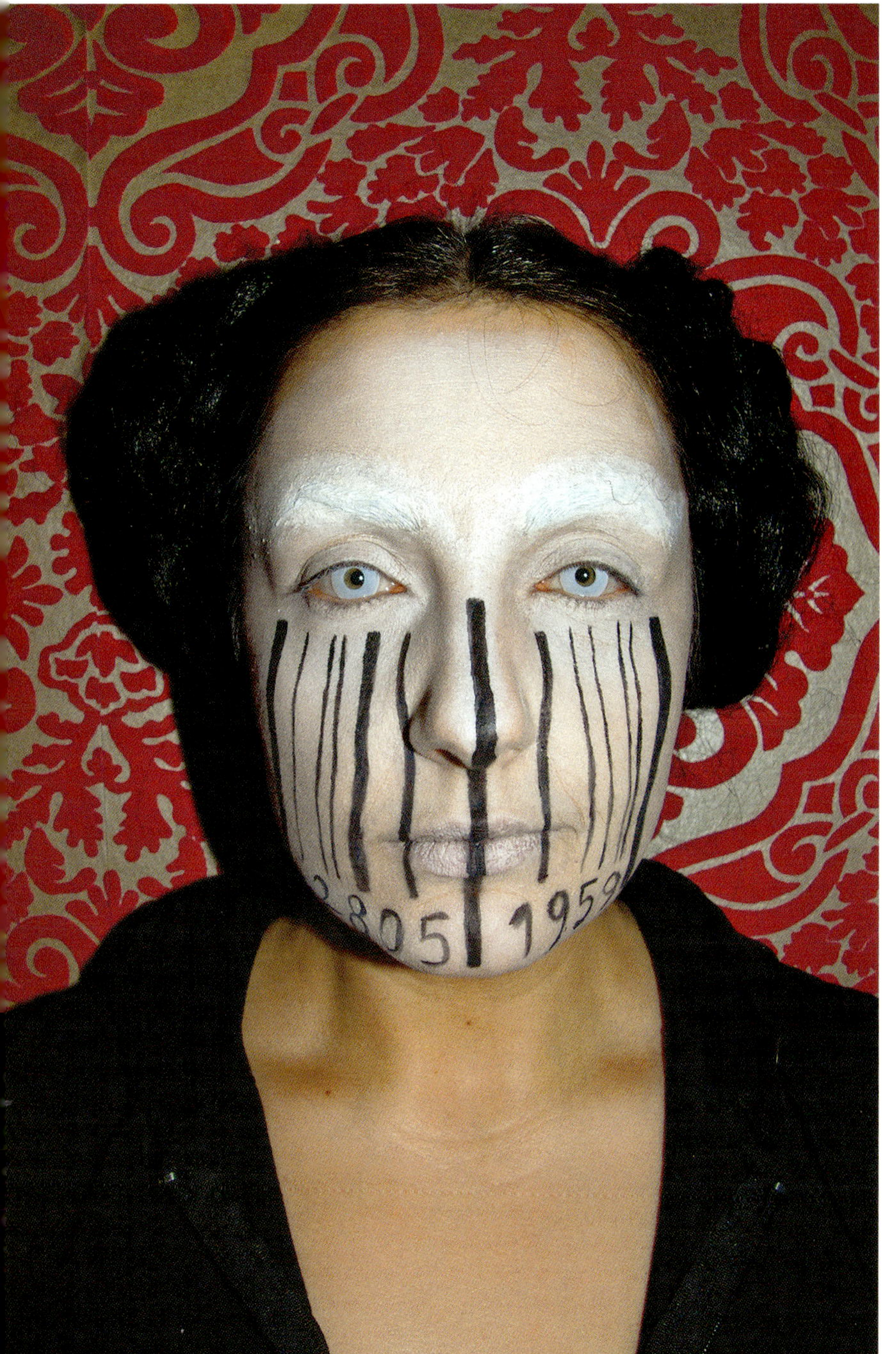

The Face – May 2010

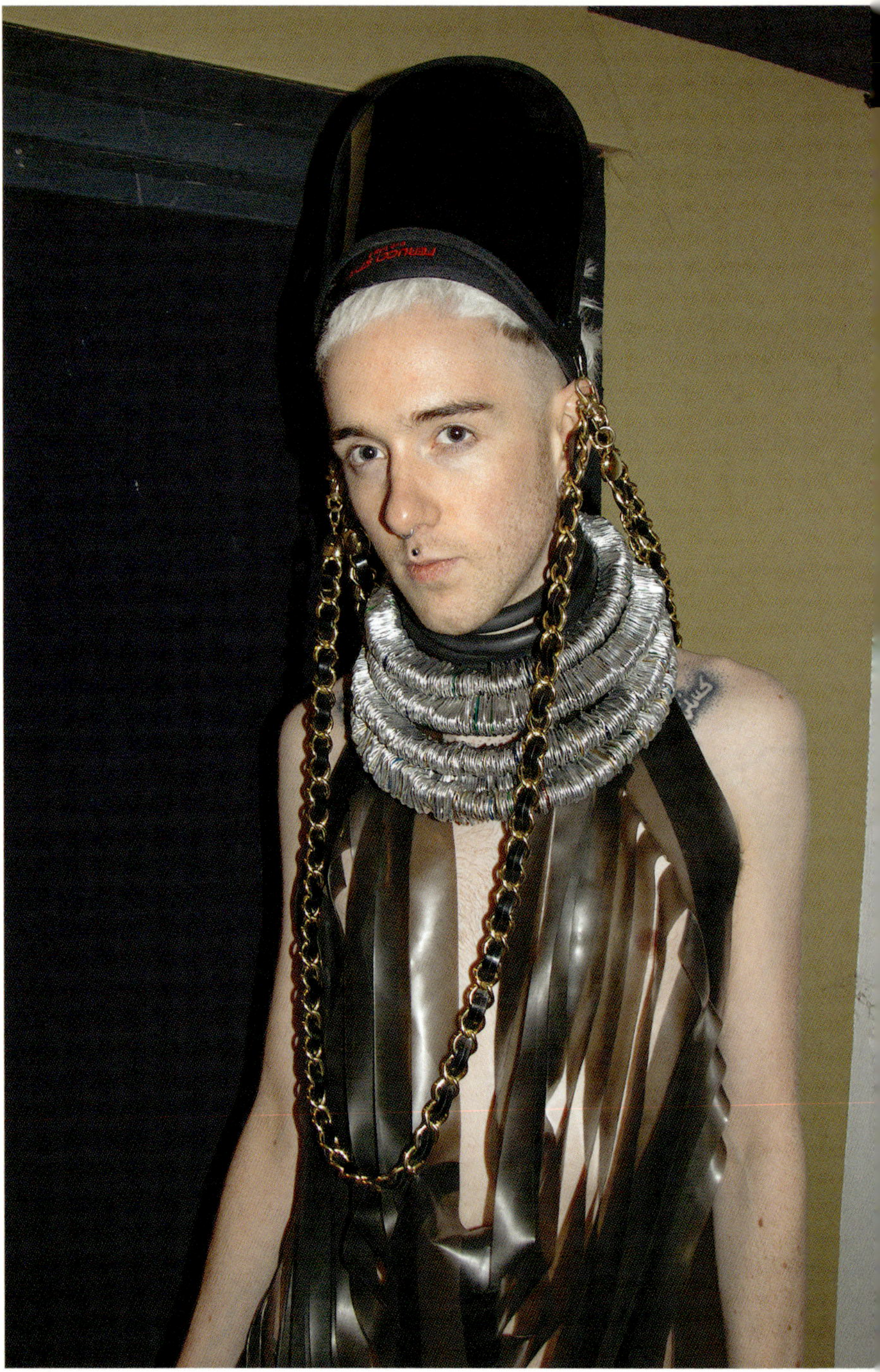

Wearable Art@Egg – Sept 2010

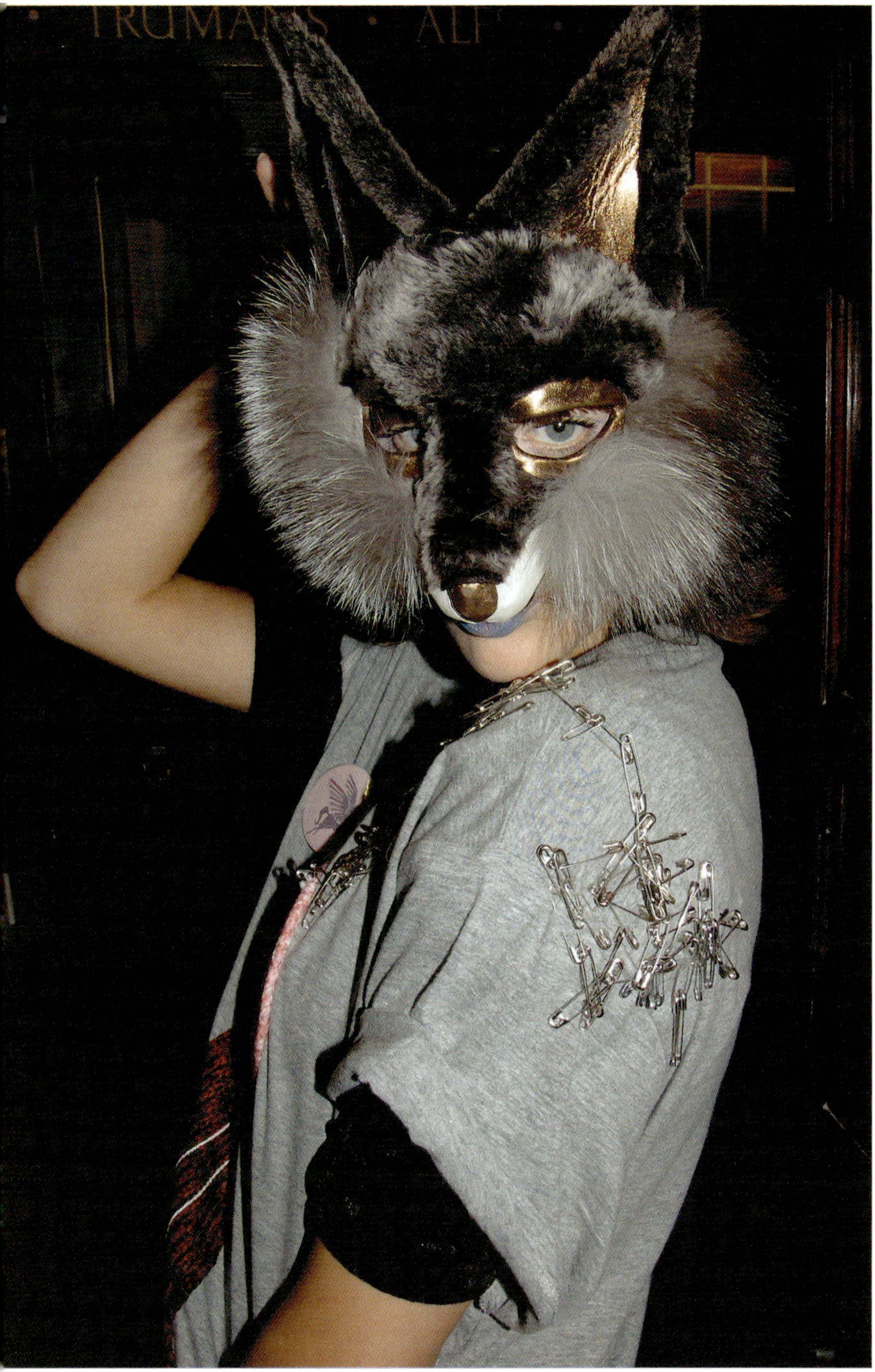

House of Blue Eyes – Sept 2010

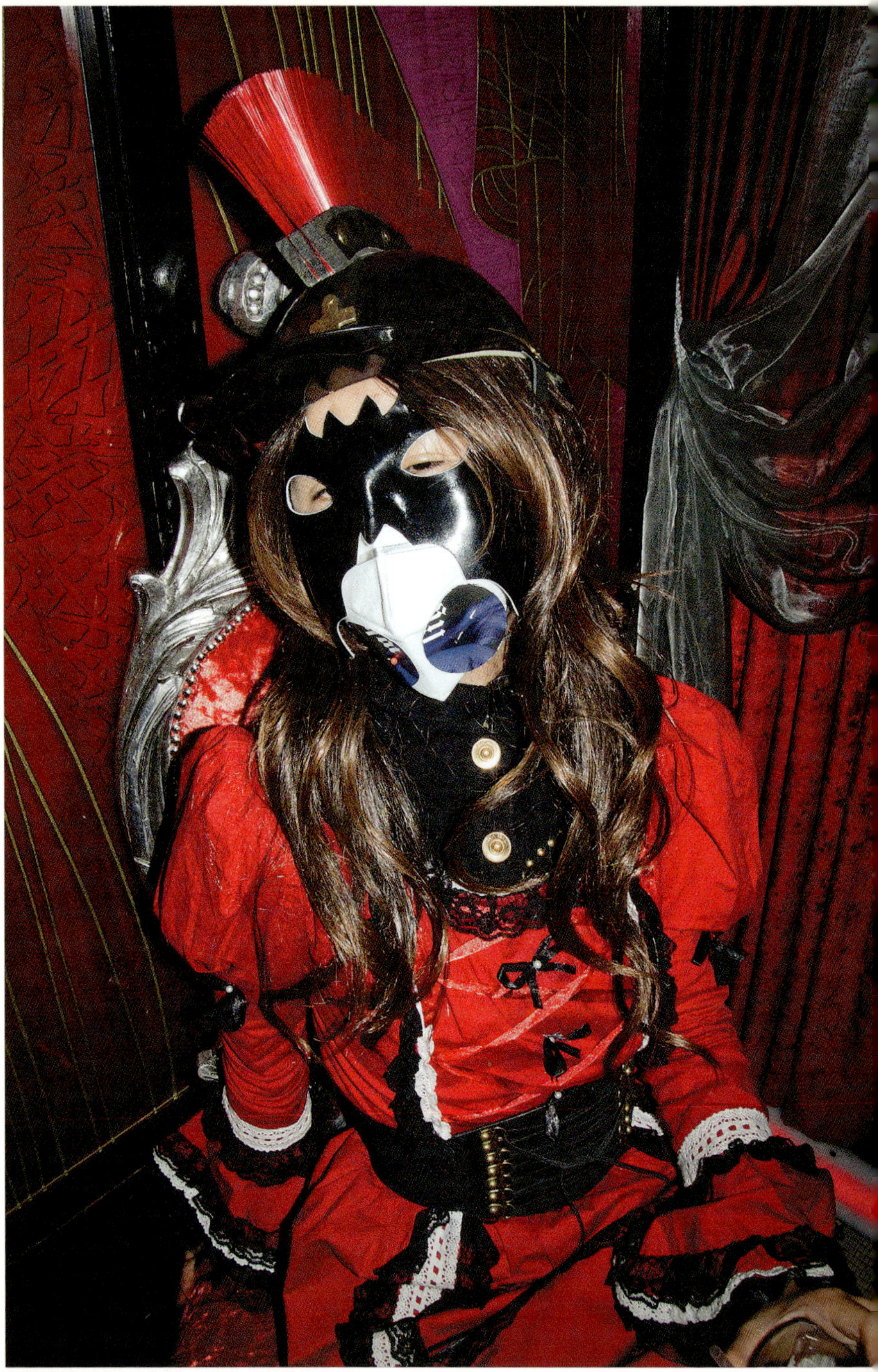

Shabba Dabba Da – Oct 2010

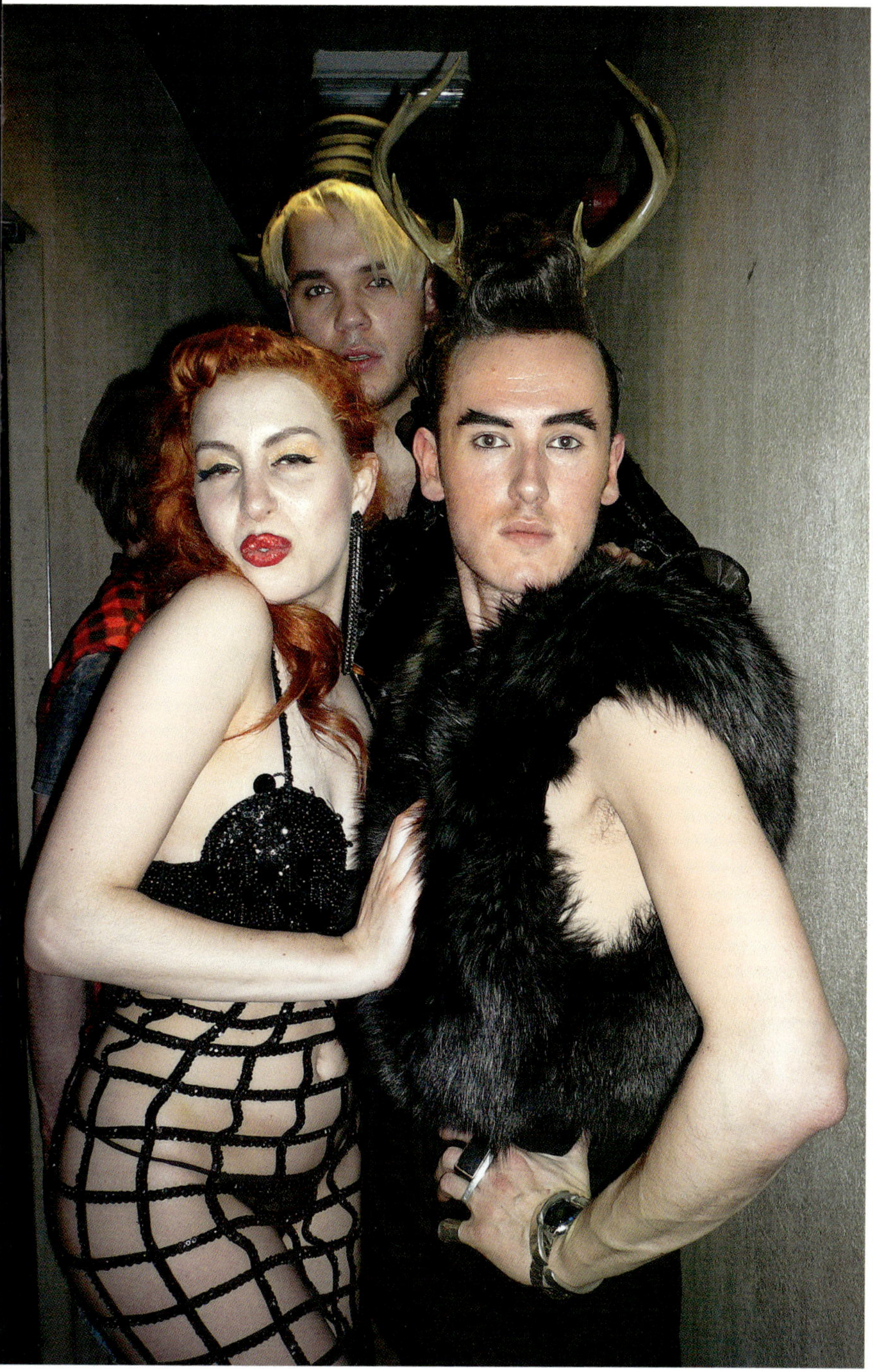

Boombox – Feb 2007

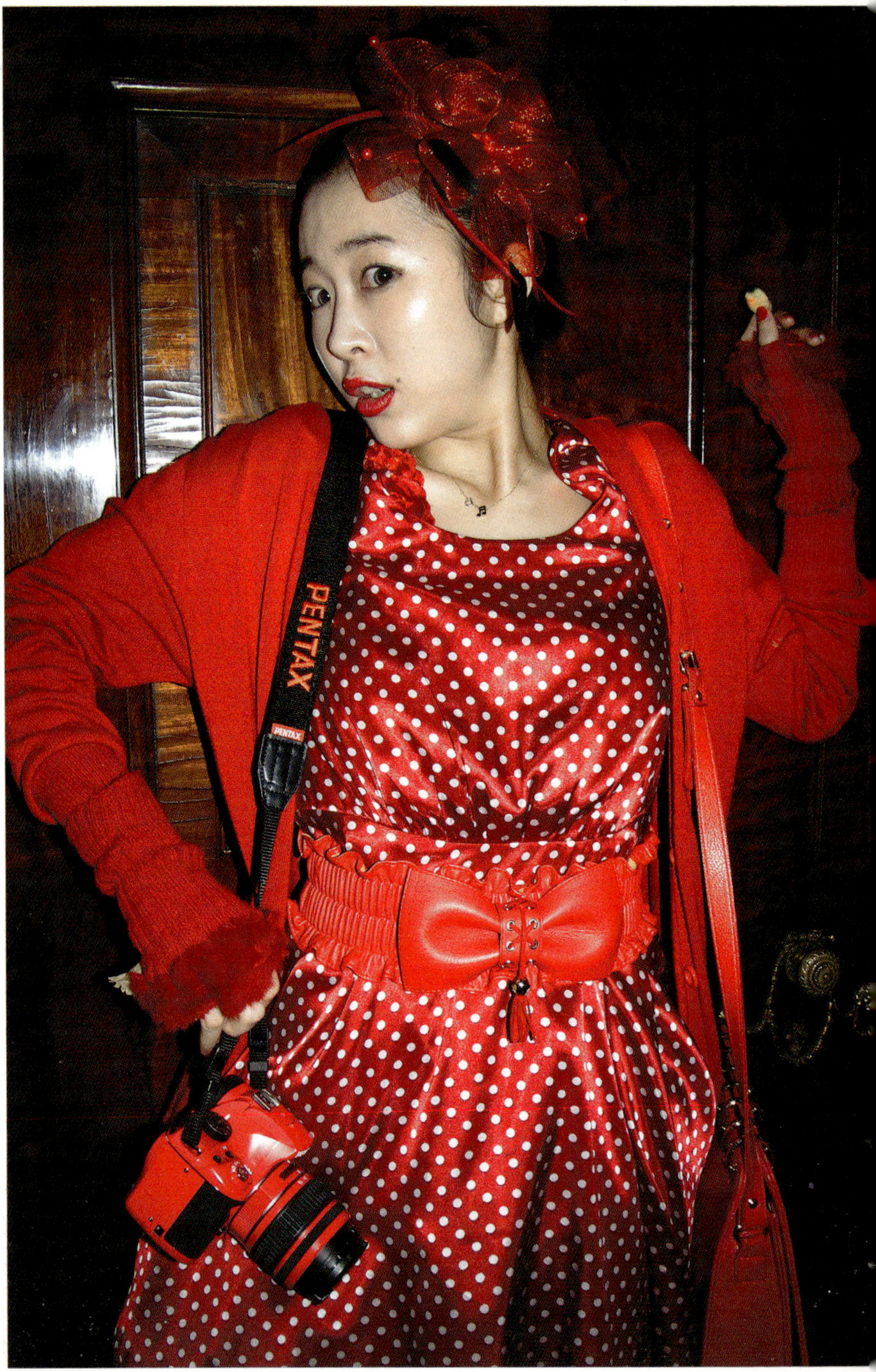

Home House – Nov 2010

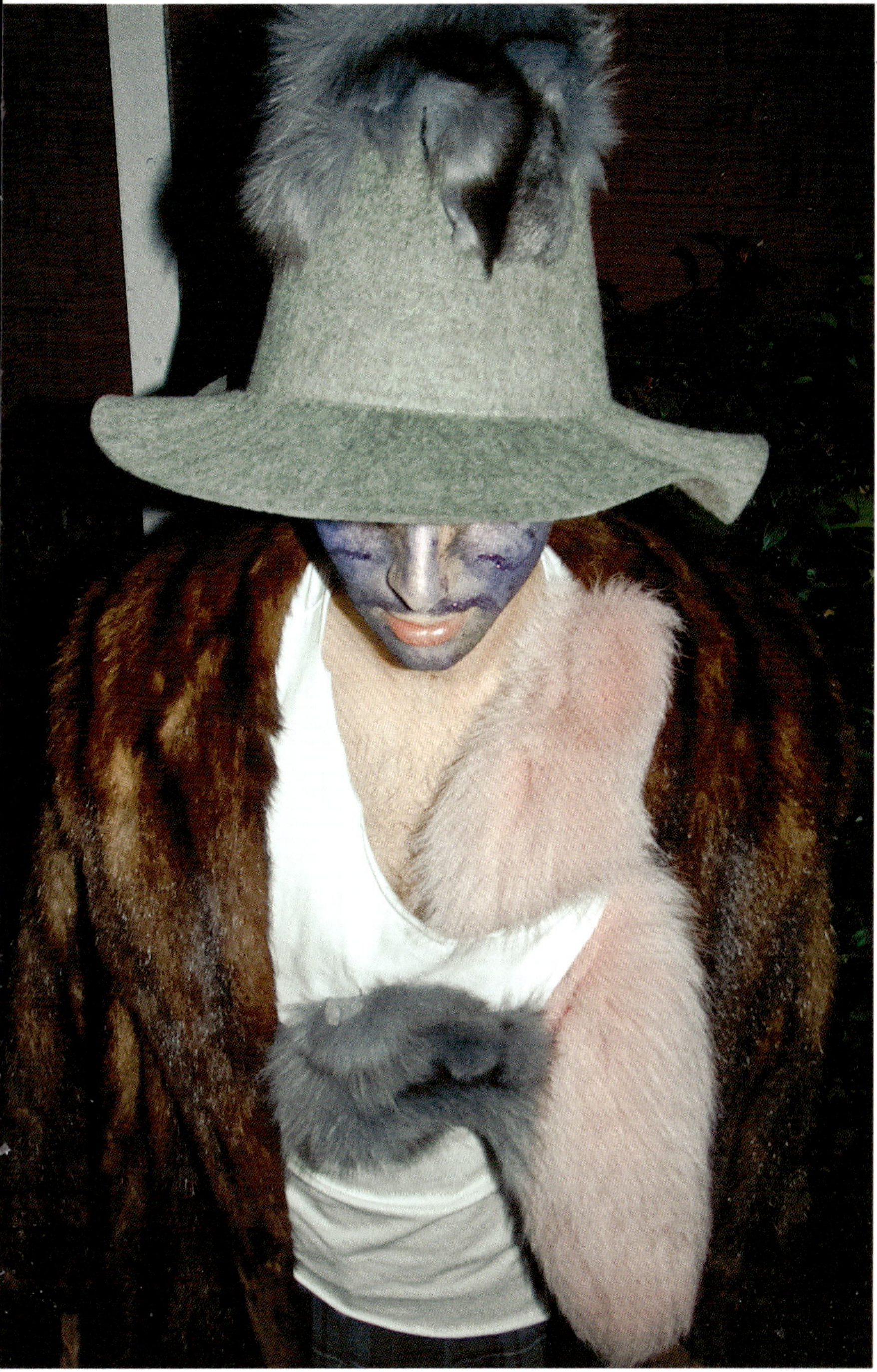

Caligula – Sept 2010

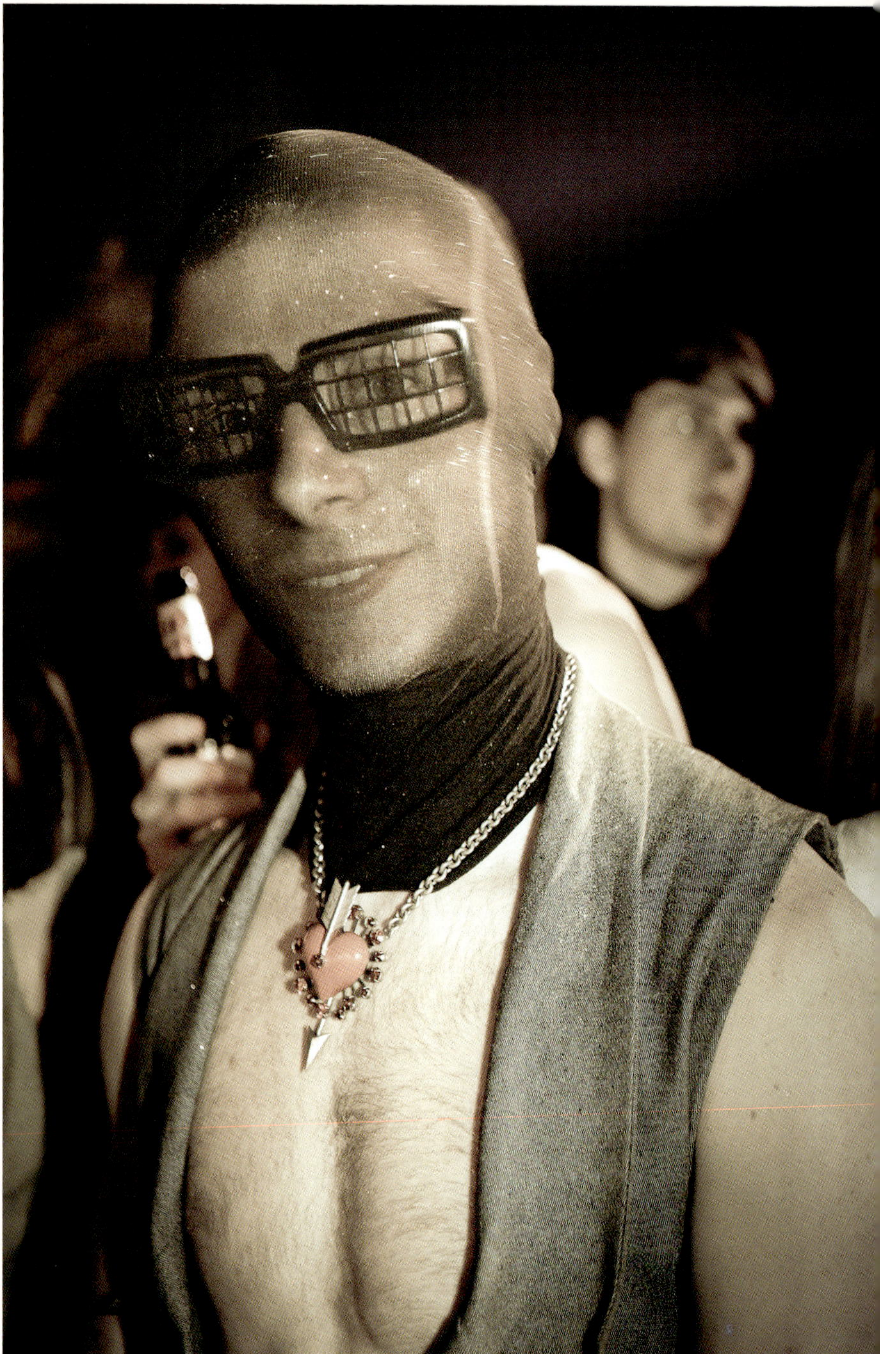

Circus – Sept 2006

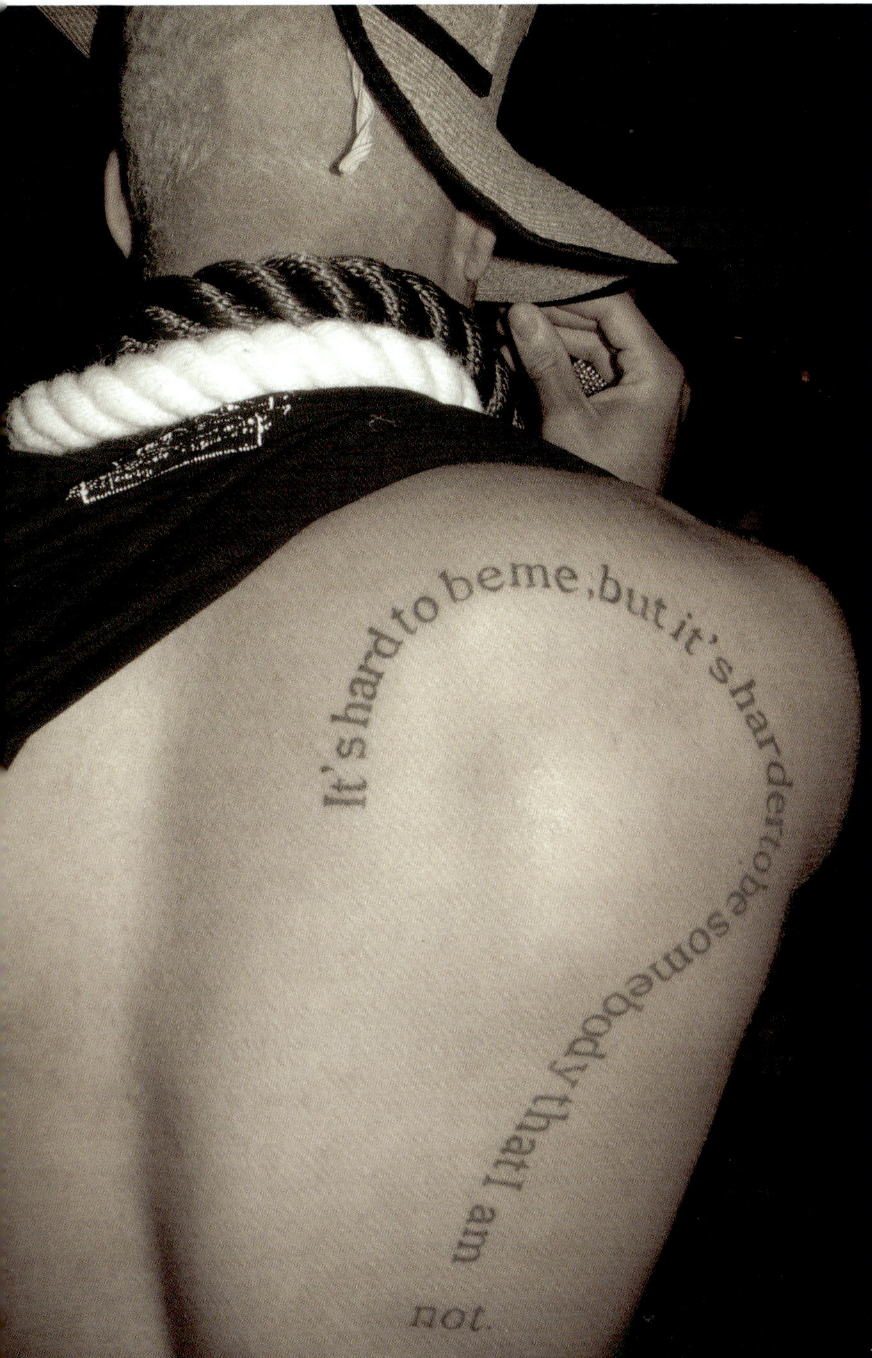

Shoreditch House – May 2010

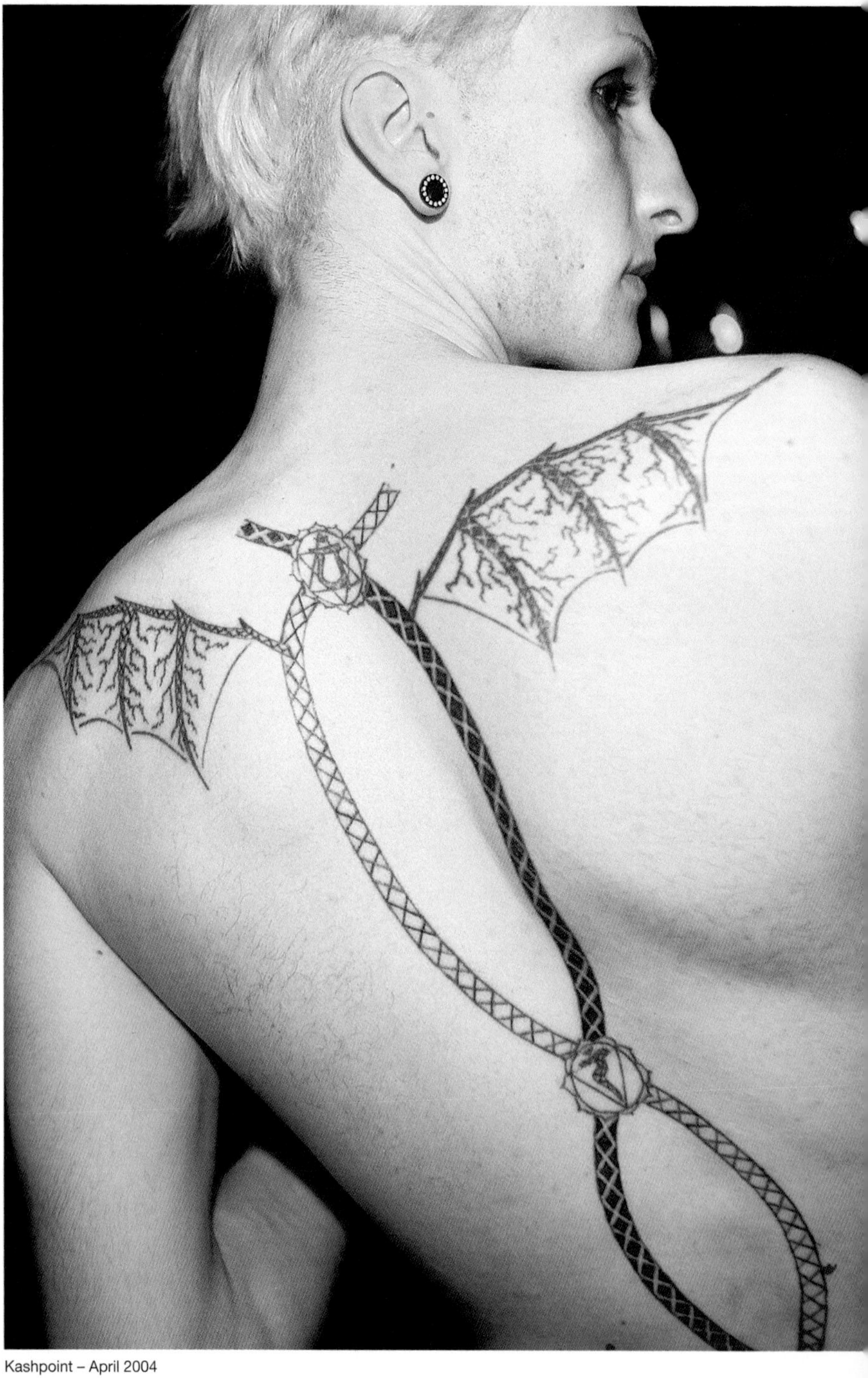

Kashpoint – April 2004

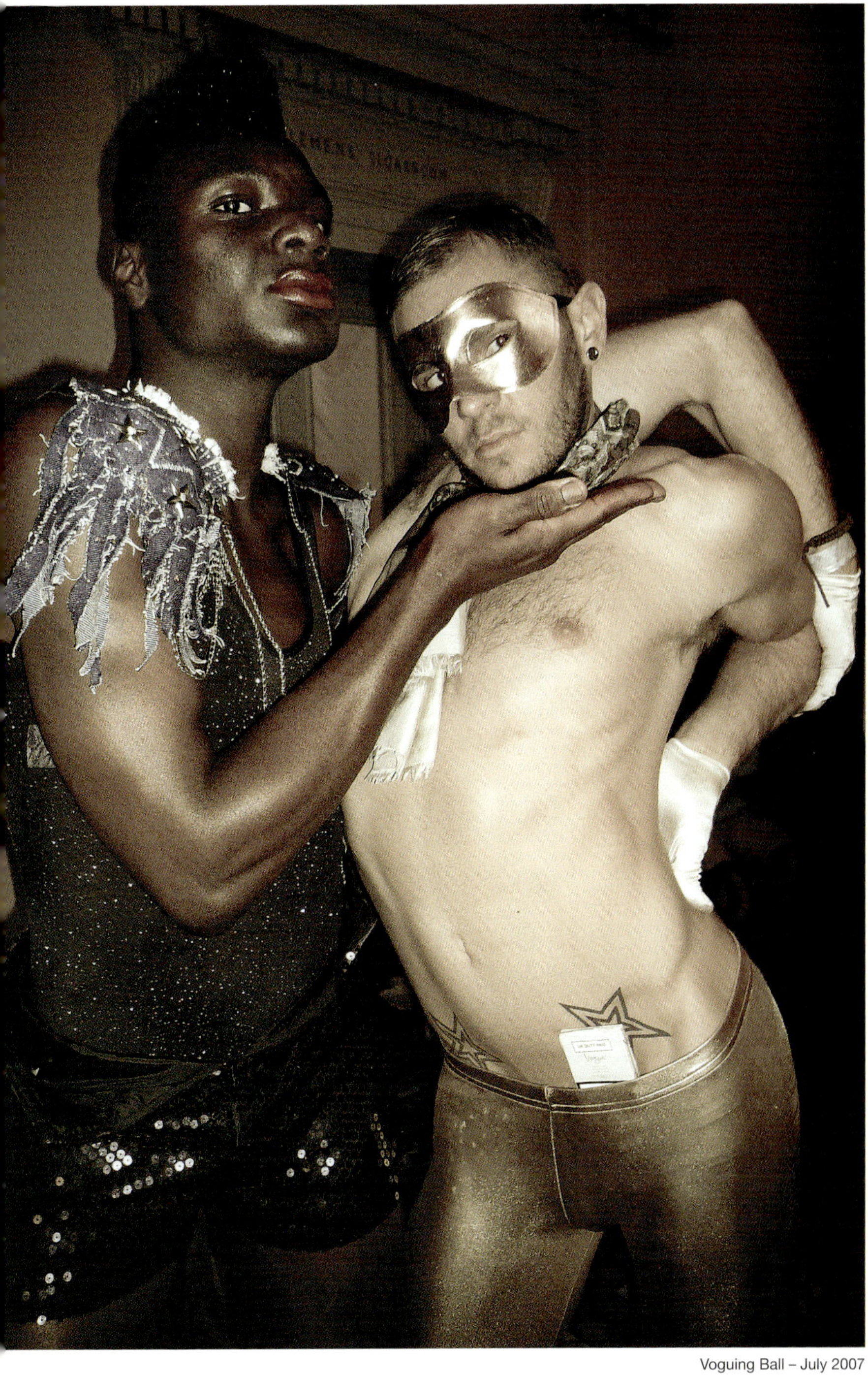

Voguing Ball – July 2007

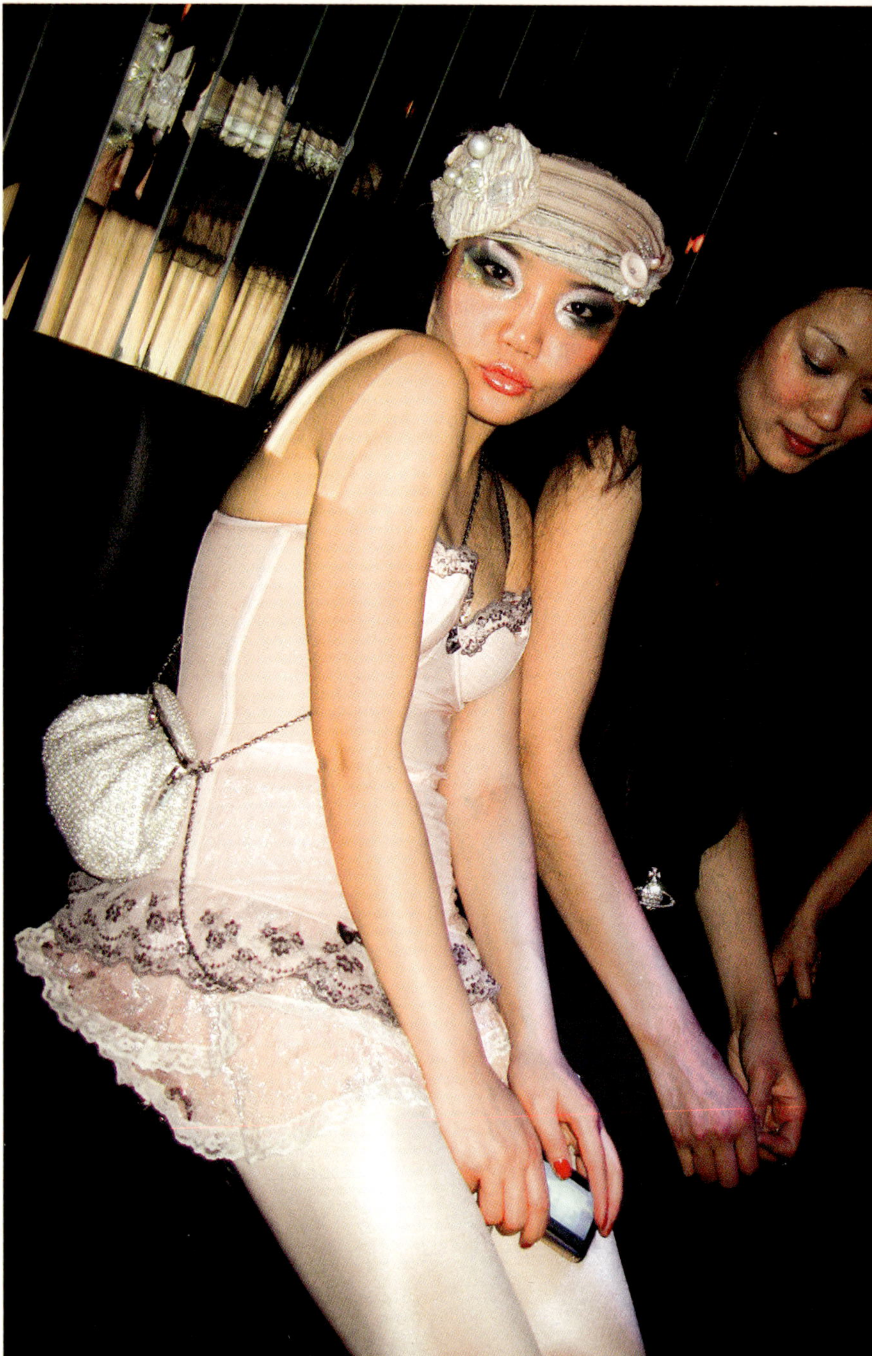

Kashpoint – June 2003

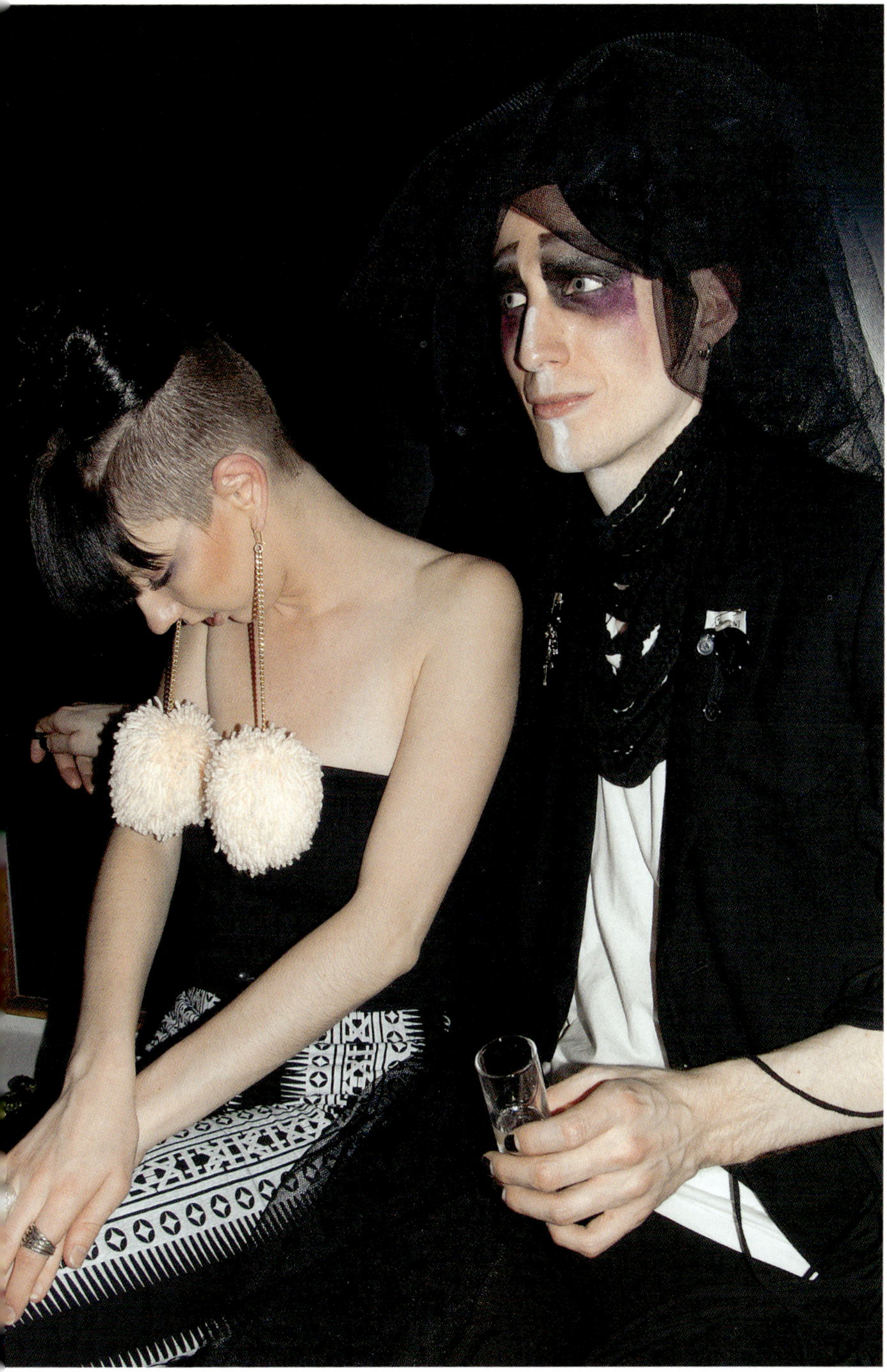

Paramount – July 2010

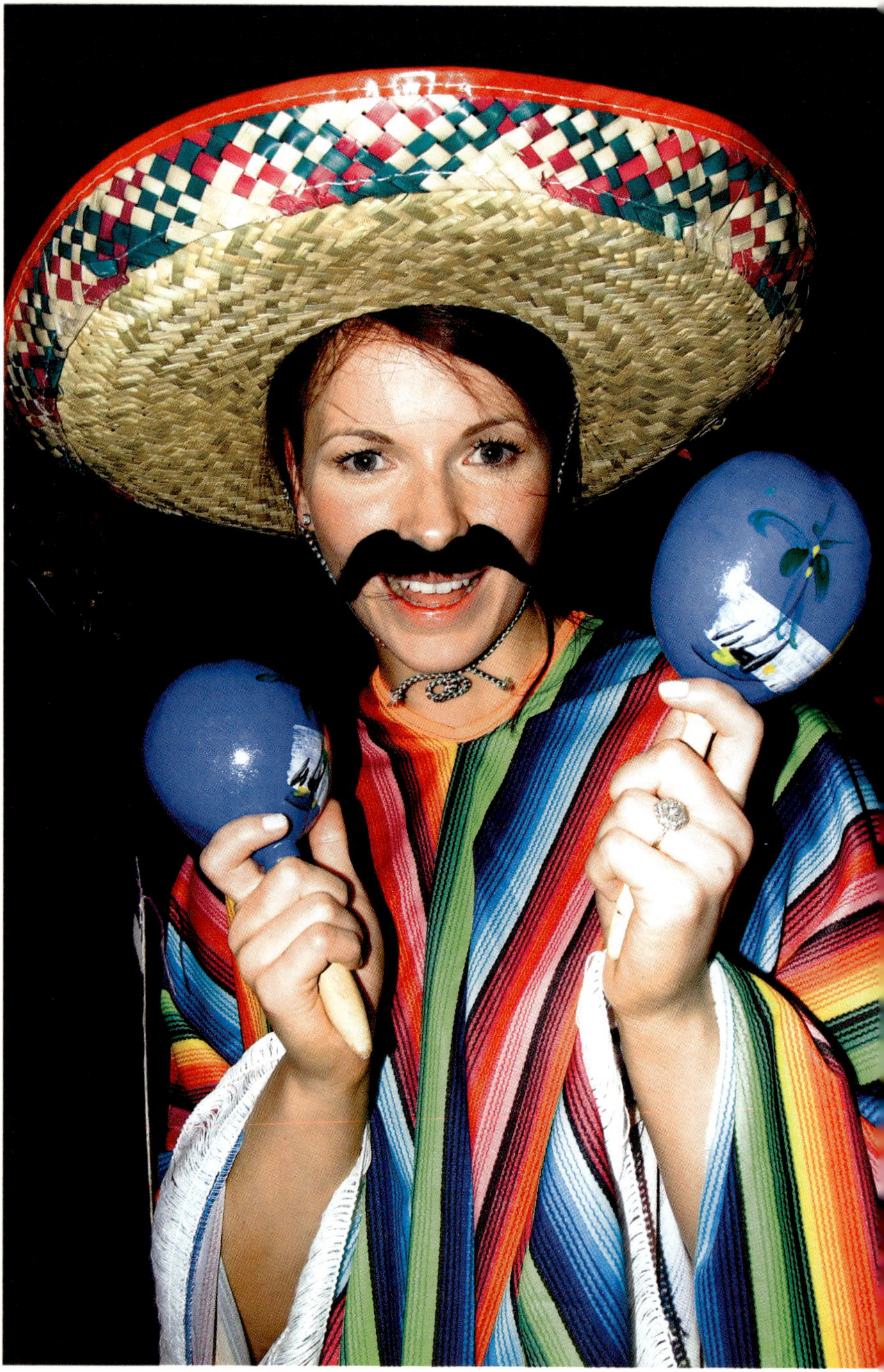

Nag Nag Nag – May 2003

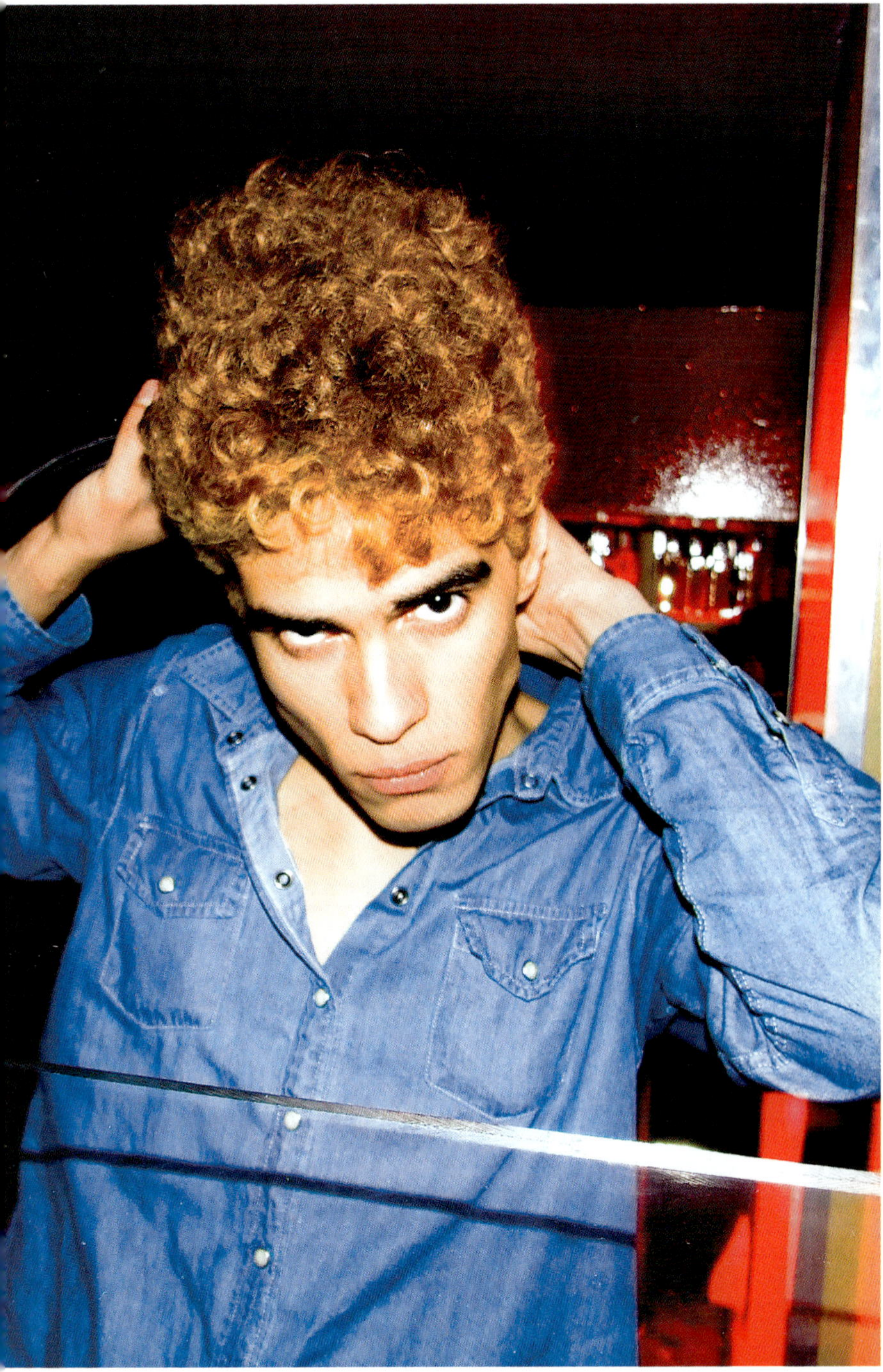

Your Mum's House – Jan 2010

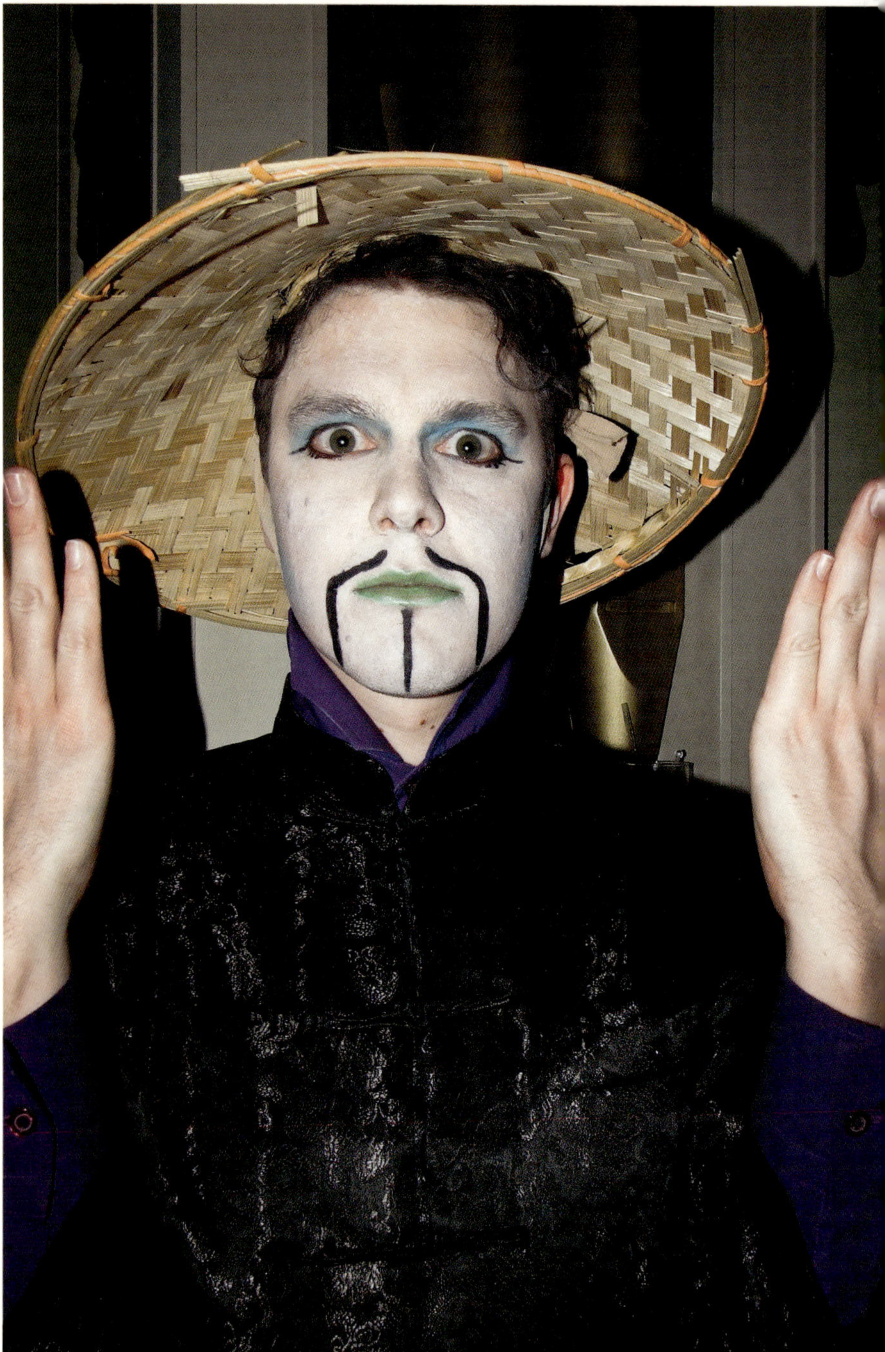

Home House – Jan 2010

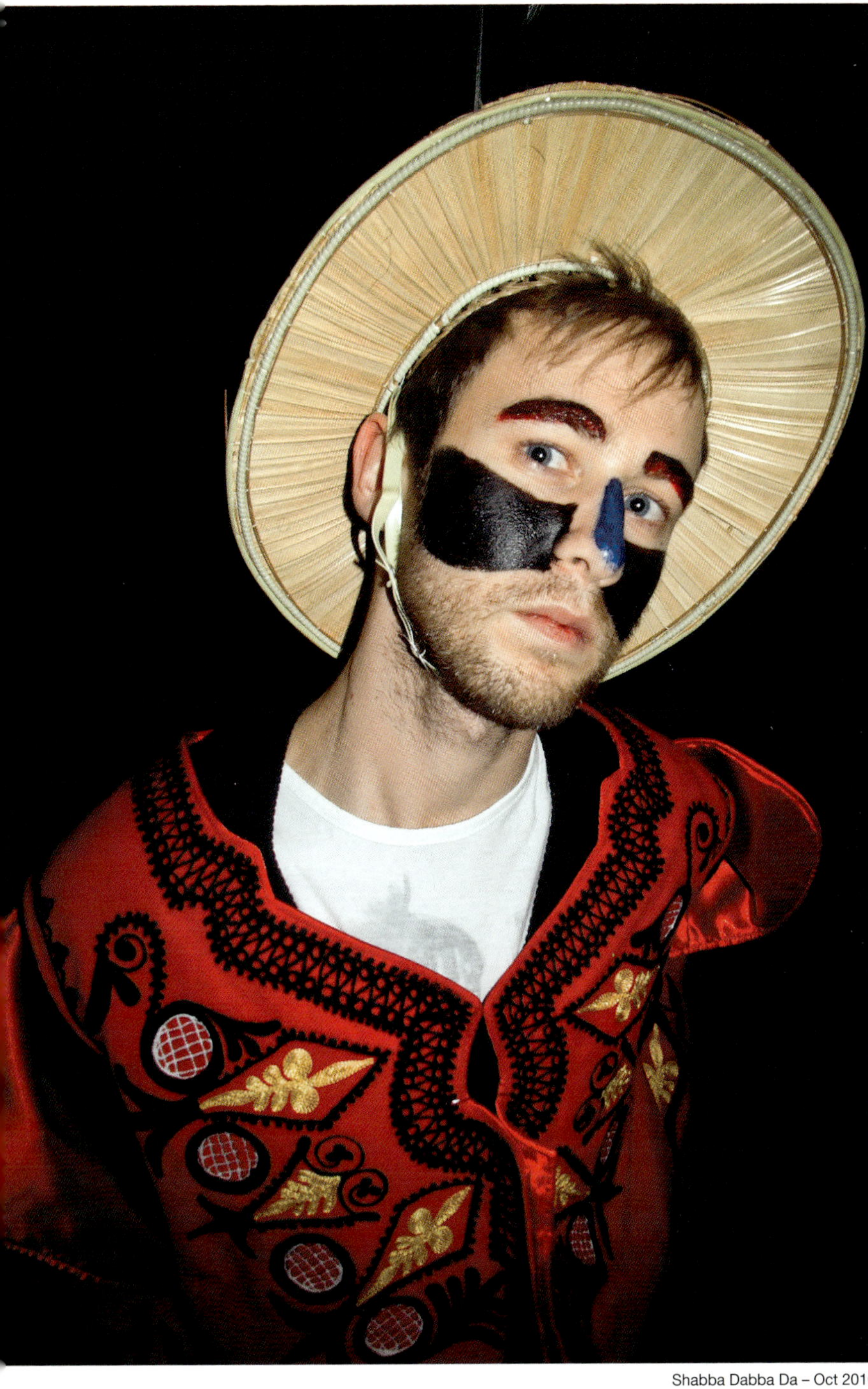

Shabba Dabba Da – Oct 2010

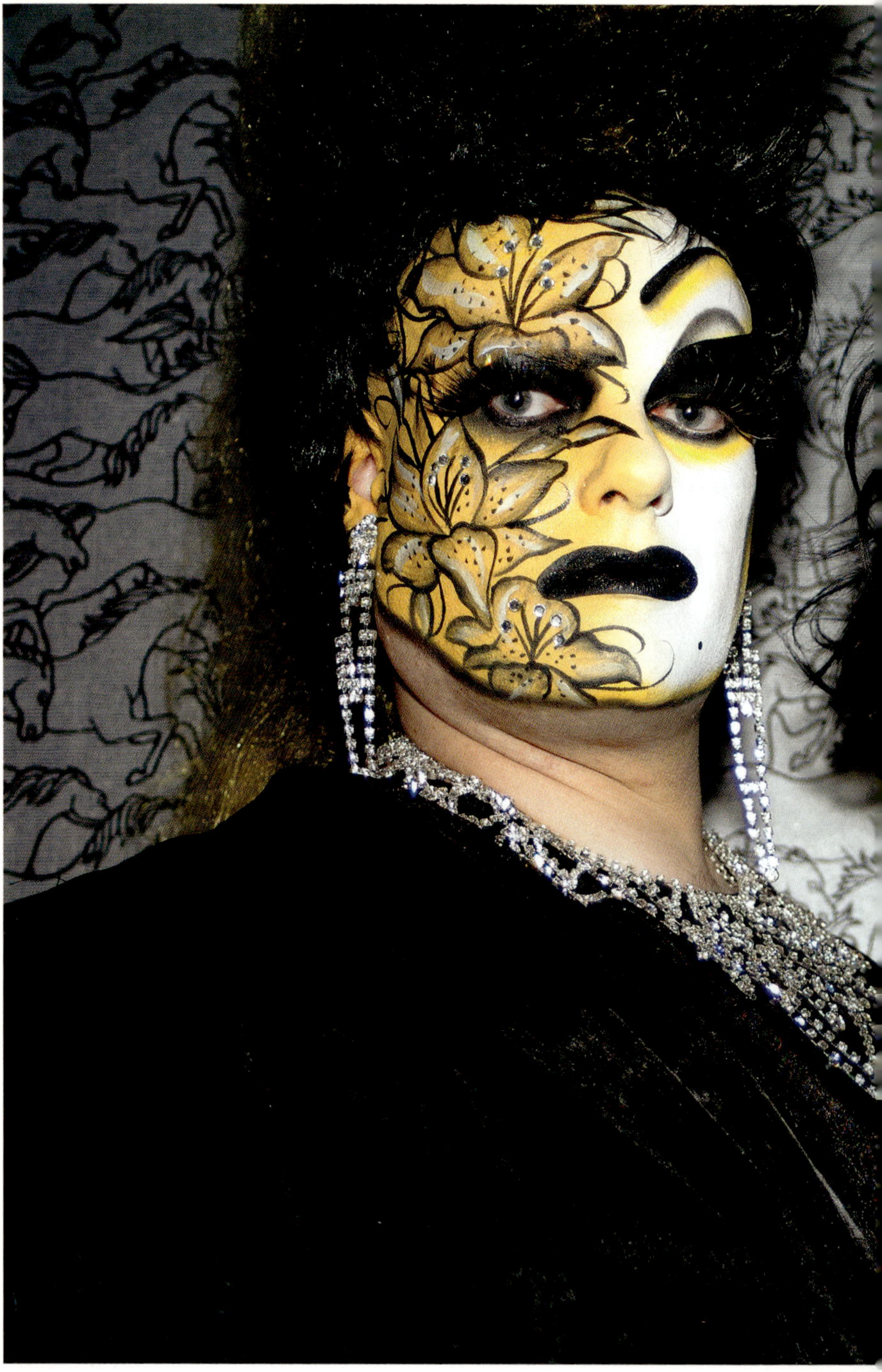

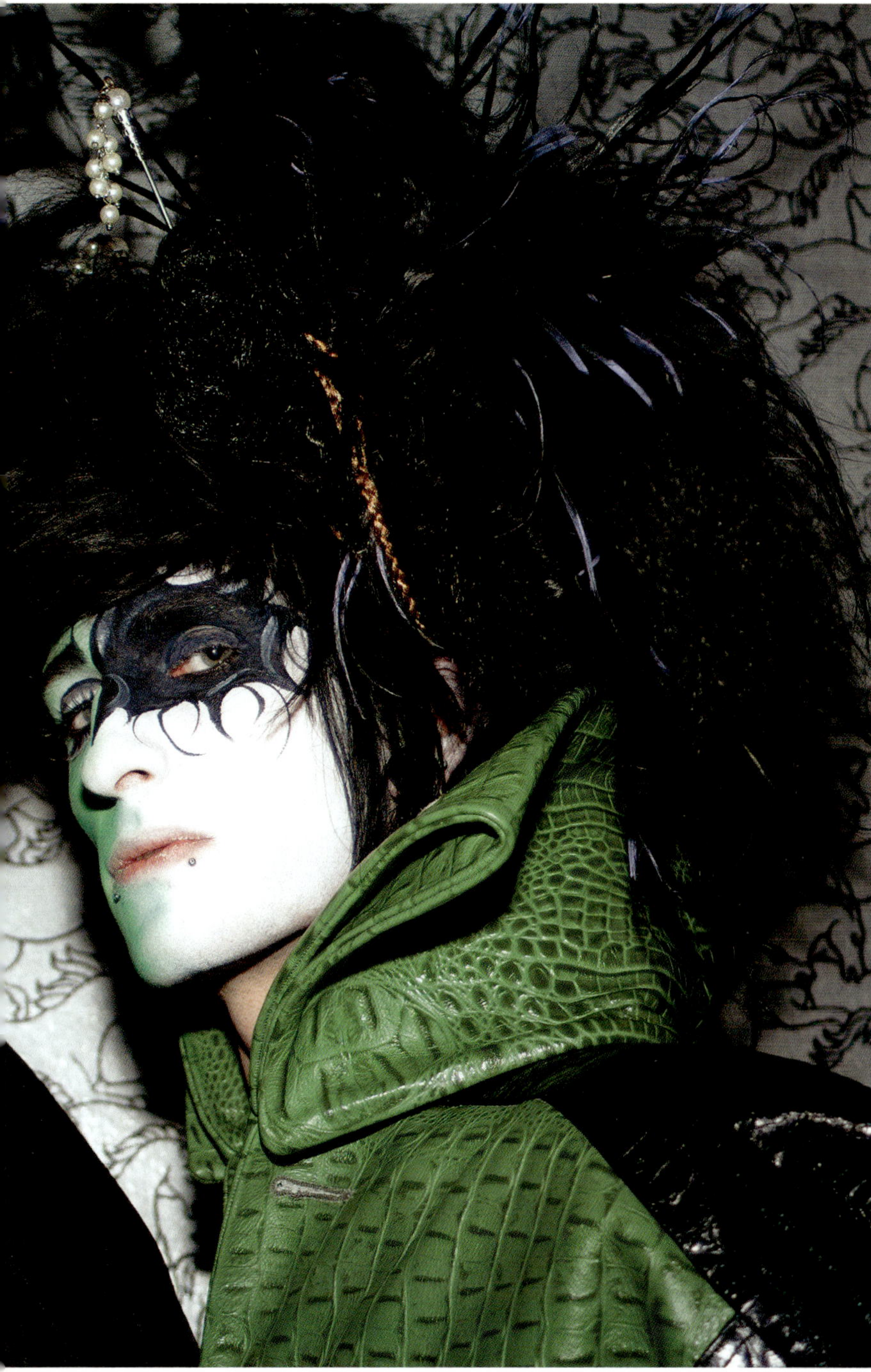

Madame Jojo's – Dec 2009

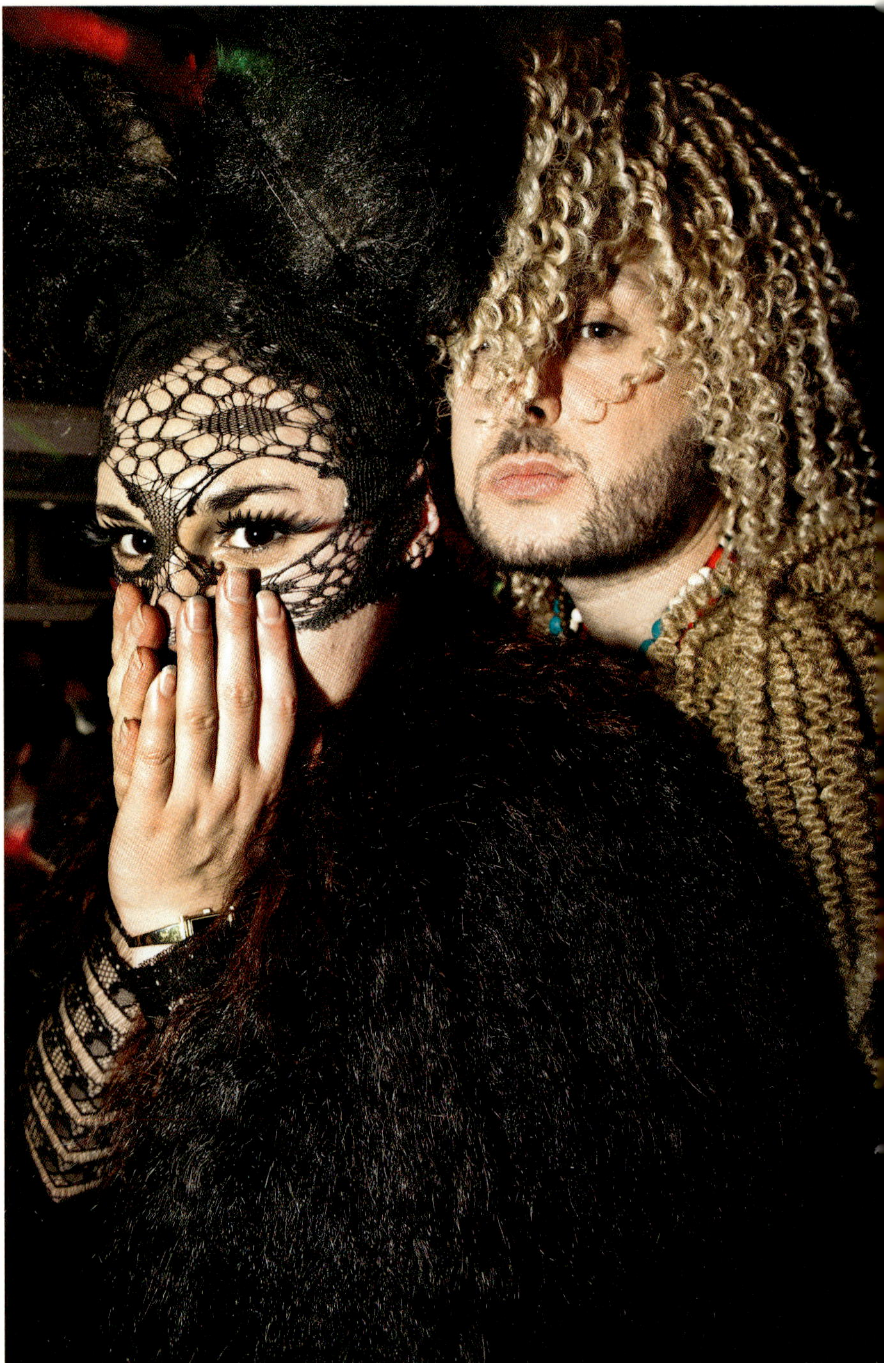

Circus – May 2010

Thanks to all the amazing people who inspired me to do this book, your efforts to look ever so fierce will be remembered; to my loyal friends who helped me immensely – Killian, your stylistic input was precious; Tamer, you are still my muse after all these years; Koko and Robbie, we still have plenty more partying to do; Andrew, your design is bespoke. Special thanks to Princess Julia for allowing me to interview her on a particularly miserable, rainy day and Olli, for your believing in this project; Philip Sallon, Daniel Lismore, Jodie Harsh and Rosemary Turner and everyone who invited me to your amusing events; Johanna for your incredible patience and extra-ordinary beauty, you're a star. Big love to Judah Jordan and to my parents and my precious grandma for their unremitting love and understanding; to my flatmates for being quiet in the early hours and resourceful in the late nights. To all of you holding this in your hands, thank you for reading it, I know it's just a few lines but it did take a lot of effort and long hours of staring at the screen. Now turn it back and start again. Enjoy!

Front Cover: Johanna
Back Cover: Anna Swiczeniuk and Markabre Charade

Prestel Verlag, Munich
A member of Verlagsgruppe Random House GmbH

Prestel Verlag
Neumarkter Str. 28
81673 Munich
Tel. +49 (0) 89 4136-0
Fax. +49 (0) 89 4136-2335
www.prestel.de

Prestel Publishing Ltd.
4 Bloomsbury Place
London WC1A 2QA
Tel. +44 (20) 7323 5004
Fax. +44 (20) 7636 8004
www.prestel.com

Prestel Publishing Ltd.
900 Broadway, Suite 603
New York, 10003
Tel. +1 (212) 995 2720
Fax. +1 (212) 995 2733
www.prestel.com

Library of Congress Control Number is available; British Library Cataloguing-in-Publication Data: a catalogue record for this book is available from the British Library; Deutsche Nationalbibliothek holds a record of this publication in the Deutsche Nationalbibliografie; detailed bibliographical data can be found under: http://dnb.d-nb.de

Prestel books are available worldwide. Please contact your nearest bookseller or one of the above addresses for information concerning your local distributor.

Editorial direction: Oliver Barter
Production: Friederike Schirge
Art direction: Oggy Yordanov
Design and layout: zinklondon.com
Typesetting: zinklondon.com
Origination: Repro Ludwig, Zell am See
Printing and Binding: C&C Printing

FSC www.fsc.org
MIX
Paper from responsible sources
FSC® C008047

Verlagsgruppe Random House FSC-DEU-0100
The FSC®-certified paper Chinese Golden Sun matt art is produced by mill Sun Paper Group (Yanzhou Tianzhang Paper Industry Co. Ltd.) in Shandong, PRC.

Printed in China

ISBN 978-3-7913-4554-3